Efficient Multirate Teletraffic Loss Models Beyond Erlang

Efficient Multirate Teletraffic Loss Models Beyond Erlang

Ioannis D. Moscholios
University of Peloponnese, Greece

Michael D. Logothetis
University of Patras, Greece

This edition first published 2019
© 2019 John Wiley & Sons Ltd

The right of Ioannis D. Moscholios and Michael D. Logothetis to be identified as the authors of this work has been asserted in accordance with law.

Registered Offices
John Wiley & Sons, Inc., 111 River Street, Hoboken, NJ 07030, USA
John Wiley & Sons Ltd, The Atrium, Southern Gate, Chichester, West Sussex, PO19 8SQ, UK

Editorial Office
The Atrium, Southern Gate, Chichester, West Sussex, PO19 8SQ, UK

For details of our global editorial offices, customer services, and more information about Wiley products visit us at www.wiley.com.

Wiley also publishes its books in a variety of electronic formats and by print-on-demand. Some content that appears in standard print versions of this book may not be available in other formats.

Library of Congress Cataloging-in-Publication Data

Names: Moscholios, Ioannis D (Associate Professor at the University of Peloponnese), author. | Logothetis, Michael D (Professor at the University of Patras), author.
Title: Efficient multirate teletraffic loss models beyond Erlang / Ioannis D. Moscholios, University of Peloponnese, Michael D. Logothetis, University of Patras.
Description: First edition. | Hoboken, NJ : John Wiley & Sons, Inc., 2019. | Includes bibliographical references and index. |
Identifiers: LCCN 2018052862 (print) | LCCN 2018056391 (ebook) | ISBN 9781119426905 (Adobe PDF) | ISBN 9781119426912 (ePub) | ISBN 9781119426882 (hardcover)
Subjects: LCSH: Telecommunication–Traffic–Mathematical models. | Queuing theory.
Classification: LCC TK5102.985 (ebook) | LCC TK5102.985 .L64 2019 (print) | DDC 621.38201/51982–dc23
LC record available at https://lccn.loc.gov/2018052862

Cover Design: Wiley
Cover Image: © Wenjie Dong/iStock.com

Set in 10/12pt WarnockPro by SPi Global, Chennai, India

Printed in Singapore by C.O.S. Printers Pte Ltd

10 9 8 7 6 5 4 3 2 1

To our families

Contents

List of Figures

List of Tables

Preface

The title: In the title of this book, the term *efficient* means effective computer implementation of the teletraffic model that is achieved through recursive formulas. A sine qua non of nowadays multi-dimensional telecom traffic is the term *multirate*, which shows that not only a single traffic service-class is accommodated in a service system but many traffic-classes. The term *teletraffic loss models* certainly reflects the content of this book, since it comprises mainly loss models where 'lost calls are cleared' (not queueing models). Relying on the fact that the Erlang-B formula was the most famous and useful formula (teletraffic model) in the past, we have added the term *beyond Erlang* hoping that the models of this book will also become pretty useful. On the other hand, although Erlang had not studied multirate loss models, we have named 'Erlang Multirate Loss Model (EMLM)', the basic multirate loss model which became the springboard of developing all other models presented in this book. The name EMLM can be justified from the fact that it provides the same results with the Erlang-B formula for a single service-class; however, the main inventors of this key model are J. S. Kaufman (Bell Laboratories, 1981) and J. W. Roberts (France Telecom, 1981).

The Subject: Teletraffic models are an inseparable part of the telecommunications and Information and Communication Technology (ICT) infrastructure from the very beginning of their existence. No matter what changes new networking technologies toward 5G may bring, the essential task of teletraffic models remains the same: To determine and evaluate the relationship between (1) the QoS parameters (i.e., call blocking probability), (2) the parameters that determine the intensity of connection requests and the demanded resources (traffic load), and (3) the parameters that describe available network resources (capacity). The global network of either 4G or 5G consisting of many interacting heterogeneous systems supports widely used broadband mobile devices and cloud computing that have given rise not only to a tremendous growth of network traffic but also to a high diversity of traffic streams. The latter more than ever necessitates the development of specialized teletraffic models according to the input traffic stream.

As we describe in the Introduction, Section 'I.13 Classification of Teletraffic Loss Models' (reading this Section is strongly recommended), the models are distinguished according to the:

i)   call arrival process
ii) call bandwidth requirements upon arrival, (i.e., service-classes) and
iii) call behavior while they are in service.

The combination of the characteristics of (i), (ii) and (iii) lead to different teletraffic models. We only present those combinations/models which are realistic and therefore interesting.

The Motivation: The motivation for developing new teletraffic models was the fact that the accuracy of network optimization/dimensioning strongly depends on the accuracy of the incorporated teletraffic model which, in turn, depends on the accurate modelling of the service-classes of network traffic. Dimensioning is considered an endless, on-going process of network performance analysis and design. To accomplish it effectively, it is necessary to work out models that incorporate the parameters of a designed network in a reliable way. Besides, teletraffic models are of great assistance for call admission control (CAC), that is, the access control of different service-classes to network resources and the bandwidth allocation among service-classes. The latter has been widely recognized as a necessary solution for QoS guarantee both in existing and future networks. Call-level multi-rate teletraffic loss models aim at assessing the call-level QoS of networks with resource reservation capabilities, as well as of the emerging and future all-optical core networks. Our ultimate aim is to contribute (through this book) to the upgrading of teletraffic models incorporated in commercial packages/tools for network configuration, optimization and planning. To the best of our knowledge, most of such tools utilize only basic (old) teletraffic models. Comparison of new teletraffic models against the basic teletraffic models is included in the book to show the necessity of the new models.

The Audience: This book is directed primarily at telecommunication engineers, professionals who are experienced with optimization and dimensioning of telecom networks, and especially to those who are responsible for QoS assessment/guarantee, or for planning and designing transmission networks. The book is also useful for telecom operators or managers on the higher and average levels, because it will help them to assess the network performance (e.g., of a transmission link), and take proper decisions on network dimensioning and traffic management that result in an increase profit, or investment savings; thus, they can gain competition advantage.

On the other hand, thinking that this book has been resulted from academic research over many years, we certainly recommend this book to PhD students (and modelers) who are involved in related research, as a valuable reference book. Besides, given that we write it in a very simple and explanatory manner, we propose this book as a textbook. It can be adopted as a textbook for a specialized course on a master/PhD level.

Our Vision: Having a bad experience of reading several contemporary books which do not offer more information than one can find, for instance, in the cited journals, we envisioned our book being unique by providing to a reader not only a collection of teletraffic models but also a detailed explanation on how efficient multirate teletraffic loss models are extracted and applied, as well as complete numerical examples. We also guide the readers through many network technologies and services. However, this is accomplished at the end of each chapter as an application example. When presenting a teletraffic model, we do not refer to technologies. The reason is that the models are abstracted from various network technologies and are not dedicated to a specific technology.

Starting from the basics, the book steadily increases in difficulty to include complex teletraffic models so as to keep the book self-contained and to provide a better understanding to those who might be new to the subject. Readers who are not familiar with the teletraffic theory may find helpful the following analogy: For a sales store, the traffic load (i.e., the number of available products each day) is a key element of its size (number of cashiers/servers, store and parking place, etc.). Traffic load is an important element for network/system dimensioning and can be estimated through a teletraffic model. The sales store example is even more important than for understanding purposes, because of the fact that the same teletraffic model can be used to estimate the traffic-load offered either to a communication system or to the sales store. Thus, we can recommend this book to a wider audience, because of the applicability of traffic theory to many other scientific fields (for instance, we mention the applicability of teletraffic models to smart grid in chapters 1, 2 and 6).

The Structure: The book comprises an Introduction (background knowledge) and three parts (Part I: chapters 1–5, Part II: chapters 6–9, Part III: chapters 10–11), including 198 examples, 191 figures, and 65 tables. The majority of the examples are of a tutorial type (accompanied by intermediate results and figures). Because of the high number of examples, there is no need to include exercises. To locate a suitable model in the book, a reader needs to know the input first; that is, if the number of traffic sources can be considered infinite (random) then a reader should resort to Part I of the book; if the number of traffic sources is finite, a reader should resort to Part II, while, if calls arrive in batches, a reader should resort to Part III. At the beginning of each part, we include a small 'preface' to further facilitate the right model localization. In each chapter, the service systems are first described and then the corresponding analytical models are presented, followed by various performance metrics. Each chapter ends with applications and further reading. The book ends with an Appendix where the interdependency of the models is demonstrated. Furthermore, the book is accompanied by a website (*www.wiley.com/go/logocode*), where a reader can find a link in order to run software of the computer implementation of the main teletraffic models.

Acknowlededgments

We would like to thank many professional colleagues and researchers for the assistance given to us over the years. Particularly, we are grateful to Dr Vassilios Vassilakis (University of York, York, UK) and Dr John Vardakas (Iquadrat Informatica S.L., Barcelona, Spain), co-authors of many of our research papers related to efficient teletraffic loss models. We are also grateful to our Polish colleagues Prof. Maciej Stasiak, Prof. Mariusz Glabowski and Prof. Piotr Zwierzykowski (Poznan University of Technology, Poznan, Poland) for the impetus they have given us in the spirit of a noble competition for the development of new teletraffic models. Besides, we ought special thanks to Mr. Panagiotis Panagoulias, PhD student at the Department of Informatics and Telecommunications of University of Peloponnese, Greece, for his valuable time spent for making the software implementation of the main teletraffic models available to the companion website.

Our heartfelt thanks to our families for the unlimited and constant encouragement we received from them especially while writing this book.

Finally, we would like to express our special appreciation to all staff of John Wiley & Sons for their support in the final formulation of this book.

Ioannis D. Moscholios
Michael D. Logothetis
March 2019

Acronyms

ABR	Available bit rate
API	Application programming interface
ASTA	Arrivals see time averages
ATM	Asynchronous transfer mode
AWG	Array waveguide grating
b.u.	Bandwidth unit
BBP	Burst blocking probability
BBU	Baseband unit
BER	Bit error rate
BHCA	Busy hour call attempts
BPP	Bernoulli–Poisson–Pascal
bps	Bits per second
BR	Bandwidth reservation
BS	Base station
CAC	Call/connection admission control
CBP	Call blocking probability(ies)
CC	Call congestion
CCS	Centum call seconds
CDF	Cumulative distribution function
CDMA	Code division multiple access
CDTM	Connection dependent threshold model
CFP	Connection failure probability
CPRI	Common public radio interface
cps	Chips (bits) per second
CS	Complete sharing
cSON	Centralized self-organizing network
DiffServ	Differentiated services
dSON	Distributed self-organizing network
DWA	Dynamic wavelength allocation
EMLM	Erlang multirate loss model
EnMLM	Engset multirate loss model
EPC	Evolved packet core
erl	The Erlang unit of traffic-load
E-UTRAN	Evolved terrestrial radio access network
FDD	Frequency division duplexing

FE	Forwarding element
FIFO	First in–first out
GB	Global balance
GoS	Grade of service
GSM	Global system for mobile communications
GW	Gateway
hSON	Hybrid self-organizing network
ICT	Information and communication technology
IntServ	Integrated services
IP	Internet protocol
ISDN	Integrated services digital network
ITU-T	International telecommunication unit–standardization sector
LB	Local balance
LBP	Local blocking probability
LEO	Low earth orbit
LF	Load factor
LHS	Left-hand side
LIFO	Last in–first out
LO-GW	Local offload gateway
LSC	Local SDN controller
LTE	Long-term evolution
MAC	Medium access control
MBS	Macro base station
MCC	Mobile cloud computing
M-CDN	Mobile content delivery network
MCN	Mobile core network
MEC	Mobile edge computing
MPLS	Multiple protocol labeling switching
MRM	Multi-retry model
MSS	Mobile satellite system
MTM	Multi-threshold model
MU	Mobile user
NFV	Network function virtualization
NFVI	Network function virtualization infrastructure
OBS	Optical burst switching
OCDMA	Optical code division multiple access
OFDM	Orthogonal frequency division multiplexing
OLT	Optical line terminal
ONU	Optical network unit
PASTA	Poisson arrivals see time averages
pdf	Probability density function
PDF	Probability distribution function
PDN	Packet data network
PFS	Product form solution
PON	Passive optical network
QoS	Quality of service
r.v.	Random variable

RAN	Radio access networks
RAT	Radio access technology
RED	Random early detection
RHS	Right-hand side
RLA	Reduced load approximation
RRA	Radio resource allocation
RRH	Remote radio head
RRM	Radio resource management
RU	Resource unit
SBS	Small cell base station
SDN	Software defined networking
SIRO	Service in random order
SNR	Signal-to-noise ratio
SON	Self-organizing network
SRM	Single-retry model
STM	Single-threshold model
TC	Time congestion
TCP	Transport control protocol
TDMA	Time division multiple access
TH	Threshold
UDP	User datagram protocol
UE	User equipment
UMTS	Universal mobile telecommunication system
VBS	Virtual base station
VNF	Virtual network function
WCDMA	Wideband code division multiple access
WDM	Wavelength division multiplexing

Symbols

α	Traffic-load
B	Blocking probability
b	Number of bandwidth units requested by a call
C	System capacity
$\Gamma(\cdot)$	Gamma function
γ	Binary parameter
δ	Binary parameter
η	Trunk (channel) efficiency
$E_C(\alpha)$	Erlang-B formula
$E_C^{\text{delay}}(\alpha)$	Erlang-C formula
$E[X]$	Expected/mean value of a random variable X
$f(\ )$	Mathematical function
G	Normalization constant
h	Mean holding time
j	Total number of occupied bandwidth units of all in-service calls
K	Number of service-classes
λ	Mean arrival rate
μ	Mean service rate (departure rate)
n	Number of calls/flows
$\bar{n}$	Mean number of calls
P	Probability
$Prob$	Probability
$q(j)$	Unnormalized link occupancy distribution
$Q(j)$	Link occupancy distribution
T_{h}	Throughput
t	Trunk/bandwidth reservation parameter
U	Utilization
$Var[X]$	Variance of a random variable X
$y_k(j)$	Average number of calls of service-class k in state j
$\mathbf{\Omega}$	State space

About the Companion Website

This book is accompanied by a companion website:

www.wiley.com/go/logocode

The website includes:

(1) The description and the structure of the book
(2) A link in order to run software of the computer implementation of the main teletraffic models.

Scan this QR code to visit the companion website.

Introduction

The word *traffic* becomes *teletraffic* in telecommunications, as communications becomes telecommunications to indicate technology use, e.g., conversation from some distance through phones or the Internet. The term "teletraffic" covers all kinds of computer communication traffic and telecom traffic. This book includes teletraffic loss models.

What is a *model*? Searching the Internet one can find several definitions for the word model:

- A representation of a system, process, etc. in mathematical terms.
- A representation of the essential aspects of an existing system (or a system to be constructed) which presents knowledge of that system in usable form.
- A mathematical representation of a process, device, or concept by means of a number of variables which are defined to represent the inputs, outputs, and internal states of the device or process, and a set of equations and inequalities describing the interaction of these variables.

All these definitions are well fitted to the models presented in this book. Teletraffic models determine mathematical relationships among three key factors of a communication system:

1. the offered *traffic-load*, α
2. the *grade of service* (*GoS*), which is related to *quality of service* (*QoS*)
3. the *system capacity*, C.

There are many cases in which the size of an establishment is directly related to the throughput of the establishment. For example, considering the size of a store (system capacity), a defining factor comprises the number of products (traffic-load) available for sale per day (GoS). Likewise, the volume of traffic carried constitutes a defining factor of the capacity of a communication system. Considering that a communication system can be a single link between two switching nodes (such as routers or telephone exchanges), the link capacity can be denoted either by the number of trunks[1] of the link or by the transmission speed in the link. For example, assuming that 1 trunk corresponds to a transmission speed of 64 kbps, we can say that a communication link of 2.048 Mbps has

---

1 The term *trunk* is quite general. For example, a trunk can be an international circuit thousands of kilometers long, or a wire of a few meters connecting two switches in a telephone exchange, or a conductive pathway of some millimeters long connecting a central processing unit with an output port on a printed circuit board, etc.

a bandwidth capacity of 32 trunks, or 32 bandwidth units (b.u.). That is, in this book, because of this correspondence, we measure the system capacity in b.u. Alternatively, the term "channel" could be used, since a trunk is a single transmission channel between two points.

I.1 Traffic-load Definition

Traffic is generated by *calls*. A call is defined as the demand for connection to a communication system. The duration of a call is called *holding time* or *service time*.

- *Traffic-load* is, by definition, the holding time of all calls during an observation time-interval divided by the observation time-interval.

Based on the above definition, it follows that traffic-load is a dimensionless quantity. However, the *Erlang* (*erl*) has been set as the unit measuring traffic-load, in honour of the Danish mathematician Agner Krarup Erlang (1878–1929), founder of teletraffic theory [1].

Example I.1 Figure I.1 shows a transmission link of three trunks. Within an observation interval of 1 hour, the first trunk is occupied by three calls for $(15 + 20 + 10)$ min $= 45$ min, the second trunk is occupied by one call for 30 min, and the third trunk by three calls for $(15 + 15 + 15)$ min $= 45$ min. What is the measured traffic-load in this link?

According to the definition, the traffic-load, α, is: $\alpha = \dfrac{(45 + 30 + 45) \text{ min}}{60 \text{ } min} = 2$ erl.

Example I.2 Other than the Erlang unit, the traffic-load is measured in *centum call seconds* (*CCS*). In this case, the unit of time interval is considered to be one hundred seconds (100 sec). That is to say, CCS measures how many hundreds of seconds a trunk was occupied.

(a) Find a relation between CCS and erl. If a trunk is continually occupied for 1 hour, express the traffic-load in erl and CCS.

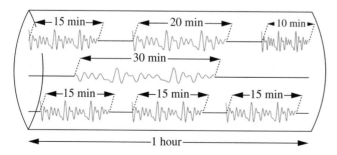

Figure I.1 Traffic-load in a link of three trunks (Example I.1).

(b) On a transmission line, we measure a traffic-load of 18 CCS. On another transmission line, we measure a traffic-load of 1 erl. What conclusion can we draw on the total holding time in these two transmission lines?

(a) *CCS versus erl*: To find a relation between CCS and erl, let us measure the traffic-load in one trunk, within a time interval of 1 hour:

Traffic-load in erl = (total holding time in sec)/3600
Traffic-load in CCS = (total holding time in sec)/100

If the trunk is continually occupied for 1 hour, then: traffic-load = 1 erl = 36 CCS.

(b) *Conclusion on the total holding time*: The transmission line of 18 CCS is occupied for $18 \cdot 100$ CCS = 1800 sec = 30 min. The transmission line of 1 erl is occupied for the entire duration of the observation time.

I.2 Traffic Congestion and GoS/QoS

To supply a telecommunication system with as many resources (switches, bandwidth, etc.) as are necessary for handling the maximum volume of traffic has proven to be infeasible financially. In many cases, it would be technically possible to dimension a central office so that all users can make telephone calls simultaneously. However, the cost to satisfy such a demand is prohibitive, especially since the probability of such an occurrence is very close to zero.

What can actually occur (and frequently does) is for all trunks in a group of trunks to be occupied, therefore not allowing this group to accept more calls. This situation is known as *congestion*. In such a situation, calls are frequently blocked and the actual traffic carried is less than the traffic offered, reduced by the quantity of traffic lost:

$$\text{carried traffic} = \text{offered traffic - lost traffic} \tag{I.1}$$

A system where an incoming call is blocked and abandons the system (we often say *blocked and lost*), upon congestion occurrence, is called a *loss system*. If, however, a call can wait for a connection, the system is called a *delay* (or *queueing*) *system*. The percentage of calls lost or delayed due to system congestion indicates the GoS provided by the system. The GoS is a (teletraffic) component of the QoS,[2] which determines the degree of the user/customer satisfaction on the service offered. For a loss system, the GoS, *B*, expressing blocking (loss) and specifically *call blocking probability* (*CBP*), is defined as follows:

$$B = \frac{\text{total number of lost calls}}{\text{total number of offered calls}} \tag{I.2a}$$

$$B = \frac{\text{lost traffic}}{\text{offered traffic}} \tag{I.2b}$$

---

2 According to ITU-T Recommendation E.800, the term QoS comprises both network related performance (e.g., GoS, bit error rate, security performance) and non-network related performance (e.g., provision time, repair time, complaints resolution time).

Also, the following expressions hold (depending on the teletraffic modeling details):

$$B \equiv \text{percentage of time during which the system is congested, or}$$
$$B \equiv \text{call blocking probability due to congestion, or} \qquad (\text{I.3})$$
$$B \equiv \text{probability of congestion.}$$

If traffic-load α is offered to a group of trunks with GoS $= B$, then the traffic lost α_{lost} and the traffic carried α_c are given by:

$$\alpha_{\text{lost}} = \alpha \cdot B \qquad\qquad\qquad \alpha_c = \alpha \cdot (1 - B) \qquad (\text{I.4})$$

Example I.3 The capacity of a help desk has been designed to offer a GoS of $B = 2\%$ during the rush hour (busy hour). The total number of offered calls during this time-interval is 300 (requests for help) on average.

(a) What is the total number of lost calls on average?
(b) For how many minutes is the help desk congested during the busy hour?

(a) From (I.2a) we get:
   total number of lost calls $= B \cdot$ (total number of offered calls) $= 0.02 \cdot 300 =$ 6 calls.
(b) According to (I.3),
   $B =$ percentage of time during which the system is congested. Therefore:
   $B = 2\%$ of the busy hour the system is congested, that is, for $0.02 \cdot 60 = 1.2\text{min}$.

The definition of a particular value of GoS is a matter of judgement. A high GoS (high probability of congestion) will result in users complaining of calls frequently failing to be put through. On the contrary, an extremely low GoS (low probability of congestion) will result in waste of capital investment because the system will be under-operating and the equipment will be excessive. It is therefore more practical for GoS to vary according to the different parts of a system.

I.3 System Capacity

The basic problem in communications, aside from achieving communication, is calculating the capacity of a system, known as the dimensioning problem. It is stated as follows:

- Knowing the offered traffic-load α and the desired GoS, find the required system capacity C.

Nowadays, the dimensioning problem is quite complex since it involves multirate networks, where more than one services are accommodated, each of which usually requires a different QoS; thus, QoS (GoS) and traffic-load are denoted as vectors.

An alternative form of the dimensioning problem is the performance evaluation problem, which is stated as follows:

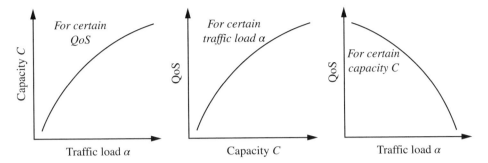

Figure I.2 Qualitative relationships between traffic-load, system capacity and GoS.

- Knowing the system capacity C and the offered traffic-load α, find the GoS offered by the system.

Qualitatively, the relationships between α, C, and QoS[3] are shown in Figure I.2. The left curve expresses the dimensioning problem, while the middle and the right curves express the performance evaluation problem, depending on what is fixed, the offered traffic-load or the system capacity, respectively.

A communication system is not dimensioned to cover the ever possible peak of traffic-load; it seems to be impossible. It is traditionally established from the world of telephony, to determine the system capacity based on the busy hour traffic-load. The term *busy hour* is a well-established term that refers to the 1-hour time interval where the traffic-load reaches its (ordinary) peak. For instance, for the telephone service, the time between 11:00 and 12:00 (day hours) has been observed as the busy hour in most measures. Since a communication system is designed to face the busy-hour traffic, it will mostly under-operate the rest of the time. This explains why telecom companies have low-price offers for calls during low-traffic hours (late at night or on Sundays), since it costs next to nothing to convey calls at times outside the busy hour. Moreover, if clients were given adequate motivation for avoiding calls during the busy hour, the peak traffic-load would be less, allowing communications companies to keep the system capacity within the planning limits and save capital investment.

I.4 Teletraffic Models

Teletraffic models express the aforementioned relationships between the offered traffic-load α, the system capacity C, and the GoS, quantitatively. Referring to models, we should also refer to a related quotation of Prof. George Box,[4]. which says that:

> *"Essentially, all models are wrong, but some are useful"*

This quotation certainly includes teletraffic models, especially because they include the notion of traffic, whose nature is stochastic. For example, consider that traffic

---

3 For an easy understanding, the general term QoS is used instead of GoS because GoS has a reverse meaning, i.e., the better the GoS, the smaller its value is (a GoS of 1% is better than a GoS of 10%).
4 George E.P. Box (1919–2013), British statistician. Another quotation by him, related to models, is: "the practical question is how wrong do they have to be to not be useful".

is originated by calls; the number of calls varies at random, as calls begin and end at random. Therefore, by expressing the traffic-load with a single number, which is the average (mean) traffic-load,[5] it is clear that the resultant model could be right on *"average"* only. Teletraffic models are created based on essential assumptions, whereby we try to describe a communication system. Since it is difficult to find an one-to-one correspondence between the parts of a communication system and a teletraffic model, in that sense a teletraffic model is wrong. On the other hand, if the assumptions are valid, then the resultant teletraffic model can be an accurate model or an approximate one. The latter results from purely mathematical approximations (e.g., rounding).

Let us concentrate on the usefulness of teletraffic models. They are useful because they help us design a system, or assess its key performance metrics, and predict its behavior even under strange conditions; the more complex the system, the more useful is the model. Having created a teletraffic model, you can implement it into your computer as a program (or tool) of a small size, and have a robust way to study a communication system in a short time, using small computer memory. Thus, one can be facilitated at most in the study of the system and produce safe conclusions.

Example I.4   Some benefits that can result from teletraffic models, when we concentrate on GoS/QoS assessment through a teletraffic model, are:

- Through a teletraffic model, bandwidth can properly be allocated among services so that the required bandwidth is assigned to each service and thus specific GoS per service is guaranteed.
- When assessing the GoS offered by a network (through a teletraffic model), we can avoid too costly over-dimensioning of the network.
- Given that by using a teletraffic model we can assess the GoS of a network in time (e.g., by measuring the offered traffic-load in fixed time intervals), excessive network throughput degradation can be prevented through traffic engineering mechanisms.

We characterise a teletraffic model as efficient when it is recurrent. Then, its computer implementation is efficient in the sense that the applicability range of the model is extended enormously, in comparison to the applicability range of the same model in a closed form. This is due to the fact that teletraffic models in a closed form usually contain factorials and exponentials, which restrict the calculation range to relatively small numbers and make the models useless in practice. In this book, all the presented teletraffic models are recurrent; this feature, together with the fact that computers are ubiquitous and in daily use, makes the presented models very useful. In the past, teletraffic models were useful/available through tables or charts containing their values.

Example I.5   Consider that calls arrive at random to a communication system of fixed bandwidth capacity of C b.u., while requesting 1 b.u. per call. If the offered traffic-load is α erl, then the CBP, B (because the system is fully congested and no b.u. are available

---

5 In most cases, the traffic-load is considered a stationary random process, i.e., with a fixed mean and variance.

upon a call arrival), is determined by the famous *Erlang-B formula* ($E_C(\alpha)$) – since 1917! In a closed form, it is written as:

$$B = E_C(\alpha) = \frac{\frac{\alpha^C}{C!}}{\sum_{i=0}^{C} \frac{\alpha^i}{i!}} \tag{I.5}$$

Convert (I.5) to a recurrent formula, so that $E_C(\alpha)$ is calculated based on $E_{C-1}(\alpha)$.

For the same system with bandwidth capacity of $C - 1$ b.u., the Erlang-B formula takes the form:

$$E_{C-1}(\alpha) = \frac{\frac{\alpha^{C-1}}{(C-1)!}}{\sum_{i=0}^{C-1} \frac{\alpha^i}{i!}} \tag{I.6}$$

Note that $E_0(\alpha) = 1$, i.e., the blocked and lost condition certainly happens for any traffic-load when the system capacity is zero. As is proved below, in the case of the Erlang-B formula it is possible to calculate $B = E_C(\alpha)$ based on $E_{C-1}(\alpha)$. If it is true, starting from $E_0(\alpha)$ one can calculate $E_1(\alpha)$ based on $E_0(\alpha)$, and so on, step by step, $B = E_C(\alpha)$ based on $E_{C-1}(\alpha)$. To this end, from (I.5), taking into account (I.6), we obtain:

$$E_C(\alpha) = \frac{\frac{\alpha}{C}\frac{\alpha^{C-1}}{(C-1)!}}{\sum_{i=0}^{C-1}\frac{\alpha^i}{i!} + \frac{\alpha^C}{C!}} = \frac{\frac{\alpha}{C}\frac{\alpha^{C-1}}{(C-1)!}}{\sum_{i=0}^{C-1}\frac{\alpha^i}{i!} + \frac{\alpha}{C}\frac{\alpha^{C-1}}{(C-1)!}} = \frac{\frac{\alpha}{C}\frac{\alpha^{C-1}}{(C-1)!} / \sum_{i=0}^{C-1}\frac{\alpha^i}{i!}}{1 + \frac{\alpha}{C}\frac{\alpha^{C-1}}{(C-1)!} / \sum_{i=0}^{C-1}\frac{\alpha^i}{i!}}$$

$$= \frac{\frac{\alpha}{C}E_{C-1}(\alpha)}{1 + \frac{\alpha}{C}E_{C-1}(\alpha)} \tag{I.7}$$

or

$$B = E_C(\alpha) = \frac{\alpha E_{C-1}(\alpha)}{C + \alpha E_{C-1}(\alpha)}, \qquad \text{where} \quad C \geq 1. \tag{I.8}$$

Equation (I.8) is the recurrent form of the Erlang-B formula.

Computationally, the applicability range of (I.5) is restricted to systems with $C \leq 170$ b.u. in a contemporary PC with double-precision arithmetic (without admeasurement of the restrictions due to the exponential of the traffic-load). Thinking that 1 b.u. $= 64$ kbps, then $C = 10.88$ Mbps only; even if 1 b.u. $= 1$ Mbps, then $C = 170$ Mbps is not a high bandwidth capacity, nowadays. Instead, by using the recurrent model of (I.8), the applicability range of the Erlang-B formula is extended to cover any C in practice.

Example I.6 Consider that calls arrive at random to a communication system of fixed bandwidth capacity of 3 b.u., while requesting 1 b.u. per call. The offered traffic-load is 2 erl.

(a) Calculate the CBP, B, through the closed form of the Erlang-B formula.
(b) Increase the bandwidth capacity to 6 b.u. and find the new CBP, B_{new}, through the recurrent form of the Erlang-B formula.
(c) Finally, recalculate B_{new} using the recurrent Erlang-B formula only.

(a) From (I.5), we get:

$$B = E_3(2) = \frac{\frac{2^3}{3!}}{\sum\limits_{i=0}^{3} \frac{2^i}{i!}} = \frac{\frac{2^3}{3!}}{\frac{2^0}{0!} + \frac{2^1}{1!} + \frac{2^2}{2!} + \frac{2^3}{3!}} = \frac{\frac{8}{6}}{1 + 2 + 2 + \frac{8}{6}} = \frac{\frac{4}{3}}{\frac{19}{3}} = 21.05\%$$

(b) Having determined $E_3(2) = 21.05\%$, we obtain B_{new} by applying three times (I.8), as follows:

$$E_3(2) = 0.2105$$

$$E_4(2) = \frac{2 \cdot E_3(2)}{4 + 2 \cdot E_3(2)} = \frac{2 \cdot 0.2105}{4 + 2 \cdot 0.2105} = 0.0952 = 9.52\%$$

$$E_5(2) = \frac{2 \cdot E_4(2)}{5 + 2 \cdot E_4(2)} = \frac{2 \cdot 0.0952}{5 + 2 \cdot 0.0952} = 0.0367 = 3.67\%$$

$$B_{new} = E_6(2) = \frac{2 \cdot E_5(2)}{6 + 2 \cdot E_5(2)} = \frac{2 \cdot 0.0367}{6 + 2 \cdot 0.0367} = 0.0121 = 1.21\%$$

(c) Alternatively, starting from $E_0(2) = 1$, and based on the recursion denoted by (I.8), successively we get:

$$E_0(2) = 1$$

$$E_1(2) = \frac{2 \cdot E_0(2)}{1 + 2 \cdot E_0(2)} = \frac{2 \cdot 1}{1 + 2 \cdot 1} = \frac{2}{3} = 66.67\%$$

$$E_2(2) = \frac{2 \cdot E_1(2)}{2 + 2 \cdot E_1(2)} = \frac{2 \cdot 0.6667}{2 + 2 \cdot 0.6667} = 0.4 = 40.00\%$$

$$E_3(2) = \frac{2 \cdot E_2(2)}{3 + 2 \cdot E_2(2)} = \frac{2 \cdot 0.40}{3 + 2 \cdot 0.40} = 0.2105 = 21.05\%$$

$$E_4(2) = \frac{2 \cdot E_3(2)}{4 + 2 \cdot E_3(2)} = \frac{2 \cdot 0.2105}{4 + 2 \cdot 0.2105} = 0.0952 = 9.52\%$$

$$E_5(2) = \frac{2 \cdot E_4(2)}{5 + 2 \cdot E_4(2)} = \frac{2 \cdot 0.0952}{5 + 2 \cdot 0.0952} = 0.0367 = 3.67\%$$

$$B_{new} = E_6(2) = \frac{2 \cdot E_5(2)}{6 + 2 \cdot E_5(2)} = \frac{2 \cdot 0.0367}{6 + 2 \cdot 0.0367} = 0.0121 = 1.21\%$$

I.5 Traffic-load Properties

In teletraffic models, traffic-load is the dominant factor and therefore it is worthwhile to discuss it in depth. Instead of traffic-load, the term *traffic intensity* is used occasionally, with just the same meaning. Important traffic-load properties follow.

(1) If n is the number of calls in a communication system and h their mean holding time, then the traffic-load α will be:

$$\alpha = nh \tag{I.9}$$

From the definition of traffic-load, it follows that dividing the total holding time of all calls by the number of calls yields the mean call holding time. Therefore, the product of the number of calls and their mean holding time provides the total call holding time (per observation interval), which is the traffic-load. If n counts for calls under service only, then the traffic estimated by (I.9) is the carried traffic. If n counts for all call arrivals, then (I.9) stands for the offered traffic.

Example I.7 In the transmission link of Figure I.1, we measure $n = 7$ calls under service within the observation time-interval of 1 hour, while their mean holding time is:

$$h = \frac{15+20+10+30+15+15+15}{7} = \frac{120}{7} \text{ min. Therefore } \alpha = nh = \frac{7}{60} \cdot \frac{120}{7} = 2 \text{ erl.}$$

(2) The traffic-load is equal to the number of calls within an observation time-interval, which is equal to the mean call holding time.
Indeed, when the observation time-interval is h, during which the number of calls in the system is n, then from (I.9), $\alpha = \frac{n}{h} \cdot h = n$. Another way to understand the above statement is by assuming $h = 1$ in (I.9).

Example I.8 Suppose that a telephone office is located in a business region in which the mean call holding time has been estimated to be 100 sec. In telephone offices, a digital switch bears a counter which shows the number of existing connections in the switch. Usually, the counter changes very often. We can measure the (instant) carried traffic in the switch as follows:

According to property (2), we have to measure the number of calls (i.e., connections) in the digital switch within a time-interval of 100 sec. We can measure this number by reading the counter every few seconds (to catch the changes). For instance, we read the counter every 10 sec and record:

20 24 19 22 17 21 20 23 18 16

That is, the mean number of calls in the switch is:

$$n = \frac{20 + 24 + 19 + 22 + 17 + 21 + 20 + 23 + 18 + 16}{10} = \frac{200}{10} = 20 \Rightarrow \alpha = 20 \text{ erl.}$$

(3) The traffic-load carried by a single b.u. expresses the probability that the b.u. is occupied.
By definition, the traffic-load is the percentage of time during which a b.u. is occupied, that is to say the traffic-load equals the probability that the b.u. is occupied. Since the maximum probability is 1, a b.u. can only carry up to 1 erl traffic-load.

Example I.9 A simple way to describe user activity in telecommunications is by expressing the percentage of time that the user is active or idle in a communication system. Equivalently, we refer to the traffic-load offered by a user, or the traffic-load per user, which, of course, cannot exceed 1; usually it is very small (e.g., 0.02 erl).

Table I.1 Measurements on b.u.

Number of occupied b.u.	0	1	2	3
Number of occurrences	55	95	100	50

(4) The traffic-load carried by a group of b.u. is equivalent to the mean number of occupied b.u. (of the particular group).

Assuming that a group of r b.u. carries a traffic-load of α erl, then the mean traffic-load carried per b.u. is $\frac{\alpha}{r}$ erl, which is equivalent to the probability that the b.u. is occupied (based on property (3)). Because of this, according to the probability theory, the mean number of occupied b.u., $\bar{r}$, is calculated by multiplying the total number of trunks r, by the probability of one b.u. being occupied, $\frac{\alpha}{r}$. Thus, $\bar{r} = r \cdot \frac{\alpha}{r} = \alpha$.

Example I.10 Calculate the carried traffic-load, α_c, in a transmission link of 3 b.u., based on the measurements of Table I.1, taken every 1 min within an observation time-interval of 5 hours (i.e., 300 measurements):

The mean number of occupied b.u. according to the measurements is:
$$\bar{r} = \frac{0 \cdot 55 + 1 \cdot 95 + 2 \cdot 100 + 3 \cdot 50}{55 + 95 + 100 + 50} = \frac{445}{300} = 1.48 \Rightarrow \alpha_c = 1.48 \text{ erl.}$$

Example I.11 According to property (4), the knowledge of the carried traffic by a transmission link gives us an estimation of the bandwidth capacity of the link. For example, if the carried traffic is 100 erl, then the link bandwidth capacity is at least 100 b.u.

I.6 Call Arrival Process

Naturally, a call arrival process is the input of a teletraffic model. As will be shown subsequently, there are several processes for call arrival. Herein, we will consider the random call arrival process, explaining what it actually means for a call to be characterized as random from a mathematical point of view. Of course, this characterization will be in accordance with the common sense of randomness. Random arriving calls at a system must meet the following conditions (axioms) for any time interval Δt approaching 0 ($\Delta t \to 0$):

* Calls arrive independent to one another.
* The probability of a call arriving at a system within Δt is proportional to Δt and independent from time t :
  $P_1(t, t + \Delta t] = P_1(\Delta t) \to \lambda \Delta t$, where λ is a proportionality constant. (I.10)
* The probability of two or more calls arriving at a system within Δt approaches zero : $P_{+2}(t, t + \Delta t] = P_{+2}(\Delta t) \to 0$.

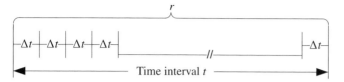

Figure I.3 Call generation process.

Assuming that calls originate from an infinite number of traffic sources (or, in practice, from a number much greater than the system capacity), this is a sufficient condition in order for the first of the above axioms to hold. The second axiom is a logical anticipation expressing the fact that the longer the time interval, the more probable a call arrival is. Although simultaneous arrivals are not excluded from the common sense of randomness, according to the last axiom they are actually excluded because time can be arbitrarily discretized to such an extent that call arrival events can always be at different (distinct) time points.

Knowing the probability of a random arriving call at a system within the infinitesimal time Δt, let us now calculate the probability $P_n(t)$ of n random call arrivals occurring within a much larger time period, $(0, t]$. We proceed by dividing the time interval t into a large number of r equal parts Δt, that is, $\Delta t = \frac{t}{r}$ (Figure I.3).

The probability $P_n^{\text{one}}(t)$ of having exactly one call arrival in n of the r parts and no call arrivals in the $r - n$ remaining parts (i.e., to have n calls in n very small time-intervals) equals:

$$P_n^{\text{one}}(t) = P_1(\Delta t)^n P_0(\Delta t)^{r-n} = P_1(\Delta t)^n [1 - P_1(\Delta t) - P_{+2}(\Delta t)]^{r-n}$$
$$= (\lambda \Delta t)^n (1 - \lambda \Delta t - 0)^{r-n} = \left(\frac{\lambda t}{r}\right)^n \left(1 - \frac{\lambda t}{r}\right)^{r-n} \tag{I.11}$$

There are $\binom{r}{n} = \frac{r!}{n!(r-n)!} = \frac{r(r-1)(r-2)\ldots(r-n+1)}{n!}$ different ways for n parts to be selected among the r parts in which we have divided the period of time t. Therefore the requested probability equals:

$$P_n(t) = \lim_{r \to \infty} \binom{r}{n} P_n^{\text{one}}(t) = \lim_{r \to \infty} \frac{r(r-1)(r-2)\ldots(r-n+1)}{n!} \left(\frac{\lambda t}{r}\right)^n \left(1 - \frac{\lambda t}{r}\right)^{r-n}$$
$$= \lim_{r \to \infty} \frac{r}{r} \frac{r-1}{r} \frac{r-2}{r} \ldots \frac{r-(n-1)}{r} \frac{(\lambda t)^n}{n!} \left(1 - \frac{\lambda t}{r}\right)^{r-n} = \frac{(\lambda t)^n}{n!} \lim_{r \to \infty} \left(1 - \frac{\lambda t}{r}\right)^{r-n} \tag{I.12}$$

or

$$P_n(t) = \frac{(\lambda t)^n}{n!} e^{-\lambda t} \qquad \text{for} \quad n = 0, 1, 2, \ldots \tag{I.13}$$

Equation (I.13) is the famous *Poisson*[6] *distribution*. It is called a distribution since it holds for all integer values of n. As was proved by the derivation of (I.13), random arriving calls follow a Poisson distribution; in other words, the expressions "Poisson distribution" and "random call arrival process" are synonyms. An example of a Poisson process in our daily life is the number of cars reaching the entrance of a narrow tunnel,

---

6 Siméon Denis Poisson, French mathematician and physicist, 1781–1840.

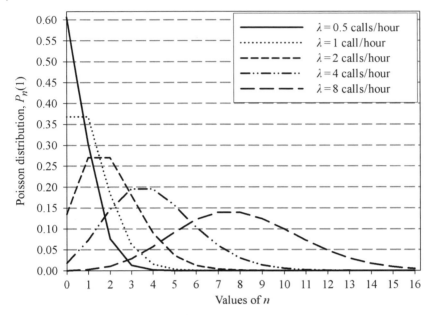

Figure I.4 Poisson distribution with rate λ calls/hour.

but not the number of cars coming out from it because the narrowness of the tunnel disturbs the randomness of the process. Another example is the number of telephone calls reaching the high usage group of trunks of a central office during the busy hour, but not the number of calls being transferred from the high usage group of trunks to an alternative route; the transferring procedure destroys the randomness of the process.

For a Poisson distribution, the mean value equals the variance, λt, where λ is the *arrival rate*. Since this coincidence holds only to a Poisson process among other *counting processes*, it can be used to identify random call arrivals by measuring the mean value and the variance of arrivals. If the unit of measuring time is 1 hour (often referred to as the busy hour), then the call arrival rate is measured in *busy hour call attempts* (BHCA).[7]

Figure I.4 shows graphs of (I.13), i.e., the probability of having n arrivals (number of occurrences) during one hour, for several arrival rates (calls/hour). Note that the graphs are discrete, that is, they are only defined at discrete values of $n = 0, 1, 2, \ldots$; they are shown as continuous for presentation purposes only.

Example I.12 Determine (a) the mean and (b) the variance of the Poisson distribution.

(a) *Mean*: If $p_X(x)$ is the probability mass function of the event x of a discrete random variable (r.v.) X, then the mean value $E[X]$ is determined by:

$$E[X] = \sum_x x p_X(x) \tag{I.14}$$

---

7 Sometimes the arrival rate in BHCA is used to express traffic-load, erroneously, of course.

Table I.2 Measurements of arrivals.

Number of arrivals, n	1	2	3	4	5	6	7	8	9	10	11	12
Number of occurrences, $o(n)$	6	9	30	42	60	36	36	27	24	18	6	6

When $p_X(x)$ follows a Poisson distribution, from (I.13) we get:

$$E[X] = \sum_{n=0}^{\infty} n \frac{(\lambda t)^n}{n!} e^{-\lambda t} = e^{-\lambda t} \sum_{n=1}^{\infty} \frac{(\lambda t)^n}{(n-1)!} =$$
$$= e^{-\lambda t} \lambda t \sum_{n=1}^{\infty} \frac{(\lambda t)^{(n-1)}}{(n-1)!} = e^{-\lambda t} \lambda t e^{\lambda t} = \lambda t \tag{I.15}$$

(b) *Variance*: The variance $Var[X]$ of a r.v. X is determined by:

$$Var[X] = E[X^2] - (E[X])^2 \tag{I.16}$$

To determine the mean value of X^2, we resort to the *moment generating function* $\Phi_X(s)$ of the r.v. X: $\Phi_X(s) = E[e^{sX}]$. For a discrete X, it holds:

$$\Phi_X(s) = \sum_x e^{sx} p_X(x) \tag{I.17}$$

where s is a proper subset of real numbers, so that the summation converges. The following property justifies the name "moment generating", when $m \geq 1$:

$$E[X^m] = \frac{d^m}{ds^m} \Phi_X(s), \qquad \text{for} \quad s = 0. \tag{I.18}$$

The moment generating function for a Poisson distribution is:

$$\Phi_X(s) = \sum_{n=0}^{\infty} e^{sn} \frac{\lambda t}{n!} e^{-\lambda t} = e^{-\lambda t} \sum_{n=0}^{\infty} \frac{(\lambda t e^s)^n}{n!} = e^{-\lambda t} e^{\lambda t e^s} = e^{\lambda t(e^s - 1)} \tag{I.19}$$

From (I.19) we obtain: $\frac{d}{ds} \Phi_X(s) = \lambda t e^s$ and $\frac{d^2}{ds^2} \Phi_X(s) = (\lambda t e^s)^2 + \lambda t e^s$, from which, for $s = 0$, we determine $E[X] = \lambda t$ (true!) and $E[X^2] = (\lambda t)^2 + \lambda t$, respectively. Therefore, from (I.16) we determine $Var[X] = (\lambda t)^2 + \lambda t - (\lambda t)^2 = \lambda t$.

Example I.13 Table I.2 presents measurements of the number of arrivals taken every 1 min within an observation interval of 5 hours (i.e., 300 measurements). Can we assume that the arrivals form a Poisson process?

From Table I.2 we calculate the mean number of arrivals $E[n]$ as: $E[n] = \overline{n} = \frac{\sum_{n=1}^{12} n \cdot o(n)}{\sum_{n=1}^{12} o(n)} = \frac{1800}{300} = 6$ arrivals per minute. Also, we calculate the variance $Var[n]$ as a sample variance:

$$Var[n] = \frac{1}{N-1} \sum_{i=1}^{N} (n_i - \overline{n})^2 \tag{I.20}$$

where $N \equiv$ the total number of measurements (300) and $n_i \equiv$ the ith measurement. From (I.20) we calculate $Var[n] = 6.04$, which is pretty close to the value of $E[n] = 6.0$ and, therefore, the hypothesis that the arrivals form a Poisson process is valid. Otherwise, we should resort to the standard statistical way for hypothesis testing, the *chi-squared test* for goodness of fit [2].

Given that the mean number of calls arriving at a system within the time interval $(0, t]$ and with arrival rate λ is λt, λ can stand for the mean value of n in (I.9) and, therefore, property (1) of traffic-load can be expressed as:

$$\alpha = \lambda h \tag{I.21}$$

Resulting from the Poisson distribution (I.15), the probability of zero call arrivals during the time interval $(0, t]$ is:

$$P_0(t) = \frac{(\lambda t)^0}{0!} e^{-\lambda t} = e^{-\lambda t} \tag{I.22}$$

Therefore the probability of the call *interarrival time* not exceeding t, $I(t)$, is:

$$I(t) = 1 - P_0(t) = 1 - e^{-\lambda t} \tag{I.23}$$

In probability theory, (I.23) is a probability distribution function (PDF) since it gives the probability that a continuous r.v. (in our case, the interarrival time) is no larger than a specific value (t). The derivative of a PDF provides the probability density function (pdf).[8] From (I.23), we obtain $\lambda e^{-\lambda t}$ as the pdf and, therefore, say that the call interarrival time follows the (negative) *exponential distribution* with mean $\frac{1}{\lambda}$.

Example I.14 Determine (a) the mean and (b) the variance of the (negative) exponential distribution $\lambda e^{-\lambda t}$.

The moment generating function for an exponentially distributed r.v. X is determined through (I.17), while substituting the summation with an integral since X is continuous:

$$\Phi_X(s) = \int_{-\infty}^{\infty} e^{sx} \lambda e^{-\lambda x} dx = \int_{0}^{\infty} e^{sx} \lambda e^{-\lambda x} dx = \lambda \int_{0}^{\infty} e^{-(\lambda-s)x} dx = \frac{\lambda}{\lambda - s} \tag{I.24}$$

which holds only if $s < \lambda$.

(a) *Mean*: From (I.24) we obtain $\frac{d}{ds}\Phi_X(s) = \frac{\lambda}{(\lambda-s)^2} \Rightarrow E[X] = \frac{d}{ds}\Phi_X(0) = \frac{1}{\lambda}$.

(b) *Variance*: From $\frac{d^2}{ds^2}\Phi_X(s) = \frac{d}{ds}\frac{\lambda}{(\lambda-s)^2} = \frac{2\lambda}{(\lambda-s)^3} \Rightarrow E[X^2] = \frac{d^2}{ds^2}\Phi_X(0) = \frac{2}{\lambda^2}$. Therefore, from (I.16) we determine $Var[X] = \frac{2}{\lambda^2} - (\frac{1}{\lambda})^2 = \frac{1}{\lambda^2}$.

---

8 The integral of the pdf over a region determines the probability for a continuous r.v. to fall within this region.

The fact that λ is a (time-independent) constant constitutes the first characteristic of a random call arrival process,[9] while its second characteristic is the exponential distribution of call interarrival time. The latter is exploited in time-tracing simulations in order for the notion of time to be introduced in the input process, that is, instead of having a number of calls arriving at random within a time-interval (according to (I.13)), distinct time-points of the arriving calls are considered (according to (I.23)).

I.6.1 Superposition and Decomposition of Poisson Processes

The sum of two independent Poisson processes with rates λ_1 and λ_2 forms a Poisson process with rate $\lambda_1 + \lambda_2$. It can readily be proved based on an easy-to-prove property of the moment generating function. The property says that the moment generating function $\Phi_{X+Y}(s)$ of the sum of two independent r.v.s X and Y is the product of the individual generating functions, $\Phi_X(s)$ and $\Phi_Y(s)$:

$$\Phi_{X+Y}(s) = E[e^{s(X+Y)}] = E[e^{sX}e^{sY}] = E[e^{sX}]E[e^{sY}] = \Phi_X(s)\Phi_Y(s). \tag{I.25}$$

This property can be verified for Poisson processes, according to (I.19):

$$\Phi_X(s)\Phi_Y(s) = e^{\lambda_1 t(e^s - 1)}e^{\lambda_2 t(e^s - 1)} = e^{(\lambda_1 + \lambda_2)t(e^s - 1)} = \Phi_{X+Y}(s).$$

Example I.15 From two independent Poisson processes X and Y with respective rates λ_1 and λ_2, a Poisson process $X + Y$ is formed with rate $\lambda_1 + \lambda_2$. Show that the conditional distribution of X given the sum $X + Y$ is a binomial distribution.

The conditional probability of having $X = r$ arrivals (within a time-interval t) given that the total arrivals are $X + Y = n$ is:

$$P[X = r \mid X + Y = n] = \frac{P[X = r \cap X + Y = n]}{P[X + Y = n]} = \frac{P[X = r \cap Y = n - r]}{P[X + Y = n]}$$

$$= \frac{(\lambda_1 t)^r e^{-\lambda_1 t}}{r!} \frac{(\lambda_2 t)^{n-r} e^{-\lambda_2 t}}{(n - r)!} \bigg/ \frac{((\lambda_1 + \lambda_2)t)^n e^{(-\lambda_1 - \lambda_2)t}}{n!} \tag{I.26}$$

$$= \frac{n!}{r!(n - r)!} \frac{(\lambda_1 t)^r (\lambda_2 t)^{n-r}}{(\lambda_1 t + \lambda_2 t)^r (\lambda_1 t + \lambda_2 t)^{n-r}} = \binom{n}{r} p^r (1 - p)^{n-r}$$

which is a binomial distribution with parameters n and $p = \frac{\lambda_1 t}{\lambda_1 t + \lambda_2 t}$.

The sum can be extended to r independent Poisson processes with rates λ_i, $i = 1, 2, \ldots, r$, and form a Poisson process with rate $\lambda = \lambda_1 + \lambda_2 + \cdots + \lambda_r$, as denoted in the LHS of Figure I.5 by the term *superposition*. Only the superposition of Poisson processes results in a Poisson process. The RHS of Figure I.5 shows the reverse procedure, which is called *decomposition* and can be considered a consequence of the superposition. A Poisson process of rate λ is decomposed into a number of r sub-processes, which are also Poisson processes. More precisely, Poisson arrivals split at point D (RHS of Figure I.5) to r subsequent routes; each route i ($i = 1, 2, \ldots, r$) is

---

9 Also named Poisson input, or Poisson arrival process, or simply Poisson process.

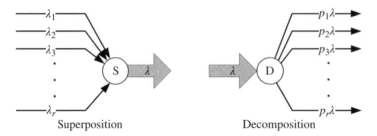

Figure I.5 Superposition and decomposition of Poisson processes.

selected with a probability p_i ($\sum_i p_i = 1$). In this way, a Poisson process results in route i with rate $p_i \lambda$.

Random selection is a different way to express the decomposition property of Poisson arrivals (with rate λ). Suppose that an arrival is selected at random with probability p. By this selection, a Poisson process is formed with rate $p\lambda$, while the remaining arrivals also constitute a Poisson process with rate $(1 - p)\lambda$.

I.6.2   Poisson Arrivals See Time Averages

In (I.3), various expressions of GoS, B, are mentioned. The first measures congestion and estimates B by the percentage of time during which the system is congested, while the second expression estimates B by counting the number of lost calls (due to congestion) over the total number of offered calls. First of all, one may observe that the first measure of B is appropriate for an outside observer of the system, while the second measure of B is appropriate for an inside observer, that is, for an arrival. In general, these two measures do not result in the same value of B. However, in the case of Poisson arrivals an inside observer measures the same value of B as that of an outside observer, who determines time averages. Therefore, we say that *Poisson arrivals see time averages (PASTA)*.[10] As far as the third expression of B is concerned, i.e., the probability of congestion, this means that B can be estimated by all the ways that a probability is estimated, as, for instance, by the relative frequency.

Example I.16   Equation (I.27) shows definitions whereby we can understand the different estimation of B by an inside and an outside observer of the system:

$$B \equiv \Pi_C = Prob\{C \mid \text{upon a call arrival}\} \qquad \text{versus} \qquad B \equiv P_C \qquad (I.27)$$

An arriving call finds the system congested (C b.u. are occupied) at the time-point of its arrival, therefore a conditional probability (Π_C) should be used for CBP calculation by an inside observer. Instead, an outside observer calculates the unconditional probability of C occupied b.u. (P_C).

Example I.17   In a system with periodic arrivals (non-Poisson) with time-period T, the service time lasts exactly for $T/2$. Show that PASTA does not hold.

---

10 In queuing networks, when non-Poisson arrivals see time averages is called ASTA.

For an observation interval T, an outside observer counts $B = 50\%$, since for half of this interval the system is occupied. An inside observer, however (i.e., a periodic arrival), finds the system always empty, and thus $B = 0\%$.

I.7 Call Service Time

After having studied the call arrival process, the call service time distribution is examined. In a loss system, an accepted call enters service immediately, and when service is completed, the call immediately departs from the system. Let us concentrate on random departures. For a random call departure within an infinitesimal time-interval Δt, the same three conditions hold axiomatically, as in the case of a random call arrival. Therefore, the probability of a particular call departure from the system in a period of time $(t, t + \Delta t]$ is proportional to Δt for any time t, with a proportionality constant μ. Of course, this departure occurs independently from other in-service calls, while the probability of simultaneous departures (two or more in Δt) is zero.

Based on these considerations, it is easy to determine the probability of call service time exceeding t, as it equals the probability of a call not departing from the system within the time interval $(0, t]$. Since we know that when referring to the infinitesimal time Δt the said probability equals $(1 - \mu\Delta t)$, we divide the time interval $(0, t]$ into a relatively great number of r equal parts Δt, as in Figure I.3, where $\Delta t = \frac{t}{r}$, $r \to \infty$. Then, the probability of call service time exceeding t, $S(t)$, will be:

$$S(t) = \lim_{r \to \infty} (1 - \mu \frac{t}{r})^r = e^{-\mu t} \tag{I.28}$$

The PDF of call service time, that is, the probability of call service time not exceeding t is $1 - S(t) = 1 - e^{-\mu t} \Rightarrow \mathrm{pdf} = \mu e^{-\mu t}$. Hence, the call service time is exponentially distributed with mean $h = \frac{1}{\mu}$, where μ is the *service rate* or *departure rate*. Based on μ, we write (I.21) as follows (the offered traffic-load is the ratio of the rates):[11]

$$\alpha = \frac{\lambda}{\mu} \tag{I.29}$$

Figure I.6 shows the graph of (I.28) for normalized values of time over h. When $t = h$, we get the probability of holding time to exceed its mean value; it is $S(1) = e^{-1} = 36.79\%$.

I.7.1 Markov Property

The *Markov property* is also known as the *memoryless property*, which is a much more descriptive term. To present the property, let us consider the duration of a process X (r.v.) (Figure I.7). If the r.v. X follows an exponential distribution, as happens to the call service time, with mean $h = \frac{1}{\mu}$, then we know that the probability of the said process exceeding time t is given by $P[X > t] = e^{-\mu t}$.

---

11 Mnemonic rule: all symbols are Greek letters; note that λ and μ are successive letters in the Greek alphabet.

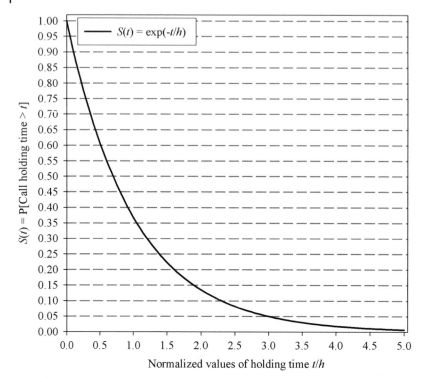

Figure I.6 Exponential distribution $e^{-\mu t}$.

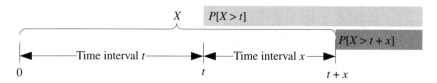

Figure I.7 Markov/memoryless property.

The question is, what is the probability of the process exceeding more time, $t + x$, given that it has already lasted up to the time instant t? Here is the answer:

$$
P[X > t + x | X > t] = \frac{P[X > t + x \cap X > t]}{P[X > t]} = \frac{P[X > t + x]}{P[X > t]} =
$$

$$
= \frac{e^{-\mu(t+x)}}{e^{-\mu t}} \qquad\qquad = e^{-\mu x} \qquad\qquad = P[X > x]
$$

(I.30)

Equation (I.30) says that the given information at time instant t is useless, since the conditional probability becomes unconditional. The process X has evolved to the time instant t; at this point we try to estimate the future behavior of the process. Equation (I.30) shows that the knowledge of the past does not influence the future. The probability that X will last more than the time instant $t + x$ depends only on the present, and therefore only on the anticipated time interval x (Figure I.7). This is the meaning of the memoryless property. A stochastic process[12] with this property is called the *Markov process*.

Example I.18 In a loss system, the mean call service time is 2 min. A call is under service for 4 min.

(a) What is the probability of the call lasting at least 4 min more?
(b) What is the probability of departure within the next 4 min?

(a) $P[X > (4 + 4) \mid X > 4] = P[X > 4] = e^{-\frac{1}{2}4} = 0.135 = 13.5\%.$
(b) $P[X \leq 4] = 1 - P[X > 4] = 1 - 0.135 = 0.865 = 86.5\%.$

The Markov/memoryless property comes out as a special characteristic of the exponential distribution. The latter appears not only in random call service time but also in random call arrivals when considering interarrival times, therefore both these processes (input and service) are Markov processes. Systems in which all processes are Markov processes are called *Markovian systems* or, comprehensively, *Markovian models*.

In this book, we especially concentrate on a Markov process $X(t)$ which changes one step at a time and is called the *birth-death process*. Its mathematical definition is:

$$P[\,X(t + \Delta t) = i \mid X(t) = j\,] = \begin{cases} \lambda_j \Delta t & \text{if} \quad i = j + 1 \\ \mu_j \Delta t & \text{if} \quad i = j - 1 \\ 0 & \text{if} \quad |i - j| \geq 2 \end{cases} \qquad i, j = 0, 1, 2, \ldots$$

(I.31)

where λ_j and μ_j are the birth and death rates, respectively.

I.8 Service Systems

Figure I.8 shows the representation of the two basic service systems: the loss system on the LHS and the queuing system on the RHS. As shown, they could be of open or closed loop type.

The core system has a capacity of C trunks (b.u.). An arrival reaching the input must access at least one free trunk in order to be serviced with a service rate μ. If it is possible to access any free trunk, the system is called a *full availability* system; otherwise it is called a *restricted availability* system. Figure I.8 shows full availability service systems.

Example I.19 In Figure I.9, the LHS system is an example of a full availability system. There is a (4×4) switch, where all outputs are accessible from all inputs. At the RHS, the (4×4) switch is an example of a restricted availability system. Only the first two inputs can access all four outputs; the last two inputs can access only two outputs.

---

12 A set of r.v.s which usually represent the evolution of a system over time.

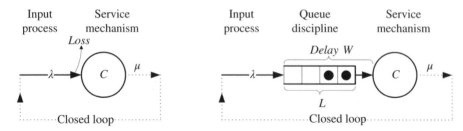

Figure I.8 Representation of service systems.

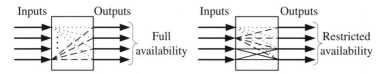

Figure I.9 Service systems of full and restricted availability (Example I.19).

As well as the schematic representation of a service system, a descriptive representation can be made using *Kendall's notation*,[13] which is mainly used to cover queuing systems:

$$A/B/C/D \quad E$$

A ≡ input process or interarrival time distribution
B ≡ service time distribution
C ≡ system capacity
D ≡ maximum number of calls in the system (in service + waiting)
E ≡ queuing discipline

The usual symbols for A and B are M for exponential (Markov), D for deterministic (fixed), G for general (arbitrary), and E for Erlang, $M(N)$ for a quasi-random input process in which the traffic-source population is N[14]. The default value of D is ∞ and refers to the queue size (waiting places in the queue). The default queuing discipline is first in, first out (FIFO), while other values of E could be random early detection (RED), last in, first out (LIFO), service in random order (SIRO), etc.

Example I.20 Examples of Kendall's notation, with which we can describe service systems, are:

- $M/M/1$ queue or $M/M/1$ FIFO: A single-server system with infinite queue size. The system accepts Poisson arrivals, while the service time is exponentially distributed.
- $M/M/\infty$: A Poisson model.
- $M/M/C/C$: An Erlang model (loss system – the Erlang-B formula is applicable).
- $M(N)/M/C/C$: An Engset model, $C < N$ (loss system).
- $M(C)/M/C/C$: A binomial model (lossless system – as many servers as traffic sources).

---

13 David George Kendall (1918–2007), English mathematician, who published the notation in 1953.
14 Because of the non-infinite population, the assumption of independent call arrivals does not hold, but the other two axioms of random call arrivals hold.

The last two cases are examples of closed-loop service systems (in order to show that the number of traffic sources is not infinite, but restricted).

I.9 Little's Law

In a delay system (RHS of Figure I.8), under steady state[15] conditions, if λ is the mean call arrival rate and W is the mean call waiting time in the queue (delay before service), then the mean number L of calls queuing for service is given by the following simple formula:

$$L = \lambda W \tag{I.32}$$

Thanks to its simplicity, but mostly because it is valid for all queuing systems regardless of the input process, service mechanism, or queue discipline, (I.32) is called *Little's law*.[16] Surprisingly, it is not required to know how much the system capacity is, whether there is a common queue, or if each trunk is fed by its own queue, or what the interarrival and service time distributions are, etc.

Proof: At first, in the RHS of (I.32), the traffic-load property (1) appears to repeat itself (e.g., (I.21)). This, however, is not entirely accurate, since L in the LHS of (I.32) is an amount measured by an external observer, while W is an amount that can be measured by those in queue. Because of this situation, the proof of Little's law requires numerous analyses; based on the traffic-load properties, however, they can be avoided as follows (according to [3]). The mean call waiting time in the queue, W, can also be thought of as the mean service time in a group of trunks, that is, the waiting places of the queue. Then, the RHS of (I.32) gives the traffic-load carried by this group of trunks and, because of property (4) of traffic-load, it equals the mean number of occupied trunks, thus, in this case, the mean number L of calls in the queue (assuming that one call occupies one waiting place).

Q.E.D.

Example I.21 In an access network, four traffic flows arrive with mean rate $\lambda_1 = 100$, $\lambda_2 = 200$, $\lambda_3 = 300$, and $\lambda_4 = 400$ packets/sec. The number of packets measured in this access network is 1000 packets on average. What is the average time taken for a packet to access this network?

The access network can be thought of as a queuing system accepting all four traffic flows, as illustrated in Figure I.10. Thus, the total arrival rate is $\lambda = 100 + 200 + 300 + 400 = 1000$ packets/sec, while the average number of packets in the access network stands for the mean number of packets queuing there, that is, $L = 1000$, and the average time for a packet to access the network is given by W, through Little's law: $W = \frac{L}{\lambda} = \frac{1000}{1000}$ sec = 1 sec.

---

15 After a long run of the system, not in a transition state.
16 John D.C. Little (1928–), a physicist from Boston (USA), published the formula in 1961.

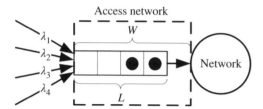

Access network

W

L

Network

λ_1
λ_2
λ_3
λ_4

Figure I.10 An access network as a queuing system (Example I.21).

Furthermore, on average, the total sojourn time of a call in a service system, T, and the total number of calls in the system, $\overline{N}$, are related to the arrival rate λ, as follows:

$$\overline{N} = \lambda T \tag{I.33}$$

Equation (I.32) is called an *extension of Little's law* and can be readily derived, thinking that T equals the mean waiting time W plus the mean service time h, and $\overline{N}$ is the number of calls waiting in the queue (L) plus the number of in-service calls, which equals the carried traffic-load according to property (4) of traffic-load. Thus, the RHS of (I.32) becomes $\lambda(W + h) = \lambda W + \lambda h = L + \alpha = \overline{N}$.

Example I.22   As a continuation of Example I.21, what is the total number of packets $\overline{N}$ in the access network and in the network if it is assumed that the mean life cycle of a packet in the network is 1 sec?

Through the extension of Little's law, we get $\overline{N} = \lambda T = \lambda(W + h) = 1000(1 + 1) = 2000$ packets, or $\overline{N} = L + \alpha = L + \lambda h = 1000 + 1000 \cdot 1 = 2000$ packets.

I.10   Other Performance Metrics of Loss Systems

Other than the GoS (B), the following performance metrics are usually considered and are very similar to each other:

- Utilization: The average number of occupied b.u. in the system is called *utilization*, U, and it is equal to the traffic-load carried by the system. This is in accordance with property (4) of traffic-load:

$$U = \alpha_c = \alpha(1 - B) \tag{I.34}$$

- Trunk efficiency: The average traffic-load carried per trunk in a system of C trunks is called *trunk efficiency*, η. Since U is the carried traffic-load by the whole system capacity of C trunks, the carried traffic-load per trunk will be U/C. Therefore:

$$\eta = \frac{U}{C} = \frac{\alpha(1 - B)}{C} \tag{I.35}$$

- Throughput: The percentage of the occupied b.u. over the system capacity is called *throughput*, T_h. On average, T_h coincides with η. However, T_h can be an instantaneous (not an average) quantity.

I.11   General Examples

The aim of the following examples is to show that although we have covered only the introductory part of teletraffic theory, many engineering problems can be answered.

Example I.23   During the busy hour, 1200 calls are offered to a transmission link, but six of them are not conveyed (are lost). The mean call holding time is 3 min. Estimate:

(a) the offered traffic-load
(b) the carried traffic
(c) the lost traffic
(d) the GoS.

(a) *Offered traffic-load*: According to (I.21), the offered traffic-load is:

$$\alpha = \lambda h = \frac{1200}{60} \, 3 = 60\text{erl}$$

(b) *Carried traffic*: According to (I.9), the carried traffic is:

$$\alpha_c = nh = \frac{1200 - 6}{60} \, 3 = 59.7\text{erl}$$

(c) *Lost traffic*: The lost traffic is determined by (I.1):

$$\alpha_{\text{lost}} = \alpha - \alpha_c = 0.3\text{erl}$$

Alternatively, it is determined based on (I.9) from the number of calls lost (during the busy hour) multiplied by the expected holding time, if they were served:

$$\alpha_{\text{lost}} = \frac{6}{60} \, 3 = 0.3\text{erl}$$

(d) *GoS*: According to (I.2a), the GoS, B, is:

$$B = \frac{\text{total number of lost calls}}{\text{total number of offered calls}} = \frac{6}{1200} = 0.5\%$$

or, according to (I.2b):

$$B = \frac{\text{lost traffic}}{\text{offered traffic}} = \frac{0.3}{60} = 0.5\%$$

Example I.24   In the transmission link of three trunks in Example I.10, we determined the carried traffic-load 1.48 erl. Also, in addition to the measurements of Table I.1, consider one more measurement: 25 arriving calls were blocked and lost during the observation time-interval of 5 hours.

(a) What is the GoS in this link?
(b) What is the offered traffic-load to the link?
(c) Although none of the measurements on this link includes time, can the mean call holding time be estimated?

(a) *GoS:* The GoS is the probability of congestion B, i.e., the probability that the transmission link is completely occupied, which is expressed by the relative frequency of 50 over 300 times: $B = \frac{50}{300} = 16.67\%$.

(b) *Carried traffic-load:* From (I.4): $\alpha_c = \alpha(1 - B) \Rightarrow \alpha = \frac{\alpha_c}{1-B} = \frac{1.48}{0.83} = 1.78$ erl.

(c) *Mean holding time:* According to (I.9), if n counts for the number of calls under service within 5 hours, then: $\alpha_c = nh \Rightarrow h = \frac{\alpha_c}{n}$.

To estimate n, resort to (I.2a) in order to determine, first, the total number of offered calls, N, which is $B = \frac{\text{Total number of lost calls}}{N} \Rightarrow N = \frac{25}{0.1667} \simeq 150$ calls, and then $n = N - 25 = 125$ calls. Finally, $h = \frac{1.48}{125/5}$ hours $\simeq 3.55$ min.

Example I.25 Consider a cell of a mobile telephone network. Call connection requests arrive in the base station (BS) from: (i) new call arrivals and (ii) *handover calls*, i.e., calls already connected to a neighboring cell which, because of their mobility, arrive in the cell. Obviously, the BS should give priority to handover calls in order to be served without interruption. Suppose that handover calls are not blocked. Every accepted call in the cell occupies a free channel (trunk). Measurements during the busy hour in the cell have shown a total number of 52 in-service calls (on average), mean call holding time of 1.64 min (regardless of the type of calls, i.e., new or handover), and losses of 2% (over new call connection requests). The mean interarrival time of new calls is 3 sec. What are the arrival rates of new and handover calls?

Let us express by "known" symbols the variables of the problem:
$\overline{N} = 52$, $T = 1.64$ min, $B = 0.02$, $\lambda_{\text{new}} \equiv$ the arrive rate of new calls, $\lambda_{\text{hand}} \equiv$ the arrive rate of handover calls, and $B_{new} \equiv$ GoS of new calls.
The arrival rate of new calls is given as $\lambda_{\text{new}} = \frac{60}{3} = 20$ calls/min.
The total arrival rate in the cell is $\lambda_{\text{new}} + \lambda_{\text{hand}}$.
Because of losses, the call acceptance rate is $\lambda = \lambda_{\text{new}}(1 - B) + \lambda_{\text{hand}}$.
Through (I.33), we get $\lambda = \frac{\overline{N}}{T} \Rightarrow \lambda_{\text{hand}} = \frac{\overline{N}}{T} - \lambda_{\text{new}}(1 - B) \Rightarrow$
$\lambda_{\text{hand}} = \frac{52}{1.64} - 20(1 - 0.02) = 12.1$ calls/min.

I.12   Service-classes – Bandwidth Sharing Policies

A *service-class*[17] is a class of calls with the same traffic characteristics. We use the term service-class to classify calls to service categories, according to the required number of b.u., that is, a service-class consists of calls which require the same number of b.u. Since this book is targeted to teletraffic loss models for multiple service-classes, we have to discuss different policies whereby the bandwidth capacity of a system can be allocated to a service-class. The prerequisites are:

- The system capacity is restricted to C b.u.
- The number of service-classes, K, is fixed.

---

17 Also called a *traffic stream* by the ITU-T.

- Each service-class call $k, (k = 1, 2, \ldots, K)$ requires b_k b.u. upon arrival in order to be served.
- A call is accepted if any b_k b.u. are available in the system; otherwise the call is blocked and lost. Contiguous assignment of b.u. is not required. The call departs from the system after having completed service, and the assigned b.u. become immediately available to a new call.

The most common bandwidth sharing policy is the *complete sharing* (CS) policy. It is characterized as complete, since the only restriction is the "complete" system capacity C. Let n_k denote the number of calls of service-class k in the system, in steady state. The total number of calls in the system is denoted by the vector $\mathbf{n} = (n_1, n_2, \ldots, n_k, \ldots, n_K)$. Vector n denotes a system state. Vector $\mathbf{b} = (b_1, b_2, \ldots, b_k, \ldots, b_K)$ denotes the required b.u. per call of each service-class.

Let Ω denote the set of all possible states of the system. The set Ω, also called the *state space*, strongly depends on the bandwidth sharing policy. For the CS policy, we have:

$$\Omega = \{\mathbf{n} : 0 \leq \mathbf{nb} \leq C\} \tag{I.36}$$

where $\mathbf{nb} = \sum_{k=1}^{K} n_k b_k$, that is, in state $\mathbf{n}$ there are n_1 calls occupying b_1 b.u. per call of service-class 1, n_2 calls occupying b_2 b.u. per call of service-class 2, etc.

Example I.26 Let $C = 8$ b.u., $K = 2$, $b_1 = 1$ b.u., $b_2 = 2$ b.u. and a system state is (n_1, n_2). The set Ω consists of all pairs of integers (n_1, n_2) that satisfy (I.36):

$$n_1 b_1 + n_2 b_2 \leq C \;\Rightarrow\; n_1 + 2b_2 \leq 8.$$

Ω is shown in Figure I.11 as a set of 25 bullets; each bullet stands for (n_1, n_2).

The CS policy is an easy to apply policy and can be taken as the default policy, but it has the following drawbacks in comparison to other policies. Although it seems that under the CS policy the bandwidth is efficiently utilized, because all b.u. are shared to all calls of all service-classes, this is not true in the multi-service environment. Also, as it is explained below, in the multi-service environment the absence of a kind of arbitration leads to an unfair bandwidth allocation among service-classes.

The so-called *complete sharing with an ordering constraint* policy seems to be similar to the CS policy, but peculiar conditions appear, as explained in Example I.27. The system capacity is completely shared among the service-classes along with a restriction that $n_k b_k \leq n_{k+1} b_{k+1}$. The set Ω is:

$$\Omega = \{\mathbf{n} : 0 \leq \mathbf{nb} \leq C, \; n_k b_k \leq n_{k+1} b_{k+1}, \quad k = 1, 2, \ldots, K-1\} \tag{I.37}$$

Figure I.11 The CS policy (Example I.26).

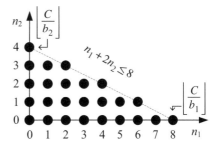

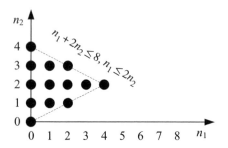

Figure I.12 A CS policy with ordering constraint (Example I.27).

Example I.27   Let $C = 8$ b.u., $K = 2$, $b_1 = 1$ b.u., $b_2 = 2$ b.u., and $n_1 \leq 2n_2$. The set Ω is graphically shown in Figure I.12. Since the restriction $(n_1 \leq 2n_2)$ must hold at any time, service-class 2 calls may delay their departure from the system! For instance, a service-class 2 call that completes its service cannot depart from state $(3, 2)$ unless the system state becomes $(2, 2)$, that is, after the service completion of a service-class 1 call.

On the other side of the CS policy is the *complete partitioning* policy, where a part of the system capacity is allocated to each service-class so that $n_k b_k \leq C_k$, $k = 1, 2, \ldots, K$, and $C_1 + C_2 + \cdots + C_k + \cdots + C_K = C$. The only benefit of this policy is to guarantee a certain GoS to a service-class, since a certain amount of bandwidth is dedicated to the service-class. However, this dedication causes resource management (and bandwidth control) problems in a multi-service environment and must be avoided.

The *threshold* (*TH*) policy combines the advantage of the complete partitioning policy for bandwidth guarantee with the unrestricted sharing of the CS policy through the following definition of Ω:

$$\Omega = \{\mathbf{n} : 0 \leq \mathbf{nb} \leq C = \sum_{k=1}^{K} C_k + C_0, \ 0 \leq n_k b_k \leq C_k + C_0, \quad k = 1, 2, \ldots, K \ \}$$

(I.38)

When $C_k = 0$, for all $k = 1, 2, \ldots, K$, then the CS policy arises. When $C_0 = 0$, then the complete partitioning policy arises.

Example I.28   A link of bandwidth capacity $C = 8$ b.u. accommodates $K = 2$ service-classes with $b_1 = 1$ b.u. and $b_2 = 2$ b.u. Let us split the capacity C to $C_0 = 4, C_1 = 2$, and $C_2 = 2$ b.u. Devote C_1 b.u. to service-class 1, and C_2 b.u. to service-class 2; C_0 b.u. are commonly shared. The set Ω is graphically shown in Figure I.13.

A favorite policy in the multi-service environment is the *bandwidth reservation* (*BR*) policy.[18] According to the BR policy, the system capacity is shared among service-classes in such a way that each service-class meets its own bandwidth capacity. An amount of t_k b.u. is reserved by the system so that service-class k meets $C - t_k$ b.u. as a system capacity. Although the parameters t_k can be arbitrarily defined (so that a reasonable

---

18 The BR policy coincides with the well-known *trunk reservation* method, which is applied in telephone networks for traffic savings in routing, and the *guard channel* policy to improve CBP of handover calls in a cell.

Figure I.13 The TH policy (Example I.28).

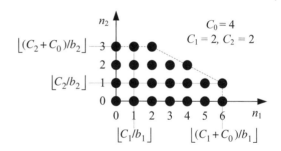

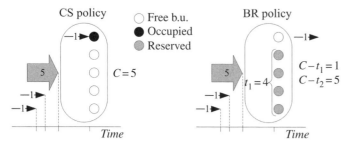

CS policy · Free b.u. · BR policy

○ Free b.u.
● Occupied
◐ Reserved

Figure I.14 Comparison of the BR policy with the CS policy (Example I.29).

amount of bandwidth capacity arises for each service-class), they are usually chosen in accordance to the required bandwidth per call for each service-class so that $b_1 + t_1 = b_2 + t_2 = \cdots = b_k + t_k = \cdots = b_K + t_K$. In this case, GoS equalization is achieved among service-classes ($B_1 = B_2 = \cdots = B_k = \cdots = B_K$). We always consider this case of the BR policy in this book (even if it is not explicitly mentioned). The set Ω of the BR policy is:

$$\Omega = \{\mathbf{n} : 0 \leq \mathbf{nb} \leq C - t_k, \ \forall k, \quad b_i + t_i = b_k + t_k, \quad i \neq k, \quad i, k = 1, 2, \dots, K\}$$

(I.39)

Example I.29 Consider a system of $C = 5$ b.u. that accommodates two service-classes with bandwidth per call requirements $b_1 = 1$ b.u. and $b_2 = 5$ b.u., respectively. Explain why $B_1 < B_2$ under the CS policy and why $B_1 = B_2$ under the BR policy.

When the system operates under the CS policy, as the LHS of Figure I.14 portrays, there is a little chance for a service-class 2 call to be serviced (although only one call of service-class 1 is under service) because it requires the entire system capacity of 5 b.u. The thin arrows bearing "1" stand for service-class 1 calls, whereas the thick arrow bearing "5" stands for a service-class 2 call. Instead, service-class 1 calls enjoy service. It is intuitively understood that under the CS policy, $B_1 \ll B_2$.

When the system operates under the BR policy so that $B_1 = B_2$, $t_1 = 4$ b.u. are reserved by the system to benefit service-class 2, while $t_2 = 0$ b.u. ($b_1 + t_1 = b_2 + t_2 = 5$). In this way, service-class 1 meets the system with a capacity of $C - t_1 = 1$ b.u., while service-class 2 meets the system with a capacity of $C - t_2 = 5$ b.u. As the RHS of Figure I.14 portrays, the system capacity (free b.u.) under the BR policy actually consists of just 1 b.u. To simplify the matter, consider the same arrival rate between the service-classes, even for different offered traffic-loads. Then, when the b.u. is free, there is a 50% chance of being occupied by a service-class 1 call and a 50% chance of being occupied by a service-class 2 call; the latter is now possible because the system has reserved four more b.u. to benefit service-class 2, exclusively. Moreover, the success of the one service-class is the failure of the other service-class. Therefore, $B_1 = B_2$. Note that $B_1 + P[\text{empty system}] = 1$ (for this particular system). By the way, it is worthwhile understanding that the offered traffic-load (or the call arrival rate) of each service-class does not influence the CBP relation of the service-classes, since CBP is a ratio (of either calls or traffic-loads); only the number of blocking states influences the CBP relation among the service-classes.

Figure I.15 graphically presents the set Ω under the CS and BR policies. Under the CS policy the system has seven states, while under the BR policy it has just three states. Based on Ω we can show for this extreme system in a more concrete way that the BR policy results in $B_1 = B_2$, whereas under the CS policy $B_1 < B_2$ is always true, given that $b_1 < b_2$.

Suppose that the probability $P(n_1, n_2)$ of being in state (n_1, n_2) is known for every state in Ω. Call blocking occurs when the system is full or when the number of available b.u. is not enough to serve a call upon arrival (in this example, a call of service-class 2). Thus, under the CS policy, call blocking of service-class 1 occurs in states $(5, 0)$ and $(0, 1)$ where the system is full. Therefore,

$$B_1 = P(5, 0) + P(0, 1)$$

Call blocking of service-class 2 occurs not only when the system is full, i.e., in states $(5, 0), (0, 1)$, but also in states $(1, 0), (2, 0), (3, 0), (4, 0)$. So,

$$B_2 = B_1 + P(1, 0) + P(2, 0) + P(3, 0) + P(4, 0)$$

which clearly proves that $B_1 < B_2$.

Under the BR policy, according to the set Ω, call blocking of service-class 1 occurs in state $(1, 0)$ because of the reservation of 4 b.u. (to benefit service-class 2), and in state $(0, 1)$ where the system is full. Thus,

$$B_1 = P(1, 0) + P(0, 1)$$

Call blocking of service-class 2 occurs in states $(0, 1)$ (system full) and $(1, 0)$ (not enough b.u. for service-class 2). So,

$$B_2 = P(0, 1) + P(1, 0)$$

That is, $B_1 = B_2$.

Having the graphical representation of Ω, we distinguish the state space of a system into two categories according to their shape:

- *Coordinate convex state space*: The orthogonal projections from any state n to the coordinate axes are on states which belong to Ω. More precisely, if $n \in \Omega$ with $n_k \geq 1$, then $\mathbf{n}_k^- = (n_1, n_2, \ldots, n_{k-1}, n_k - 1, n_{k+1}, \ldots, n_K) \in \Omega$, $\forall\, k = 1, 2, \ldots, K$.

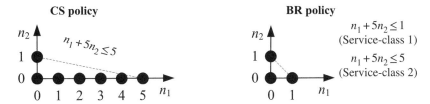

Figure I.15 System states in the CS and the BR policies (Example I.29).

- *Non-coordinate convex state space*: The orthogonal projections from any state n to the coordinate axes are on states which do not necessarily belong to Ω.

Example I.30 Figures I.11, I.13, and I.15 show examples of coordinate convex state spaces, while Figure I.12 presents an example of a non-coordinate convex policy.

For instance, from any state of Figure I.11 or Figure I.13 with $n_k \geq 1$, say $(3, 2)$ where $n_2 = 2$, both $(3, 1) \in \Omega$ and $(3, 0) \in \Omega$. On the contrary, in Figure I.12, the corresponding states $(3, 1) \notin \Omega$ and $(3, 0) \notin \Omega$. As discussed in Example I.27, a call while being in such a state (e.g., $(3, 2)$) of a non-coordinate convex state-space may delay its departure from the system.

A coordinate convex state-space has the following essential and desired features:

(a) *No blocking at call departure*: Calls that have completed their service and are ready to depart from the system are not blocked.
(b) *Call/connection admission control* (*CAC*): A new call of service-class k that finds the system in state $\mathbf{n} \in \Omega$ is accepted in the system if $\mathbf{n}_k^+ \in \Omega$, where $\mathbf{n}_k^+ = (n_1, n_2, \ldots, n_{k-1}, n_k + 1, n_{k+1}, \ldots, n_K) \ \forall \ k = 1, 2, \ldots, K$.
(c) *Product form solution* (*PFS*): The probability $P(\mathbf{n})$ that the system is in state $\mathbf{n}$ in steady state has a PFS for any value of $\mathbf{n} \in \Omega$. PFS means that $P(\mathbf{n})$ is determined as the product of K factors. This is possible because n is composed of K subcomponents:

$$P(\mathbf{n}) \equiv P(n_1, n_2, \ldots, n_k, \ldots, n_K) = \frac{\prod_{k=1}^{K} f(P(n_k))}{G} \tag{I.40}$$

where $f(P(n_k))$ is a function of the probability that the system is in state n_k, if only one service-class k is accommodated in the system; G is the normalization condition so that $\sum_{\mathbf{n} \in \Omega} P(\mathbf{n}) = 1$.
We further explain PFS mainly in Sections 1.2.1 and 1.2.2.1 of Part I.

According to the above discussion, in this book we concentrate on the CS policy, since it is the default policy, and on the BR policy because it is a sine qua non policy in the multi-service environment. A few models are presented that assume the TH policy. Needless to say, different teletraffic models are required for a service-system with different bandwidth sharing policies.

I.13 Classification of Teletraffic Loss Models

After having presented the preliminaries of teletraffic theory, we now proceed with the classification of teletraffic loss models, as they are presented in the following chapters of this book, apart from the distinction according to the aforementioned bandwidth sharing policies. For the models classification, three are the key considerations:

(a) the call arrival process
(b) the service-classes
(c) the behavior of in-service calls regarding the amount of occupied b.u. per call over time.

A call plays a dominant role in a teletraffic model, so different call characteristics lead to different teletraffic models. In what follows we describe in more detail several call attributes, each of which leads to a different teletraffic model (presented in this book).

- According to the arrival process (Figure I.16), calls are classified as:
  (i) random calls: random traffic (infinite number of traffic sources)
  (ii) quasi-random calls: quasi-random traffic (finite number of traffic sources)
  (iii) batch Poisson arrivals (infinite number of traffic sources), with calls from different service-classes arriving in batches and batches arriving randomly following a Poisson process.
- According to the bandwidth requirements upon call arrival (Figure I.17), calls are classified as:
  (i) calls with fixed bandwidth requirements
  (ii) calls with several alternative, contingency, fixed bandwidth requirements, called elastic bandwidth requirements.
- According to their behavior when calls are in service (Figure I.18), calls are classified to:
  (i) calls with fixed bandwidth allocation (stream traffic)
  (ii) calls tolerant to bandwidth compression or expansion (elastic traffic/bandwidth)
  (iii) calls that alternate between transmission periods of fixed bandwidth (ON) and no transmission periods (OFF) (ON–OFF traffic).

Then, according to the call arrival process, the bandwidth requirement upon call arrival, and the in-service behavior of a call, the teletraffic models presented in this book fall into the following three categories:

(I) *Teletraffic models of random input*
  - Random arriving calls with fixed or elastic bandwidth requirements and fixed bandwidth allocation during service.

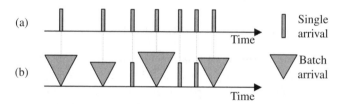

Figure I.16 Visualization of (a) random/quasi-random and (b) batch Poisson arrivals.

Figure I.17 Visualization of (a) fixed and (b) elastic bandwidth requirements.

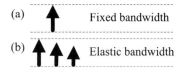

(a) ↑ Fixed bandwidth

(b) ↑↑↑ Elastic bandwidth

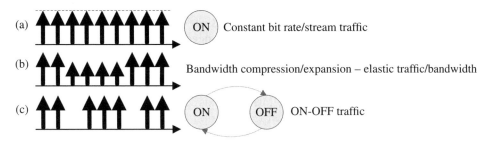

(a) ON Constant bit rate/stream traffic

(b) Bandwidth compression/expansion – elastic traffic/bandwidth

(c) ON OFF ON-OFF traffic

Figure I.18 Visualization of (a) stream, (b) elastic, and (c) ON–OFF traffic.

- Random arriving calls with fixed or elastic bandwidth requirements and elastic bandwidth during service.
- Random arriving calls with fixed or elastic bandwidth requirements and ON–OFF traffic behavior during service.

(II) *Teletraffic models of quasi-random input*

- Quasi-random arriving calls with fixed or elastic bandwidth requirements and fixed bandwidth allocation during service.
- Quasi-random arriving calls with fixed bandwidth requirements and elastic bandwidth during service.
- Quasi-random arriving calls with fixed bandwidth requirements and ON–OFF traffic behavior during service.

(III) *Teletraffic models of batched Poisson input*

- Batched Poisson arriving calls with fixed bandwidth requirements and fixed bandwidth allocation during service.
- Batched Poisson arriving calls with fixed bandwidth requirements and elastic bandwidth during service.

The above categories correspond to the three parts of this book. Each part includes several chapters, but the number of book chapters does not correspond to the number of bullets shown in each category above. For smooth transition to multi-dimensional traffic we first present models of single service-class.

I.14   Teletraffic Models and the Internet

Teletraffic models have been an inseparable part of the development of telecommunications and information and communication technology (ICT) infrastructure from the very beginning of their existence. Each and every newly introduced type of network technology is followed by a substantial increase in both the number and the complexity of teletraffic problems that need to be resolved. No matter what changes the new technologies may bring, the essential task for teletraffic theory remains the same:

- To determine and evaluate the relationship between the QoS parameters, the parameters that determine the intensity of connection requests and the demanded resources, and the parameters that describe available network resources (capacity).

These relationships provide a basis for developing teletraffic models used for designing, performance analysis, and optimization of telecom systems and networks.

Since the Internet is the global "ubiquitous network", we will pay special attention here to how teletraffic models are related to it. The need for a teletraffic model in packet switching networks, like the Internet, arises from the necessity to support and guarantee the QoS of the various network services. In the past, the Internet was engineered more by the use of pragmatic rules of thumb than by applying soundly based mathematical models [4], like the Erlang-B formula (Example I.5). Over-provisioning (e.g., over-dimensioning of the bandwidth of transmission links) is an inadequate solution because the network is not able to ensure low latency for packets (e.g., of real-time services) while maintaining sufficiently high throughput. Besides, according to forecasts [5], in the near future the Internet traffic-load will be so high that it is questionable whether we could provide ample bandwidth and over-dimensioning. Fortunately, the so-called best-effort Internet (i.e., without QoS guarantee) can be enhanced/substituted by two resource (e.g., bandwidth) allocation strategies whereby QoS can be guaranteed:

- integrated services (IntServ)
- differentiated services (DiffServ).

Before looking at these two strategies in detail, we will describe Internet traffic because the notion of call varies (and of course it does not coincide with a packet).

Although Internet traffic is too complicated to be modeled using traditional techniques (developed for telephone networks or computer systems), the teletraffic models in this book are applicable to the Internet and provide handy tools for performance evaluation. To this end, we need to identify which Internet traffic characteristics are essential and which can be ignored. Depending on the time scale of traffic measurements, one can measure packets, bursts, flows, sessions or connections. As has been well investigated, the packet arrival process (e.g., Ethernet traffic) is self-similar, that is, it has some statistical properties which repeat themselves (i.e., fractals appear) at many time scales [6]. Doubtless, a different level of abstraction than that of streams of packets that actually cross the network is needed, since the teletraffic models in this book are not conducive to self-similar traffic but basically to Poisson traffic (or to quasi-random traffic). From the traffic engineering point of view, it is more effective when Internet traffic is thought at a flow level [7]. Packets (usually forming bursts) belong to flows, which in turn belongs to sessions (in terms of the Internet). So, the flow level is the essential level of Internet traffic and readily distinguishable, given that packets of the same flow have the same identifier (e.g., addresses, port numbers, etc.). Flows in a session are separated with random (exponentially distributed) time-intervals (in the order of seconds), thus the flow arrival process can be considered random or quasi-random (sessions also occur randomly or quasi-randomly). According to our classification of teletraffic models, we can distinguish three service-classes for flows: stream traffic (i.e., streaming flows), elastic traffic (i.e., elastic flows), and ON–OFF traffic (i.e., bursts of steaming traffic).

For streaming traffic, the network (e.g., a router) accepts or rejects a new flow based on the required constant bandwidth of the flow and depending on whether or not the required QoS can be guaranteed. The flow can be either an individual flow or an aggregation of flows, corresponding to IntServ or DiffServ resource allocation strategies. To ensure that the traffic characteristics are not altered during the duration of a session, or on a per-flow basis, a policing function is needed. Streaming flows typically are generated under the user datagram protocol (UDP).

For elastic traffic (i.e., flows with a variable bandwidth up to a maximum value), the network accepts or rejects a new flow depending not only on the required maximum bandwidth of the flow but also on whether the bandwidth it would receive falls below a threshold (e.g., due to congestion). When the traffic load is normal, the admittance threshold should be small enough, whereas under overload traffic conditions the admittance threshold should be large enough (to ensure satisfactory throughput for accepted flows). Thus, a multi-threshold CAC scheme would be preferable, while teletraffic models considering thresholds, or bandwidth compression, are necessary for network performance evaluation in the case of elastic traffic. Elastic flows typically are generated under the transport control protocol (TCP).

For ON–OFF traffic (i.e., flows of well distinguished active and passive periods or, in other words, where burstiness cannot be ignored), the network accepts or rejects a new flow based on the required peak bandwidth of the flow, while, for network performance, sophisticated teletraffic models incorporating the ON–OFF traffic characteristics are required. ON–OFF traffic typically is a variance of elastic flows.

As far as the traffic load in the Internet is concerned, although it varies very much during the day, nevertheless a busy period can be detected where the traffic load can be considered constant (i.e., a stationary stochastic process having constant mean) and this is crucial for QoS assessment. Having discussed Internet traffic, in what follows we present the aforementioned two resource allocation strategies which enable QoS guarantee in the Internet:

- IntServ is a resource separation strategy (Figure I.19a) that allows a prioritized flow to occupy its own network resource, which is physically or logically separated from resources used by other flows. Per-flow traffic classification and scheduling functions are implemented at routers, while they are required to keep per-flow state and process per-flow reservation messages; thus, the scalability of the IntServ Internet architecture is limited. To implement this strategy, a connection setup phase is required, where each flow explicitly must specify its QoS requirements. Based on these, the CAC, through a teletraffic model, evaluates the number of resources (capacity) necessary for guaranteeing the QoS requirements, and then the necessary resources are reserved along the path where the connection is established.
- DiffServ is a resource sharing strategy (Figure I.19b) that aims to realize a scalable QoS assurance rather than strict QoS guarantee. It follows the philosophy that complexity is placed to the network edges, while simplicity should characterize the core network. In the DiffServ Internet, datagrams (Internet protocol (IP) packets) are marked with a priority level (QoS requirement) at the network edges (end-systems) and thus are classified into coarse-grained QoS classes (groups); an 8-bit field in the packet header (type of service in IPv4 or traffic class in IPv6) is used to identify the QoS class. Then packets are scheduled and forwarded at each router on a per-class basis, that is, aggregated flows are formed. Since no state information per flow is maintained at routers, the scalability of DiffServ architecture is much better than that of IntServ architecture.

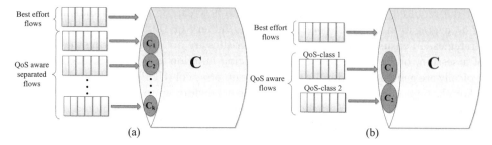

Figure I.19 (a) Resource separation (*k* QoS-aware flows) and (b) resource sharing (two QoS classes).

For each aggregated flow (QoS class), network resources (capacity) are reserved, and thus QoS (averaged over QoS-class traffic) can be assured, if there is some CAC function for limiting the traffic load of the classes. Thus, again, there is a need to combine capacity, QoS, and traffic-load through a teletraffic model.

Which strategy is preferable (resource reservation, or resource sharing) depends on various conditions, such as the specific QoS requirement [8]. IntServ and DiffServ are not the only architectures whereby we can guarantee QoS in the Internet; multiple protocol labeling switching (MPLS) is another such technology applicable to IP-based networks.

References

1 E. Brockmeyer, H.L. Halstrom, and A. Jensen, The life and works of A.K. Erlang. *Transactions of the Danish Academy of Technical Science*, No. 2, 1948.

2 Y. Viniotis, *Probability and Random Processes for Electrical Engineers*, McGraw-Hill, 1998.

3 H. Akimaru and K. Kawashima, *Teletraffic – Theory and Applications*, 2nd edn, Springer, Berlin, 1999.

4 T. Bonald and J. Roberts, Internet and the Erlang Formula. *ACM SIGCOMM Computer Communication Review*, 42(1):23–30, January 2012.

5 Cisco® *The Zettabyte Era: Trends and Analysis* (White Paper). https://www.cisco.com/c/en/us/solutions/collateral/service-provider/visual-networking-index-vni/vni-hyperconnectivity-wp.html (accessed November 2018).

6 K. Park and W. Willinger, Self-Similar Network Traffic: An Overview, in *Self-Similar Network Traffic and Performance Evaluation*, K. Park and W. Willinger (eds), John Wiley & Sons, 2000.

7 J. Roberts, Traffic Theory and the Internet. *IEEE Communications Magazine*, 39(1):94–99, January 2001.

8 S. Shioda, Fundamental trade-offs between resource separation and resource share for quality of service guarantees. *IET Networks*, 3(1):4–15, March 2014.

Part I

Teletraffic Models of Random Input

Part I, includes teletraffic loss models of:

(A) Random arriving calls with fixed or elastic bandwidth requirements and fixed bandwidth allocation during service.
(B) Random arriving calls with fixed or elastic bandwidth requirements and elastic bandwidth during service.
(C) Random arriving calls with fixed or elastic bandwidth requirements and ON–OFF traffic behavior during service.

1

The Erlang Multirate Loss Model

We start with random arriving calls of fixed bandwidth requirements and fixed bandwidth allocation during service.
Before the study of multirate teletraffic loss models where multiple service-classes of different bandwidth per call requirements are accommodated in a service system, let us begin with the simpler case where all calls belong to just one service-class, and afterwards consider the multi-service system.

1.1 The Erlang Loss Model

1.1.1 The Service System

Consider that a single service-class (e.g., telephone service) is accommodated to a loss system, say a transmission link, of capacity C b.u. Each call arrives in the system according to a Poisson process with mean value λ and requires 1 b.u. to be serviced. If this bandwidth is available, then a call is accepted in the system and remains under service for an exponentially distributed service time, with mean value $h = \mu^{-1}$. Otherwise, when all b.u. are occupied, a call is blocked and lost without further affecting the system (e.g., a blocked call is not allowed to retry).

Now, let $X(t)$ be the number of in-service calls at the time instant t. Since each call occupies 1 b.u. then $X(t)$ also expresses the number of occupied b.u. at the time instant t, i.e., $0 \leq X(t) \leq C$. Assume that at time instant $t + \Delta t$, $(\Delta t \to 0)$, the number of in-service calls is n, that is, $X(t + \Delta t) = n$; in the teletraffic jargon, we say that the system is in state n. Let $P_n(t + \Delta t)$ denote the probability of being in state n. Since calls arrive at random, based on (I.10) the system's state becomes n at $t + \Delta t$, if one of the following events takes place:

(a) $X(t) = n$ and (no arrival or departure occurs in Δt).
(b) $X(t) = n - 1$ and (one new call arrives in Δt).
(c) $X(t) = n + 1$ and (one in-service call departs from the system in Δt).

The probability of the first event equals $P_n(t)(1 - \lambda \Delta t - n\mu \Delta t)$. Note that the probability for a specific call to depart within Δt is $\mu \Delta t$; given that there are n in-service calls, one departure is possible due to the first or the second or the nth call, and therefore the probability of one departure becomes the sum of n probabilities: $n\mu \Delta t$.

Efficient Multirate Teletraffic Loss Models Beyond Erlang, First Edition.
Ioannis D. Moscholios and Michael D. Logothetis.
© 2019 John Wiley & Sons Ltd. Published 2019 by John Wiley & Sons Ltd.
Companion website: www.wiley.com/go/logocode

The probability of the second event equals $P_{n-1}(t)\lambda\Delta t$, while the probability of the last event equals $P_{n+1}(t)(n+1)\mu\Delta t$ (because of the $n+1$ in-service calls).

Therefore, because the above events are exclusive, we take:

$$P_n(t+\Delta t) = P_n(t)(1 - \lambda\Delta t - n\mu\Delta t) + P_{n-1}(t)\lambda\Delta t + P_{n+1}(t)(n+1)\mu\Delta t =$$
$$= [\lambda P_{n-1}(t) + (n+1)\mu P_{n+1}(t) - (\lambda + n\mu)P_n(t)]\Delta t + P_n(t) \qquad (1.1)$$

or

$$P_n(t+\Delta t) - P_n(t) = [\lambda P_{n-1}(t) + (n+1)\mu P_{n+1}(t) - (\lambda + n\mu)P_n(t)]\Delta t \Rightarrow$$
$$\frac{P_n(t+\Delta t) - P_n(t)}{\Delta t} = \lambda P_{n-1}(t) + (n+1)\mu P_{n+1}(t) - (\lambda + n\mu)P_n(t) \qquad (1.2)$$

In (1.2), when $\Delta t \to 0$, the limit of the LHS defines the derivative of $P_n(t)$:

$$\lim_{\Delta t \to 0} \frac{P_n(t+\Delta t) - P_n(t)}{\Delta t} \equiv \frac{d}{dt}P_n(t) = \lambda P_{n-1}(t) + (n+1)\mu P_{n+1}(t) - (\lambda + n\mu)P_n(t)$$
$$(1.3)$$

According to the notion of derivative, (1.3) shows the rate of changes of the instantaneous value of $P_n(t)$, which is of little interest. Instead, of great interest is to find the state probability in the steady state, that is, when the system operates normally for a long time period. Service systems normally have a steady state; this means that as $t \to \infty \Rightarrow \frac{d}{dt}P_n(t) \to 0$. Then, the probability $P_n(t)$ approaches a limiting value P_n, which is constant over time and is determined through (1.3) when the LHS is zero:

$$0 = \lambda P_{n-1} + (n+1)\mu P_{n+1} - (\lambda + n\mu)P_n \quad \Rightarrow \quad (\lambda + n\mu)P_n = \lambda P_{n-1} + (n+1)\mu P_{n+1}$$
$$(1.4)$$

where $n = 0, 1, 2, \ldots, C$ and $P_{-1} = 0 = P_{C+1}$.

Since (1.4) holds for all n, we say that the system is in *statistical equilibrium*. To find the *limiting probabilities* P_n, also called *steady state probabilities*, we solve (1.4) by applying the so-called *ladder method*:

For $n = 0$: $\lambda P_0 = \mu P_1$

For $n = 1$: $\lambda P_1 + \mu P_1 = \lambda P_0 + 2\mu P_2$

For $n = 2$: $\lambda P_2 + 2\mu P_2 = \lambda P_1 + 3\mu P_3$

$\cdots$

For $n = n-2$: $\lambda P_{n-2} + (n-2)\mu P_{n-2} = \lambda P_{n-3} + (n-1)\mu P_{n-1}$

For $n = n-1$: $\lambda P_{n-1} + (n-1)\mu P_{n-1} = \lambda P_{n-2} + n\mu P_n$

By adding these equations side by side, we obtain the following recurrent formula:

$$P_n = \frac{\alpha}{n}P_{n-1}, \qquad \text{for} \quad n = 1, \ldots, C \qquad (1.5)$$

where $\alpha = \frac{\lambda}{\mu}$ is the offered traffic-load in erl.

From (1.5), by successive substitutions, we relate P_n to the probability that the system is empty, P_0:

$$P_n = \frac{\alpha}{n}P_{n-1} = \frac{\alpha}{n}\frac{\alpha}{n-1}P_{n-2} = \frac{\alpha}{n}\frac{\alpha}{n-1}\frac{\alpha}{n-2}P_{n-3} = \cdots = \frac{\alpha^n}{n!}P_0 \qquad (1.6)$$

One more equation is needed between P_n and P_0 to formulate a system of two equations with two unknowns. Since the system will always be in one of the states $n = 0, 1, 2, \ldots, C$, we have:

$$\sum_{n=0}^{C} P_n = 1 \Rightarrow \sum_{n=0}^{C} \frac{\alpha^n}{n!} P_0 = 1 \Rightarrow P_0 \sum_{n=0}^{C} \frac{\alpha^n}{n!} = 1 \qquad (1.7)$$

that is,

$$P_0 = \left[\sum_{n=0}^{C} \frac{\alpha^n}{n!} \right]^{-1} \qquad (1.8)$$

By substituting (1.8) to (1.6), we determine P_n:

$$P_n = \frac{\frac{\alpha^n}{n!}}{\sum_{i=0}^{C} \frac{\alpha^i}{i!}} \qquad \text{for } n = 0, 1, 2, \ldots, C \qquad (1.9)$$

which is the well-known *Erlang distribution*.[1]

Example 1.1 Assume that the system capacity becomes $C \to \infty$. How does the Erlang distribution (1.9) change?

In a system of infinite capacity all arrivals are accepted for service; this means that the probability of having n in-service calls coincides with the probability of having n arrivals, which is given by the Poisson distribution (I.13). In fact, in (1.9), the denominator becomes $\sum_{n=0}^{\infty} \frac{\alpha^n}{n!} = e^{-\alpha}$, and then $P_n = \frac{\alpha^n}{n!} e^{-\alpha}$. In other words, a Poisson process truncated by the system capacity becomes an Erlang process; thus, the Erlang distribution is also called the *truncated Poisson distribution*.

1.1.2 Global and Local Balance

It is important at this point to interpret (1.4) and (1.5). Let us rewrite them as follows, while multiplying them by Δt:

$$(\lambda \Delta t + n\mu \Delta t) P_n = \lambda \Delta t P_{n-1} + (n + 1)\mu \Delta t P_{n+1} \qquad \text{global balance} \qquad (1.10a)$$

$$n\mu \Delta t P_n = \lambda \Delta t P_{n-1} \qquad \text{local balance} \qquad (1.10b)$$

The LHS of (1.10a) shows the probability sum of two events while the system is in state n: a call arrival ($\lambda \Delta t$) and a call departure ($n\mu \Delta t$), which transfer the system out of state n, obviously to the adjacent state $n + 1$ or $n - 1$, respectively. Likewise, the RHS of (1.10a) shows the probability of moving to state n from the adjacent states $n - 1$ and $n + 1$, due to a call arrival and a call departure, respectively. Let us remove Δt from this equation. Then, (1.10a) denotes the fact that *rate-out = rate-in* and is named the *global balance (GB)* equation of state n.

Even more interesting is the interpretation of (1.10b), where the RHS shows the probability of moving up, from state $n - 1$ to state n, due to a call arrival, while the LHS shows

---

1 It is also known as Erlang's first formula.

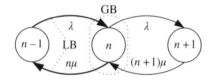

Figure 1.1 State transition diagram for the Erlang loss model (*M/M/C/0*).

the probability of moving down, from state n to state $n - 1$, due to a call departure. When removing Δt, this equation denotes the fact that *rate-down* = *rate-up* and is named the *local balance* (*LB*) equation between the adjacent states n and $n - 1$.

Having removed Δt from (1.10a), its graphical representation is shown in Figure 1.1 by the *state transition diagram* of the system. Two LB equations are presented (the first one between states $n - 1$ and n and the second one between states n and $n + 1$). Note at this point that the existence of GB between adjacent states does not guarantee the existence of LB. The opposite holds.

Equations (1.10) introduce the following methodology, called *classical methodology*, in analyzing a service system in equilibrium, i.e., in determining its steady state probabilities:

(i) Start with the state transition diagram of the system.
(ii) Write the GB equations.
(iii) Apply the ladder method to the GB equations in order to obtain simpler equations, usually the LB equations.
(iv) If steps (ii) and (iii) are too complicated, assume that LB equations hold and go on, but check for atopy.
(v) Consider the normalization condition.[2]
(vi) Solve the resultant linear system of equations of the steady state probabilities.

Example 1.2 Consider the queuing system of Figure 1.2, as an *M/M/C/∞* FIFO system. Determine:

(a) the probability of having n calls in the system (both in the queue and in the service mechanism) in steady state
(b) the probability that a call delays (i.e., enters the queue)
(c) the mean queue length L
(d) the mean call waiting time W.

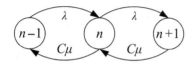

Figure 1.2 *M/M/C/∞* FIFO – state transition diagram for $n > C$ (Example 1.2).

---

2 The sum of all probabilities equals 1.

(a) *To determine the steady state probabilities P_n*

    (i) Starting with the state transition diagram of this system, we have to consider two cases: (a) when $n \leq C$ and (b) when $n > C$. This is due to the fact that in the latter case the rate whereby calls depart from the system remains constant and equals $C\mu$, while in case (a) this rate depends on the number of in-service calls and equals $n\mu$. The state transition diagram of Figure 1.1 stands for case (a). Case (b) is shown in Figure 1.2.

    (ii) According to the two state transition diagrams, the GB equations are:

$$\text{For} \quad n \leq C : \quad (\lambda + n\mu)P_n = \lambda P_{n-1} + (n+1)\mu P_{n+1}$$
$$\text{For} \quad n > C : \quad (\lambda + C\mu)P_n = \lambda P_{n-1} + C\mu P_{n+1} \tag{1.11}$$

    (iii) The applicability of the ladder method on (1.11) for $n \leq C$ results in (1.5) and finally in (1.6). Let us rewrite (1.6) (remembering that $\alpha = \frac{\lambda}{\mu}$):

$$\text{For} \quad n \leq C : \quad P_n = \frac{\alpha^n}{n!}P_0 \quad \Rightarrow \quad P_C = \frac{\alpha^C}{C!}P_0 \tag{1.12}$$

    (iv) To speed up the procedure for $n > C$, let us consider that the LB equation between states $n - 1$ and n holds:

$$\text{For} \quad n > C : \quad C\mu P_n = \lambda P_{n-1} \quad \Rightarrow \quad P_n = \frac{\alpha}{C}P_{n-1} \tag{1.13}$$

From (1.13), by successive substitutions and based on (1.12), we obtain:

$$\text{For} \quad n = C + 1 : \quad P_{C+1} = \frac{\alpha}{C}P_C = \frac{\alpha}{C}\frac{\alpha^C}{C!}P_0$$

$$\text{For} \quad n = C + 2 : \quad P_{C+2} = \frac{\alpha}{C}P_{C+1} = \frac{\alpha}{C}\frac{\alpha}{C}\frac{\alpha^C}{C!}P_0 = \left(\frac{\alpha}{C}\right)^2\frac{\alpha^C}{C!}P_0$$

$$\text{For} \quad n = C + 3 : \quad P_{C+3} = \frac{\alpha}{C}P_{C+2} = \frac{\alpha}{C}\left(\frac{\alpha}{C}\right)^2\frac{\alpha^C}{C!}P_0 = \left(\frac{\alpha}{C}\right)^3\frac{\alpha^C}{C!}P_0$$

$$\cdots$$

$$\text{For} \quad n = C + i : \quad P_{C+i} = \left(\frac{\alpha}{C}\right)^i\frac{\alpha^C}{C!}P_0$$

Or, since $i = n - C$,

$$\text{For} \quad n > C : \quad P_n = \frac{\alpha^C}{C!}\left(\frac{\alpha}{C}\right)^{n-C}P_0 \tag{1.14}$$

    (v) The normalization condition is:

$$\sum_{n=0}^{C}\frac{\alpha^n}{n!}P_0 + \sum_{n=C+1}^{\infty}\frac{\alpha^C}{C!}\left(\frac{\alpha}{C}\right)^{n-C}P_0 = 1 \Rightarrow P_0\left[\sum_{n=0}^{C}\frac{\alpha^n}{n!} + \frac{\alpha^C}{C!}\sum_{n=C+1}^{\infty}\left(\frac{\alpha}{C}\right)^{n-C}\right] = 1$$

$$\Rightarrow P_0\left[\sum_{n=0}^{C-1}\frac{\alpha^n}{n!} + \frac{\alpha^C}{C!} + \frac{\alpha^C}{C!}\sum_{n=1}^{\infty}\left(\frac{\alpha}{C}\right)^n\right] = P_0\left[\sum_{n=0}^{C-1}\frac{\alpha^n}{n!} + \frac{\alpha^C}{C!}\sum_{n=0}^{\infty}\left(\frac{\alpha}{C}\right)^n\right] = 1 \Rightarrow$$

$$P_0 = \left[\sum_{n=0}^{C-1}\frac{\alpha^n}{n!} + \frac{\alpha^C}{C!}\sum_{n=0}^{\infty}\left(\frac{\alpha}{C}\right)^n\right]^{-1} = \left[\sum_{n=0}^{C-1}\frac{\alpha^n}{n!} + \frac{\alpha^C}{C!}\frac{C}{C-\alpha}\right]^{-1} \tag{1.15}$$

Let us emphasize that the summation in (1.15) converges if and only if $\alpha < C$. Only under this condition can we determine P_0 and, consequently, P_n. To summarize:

$$
P_n = \begin{cases}
\dfrac{\alpha^n}{n!} P_0 & \text{for } n \leq C \\[2ex]
\dfrac{\alpha^C}{C!} \left(\dfrac{\alpha}{C}\right)^{n-C} P_0 & \text{for } n > C
\end{cases}
\tag{1.16}
$$

where P_0 is given by (1.15).

(b) *The probability that a call delays, P_D:* This equals the probability that the system is in state n, where $n \geq C$:

$$
P_D = \sum_{n=C}^{\infty} P_n = \frac{\alpha^C}{C!} P_0 \sum_{n=0}^{\infty} \left(\frac{\alpha}{C}\right)^n \quad \Rightarrow \quad P_D = \frac{\alpha^C}{C!} \frac{C}{C-\alpha} P_0
\tag{1.17}
$$

Again, only when $\alpha < C$, can P_D be determined via (1.17), which is the well-known *Erlang-C formula*.[3] It is worth mentioning the following recursive form of the Erlang-C formula ($E_C^{\text{delay}}(\alpha)$), which is based on the Erlang-B recursion (I.8):

$$
P_D \equiv E_C^{\text{delay}}(\alpha) = \frac{\dfrac{\alpha^C}{C!} \dfrac{C}{C-\alpha}}{\displaystyle\sum_{n=0}^{C-1} \dfrac{\alpha^n}{n!} + \dfrac{\alpha^C}{C!} \dfrac{C}{C-\alpha}} = \frac{E_C(\alpha) \dfrac{C}{C-\alpha}}{1 - E_C(\alpha) + E_C(\alpha) \dfrac{C}{C-\alpha}}
$$

$$
= \frac{C E_C(\alpha)}{C - \alpha(1 - E_C(\alpha))}
\tag{1.18}
$$

(c) *To determine the mean queue length, L:* We apply the definition of the expected value of the number of calls waiting in the queue, as follows:

$$
L = \sum_{n=C}^{\infty} (n-C) P_n = \frac{\alpha^C}{C!} P_0 \sum_{n=0}^{\infty} n \left(\frac{\alpha}{C}\right)^n = \frac{\alpha^C}{C!} P_0 \frac{\dfrac{\alpha}{C}}{\left(1 - \dfrac{\alpha}{C}\right)^2} = \frac{\dfrac{\alpha^{C+1}}{(C-1)!}}{(C-\alpha)^2} P_0
\tag{1.19}
$$

since $\sum_{r=0}^{\infty} r x^r = x(1 + 2x^1 + 3x^2 + \cdots) = x \frac{d}{dr} \sum_{r=0}^{\infty} x^r = x \frac{d}{dr} \frac{1}{1-x} = \frac{x}{(1-x)^2}$, if $x < 1$. From (1.17), $P_0 = \frac{C-\alpha}{C} \frac{C!}{\alpha^C} P_D$, then (1.19) can be written as:

$$
L = \frac{\alpha}{C-\alpha} P_D
\tag{1.20}
$$

(d) *To determine the mean call waiting time W (mean delay in the queue):* We apply Little's law (I.32):

$$
W = \frac{L}{\lambda} = \frac{\alpha P_D}{(C-\alpha)\lambda} = \frac{P_D}{C-\alpha} h
\tag{1.21}
$$

where h is the mean call holding time (in the service mechanism).

1.1.3 Call Blocking Probability

The most important question in a loss system is "What is the CBP?" or, equivalently, "What is the GoS?". Call blocking occurs when the system is fully occupied, that is, CBP

---

3 In the Erlang-B formula, a call is blocked and lost. In the Erlang-C formula, a call may enter a queue.

equals P_C, the probability that the system is in state C. From (1.9) we have

$$P_C \equiv E_C(\alpha) = \frac{\frac{\alpha^C}{C!}}{\sum_{i=0}^{C} \frac{\alpha^i}{i!}} \tag{1.22}$$

Equation (1.22) is the famous Erlang-B formula also met in (I.5). As we discussed there (Example I.5), the closed form of the Erlang-B formula is not appealing for large values of α and C, instead its recurrent form (I.8) is not only preferred but necessary.

It is worth mentioning at this point that, as has been investigated (e.g., [1–3]), (1.9) and consequently (1.22) are insensitive to the distribution of service time, and depend only on the mean holding time, $h = \mu^{-1}$, which is inherently included in the traffic-load ($\alpha = \frac{\lambda}{\mu}$). Besides, (1.22) refers to the proportion of time that all C b.u. are occupied (i.e., the system is congested). This probability is named *time congestion* (TC) probability and can be measured by an outside observer. Due to the PASTA property, an inside observer sees the same probability, therefore (1.22) is also called *call congestion* (CC) probability or CBP.

Example 1.3 Consider an Erlang loss system of capacity C b.u. and let P_n be the probability that there exist n users in the system occupying n b.u. at a chosen time, randomly selected.

(a) Assuming a long time interval $(0, T)$, determine the portion of time that the system accommodates n users.
(b) Assume that users arrive in the system according to a Poisson process with rate λ. Show that the probability Π_n seen by an arriving user, that n users exist in the system just prior to its arrival, equals P_n.

(a) The portion of time that the system accommodates n users is $P_n T$.
(b) Based on the *Bayes'* and the *total probability* theorems, we have:

$$\Pi_n = P(n \text{ users}|\text{an arrival}) = \frac{P(n \text{ users})P(\text{an arrival}|n \text{ users})}{\sum_{i=0}^{C} P(i \text{ users})P(\text{an arrival}|i \text{ users})} =$$

$$= \frac{P(n \text{ users})P(\text{an arrival})}{\sum_{i=0}^{C} P(i \text{ users})P(\text{an arrival})} = \frac{P_n \lambda \Delta t}{\sum_{i=0}^{C} P_i \lambda \Delta t} = \frac{P_n \lambda \Delta t}{\lambda \Delta t \sum_{i=0}^{C} P_i} = P_n \tag{1.23}$$

where $P(\text{an arrival}) = \lambda \Delta t$, according to (I.10).

Having found a relationship between α, C and GoS, i.e., CBP $= E_C(\alpha)$, let us now provide graphs of them (Figure 1.3) in order to compare them with the qualitative graphs of Figure I.2. The first graph of Figure 1.3 presents the required system capacity C versus the offered traffic-load α (for two certain values of GoS: 1% and 3%) and corresponds to the LHS graph of Figure I.2. However, the anticipated curve of Figure I.2 is hardly followed in Figure 1.3; the function $C = f(\alpha)$ is rather a straight line in a wide range of the presented values of traffic-load. The second graph of Figure 1.3 presents CBP versus C, for $\alpha = 10$ erl and $\alpha = 15$ erl, and corresponds to the middle graph of Figure I.2. Due

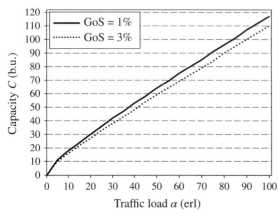

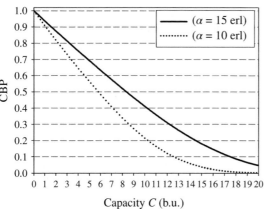

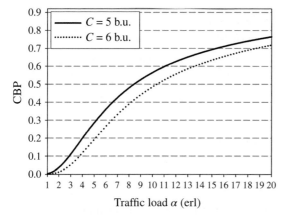

Figure 1.3 Quantitative relationships between traffic-load, system capacity, and CBP.

to the reverse meaning of CBP,[4] the convex curvature of the middle graph in Figure I.2 appears in the middle graph of Figure 1.3, as a concave (reverse) curvature. The third graph of Figure 1.3 presents CBP versus traffic-load α for two values of C: 5 and 6 b.u. Herein, the corresponding qualitative graph of Figure I.2 (RHS) is followed pretty well.

Example 1.4 The terms GoS and CBP are not always interchangeable, although they both express blocking probability in loss systems. The different use of these terms arises when integer values of the system capacity C are considered. For instance, we say: Determine C when $\alpha = 10$ erl, for GoS = 1%; we cannot say for CBP = 1%, because it is extremely seldom that it completely satisfies this CBP equality. By using the term GoS, we actually mean that the resultant CBP must not exceed 1%. Indeed, CBP = $E_C(10) \leq$ 1% $\Rightarrow C = 18$ (Figure 1.3, first) and CBP = $E_{18}(20) = 0.007142 < 1\%$ (Figure 1.3, middle).

1.1.4 Other Performance Metrics

- Utilization: The utilization, U, is expressed by the average number of occupied b.u.:

$$U = \sum_{n=1}^{C} n P_n = \sum_{n=1}^{C} n \frac{\alpha^n}{n!} P_0 \Rightarrow$$

$$U = \alpha P_0 \sum_{n=1}^{C} \frac{\alpha^{n-1}}{(n-1)!} = \alpha P_0 \left[\sum_{n=0}^{C} \frac{\alpha^n}{n!} - \frac{\alpha^C}{C!} \right] = \alpha \left[\sum_{n=0}^{C} \frac{\alpha^n}{n!} \right]^{-1} \left[\sum_{n=0}^{C} \frac{\alpha^n}{n!} - \frac{\alpha^C}{C!} \right] \Rightarrow$$

$$U = \alpha(1 - E_C(\alpha))$$

(1.24)

Equation (1.24) verifies (I.34). Because of property (4) of traffic-load, $U \leq C$.

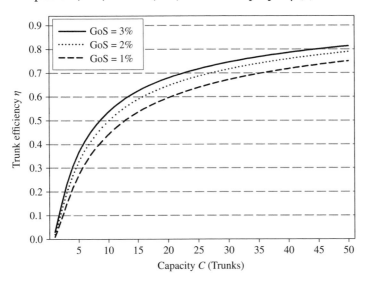

Figure 1.4 Trunk efficiency for various values of GoS and C.

---

4 The better CBP, the lower its value.

- Trunk efficiency: According to (I.35), the trunk efficiency η is:

$$\eta = \frac{U}{C} = \frac{\alpha}{C}(1 - E_C(\alpha)) \tag{1.25}$$

Since η expresses traffic-load per trunk, $\eta \leq 1$ (property (3) of traffic-load). Thus, again, $U \leq C$. As Figure 1.4 shows, the trunk efficiency increases as the system capacity increases, for a certain GoS. This is called the *large-scale effect* and leads to the conclusion that loss systems must be designed with the greatest possible capacity in order for trunks to be used efficiently. The latter happens because the larger the system capacity, the greater the carried traffic conveyed under a certain GoS.

Example 1.5

(a) A transmission link is designed for GoS = 1% to convey an offered traffic-load of 2.5 erl in one traffic-flow direction. For the reverse traffic-flow direction, another transmission link with the same characteristics is used. What is the trunk efficiency in these two links?
(b) The two links are replaced by one bi-directional link, which is designed to convey the sum of the traffic-loads with the same GoS. What is the trunk efficiency of the bi-directional link?

(a) *Using uni-directional links*: In each transmission link for each traffic-flow direction, the capacity is determined as $C = 7$ b.u., so that GoS = 1% is guaranteed. Indeed, $E_7(2.5) = 0.01$. By applying (1.25), we have $\eta = \frac{2.5}{7}(1 - 0.01) \simeq 35\%$.
(b) *Using bi-directional links*: The bi-directional link will have a greater capacity than the uni-directional link in order to accommodate the same total offered traffic-load with the same GoS, thus the large-scale effect takes place and a better η is anticipated for the bi-directional link. The total offered traffic-load is 5.0 erl and the capacity is determined as $C = 11$ b.u. for GoS = 1%. Note that $E_{11}(5.0) < 0.01$, while $E_{10}(5.0) > 0.01$. Precisely, $E_{11}(5.0) = 0.008$. By applying (1.25), we have $\eta = \frac{5.0}{11}(1 - 0.008) = 45\%$; indeed, clearly better than 35%.
On the other hand, this example reveals the importance of the large-scale effect through the savings in system capacity, when a system of a larger capacity replaces smaller systems. The bi-directional transmission link requires a capacity of 11 b.u., which is less than the total capacity of 14 b.u. required by the two uni-directional transmission systems.

- A low bound of $E_C(\alpha)$: Since $U \leq C$ always, we have:

$$U \leq C \quad \Rightarrow \quad \alpha(1 - E_C(\alpha)) \leq C \quad \Rightarrow \quad E_C(\alpha) \geq 1 - \frac{C}{\alpha} \tag{1.26}$$

Equation (1.26) can be used for a fast evaluation of CBP measurements or CBP calculations, given that the offered traffic-load α estimation is correct. For instance, according to (1.26), if $C = 10$ b.u. and $\alpha = 15$ erl, the anticipated CBP = 33.33% at least. Note that the actual CBP value is $E_{10}(15)) = 41.03\%$. The interested reader may resort to [4] and the references therein for an in-depth analysis of the lower and upper bounds on the Erlang-B and Erlang-C formulas.

1.2 The Erlang Multirate Loss Model

1.2.1 The Service System

Let us now consider the multi-service system or, as we call it, the *Erlang multirate loss model (EMLM)*. A single link of capacity C b.u. accommodates calls of K different service-classes under the CS policy. Each call of service-class k $(k = 1, \ldots, K)$ arrives in the system following a Poisson process with mean rate λ_k and requires b_k b.u. to be serviced. If the requested bandwidth is available, then a call is accepted in the system and remains under service for an exponentially distributed service time, with mean μ_k^{-1}. Otherwise, the call is blocked and lost, without further affecting the system. After service completion, the b_k b.u. are released and become available to new arriving calls.

Let n_k denote the number of in-service calls of service-class k in the steady state, $\mathbf{n} = (n_1, n_2, \ldots, n_k, \ldots, n_K)$ the corresponding vector of all in-service calls of all service-classes, and $\mathbf{b} = (b_1, b_2, \ldots, b_k, \ldots, b_K)$ the corresponding vector of the required bandwidth per call of all service-classes in the system. Because of the CS policy, the set $\mathbf{\Omega}$ of the system (state space) is given by (I.36). The product $\mathbf{nb} = \sum_{k=1}^{K} n_k b_k$ expresses the occupied link bandwidth in system state $\mathbf{n}$ and plays a decisive role in CAC:

$$\mathbf{nb} + b_k \leq C \; \forall \; k \tag{1.27}$$

In terms of $\mathbf{\Omega}$, the CAC is expressed as follows. A new call of service-class k that finds the system in state $\mathbf{n}$ is accepted in the system if $\mathbf{n}_k^+ \in \mathbf{\Omega} = \{\mathbf{n} : 0 \leq \mathbf{nb} \leq C\}$, where $\mathbf{n}_k^+ = (n_1, n_2, \ldots, n_{k-1}, n_k + 1, n_{k+1}, \ldots, n_K) \; \forall \; k = 1, 2, \ldots, K$.

Example 1.6 Consider a single link with $C = 5$ b.u. The link accommodates $K = 2$ service-classes with $b_1 = 1$ b.u. and $b_2 = 2$ b.u. Figure 1.5 illustrates this service system under the CS policy.

(a) Draw the complete state transition diagram of the system.
(b) Is there an indication that the system has a PFS?

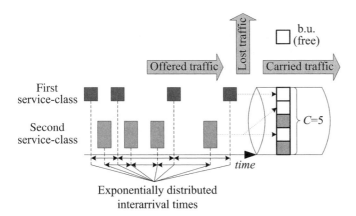

Figure 1.5 A service system of $C = 5$ b.u. and two service-classes under the CS policy (Example 1.6).

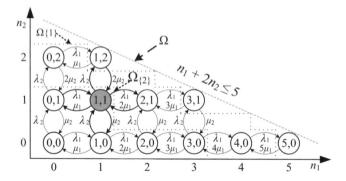

Figure 1.6 The state space Ω (CS policy) and the state transition diagram (Example 1.6).

(a) *State transition diagram*: According to the CS policy, $\Omega = \{\mathbf{n} : 0 \leq \mathbf{nb} \leq C\}$, each state $\mathbf{n} = (n_1, n_2)$ should satisfy the inequality $n_1 + 2n_2 \leq 5$. Figure 1.6 shows the state space Ω (12 states), together with the complete state transition diagram of the system.

(b) *Indication of the PFS*: As we discussed in Section I.12, the state space of this example satisfies the coordinate convexity conditions and the steady state probability $P(\mathbf{n})$ can be expressed by the PFS (I.40). Based on Figure 1.6, we can intuitively understand the existence of a PFS. If only one service-class exists in the system, say service-class 1, then the steady state probability P_{n_1} will be given by the Erlang distribution (1.9). Likewise, if this system accommodates only service-class 2, its steady state probability P_{n_2} will be given again by the Erlang distribution, under the assumption that each call of service-class 2 requests 1 b.u. (instead of two), while the system capacity is half (suppose that $C/2$ is integer). That is:

$$P_{n_1} = \frac{\frac{\alpha_1^{n_1}}{n_1!}}{\sum\limits_{i=0}^{C} \frac{\alpha_1^i}{i!}} \Rightarrow \frac{\alpha_1^{n_1}}{n_1!} \equiv f(P_{n_1}) \quad \text{and} \quad P_{n_2} = \frac{\frac{\alpha_2^{n_2}}{n_2!}}{\sum\limits_{i=0}^{C/2} \frac{\alpha_2^i}{i!}} \Rightarrow \frac{\alpha_2^{n_2}}{n_2!} \equiv f(P_{n_2}) \quad (1.28)$$

where $\alpha_1 = \frac{\lambda_1}{\mu_1}$ and $\alpha_2 = \frac{\lambda_2}{\mu_2}$.

The steady state probability $P(n_1, n_2)$ is the joint probability that n_1 calls of service-class 1 coexist in the system with n_2 calls of service-class 2, by sharing the bandwidth C under the CS policy. Thanks to the CS policy, the two service-classes do not further influence each other; in this sense, the events n_1 and n_2 can be considered independent. Therefore, their joint probability is expressed by the product of marginal (individual) probabilities. This consideration would be absolutely correct if $C = \infty$. Now, because of the restricted C, the presence of calls of one service-class does influence the number of calls of the other service-class at the borders of the system (only). For this reason, we can accept the principle of independency (i.e., multiplication of probabilities), but we have to reconsider the normalization condition, so that the state probabilities of all possible states sum up to 1. Thus, we multiply not the marginal probabilities but a proper function of them:

$$P(n_1, n_2) = \frac{f(P_{n_1})f(P_{n_2})}{G} = \frac{\frac{\alpha_1^{n_1}}{n_1!} \frac{\alpha_2^{n_2}}{n_2!}}{G} \tag{1.29}$$

where G is a normalization constant (to be determined).

In any case, the best way to prove that a system has a PFS,[5] is to find it!

1.2.2 The Analytical Model

1.2.2.1 Steady State Probabilities

In analyzing a service system, the first target is to determine the steady state probability $P(\mathbf{n})$. For the EMLM, it can be determined, obviously, by extending the PFS (1.29) of Example 1.6 to K service-classes, as follows:

$$P(\mathbf{n}) = \frac{\prod_{k=1}^{K} \frac{\alpha_k^{n_k}}{n_k!}}{G} \tag{1.30}$$

where $G \equiv$ the normalization constant, which is determined through $\sum_{\mathbf{n} \in \Omega} P(\mathbf{n}) = 1$:

$$\sum_{\mathbf{n} \in \Omega} \frac{\prod_{k=1}^{K} \frac{\alpha_k^{n_k}}{n_k!}}{G} = 1 \Rightarrow \frac{1}{G} \sum_{\mathbf{n} \in \Omega} \prod_{k=1}^{K} \frac{\alpha_k^{n_k}}{n_k!} = 1 \Rightarrow G = \sum_{\mathbf{n} \in \Omega} \prod_{k=1}^{K} \frac{\alpha_k^{n_k}}{n_k!} \tag{1.31}$$

Of course, the PFS (1.30) must satisfy the set of GB and LB equations of the system. To verify it, follow the aforementioned classical methodology:

(i) Draw the state transition diagram and write the GB equations. Figure 1.7 shows the one-dimensional state transition diagram of the EMLM when a general state $\mathbf{n}$ is considered. Normally, the state transition diagram has as many dimensions (axes) as the number of service-classes K; see the LHS of Figure 1.8. To be converted to a one-dimensional diagram, we define the equivalent diagram at the RHS of Figure 1.8. This consideration is justified because both diagrams lead to the same GB equation (see (1.32)). Thus, the GB equation (*rate in = rate out*) for state $\mathbf{n} = (n_1, n_2, \dots, n_k, \dots, n_K)$ is given by:

$$\sum_{k=1}^{K} \lambda_k \delta_k^-(\mathbf{n}) P(\mathbf{n}_k^-) + \sum_{k=1}^{K} (n_k + 1) \mu_k \delta_k^+(\mathbf{n}) P(\mathbf{n}_k^+) =$$
$$= \sum_{k=1}^{K} \lambda_k \delta_k^+(\mathbf{n}) P(\mathbf{n}) + \sum_{k=1}^{K} n_k \mu_k \delta_k^-(\mathbf{n}) P(\mathbf{n}) \tag{1.32}$$

---

5 As we discuss in Section 1.3.2, another indication of PFS is the existence of LB between all the adjacent states of the system or, equivalently, the Markov chain reversibility.

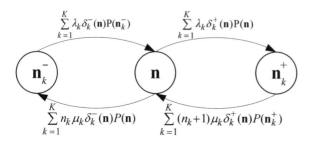

$$\sum_{k=1}^{K} \lambda_k \delta_k^-(\mathbf{n}) P(\mathbf{n}_k^-) \qquad \sum_{k=1}^{K} \lambda_k \delta_k^+(\mathbf{n}) P(\mathbf{n})$$

$$\sum_{k=1}^{K} n_k \mu_k \delta_k^-(\mathbf{n}) P(\mathbf{n}) \qquad \sum_{k=1}^{K} (n_k+1)\mu_k \delta_k^+(\mathbf{n}) P(\mathbf{n}_k^+)$$

Figure 1.7 State transition diagram of the EMLM.

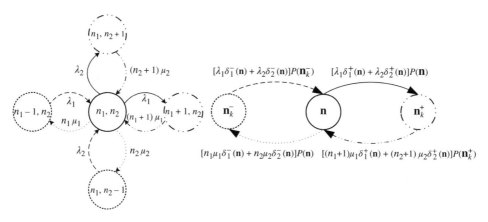

Figure 1.8 GB in the system of Example 1.6 (Example 1.7).

where $P(\mathbf{n}_k^-), P(\mathbf{n}_k^+)$ are the probability distributions of the corresponding states $\mathbf{n}_k^-, \mathbf{n}_k^+$; parameters δ validate a state transition through the following expressions:

$$\delta_k^-(\mathbf{n}) = \begin{cases} 1 & \text{if } \mathbf{n}_k^- \in \mathbf{\Omega} \\ 0 & \text{otherwise} \end{cases} \qquad \delta_k^+(\mathbf{n}) = \begin{cases} 1 & \text{if } \mathbf{n}_k^+ \in \mathbf{\Omega} \\ 0 & \text{otherwise} \end{cases} \qquad (1.33)$$

Example 1.7 Explanation of (1.32) and the usage of parameters δ.

Figure 1.8 illustrates the GB equation (1.32) of Example 1.6. As far as the use of parameters δ is concerned, if state $\mathbf{n}$ (Figure 1.8) stands for $(1,1)$ (Figure 1.6), then both δ_k^- and δ_k^+ equal 1 because all transfers to all adjacent states are permitted from $(1,1)$. However, if $\mathbf{n}$ stands for any other state, not all transfers are possible, and therefore parameters δ should properly be used (0 or 1). For instance, if $\mathbf{n} = (3,1)$, then according to (1.32), we have:

$$[\lambda_1 \cdot 1 \cdot P(2,1) + \lambda_2 \cdot 1 \cdot P(3,0)] + [4\mu_1 \cdot 0 \cdot P(4,1) + 2\mu_2 \cdot 0 \cdot P(3,2)] =$$
$$= [\lambda_1 \cdot 0 \cdot P(3,1) + \lambda_2 \cdot 0 \cdot P(3,1)] + [3\mu_1 \cdot 1 \cdot P(3,1) + \mu_2 \cdot 1 \cdot P(3,1)] \Rightarrow$$
$$\lambda_1 \cdot P(2,1) + \lambda_2 \cdot P(3,0) = 3\mu_1 \cdot P(3,1) + \mu_2 \cdot P(3,1)$$

On the other hand, the use of parameter δ in each arrow of Figure 1.8 denotes that only one term at a time occurs, e.g., the pair of δ can be $(1,0)$ or $(0,1)$.

(ii) Assume that LB exists and check for atopy.

Assuming the existence of LB between any adjacent states ($\mathbf{n}_k^-$ and $\mathbf{n}$, or $\mathbf{n}$ and $\mathbf{n}_k^+$, for $k = 1, 2, \ldots, K$), then the following LB equations (*rate up = rate down*) are extracted from the state transition diagram (Figure 1.8, LHS) (correspondingly):

$$\lambda_k \delta_k^-(\mathbf{n})P(\mathbf{n}_k^-) = n_k \mu_k \delta_k^-(\mathbf{n})P(\mathbf{n}) \tag{1.34a}$$

$$\lambda_k \delta_k^+(\mathbf{n})P(\mathbf{n}) = (n_k + 1)\mu_k \delta_k^+(\mathbf{n})P(\mathbf{n}_k^+) \tag{1.34b}$$

(iii) Solve the resultant linear system of equations of the equilibrium probabilities, while considering the normalization condition. Check for atopy, again.

It can be verified that the probability distribution $P(\mathbf{n})$ has a PFS by substituting (1.30) into (1.34a) or (1.34b).

Example 1.8 Let us verify that the PFS (1.30) stands for the state probability $P(\mathbf{n}) = P(n_1, n_2)$ of Example 1.6. For simplicity reasons, let $\lambda_1 = \lambda_2 = \mu_1 = \mu_2 = 1 \text{ min}^{-1}$.

The steady state probabilities (1.29) result from (1.30) when $K = 2$, while G is given by (1.31). From Figure 1.6, the state space Ω is:

$\Omega = \{(0,0), (0,1), (0,2), (1,0), (1,1), (1,2), (2,0), (2,1), (3,0), (3,1), (4,0), (5,0)\}$.

Thus, we have to verify that:

$$P(\mathbf{n}) = P(n_1, n_2) = \frac{\dfrac{\alpha_1^{n_1} \alpha_2^{n_2}}{n_1! \, n_2!}}{\displaystyle\sum_{(n_1, n_2) \in \Omega} \dfrac{\alpha_1^{n_1} \alpha_2^{n_2}}{n_1! \, n_2!}} \tag{1.35}$$

satisfies the LB equations obtained via (1.34), when considering any pair of states and any service-class.

For instance, for the pair $(\mathbf{n}_1^-, \mathbf{n}) = ((0,0), (0,1))$ (Figure 1.6), the LB equation is:

$$\lambda_1 P(0,0) = \mu_1 P(0,1) \Rightarrow P(0,0) = P(0,1)$$

Since $\alpha_1 = \frac{\lambda_1}{\mu_1} = 1 = \alpha_2 = \frac{\lambda_2}{\mu_2}$, the denominator of (1.35) becomes:

$$\sum_{(n_1, n_2) \in \Omega} \frac{\alpha_1^{n_1} \alpha_2^{n_2}}{n_1! \, n_2!} = \frac{\alpha_1^0 \alpha_2^0}{0! \, 0!} + \frac{\alpha_1^0 \alpha_2^1}{0! \, 1!} + \frac{\alpha_1^0 \alpha_2^2}{0! \, 2!} + \cdots + \frac{\alpha_1^5 \alpha_2^0}{5! \, 0!} = 6.38333$$

Then:

$$P(0,0) = \frac{\frac{\alpha_1^0 \alpha_2^0}{0! \, 0!}}{G} = \frac{1}{6.38333} = 0.156658 \quad \text{and} \quad P(0,1) = \frac{\frac{\alpha_1^0 \alpha_2^1}{0! \, 1!}}{G} = \frac{1}{6.38333}$$
$$= 0.156658$$

For the pair $(\mathbf{n}_2^+, \mathbf{n}) = ((1,2), (1,1))$ (Figure 1.6), the LB equation is:

$$\lambda_2 P(1,1) = 2\mu_2 P(1,2) \Rightarrow P(1,1) = 2P(1,2)$$

Indeed:

$$P(1,1) = \frac{\frac{\alpha_1^1 \alpha_2^1}{1! \, 1!}}{G} = \frac{1}{6.38333} = 0.156658 \quad \text{and} \quad P(1,2) = \frac{\frac{\alpha_1^1 \alpha_2^2}{1! \, 2!}}{G} = \frac{\frac{1}{2}}{6.38333}$$
$$= \frac{1}{2}P(1,1), \text{ etc.}$$

Having calculated the steady state probability $P(\mathbf{n})$, we proceed to determine the CBP. To this end, we denote by $\mathbf{\Omega}_{\{k\}}$ the admissible state space of service-class k: $\mathbf{\Omega}_{\{k\}} = \{\mathbf{n} \in \mathbf{\Omega} : \mathbf{nb} \leq C - b_k\}$, $k = 1, 2, \ldots, K$. A new service-class k call is accepted in the system, if, at the time point of its arrival, the system is in a state $\mathbf{n} \in \mathbf{\Omega}_{\{k\}}$. Hence, the CBP of service-class k is determined by the state space $\mathbf{\Omega} - \mathbf{\Omega}_{\{k\}}$, as follows:

$$B_k = \sum_{\mathbf{n} \in (\mathbf{\Omega} - \mathbf{\Omega}_{\{k\}})} P(\mathbf{n}) \Rightarrow B_k = 1 - \sum_{\mathbf{n} \in \mathbf{\Omega}_{\{k\}}} P(\mathbf{n}) \Rightarrow B_k = 1 - \frac{\displaystyle\sum_{\mathbf{n} \in \mathbf{\Omega}_{\{k\}}} \prod_{k=1}^{K} \frac{\alpha_k^{n_k}}{n_k!}}{\displaystyle\sum_{\mathbf{n} \in \mathbf{\Omega}} \prod_{k=1}^{K} \frac{\alpha_k^{n_k}}{n_k!}} \tag{1.36}$$

Example 1.9 In Example 1.6 ($C = 5, K = 2, b_1 = 1, b_2 = 2$), assume that $\alpha_1 = \alpha_2 = 1$. Find both the admissible and blocking states of each service-class and, based on (1.36), determine the CBP.

As shown in Figure 1.6:

$\mathbf{\Omega}_{\{1\}} = \{(0,0), (0,1), (0,2), (1,0), (1,1), (2,0), (2,1), (3,0), (4,0)\}$

$\mathbf{\Omega}_{\{2\}} = \{(0,0), (0,1), (1,0), (1,1), (2,0), (3,0)\}$

According to (1.36), the CBP are determined as the summation of the probabilities of (blocking) states: $B_1 \Rightarrow \mathbf{\Omega} - \mathbf{\Omega}_{\{1\}} = \{(1,2), (3,1), (5,0)\}$ and $B_2 \Rightarrow \mathbf{\Omega} - \mathbf{\Omega}_{\{2\}} = \{(1,2), (3,1), (5,0), (0,2), (2,1), (4,0)\}$. Hence,

$B_1 = P(1,2) + P(3,1) + P(5,0) = \frac{1}{6.38333}\left(\frac{1}{2} + \frac{1}{6} + \frac{1}{120}\right) = 10.57\%.$

$B_2 = B_1 + P(0,2) + P(2,1) + P(4,0) = 0.1057 + \frac{1}{6.38333}\left(\frac{1}{2} + \frac{1}{2} + \frac{1}{24}\right) = 26.89\%.$

Equation (1.35) provides the CBP of the EMLM based on a PFS. A recurrent form for the CBP calculation can be obtained by expressing (1.36), as follows:

$$B_k = 1 - \frac{G(C - K, K)}{G(C, K)} \tag{1.37}$$

where $G(C, K) \equiv \mathbf{\Omega}$; the values of $G(C, K)$ can be determined recursively via:

$$G(j, k) = \sum_{l=0}^{\lfloor j/b_k \rfloor} \frac{\alpha_k^l}{l!} G(j - lb_k, k - 1) \quad k = 2, \ldots, K, \quad j = 0, 1, 2, \ldots, C$$

$$G(j, 1) = \sum_{l=0}^{\lfloor j/b_1 \rfloor} \frac{\alpha_1^l}{l!} \tag{1.38}$$

For large values of C, K the computational complexity of (1.38) is $O(C^K)^6$. A simpler formula follows with a computational complexity $O(CK)$,[7] for the determination of the state probabilities of the system, when the system state is represented not by the number of in-service calls of each service-class, but by the total occupied b.u. j in the link, where $j = 0, 1, 2, \ldots, C$. This state representation is more effective when aimed at calculating

---

6 This big O notation, also called Landau's symbol, shows that the computational complexity increases exponentially, according to C^K.

7 Proportional to the product CK.

the key performance metrics of the system, like CBP and link utilization. The unnormalized values $q(j)$ of the *link occupancy distribution*, i.e., the probability that j out of C b.u. are occupied, are given by:

$$q(j) = \begin{cases} 1 & \text{if} \quad j = 0 \\ \dfrac{1}{j} \sum_{k=1}^{K} \alpha_k b_k q(j - b_k) & j = 1, 2, \dots, C \\ 0 & \text{otherwise} \end{cases} \tag{1.39}$$

Equation (1.39), known in the literature as the *Kaufman–Roberts*[8] *recursion*, is accurate and computationally efficient with an easy computer implementation. Because of this, it is the springboard to derive other more complex but efficient teletraffic models. In order for the $q(j)$ values of (1.39) to become probabilities, they must be normalized through division by the sum of them, G:

$$G = \sum_{j=0}^{C} q(j) \tag{1.40}$$

Note that $q(j)$ denotes either a normalized or unnormalized value of the link occupancy distribution, but, in any case, it will be explicitly mentioned (unless it is clear), while $Q(j) = q(j)/G$ denotes a normalized value of the link occupancy distribution.

Proof of (1.39): According to [5], let us consider the occupied link bandwidth j ($j = 0, 1, 2, \dots, C$), as a system state. Thus, the system can be seen either via state $\mathbf{n}$ (multi-dimensional system) or via the new (aggregate) state j (one-dimensional system). The link occupancy distribution $q(j)$ is defined as:

$$q(j) = \sum_{\mathbf{n} \in \Omega_j} P(\mathbf{n}) \tag{1.41}$$

where Ω_j is the set of states in which exactly j b.u. are occupied by all in-service calls: $\Omega_j = \{\mathbf{n} \in \Omega : \mathbf{nb} = j\}$ (Figure 1.9).

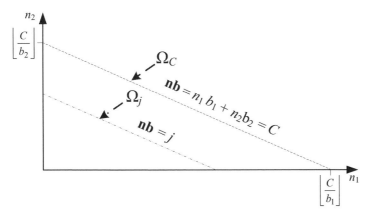

Figure 1.9 Sets Ω_C and Ω_j for the EMLM of two service-classes, under the CS policy.

8 Joseph S. Kaufman, Bell Laboratories (1981) and Jim W. Roberts, France Telecom (1981).

The key point for the recursive calculation of $q(j)$ is to associate the values of $q(j)$ values with the "previous" values of $q(j - b_k)$. In other words, we have to relate the values of $P(\mathbf{n})$ with the ("previous") values of $P(\mathbf{n}_k^-)$, since in state j there are n_k in-service calls of service-class k, while in state $j - b_k$ there are $n_k - 1$ in-service calls (assuming that $n_k - 1 \geq 0$). This relation will be achieved by the use of the LB equation (1.34a), as we will shortly show.

Since $j = \mathbf{nb} = \sum_{k=1}^{K} n_k b_k$, we can write (1.41) as follows:

$$jq(j) = \sum_{k=1}^{K} n_k b_k \sum_{\mathbf{n} \in \Omega_j} P(\mathbf{n}) \Rightarrow jq(j) = \sum_{k=1}^{K} b_k \sum_{\mathbf{n} \in \Omega_j} n_k P(\mathbf{n}) \tag{1.42}$$

From the LB equation (1.34a), the product $n_k P(\mathbf{n})$ is determined by:

$$\frac{\lambda_k}{\mu_k} \delta_k^-(\mathbf{n}) P(\mathbf{n}_k^-) = n_k \delta_k^-(\mathbf{n}) P(\mathbf{n}) \Rightarrow \alpha_k \gamma_k(\mathbf{n}) P(\mathbf{n}_k^-) = n_k P(\mathbf{n}) \tag{1.43}$$

where the parameter δ is replaced by γ (another binary parameter) to denote that:

$$\gamma_k(\mathbf{n}) = \begin{cases} 1 & \text{if} \quad n_k \geq 1 \\ 0 & \text{if} \quad n_k = 0 \end{cases} \quad \forall k \tag{1.44}$$

We take sums of both sides of (1.43) over Ω_j to have:

$$\alpha_k \sum_{\mathbf{n} \in \Omega_j} \gamma_k(\mathbf{n}) P(\mathbf{n}_k^-) = \sum_{\mathbf{n} \in \Omega_j} n_k P(\mathbf{n}) \tag{1.45}$$

Equation (1.43) has no meaning when $n_k = 0$; since the RHS of (1.45) refers to state $\mathbf{n} \in \Omega_j$, the previous state $\mathbf{n}_k^-$ (in which the LHS of (1.45) refers to) belongs to Ω_{j-b_k} given that $n_k \geq 1$. This is expressed through the parameters γ_k. More formally, when $n_k \geq 1$, the LHS of (1.45) is written as:

$$\alpha_k \sum_{\mathbf{n} \in \Omega_j} \gamma_k(\mathbf{n}) P(\mathbf{n}_k^-) = \alpha_k \sum_{\mathbf{n} \in \Omega_j \wedge (n_k \geq 1)} P(\mathbf{n}_k^-) \tag{1.46}$$

and the set $\Omega_j \wedge (n_k \geq 1) = \{\mathbf{n} : \sum_{l \neq k} n_l b_l + (n_k - 1) b_k = j - b_k, \ n_k \geq 1, \ k = 1, 2, \ldots,$ $K\}$ defines the state space Ω_{j-b_k}. To individuate the case where $l = k$, we introduce the following variable:

$$\hat{\mathbf{n}}_l = \begin{cases} \mathbf{n}_l & \text{if} \quad l \neq k \\ \mathbf{n}_l - 1 & \text{if} \quad l = k \end{cases} \tag{1.47}$$

By using (1.47), and because of the definition (1.41), we can write (1.46) as follows:

$$\alpha_k \sum_{\mathbf{n} \in \Omega_j \wedge (n_k \geq 1)} P(\mathbf{n}_k^-) = \alpha_k \sum_{\hat{\mathbf{n}} \in \Omega_{j-b_k}} P(\hat{\mathbf{n}}) = \alpha_k q(j - b_k) \tag{1.48}$$

From (1.45), (1.46), and (1.48), we obtain:

$$\alpha_k q(j - b_k) = \sum_{\mathbf{n} \in \Omega_j} n_k P(\mathbf{n}) \tag{1.49}$$

Based on (1.49), (1.42) is written as:

$$jq(j) = \sum_{k=1}^{K} \alpha_k b_k q(j - b_k) \tag{1.50}$$

Figure 1.10 The Kaufman–Roberts recursion as a birth–death process.

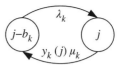

which is the Kaufman–Roberts recursion (1.39). For an alternative proof see Example 1.12.

Q.E.D.

According to [5], (1.39) can be used for arbitrary distributed service times. An interesting interpretation of (1.39) is that it stands for an LB equation of a birth–death process, in which $\lambda_k q(j - b_k)$ is the birth rate of service-class k calls, $y_k(j)\mu_k q(j)$ is the corresponding death rate, and $y_k(j)$ is the mean number of service-class k calls in state j (Figure 1.10):

$$\alpha_k q(j - b_k) = y_k(j)q(j) \qquad j = 1, 2, \dots, C \tag{1.51}$$

Indeed, (1.51) is derived from (1.49) because the RHS of (1.49) is written as follows:

$$\sum_{\mathbf{n} \in \Omega_j} n_k P(\mathbf{n}) = \sum_{\mathbf{n} \in \Omega_j} n_k \frac{P(\mathbf{n})}{q(j)} q(j) = \left(\sum_{\mathbf{n} \in \Omega_j} n_k P(\mathbf{n}|j) \right) q(j) = y_k(j)q(j) \tag{1.52}$$

Note that (1.39) can be derived from (1.51) by multiplying both sides of (1.51) by b_k and summing over k.

1.2.2.2 CBP, Utilization, and Mean Number of In-service Calls

The following performance measures are determined based on (1.39):

- CBP: The determination of CBP of service-class k, B_k, is given by:

$$B_k = \sum_{j=C-b_k+1}^{C} \frac{q(j)}{G} \qquad \text{or} \qquad B_k = \sum_{j=0}^{b_k-1} \frac{q(C-j)}{G} \tag{1.53}$$

where G is given by (1.40).

Figure 1.11 depicts a helpful visualization regarding (1.53).

Note that (1.53) refers to the TC probabilities of service-class k calls. These probabilities coincide with the CBP due to the PASTA property.

Needless to say that in the case of one service-class in the system, the CBP obtained by (1.53) coincides with the results of the Erlang-B formula; hence, we name this model the Erlang multirate loss model.

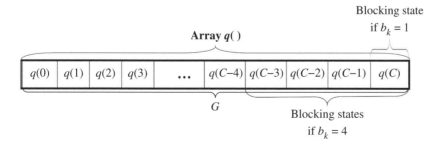

Figure 1.11 Visualization of CBP calculation.

- Utilization: The link utilization, U, is calculated by:

$$U = \sum_{j=1}^{C} j \frac{q(j)}{G} \tag{1.54}$$

- Mean number of in-service calls in state j: The mean number of in-service calls of service-class k in state j ($q(j) > 0$), $y_k(j)$ is given (because of (1.51)) by:

$$y_k(j) = \alpha_k \frac{q(j - b_k)}{q(j)} \qquad j = 1, 2, \dots, C \tag{1.55}$$

Note that $y_k(j) = 0$, if $j < b_k$.

- Mean number of in-service calls in the system: The mean number of in-service calls for service-class k in the system, $\bar{n}_k$, is given by:

$$\bar{n}_k = \sum_{j=1}^{C} y_k(j) \frac{q(j)}{G} \tag{1.56}$$

Example 1.10 In the system of Example 1.6 ($C = 5$, $K = 2$, $\alpha_1 = \alpha_2 = 1$, $b_1 = 1$, $b_2 = 2$):

(a) Calculate the state probabilities $Q(j)$, by applying the Kaufman–Roberts recursion.
(b) Verify the probability $Q(5)$ (that 5 b.u. are occupied) through the state probabilities $P(n_1, n_2)$ obtained from Example 1.9.
(c) Calculate the CBP of the two service-classes through (1.53).
(d) Calculate the link utilization.
(e) Calculate the trunk efficiency.
(f) Calculate the mean number of in-service calls of the two service-classes when the system is full.
(g) Calculate the mean number of in-service calls of the two service-classes in the system.
(h) Apply the classical methodology of solving the system of GB equations to check the accuracy of the state probabilities calculated by the Kaufman–Roberts recursion.

(a) *State probabilities through the Kaufman–Roberts recursion:* For $C = 5, K = 2, \alpha_1 = \alpha_2 = 1, b_1 = 1$, and $b_2 = 2$, the Kaufman–Roberts recursion is written as:

$$jq(j) = \alpha_1 b_1 q(j - b_1) + \alpha_2 b_2 q(j - b_2) \Rightarrow jq(j) = q(j - 1) + 2q(j - 2)$$

Starting with $q(0) = 1$, we recursively calculate the $q(j)$ values for $j = 1, \dots, 5$:

$$j = 1 : \quad q(1) = q(0) + 0 = 1.0 \qquad\qquad \Rightarrow \quad q(1) = 1.0$$
$$j = 2 : \quad 2q(2) = q(1) + 2q(0) = 3.0 \qquad\quad \Rightarrow \quad q(2) = 1.5$$
$$j = 3 : \quad 3q(3) = q(2) + 2q(1) = 3.5 \qquad\quad \Rightarrow \quad q(3) = 1.1667$$
$$j = 4 : \quad 4q(4) = q(3) + 2q(2) = 4.1667 \quad \Rightarrow \quad q(4) = 1.0417$$
$$j = 5 : \quad 5q(5) = q(4) + 2q(3) = 3.3751 \quad \Rightarrow \quad q(5) = 0.675$$

The normalization constant is $G = \sum_{j=0}^{5} q(j) = 6.3834$.

The state probabilities (link occupancy distribution) are:

$$Q(0) = \frac{1}{6.3834} = 15.67\%, \quad Q(1) = \frac{1}{6.3834} = 15.67\%, \quad Q(2) = \frac{1.5}{6.3834} = 23.49\%,$$

$$Q(3) = \frac{1.1667}{6.3834} = 18.28\%, \quad Q(4) = \frac{1.0417}{6.3834} = 16.32\%, \quad Q(5) = \frac{0.675}{6.3834} = 10.57\%.$$

(b) *Comparison–verification between the state probabilities $Q(5)$ and $P(n_1, n_2)$*: From Figure 1.6, we have that $Q(5) = P(1, 2) + P(3, 1) + P(5, 0)$. In Example 1.9, we have calculated that $P(1, 2) + P(3, 1) + P(5, 0) = 10.57\%$, which coincides with $Q(5)$ calculated in (a) in this example.

(c) *CBP calculation*: According to (1.53), the CBP of each service-class is:

$$B_1 = \sum_{j=C-b_1+1}^{C} \frac{q(j)}{G} = \sum_{j=5-1+1}^{5} \frac{q(j)}{G} = \frac{q(5)}{G} = \frac{0.675}{6.3834} = 10.57\%$$

$$B_2 = \sum_{j=C-b_2+1}^{C} \frac{q(j)}{G} = \sum_{j=5-2+1}^{5} \frac{q(j)}{G} = \frac{q(4) + q(5)}{G} = \frac{1.0417 + 0.675}{6.3834} = 26.89\%$$

(d) *Utilization*: According to (1.54), the link utilization is:

$$U = \sum_{j=1}^{5} j \frac{q(j)}{G} = 1\frac{q(1)}{G} + 2\frac{q(2)}{G} + 3\frac{q(3)}{G} + 4\frac{q(4)}{G} + 5\frac{q(5)}{G} =$$

$$= 1 \cdot Q(1) + 2 \cdot Q(2) + 3 \cdot Q(3) + 4 \cdot Q(4) + 5 \cdot Q(5) =$$

$$= 1 \cdot 0.1567 + 2 \cdot 0.2349 + 3 \cdot 0.1828 + 4 \cdot 0.1632 + 5 \cdot 0.1057 = 2.3562 \quad \text{b.u.}$$

(e) *Trunk efficiency*: On average, 2.3562 b.u. (out of 5 b.u.) are occupied, that is, a percentage of $\eta = \frac{2.3562}{5} = 47.12\%$, which is the trunk efficiency.

In case of two service-classes, an alternative estimation of the trunk efficiency is achieved by considering an equivalent single service-class in the link, with the following offered traffic-load and CBP:

$\alpha = (\alpha_1 b_1 + \alpha_2 b_2) = 3$ erl and $B = \frac{(\alpha_1 b_1)B_1 + (\alpha_2 b_2)B_2}{(\alpha_1 b_1 + \alpha_2 b_2)} = \frac{0.1057 + 2 \cdot 0.2689}{3} = 21.45\%$

Then, $\eta = \frac{\alpha(1-B)}{C} = \frac{3(1-0.2145)}{5} = 47.13\%$.

(f) *Mean number of calls, when the system is full*: The system is full in state $j = 5$ ($(n_1, n_2) = (5, 0)$, or$(3, 1)$, or$(1, 2)$). Then, according to (1.55), we have:

$$y_1(5) = \alpha_1 \frac{q(5 - b_1)}{q(5)} = \frac{q(4)}{q(5)} = \frac{1.0417}{0.675} = 1.54$$

$$y_2(5) = \alpha_2 \frac{q(5 - b_2)}{q(5)} = \frac{q(3)}{q(5)} = \frac{1.1667}{0.675} = 1.73$$

Indeed, $y_1(5) \cdot b_1 + y_2(5) \cdot b_2 = j = 5$.

(g) *Mean number of calls in the system*: Based on (1.56), the mean numbers of calls of the first and second service-classes are $\bar{n}_1 = 0.894$ and $\bar{n}_2 = 0.731$, respectively.

(h) *Accuracy of the Kaufman–Roberts recursion, examined by classical methodology*: According to classical methodology, we have to formulate a linear system of equations obtained from the GB equations of the system, together with the normalization condition that all state probabilities $P(n_1, n_2)$ sum up to 1. Therefore, for each of the 12 states of Figure 1.6, we write the corresponding GB equation (*rate in = rate out*):

$(0,0):\quad \mu_1 P(1,0) + \mu_2 P(0,1) = (\lambda_1 + \lambda_2)P(0,0)$

$(0,1):\quad \lambda_2 P(0,0) + 2\mu_2 P(0,2) + \mu_1 P(1,1) = (\lambda_1 + \lambda_2 + \mu_2)P(0,1)$

$(0,2):\quad \lambda_2 P(0,1) + \mu_1 P(1,2) = (\lambda_1 + 2\mu_2)P(0,2)$

$(1,0):\quad \lambda_1 P(0,0) + \mu_2 P(1,1) + 2\mu_1 P(2,0) = (\lambda_1 + \lambda_2 + \mu_1)P(1,0)$

$(1,1):\quad \lambda_1 P(0,1) + \lambda_2 P(1,0) + 2\mu_1 P(2,1) + 2\mu_2 P(1,2) = (\lambda_1 + \lambda_2 + \mu_1 + \mu_2)P(1,1)$

$(1,2):\quad \lambda_1 P(0,2) + \lambda_2 P(1,1) = (\mu_1 + 2\mu_2)P(1,2)$

$(2,0):\quad \lambda_1 P(1,0) + \mu_2 P(2,1) + 3\mu_1 P(3,0) = (\lambda_1 + \lambda_2 + 2\mu_1)P(2,0)$

$(2,1):\quad \lambda_1 P(1,1) + \lambda_2 P(2,0) + 3\mu_1 P(3,1) = (\lambda_1 + \mu_2 + 2\mu_1)P(2,1)$

$(3,0):\quad \lambda_1 P(2,0) + \mu_2 P(3,1) + 4\mu_1 P(4,0) = (\lambda_1 + \lambda_2 + 3\mu_1)P(3,0)$

$(3,1):\quad \lambda_1 P(2,1) + \lambda_2 P(3,0) = (\mu_2 + 3\mu_1)P(3,1)$

$(4,0):\quad \lambda_1 P(3,0) + 5\mu_1 P(5,0) = (\lambda_1 + 4\mu_1)P(4,0)$

$(5,0):\quad \lambda_1 P(4,0) = 5\mu_1 P(5,0)$

To finalize the formation of the system of equations, let us now replace the longest, the GB equation of (1,1), with the normalization condition:

$(0,0):\quad \Rightarrow \quad P(1,0) + P(0,1) - 2P(0,0) = 0$

$(0,1):\quad \Rightarrow \quad P(0,0) + 2P(0,2) + P(1,1) - 3P(0,1) = 0$

$(0,2):\quad \Rightarrow \quad P(0,1) + P(1,2) - 3P(0,2) = 0$

$(1,0):\quad \Rightarrow \quad P(0,0) + P(1,1) + 2P(2,0) - 3P(1,0) = 0$

$(1,2):\quad \Rightarrow \quad P(0,2) + P(1,1) - 3P(1,2) = 0$

$(2,0):\quad \Rightarrow \quad P(1,0) + P(2,1) + 3P(3,0) - 4P(2,0) = 0$

$(2,1):\quad \Rightarrow \quad P(1,1) + P(2,0) + 3P(3,1) - 4P(2,1) = 0$

$(3,0):\quad \Rightarrow \quad P(2,0) + P(3,1) + 4P(4,0) - 5P(3,0) = 0$

$(3,1):\quad \Rightarrow \quad P(2,1) + P(3,0) - 4P(3,1) = 0$

$(4,0):\quad \Rightarrow \quad P(3,0) + 5P(5,0) - 5P(4,0) = 0$

$(5,0):\quad \Rightarrow \quad P(4,0) - 5P(5,0) = 0$

$\qquad\qquad$ and $\quad \sum_{n\in\Omega} P(n_1, n_2) = 1.$

Although the above linear system can be solved on paper by the simple method of successive substitutions, the procedure is tedious and therefore a computer program is used to obtain the results:

$P(0,0) = 0.156658$	$P(0,1) = 0.156658$	$P(0,2) = 0.078329$	$P(1,0) = 0.156658$
$P(1,1) = 0.156658$	$P(1,2) = 0.078329$	$P(2,0) = 0.078329$	$P(2,1) = 0.078329$
$P(3,0) = 0.026110$	$P(3,1) = 0.026110$	$P(4,0) = 0.006527$	$P(5,0) = 0.001305$

These results verify the results of the Kaufman–Roberts recursion in (a), since:

$Q(0) = P(0,0) \checkmark$

$Q(1) = P(1,0) \checkmark$

$Q(2) = P(2,0) + P(0,1) \checkmark$

$Q(3) = P(3,0) + P(1,1) \checkmark$

$Q(4) = P(4,0) + P(2,1) + P(0,2) \checkmark$

$Q(5) = P(5,0) + P(3,1) + P(1,2) \checkmark$

Example 1.11   Based on Example 1.6 ($C = 5$, $K = 2$, $\alpha_1 = \alpha_2 = 1$, $b_1 = 1$, $b_2 = 2$), show that:

(a) The Kaufman–Roberts recursion holds for any initial value of $q(0) > 0$ (not only for $q(0) = 1$).
(b) Find a way to reduce the value of G so that register overflow is avoided in the computer implementation of the Kaufman–Roberts recursion.

(a) *Initial value of $q(j)$ for the Kaufman–Roberts recursion*: Let $q(0) > 0$ and apply the Kaufman–Roberts recursion (1.39), or (1.50), for $j = 1, 2, \ldots, C$:

$j = 1$: $q(1) = q(0)$

$j = 2$: $2q(2) = q(1) + 2q(0) = 3q(0)$ $\Rightarrow$ $q(2) = 1.5q(0)$

$j = 3$: $3q(3) = q(2) + 2q(1) = 1.5q(0) + 2q(0) = 3.5q(0)$ $\Rightarrow$ $q(3) = 1.1667q(0)$

$j = 4$: $4q(4) = q(3) + 2q(2) = 1.1667q(0) + 3q(0) = 4.1667q(0)$ $\Rightarrow$ $q(4) = 1.0417q(0)$

$j = 5$: $5q(5) = q(4) + 2q(3) = 1.0417q(0) + 2.3333q(0) = 3.375q(0)$ $\Rightarrow$ $q(5) = 0.675q(0)$

The normalization constant becomes $G = \sum_{j=0}^{5} q(j) = 6.3834q(0)$.
By dividing the $q(j)$ values by G, we have exactly the same results as if $q(0) = 1$.

(b) *Method of reducing the value of G*: Since G is a product of $q(0)$, by choosing a small value for $q(0)$, for instance $q(0) = 10^{-6}$, G is reduced. Furthermore, thanks to the recurrent calculations, it is possible to check the value of G in each iteration, and if G exceeds a threshold, then (at that iteration) all the already determined values (including $q(0)$) can be divided by a large number to obtain smaller values (without affecting the final probabilities). For instance, starting with $q(0) = 1$ and setting the threshold value of G at 4, we find that $G > 4$ just after the iteration for $j = 3$. Before continuing, we can divide by 10 in order to take smaller values: $q(0) = 0.1$, $q(1) = 0.1$, $q(2) = 0.15$ and $q(3) = 0.11667$. When continuing, we have $q(4) = 0.10417$ and $q(5) = 0.0675$, resulting in $G = 0.63834$. This technique is useful for systems with a large capacity C and many service-classes.

Example 1.12   Prove (1.39), based on the CBP definition (I.2b) and property (4) of the traffic-load.

Proof: An alternative proof of the Kaufman–Roberts recursion (1.39) (and consequently of (1.53)) is given in [6]. Since call blocking of service-class k occurs when the total occupied link bandwidth $j = \mathbf{nb} > C - b_k$, the CBP of service-class k becomes:

$$B_k = \sum_{\mathbf{n} \in \Omega:\ \mathbf{nb} > C - b_k} P(\mathbf{n}) \tag{1.57}$$

From the definition ((I.2b)), $B_k = \frac{\alpha_k - \alpha_{ck}}{\alpha_k}$, and property (4) of traffic-load, i.e., the mean number of service-class k calls under service, $\bar{n}_k$, equals the carried traffic α_{ck} of service-class k, so we have:

$$\bar{n}_k = \alpha_k(1 - B_k) = \alpha_{ck} \tag{1.58}$$

From (1.58), we have the mean number of occupied b.u. in the link, $E[j]$:

$$E[j] = \sum_{k=1}^{K} b_k \bar{n}_k \tag{1.59}$$

which is also written as (according to the probabilistic notion of mean value):

$$E[j] = \sum_{j=0}^{C} j q(j) \tag{1.60}$$

Because of (1.57), (1.58) can be rewritten as (see also (1.36)):

$$\bar{n}_k = \alpha_k (1 - \sum_{n \in \Omega: \ nb > C - b_k} P(\mathbf{n})) = \alpha_k \sum_{n \in \Omega_{\{k\}}: \ nb \leq C - b_k} P(\mathbf{n}) = \alpha_k \sum_{j=0}^{C - b_k} q(j) \tag{1.61}$$

where $\mathbf{n} \in \Omega_{\{k\}}$ is the set of all admissible states of service-class k (e.g., $\Omega_{\{1\}}$ for service-class 1, in Figure 1.6).

By multiplying the LHS and RHS of (1.61) by b_k and summing up to K, we have:

$$\sum_{k=1}^{K} b_k \bar{n}_k = \sum_{k=1}^{K} b_k \alpha_k \sum_{j=0}^{C - b_k} q(j) \Rightarrow E[j] = \sum_{k=1}^{K} b_k \alpha_k \sum_{j=0}^{C} q(j - b_k) \tag{1.62}$$

Combining (1.60) with (1.62), we have:

$$\sum_{j=0}^{C} j q(j) = \sum_{k=1}^{K} \alpha_k b_k \sum_{j=0}^{C} q(j - b_k) = \sum_{j=0}^{C} \sum_{k=1}^{K} \alpha_k b_k q(j - b_k) \tag{1.63}$$

From the LHS and RHS of (1.63), we have (1.39).

Q.E.D.

Although this proof is more tractable, the proof given by Kaufman in [5] provides interesting insights of the EMLM, like the interpretation of a multi-dimensional system by an one-dimensional Markov chain through the parameters δ and (1.49).

Example 1.13 Consider again Example 1.6 ($C = 5, K = 2$, $b_1 = 1, b_2 = 2$) and let $\lambda_1 = \lambda_2 = \mu_1 = \mu_2 = 1 \quad \text{min}^{-1}$. Herein, we determine the CBP of both service-classes by using an alternative approach, called *convolution algorithm* [7]. The same CBP results as in Example 1.10 are provided.

The convolution algorithm for $K = 2$ service-classes is as follows.

(a) For each service-class k ($k = 1, 2$) calculate the link occupancy distribution $q_k(j)$, $j = 0, 1, \ldots, C$, assuming that only one (the kth) service-class is accommodated in the link, $q_k(j) = q_k(0) \frac{\alpha_k^i}{i!}$ for $1 \leq i \leq \lfloor C/b_k \rfloor$ and $j = ib_k$, while $q_k(0) = 1$ ($j = 0$).
   - First *service-class* ($\alpha_1 = 1$ erl, $b_1 = 1$ b.u.). For $1 \leq i \leq 5$, we have:

$$j = 0 : \qquad q_1(0) = 1$$

$$i = 1, \quad j = 1 : \qquad q_1(1) = \frac{\alpha_1^1}{1!} q_1(0) \quad \Rightarrow \quad q_1(1) = 1.0$$

$i = 2, \quad j = 2 \; : \quad q_1(2) = \dfrac{\alpha_1^2}{2!} q_1(0) \quad \Rightarrow \quad q_1(2) = 0.5$

$i = 3, \quad j = 3 \; : \quad q_1(3) = \dfrac{\alpha_1^3}{3!} q_1(0) \quad \Rightarrow \quad q_1(3) = 0.16667$

$i = 4, \quad j = 4 \; : \quad q_1(4) = \dfrac{\alpha_1^4}{4!} q_1(0) \quad \Rightarrow \quad q_1(4) = 0.04167$

$i = 5, \quad j = 5 \; : \quad q_1(5) = \dfrac{\alpha_1^5}{5!} q_1(0) \quad \Rightarrow \quad q_1(5) = 0.00833$

Therefore: $G = \sum_{j=0}^{5} q_1(j) = 2.71667$, and the normalized values of $q_1(j)$ are:

$Q_1(0) = q_1(0)/G = 0.3681 \quad Q_1(1) = q_1(1)/G = 0.3681 \quad Q_1(2) = q_1(2)/G = 0.1840$

$Q_1(3) = q_1(3)/G = 0.0614 \quad Q_1(4) = q_1(4)/G = 0.0153 \quad Q_1(5) = q_1(5)/G = 0.0031$

- Second *service-class* ($\alpha_2 = 1$ erl, $b_2 = 2$ b.u.). For $1 \le i \le 2$, we have:

$j = 0 \; : \qquad\quad q_2(0) = 1$

$i = 1, \quad j = 2 \; : \quad q_2(2) = \dfrac{\alpha_2^1}{1!} q_2(0) \quad \Rightarrow \quad q_2(2) = 1.0$

$i = 2, \quad j = 4 \; : \quad q_2(4) = \dfrac{\alpha_2^2}{2!} q_2(2) \quad \Rightarrow \quad q_2(4) = 0.5$

Therefore $G = \sum_{j=0}^{5} q_2(j) = 2.5$, and the normalized values of $q_2(j)$ are:

$Q_2(0) = q_2(0)/G = 0.4 \qquad Q_2(2) = q_2(2)/G = 0.4 \qquad Q_2(4) = q_2(4)/G = 0.2$

(b) By applying successive convolutions we calculate the link occupancy distribution $q(j)$ for all states $j = 0, 1, \ldots, C$. Letting the symbol $*$ denote the convolution operator, we have the following formula for the calculation of $q(j)$ for both service-classes:
$q(j) = Q_1(j) * Q_2(j) = \sum_{i=0}^{j} Q_1(i) Q_2(j - i)$. Thus:

$j = 0 \; : \; q(0) = Q_1(0) \; * \; Q_2(0) = Q_1(0) Q_2(0) = 0.1472$

$j = 1 \; : \; q(1) = Q_1(1) \; * \; Q_2(1) = \displaystyle\sum_{i=0}^{1} Q_1(i) Q_2(1 - i) = Q_1(0) Q_2(1) + Q_1(1) Q_2(0) = 0.1472$

$j = 2 \; : \; q(2) = Q_1(2) \; * \; Q_2(2) = \displaystyle\sum_{i=0}^{2} Q_1(i) Q_2(2 - i) = Q_1(0) Q_2(2) + Q_1(1) Q_2(1) + Q_1(2) Q_2(0)$

$\qquad\qquad = 0.2209$

$j = 3 \; : \; q(3) = Q_1(3) \; * \; Q_2(3) = \displaystyle\sum_{i=0}^{3} Q_1(i) Q_2(3 - i) = Q_1(0) Q_2(3) + Q_1(1) Q_2(2) + Q_1(2) Q_2(1)$

$\qquad\qquad + Q_1(3) Q_2(0) = 0.1718$

$j = 4 \; : \; q(4) = Q_1(4) \; * \; Q_2(4) = \displaystyle\sum_{i=0}^{4} Q_1(i) Q_2(4 - i) = Q_1(0) Q_2(4) + Q_1(1) Q_2(3) + Q_1(2) Q_2(2)$

$\qquad\qquad + Q_1(3) Q_2(1) + Q_1(4) Q_2(0) = 0.1534$

$j = 5 \; : \; q(5) = Q_1(5) \; * \; Q_2(5) = \displaystyle\sum_{i=0}^{5} Q_1(i) Q_2(5 - i) = Q_1(0) Q_2(5) + Q_1(1) Q_2(4) + Q_1(2) Q_2(3)$

$\qquad\qquad + Q_1(3) Q_2(2) + Q_1(4) Q_2(1) + Q_1(5) Q_2(0) = 0.0994$

Thus, $G = \sum_{j=0}^{5} q(j) = 0.9399$. The CBP are exactly the same as in Example 1.10(c):
$B_1 = Q(5) = \frac{q(5)}{G} = \frac{0.0994}{0.9394} = 10.57\%, B_2 = Q(4) + Q(5) = \frac{q(4)+q(5)}{G} = \frac{0.2528}{0.9399} = 26.89\%.$

In general, convolution algorithms can be applied only in PFS models. If a PFS does not hold, there are other methods that are computationally more effective. As an example, consider the application of the BR policy in the EMLM. As we will see in Section 1.3.2, this policy destroys the PFS of the steady state probabilities, but the CBP calculation can be easily determined through recursive formulas. However, the CBP calculation based on convolution algorithms is much more complex, as [8] and [9] reveal.

Example 1.14   Consider a single link of capacity $C = 100$ b.u. that accommodates calls of $K = 2$ service-classes with the following traffic characteristics: first service-class $\alpha_1 = 1$ erl, $b_1 = 1$ b.u., second service-class $\alpha_2 = 2$ erl, $b_2 = 16$ b.u. Calculate the CBP B_1, B_2 of the two service-classes, when α_1 increases in steps of 1 erl (up to 40 erl), while α_2 remains constant. Observe how each CBP varies versus the offered traffic-load. In particular, the graph of B_1 differs a lot from the corresponding graph of Figure 1.3 (last) because of the observed oscillations. Such oscillations are a characteristic of the CS policy, especially when $K = 2$ and the bandwidth per call requirements between the service-classes highly differ.

We present the exact CBP B_1 and B_2 in Figure 1.12. The oscillations that occur in the CBP of the first service-class can be intuitively explained. The fact that B_1 does not increase (actually decreases) when, for instance, α_1 increases from 4 to 7 erl can be justified by the great number (15) of b.u. which become available to the first service-class calls at the time points that the second service-class calls suffer from blocking. An in-depth analysis of this phenomenon is found in [10].

1.3   The Erlang Multirate Loss Model under the BR policy

1.3.1   The Service System

We consider again the multi-service system of the EMLM, but with the following CAC. A new service-class k call is accepted in the link if, after its acceptance, the link has at least t_k b.u. available to serve calls of other service-classes. This service system is called *EMLM under the BR policy (EMLM/BR)*. By properly selecting the BR parameters t_k, we can achieve CBP equalization among service-classes; this is the main target of the BR policy. Assuming that $b_K > \ldots > b_k > \ldots > b_2 > b_1$, then for CBP equalization the parameters t_k are chosen so that $b_1 + t_1 = b_2 + t_2 = \ldots = b_k + t_k = \ldots = b_K$, that is, $t_K = 0$, since it is reasonable not to reserve bandwidth against the service-class which requires the maximum bandwidth per call. Obviously, due to CBP equalization, we avoid the CBP oscillations observed in the EMLM under the CS policy.

Figure 1.13 illustrates the case of a single link with $C = 5$ that accommodates calls of two service-classes with $b_1 = 1$ and $b_2 = 2$ b.u. To achieve CBP equalization we reserve $t_1 = 1$ b.u. in favor of calls of the second service-class.

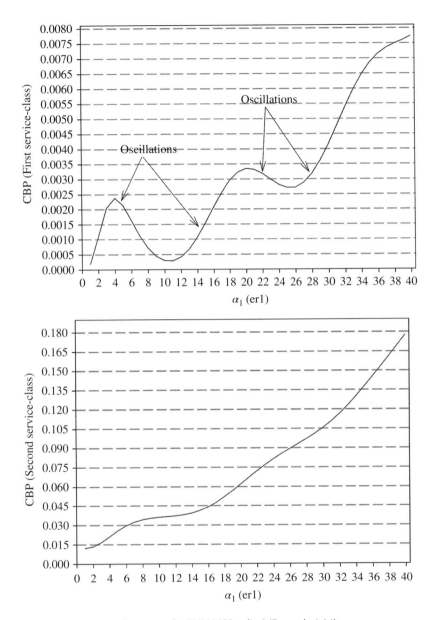

Figure 1.12 CBP oscillations in the EMLM (CS policy) (Example 1.14).

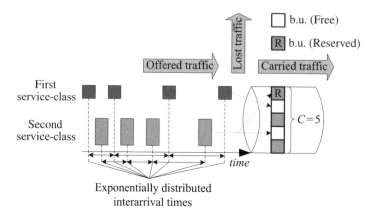

Figure 1.13 An example of the EMLM under the BR policy.

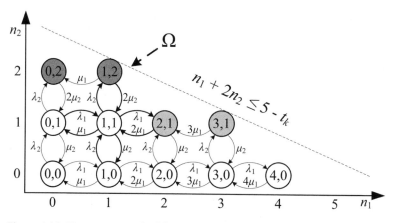

Figure 1.14 The state space Ω of the EMLM under the BR policy (Example 1.15).

1.3.2 The Analytical Model

The basic characteristic of the BR policy is that the steady state probabilities cannot be calculated via a PFS. This is because LB between some adjacent states is destroyed (see the following example).

Example 1.15 Consider a single link of capacity $C = 5$ b.u. which accommodates calls of two service-classes, under the BR policy, with $b_1 = 1$ b.u. and $b_2 = 2$ b.u. The BR parameters are $t_1 = 1$ and $t_2 = 0$. Let $\lambda_1, \mu_1, \lambda_2,$ and μ_2 be the corresponding traffic parameters of each service-class; for simplicity suppose that $\lambda_1 = \mu_1 = \lambda_2 = \mu_2 = 1$. Present graphically the state space Ω of this system and show the states in which the LB does not exist.

The state space Ω of this system consists of 11 states and is presented in Figure 1.14. Each state $\mathbf{n} = (n_1, n_2)$ satisfies the inequality $n_1 + 2n_2 \leq 5 - t_k, \quad k = 1, 2.$

LB is destroyed between the adjacent states: (a) (0,2) and (1,2) and (b) (2,1) and (3,1). For instance, consider that the system is in state $(0, 2)$ when a call of the first service-class arrives; due to the BR policy, the call is blocked and lost. On the other hand, let the system state be $(1, 2)$. In that case, the first service-class call may complete its service and leave the system. Then, the system state becomes $(0, 2)$.

1.3.2.1 Accurate CBP Calculation

The absence of a PFS in the EMLM/BR leads to approximate solutions as far as the recursive calculation of the state probabilities (and consequently the CBP) is concerned. An accurate CBP calculation is achieved only by solving the linear system of GB equations; however, this is applicable only to small systems with a few service-classes. Otherwise, the computational requirements become quite excessive.

Example 1.16 Consider Example 1.15 ($C = 5$, $K = 2$, $b_1 = 1$, $b_2 = 2$, $t_1 = 1$, $t_2 = 0$, $\lambda_1 = \mu_1 = \lambda_2 = \mu_2 = 1$) and determine the CBP of both service-classes based on the GB equations.

For each of the 11 states of Figure 1.14, we write the corresponding GB equation (*rate in = rate out*):

$(0,0)$: $\mu_1 P(1,0) + \mu_2 P(0,1) = (\lambda_1 + \lambda_2)P(0,0)$

$(0,1)$: $\lambda_2 P(0,0) + 2\mu_2 P(0,2) + \mu_1 P(1,1) = (\lambda_1 + \lambda_2 + \mu_2)P(0,1)$

$(0,2)$: $\lambda_2 P(0,1) + \mu_1 P(1,2) = 2\mu_2 P(0,2)$

$(1,0)$: $\lambda_1 P(0,0) + \mu_2 P(1,1) + 2\mu_1 P(2,0) = (\lambda_1 + \lambda_2 + \mu_1)P(1,0)$

$(1,1)$: $\lambda_1 P(0,1) + \lambda_2 P(1,0) + 2\mu_1 P(2,1) + 2\mu_2 P(1,2) = (\lambda_1 + \lambda_2 + \mu_1 + \mu_2)P(1,1)$

$(1,2)$: $\lambda_2 P(1,1) = (\mu_1 + 2\mu_2)P(1,2)$

$(2,0)$: $\lambda_1 P(1,0) + \mu_2 P(2,1) + 3\mu_1 P(3,0) = (\lambda_1 + \lambda_2 + 2\mu_1)P(2,0)$

$(2,1)$: $\lambda_1 P(1,1) + \lambda_2 P(2,0) + 3\mu_1 P(3,1) = (\mu_2 + 2\mu_1)P(2,1)$

$(3,0)$: $\lambda_1 P(2,0) + \mu_2 P(3,1) + 4\mu_1 P(4,0) = (\lambda_1 + \lambda_2 + 3\mu_1)P(3,0)$

$(3,1)$: $\lambda_2 P(3,0) = (\mu_2 + 3\mu_1)P(3,1)$

$(4,0)$: $\lambda_1 P(3,0) = 4\mu_1 P(4,0)$

By setting the numerical values, the linear system of equations becomes:

$(0,0)$: $P(1,0) + P(0,1) - 2P(0,0) = 0$

$(0,1)$: $P(0,0) + 2P(0,2) + P(1,1) - 3P(0,1) = 0$

$(0,2)$: $P(0,1) + P(1,2) - 2P(0,2) = 0$

$(1,0)$: $P(0,0) + P(1,1) + 2P(2,0) - 3P(1,0) = 0$

$(1,1)$: $P(0,1) + P(1,0) + 2P(2,1) + 2P(1,2) - 4P(1,1) = 0$

$(1,2)$: $P(1,1) - 3P(1,2) = 0$

$(2,0)$: $P(1,0) + P(2,1) + 3P(3,0) - 4P(2,0) = 0$

$(2,1)$: $P(1,1) + P(2,0) + 3P(3,1) - 3P(2,1) = 0$

$(3,0)$: $P(2,0) + P(3,1) + 4P(4,0) - 5P(3,0) = 0$

$(3,1)$: $P(3,0) - 4P(3,1) = 0$

$(4,0)$: $P(3,0) - 4P(4,0) = 0$

To finalise the formation of the linear system of equations, we have to replace one of the above equations with the normalization condition $\sum_{n\in\Omega}P(n_1,n_2) = 1$. The solution of the system of the 11 equations with the 11 variables (state probabilities) is:

$P(0,0) = 0.1686,$ $P(0,1) = 0.1831,$ $P(0,2) = 0.1163,$ $P(1,0) = 0.1541,$

$P(1,1) = 0.1483,$ $P(1,2) = 0.0494,$ $P(2,0) = 0.0727,$ $P(2,1) = 0.0785,$

$P(3,0) = 0.0194,$ $P(3,1) = 0.0048,$ $P(4,0) = 0.0048.$

The CBP are determined based on the state probabilities. New calls of the first service-class are blocked whenever the occupied link bandwidth is $j \geq C - t_1 \rightarrow j = 4, 5$. Hence:

$$B_1 = P(0,2) + P(2,1) + P(4,0) + P(1,2) + P(3,1) = 25.38\%$$

Similarly, new calls of the second service-class are blocked if less than 2 b.u. are available in the link, hence:

$$B_2 = P(0,2) + P(2,1) + P(4,0) + P(1,2) + P(3,1) = 25.38\%$$

As anticipated, $B_1 = B_2$, since $b_1 + t_1 = b_2 + t_2$.

1.3.2.2 Approximate CBP Calculation based on the Roberts Method

In the EMLM/BR, the link occupancy distribution, $q(j)$, is given in an approximate way by the following recursive formula [11]:

$$q(j) = \begin{cases} 1 & \text{if} \quad j = 0 \\ \dfrac{1}{j}\sum_{k=1}^{K} \alpha_k D_k(j - b_k)q(j - b_k) & j = 1, 2, \ldots, C \\ 0 & \text{otherwise.} \end{cases} \tag{1.64}$$

where:

$$D_k(j - b_k) = \begin{cases} b_k & \text{for} \quad j \leq C - t_k \\ 0 & \text{for} \quad j > C - t_k \end{cases} \tag{1.65}$$

This formula has a form similar to the Kaufman–Roberts recursion (1.39), and its existence is based on the assumption that, for a service-class k with $t_k > 0$, the mean number of service-class k calls in state j, $y_k(j)$, is zero in all states j which belong to the prohibitive space of this service-class: $j \in [C - t_k + 1, \ldots, C]$. Thanks to this assumption, which is reflected in the variable $D_k(j - b_k)$, the one-dimensional Markov chain of the system is transformed to an approximate reversible Markov chain,[9] which leads to the recurrent formula (1.64). Markov chain reversibility is a strong indication of the existence of a PFS.

Example 1.17 In Example 1.15 ($C = 5$, $K = 2$, $b_1 = 1$, $b_2 = 2$, $t_1 = 1$, $t_2 = 0$, $\lambda_1 = \mu_1 = \lambda_2 = \mu_2 = 1$), find in which (macro-) states j the population of calls is negligible ($y_k(j) = 0$), for each service-class, according to the Roberts' assumption.

---

9 A Markov chain is *reversible* when LB holds between all the adjacent states.

According to the Roberts' assumption, the population of calls of the first service-class is negligible in states $j > C - t_1 = 4$, that is, in state $j = 5$ we have $y_1(5) = 0$. However, state $j = 5$ corresponds to the detailed states $(n_1, n_2) = (1, 2)$ and $(3, 1)$, which both belong to the state space of the system (Figure 1.14). In both states, the value of $n_1 > 0$; this shows why Roberts' formula provides an approximate way for the calculation of $q(j)$. For the second service-class, the assumption does not hold, since $t_2 = 0$.

The CBP of service-class k, B_k, is given by:

$$B_k = \sum_{j=C-b_k-t_k+1}^{C} \frac{q(j)}{G} \tag{1.66}$$

where G is the normalization constant, given by (1.40).

The link utilization, U, is given by (1.54).

The mean number of service-class k calls, in state j $(q(j) > 0)$, $y_k(j)$, is determined by:

$$y_k(j) = \begin{cases} \dfrac{\alpha_k q(j - b_k)}{q(j)} & \text{for} \quad j \leq C - t_k \\ 0 & \text{for} \quad j > C - t_k \end{cases} \tag{1.67}$$

The mean number of service-class k calls in the system, $\overline{n}_k$, is given by (1.56).

Example 1.18 For the system of Example 1.15 $(C = 5, K = 2, \alpha_1 = \alpha_2 = 1, b_1 = 1, b_2 = 2, t_1 = 1, t_2 = 0)$, draw the state transition diagram (one-dimensional Markov chain) for all states $j = 0, 1, \ldots, C$ and calculate the CBP of the service-classes by using the Roberts' method.

The state transition diagram of this example is depicted in Figure 1.15. In state $j = 5$, due to the BR parameters, there is no rate in of the first service-class from state $j = 4$. Also, in state $j = 5$, there is no rate out of the first service-class (backward to state $j = 4$) because of the Roberts' assumption that $y_1(5) = 0$. To calculate CBP, from (1.64) and (1.65), we obtain that:

$$jq(j) = \begin{cases} q(j - 1) + 2q(j - 2) & \text{if} \quad j = 1, 2, 3, 4 \\ 2q(j - 2) & \text{if} \quad j = 5 \end{cases}$$

Thus, starting with $q(0) = 1$, we recursively calculate the $q(j)$ values for $j = 1, \ldots, 5$:

$$\begin{array}{llll}
j = 1: & q(1) & = q(0) + 0 = 1.0 & \Rightarrow & q(1) = 1.0 \\
j = 2: & 2q(2) & = q(1) + 2q(0) = 3.0 & \Rightarrow & q(2) = 1.5 \\
j = 3: & 3q(3) & = q(2) + 2q(1) = 3.5 & \Rightarrow & q(3) = 1.1667 \\
j = 4: & 4q(4) & = q(3) + 2q(2) = 4.1667 & \Rightarrow & q(4) = 1.0417 \\
j = 5: & 5q(5) & = 2q(3) = 2.3333 & \Rightarrow & q(5) = 0.4667
\end{array}$$

The normalization constant is

$$G = \sum_{j=0}^{5} q(j) = 6.1751.$$

Then, from (1.66) we have:

$$B_1 = \sum_{j=C-b_1-t_1+1}^{C} q(j) = \frac{q(4) + q(5)}{G} = 24.43\% \quad \text{and} \quad B_2 = \sum_{j=C-b_2-t_2+1}^{C} q(j) = \frac{q(4)+q(5)}{G} = 24.43\%$$

which are close to the accurate values of 25.38% (calculated in Example 1.16).

1.3.2.3 CBP Calculation Recursively based on the Stasiak–Glabowski Method

When aiming at QoS equalization among service-classes, the recursive CBP calculation of the EMLM/BR according to the Roberts method can be improved by the following method proposed by Stasiak and Glabowski[10] [12]. The average number of service-class k calls, $y_k(j)$, in state $j \in [C - t_k + 1, \ldots, C]$ is not zero but positive, and can be determined approximately in a recurrent way by:

$$y_k(j) \equiv y_k^*(j) = \begin{cases} \dfrac{\alpha_k q(j - b_k)}{q(j)} & \text{for} \quad j \leq C - t_k \\[2em] \displaystyle\sum_{i=1, i\neq k}^{K} y_k^*(j - b_i) w_{k,i}(j) & \text{for} \quad j > C - t_k \end{cases} \tag{1.68}$$

where for the calculation of $q(j)$ the corresponding EMLM system under the CS policy is assumed (i.e., the Kaufman–Roberts recursion (1.39)), while $w_{k,i}(j)$ is a weight given by:

$$w_{k,i}(j) = \frac{\alpha_i b_i}{\displaystyle\sum_{r=1, r\neq k}^{K} \alpha_r b_r} \tag{1.69}$$

The weight $w_{k,i}(j)$ determines the proportion of $y_k^*(j)$ that is transferred in state j by a call of service-class i (other than k), assuming that $j \leq C - t_i$. Although the system cannot be in state j due to an arriving call of service-class k (because of the BR policy), the system can be in state j due to arriving calls of other service-classes (calls of other service-classes may coexist in previous states together with service-class k calls). Thus,

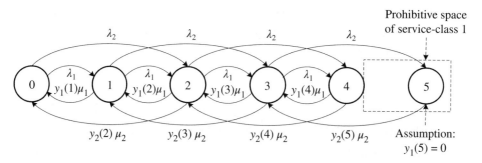

Figure 1.15 The one-dimensional Markov chain of the EMLM/BR (Roberts' assumption, Example 1.18).

10 Maciej Stasiak and Mariusz Glabowski, Polish professors at the Poznan University of Technology, Poland.

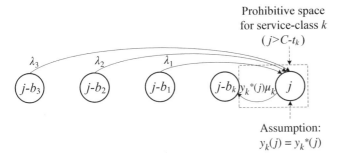

Figure 1.16 Calls of service-classes $i = 1, 2, 3$ contribute in $y_k^*(j)$ by transferring the population of service-class $k \neq i$ to state j.

when the system is transferred to state j by a service-class i call, this call also transfers to state j the population of service-class k. Therefore, the assumption that the average number of calls is positive even in a prohibitive state of a service-class is more realistic compared to the Roberts assumption. Figure 1.16 illustrates the fact that calls from different service-classes may contribute in transferring the population of service-class k to a prohibitive state $j > C - t_k$. Consequently, given that in state j the population of service-class k does exist, a backward transition to state $j - b_k$ is true.

Having determined the average number of calls in each state j via (1.68), then the Roberts method is followed by replacing $1/j$ in the RHS of $q(j)$ in (1.64) by $1/j^*$, in order for the average number of calls of each service-class in state j to be determined:

$$j^* = \sum_{k=1}^{K} y_k^*(j)b_k \tag{1.70}$$

The philosophy behind this method is that the approximated reversible Markov chain of the Roberts method is kept, but each state j of the prohibited state space is now substituted by state j^*. The Stasiak–Glabowski method is summarized in the following procedure:

Step 1: Assuming that the system is under the CS policy (instead of the BR policy), calculate $q(j)$ via (1.39).
Step 2: Calculate the average number of service-class k calls in state j, $y_k^*(j)$, according to (1.68) and (1.69).
Step 3: Determine $q(j)$ for the EMLM/BR, as follows:

$$q(j) = \begin{cases} 1 & \text{if } j = 0 \\ \dfrac{1}{j^*} \displaystyle\sum_{k=1}^{K} \alpha_k D_k(j - b_k)q(j - b_k) & \text{if } j = 1, 2, \ldots, C \\ 0 & \text{otherwise.} \end{cases} \tag{1.71}$$

where j^* is given by (1.70) and $D_k(j - b_k)$ is given by (1.65).
Step 4: Determine the CBP of each service-class according to (1.66).

Example 1.19 For the system of Example 1.15 ($C = 5, K = 2, \lambda_1 = \lambda_2 = \mu_1 = \mu_2 = 1, b_1 = 1, b_2 = 2, t_1 = 1, t_2 = 0$), explain the Stasiak–Glabowski assumption by properly

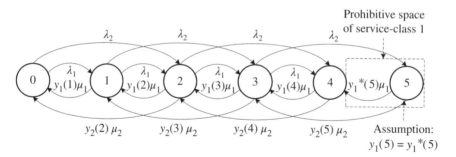

Figure 1.17 The one-dimensional Markov chain of the EMLM/BR under the Stasiak–Glabowski assumption (Example 1.19).

modifying the one-dimensional Markov chain of Figure 1.15, and calculate the CBP of both service-classes by using the Stasiak–Glabowski method.

Let the system be in state $j = 3$, in which there are in-service calls of the first service-class. Assume now that a new call of the second service-class arrives in the system and requires $b_2 = 2$ b.u. After the acceptance of this call in the system, the population not only of the second service-class but also of the first service-class is transferred in the new state $j = 5$. Thus, since it is realistic to assume that the average population of first service-class calls in state $j = 5$ is positive, we also assume the backward transition to state $j = 4$, due to a first service-class call departure. This transition is shown in Figure 1.17 as a modification of Figure 1.15. To calculate the CBP according to the Stasiak–Glabowski method, we proceed as follows:

Step 1: Assuming that the system is under the CS policy, we calculate $q(j)$ via (1.39). These results have been obtained in Example 1.10:

$$q(0) = 1 \quad q(1) = 1.0 \quad q(2) = 1.5 \quad q(3) = 1.1667 \quad q(4) = 1.0417 \quad q(5) = 0.675$$

with normalization constant: $G = 6.3834$.

Step 2: The average number of service-class k calls in state j, $y_k^*(j)$, according to (1.68) and (1.69), is:

$$y_1^*(1) = 1 \qquad y_2^*(1) = 0 \qquad y_1^*(4) = 1.12 \qquad y_2^*(4) = 1.44$$
$$y_1^*(2) = 0.666667 \qquad y_2^*(2) = 0.666667 \qquad y_1^*(5) = \mathbf{1.285714} \qquad y_2^*(5) = 1.728395$$
$$y_1^*(3) = 1.285714 \qquad y_2^*(3) = 0.857143$$

The value of $y_1^*(5)$ (in bold) is positive, while it is zero according to the Roberts method. All other values are exactly the same in both methods.

Step 3: We determine $q(j)$ for the EMLM/BR via (1.71): $j = 0 \Rightarrow q(0) = 1$

$j = 1$:	$j^* = 1$	$q(1) = q(0) + 0 = 1$	$\Rightarrow$	$q(1) = 1.0$
$j = 2$:	$j^* = 2$	$2q(2) = q(1) + 2q(0) = 3$	$\Rightarrow$	$q(2) = 1.5$
$j = 3$:	$j^* = 3$	$3q(3) = q(2) + 2q(1) = 3.5$	$\Rightarrow$	$q(3) = 1.1667$
$j = 4$:	$j^* = 4$	$4q(4) = q(3) + 2q(2) = 4.1667$	$\Rightarrow$	$q(4) = 1.0417$
$j = 5$:	$j^* = 4.7425$	$4.7425q(5) = 2q(3) = 2.3333$	$\Rightarrow$	$q(5) = 0.492$

The normalization constant is $G = \sum_{j=0}^{5} q(j) = 6.2004$.

Step 4: The CBP of each service-class is calculated according to (1.66):

$$B_1 = \sum_{j=C-b_1-t_1+1}^{C} q(j) = \frac{q(4) + q(5)}{G} = 24.74\% \text{ and } B_2 = \sum_{j=C-b_2-t_2+1}^{C} q(j) = \frac{q(4) + q(5)}{G} = 24.74\%$$

which are closer to the accurate values of 25.38% (calculated in Example 1.16) than the results of the Roberts method (24.43%, calculated in Example 1.18).

Example 1.20 A single link of capacity $C = 30$ b.u. accommodates three service-classes under the BR policy, with $(b_1, b_2, b_3) = (1, 2, 14)$ b.u. and offered traffic-load of $(\alpha_1, \alpha_2, \alpha_3) = (5, 2.5, 0.3571)$ erl (so that $\alpha_1 b_1 = \alpha_2 b_2 = \alpha_3 b_3$). Determine the CBP of each service-class, according to the Roberts method and the Stasiak–Glabowski method, for the following three sets of the BR parameters (t_1, t_2, t_3): (A) (7, 6, 0), (B) (9, 8, 0), and (C) (13, 12, 0) (obtained from [12]). Compare the CBP results with the corresponding CBP results when the CS policy is applied in the link.

Observe that only the last set of BR parameters leads to CBP equalization among these three service-classes, while both sets (A) and (B) lead to CBP equalization between the first and second service-classes only (since $b_1 + 7 = b_2 + 6 = 8$ b.u. and $b_1 + 9 = b_2 + 8 = 10$ b.u.). In respect of CBP, the last set of BR parameters benefits the third service-class most, while the least benefit for the third service-class is anticipated by set (A). Notice that by set (A), less b.u. (than set (B) or (C)) are reserved to benefit the third service-class.

The following table contains the CBP results under the CS policy and the BR policy for each set of BR parameters:

	B_1 (%)	B_2 (%)	B_3 (%)
CS policy	0.82	1.90	29.18
Set (A) Roberts	10.74	10.74	25.22
Set (A) Stasiak–Glabowski	10.79	10.79	25.27
Set (A) Simulation	9.91± 0.10	9.90± 0.18	28.27± 0.27
Set (B) Roberts	14.32	14.32	23.32
Set (B) Stasiak–Glabowski	14.42	14.42	23.40
Set (B) Simulation	14.38± 0.10	14.36± 0.15	27.86± 0.24
Set (C) Roberts	19.70	19.70	19.70
Set (C) Stasiak–Glabowski	20.44	20.44	20.44
Set (C) Simulation	24.28± 0.23	24.29± 0.19	24.30± 0.13

The rows referring to "Simulation" provide CBP results from simulation as mean values of 12 runs with a confidence interval of 95%. These values are considered reference values in order to check the accuracy of the other CBP results. Thus, based on simulation, we found that, indeed, the Stasiak–Glabowski method provides better results than the Roberts method for CBP equalization (set (C)), but not for set (A). For set (B) the CBP results of the two methods are pretty close to each other.

Comparing the CBP results under the CS and BR policies (set (C)), it is worth noticing that the BR policy achieves CBP equalization at the expense of high traffic losses of low-speed calls (while the traffic savings of the high-speed calls are relatively low).

1.4 The Erlang Multirate Loss Model under the Threshold Policy

1.4.1 The Service System

We consider again the multi-service system of the EMLM and adopt a TH-type CAC, as follows: A new call of service-class k is accepted in the system, of C b.u., if:

(i) its bandwidth requirement, b_k b.u., is less or equal to the available link bandwidth
(ii) the number n_k of in-service calls of service-class k does not exceed a predefined threshold parameter, after its acceptance. Otherwise, the call is blocked and lost without affecting the system.

By definition a policy is called a TH policy if there exists a set of positive integers $\{C_1, C_2, \ldots, C_k, \ldots, C_K\}$ such that a service-class k call is accepted in the system when in state $\mathbf{n}$, if and only if the new system state fulfils the relations $b_k(n_k + 1) \leq C_k$ and $\mathbf{nb} + b_k \leq C$ [13].

Example 1.21 A single link of $C = 5$ b.u. accommodates calls of two service-classes with $b_1 = 1$ and $b_2 = 2$ b.u., respectively. The TH policy is applied only to calls of service-class 1, by assuming that in-service calls of that service-class can be at most three, i.e., $n_{1,\max} = 3$. For example, because of this threshold, a new service-class 1 call will be blocked even if there are two available b.u. in the link, upon the call's arrival. Describe this TH policy according to (I.38).

For $C_0 = 3$, $C_1 = 0$, $C_2 = 2$, we have $\Omega = \{\mathbf{n} : 0 \leq \mathbf{nb} \leq 5, \quad 0 \leq n_1 b_1 \leq 3, \quad k = 1, 2\}$.

Example 1.22 The following example shows an interesting application of the TH policy in the case of tree networks. Consider calls of K service-classes accommodated in a tree network. The network consists of K access links of capacity C_k, $(k = 1, \ldots, K)$ b.u. and a common link of capacity C b.u. Calls of service class k $(k = 1, \ldots, K)$ follow a Poisson process with mean arrival rate λ_k and have an exponentially distributed service time with mean μ_k^{-1}. The offered traffic-load of service-class k is $\alpha_k = \lambda_k / \mu_k$ (in erl). Calls of service class k request b_k b.u. simultaneously on the kth access link and the common link (Figure 1.18). Without loss of generality, we assume that C_k is a multiple integer of b_k for all $k = 1, \ldots, K$. If these b_k b.u. are available, then the call is accepted in the system,

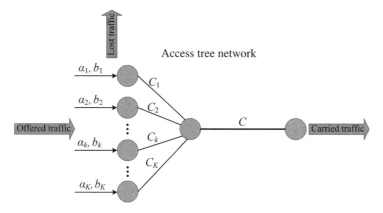

Figure 1.18 A multirate access tree network that accommodates K service-classes of Poisson input (Example 1.22).

otherwise the call is blocked and lost. Show how the tree network of Figure 1.18 can be described by the EMLM/TH.

If $\mathbf{n} = (n_1, n_2, \ldots, n_k, \ldots, n_K)$ denotes the vector of all in-service calls, then the state space Ω of the tree network is written as $\Omega = \{\mathbf{n} \: : \: 0 \leq \mathbf{nb} \leq C, \quad n_k b_k \leq C_k, \quad k = 1, \ldots, K\}$, with $\mathbf{b} = (b_1, b_2, \ldots, b_k, \ldots, b_K)$ and $\mathbf{nb} = \sum_{k=1}^{K} n_k b_k$.

Now, let $n_{k,\max} = \frac{C_k}{b_k}$ be the maximum number of service-class k calls serviced by the tree network. Then, we rewrite the state space as $\Omega = \{\mathbf{n} \: : \: 0 \leq \mathbf{nb} \leq C, \quad n_k \leq n_{k,\max}, \quad k = 1, \ldots, K\}$. This form of Ω represents a link of capacity C b.u. that accommodates calls of K service-classes, which compete for the available bandwidth under the EMLM/TH.

According to the aforementioned definition of the TH policy, the topology of Figure 1.18 can be replaced by the single link of Figure 1.19, and the analytical formulas obtained for the first topology can be used in the second one and vice versa. For simplicity, we adopt the topology of Figure 1.19, which corresponds to the EMLM/TH.

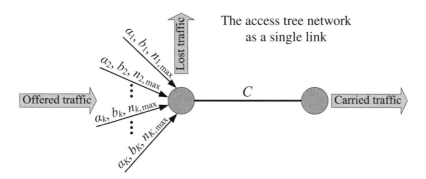

Figure 1.19 A single link that accommodates K service-classes of Poisson input described by the EMLM/TH (Example 1.22).

1.4.2 The Analytical Model

1.4.2.1 Steady State Probabilities

Due to the fact that the TH policy is a coordinate convex policy (as the CS policy is) the steady state probabilities in the EMLM/TH have a PFS whose form is the same as that of the EMLM (only the definition of Ω differs):

$$P(\mathbf{n}) = \frac{\prod_{k=1}^{K} \frac{\alpha_k^{n_k}}{n_k!}}{G} \qquad (1.72)$$

where $G = \sum_{\mathbf{n} \in \Omega} \prod_{k=1}^{K} \frac{\alpha_k^{n_k}}{n_k!}$ and $\Omega = \{\mathbf{n} : 0 \leq \mathbf{nb} \leq C, n_k \leq n_{k,\max}, k = 1, \ldots, K\}$.

Example 1.23 Consider again Example 1.6 ($C = 5$, $K = 2$, $b_1 = 1$, $b_2 = 2$) and assume that the TH policy is applied to calls of service-class 1, with $n_{1,\max} = 3$. By assuming that $\lambda_1 = \lambda_2 = \mu_1 = \mu_2 = 1$:

(a) Present graphically the state space Ω and calculate the state probabilities $P(n_1, n_2)$ and, based on them, the corresponding values of $Q(j)$.
(b) Verify that the PFS of (1.72) results in the same values of $P(n_1, n_2)$ as those obtained in (a).
(c) Calculate the CBP of both service-classes.
(d) Assume an increase in α_2 from 0.1 to 1.0 erl in steps of 0.1 erl. Present graphically the CBP of each service-class obtained by the EMLM, the EMLM/BR (let $t_1 = 1$ and $t_2 = 0$, for CBP equalization), and the EMLM/TH when $n_{1,\max} = 2$, 3, 4. Comment on the results.

(a) The state space Ω of this system consists of 10 states and is presented in Figure 1.20. This state space is actually a subset of the EMLM presented in Example 1.6. Each state $\mathbf{n} = (n_1, n_2)$ satisfies the inequalities $n_1 + 2n_2 \leq 5$, $n_1 \leq 3$. To determine the state probabilities, we write the GB equations for the 10 states $\mathbf{n} = (n_1, n_2)$ of Figure 1.20:

$(0,0):$ $\mu_1 P(1,0) + \mu_2 P(0,1) = (\lambda_1 + \lambda_2)P(0,0) \Rightarrow P(1,0) + P(0,1) - 2P(0,0) = 0$

$(0,1):$ $\lambda_2 P(0,0) + 2\mu_2 P(0,2) + \mu_1 P(1,1) = (\lambda_1 + \lambda_2 + \mu_2)P(0,1)$
          $\Rightarrow P(0,0) + 2P(0,2) + P(1,1) - 3P(0,1) = 0$

$(0,2):$ $\lambda_2 P(0,1) + \mu_1 P(1,2) = (\lambda_1 + 2\mu_2)P(0,2) \Rightarrow P(0,1) + P(1,2) - 3P(0,2) = 0$

$(1,0):$ $\lambda_1 P(0,0) + \mu_2 P(1,1) + 2\mu_1 P(2,0) = (\lambda_1 + \lambda_2 + \mu_1)P(1,0)$
          $\Rightarrow P(0,0) + P(1,1) + 2P(2,0) - 3P(1,0) = 0$

$(1,1):$ $\lambda_1 P(0,1) + \lambda_2 P(1,0) + 2\mu_1 P(2,1) + 2\mu_2 P(1,2) = (\lambda_1 + \lambda_2 + \mu_1 + \mu_2)P(1,1)$
          $\Rightarrow P(0,1) + P(1,0) + 2P(2,1) + 2P(1,2) - 4P(1,1) = 0$

$(1,2):$ $\lambda_1 P(0,2) + \lambda_2 P(1,1) = (\mu_1 + 2\mu_2)P(1,2) \Rightarrow P(0,2) + P(1,1) - 3P(1,2) = 0$

$(2,0):$ $\lambda_1 P(1,0) + \mu_2 P(2,1) + 3\mu_1 P(3,0) = (\lambda_1 + \lambda_2 + 2\mu_1)P(2,0)$
          $\Rightarrow P(1,0) + P(2,1) + 3P(3,0) - 4P(2,0) = 0$

$(2,1):$ $\lambda_1 P(1,1) + \lambda_2 P(2,0) + 3\mu_1 P(3,1) = (\lambda_1 + \mu_2 + 2\mu_1)P(2,1)$
          $\Rightarrow P(1,1) + P(2,0) + 3P(3,1) - 4P(2,1) = 0$

$(3,0):$ $\lambda_1 P(2,0) + \mu_2 P(3,1) = (\lambda_2 + 3\mu_1)P(3,0) \Rightarrow P(2,0) + P(3,1) - 4P(3,0) = 0$

$(3,1):$ $\lambda_1 P(2,1) + \lambda_2 P(3,0) = (\mu_2 + 3\mu_1)P(3,1) \Rightarrow P(2,1) + P(3,0) - 4P(3,1) = 0$

By replacing a GB equation (e.g., of $(1,1)$) with the normalization condition $\sum_{\mathbf{n} \in \Omega} P(n_1, n_2) = 1$, we have the solution of this linear system of 10 equations:

$P(0,0) = 0.157895$ $P(0,1) = 0.157895$ $P(0,2) = 0.078947$ $P(1,0) = 0.157895$

$P(1,1) = 0.157895$ $P(1,2) = 0.078947$ $P(2,0) = 0.078947$ $P(2,1) = 0.078947$

$P(3,0) = 0.026316$ $P(3,1) = 0.026316$

Based on the values of $P(n_1, n_2)$ we have:

$Q(0) = P(0,0) = 0.157895$ $Q(3) = P(3,0) + P(1,1) = 0.184211$

$Q(1) = P(1,0) = 0.157895$ $Q(4) = P(2,1) + P(0,2) = 0.157894$

$Q(2) = P(2,0) + P(0,1) = 0.236842$ $Q(5) = P(3,1) + P(1,2) = 0.105263$

(b) It is easy to verify that the PFS of $P(n_1, n_2) = \dfrac{\frac{\alpha_1^{n_1}}{n_1!} \frac{\alpha_2^{n_2}}{n_2!}}{\sum_{\mathbf{n} \in \Omega} \frac{\alpha_1^{n_1}}{n_1!} \frac{\alpha_2^{n_2}}{n_2!}}$, where $\Omega = \{\mathbf{n} : 0 \leq \mathbf{nb} \leq C,\ n_1 \leq n_{1,\max}\}$ gives exactly the same results as those obtained in (a).

(c) The CBP of service-class 1 is given by the formula:

$$B_1 = \sum_{j=C-b_1+1}^{C} Q(j) + \sum_{x=n_{1,\max} b_1}^{C-b_1} Prob[x = j,\ n_1 = n_{1,\max}] = Q(5) + P(3,0) = 0.131579$$

where the second summation refers to the TH policy.
The CBP of service-class 2 is given by the formula:

$$B_2 = \sum_{j=C-b_2+1}^{C} Q(j) = Q(4) + Q(5) = 0.263157$$

Note that exactly the same CBP are obtained when considering two concatenated links with $C_1 = 3$ and $C_2 = 5$ b.u. (substituting the single link of $C = 5$ b.u.), and calls of the first service-class traverse both links, while calls of the second service-class utilize only the second link of $C_2 = 5$ b.u. (see Section 1.5 and Example 1.25 where the similar case of $C_1 = 4$ and $C_2 = 5$ b.u. is examined).

(d) Figure 1.21 presents B_1 and B_2, in the LHS and the RHS, respectively, for the EMLM, the EMLM/BR, and the EMLM/TH. Based on Figure 1.21, we see that:

- increasing the value of $n_{1,\max}$ decreases the CBP of service-class 1 and increases the CBP of service-class 2
- the EMLM and the EMLM/BR cannot capture the behavior of the EMLM/TH. Especially for the case of $n_{1,\max} = 4$ one would expect that the CBP of service-class 1 for the EMLM/BR and the EMLM/TH would be quite close due to the selection of the BR parameter $t_1 = 1$, which prevents $n_{1,\max}$ becoming 5. However, this is not the case since $B_1 = Q(5) + P(4,0)$ for the EMLM/TH, while $B_1 = Q(5) + Q(4) = Q(5) + P(0,2) + P(2,1) + P(4,0)$ for the EMLM/BR.

For the determination of the unnormalized values of $q(j)$, the following accurate and recursive formula can be used [14]:

$$q(j) = \begin{cases} 1, & \text{if } j = 0 \\ \dfrac{1}{j} \sum_{k=1}^{K} \alpha_k b_k [q(j - b_k) - \Theta_k(j - b_k)], & j = 1, ..., C \\ 0, & \text{otherwise} \end{cases} \tag{1.73}$$

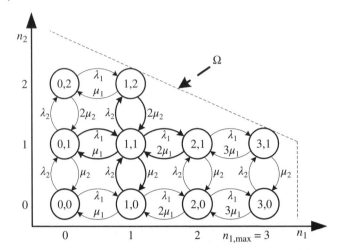

Figure 1.20 The state space Ω of system under the TH policy (Example 1.23).

where $\Theta_k(x)$ is the probability that x b.u. are occupied, while the number of service-class k calls is $n_{k,\max}$ or:

$$\Theta_k(x) := Prob[j = x, \quad n_k = n_{k,\max}] \tag{1.74}$$

In (1.73) the fact that $n_k = n_{k,\max}$ implies that:

(i) $j \geq n_{k,\max}b_k$ and therefore $\Theta_k(x) = 0$ for $x = 0, 1, \ldots, n_{k,\max}b_k - 1$ and
(ii) $\Theta_k(x)$ is a blocking probability factor for service-class k calls.

The proof of (1.73) is similar to the proof of the Kaufman–Roberts formula (see e.g., [14]). The only difference is that (1.48) now takes the form:

$$\alpha_k \sum_{\hat{n} \in \Omega_{j-b_k}} P(\hat{n}) = \alpha_k(q(j - b_k) - Prob[x = j - b_k, \quad n_k = n_{k,\max}]) \tag{1.75}$$

due to the existence of the TH policy.

Intuitively, the form of (1.75) is expected, since the term $Prob[x = j - b_k, \quad n_k = n_{k,\max}]$ is a factor that blocks a new service-class k call from being accepted in the system and therefore blocks the transition from state $j - b_k$ to state j.

1.4.2.2 CBP, Utilization and Mean Number of In-service Calls

The following performance measures can be determined:

- To determine the CBP of service-class k, B_k, we consider two groups of macro-states:
  (i) those where there is no available bandwidth to accept a new service-class k call; this happens when $C - b_k + 1 \leq j \leq C$
  (ii) those where available bandwidth exists, i.e., $j \leq C - b_k$ but $n_k = n_{k,\max}$; the latter implies that $j \geq n_{k,\max}b_k$.

The values of B_k are given by:

$$B_k = \sum_{j=C-b_k+1}^{C} \frac{q(j)}{G} + \sum_{j=n_{k,\max}b_k}^{C-b_k} \frac{\Theta_k(j)}{G} \tag{1.76}$$

where $G = \sum_{j=0}^{C} q(j)$ is the normalization constant.

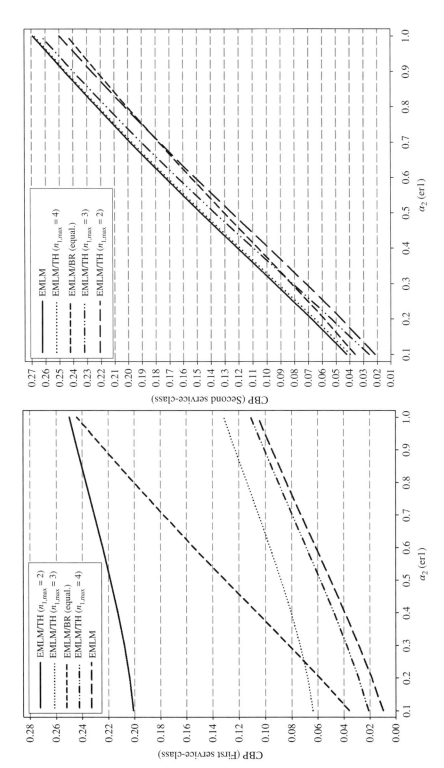

Figure 1.21 Comparison of the EMLM, the EMLM/BR, and the EMLM/TH (Example 1.23).

- The link utilization is given by (1.54).
- The mean number $y_k(j)$ of service-class k calls, in state j $(q(j) > 0)$, is given by:

$$y_k(j) = \frac{\alpha_k[q(j - b_k) - \Theta_k(j - b_k)]}{q(j)} \tag{1.77}$$

- The mean number of service-class k calls in the system is given by (1.56).

Equations (1.76) and (1.77) require knowledge of $\Theta_k(j)$. The latter takes positive values when $j = n_{k,max}b_k, \ldots, C - b_k$. Thus, we consider a subsystem of capacity $F_k = C - b_k - n_{k,max}b_k$ that accommodates all service-classes but service-class k. For this subsystem, we define $\vartheta_k(j)$, $(j = 0, \ldots, F_k)$, which is analogous to $q(j)$ of (1.73):

$$\vartheta_k(j) = \begin{cases} 1, & \text{if } j = 0 \\ \dfrac{1}{j} \displaystyle\sum_{i=1, \ i\neq k}^{K} \alpha_i b_i[\vartheta_k(j - b_i) - \Theta_i(j - b_i)], & j = 1, \ldots, F_k \\ 0, & \text{otherwise} \end{cases} \tag{1.78}$$

We can now compute $\Theta_k(j)$ for $j = n_{k,max}b_k, \ldots, C - b_k$, as follows:

$$\Theta_k(j) = \frac{\alpha_k^{n_{k,max}}}{n_{k,max}!} \vartheta_k(j - n_{k,max}b_k) \tag{1.79}$$

In (1.79), the term $\frac{\alpha_k^{n_{k,max}}}{n_{k,max}!}$ is expected, since for states $j = n_{k,max}b_k, \ldots, C - b_k$, the number of in-service calls of service-class k is always $n_{k,max}$.

The computational complexity of the EMLM/TH is in the order of $O\{K^m C\}$, where $m := \max\{\lceil C/C_k \rceil : k = 1, \ldots, K\}$; for more details, see [14].

Note: In (1.78), each time that the calculation of $\vartheta_k(j)$ requires knowledge of $\Theta_i(j - b_i)$ (this happens when $\Theta_i(j - b_i) > 0$, $(j = 1, \ldots, F_k)$), for $i \neq k$, an extra subsystem is needed for the calculation of $\vartheta_i(j)$ and $\Theta_i(j)$ via (1.78) and (1.79) (see also Section IV, pp. 12–69 in [14]). Instead of using subsystems, we may calculate $\vartheta_k(j)$ for those values of j that result in $\Theta_i(j - b_i) = 0$ (in (1.78)), while for the rest values of j we can use the following formula (which is based on the fact that the EMLM/TH has a PFS):

$$\Theta_k(j) = \frac{\alpha_k^{n_{k,max}}}{n_{k,max}!} \prod_{i=1, i\neq k}^{K} \frac{\alpha_i^{n_i}}{n_i!} \tag{1.80}$$

for $\mathbf{n} = (n_1, n_2, \ldots, n_{k,max}, \ldots, n_K)$ and $\mathbf{nb} = j$.

This method can be useful especially for systems with small to moderate state spaces (see Example 3.10). This topic remains open to investigation.

1.5 The Erlang Multirate Loss Model in a Fixed Routing Network

1.5.1 The Service System

According to ITU-T, a *fixed routing network* is a network in which a route[11] providing a connection between an originating node and a destination node is fixed for every service-class (or for every traffic flow of the same service-class). Let us consider that a

---

11 A concatenation of links.

fixed routing network consists of L links. Each link l $(l = 1, \ldots, L)$ has a fixed capacity of C_l b.u. The network accommodates calls of K service-classes under the CS policy. Calls of service-class k follow a Poisson process with rate λ_k, require b_k b.u. and have a generally distributed service time with mean μ_k^{-1}. Let R_k be the fixed route of service-class k calls in the network, where $R_k \subseteq \{1, \ldots, L\}$. A call of service-class k is accepted in the network if its b_k b.u. are available in every link $l \in R_k$, otherwise the call is blocked and lost.

1.5.2 The Analytical Model

Let n_k be the number of in-service calls of service-class k in the steady state of the system and $\mathbf{n} = (n_1, n_2, \ldots, n_K)$ be the corresponding steady state vector of all service-classes in the fixed routing network. If K_l is the set of service-classes whose calls are accommodated in link l, i.e., $K_l = \{k \in K : l \in R_k\}$, then the state space Ω of the system is given by:

$$\Omega = \left\{ \mathbf{n} : 0 \leq \sum_{k \in K_l}^{K} n_k b_k \leq C_l, \quad l = 1, \ldots, L \right\} \tag{1.81}$$

Example 1.24 Consider two service-classes whose calls require b_1 and b_2 b.u., respectively. All calls are accommodated to a network of three sequential links of capacity C_1, C_2 and C_3 b.u., respectively. Draw the bounds of the state space Ω of this system.

The bounds of the state space Ω consist of three linear constraints; they are drawn in Figure 1.22, where n_1 and n_2 are the numbers of calls of the two service- classes, respectively, $\lfloor x \rfloor$ is the largest integer not exceeding x, and $b_{kl} = \begin{cases} b_k, & \text{if } l \in R_l \\ 0, & \text{otherwise} \end{cases}$.

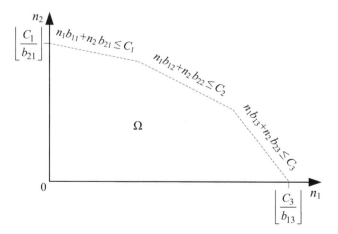

Figure 1.22 The state space Ω of the three link network (Example 1.24).

1.5.2.1 Steady State Probabilities

The steady state probabilities $P(\mathbf{n})$ have a PFS whose form is the following [13, 15]:

$$P(\mathbf{n}) = G^{-1} \prod_{k=1}^{K} \frac{\alpha_k^{n_k}}{n_k!} \tag{1.82}$$

where $G \equiv G(\Omega) = \sum_{\mathbf{n} \in \Omega} \left(\prod_{k=1}^{K} \frac{\alpha_k^{n_k}}{n_k!} \right)$ is the normalization constant, and $\alpha_k = \frac{\lambda_k}{\mu_k}$ is the offered traffic-load of service-class k calls.

If we denote by j_l the occupied b.u. of link l, where $j_l = n_1 b_{1l} + n_2 b_{2l} + \dots + n_K b_{Kl}$, and $\mathbf{j} = (j_1, j_2, \dots, j_l, \dots, j_L)$ is the corresponding vector of the entire fixed routing network, then the unnormalized values of the occupancy distribution $q(\mathbf{j})$ in the fixed routing network are given by the following L-dimensional accurate recursive formula [15]:

$$q(\mathbf{j}) = \begin{cases} 1 & \text{if } \mathbf{j} = \mathbf{0} \\ \frac{1}{j_l} \sum_{k=1}^{K} \alpha_k b_{kl} q(\mathbf{j} - \mathbf{b}_k) & j_l = 1, \dots, C_l, \quad \text{for} \quad l = 1, \dots, L \\ 0 & \text{otherwise} \end{cases} \tag{1.83}$$

where $b_{kl} = \begin{cases} b_k & \text{if } l \in R_k \\ 0 & \text{otherwise} \end{cases}$, $\mathbf{b}_k = (b_{k1}, b_{k2}, \dots, b_{kl}, \dots, b_{kL})$ is the kth row of a $(K \times L)$ matrix (routing table), and shows the route (sequence of links) for the kth service-class.

Note: In the case of a single link, (1.83) becomes the Kaufman–Roberts recursion (1.39).

1.5.2.2 CBP, Utilization, and Mean Number of In-service Calls in the System

Having determined the values of $q(\mathbf{j})$, the following performance measures can be determined:

- We calculate the CBP of service-class k, B_k, as follows:

$$B_k = \sum_{\left\{ \mathbf{j} \left| \bigcup_{l=1}^{L} [(b_{kl} + j_l) > C_l] \right. \right\}} G^{-1} q(\mathbf{j}) \tag{1.84}$$

where $G = \sum_{\mathbf{j} \in \Omega} q(\mathbf{j})$.
- The utilization of link l, U_l, is given by the following formula:

$$U_l = \sum_{\tau=1}^{C_l} G^{-1} \tau q_l(\tau) \tag{1.85}$$

where $q_l(\tau) = \sum_{\{\mathbf{j} | j_l = \tau\}} q(\mathbf{j})$.
- The mean number of service-class k calls in state $\mathbf{j}$, $y_k(\mathbf{j})$, is determined by the formula:

$$y_k(\mathbf{j}) = \frac{\alpha_k q(\mathbf{j} - \mathbf{b}_k)}{q(\mathbf{j})} \tag{1.86}$$

- The mean number of service-class k calls in the system, $\bar{n}_k$, is given by:

$$\bar{n}_k = \sum_{\mathbf{j} \in \Omega} y_k(\mathbf{j}) \frac{q(\mathbf{j})}{G} \tag{1.87}$$

Example 1.25 Consider the fixed routing network of Figure 1.23. The first link has a capacity of $C_1 = 4$ b.u. while the second one has a capacity of $C_2 = 5$ b.u. This system accommodates calls of $K = 2$ service-classes, with $b_1 = 1$ and $b_2 = 2$ b.u., respectively. Calls of service-class 1 traverse both links, while calls of service-class 2 traverse only the second link.

(a) Calculate the CBP of both service-classes via (1.83) and (1.84), when $\alpha_1 = \alpha_2 = 1$ erl.
(b) Calculate the utilization of each link.

(a) Since calls of service-class 1 traverse both links, while calls of service-class 2 traverse the second link, the (2×2) matrix of this example is $\begin{bmatrix} b_{11} & b_{12} \\ b_{21} & b_{22} \end{bmatrix} = \begin{bmatrix} 1 & 1 \\ 0 & 2 \end{bmatrix}$. According to (1.83), we have $\mathbf{j} = (j_1, j_2)$, with $j_1 = 0, 1, \ldots, 4$ and $j_2 = 0, 1, \ldots, 5$.
Starting with $q(0,0) = 1$ and considering the second link only (i.e., $l = 2$ in (1.83)), we recursively calculate $q(0, j_2)$ for $j_2 = 1, \ldots, 5$:

$1q(0,1) = a_2 b_{22} q(0, 1 - b_{22}) = 2q(0, -1)$	$=$	0.0	$\Rightarrow$	$q(0,1) = 0.0$
$2q(0,2) = a_2 b_{22} q(0, 2 - b_{22}) = 2q(0,0)$	$=$	2.0	$\Rightarrow$	$q(0,2) = 1.0$
$3q(0,3) = a_2 b_{22} q(0, 3 - b_{22}) = 2q(0,1)$	$=$	0.0	$\Rightarrow$	$q(0,3) = 0.0$
$4q(0,4) = a_2 b_{22} q(0, 4 - b_{22}) = 2q(0,2)$	$=$	2.0	$\Rightarrow$	$q(0,4) = 0.5$
$5q(0,5) = a_2 b_{22} q(0, 5 - b_{22}) = 2q(0,3)$	$=$	0.0	$\Rightarrow$	$q(0,5) = 0.0$

Indeed, given that $b_2 = 2$ b.u., when the second link is occupied by calls of the second service-class only, we cannot have an odd number of occupied b.u., hence $q(0,1) = q(0,3) = q(0,5) = 0.0$. Likewise, since calls of the first service-class occupy b.u. in both links, we have $q(1,0) = q(2,0) = q(3,0) = q(4,0) = 0.0$.
We now consider the first link (i.e., $l = 1$ in (1.83)), and we recursively calculate $q(j_1, j_2)$ (for $j_1 = 1, \ldots, 4$ and $j_2 = 1, \ldots, 5$) as follows: $q(1,1) = a_1 b_{11} q(j_1 - b_{11}, j_2 - b_{12}) + a_2 b_{21} q(j_1 - b_{21}, j_2 - b_{22}) = q(0,0) + 0q(1,-1) = 1.0 \Rightarrow q(1,1) = 1.0$
Since $b_{21} = 0$, the term $a_2 b_{21} q(j_1 - b_{21}, j_2 - b_{22})$ is not included in the rest of the calculations:

$q(1,2)$	$=$	$a_1 b_{11} q(0,1)$	$=$	0.0	$\Rightarrow$	$q(1,2) = 0.0$
$q(1,3)$	$=$	$a_1 b_{11} q(0,2)$	$=$	1.0	$\Rightarrow$	$q(1,3) = 1.0$
$q(1,4)$	$=$	$a_1 b_{11} q(0,3)$	$=$	0.0	$\Rightarrow$	$q(1,4) = 0.0$
$q(1,5)$	$=$	$a_1 b_{11} q(0,4)$	$=$	0.5	$\Rightarrow$	$q(1,5) = 0.5$
$2q(2,1)$	$=$	$a_1 b_{11} q(1,0)$	$=$	0.0	$\Rightarrow$	$q(2,1) = 0.0$
$2q(2,2)$	$=$	$a_1 b_{11} q(1,1)$	$=$	1.0	$\Rightarrow$	$q(2,2) = 0.5$
$2q(2,3)$	$=$	$a_1 b_{11} q(1,2)$	$=$	0.0	$\Rightarrow$	$q(2,3) = 0.0$
$2q(2,4)$	$=$	$a_1 b_{11} q(1,3)$	$=$	1.0	$\Rightarrow$	$q(2,4) = 0.5$
$2q(2,5)$	$=$	$a_1 b_{11} q(1,4)$	$=$	0.0	$\Rightarrow$	$q(2,5) = 0.0$
$3q(3,1)$	$=$	$a_1 b_{11} q(2,0)$	$=$	0.0	$\Rightarrow$	$q(3,1) = 0.0$
$3q(3,2)$	$=$	$a_1 b_{11} q(2,1)$	$=$	0.0	$\Rightarrow$	$q(3,2) = 0.0$
$3q(3,3)$	$=$	$a_1 b_{11} q(2,2)$	$=$	0.5	$\Rightarrow$	$q(3,3) = 0.16667$
$3q(3,4)$	$=$	$a_1 b_{11} q(2,3)$	$=$	0.0	$\Rightarrow$	$q(3,4) = 0.0$

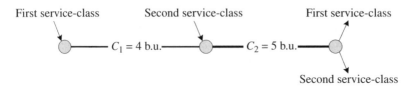

Figure 1.23 Two service-classes accommodated in a fixed routing network of two links (Example 1.25).

$3q(3,5)$	$=$	$\alpha_1 b_{11} q(2,4)$	$=$	0.5	$\Rightarrow$	$q(3,5) = 0.16667$
$4q(4,1)$	$=$	$\alpha_1 b_{11} q(3,0)$	$=$	0.0	$\Rightarrow$	$q(4,1) = 0.0$
$4q(4,2)$	$=$	$\alpha_1 b_{11} q(3,1)$	$=$	0.0	$\Rightarrow$	$q(4,2) = 0.0$
$4q(4,3)$	$=$	$\alpha_1 b_{11} q(3,2)$	$=$	0.0	$\Rightarrow$	$q(4,3) = 0.0$
$4q(4,4)$	$=$	$\alpha_1 b_{11} q(3,3)$	$=$	0.16667	$\Rightarrow$	$q(4,4) = 0.04168$
$4q(4,5)$	$=$	$\alpha_1 b_{11} q(3,4)$	$=$	0.0	$\Rightarrow$	$q(4,5) = 0.0$

The normalization constant is $G = \sum_{j \in \Omega} q(j) = 6.375$. Thus:

$$B_1 = \sum_{\left\{ j \left| \bigcup_{l=1}^{L} [(b_{1l} + j_l) > C_l] \right. \right\}} G^{-1} q(j) = \frac{q(1,5) + q(3,5) + q(4,4)}{G} = 0.11111$$

$$B_2 = \sum_{\left\{ j \left| \bigcup_{l=1}^{L} [(b_{2l} + j_l) > C_l] \right. \right\}} G^{-1} q(j) = \frac{q(0,4) + q(1,5) + q(2,4) + q(3,5) + q(4,4)}{G} = 0.26797$$

It is worth mentioning that exactly the same B_1 and B_2 are obtained by the EMLM/TH when assuming a single link of capacity $C = 5$ b.u. and $n_{1,max} = \frac{C_1}{b_1} = 4$.

(b) $U_1 = \sum_{\tau=1}^{C_1} G^{-1} \tau q_1(\tau) = \sum_{\tau=1}^{4} G^{-1} \tau q_1(\tau) = 0.8888$ where:

$q_1(1) = q(1,0) + q(1,1) + q(1,2) + q(1,3) + q(1,4) + q(1,5) = 2.5$
$q_1(2) = q(2,0) + q(2,1) + q(2,2) + q(2,3) + q(2,4) + q(2,5) = 1.0$
$q_1(3) = q(3,0) + q(3,1) + q(3,2) + q(3,3) + q(3,4) + q(3,5) = 1/3$
$q_1(4) = q(4,0) + q(4,1) + q(4,2) + q(4,3) + q(4,4) + q(4,5) = 1/24$

Similarly, $U_2 = \sum_{\tau=1}^{C_2} G^{-1} \tau q_2(\tau) = \sum_{\tau=1}^{5} G^{-1} \tau q_2(\tau) = 2.3529$ where:

$q_2(1) = q(0,1) + q(1,1) + q(2,1) + q(3,1) + q(4,1) = 1.0$
$q_2(2) = q(0,2) + q(1,2) + q(2,2) + q(3,2) + q(4,2) = 1.5$
$q_2(3) = q(0,3) + q(1,3) + q(2,3) + q(3,3) + q(4,3) = 7/6$
$q_2(4) = q(0,4) + q(1,4) + q(2,4) + q(3,4) + q(4,4) = 25/24$
$q_2(5) = q(0,5) + q(1,5) + q(2,5) + q(3,5) + q(4,5) = 4/6$

Although (1.83) determines CBP in an accurate way, it has a high computational complexity of the order $O(K \prod_{l=1}^{L} C_l)$ [16]. The latter shows the necessity for approximate methods that can be used instead of (1.83), especially in the case of large networks. The most popular method is the *reduced load approximation* (*RLA*) (see e.g., [13, 15, 17], and [18]) and is the subject of the next subsection.

1.5.3 CBP Calculation by the RLA Method

1.5.3.1 A Fixed Routing Network Supporting a Single Service-class

We assume that a fixed routing network supports K different traffic flows of a single service-class requiring 1 b.u. per traffic flow, that is, $b_k = 1$, $k = 1, \ldots, K$. Traffic flows are distinguished by the different sequence of links traversing the various end-to-end connections in a fixed routing network. Let $\bar{\alpha}_l$ be the total offered traffic-load to a link l, where $l \in \{1, 2, \ldots, L\}$:

$$\bar{\alpha}_l = \sum_{k \in K_l} \alpha_k \tag{1.88}$$

where K_l is the set of traffic flows utilizing link l.

The CBP of traffic-flow k, B_k, can be upper bounded by the following product (based on the Erlang-B formula) [19]:

$$B_k \leq 1 - \prod_{l \in R_k} (1 - E_{C_l}(\bar{\alpha}_l)) \tag{1.89}$$

This product-bound provides a good CBP approximation only if the number of links used by traffic flows in the network is small. If not, this bound is unreliable, for example consider only one traffic flow traversing L links of the same capacity C. Then, from (1.89), we have [13]:

$$B_1 \leq 1 - (1 - E_C(\alpha_1))^L \tag{1.90}$$

where $\alpha_1 = \bar{\alpha}_l$ for every link $l = 1, \ldots, L$.

The bound of (1.90) approaches unity when L increases, although $B_1 = E_C(\alpha_1)$ for every link and, consequently, for the entire fixed routing network.

A better CBP approximation is achieved by reducing the offered traffic-load $\bar{\alpha}_l$ so that blocking in the other links (excluding l) is taken into account. Specifically, this is done by substituting in (1.88) the term α_k with $\alpha_k r_k(l)$, where the reduced factor $r_k(l)$ is the probability that there is at least 1 b.u. available in every link of the route $R_k - \{l\}$. Denoting the approximate CBP in link l by V_l, we obtain:

$$V_l = E_{C_l}(\bar{\alpha}_l) = E_{C_l}\left(\sum_{k \in K_l} \alpha_k r_k(l)\right), \quad l = 1, \ldots, L \tag{1.91}$$

Assuming that blocking is independent from link to link (an assumption that is incorrect), we have [13]:

$$r_k(l) = \prod_{i \in R_k - \{l\}} (1 - V_i) \tag{1.92}$$

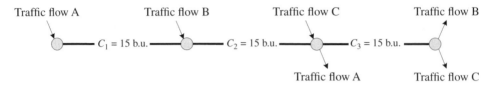

Figure 1.24 Application of the RLA method in a telephone network of three links (Example 1.26).

The combination of (1.91) and (1.92) gives the following *fixed-point equation*[12] for the approximate CBP determination in link l:

$$V_l = E_{C_l}\left(\sum_{k\in K_l} \alpha_k \prod_{i\in R_k-\{l\}} (1 - V_i)\right), \quad l = 1, ..., L \tag{1.93}$$

Assuming again that blocking is independent from link to link, we approximate the CBP of traffic flow k, B_k, as follows [13]:

$$B_k \approx 1 - \prod_{l\in R_k}(1 - V_l), \quad k = 1, ..., K \tag{1.94}$$

The combination of (1.93) and (1.94) constitutes the RLA method (or the so-called *Erlang fixed point equation*, see e.g., [20]) for fixed routing networks that support traffic flows of a single service-class.

Note that the fixed point equation has a unique solution (see e.g., Theorem 5.9 in [13]) which satisfies the bound:

$$V_l^* \leq E_{C_l}\left(\sum_{k\in K_l} \alpha_k\right) \tag{1.95}$$

This solution can be obtained via a simple method that relies on repeated substitutions, as the following example shows.

Example 1.26 Consider the telephone network of Figure 1.24 that accommodates $K = 3$ telephone traffic flows of equal offered traffic-load: $\alpha_A = \alpha_B = \alpha_C = 5$ erl. Estimate the CBP for each traffic flow ($b_A = b_B = b_C = 1$ b.u.), as well as each link.

According to (1.91) and (1.92), for $l = 1, 2, 3$, we have:

$V_1 = E_{C_1}(\alpha_A r_A(1))$ $r_A(1) = 1 - V_2$

$V_2 = E_{C_2}(\alpha_A r_A(2) + \alpha_B r_B(2))$ $r_A(2) = 1 - V_1$ $r_B(2) = 1 - V_3$

$V_3 = E_{C_3}(\alpha_B r_B(3) + \alpha_C r_C(3))$ $r_B(3) = 1 - V_2$ $r_C(3) = 1$

Thus, we can proceed according to (1.93) and (1.94):

$V_1 = E_{C_1}(\alpha_A(1 - V_2))$ $B_A \approx 1 - (1 - V_1)(1 - V_2)$

$V_2 = E_{C_2}(\alpha_A(1 - V_1) + \alpha_B(1 - V_3))$ $B_B \approx 1 - (1 - V_2)(1 - V_3)$

$V_3 = E_{C_3}(\alpha_B(1 - V_2) + \alpha_C)$ $B_C \approx 1 - (1 - V_3)$ $\Rightarrow$ $B_C \approx V_3$

---

12 This term implies a unique solution of the equation.

To solve the above system of equations, we initially set $V_1 = V_2 = V_3 = 1$ and calculate the new values of $(V_1, V_2, V_3) = (0, 0, 0.000157)$ and the corresponding values of $(B_A, B_B, B_C) \approx (1, 0.000157, 0.000157)$. We repeat the calculations by considering the new values as initial values and so on. We terminate this iterative process when the new values differ from the previous values by less than a predefined value, say 0.00001; in this example, we need eight repetitions. The results are:

Repetition	V_1	V_2	V_3	B_A	B_B	B_C
1	0.000000	0.000000	0.000157	1.000000	0.000157	0.000157
2	0.000157	0.036466	0.180316	0.036618	0.210207	0.180316
3	0.000013	0.010778	0.168421	0.010791	0.177384	0.168421
4	0.000020	0.019001	0.176808	0.019021	0.192450	0.176808
5	0.000018	0.011104	0.176442	0.011122	0.185557	0.176442
6	0.000018	0.011138	0.176701	0.011156	0.185871	0.176701
7	0.000018	0.011114	0.176690	0.011133	0.185841	0.176690
8	**0.000018**	**0.011158**	**0.176698**	**0.011176**	**0.185885**	**0.176698**

1.5.3.2 A Fixed Routing Network Supporting Multiple Service-classes

Consider now that K service-classes are accommodated in a fixed routing network of L links, according to the service system described in Section 1.5.1. Suppose that a service-class k traverses a link l of capacity C_l b.u. and experiences there CBP, B_{lk}. B_{lk} can be determined approximately by:

$$B_{lk}[C_l; \alpha_x, \quad x \in K_l] = \sum_{j=C_l-b_k+1}^{C_l} G^{-1}q(j) \tag{1.96}$$

where it is assumed that the offered traffic-load α_x of service-class x to the whole fixed routing network is the same as the offered traffic-load of service-class x in link l; $q(j)$ is the unnormalized probability of having j occupied b.u. in this link (calculated by the Kaufman–Roberts recursion, (1.39), over all $x \in K_l = \{x \in K : l \in R_x\}$) and G is the corresponding normalization constant.

The CBP expression (1.96) can be improved by considering that the offered traffic-load of a service-class to a link is actually reduced when traversing through a sequence of links. Let us denote by V_{lk} the improved CBP of service-class k in link l. Based on (1.92), the offered traffic-load α_x is reduced to $\alpha_x \prod_{i \in R_x - \{l\}}(1 - V_{ix})$. Then, V_{lk} is given by [13]:

$$V_{lk} = B_{lk}\left[C_l; \alpha_x \prod_{i \in R_x - \{l\}}(1 - V_{ix}), \quad x \in K_l\right], \quad k \in K_l, \quad l = 1, ..., L \tag{1.97}$$

Based on (1.97), the approximate CBP calculation of service- class k, B_k, in the entire route R_k, is given by:

$$B_k \approx 1 - \prod_{l \in R_k}(1 - V_{lk}), \quad k = 1, ..., K \tag{1.98}$$

The combination of (1.97) and (1.98) constitutes the RLA method for fixed routing networks that support calls of different service-class. The values of V_{lk} can be obtained via repeated substitutions as Example 1.27 shows.

The extension of the RLA method to include different service- classes appears in the literature as the *knapsack approximation* [21]. This term is justified by the fact that the EMLM resembles the stochastic knapsack/problem in combinatorial optimization [22]. The *knapsack approximation* does not always lead to a unique solution (for an analytical example see [13]), however in most cases it approximates CBP quite satisfactorily.

Example 1.27 Consider again Example 1.25 (Figure 1.23, $C_1 = 4$, $C_2 = 5$, $K = 2$, $\alpha_1 = \alpha_2 = 1$, $b_1 = 1$, $b_2 = 2$) and calculate the CBP of both service-classes by applying the RLA method.

Let B_{11} and B_{21} be the CBP of service- class 1 in the first and second links, respectively, and B_{22} the CBP of service-class 2 in the second link. Then, according to (1.96), we have:

$$B_{11}[C_1; \alpha_x, \ x \in K_1] = \sum_{j=C_1-b_1+1}^{C_1} G^{-1}q(j) \tag{1.99a}$$

$$B_{21}[C_2; \alpha_x, \ x \in K_2] = \sum_{j=C_2-b_1+1}^{C_2} G^{-1}q(j) \tag{1.99b}$$

$$B_{22}[C_2; \alpha_x, \ x \in K_2] = \sum_{j=C_2-b_2+1}^{C_2} G^{-1}q(j) \tag{1.99c}$$

where the values of $q(j)$ are determined by the Kaufman–Roberts recursion (1.39).

Based on (1.92), we determine the reduced offered traffic-load of service-class 1 to the first and second links by (1.100a) and (1.100b), respectively, and the reduced offered traffic- load of service-class 2 to the second link by (1.100c):

$$\alpha_x \prod_{i \in R_x - \{l\}} (1 - V_{ix}) \overset{x=1, \ l=1}{=} \alpha_1 \prod_{i \in R_1 - \{1\}} (1 - V_{i1}) = \alpha_1(1 - V_{21}) \tag{1.100a}$$

$$\alpha_x \prod_{i \in R_x - \{l\}} (1 - V_{ix}) \overset{x=1, \ l=2}{=} \alpha_1 \prod_{i \in R_1 - \{2\}} (1 - V_{i1}) = \alpha_1(1 - V_{11}) \tag{1.100b}$$

$$\alpha_x \prod_{i \in R_x - \{l\}} (1 - V_{ix}) \overset{x=2, \ l=2}{=} \alpha_2 \prod_{i \in R_2 - \{2\}} (1 - V_{i1}) = \alpha_2 \tag{1.100c}$$

Then, according to (1.97), the improved CBP of service-class 1 in the first and second links, V_{11} and V_{21}, respectively, and the improved CBP of service-class 2 in the second link, V_{22}, are:

$$V_{11} = B_{11}[C_1; \ \alpha_1(1 - V_{21})] \tag{1.101a}$$

$$V_{21} = B_{21}[C_2; \ \alpha_1(1 - V_{11}), \ \alpha_2] \tag{1.101b}$$

$$V_{22} = B_{22}[C_2; \ \alpha_1(1 - V_{11}), \ \alpha_2] \tag{1.101c}$$

In the following, we calculate V_{11}, V_{21} and V_{22} by repeated substitutions, starting with $V_{11} = V_{21} = V_{22} = 1$:

Repetition 1

$V_{11} = B_{11}[C_1; \ 0] = 0.0$

$V_{21} = B_{21}[C_2; \ 0, \alpha_2] = 0.0$

$V_{22} = B_{22}[C_2; \ 0, \alpha_2] = \displaystyle\sum_{j=C_2-b_2+1}^{C_2} G^{-1}q(j) = \dfrac{q(4)+q(5)}{G} = \dfrac{0.5}{2.5} = 0.20 \Rightarrow V_{22} = 0.20$

Repetition 2

$V_{11} = B_{11}[C_1; \ \alpha_1] = \displaystyle\sum_{j=C_1-b_1+1}^{C_1} G^{-1}q(j) = \dfrac{q(4)}{G} = \dfrac{0.041667}{2.70833} = 0.01538 \Rightarrow V_{11} = 0.01538$

$V_{21} = B_{21}[C_2; \ \alpha_1, \alpha_2] = \displaystyle\sum_{j=C_2-b_1+1}^{C_2} G^{-1}q(j) = \dfrac{q(5)}{G} = \dfrac{0.675}{6.38333} = 0.10574 \Rightarrow V_{21} = 0.10574$

$V_{22} = B_{22}[C_2; \ \alpha_1, \alpha_2] = \displaystyle\sum_{j=C_2-b_2+1}^{C_2} G^{-1}q(j) = \dfrac{q(4)+q(5)}{G} = \dfrac{1.71667}{6.38333} = 0.26893 \Rightarrow V_{22} = 0.26893$

Repetition 3

$V_{11} = B_{11}[C_1; \ \alpha_1(1-0.10574)] \Rightarrow V_{11} = 0.01092$

$V_{21} = B_{21}[C_2; \ \alpha_1(1-0.01538), \alpha_2] \Rightarrow V_{21} = 0.10469$

$V_{22} = B_{22}[C_2; \ \alpha_1(1-0.01538), \alpha_2] \Rightarrow V_{22} = 0.26731$

...

Repetition 6

$V_{11} = 0.01095 \quad V_{21} = 0.10499 \quad V_{22} = 0.26777$

We stop at Repetition 6 since the values of V_{11}, V_{21} and V_{22} are pretty close to those obtained in the previous step.
   Then, we calculate the CBP according to (1.98):

$B_1 \approx 1 - (1-V_{11})(1-V_{21}) = 1 - (1-0.010945)(1-0.10499) = 0.11479$

$B_2 \approx 1 - (1-V_{22}) = V_{22} = 0.26777$

which are quite close to the accurate values of Example 1.25:

$B_1 = 0.11111 \qquad B_2 = 0.26797.$

Example 1.28   Consider the ring network of Figure 1.25 that accommodates $K = 4$ service-classes with the following traffic characteristics: $(\lambda_1, \mu_1^{-1}, b_1) = (60, 1, 1)$, $(\lambda_2, \mu_2^{-1}, b_2) = (30, 1, 1)$, $(\lambda_3, \mu_3^{-1}, b_3) = (2, 1, 30)$, and $(\lambda_4, \mu_4^{-1}, b_4) = (1, 1, 30)$, respectively. Calls of service-class 1 follow the routes AB and EA, calls of service-class 2 follow the routes ABC, BCD, CD, DE, and DEA, calls of service-class 3 follow the routes AB, ABC, BCD, DE, DEA, and EA, while calls of service-class 4 follow the route CD. Calculate the CBP of all service-classes in their routes, assuming the existence of the BR policy with BR parameters $t_1 = 29, t_2 = 29, t_3 = 0$, and $t_4 = 0$, and compare the analytical with simulation results.

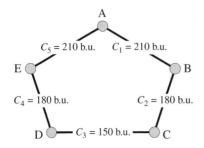

Figure 1.25 A ring network supporting service-classes under the BR policy (Example 1.28).

Table 1.1 Equalized CBP under the BR policy in the network of Figure 1.25.

Route	Offered traffic (erl)	RLA method CBP (%)	Simulation CBP (%)	Route	Offered traffic (erl)	RLA method CBP (%)	Simulation CBP (%)
AB	60.0	20.48	22.03±0.49	AB	2.0	20.48	22.11±0.64
ABC	30.0	34.02	33.41±0.63	ABC	2.0	34.02	33.04±0.59
BCD	30.0	36.68	36.89±0.55	BCD	2.0	36.68	36.74±0.54
CD	30.0	23.69	26.92±0.50	CD	1.0	23.69	27.12±0.59
DE	30.0	22.24	24.10±0.59	DE	2.0	22.24	24.00±0.52
DEA	30.0	37.29	37.60±0.39	DEA	2.0	37.29	38.14±0.87
EA	60.0	19.36	20.11±0.24	EA	2.0	19.36	20.35±0.46

For the analytical calculation of $q(j)$, we apply the Roberts method (see recursive formula (1.64)). Equations (1.97) and (1.98) remain unchanged, while (1.96) becomes:

$$B_{lk}[C; a_x, \; x \in K_l] = \sum_{j=C_l-b_k-t_k+1}^{C_l} G^{-1}q(j) \tag{1.102}$$

in order to take into account the BR parameters t_k, $(k = 1, \ldots, 4)$. Observe that $b_1 + t_1 = b_2 + t_2 = b_3 + t_3 = b_4 + t_4$, and therefore the CBP among the service-classes are equalized.

In Table 1.1 we present the equalized CBP of all service-classes for all routes. The differences between the analytical CBP results (obtained by the RLA method) and the simulation results (mean values of 12 runs with 95% confidence interval), are within an acceptable range for the call-level network performance. The simulation language used is SIMSCRIPT III [23].

1.6 Applications

1.6.1 The Erlang-B Formula

Although the Erlang loss model is now obsolete, since it is applicable to single service-class systems only, it is still useful when a network operator wants to guarantee a specific QoS for a service (of streaming traffic) and, to achieve it, reserves a certain amount of bandwidth, C b.u. for this service (not recommended, because of no statistical multiplexing gain [24]). For the applicability of the Erlang-B formula (1.22) when a call requires a service rate $b > 1$ b.u., we have to consider a system capacity of $\lfloor \frac{C}{b} \rfloor$ and traffic-load α: $E_{\lfloor C/b \rfloor}(\alpha)$. Thus, we transform the system as if it were $b = 1$. When the system capacity is a real number, $E_C(\alpha)$ is determined through the gamma function $\Gamma(\cdot)$ [25]:

$$E_C(\alpha) = \frac{e^C e^{-\alpha}}{\Gamma(\alpha + 1)} \tag{1.103}$$

1.6.2 The Erlang-C Formula

For the Internet, more interesting is the case of the Erlang-C formula (1.18). As has been investigated (e.g., [26], [27]), the Erlang-C formula can provide an upper bound of the congestion probability in a lightly loaded link of the Internet with C b.u., when a max−min fairness policy is applied among traffic flows sharing the link (see [28] and [29]). Assume that we can distinguish K different peak rates $b_1, b_2, \ldots, b_K$ (in increasing order) among the flows traversing the link. Let α_k be the offered traffic-load of flows which corresponds to peak rate b_k, $(k = 1, 2, \ldots, K)$; then, the overall traffic-load is $\alpha = \sum_{k=1}^{K} \alpha_k < C$ (for a steady state).[13] If n_k is the number of active flows (calls) with peak rate b_k, then congestion occurs when $\sum_k n_k b_k > C$. In this case, when a fair rate r^* is determined based on the max−min fairness policy, flows of higher rates (say, all flows with peak rates from b_j to b_K, $j \leq K$) must reduce their bandwidth to the fair rate r^* (so that $r^* = b_K = \cdots = b_j > b_{j-1}$) in order for the total rate to satisfy the link bandwidth capacity C. The proportion of time where any active flow of rate r would suffer loss or has to reduce its bandwidth should be less than a targeted value (i.e., the GoS); this proportion of time is defined as the rate-r congestion probability[14] [26]:

$$Prob \left[\sum_{k=1}^{K} n_k \min(b_k, r) \geq C \right] < \text{GoS} \tag{1.104}$$

Equivalently, the rate-r congestion probability is the probability that the max−min fair rate r^* is less than r (because r^* is determined so that the system capacity C is not violated). This probability increases when all higher peak rates are reduced to r (or all lower peak rates increase to r), while keeping constant the overall traffic-load $\alpha < C$. When the peak rates of higher peak rates are reduced to r, the number n_k of flows increases to n_k^{new} (suppose for all k), so that the overall traffic-load remains constant. Thus, the corresponding probability of rate-r congestion also increases:

$$Prob \left[\sum_{k=1}^{K} n_k^{new} \min(b_k, r) \geq C \right] > Prob \left[\sum_{k=1}^{K} n_k \min(b_k, r) \geq C \right] \tag{1.105}$$

---

13 Although it is hard to know α_k, the total load, α, can readily be determined, e.g., by measuring the total time that the link is busy, on average.

14 For dimensioning purposes, provide the necessary capacity C so that the overall traffic-load α is conveyed while the rate-r congestion probability is less than the GoS.

Intuitively, the max–min fair rate of the original system cannot be less than that of the new system (since $n_k^{new} > n_k$ and higher peak rates have been reduced in the new system).

The worst case of the distribution of the peak rates in the link for the rate-*r* congestion probability under the max–min fair policy is the case where all flows have an equal peak rate *r*. In that case, the rate-*r* congestion probability cannot be increased since the max-min fair rate cannot be reduced, and therefore it becomes an upper bound of the congestion probability. The total number of flows $\sum_k n_k = n$ (each flow with the same peak rate *r* bps) offering a total traffic-load α in the link of capacity *C* (bps) resembles a FIFO queuing system with no loss (if it is lightly loaded), and thus can be modeled as $M/M/C/\infty$. Specifically, if C/r is an integer and $\alpha < C$, then the probability of congestion (i.e., the proportion of time where $nr \geq C$) is given by the Erlang-C formula (1.18) when the system capacity is $\frac{C}{r}$ and the offered traffic-load is $\frac{\alpha}{r}$. Thus, we have:

$$Prob\left[\sum_{k=1}^{K} n_k \min(b_k, r) \geq C\right] \leq Prob[nr \geq C] = E_{C/r}^{delay}(\alpha/r) \qquad (1.106)$$

The applicability of the Erlang-C formula in the Internet fits well to the IntServ resource (bandwidth) allocation strategy, but not to the DiffServ strategy (see Section I.14). Max–min fairness can be implemented through TCP congestion control.

1.6.3 The Kaufman–Roberts Recursion

Applications of the EMLM (Kaufman–Roberts recursive formula (1.39)) in contemporary communications networks are numerous. Its applicability to integrated services digital networks (ISDN) or global system for mobile (GSM) communications networks is straightforward and there is no need for additional explanation.

In optical networks of wavelength division multiplexing (WDM) technology, each fiber supports multiple communication channels, each one operating at a different wavelength. In view of the fact that only a small number of network users necessitate the entire bandwidth of the channel (e.g., up to $40 \cdot 10^9$ bps data rate), the network mostly supports traffic demands with data rates significantly lower than the full wavelength capacity. Therefore, the channel bandwidth is divided into lower sub-rate units (called *traffic grooming*), while traffic streams use one or multiple of these units, i.e., b.u. Considering a single link and a certain capacity (in b.u.) in each wavelength of the link supporting several service-classes, the application of (1.39) for the calculation of the occupancy distribution of each separate wavelength is also straightforward under the Poisson traffic assumption [30].

Let us concentrate now on wideband code division multiple access (WCDMA) wireless networks like the Universal Mobile Telecommunication System (UMTS) in Europe [31]. In a WCDMA cell, all users transmit in the same frequency band by using (pseudo) orthogonal codes to have their signals separated. The basic idea is that a user considers interference (noise) all other signals of all other users. The interference increases as the number of users increases, whereas the cell capacity of the uplink decreases; thus, the applicability of the EMLM is not straightforward but possible. We need to interpret the several sources of noise in terms of the EMLM (see also Section 2.11). The maximum cell load (c_{max}) can be seen as the system capacity *C*, while the required bandwidth per call

b_k corresponds to the occupied cell's resources per call/user (*load factor*, LF_k). The latter is determined by the *bit-error-rate* (BER) parameter, $(E_b/N_0)_k$,[15] and the transmission bit rate TR_k of the corresponding mobile station k [32], [33]:

$$LF_k = \frac{(E_b/N_0)_k \cdot TR_k}{W + [(E_b/N_0)_k \cdot TR_k]} \tag{1.107}$$

where W is the chip rate of the WCDMA carrier.[16]

Since discretization is necessary to apply (1.39), this is achieved through the introduction of a cell load unit g: $C = \frac{C_{max}}{g}$, $b_k = \frac{LF_k}{g}$. The g controls the granularity of the state space of the system, which increases as g decreases. On the other hand, the smaller the g, the better the analytical results (CBP on the uplink) we obtain. For a thorough study, several other parameters (such as *local blocking* (expressing the fact that a call may be blocked due to noise even if the cell accommodates a very few number of users), user activity, interference from other cells) must be incorporated in the EMLM for WCDMA networks [32]. Having understood the applicability of the EMLM to WCDMA systems, then it can readily be applied to more complex systems like the one presented in [34].

We concentrate now on the downlink of an orthogonal frequency division multiplexing (OFDM)-based cell that services calls from different service-classes with different traffic description parameters and consequently different QoS requirements. The cell has M subcarriers and let R, P and S_B be the average data rate per subcarrier, the available power in the cell and the system's bandwidth, respectively. Let the entire range of channel gains or signal-to-noise ratios per unit power be partitioned into K consecutive (but non-overlapping) intervals and denoted as γ_k, $k = 1, \ldots, K$ the average channel gain of the kth interval. Considering L subcarrier requirements and K average channel gains, there are $L \cdot K$ service-classes. A newly arriving service-class (k, l) call ($k = 1, \ldots, K$ and $l = 1, \ldots, L$) requires b_l subcarriers in order to be accepted in the cell (i.e., the call has a data rate requirement $b_l R$) and has an average channel gain γ_k. If these subcarriers are not available, the call is blocked and lost. Otherwise, the call remains in the cell for a generally distributed service time with mean μ^{-1}. To calculate the power p_k required to achieve the data rate R of a subcarrier assigned to a call whose average channel gain is γ_k, we use the Hartley–Shannon theorem: $R = (S_B/M)\log_2(1 + \gamma_k p_k)$. Assuming that calls follow a Poisson process with rate λ_{kl} and that n_{kl} is the number of in-service calls of service-class (k, l), then the system can be described as a multirate loss model with a PFS for the steady state probabilities $\pi(\mathbf{n})$ [35]:

$$\pi(\mathbf{n}) = G^{-1}\left(\prod_{k=1}^{K}\prod_{l=1}^{L}\frac{p_{kl}^{n_{kl}}}{n_{kl}!}\right) \tag{1.108}$$

where $\mathbf{n} = (n_{11}, \ldots, n_{k1}, \ldots, n_{K1}, n_{12}, \ldots, n_{k2}, \ldots, n_{K2}, \ldots, n_{1L}, \ldots, n_{kL}, \ldots, n_{KL})$, $\Omega = \{\mathbf{n} : 0 \leq \sum_{k=1}^{K}\sum_{l=1}^{L}n_{kl}b_l \leq M, \quad 0 \leq \sum_{k=1}^{K}\sum_{l=1}^{L}p_k n_{kl}b_l \leq P\}$ is the state space of the system, $G = \sum_{\mathbf{n}\in\Omega}\left(\prod_{k=1}^{K}\prod_{l=1}^{L}\frac{p_{kl}^{n_{kl}}}{n_{kl}!}\right)$ is the normalization constant, and $p_{kl} = \lambda_{kl}/\mu$ is the offered traffic-load (in erl) of service-class (k, l) calls.

---

15 BER parameter $\equiv$ bit-energy-to-noise ratio $(E_b/N_0)_k$ for service-class k calls received by the cell controller.

16 Chip rate stands for the bit rate used in the encoding process of the data bits. In WCDMA, typically $W = 3.84 \cdot 10^6$ cps over 5 MHz frequency band and roll-off factor 0.3.

Note that the derivation of (1.108) requires that P and p_k are integers (which is generally not true). In order to have an equivalent representation of the constraint $0 \le \sum_{k=1}^{K} \sum_{l=1}^{L} p_k n_{kl} b_l \le P$, we multiply both sides of this expression by a constant to get $\sum_{k=1}^{K} \sum_{l=1}^{L} p_k' n_{kl} b_l \le P'$, where P' and p_k' are integers [35]. Thus, without loss of generality, we assume that P and p_k are integers. Now, let $j_1 = \sum_{k=1}^{K} \sum_{l=1}^{L} n_{kl} b_l$ (i.e., $j_1 = 0, \dots, M$) be the occupied subcarriers and $j_2 = \sum_{k=1}^{K} \sum_{l=1}^{L} p_k n_{kl} b_l$ (i.e., $j_2 = 0, 1, \dots, P$) the occupied power in the cell. Then, it is proved in [36] that there exists a recursive formula, which resembles the Kaufman–Roberts recursion, for the determination of $q(\mathbf{j}) = q(j_1, j_2)$ and consequently all performance measures.

Finally, it is worth mentioning a remarkable application of the EMLM on *smart grid*, which is an example showing the wide applicability range of the model. To control energy consumption, all appliances are connected to a central controller. Each appliance has a power demand (in power units), while the appliances are distinguished into different types according to the demand. For a specific type of appliance, the power demand arrival processes (to the controller) can be assumed Poisson. The controller activates each power demand request upon arrival, if it is possible, given that the total amount of power (capacity in total power units) that can be distributed to the appliances is limited. Each appliance operates for an operating time (depending on its type), which is generally distributed. Assuming that the amounts of power can be discretized, the analogy between a communication link and the smart grid case becomes obvious: the total amount of power corresponds to the link bandwidth capacity, the various types of appliances to service- classes, the power demand of a specific appliance to the required bandwidth per service-class call, the arrival process for power request to the call arrival process, and the operating time of appliances to the service time of calls. In this way, the probability distribution of the total power units devoted to the appliances can be determined through the EMLM. Alternatively, the EMLM can be used as a tool to calculate the total amount of power needed for guaranteeing power demands under a specific GoS per type of appliances [37].

1.7 Further Reading

There is a vast number of papers related to extensions and applications of the models presented in this chapter. In this section we present only an indicative list of papers for further reading in various directions.

Although we would like to focus on works beyond the Erlang-B formula, it would be an omission if we did not mention several extensions of the Erlang-B formula in wireless ([38], [39]), optical ([40], [41]), and satellite networks [42] that have emerged in recent years. In [38], a multi-cell mobility model for cellular networks is considered and a two-dimensional Erlang loss model is proposed for the determination of loss probabilities. In [39], the Erlang-B formula has been adopted in order to provide approximate CBP in a two WiFi access link system in which the two links share their bandwidth. In [40], an analytical model is proposed for the determination of burst blocking probabilities in optical burst switching (OBS) networks. The model extends the Erlang-B formula by considering multiple priority classes and the notion of preemption. In [41], an analytical model, based on the Erlang fixed point approximation, is proposed for the approximate network-wide blocking probability determination in any cast routing and wavelength assignment optical WDM networks. In [42], a fixed point approximation method is proposed for the CBP calculation in a low earth orbit (LEO) satellite network. The CBP calculation uses the Erlang-B formula, but the offered traffic-load is modified in order to take into account the time and location in which the calls are made.

Many remarkable extensions of the EMLM in wired ([43–57]), wireless ([58–66]), optical ([67–69]), and satellite networks ([70–72]) have been published. In [43], a recursive formula is proposed for the determination of the link occupancy distribution in a link that accommodates Bernoulli–Poisson–Pascal (BPP) traffic. In [44] and [45], and [46] and [47], the EMLM is extended to handle unicast/multicast connections in a single link and a network, respectively. In [48–51] and [52], CBP derivatives with respect to offered traffic-load, arrival rate or service rate are studied in the EMLM and in the EMLM/BR, respectively. CBP derivatives are significant in multirate loss systems since they enable the study of the interaction between different service-classes that share the same link. In [53–56], the EMLM is extended to handle overflow traffic, i.e., traffic that is lost in a primary link and is routed to a secondary link. In [57], a recent review on loss networks is presented. In [58], the EMLM/BR is extended to include a reservation policy in which the reserved b.u. can have a real (not integer) value. In [59], an EMLM-based model is proposed for the CBP determination in the X2 interface that interconnects neighboring eNBs in a LTE network. In [60] and [61], the EMLM is applied to the CBP calculation in the downlink of orthogonal frequency division multiple access cellular networks. In [62], an EMLM-based model is proposed for the CBP calculation in a multicast 3G network. The authors of [63] investigated strategies for active sharing of radio access among multiple operators, assuming the existence of Cloud-RAN. For their analysis a BPP multirate loss model is considered. In [64], the EMLM is used in the call- level analysis of the access part of a 3G mobile network that incorporates priorities between calls of different service-classes. In [65], a probabilistic threshold policy is proposed that extends the EMLM/TH. In [66], the two WiFi access link system of [39] (which accommodates a single service-class) has been extended to include the case of multiple service-classes. In [67], EMLM-based models are proposed for calculating connection failure probabilities (due to unavailability of a wavelength) and CBP (due to the restricted bandwidth capacity of a wavelength) in hybrid TDM-WDM passive optical networks with dynamic wavelength allocation (DWA). In [68], an analytical methodology for computing approximate blocking probabilities in multirate optical WDM networks is proposed which is based on the EMLM and the RLA. In [69], the EMLM is applied in elastic optical networks. Based on the EMLM, an analytical framework is proposed for evaluating the performance of the CS and the fixed channel reservation policies [70] as well as the complete partitioning and the threshold call admission policies [71] that are applied in LEO mobile satellite systems. An extension of [70] and [71] that includes efficient formulas for various performance measures (including CBP and handover failure probabilities) has been proposed in [72].

References

1 B. Sevastyanov, An ergodic theorem for Markov processes and its application to telephone systems with refusals. *Theory of Probability & Its Applications*, 2(1): 104–112, 1957.

2 L. Takacs, On Erlang's Formula. *The Annals of Mathematical Statistics*, 40(1): 71–78, 1969.

3 P. Taylor, Insensitivity in Stochastic Models, Chapter 3 in *Queueing Networks: A Fundamental Approach*, N. van Dijk and R. J. Boucherie (eds.), Springer-Verlag, pp. 121–140, 2011.

4 A. Harel, Sharp and simple bounds for the Erlang delay and loss formulae. *Queueing Systems*, 64(2):119–143, February 2010.

5 J. Kaufman, Blocking in a shared resource environment. *IEEE Transactions on Communications*, 29(10): 1474–1481, October 1981.

6 M. Schwartz and B. Kraimeche, An analytic control codel for an integrated node. *Proceedings of the IEEE Infocom*, pp. 540–545, 1983.

7 V. Iversen, The exact evaluation of multi-service loss system with access control. *Teleteknik* [English edn], 31(2): 56–61, 1987.

8 M. Glabowski, A. Kaliszan and M. Stasiak, Asymmetric convolution algorithm for blocking probability calculation in full-availability group with bandwidth reservation. *IET Circuits Devices & Systems*, 2(1): 87–94, February 2008.

9 Q. Huang, K. Ko and V. Iversen, A new convolution algorithm for loss probability analysis in multiservice networks. *Performance Evaluation*, 68(1):76–87, January 2011.

10 S. Johnson, A performance analysis of integrated communications systems. *British Telecom Technology Journal*, 3(4): 36–45, 1985.

11 J. Roberts, Teletraffic models for the Telecom 1 Integrated Services Network. *Proceedings of ITC-10*, Montreal, Canada, 1983.

12 M. Stasiak and M. Glabowski, A simple approximation of the link model with reservation by a one-dimensional Markov chain. *Performance Evaluation*, 41(2–3):195–208, July 2000.

13 K. Ross, *Multiservice Loss Models for Broadband Telecommunication Networks*, Springer, Berlin, 1995.

14 D. Tsang and K. Ross, Algorithms to determine exact blocking probabilities for multirate tree networks. *IEEE Transactions on Communications*, 38(8):1266–1271, August 1990.

15 Z. Dziong and J. Roberts, Congestion probabilities in a circuit switched integrated services network. *Performance Evaluation*, 7(4):267–284, November 1987.

16 G. Awater and H. van de Vlag, Exact computation of time and call blocking probabilities in large, multi-traffic, multi-resource loss systems. *Performance Evaluation*, 25(1): 41–58, March 1996.

17 D. Bear, *Principles of Telecommunication-Traffic Engineering*, Peter Peregrinus Ltd, 1976.

18 A. Girard, *Routing and Dimensioning in Circuit Switched Networks*, Addison Wesley, 1990.

19 W. Whitt, Blocking when service is required from several facilities simultaneously. *AT&T Technical Journal*, 64:1807–1856, 1985.

20 F. Kelly, Loss networks. *Annals of Applied Probability*, 1(3):319–378, August 1991.

21 S. Chung and K. Ross, Reduced load approximations for multirate loss networks. *IEEE Transactions on Communications*, 41(8):1222–1231, August 1993.

22 H. Wagner, *Principles of Operations Research*, Prentice-Hall, 1969.

23 SIMSCRIPT III, http://www.simscript.com/.

24 H. Saito, *Teletraffic Technologies in ATM Networks*, Artech House, 1994.

25 H. Akimaru and K. Kawashima, *Teletraffic – Theory and Applications*, 2nd edn, Springer, Berlin, 1999.

26 T. Bonald and J. Roberts, Internet and the Erlang formula. *ACM SIGCOMM Computer Communication Review*, 42(1):23–30, January 2012.

27 V.B. Iversen, The Internet Erlang formula, in *NEW2AN/ruSMART 2012*, S. Andreev et al. (eds), LNCS 7469, pp. 328–337, Springer-Verlag, Berlin, Heidelberg, 2012.

28 I. Moscholios and M. Logothetis, New algorithm for the generalized max–min fairness policy based on linear programming. *IEICE Transactions on Communications*, E88-B(2):775–780, February 2005.

29 M. Logothetis, I. Moscholios and G. Kokkinakis, The generalized max–min fairness policy based on linear programming. *Mediterranean Journal of Electronics and Communications*, 2(1):1–10, 2006.

30 J.S. Vardakas, V.G. Vassilakis and M.D. Logothetis, Calculating blocking probabilities in single-hop WDM traffic groomed optical networks. *Proceedings of the International Conference on Transparent Optical Networks (ICTON 2007)*, Rome, 1–5 July, 2007.

31 H. Holma and A. Toskala (eds), *WCDMA for UMTS*, 5th edn, John Wiley & Sons Ltd, 2010.

32 D. Staehle and A. Mäder, An analytic approximation of the uplink capacity in a UMTS network with heterogeneous traffic. *Proceedings of the 18th International Teletraffic Congress (ITC18)*, Berlin, September 2003.

33 M. Logothetis, V. Vassilakis and I. Moscholios, Call-level performance modeling and QoS assessment of W-CDMA networks, in *Wireless Networks: Research, Technology and Applications*, pp. 57–90, Nova Science Publishers, New York, 2009.

34 J.S. Vardakas, V.G. Vassilakis and M.D. Logothetis, Call-level analysis of hybrid WDM-OCDMA PONs. *Proceedings of the International Conference on Transparent Optical Networks (ICTON 2008)*, Athens, Greece, June 22–26, 2008.

35 C. Paik and Y. Suh, Generalized queueing model for call blocking probability and resource utilization in OFDM wireless networks. *IEEE Communication Letters*, 15(7):767–769, July 2011.

36 I. Moscholios, V. Vassilakis, P. Panagoulias and M. Logothetis, On call blocking probabilities and resource utilization in OFDM wireless networks. *Proceedings of the IEEE/IET CSNDSP*, Budapest, Hungary, 18–20 July 2018.

37 J.S. Vardakas, N. Zorba and C.V. Verikoukis, Performance evaluation of power demand scheduling scenarios in a smart grid environment. *Applied Energy*, 142:164–178, March 2015.

38 K. Kim and H. Choi, A mobility model and performance analysis in wireless cellular network with general distribution and multi-cell model. *Wireless Personal Communications*, 53(2):179–198, April 2010.

39 V. Burger, M. Seufert, T. Hossfeld and P. Tran-Gia, Performance evaluation of back-haul bandwidth aggregation using a partial sharing scheme. *Physical Communication*, 19:135–144, June 2016.

40 G. Zeng, A review on a new conservation law in optical burst switching networks. *Mathematical and Computer Modelling*, 57(5–6):1504–1513, March 2013.

41 Y. Cui and V. Vokkarane, Analytical blocking model for anycast RWA in optical WDM networks. *IEEE/OSA Journal of Optical Communications and Networking*, 8(10):787–799, October 2016.

42 D. Yiltas and A. Zaim, Evaluation of call blocking probabilities in LEO satellite networks. *International Journal of Satellite Communications and Networking*, 27(2):103–115, March/April 2009.

43 L. Delbrouck, On the steady-state distribution in a service facility carrying mixtures of traffic with different peakedness factors and capacity requirements. *IEEE Transactions on Communications*, 31(11):1209–1211, November 1983.

44 K. Boussetta and A. Beylot, Multirate resource sharing for unicast and multicast connections, in *Broadband Communications – Convergence of Network Technologies*, Volume 30 of the IFIP series, pp. 561–570, 2000.

45 I. Gudkova and O. Plaskina, Performance measures computation for a single link loss network with unicast and multicast traffics, in *Lecture Notes in Computer Science*, Volume 6294, Springer, Berlin, 2010.

46 K. Samouylov and N. Yarkina, Blocking probabilities in multiservice networks with unicast and multicast connections. *Proceedings of the 8th International Conference on Telecommunications (ConTEL)*, Zagreb, Croatia, June 2005.

47 M. Glabowski, M. Stasiak and P. Zwierzykowski, Modeling of virtual-circuit switching nodes with multicast connections. *European Transactions on Communications*, 20(2):123–137, March 2009.

48 J. Virtamo, Reciprocity of blocking probabilities in multiservice loss systems. *IEEE Transactions on Communications*, 36(10):1257–1260, October 1988.

49 S. Jordan and P. Varaiya, Throughput in multiple service multiple resource communications networks. *IEEE Transactions on Communications*, 39(8):1216–1222, August 1991.

50 C. Aswakul and J. Barria, Error analysis of multiservice single-link system studies using linear approximation model. *Proceedings of the IEEE ICC*, Seoul, South Korea, May 2005.

51 V. Iversen and S. Stepanov, Derivatives of blocking probabilities for multi-service loss systems and their applications, in *Lecture Notes in Computer Science*, Volume 4712, Springer, Berlin, 2007.

52 I. Moscholios, J. Vardakas, M. Logothetis and A. Boucouvalas, New algorithms for performance measures derivatives in the Erlang multirate loss model including the bandwidth reservation policy. *Mediterranean Journal of Computers and Networks*, 7(4):304–316, October 2011.

53 Q. Huang, K. Ko and V. Iversen, Approximation of loss calculation for hierarchical networks with multiservice overflows. *IEEE Transactions on Communications*, 56(3):466–473, March 2008.

54 M. Glabowski, K. Kubasik and M. Stasiak, Modeling of systems with overflow multi-rate traffic. *Telecommunication Systems*, 37(1–3):85–96, March 2008.

55 M. Glabowski, S. Hanczewski, and M. Stasiak, Modelling of cellular networks with traffic overflow. *Mathematical Problems in Engineering*, article ID 286490, 15 pp, 2015, doi: 10.1155/2015/286490.

56 M. Glabowski, A. Kaliszan and M. Stasiak, Modelling overflow systems with distributed secondary resources. *Computer Networks*, 108:171–183, October 2016.

57 S. Zachary and I. Ziedins, Loss networks, in *Queueing Networks: A fundamental approach*, R. Boucherie and N. van Dijk (eds), pp. 701–728, Springer, Berlin, 2011.

58 F. Cruz-Pérez, J. Vázquez-Ávila and L. Ortigoza-Guerrero, Recurrent formulas for the multiple fractional channel reservation strategy in multiservice mobile cellular networks. *IEEE Communication Letters*, 8(10): 629–631, October 2004.

59 I. Widjaja and H. La Roche, Sizing X2 bandwidth for inter-connected eNBs. *Proceedings of the IEEE Vehicle Technology Conference*, Fall, Anchorage, USA, September, 2009.

60 B. Blaszczyszyn and M. Karray, Dimensioning of the downlink in OFDMA cellular networks via an Erlang's loss model. *Proceedings of the European Wireless Conference*, Aalborg, Denmark, May 2009.

61 M. Karray, Analytical evaluation of QoS in the downlink of OFDMA wireless cellular networks serving streaming and elastic traffic. *IEEE Transactions on Wireless Communications*, 9(5):1799–1807, May 2010.

62 D. Parniewicz, M. Stasiak and P. Zwierzykowski, Traffic engineering for multicast connections in multiservice cellular networks. *IEEE Transactions on Industrial Informatics*, 9(1):262–270, February 2013.

63 A. Avramova and V. Iversen, Radio access sharing strategies for multiple operators in cellular networks. *IEEE ICC Workshop on 5G & Beyond,*London, UK, June 2015.

64 S. Hanczewski, M. Stasiak and P. Zwierzykowski, Modelling of the access part of a multi-service mobile network with service priorities. *Eurasip Journal on Wireless Communications and Networking*, 2015:194, December 2015, doi: 10.1186/s13638-015-0420-4.

65 I. Moscholios, V. Vassilakis, M. Logothetis and A. Boucouvalas, A probabilistic threshold-based bandwidth sharing policy for wireless multirate loss networks. *IEEE Wireless Communication Letters*, 5(3):304–307, June 2016.

66 S. Sagkriotis, S. Pantelis, I. Moscholios and V. Vassilakis, Call blocking probabilities in a two-link multi rate loss system for Poisson traffic, *IET Networks*, 7(4):233–241, July 2018.

67 J. Vardakas, V. Vassilakis and M. Logothetis, Blocking analysis in hybrid TDM-WDM passive optical networks. *Proceedings of the 5th HET-NETs*, Karlskrona, Sweden, February 2008.

68 K. Kuppuswamy and D. Lee, An analytical approach to efficiently computing call blocking probabilities for multiclass WDM networks. *IEEE/ACM Transactions on Networking*, 17(2):658–670, April 2009.

69 H. Beyranvand, M. Maier and J. Salehi, An analytical framework for the performance evaluation of node-and network-wise operation scenarios in elastic optical networks. *IEEE Transactions on Communications*, 62(5):1621–1633, May 2014.

70 Z. Wang, P.T. Mathiopoulos and R. Schober, Performance analysis and improvement methods for channel resource management strategies of LEO-MSS with multiparty traffic. *IEEE Transactions on Vehicle Technology*, 57(6):3832–3842, November 2008.

71 Z. Wang, P.T. Mathiopoulos and R. Schober, Channeling partitioning policies for multi-class traffic in LEO-MSS. *IEEE Transactions on Aerospace and Electronic Systems*, 45(4):1320–1334, October 2009.

72 I. Moscholios, V. Vassilakis, N. Sagias and M. Logothetis, On channel sharing policies in LEO mobile satellite systems. *IEEE Transactions on Aerospace and Electronic Systems*, 54(4):1628–1640, August 2018.

2

Multirate Retry Threshold Loss Models

We consider multirate loss models of random arriving calls with elastic bandwidth requirements and fixed bandwidth allocation during service. Calls may retry several times upon arrival (requiring less bandwidth each time) in order to be accepted for service. Alternatively, calls may request less bandwidth upon arrival, according to the occupied link bandwidth indicated by threshold(s).

2.1 The Single-Retry Model

2.1.1 The Service System

In the *single-retry model* (SRM), a link of capacity C b.u. accommodates Poisson arriving calls of K service-classes, under the CS policy. A new call of service-class k ($k = 1, \ldots, K$) has a peak-bandwidth requirement of b_k b.u. and an exponentially distributed service time with mean μ_k^{-1}. If the initially required b.u. are not available in the link, the call is blocked, but immediately retries to be connected with bandwidth requirement $b_{kr} < b_k$ b.u., while the mean of the new (exponentially distributed) service time increases to $\mu_{kr}^{-1} = \frac{b_k}{b_{kr}} \mu_k^{-1}$, so that the product *bandwidth requirement* by *service time* ($b_k \mu_k^{-1} = b_{kr} \mu_{kr}^{-1}$) remains constant [1, 2]. If the b_{kr} b.u. are not available, the call is blocked and lost (Figure 2.1). The CAC mechanism of a call of service-class k is depicted in Figure 2.2. A new call of service-class k is blocked with b_k b.u. if $j > C - b_k$ and is accepted with b_{kr} b.u., if $C - b_{kr} \geq j > C - b_k$, where $j = \sum_{k=1}^{K}(n_k b_k + n_{kr} b_{kr})$ and n_k, n_{kr} are the in-service calls of service-class k (in the steady state of the system) accepted with b_k, b_{kr} b.u., respectively. The comparison of the SRM with the EMLM reveals the following basic differences:

(i) The steady state probabilities in the SRM do not have a PFS, since the notion of LB between adjacent states does not hold (see Example 2.1). Because of this, the unnormalized values of $q(j)$ are determined via an approximate, but recursive, formula, as Section 2.1.2 shows.

(ii) In the EMLM, the steady state vector of all in-service calls of all service-classes is $\mathbf{n} = (n_1, n_2, \ldots, n_K)$, while in the SRM the corresponding vector becomes $\mathbf{n} = (n_1, n_{1r}, n_2, n_{2r}, \ldots, n_K, n_{Kr})$. This dimensionality increase means that only quite small problems can be solved exactly (see Example 2.1).

Efficient Multirate Teletraffic Loss Models Beyond Erlang, First Edition.
Ioannis D. Moscholios and Michael D. Logothetis.
© 2019 John Wiley & Sons Ltd. Published 2019 by John Wiley & Sons Ltd.
Companion website: www.wiley.com/go/logocode

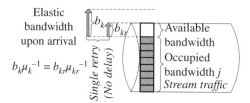

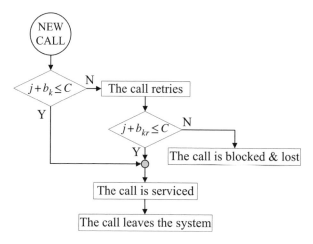

Figure 2.1 Service system of the SRM.

Figure 2.2 The CAC mechanism for a new call in the SRM.

(iii) In the EMLM, the calculation of $q(j)$ via the Kaufman–Roberts recursion (1.39) is insensitive to the service time distribution [3]. In the SRM, this insensitivity property does not hold. However, numerical examples in [2] show that the CBP obtained for various service time distributions are quite close.

Example 2.1   Consider a link of $C = 5$ b.u. The link accommodates Poisson arriving calls of $K = 2$ service-classes. Calls of service-class 1 require $b_1 = 1$ b.u., while calls of service-class 2 require $b_2 = 3$ b.u. Blocked calls of service-class 2 can immediately retry with $b_{2r} = 2$ b.u. For simplicity, assume that $\lambda_1 = \lambda_2 = 1$ call/s, $\mu_1^{-1} = \mu_2^{-1} = 1$ sec, and $\mu_{2r}^{-1} = \frac{b_2}{b_{2r}}\mu_2^{-1} = 1.5$ sec:

(a) Find the total number of permissible states $\mathbf{n} = (n_1, n_2, n_{2r})$ (state space Ω) and draw the state transition diagram.
(b) Find those adjacent states that the LB is destroyed and justify your answer.
(c) Calculate the state probabilities $P(n_1, n_2, n_{2r})$ based on the GB equations. Then, calculate $Q(j)$ (link occupancy distribution).
(d) Calculate the CBP of both service-classes including the retry probability and the link utilization.
(e) Calculate the conditional CBP of service-class 2 retry calls given that they have been blocked with their initial bandwidth requirement, b_2 b.u.

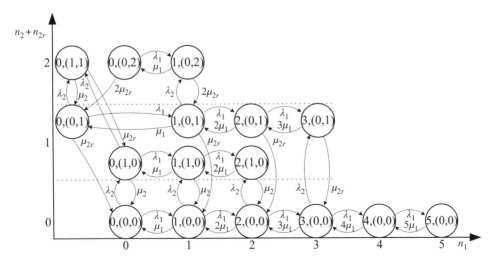

Figure 2.3 The state space Ω (CS policy) and the state transition diagram (Example 2.1).

(a) There are 16 permissible states of the form $\mathbf{n} = (n_1, n_2, n_{2r})$. The state space Ω and the state transition diagram are shown in Figure 2.3.

(b) From Figure 2.3, we see that the LB is destroyed between the following adjacent states: (We justify the first two pairs, while the justification for the other two pairs is similar.)

- (0,0,0) and (0,0,1): Assuming that the system state is (0,0,0) when a new call of service-class 2 arrives in the system. The call will be accepted with b_2 b.u. and the new state will be (0,1,0), not (0,0,1). On the other hand, if the system state is (0,0,1), then the in-service retry call of service-class 2 can depart from the system with rate μ_{2r} and the new state will be (0,0,0).

- (0,0,1) and (0,0,2): Assuming that the system state is (0,0,1), when a new call of service-class 2 arrives in the system. The call will be accepted with b_2 b.u. and the new state will be (0,1,1), not (0,0,2). On the other hand, if the system state is (0,0,2), then an in-service retry call of service-class 2 can depart from the system with rate $2\mu_{2r}$ and the new state will be (0,0,1).

- (1,0,0) and (1,0,1)

- (2,0,0) and (2,0,1)

(c) Based on Figure 2.3, we obtain the following 16 GB equations:

$(0,0,0):$ $P(0,1,0) + P(1,0,0) + 2/3P(0,0,1) - 2P(0,0,0) = 0$

$(0,0,1):$ $P(0,1,1) + P(1,0,1) + 4/3P(0,0,2) - 8/3P(0,0,1) = 0$

$(0,0,2):$ $P(1,0,2) - 7/3P(0,0,2) = 0$

$(0,1,0):$ $P(0,0,0) + 2/3P(0,1,1) + P(1,1,0) - 3P(0,1,0) = 0$

$(0,1,1):$ $P(0,1,0) + P(0,0,1) - 5/3P(0,1,1) = 0$

$(1,0,0):$ $P(0,0,0) + 2/3P(1,0,1) + 2P(2,0,0) + P(1,1,0) - 3P(1,0,0) = 0$

$(1,0,1):$ $P(0,0,1) + 4/3P(1,0,2) + 2P(2,0,1) - 11/3P(1,0,1) = 0$

$(1,0,2):$ $P(0,0,2) + P(1,0,1) - 7/3P(1,0,2) = 0$

$(1,1,0):$ $P(0,1,0) + P(1,0,0) + 2P(2,1,0) - 3P(1,1,0) = 0$

$(2,0,0):$ $P(1,0,0) + 3P(3,0,0) + P(2,1,0) + 2/3P(2,0,1) - 4P(2,0,0) = 0$

$(2,0,1):$ $P(1,0,1) + 3P(3,0,1) - 11/3P(2,0,1) = 0$

$(2,1,0):$ $P(1,1,0) + P(2,0,0) - 3P(2,1,0) = 0$

$(3,0,0):$ $P(2,0,0) + 2/3P(3,0,1) + 4P(4,0,0) - 5P(3,0,0) = 0$

$(3,0,1):$ $P(3,0,0) + P(2,0,1) - 11/3P(3,0,1) = 0$

$(4,0,0):$ $P(3,0,0) + 5P(5,0,0) - 5P(4,0,0) = 0$

$(5,0,0):$ $P(4,0,0) - 5P(5,0,0) = 0$

By replacing one GB equation (say the (1,0,0)) with the equation $\sum_{n\in\Omega} P(n_1, n_2, n_{2r}) = 1$, the solution of this linear system is:

$P(0,0,0) = 0.159428$	$P(0,0,1) = 0.054654$	$P(0,0,2) = 0.006608$	$P(0,1,0) = 0.124614$
$P(0,1,1) = 0.107561$	$P(1,0,0) = 0.157806$	$P(1,0,1) = 0.02937$	$P(1,0,2) = 0.015419$
$P(1,1,0) = 0.142709$	$P(2,0,0) = 0.07585$	$P(2,0,1) = 0.016239$	$P(2,1,0) = 0.072853$
$P(3,0,0) = 0.020639$	$P(3,0,1) = 0.010058$	$P(4,0,0) = 0.00516$	$P(5,0,0) = 0.001032$

Then, based on the values of $P(n_1, n_2, n_{2r})$, we obtain the values of $Q(j)$:

$Q(0) = P(0,0,0) = 0.159428$

$Q(1) = P(1,0,0) = 0.157806$

$Q(2) = P(0,0,1) + P(2,0,0) = 0.130504$

$Q(3) = P(0,1,0) + P(1,0,1) + P(3,0,0) = 0.174623$

$Q(4) = P(0,0,2) + P(1,1,0) + P(2,0,1) + P(4,0,0) = 0.170716$

$Q(5) = P(0,1,1) + P(1,0,2) + P(2,1,0) + P(3,0,1) + P(5,0,0) = 0.206923$

(d) The CBP of service-class 1, B_1, is given by:

$$B_1 = \sum_{j=C-b_1+1}^{C} Q(j) = Q(5) = 0.206923$$

The $Prob\{retry\}$ of service-class 2 calls, B_2, when they require b_2 b.u. upon arrival, is:

$$B_2 = \sum_{j=C-b_2+1}^{C} Q(j) = Q(3) + Q(4) + Q(5) = 0.552262$$

Let us emphasize that B_2 gives the percentage of calls which retry. The CBP of service-class 2, B_{2r}, refers to service-class 2 retry calls which require b_{2r} b.u. and is given by:

$$B_{2r} = \sum_{j=C-b_{2r}+1}^{C} Q(j) = Q(4) + Q(5) = 0.377639$$

The link utilization is determined by:

$$U = \sum_{j=1}^{C} jQ(j) = 2.66 \text{ b.u.}$$

For comparison, note that the corresponding CBP and link utilization results in the case of the EMLM are $B_1 = 0.09744$, $B_2 = 0.52077$, and $U = 2.34$ b.u.

(e) In (d), B_{2r} is determined as a percentage of blocked calls over all arriving calls of service-class 2. The conditional CBP of service-class 2 retry calls over those calls which cannot be accepted with the initial bandwidth b_2 is given by:

$$B_{2r}^* = Prob\{j > C - b_{2r} | j > C - b_2\} = \frac{B_{2r}}{B_2} = 0.68380$$

2.1.2 The Analytical Model

2.1.2.1 Steady State Probabilities

To describe the analytical model in the steady state, let us concentrate on a single link of capacity C b.u. that accommodates two service-classes with the following traffic characteristics: $(\lambda_1, \lambda_2), (\mu_1^{-1}, \mu_2^{-1}), (b_1, b_2)$. Blocked calls of service-class 2 can retry with parameters (b_{2r}, μ_{2r}^{-1}), while blocked calls of service-class 1 are not allowed to retry. Although the SRM does not have a PFS, we assume that the LB equation (1.51) proposed in the EMLM does hold, that is:

$$\lambda_k q(j - b_k) = y_k(j) \mu_k q(j)$$
$$\text{for } j = 1, \dots, C \quad \text{and} \quad k = 1, 2 \tag{2.1}$$

This assumption (approximation) is important for the derivation of an approximate but recursive formula for the calculation of $q(j)$. The aforementioned equation expresses the fact that no call blocking occurs in state $(j - b_k)$, if there are available b_k b.u. ($k = 1, 2$). If $j > C - b_2$, when a new call of service-class 2 arrives in the system, then this call is blocked and retries to be connected with b_{2r} b.u. If $j \le C - b_{2r}$, then, the retry call will be accepted in the system. To describe the latter case, we need an additional LB equation [2]:

$$\lambda_2 q(j - b_{2r}) = y_{2r}(j) \mu_{2r} q(j)$$
$$j - b_{2r} > C - b_2 \tag{2.2}$$

where $y_{2r}(j)$ is the mean number of service-class k calls accepted in the system with b_{2r} in state j.

Dividing (2.2) by μ_{2r} and multiplying by b_{2r}, we obtain [2]:

$$\alpha_{2r} b_{2r} q(j - b_{2r}) = y_{2r}(j) b_{2r} q(j)$$
$$C \ge j > C - (b_2 - b_{2r}) \tag{2.3}$$

where $\alpha_{2r} = \lambda_2 \mu_{2r}^{-1}$ is the offered traffic-load of service-class 2 calls with b_{2r}.

Equation (2.1) can be written as $\alpha_k q(j - b_k) = y_k(j) q(j)$. Then, by multiplying both sides with b_k and summing up for $k = 1, 2$, we have:

$$\alpha_1 b_1 q(j - b_1) + \alpha_2 b_2 q(j - b_2) = [y_1(j) b_1 + y_2(j) b_2] q(j)$$
$$\text{for} \quad j = 1, \dots, C \tag{2.4}$$

Adding (2.3) to (2.4), and since $y_1(j) b_1 + y_2(j) b_2 + y_{2r}(j) b_{2r} = j$, we have:

$$\alpha_1 b_1 q(j - b_1) + \alpha_2 b_2 q(j - b_2) + \alpha_{2r} b_{2r} q(j - b_{2r}) = jq(j)$$
$$C \ge j > C - (b_2 - b_{2r}) \quad \text{and} \quad j = 1, \dots, C. \tag{2.5}$$

Apart from the assumption of the LB equation (2.1), another approximation is necessary for the recursive calculation of $q(j)$ [2]:

$$y_1(j)b_1 + y_2(j)b_2 \approx j$$
$$\text{for} \quad j = 1, ..., C - (b_2 - b_{2r}) \tag{2.6}$$

Equation (2.6) expresses the so-called *migration approximation* [1, 2, 4], according to which the number of calls accepted in the system with other than the maximum bandwidth requirement is negligible within a state space, called the *migration space*. In this space, the value of $y_{2r}(j)b_{2r}$ is negligible compared to $y_1(j)b_1 + y_2(j)b_2$ when $j \le C - (b_2 - b_{2r})$. For service-class k (with $b_{kr} > 0$):

$$1 \le j \le C - (b_k - b_{kr}) \quad \text{migration space}$$
$$y_{kr}(j) = 0 \qquad\qquad\qquad \text{migration approximation} \tag{2.7}$$

Equation (2.4) due to (2.6) is written as:

$$\alpha_1 b_1 q(j - b_1) + \alpha_2 b_2 q(j - b_2) = jq(j)$$
$$j = 1, \dots, C - (b_2 - b_{2r}) \tag{2.8}$$

The combination of (2.5) and (2.8) is achieved through the use of a binary parameter (γ), and gives an approximate but recursive formula for the determination of $q(j)$ in the SRM, considering two service-classes where only calls of service-class 2 can retry [1, 2]:

$$\alpha_1 b_1 q(j - b_1) + \alpha_2 b_2 q(j - b_2) + \alpha_{2r} b_{2r} \gamma_2(j) q(j - b_{2r}) = jq(j) \tag{2.9}$$

where $j = 1, ..., C$, and $\gamma_2(j) = 1$ when $j > C - (b_2 - b_{2r})$ (otherwise $\gamma_2(j) = 0$).

The symbol γ is used to distinguish retry models, where only the migration approximation exists, from other models (e.g., thresholds models presented in Section 2.5) where the symbol δ is used and additional approximations are considered.

The generalization of (2.9) for K service-classes, where all service-classes may retry, is as follows [2]:

$$q(j) = \begin{cases} 1, & \text{if } j = 0 \\ \dfrac{1}{j}\left(\displaystyle\sum_{k=1}^{K} \alpha_k b_k q(j - b_k) + \sum_{k=1}^{K} \alpha_{kr} b_{kr} \gamma_k(j) q(j - b_{kr}) \right), & j = 1, \dots, C \\ 0, & \text{otherwise} \end{cases} \tag{2.10}$$

where $\alpha_{kr} = \lambda_{kr} \mu_{kr}^{-1}$ and $\gamma_k(j) = 1$ when $j > C - (b_k - b_{kr})$ (otherwise $\gamma_k(j) = 0$).
Note that the variable $\gamma_k(j)$ in (2.10) expresses the migration approximation, i.e., (2.7).

2.1.2.2 CBP, Utilization, and Mean Number of In-service Calls

Having determined the unnormalized values of $q(j)$, we can calculate the following performance measures:

- The CBP of service-class k calls with b_{kr} b.u. (i.e., the actual CBP of service-class k with retrial), B_{kr}, via the following formula [2]:

$$B_{kr} = \sum_{j=C-b_{kr}+1}^{C} G^{-1} q(j) \tag{2.11}$$

where $G = \sum_{j=0}^{C} q(j)$ is the normalization constant.

- The CBP of service-class k calls with b_k b.u. (i.e., the actual CBP of service-class k without retrial, or the retry probability in case of service-class k with retrial), B_k, via:

$$B_k = \sum_{j=C-b_k+1}^{C} G^{-1} q(j) \tag{2.12}$$

- The conditional CBP of service-class k retry calls given that they have been blocked with their initial bandwidth requirement b_k, B_{kr}^*, via:

$$B_{kr}^* = Prob\{j > C - b_{kr} | j > C - b_k\} = \frac{B_{kr}}{B_k} \tag{2.13}$$

- The link utilization, U, via (1.54).
- The mean number of service-class k calls with b_k b.u. in state j, $y_k(j)$, via:

$$y_k(j) = \frac{\alpha_k q(j - b_k)}{q(j)}, \quad q(j) > 0 \tag{2.14}$$

- The mean number of service-class k calls with b_{kr} b.u. in state j, $y_{kr}(j)$, via:

$$y_{kr}(j) = \frac{\alpha_{kr} \gamma_k(j) q(j - b_{kr})}{q(j)}, \quad q(j) > 0 \tag{2.15}$$

  where $\gamma_k(j) = 1$ when $j > C - (b_k - b_{kr})$ (otherwise $\gamma_k(j) = 0$).
- The mean number of in-service calls of service-class k accepted in the system with b_k, $\bar{n}_k$, via:

$$\bar{n}_k = \sum_{j=1}^{C} y_k(j) \frac{q(j)}{G} \tag{2.16}$$

- The mean number of in-service calls of service-class k accepted in the system with b_{kr}, $\bar{n}_{kr}$, via:

$$\bar{n}_{kr} = \sum_{j=1}^{C} y_{kr}(j) \frac{q(j)}{G} \tag{2.17}$$

Example 2.2 In the system of Example 2.1 ($C = 5, K = 2, b_1 = 1, b_2 = 3, b_{2r} = 2, \lambda_1 = \lambda_2 = \mu_1^{-1} = \mu_2^{-1} = 1, \mu_{2r}^{-1} = 1.5$):

(a) Calculate the values of $Q(j)$ (link occupancy distribution) based on (2.10).
(b) Calculate the CBP of both service-classes including the retry probability, as well as the conditional B_{2r}^*.

(a) To determine the values of $Q(j)$ based on (2.10) (the unnormalized link occupancy distribution), starting with $q(0) = 1$, we recursively calculate $q(j)$ for $j = 1, \ldots, 5$, while having $\alpha_1 = \alpha_2 = 1.0$ erl, $\alpha_{2r} = \frac{b_2}{b_{2r}} \alpha_2 = 1.5$ erl, and $\gamma_2(j) = 1$ for $j = 5$:

$j = 1$:	$q(1) = \alpha_1 b_1 q(1 - b_1) + 0 = 1.0$	$\Rightarrow q(1) = 1.0$
$j = 2$:	$2q(2) = \alpha_1 b_1 q(2 - b_1) + 0 = 1.0$	$\Rightarrow q(2) = 0.5$

$j = 3:$ $3q(3) = \alpha_1 b_1 q(3 - b_1) + \alpha_2 b_2 q(3 - b_2) = 3.5$ $\Rightarrow q(3) = 1.16667$

$j = 4:$ $4q(4) = \alpha_1 b_1 q(4 - b_1) + \alpha_2 b_2 q(4 - b_2) = 4.16667$ $\Rightarrow q(4) = 1.04167$

$j = 5:$ $5q(5) = \alpha_1 b_1 q(5 - b_1) + \alpha_2 b_2 q(5 - b_2) + \alpha_{2r} b_{2r} q(5 - b_{2r}) = 6.04168$ $\Rightarrow q(5) = 1.20834$

The normalization constant is

$$G = q(0) + q(1) + q(2) + q(3) + q(4) + q(5) = 5.91668.$$

Thus:

$$Q(0) = \frac{q(0)}{G} = 0.16901 \qquad Q(1) = \frac{q(1)}{G} = 0.16901 \qquad Q(2) = \frac{q(2)}{G} = 0.08451$$

$$Q(3) = \frac{q(3)}{G} = 0.19718 \qquad Q(4) = \frac{q(4)}{G} = 0.17606 \qquad Q(5) = \frac{q(5)}{G} = 0.20423$$

(b) $B_1 \equiv$ CBP of service-class 1, $B_2 \equiv Prob\{retry\}$ of service-class 2, and $B_{2r} \equiv$ CBP of service-class 2:

$B_1 = \sum_{j=C-b_1+1}^{C} Q(j)$ $= Q(5) = 0.20423$ (compare with the exact 0.20692)

$B_2 = \sum_{j=C-b_2+1}^{C} Q(j)$ $= Q(3) + Q(4) + Q(5) = 0.57745$ (compare with the exact 0.55226)

$B_{2r} = \sum_{j=C-b_{2r}+1}^{C} Q(j)$ $= Q(4) + Q(5) = 0.38028$ (compare with the exact 0.37764)

$B_{2r}^* = \frac{B_{2r}}{B_2}$ $= 0.65855$ (compare with the exact 0.68380)

It is apparent that even in small SRM examples the error introduced by the assumption of LB and the migration approximation is not significant.

2.2 The Single-Retry Model under the BR Policy

2.2.1 The Service System

In the *SRM under the BR policy (SRM/BR)*, t_k b.u. are reserved to benefit calls of all other service-classes apart from service-class k. The application of the BR policy in the SRM is similar to that of the EMLM/BR, as the following example shows.

Example 2.3   Consider Example 2.1 ($C = 5, K = 2, b_1 = 1, b_2 = 3, b_{2r} = 2, \lambda_1 = \lambda_2 = \mu_1^{-1} = \mu_2^{-1} = 1, \mu_{2r}^{-1} = 1.5$) and apply the BR parameters $t_1 = 2$ b.u. and $t_2 = 0$ b.u. to the first and second service-class, respectively.

(a) Explain the anticipated effect of these BR parameters on the CBP of both service-classes.

(b) Find the total number of permissible states $\mathbf{n} = (n_1, n_2, n_{2r})$ and those adjacent states where the LB is destroyed due to the BR policy (justify your answer). Draw the state transition diagram. (*Hint*: elaborate on Figure 2.3).

(c) Calculate the state probabilities $P(n_1, n_2, n_{2r})$ and the corresponding values of $Q(j)$ (link occupancy distribution) based on the GB equations.

(d) Calculate the CBP of both service-classes.

(a) Since $b_1 = 1$, $b_2 = 3$, and $b_{2r} = 2$, while $t_1 = 2$ and $t_2 = 0$, we have that $b_1 + t_1 = b_2 + t_2 > b_{2r} + t_2$. This means that the CBP of the first service-class becomes equal to the probability of retry of the second service-class. Because of these BR parameters, there are 3 blocking states of the first service-class, that is, more than the blocking states of the second service-class, (retry) calls of which eventually require 2 b.u. In other words, the CBP of the first service-class under this BR policy becomes worse than the CBP of the second service-class.

(b) Elaborating on Figure 2.3, we find that we have to exclude two states, namely states $(4, 0, 0)$ and $(5, 0, 0)$. So, the total number of permissible states, of the form $\mathbf{n} = (n_1, n_2, n_{2r})$, is 14, shown in Figure 2.4 together with the state transition diagram. Due to the BR policy, the LB is destroyed between adjacent states: (0,0,2) – (1,0,2), (0,1,0) – (1,1,0), (1,0,1) – (2,0,1), (1,1,0) – (2,1,0), and (2,0,1) – (3,0,1). We comment on the first pair (similar justifications exist for the other pairs and thus they are omitted).

- States: (0,0,2) – (1,0,2). Assuming that the system state is (0,0,2) when a new call of service-class 1 arrives to the system. In this state, the total occupied bandwidth is $j = 4$ b.u. Thus, the call cannot be accepted in the system because the free b.u. is reserved for calls of service-class 2 (or think that service-class 1 sees the system with capacity, $C - t_1 = 3$ b.u.).

(c) Based on the GB in each state, we write 14 GB equations:

$(0, 0, 0):$ $P(0, 1, 0) + P(1, 0, 0) + 2/3P(0, 0, 1) - 2P(0, 0, 0) = 0$

$(0, 0, 1):$ $P(0, 1, 1) + P(1, 0, 1) + 4/3P(0, 0, 2) - 8/3P(0, 0, 1) = 0$

$(0, 0, 2):$ $P(1, 0, 2) - 4/3P(0, 0, 2) = 0$

$(0, 1, 0):$ $P(0, 0, 0) + 2/3P(0, 1, 1) + P(1, 1, 0) - 2P(0, 1, 0) = 0$

$(0, 1, 1):$ $P(0, 1, 0) + P(0, 0, 1) - 5/3P(0, 1, 1) = 0$

$(1, 0, 0):$ $P(0, 0, 0) + 2/3P(1, 0, 1) + 2P(2, 0, 0) + P(1, 1, 0) - 3P(1, 0, 0) = 0$

$(1, 0, 1):$ $P(0, 0, 1) + 4/3P(1, 0, 2) + 2P(2, 0, 1) - 8/3P(1, 0, 1) = 0$

$(1, 0, 2):$ $P(1, 0, 1) - 7/3P(1, 0, 2) = 0$

$(1, 1, 0):$ $P(1, 0, 0) + 2P(2, 1, 0) - 2P(1, 1, 0) = 0$

$(2, 0, 0):$ $P(1, 0, 0) + 3P(3, 0, 0) + P(2, 1, 0) + 2/3P(2, 0, 1) - 4P(2, 0, 0) = 0$

$(2, 0, 1):$ $3P(3, 0, 1) - 8/3P(2, 0, 1) = 0$

$(2, 1, 0):$ $P(2, 0, 0) - 3P(2, 1, 0) = 0$

$(3, 0, 0):$ $P(2, 0, 0) + 2/3P(3, 0, 1) - 4P(3, 0, 0) = 0$

$(3, 0, 1):$ $P(3, 0, 0) - 11/3P(3, 0, 1) = 0$

By replacing one GB equation, say (1,0,0), with the equation of the normalization condition $\sum_{\mathbf{n} \in \Omega} P(n_1, n_2, n_{2r}) = 1$, the solution of the resultant linear system is:

$P(0, 0, 0) = 0.188861$ $P(0, 0, 1) = 0.085939$ $P(0, 0, 2) = 0.014322$ $P(0, 1, 0) = 0.189922$

$P(0, 1, 1) = 0.165517$ $P(1, 0, 0) = 0.130507$ $P(1, 0, 1) = 0.044557$ $P(1, 0, 2) = 0.019096$

$P(1, 1, 0) = 0.080640$ $P(2, 0, 0) = 0.046158$ $P(2, 0, 1) = 0.003709$ $P(2, 1, 0) = 0.015386$

$P(3, 0, 0) = 0.012089$ $P(3, 0, 1) = 0.003297$

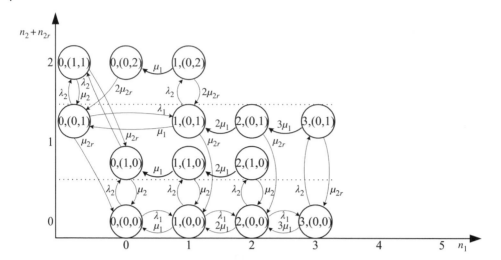

Figure 2.4 The state space Ω (BR policy) and the state transition diagram (Example 2.3).

Based on the values of $P(n_1, n_2, n_{2r})$, we have:

$Q(0) = P(0, 0, 0) = 0.188861$
$Q(1) = P(1, 0, 0) = 0.130507$
$Q(2) = P(0, 0, 1) + P(2, 0, 0) = 0.132097$
$Q(3) = P(0, 1, 0) + P(1, 0, 1) + P(3, 0, 0) = 0.246568$
$Q(4) = P(0, 0, 2) + P(1, 1, 0) + P(2, 0, 1) = 0.098671$
$Q(5) = P(0, 1, 1) + P(1, 0, 2) + P(2, 1, 0) + P(3, 0, 1) = 0.203296$

(d) The CBP of service-class 1 is given by:

$$B_1 = \sum_{j=C-b_1-t_1+1}^{C} Q(j) = Q(3) + Q(4) + Q(5) = 0.548536$$

The *Prob*{retry} of service-class 2 calls is given by:

$$B_2 = \sum_{j=C-b_2+1}^{C} Q(j) = Q(3) + Q(4) + Q(5) = 0.548536$$

Finally, the CBP of service-class 2 (calls with b_{2r}), is given by:

$$B_{2r} = \sum_{j=C-b_{2r}+1}^{C} Q(j) = Q(4) + Q(5) = 0.301968$$

We see that the BR policy has substantially increased B_1 (from 0.206923 in the SRM to 0.548536 in the SRM/BR) and as a result there is a decrease in B_{2r} (from 0.377639 in the SRM to 0.301968 in the SRM/BR).

2.2.2 The Analytical Model

2.2.2.1 Steady State Probabilities

To calculate the link occupancy distribution in the steady state of the SRM/BR, we prefer the Roberts method to the Stasiak–Glabowski method. The latter is more complex compared to the Roberts method and does not provide more accurate results (compared to simulation) in retry loss models and threshold loss models (see Section 2.6, below) [5].

Based on the Roberts method, (2.10) takes the form [4]:

$$q(j) = \begin{cases} 1, & \text{if } j = 0 \\ \frac{1}{j} \left(\sum_{k=1}^{K} \alpha_k D_k(j - b_k) q(j - b_k) + \sum_{k=1}^{K} \alpha_{kr} D_{kr}(j - b_{kr}) \gamma_k(j) q(j - b_{kr}) \right), \\ \quad \text{for } j = 1, \dots, C \\ 0, & \text{otherwise} \end{cases}$$

(2.18)

where $\alpha_{kr} = \lambda_{kr} \mu_{kr}^{-1}$, $\gamma_k(j) = 1$, when $j > C - (b_k - b_{kr})$ (otherwise $\gamma_k(j) = 0$), $D_k(j - b_k)$ is given by (1.65) and, similarly, $D_{kr}(j - b_{kr})$ by:

$$D_{kr}(j - b_{kr}) = \begin{cases} b_{kr} & \text{for } j \le C - t_k \\ 0 & \text{for } j > C - t_k \end{cases}$$

(2.19)

2.2.2.2 CBP, Utilization, and Mean Number of In-service Calls

Based on (2.18) and (2.19), we can calculate the following performance measures:

- The CBP of service-class k calls with b_{kr} b.u., B_{kr}, via the following formula [4]:

$$B_{kr} = \sum_{j=C-b_{kr}-t_k+1}^{C} G^{-1} q(j)$$

(2.20)

where $G = \sum_{j=0}^{C} q(j)$ is the normalization constant.
- The CBP of service-class k calls with b_k b.u., B_k (i.e., the actual CBP of service-class k without retrials, or retry probability in case of service-class k with retrials), can be determined via (1.66), while the conditional CBP of service-class k retry calls given that they have been blocked with their initial bandwidth requirement b_k, B_{kr}, via (2.13), while subtracting t_k from $C - b_{kr}$ and from $C - b_k$.
- The link utilization, U, is given by (1.54).
- The mean number of service-class k calls with b_k b.u. in state j, $y_k(j)$, is given by (1.67), while the mean number of service-class k calls with b_{kr} b.u. in state j, $y_{kr}(j)$, is given by:

$$y_{kr}(j) = \begin{cases} \dfrac{\alpha_{kr} \gamma_k(j) q(j - b_{kr})}{q(j)}, & \text{for } j \le C - t_k \\ 0, & \text{for } j > C - t_k \end{cases}$$

(2.21)

where $\gamma_k(j) = 1$ when $j > C - (b_k - b_{kr})$ (otherwise $\gamma_k(j) = 0$).
- The mean number of in-service calls of service-class k accepted in the system with b_k, $\bar{n}_k$, is calculated by (2.16), while the mean number of in-service calls of service-class k accepted in the system with b_{kr}, $\bar{n}_{kr}$, by (2.17).

Example 2.4   In the system of Example 2.3 ($C = 5, K = 2, b_1 = 1, b_2 = 3, b_{2r} = 2, t_1 = 2, t_2 = 0, \lambda_1 = \lambda_2 = \mu_1^{-1} = \mu_2^{-1} = 1, \mu_{2r}^{-1} = 1.5$):

(a) Calculate the values of $Q(j)$ (link occupancy distribution) based on (2.18).
(b) Calculate the CBP of both service-classes, including the retry probability. Compare with the exact results of Example 2.3.

(a) To determine the state probability $Q(j)$ based on (2.18), we recursively calculate $q(j)$ for $j = 1, \ldots, 5$, starting with $q(0) = 1$, while $\alpha_1 = \alpha_2 = 1.0$ erl, $\alpha_{2r} = \frac{b_2}{b_{2r}}\alpha_2 = 1.5$ erl, and $\gamma_2(j) = 1$ for $j = 5$:

$j = 1$: $q(1) = \alpha_1 b_1 q(1 - b_1) + 0 = 1.0$ $\Rightarrow q(1) = 1.0$
$j = 2$: $2q(2) = \alpha_1 b_1 q(2 - b_1) + 0 = 1.0$ $\Rightarrow q(2) = 0.5$
$j = 3$: $3q(3) = \alpha_1 b_1 q(3 - b_1) + \alpha_2 b_2 q(3 - b_2) = 3.5$ $\Rightarrow q(3) = 1.16667$
$j = 4$: $4q(4) = 0 + \alpha_2 b_2 q(4 - b_2) = 3.0$ $\Rightarrow q(4) = 0.75$
$j = 5$: $5q(5) = 0 + \alpha_2 b_2 q(5 - b_2) + \alpha_{2r} b_{2r} q(5 - b_{2r}) = 5.0$ $\Rightarrow q(5) = 1.0$

The normalization constant is $G = 5.41666$. Thus:

$$Q(0) = \frac{q(0)}{G} = 0.18462 \qquad Q(1) = \frac{q(1)}{G} = 0.18462 \qquad Q(2) = \frac{q(2)}{G} = 0.09231$$

$$Q(3) = \frac{q(3)}{G} = 0.21538 \qquad Q(4) = \frac{q(4)}{G} = 0.13846 \qquad Q(5) = \frac{q(5)}{G} = 0.18462$$

As the following results reveal, the error introduced by the assumption of LB, the migration approximation, and the Roberts method is not significant, even in small SRM/BR examples.

$$B_1 = \sum_{j=C-b_1-t_1+1}^{C} Q(j) = Q(3) + Q(4) + Q(5) = 0.53846 \quad \text{(compare with the exact 0.548536)}$$

$$B_2 = \sum_{j=C-b_2-t_2+1}^{C} Q(j) = 0.53846 = B_1 \qquad \text{(due to the values of the BR parameters)}$$

$$B_{2r} = \sum_{j=C-b_{2r}+1}^{C} Q(j) = Q(4) + Q(5) = 0.32308 \qquad \text{(compare with the exact 0.301968)}$$

Example 2.5   Consider a single link of capacity $C = 500$ b.u. that accommodates calls of four different service-classes with the following traffic characteristics:

$(\lambda_1, \mu_1^{-1}, b_1) = (8, 12, 1)$, $(\lambda_2, \mu_2^{-1}, b_2) = (4, 10, 7)$, $(\lambda_3, \mu_3^{-1}, b_3) = (2, 8, 14)$,
$(\lambda_4, \mu_4^{-1}, b_4) = (1, 6, 28)$, $(\mu_{4r}^{-1}, b_{4r}) = (12, 14)$, and $b_4 \mu_4^{-1} = b_{4r}\mu_{4r}^{-1}$.

That is, only calls of service-class 4 have the ability to retry.

(a) Present graphically the CBP of all service-classes, including the retry probability and the conditional B_{4r}^*, as well as the link utilization, when assuming the SRM under the CS policy (no BR parameters). Compare the results with those obtained by the EMLM, assuming an increase of C from 500 to 1000 b.u. in steps of 100 b.u. Provide simulation results for evaluation.

(b) Present graphically the equalized CBP of all service-classes in the SRM/BR (i.e., under the BR policy) for the following set of BR parameters: Set 1 $t_1 = 13, t_2 = 7, t_3 = t_4 = 0$ b.u., which causes CBP equalization (the same increase of C, from 500 to 1000 b.u. in steps of 100 b.u., is assumed). For comparison, include the CBP obtained by the EMLM/BR while considering not only Set 1, but also the following set of BR parameters: Set 2 $t_1 = 27, t_2 = 21, t_3 = 14, t_4 = 0$.

(c) Comment on the results.

(a) Figure 2.5 presents the corresponding CBP of all service-classes, including the retry probability and the conditional B_{4r}^*. Observe that $B_{4r} = B_3$, since $b_{4r} = b_3 = 14$ b.u. Because of this, we only present the values of B_3. In Table 2.1, we present the corresponding analytical and simulation CBP results for $C = 500$ b.u. and $C = 1000$ b.u. Simulation CBP results for the SRM are quite close to the analytical results, and therefore are not shown in Figure 2.5. Simulation results are based on SIMSCRIPT III [6], and are mean values of 12 runs with 95% confidence interval.

In Figure 2.6, we present the link utilization results for the EMLM and SRM; both models give almost the same results, a fact that is explained by the fact that the CBP decrease in service-class 4 is accompanied by the CBP increase of the other service-classes.

(b) Figure 2.7 presents the corresponding equalized CBP of all service-classes for the SRM/BR and the EMLM/BR (set 1 and set 2). Simulation CBP results for the SRM/BR are quite close to the analytical results and, therefore, are omitted. As an example, we provide in Table 2.2 the corresponding analytical and simulation equalized CBP results for $C = 500$ b.u. and $C = 1000$ b.u.

(c) Apart from the fact that all CBP decrease when C increases, we also see the following:

(1) According to Figure 2.5:

(i) The CBP of retry calls (i.e., $B_{4r} = B_3$) are much lower compared to the CBP obtained by the EMLM (i.e., B_4).

(ii) The fact that calls of service-class 4 retry, increases the CBP of service-classes 1, 2 and 3 in the SRM compared to the EMLM.

(iii) The EMLM results fail to approximate the corresponding CBP results of the SRM.

(2) Set 1 causes CBP equalization in the EMLM/BR among calls of the first three service-classes, while Set 2 causes CBP equalization in the EMLM/BR of all service-classes. According to Figure 2.7, the CBP obtained by the SRM/BR can be approximated by the EMLM/BR (Set 2), especially for high values of C, while the CBP results of the EMLM/BR (Set 1) fail to approximate the corresponding results of the SRM/BR.

2.3 The Multi-Retry Model

2.3.1 The Service System

In the multi-retry model (MRM), calls of service-class k can retry not only once, but several times, in order to be accepted in the system [1, 2]. Let $S(k)$ be the number of retrials

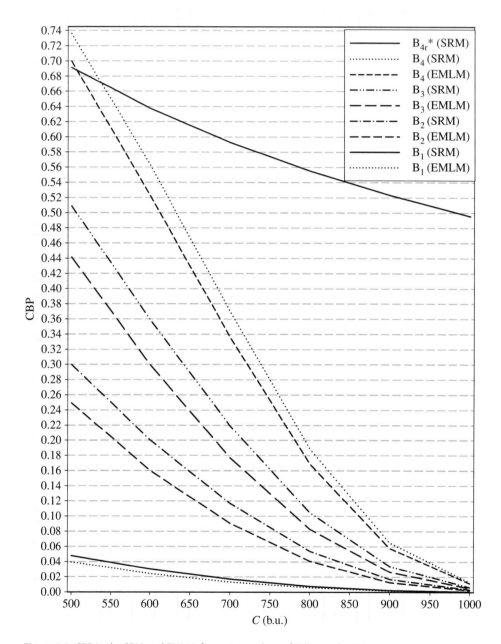

Figure 2.5 CBP in the SRM and EMLM, for various values of C (Example 2.5).

Table 2.1 CBP of Example 2.5 (SRM, $C = 500$ b.u. and $C = 1000$ b.u.).

	C = 500 b.u.		C = 1000 b.u.	
CBP	Analytical results	Simulation results	Analytical results	Simulation results
B_1	0.0479	0.0493 ± 1.2745e-4	0.0004	0.0004 ± 9.0281e-6
B_2	0.2997	0.2986 ± 5.1219e-4	0.0031	0.0029 ± 5.6690e-5
B_3	0.5089	0.5077 ± 4.7558e-4	0.0063	0.0060 ± 6.8768e-5
B_4	0.7360	0.7430 ± 4.8105e-4	0.0128	0.0125 ± 1.0325e-4
B_{4r}	0.5089	0.5081 ± 6.3207e-4	0.0063	0.0060 ± 8.0577e-5
B_{4r}^*	0.6914	0.6844 ± 1.4349e-3	0.4955	0.4871 ± 4.6728e-3

Table 2.2 CBP of Example 2.5 (SRM/BR, $C = 500$ b.u. and $C = 1000$ b.u.).

	C = 500 b.u.		C = 1000 b.u.	
CBP	Analytical results	Simulation results	Analytical results	Simulation results
B_1	0.3804	0.3825 ± 3.3290e-4	0.00485	0.00485 ± 1.1740e-4
B_2	0.3804	0.3826 ± 4.2058e-4	0.00485	0.00486 ± 1.6266e-4
B_3	0.3804	0.3824 ± 4.2857e-4	0.00485	0.00485 ± 1.3816e-4
B_4	0.3804	0.3825 ± 6.0689e-4	0.00485	0.00487 ± 1.0434e-4

for calls of service-class k, and assume that $b_k > b_{kr_1} > \ldots > b_{kr_s} > \ldots > b_{kr_{S(k)}}$, where b_{kr_s} is the required bandwidth of a service-class k call in the sth retry, $s = 1, \ldots, S(k)$. Then a service-class k call is accepted in the system with b_{kr_s} b.u. if $C - b_{kr_{s-1}} < j \leq C - b_{kr_s}$. By definition, $b_{kr_0} = b_k$ and $\alpha_{kr_0} = \alpha_k$.

Example 2.6 Consider a link of $C = 3$ b.u. The link accommodates Poisson arriving calls of two service-classes. Calls of service-class 1 require $b_1 = 1$ b.u., while calls of service-class 2 require $b_2 = 3$. Blocked calls of service-class 2, in order to be accepted in the system, can immediately retry two times with $b_{2r_1} = 2$ b.u. and $b_{2r_2} = 1$ b.u. Let $\lambda_1 = \lambda_2 = 1$ calls/sec, $\mu_1^{-1} = \mu_2^{-1} = 1$ sec, $\mu_{2r_1}^{-1} = 2.0$ sec, and $\mu_{2r_2}^{-1} = 4.0$ sec (in this example we do not assume that $b_2 \mu_2^{-1} = b_{2r_1} \mu_{2r_1}^{-1} = b_{2r_2} \mu_{2r_2}^{-1}$).

(a) Find the total number of permissible states $\mathbf{n} = (n_1, n_2, n_{2r_1}, n_{2r_2})$ (state space Ω) and draw the state transition diagram.
(b) Calculate the state probabilities $P(n_1, n_2, n_{2r_1}, n_{2r_2})$ and the corresponding values of $Q(j)$ (link occupancy distribution) based on the GB equations.
(c) Calculate the CBP of both service-classes, including the retry probabilities and the link utilization.
(d) Calculate the conditional CBP of service-class 2 retry calls with b_{2r_2} given that they have been blocked with their initial bandwidth requirement, b_2.

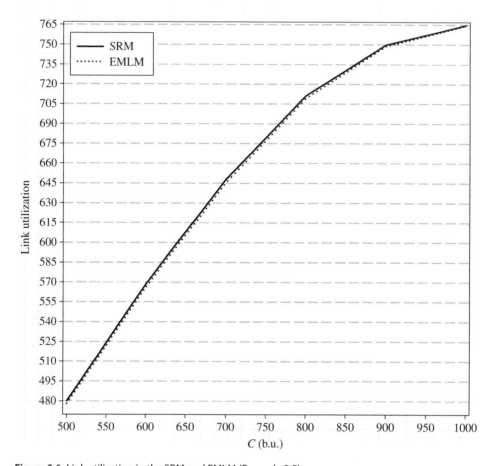

Figure 2.6 Link utilization in the SRM and EMLM (Example 2.5).

(a) The total number of permissible states, of the form $\mathbf{n} = (n_1, n_2, n_{2r_1}, n_{2r_2})$, is 14. They are shown in Figure 2.8 together with the state transition diagram.

(b) Based on Figure 2.8, the corresponding 14 GB equations are:

$(0,0,0,0)$: $0.5P(0,0,1,0) + 0.25P(0,0,0,1) + P(0,1,0,0) + P(1,0,0,0) - 2P(0,0,0,0) = 0$

$(0,0,0,1)$: $0.5P(0,0,0,2) + 0.5P(0,0,1,1) + P(1,0,0,1) - 2.25P(0,0,0,1) = 0$

$(0,0,0,2)$: $P(1,0,0,2) + 0.75P(0,0,0,3) - 2.5P(0,0,0,2) = 0$

$(0,0,0,3)$: $P(0,0,0,2) - 0.75P(0,0,0,3) = 0$

$(0,0,1,0)$: $0.25P(0,0,1,1) + P(1,0,1,0) - 2.5P(0,0,1,0) = 0$

$(0,0,1,1)$: $P(0,0,0,1) + P(0,0,1,0) - 0.75P(0,0,1,1) = 0$

$(0,1,0,0)$: $P(0,0,0,0) - P(0,1,0,0) = 0$

$(1,0,0,0)$: $0.25P(1,0,0,1) + 2P(2,0,0,0) + 0.5P(1,0,1,0) + P(0,0,0,0) - 3P(1,0,0,0) = 0$

$(1,0,0,1)$: $2P(2,0,0,1) + 0.5P(1,0,0,2) + P(0,0,0,1) - 3.25P(1,0,0,1) = 0$

$(1,0,0,2)$: $P(0,0,0,2) + P(1,0,0,1) - 1.5P(1,0,0,2) = 0$

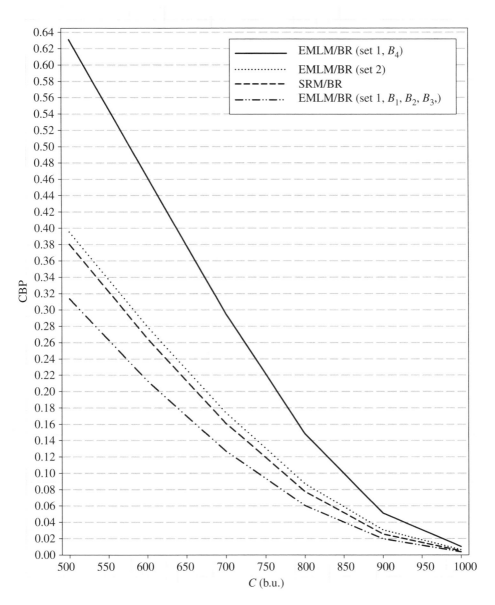

Figure 2.7 CBP in the SRM/BR and the EMLM/BR for various values of C (Example 2.5).

$(1,0,1,0):$ $P(0,0,1,0) + P(1,0,0,0) - 1.5P(1,0,1,0) = 0$

$(2,0,0,0):$ $P(1,0,0,0) + 3P(3,0,0,0) + 0.25P(2,0,0,1) - 4P(2,0,0,0) = 0$

$(2,0,0,1):$ $P(1,0,0,1) + P(2,0,0,0) - 2.25P(2,0,0,1) = 0$

$(3,0,0,0):$ $P(2,0,0,0) - 3P(3,0,0,0) = 0$

By replacing the GB equation of $(1,0,0,0)$ with the normalization condition $\sum_{\mathbf{n}\in\Omega} P(n_1, n_2, n_{2r_1}, n_{2r_2}) = 1$, the solution of this linear system is:

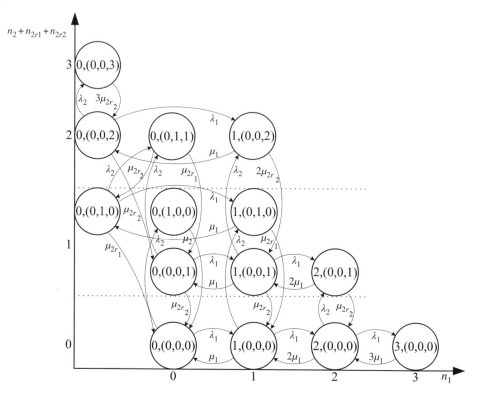

Figure 2.8 The state space Ω (CS policy) and the state transition diagram (Example 2.6).

$P(0,0,0,0) = 0.123557$	$P(0,0,0,1) = 0.070215$	$P(0,0,0,2) = 0.04398$
$P(0,0,0,3) = 0.05864$	$P(0,0,1,0) = 0.051313$	$P(0,0,1,1) = 0.162037$
$P(0,1,0,0) = 0.123557$	$P(1,0,0,0) = 0.080347$	$P(1,0,0,1) = 0.054975$
$P(1,0,0,2) = 0.065969$	$P(1,0,1,0) = 0.087774$	$P(2,0,0,0) = 0.029927$
$P(2,0,0,1) = 0.037734$	$P(3,0,0,0) = 0.009976$	

Based on the values of $P(n_1, n_2, n_{2r_1}, n_{2r_2})$, we have:

$$
\begin{aligned}
Q(0) = & \ P(0,0,0,0) && = 0.123557 \\
Q(1) = & \ P(0,0,0,1) + P(1,0,0,0) && = 0.150562 \\
Q(2) = & \ P(0,0,0,2) + P(0,0,1,0) + P(1,0,0,1) + P(2,0,0,0) && = 0.180195 \\
Q(3) = & \ P(0,0,0,3) + P(0,0,1,1) + P(0,1,0,0) + P(1,0,0,2)+ \\
& \ P(1,0,1,0) + P(2,0,0,1) + P(3,0,0,0) && = 0.545687
\end{aligned}
$$

(c) The CBP of service-class 1 is given by: $B_1 = \displaystyle\sum_{j=C-b_1+1}^{C} Q(j) = Q(3) = 0.545687$

The $Prob\{1\text{st retry}\}$ of service-class 2 is given by:

$$
B_2 = \sum_{j=C-b_2+1}^{C} Q(j) = 1 - Q(0) = 0.876443
$$

The *Prob*{2nd retry} of service-class 2, is given by:

$$B_{2r_1} = \sum_{j=C-b_{2r_1}+1}^{C} Q(j) = Q(2) + Q(3) = 0.725882$$

The CBP of service-class 2 is given by: $B_{2r_2} = \sum_{j=C-b_{2r_2}+1}^{C} Q(j) = Q(3) = 0.545687$

The link utilization is determined by: $U = \sum_{j=1}^{C} jQ(j) = 2.148$ b.u.

Compare these results with the corresponding CBP and link utilization results in the case of the EMLM: $B_1 = 0.31818,\ B_2 = 0.72727,\ U = 1.50$ b.u.

(d) The conditional CBP of service-class 2 retry calls with b_{2r_2} is given by:

$$B^*_{2r_2} = Prob\{j > C - b_{2r_2} | j > C - b_2\} = \frac{B_{2r_2}}{B_2} = 0.62262$$

2.3.2 The Analytical Model

2.3.2.1 Steady State Probabilities

Following the analysis of Section 2.1.2.1, we have to assume in the MRM the existence of both LB and the migration approximation. According to the migration approximation, the mean number of service-class k calls in state j, $y_{kr_s}(j)$, accepted with b_{kr_s} b.u., is negligible when $j \leq C - (b_{kr_{s-1}} - b_{kr_s})$, where $s = 1, \ldots, S(k)$. This means that service-class k calls with b_{kr_s} are limited in the area $j > C - (b_{kr_{s-1}} - b_{kr_s})$. Based on [1, 2], the unnormalized values of $q(j)$ can be determined by the following recursive formula:

$$q(j) = \begin{cases} 1, & \text{if } j = 0 \\ \dfrac{1}{j}\left(\displaystyle\sum_{k=1}^{K} \alpha_k b_k q(j-b_k) + \sum_{k=1}^{K}\sum_{s=1}^{S(k)} \alpha_{kr_s} b_{kr_s} \gamma_{k_s}(j)q(j-b_{kr_s})\right) \\ \qquad j = 1, \ldots, C \\ 0, & \text{otherwise} \end{cases} \tag{2.22}$$

where $\alpha_{kr_s} = \lambda_k \mu_{kr_s}^{-1}$, $\gamma_{k_s}(j) = 1$ when $j > C - (b_{kr_{s-1}} - b_{kr_s})$ (otherwise $\gamma_{k_s}(j) = 0$).

2.3.2.2 CBP, Utilization, and Mean Number of In-service Calls

Having determined the unnormalized values of $q(j)$, we can determine the following performance measures:

- The CBP of service-class k calls (with their last bandwidth requirement $b_{kr_{S(k)}}$), $B_{kr_{S(k)}}$, are determined as follows (if $G = \sum_{j=0}^{C} q(j)$ is the normalization constant) [2]:

$$B_{kr_{S(k)}} = \sum_{j=C-b_{kr_{S(k)}}+1}^{C} G^{-1}q(j) \tag{2.23}$$

- The *Prob*{1st retry} of service-class k calls of b_k b.u., B_k, is determined via (2.12), while the conditional probability of service-class k retry calls, requesting $b_{kr_{S(k)}}$ b.u.

given that they have been blocked with their initial bandwidth requirement b_k, $B^*_{kr_{S(k)}}$, is defined as:

$$B^*_{kr_{S(k)}} = Prob\{j > C - b_{kr_{S(k)}} \mid j > C - b_k\} = \frac{B_{kr_{S(k)}}}{B_k} \tag{2.24}$$

- The link utilization, U, is given by (1.54).
- The mean number of service-class k calls with b_k b.u. in state j, $y_k(j)$, is given by (2.14), while the mean number of service-class k calls with b_{kr_s} b.u. in state j, $y_{kr_s}(j)$, is given by:

$$y_{kr_s}(j) = \frac{a_{kr_s}\gamma_{k_s}(j)q(j - b_{kr_s})}{q(j)}, \quad q(j) > 0 \tag{2.25}$$

where $\gamma_{k_s}(j) = 1$ when $j > C - (b_{kr_{s-1}} - b_{kr_s})$ (otherwise $\gamma_{k_s}(j) = 0$).
- The mean number of in-service calls of service-class k accepted in the system with b_k, $\overline{n}_k$, is calculated by (2.16), while the mean number of in-service calls of service-class k accepted in the system with b_{kr_s}, $\overline{n}_{kr_s}$ is determined by:

$$\overline{n}_{kr_s} = \sum_{j=1}^{C} y_{kr_s}(j)\frac{q(j)}{G} \tag{2.26}$$

Example 2.7 In the system of Example 2.6 ($C = 3, K = 2, b_1 = 1, b_2 = 3, b_{2r_1} = 2, b_{2r_2} = 1, \lambda_1 = \lambda_2 = 1, \mu_1^{-1} = \mu_2^{-1} = 1, \mu_{2r_1}^{-1} = 2.0, \mu_{2r_2}^{-1} = 4.0$):

(a) Calculate the values of $Q(j)$ (link occupancy distribution) based on (2.22).
(b) Calculate the CBP of both service-classes, including the retry probabilities, as well as the conditional $B^*_{2r_2}$.
(c) Repeat the previous calculations assuming that $C = 4$ (instead of 3) b.u.

(a) To determine the state probability $Q(j)$ based on (2.22), we recursively calculate $q(j)$ for $j = 1, 2, 3$, starting with $q(0) = 1$, while $\alpha_1 = \alpha_2 = 1.0$ erl, $\alpha_{2r_1} = 2.0$ erl, $\alpha_{2r_2} = 4.0$, and $\gamma_{2_1}(j) = \gamma_{2_2}(j) = 1$ both for $j = 3$:

$$j = 1: \quad q(1) = \alpha_1 b_1 q(1 - b_1) + 0 + 0 + 0 = 1.0 \qquad \Rightarrow q(1) = 1.0$$
$$j = 2: \quad 2q(2) = \alpha_1 b_1 q(2 - b_1) + 0 + 0 + 0 = 1.0 \qquad \Rightarrow q(2) = 0.5$$
$$j = 3: \quad 3q(3) = \alpha_1 b_1 q(3 - b_1) + \alpha_2 b_2 q(3 - b_2) +$$
$$\alpha_{2r_1} b_{2r_1} q(3 - b_{2r_1}) + \alpha_{2r_2} b_{2r_2} q(3 - b_{2r_2}) = 9.5 \quad \Rightarrow q(3) = 3.16667$$

The normalization constant is $G = 5.66667$. Thus:

$$Q(0) = \frac{q(0)}{G} = 0.17647 \qquad\qquad Q(1) = \frac{q(1)}{G} = 0.17647$$

$$Q(2) = \frac{q(2)}{G} = 0.088235 \qquad\qquad Q(3) = \frac{q(3)}{G} = 0.55882$$

(b) $B_1 \equiv$ CBP of service-class 1, and $B_2 \equiv Prob\{1st\ retry\}$, $B_{2r_1} \equiv Prob\{2nd\ retry\}$, and $B_{2r_2} \equiv$ CBP of service-class 2.

$$B_1 = \sum_{j=C-b_1+1}^{C} Q(j) = Q(3) = 0.55882 \qquad \text{(compare with the exact 0.545687)}$$

$$B_2 = \sum_{j=C-b_2+1}^{C} Q(j) = 1 - Q(0) = 0.82353 \qquad \text{(compare with the exact 0.876443)}$$

$$B_{2r_1} = \sum_{j=C-b_{2r_1}+1}^{C} Q(j) = Q(2) + Q(3) = 0.647055 \qquad \text{(compare with the exact 0.725882)}$$

$$B_{2r_2} = \sum_{j=C-b_{2r_2}+1}^{C} Q(j) = Q(3) = 0.55882 \qquad \text{(compare with the exact 0.545687)}$$

$$B_{2r_2}^* = \frac{B_{2r_2}}{B_2} = 0.67857 \qquad \text{(compare with the exact 0.62262)}$$

In this very small example, the recursive formula (2.22) does not provide very good results compared to the exact results of Example 2.6. For an explanation, consider the effect of the migration approximation to the calculation of $q(j)$. The migration approximation assumes that service-class 2 calls with b_{2r_1} and b_{2r_2} exist only when $j = 3$. However, we have already seen in Example 2.6 that $n_{2r_1} > 0$, when $j = 2, 3$ (states $(n_1, n_2, n_{2r_1}, n_{2r_2})$: $(0,0,1,0)$, $(0,0,1,1)$ and $(1,0,1,0)$), while $n_{2r_2} > 0$, when $j = 1, 2, 3$ (states $(n_1, n_2, n_{2r_1}, n_{2r_2})$: $(0,0,0,1)$, $(0,0,0,2)$, $(0,0,0,3)$, $(0,0,1,1)$, $(1,0,0,1)$, $(1,0,0,2)$, $(2,0,0,1)$).

(c) Since $C = 4$ b.u., we have that $\gamma_{k_1}(j) = 1$ and $\gamma_{k_2}(j) = 1$ for $j = 4$:

$$j = 1 : q(1) = \alpha_1 b_1 q(1 - b_1) + 0 + 0 + 0 = 1.0 \Rightarrow q(1) = 1.0$$
$$j = 2 : 2q(2) = \alpha_1 b_1 q(2 - b_1) + 0 + 0 + 0 = 1.0 \Rightarrow q(2) = 0.5$$
$$j = 3 : 3q(3) = \alpha_1 b_1 q(3 - b_1) + \alpha_2 b_2 q(3 - b_2) + 0 + 0 = 3.5 \Rightarrow q(3) = 1.16667$$
$$j = 4 : 4q(4) = \alpha_1 b_1 q(4 - b_1) + \alpha_2 b_2 q(4 - b_2) +$$
$$\alpha_{2r_1} b_{2r_1} q(4 - b_{2r_1}) + \alpha_{2r_2} b_{2r_2} q(4 - b_{2r_2}) = 10.83333 \Rightarrow q(4) = 2.70833$$

The normalization constant is $G = 6.375$. Thus:

$$Q(0) = \frac{q(0)}{G} = 0.156863 \qquad Q(1) = \frac{q(1)}{G} = 0.156863 \qquad Q(2) = \frac{q(2)}{G} = 0.078431$$

$$Q(3) = \frac{q(3)}{G} = 0.183006 \qquad Q(4) = \frac{q(4)}{G} = 0.424836$$

$$B_1 = \sum_{j=C-b_1+1}^{C} Q(j) = Q(4) = 0.424836 \qquad \text{(compare with the exact 0.416381)}$$

$$B_2 = \sum_{j=C-b_2+1}^{C} Q(j) = Q(2) + Q(3) + Q(4) = 0.686267 \qquad \text{(compare with the exact 0.72426)}$$

$$B_{2r_1} = \sum_{j=C-b_{2r_1}+1}^{C} Q(j) = Q(3) + Q(4) = 0.607836 \qquad \text{(compare with the exact 0.59663)}$$

$$B_{2r_2} = \sum_{j=C-b_{2r_2}+1}^{C} Q(j) = Q(4) = 0.424836 \qquad \text{(compare with the exact 0.416381)}$$

$$B_{2r_2}^* = \frac{B_{2r_2}}{B_2} = 0.61905 \qquad \text{(compare with the exact 0.57491)}$$

It is worth mentioning that the exact values require the knowledge of 25 steady state probabilities of the form $P(n_1, n_2, n_{2r_1}, n_{2r_2})$. Of course, the increase of C results in a larger system (25 states vs 14 states when $C = 3$) in which the migration approximation introduces less error in the calculation of $q(j)$.

2.4 The Multi-Retry Model under the BR Policy

2.4.1 The Service System

Obviously, in the *MRM under the BR policy (MRM/BR)*, unlike the SRM/BR, blocked calls of service-class k can retry more than once to be connected in the system.

Example 2.8 Consider the system of Example 2.6 ($C = 3, K = 2, b_1 = 1, b_2 = 3, b_{2r_1} = 2, b_{2r_2} = 1, \lambda_1 = \lambda_2 = 1, \mu_1^{-1} = \mu_2^{-1} = 1, \mu_{2r_1}^{-1} = 2.0, \mu_{2r_2}^{-1} = 4.0$) under the BR policy with BR parameters $t_1 = 2$ b.u. and $t_2 = 0$ b.u. for the two service-classes, respectively, so that $b_1 + t_1 = b_2 + t_2$. In that case, CBP of service-class 1 calls is equalized with the *Prob*{1st retry} of calls of service-class 2:

(a) Find the total number of permissible states $\mathbf{n} = (n_1, n_2, n_{2r_1}, n_{2r_2})$ (state space Ω) and draw the state transition diagram. (*Hint*: elaborate on Figure 2.8).
(b) Calculate the state probabilities $P(n_1, n_2, n_{2r_1}, n_{2r_2})$ and the corresponding values of $Q(j)$ (link occupancy distribution) based on the GB equations.
(c) Calculate the CBP of both service-classes, including the probabilities of retry, and the link utilization.

(a) The total number of permissible states, of the form $\mathbf{n} = (n_1, n_2, n_{2r_1}, n_{2r_2})$, is 7. They are shown in Figure 2.9 together with the state transition diagram.
(b) Based on Figure 2.9, the corresponding 7 GB equations are:

$(0, 0, 0, 0) :$ $0.5P(0, 0, 1, 0) + 0.25P(0, 0, 0, 1) + P(0, 1, 0, 0) + P(1, 0, 0, 0) - 2P(0, 0, 0, 0) = 0$

$(0, 0, 0, 1) :$ $0.5P(0, 0, 1, 1) - 1.25P(0, 0, 0, 1) = 0$

$(0, 0, 1, 0) :$ $0.25P(0, 0, 1, 1) + P(1, 0, 1, 0) - 1.5P(0, 0, 1, 0) = 0$

$(0, 0, 1, 1) :$ $P(0, 0, 0, 1) + P(0, 0, 1, 0) - 0.75P(0, 0, 1, 1) = 0$

$(0, 1, 0, 0) :$ $P(0, 0, 0, 0) - P(0, 1, 0, 0) = 0$

$(1, 0, 0, 0) :$ $0.5P(1, 0, 1, 0) + P(0, 0, 0, 0) - 2P(1, 0, 0, 0) = 0$

$(1, 0, 1, 0) :$ $P(1, 0, 0, 0) - 1.5P(1, 0, 1, 0) = 0$

By replacing the GB equation of $(1, 0, 0, 0)$ with $\sum_{\mathbf{n} \in \Omega} P(n_1, n_2, n_{2r_1}, n_{2r_2}) = 1$, the solution of this linear system is:

$P(0, 0, 0, 0) = 0.180328$

$P(0, 0, 0, 1) = 0.104918$ $P(0, 0, 1, 0) = 0.091803$ $P(0, 0, 1, 1) = 0.262295$

$P(0, 1, 0, 0) = 0.180328$ $P(1, 0, 0, 0) = 0.108197$ $P(1, 0, 1, 0) = 0.072131$

Based on the values of $P(n_1, n_2, n_{2r_1}, n_{2r_2})$, we have:

$Q(0) = P(0, 0, 0, 0) = 0.180328$ $Q(1) = P(0, 0, 0, 1) + P(1, 0, 0, 0) = 0.213115$

$Q(2) = P(0, 0, 1, 0) = 0.091803$ $Q(3) = P(0, 0, 1, 1) + P(0, 1, 0, 0) + P(1, 0, 1, 0) = 0.514754$

(c) The CBP of service-class 1 is given by:

$$B_1 = \sum_{j=C-b_1-t_1+1}^{C} Q(j) = 1 - Q(0) = 0.819672 \qquad \text{(compare with 0.545687 in the MRM)}$$

The $Prob\{1\text{st retry}\} = B_2$ of service-class 2 is given by:

$$B_2 = \sum_{j=C-b_2+1}^{C} Q(j) = 1 - Q(0) = B_1 = 0.819672 \qquad \text{(compare with 0.876443 in the MRM)}$$

The $Prob\{2\text{nd retry}\} = B_{2r_1}$ of service-class 2 is given by:

$$B_{2r_1} = \sum_{j=C-b_{2r_1}+1}^{C} Q(j) = Q(2) + Q(3) = 0.606557 \qquad \text{(compare with 0.725882 in the MRM)}$$

The CBP of service-class 2 is given by:

$$B_{2r_2} = \sum_{j=C-b_{2r_2}+1}^{C} Q(j) = Q(3) = 0.514754 \qquad \text{(compare with 0.545687 in the MRM)}$$

The link utilization is determined by:

$$U = \sum_{j=1}^{C} jQ(j) = 1.941 \text{ b.u.} \qquad \text{(compare with 2.148 b.u. in the MRM)}$$

2.4.2 The Analytical Model

2.4.2.1 Steady State Probabilities

Based on the Roberts method, we calculate the unnormalized link occupancy distribution in the steady state of the MRM/BR by modifying (2.22) as follows [4]:

$$q(j) = \begin{cases} 1 & \text{if } j = 0 \\ \dfrac{1}{j}\left(\displaystyle\sum_{k=1}^{K} \alpha_k D_k(j - b_k)q(j - b_k) + \sum_{k=1}^{K}\sum_{s=1}^{S(k)} \alpha_{kr_s} D_{kr_s}(j - b_{kr_s})\gamma_{k_s}(j)q(j - b_{kr_s}) \right) & \\ & j = 1, \ldots, C \\ 0 & \text{otherwise} \end{cases}$$

(2.27)

where $\alpha_{kr_s} = \lambda_k \mu_{kr_s}^{-1}$, $\gamma_{k_s}(j) = 1$ when $j > C - (b_{kr_{s-1}} - b_{kr_s})$ (otherwise $\gamma_{k_s}(j) = 0$), and $D_k(j - b_k)$ is given by (1.65) and, similarly, $D_{kr_s}(j - b_{kr_s})$ by:

$$D_{kr_s}(j - b_{kr_s}) = \begin{cases} b_{kr_s} & \text{for } j \leq C - t_k \\ 0 & \text{for } j > C - t_k \end{cases}$$

(2.28)

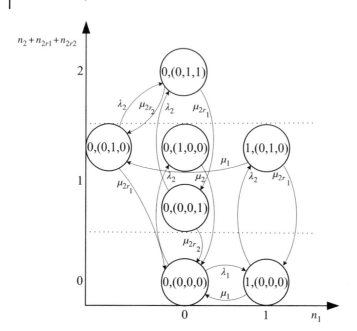

Figure 2.9 The state space Ω (BR policy) and the state transition diagram (Example 2.8).

2.4.2.2 CBP, Utilization, and Mean Number of In-service Calls

Based on (2.27) and (2.28), we can determine the following performance measures:

- The CBP of service-class k calls with $b_{kr_{S(k)}}$ b.u., $B_{kr_{S(k)}}$, by the following formula [4]:

$$B_{kr_{S(k)}} = \sum_{j=C-b_{kr_{S(k)}}-t_k+1}^{C} G^{-1} q(j) \tag{2.29}$$

where $G = \sum_{j=0}^{C} q(j)$ is the normalization constant.

- The CBP of service-class k calls with b_k b.u., B_k, via (1.66).
- The conditional CBP of service-class k retry calls, with $b_{kr_{S(k)}}$, given that they have been blocked with their initial bandwidth requirement b_k, $B^*_{kr_{S(k)}}$, via (2.24), while subtracting t_k from $C - b_{kr_{S(k)}}$ and from $C - b_k$.
- The link utilization, U, via (1.54).
- The mean number of service-class k calls with b_k b.u. in state j, $y_k(j)$, via (1.67).
- The mean number of service-class k calls with b_{kr_s} b.u. in state j, $y_{kr_s}(j)$, via:

$$y_{kr_s}(j) = \begin{cases} \dfrac{\alpha_{kr_s} \gamma_{k_s}(j) q(j - b_{kr_s})}{q(j)} & \text{for } j \leq C - t_k \\ 0 & \text{for } j > C - t_k \end{cases} \tag{2.30}$$

where $\gamma_{k_s}(j) = 1$ when $j > C - (b_{kr_{s-1}} - b_{kr_s})$ (otherwise $\gamma_{k_s}(j) = 0$).

- The mean number of in-service calls of service-class k accepted with b_k, $\bar{n}_k$, via (2.16).
- The mean number of in-service calls of service-class k accepted in the system with b_{kr_s}, $\bar{n}_{kr_s}$, via (2.26).

Example 2.9 In the system of Example 2.8 ($C = 3, K = 2, b_1 = 1, b_2 = 3, b_{2r_1} = 2, b_{2r_2} = 1, t_1 = 2, t_2 = 0, \lambda_1 = \lambda_2 = 1, \mu_1^{-1} = \mu_2^{-1} = 1, \mu_{2r_1}^{-1} = 2.0, \mu_{2r_2}^{-1} = 4.0$):

(a) Calculate the values of $Q(j)$ (link occupancy distribution) based on (2.27).
(b) Calculate the CBP of both service-classes including the retry probabilities.

(a) To determine the values of $Q(j)$ based on (2.27), we recursively calculate $q(j)$ for $j = 1, 2, 3$, starting with $q(0) = 1$, while $\alpha_1 = \alpha_2 = 1.0$ erl, $\alpha_{2r_1} = 2.0$ erl, $\alpha_{2r_2} = 4.0$, and $\gamma_{2_1}(j) = \gamma_{2_2}(j) = 1$ both for $j > 2 \Rightarrow j = 3$:

$j = 1 : q(1) = \alpha_1 b_1 q(1 - b_1) + 0 + 0 + 0 = 1.0 \Rightarrow \quad q(1) = 1.0$
$j = 2 : 2q(2) = 0 + 0 + 0 + 0 = 0 \Rightarrow \quad q(2) = 0$ (due to the BR parameter $t_1 = 2$)
$j = 3 : 3q(3) = 0 + \alpha_2 b_2 q(3 - b_2) + \alpha_{2r_1} b_{2r_1} q(3 - b_{2r_1}) + \alpha_{2r_2} b_{2r_2} q(3 - b_{2r_2}) = 7.0$

$$\Rightarrow \quad q(3) = 2.33333$$

The normalization constant is $G = q(0) + q(1) + q(2) + q(3) = 4.33333$. Thus,

$$Q(0) = \frac{q(0)}{G} = 0.23077 \quad Q(1) = \frac{q(1)}{G} = 0.23077 \quad Q(2) = \frac{q(2)}{G} = 0.0 \quad Q(3) = \frac{q(3)}{G} = 0.53846$$

(b) $B_1 \equiv$ CBP of service-class 1 $\qquad\qquad B_2 \equiv Prob\{1st\ retry\}$

$B_{2r_1} \equiv Prob\{2nd\ retry\}$ $\qquad\qquad B_{2r_2} \equiv$ CBP of service-class 2

$$B_1 = \sum_{j=C-b_1-t_1+1}^{C} Q(j) = 1 - Q(0) = 0.76923 \qquad \text{(compare with the exact 0.819672)}$$

$$B_2 = \sum_{j=C-b_2+1}^{C} Q(j) = 1 - Q(0) = 0.76923 = B_1$$

$$B_{2r_1} = \sum_{j=C-b_{2r_1}+1}^{C} Q(j) = Q(2) + Q(3) = 0.53846 \qquad \text{(compare with the exact 0.606557)}$$

$$B_{2r_2} = \sum_{j=C-b_{2r_2}+1}^{C} Q(j) = Q(3) = 0.53846 \qquad \text{(compare with the exact 0.514754)}$$

In this very small example, (2.27) does not provide good results compared to the exact values of Example 2.8. This is because, the Roberts approximation (BR policy) and the migration approximation have additively introduced errors on the results. Fortunately, in larger examples (i.e., more realistic scenarios) the results provided by (2.27) are quite good compared to simulation [4]. To be more specific, in this example, the Roberts approximation ignores the transition from state $(0, 0, 1, 0)$ to $(1, 0, 1, 0)$ for $j = 3$. On the other hand, migration approximation ignores the existence of states $(0, 0, 1, 0)$ and $(0, 0, 0, 1)$, since $\gamma_{2_1}(j) > 0$ and $\gamma_{2_2}(j) > 0$ when $j = 3$.

Example 2.10 Consider a single link of capacity $C = 300$ b.u. that accommodates calls of four different service-classes with the following traffic characteristics: $(\lambda_1, \mu_1^{-1}, b_1) = (8, 6, 1), (\lambda_2, \mu_2^{-1}, b_2) = (6, 4, 4), (\lambda_3, \mu_3^{-1}, b_3) = (4, 3, 6), (\lambda_4, \mu_4^{-1}, b_4) = (1, 1, 24), (b_{4r_1}, b_{4r_2}, b_{4r_3}, b_{4r_4}) = (20, 16, 12, 8),$ and $(\mu_{4r_1}^{-1}, \mu_{4r_2}^{-1}, \mu_{4r_3}^{-1}, \mu_{4r_4}^{-1}) = (1.2, 1.5, 2.0, 3.0)$ That is,

Table 2.3 CBP of Example 2.10 (MRM, $C = 300$ b.u.).

CBP	Analytical results	Simulation results
B_1	0.0049	0.0049± 8.3970e-5
B_2	0.0202	0.0202± 5.3021e-4
B_3	0.0273	0.0286± 4.9654e-4
B_4	0.1161	0.1142± 1.6558e-3
B_{4r_4}	0.0349	0.0374± 3.0918e-4

only calls of service-class 4 have the ability to retry four times; note that the product *bandwidth* by *service time* for service-class 4 remains constant.

(a) Present graphically the CBP of all service-classes and compare them with those obtained by the EMLM and the SRM, assuming an increase of C from 300 to 350 b.u. in steps of 10 b.u. For the SRM let $b_{4r} = 8$ b.u. and $\mu_{4r}^{-1} = 3.0$ sec.

(b) Present graphically the equalized CBP of all service-classes in the MRM/BR for the following set of BR parameters: $t_1 = 7, t_2 = 4, t_3 = 2, t_4 = 0$, which causes CBP equalization (the same increase of C, from 300 to 350 b.u. in steps of 10 b.u., is assumed). For comparison, include the equalized CBP obtained by the EMLM/BR, while considering the following set of BR parameters: $t_1 = 23, t_2 = 20, t_3 = 18, t_4 = 0$.

(c) Comment on the results.

(a) Figure 2.10 presents the CBP of the first three service-classes while Figure 2.11 presents the CBP of service-class 4. Simulation CBP results for the MRM and the MRM/BR are quite close to the analytical results and therefore are omitted. As an example, we present in Table 2.3 the corresponding analytical and simulation CBP results for $C = 300$ b.u. in the case of the MRM.

(b) Figure 2.12 presents the CBP of the MRM/BR and the EMLM/BR for the various values of C.

(c) Apart from the fact that all CBP decrease when C increases, we also see that:
- According to Figures 2.10 and 2.11:
  (i) The CBP of the first three service-classes is better when calls of service-class 4 retry only once (from $b_4 = 24$ to $b_{4r} = 8$ b.u.) instead of four times. On the contrary, the CBP of service-class 4 (not only B_4 but also B_{4r_4}) is slightly better in the MRM than in the SRM. This behavior is expected since in the MRM blocked calls of service-class 4 compete more times for the available link bandwidth than in the SRM.
  (ii) The EMLM results fail to approximate the corresponding CBP results of the MRM and SRM.
- According to Figure 2.12, the EMLM/BR results fail to approximate the corresponding results of the MRM/BR.

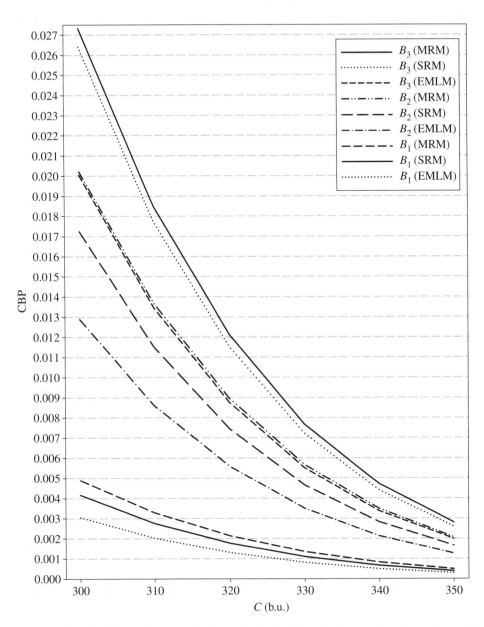

Figure 2.10 CBP of the first three service-classes in the MRM, SRM, and EMLM for various values of C (Example 2.10).

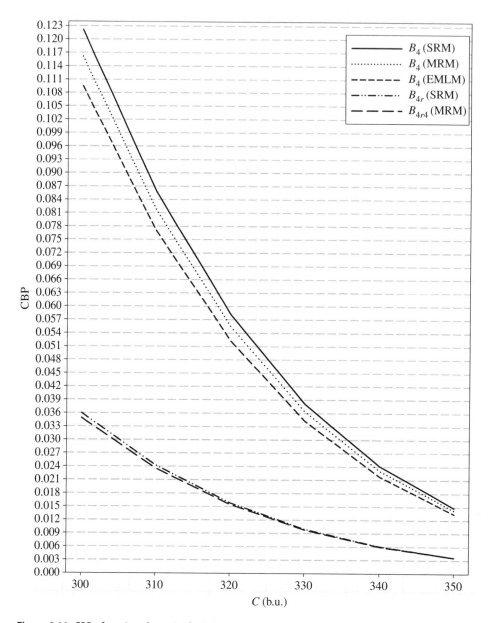

Figure 2.11 CBP of service-class 4 in the MRM, SRM, and EMLM for various values of C (Example 2.10).

2.5 The Single-Threshold Model

2.5.1 The Service System

In the *single-threshold model* (*STM*), the requested b.u. and the corresponding service time of a new call are related to the value j of the occupied link bandwidth (upon the new

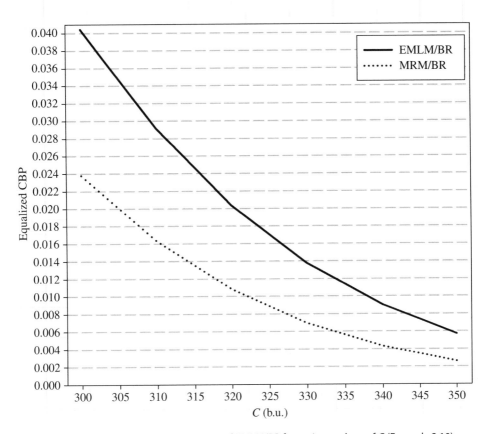

Figure 2.12 Equalized CBP in the MRM/BR and EMLM/BR for various values of C (Example 2.10).

call arrival). More precisely, the following CAC is applied. When the value of j is lower or equal to a threshold J_0, then a new call of service-class k is accepted in the system with its initial requirements (b_k, μ_k^{-1}). Otherwise, if $j > J_0$, the call tries to be connected in the system with (b_{kc}, μ_{kc}^{-1}), where $b_{kc} < b_k$ and $\mu_{kc}^{-1} = \frac{b_k}{b_{kc}} \mu_k^{-1}$, so that the product *bandwidth requirement* by *service time* remains constant [1]. This means that, contrary to the SRM, a call does not have to be blocked in order to retry with lower bandwidth requirement. If the b_{kc} b.u. are not available the call is blocked and lost.

The comparison of the STM with the SRM reveals the following basic similarities and differences:

- The steady state probabilities in the STM do not have a PFS, similar to the SRM (see Example 2.11). Thus, the unnormalized values of $q(j)$ are determined via an approximate, but recursive, formula, as Section 2.5.2 shows.
- In the STM, the steady state vector of all in-service calls of all service-classes is $\mathbf{n} = (n_1, n_{1c}, n_2, n_{2c}, \ldots, n_K, n_{Kc})$. Although a similar vector is defined for the SRM, an SRM system and an STM system that accommodate the same service-classes may have a different number of possible states, depending on the value of the threshold J_0.
- The CBP results obtained in the STM are sensitive to the service time distribution [1].

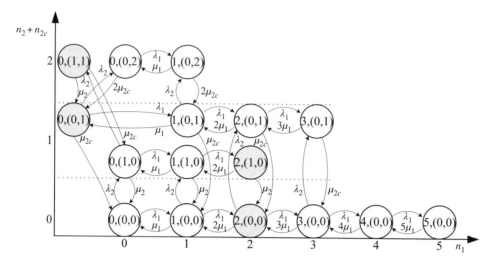

Figure 2.13 The state space Ω (CS policy) and the state transition diagram (Example 2.11).

- Setting the value of the threshold $J_0 = C - b_k$ results in the same CBP for both the SRM and STM.

Example 2.11 Consider again Example 2.1 ($C = 5, K = 2, b_1 = 1, b_2 = 3, b_{2r} = b_{2c} = 2, \lambda_1 = \lambda_2 = \mu_1^{-1} = \mu_2^{-1} = 1, \mu_{2r}^{-1} = \mu_{2c}^{-1} = 1.5$) and let $J_0 = 1$ b.u.

(a) Assume that a new call of service-class 2, having two possible bandwidth requirements $(b_2, b_{2c}) = (3, 2)$, arrives to the system where the threshold principle is applied for CAC. Find the bandwidth requirement of that call depending on the value of j.

(b) Find the total number of permissible states $\mathbf{n} = (n_1, n_2, n_{2c})$, where n_{2c} is the number of service-class 2 calls accepted in the system with b_{2c} b.u. Draw the state transition diagram.

(c) Find those adjacent states in which the LB is destroyed only due to the value of J_0 Compare with the SRM of Example 2.1.

(d) Calculate the state probabilities $P(n_1, n_2, n_{2c})$ and the corresponding values of $Q(j)$ (link occupancy distribution) based on the GB equations.

(e) Calculate the CBP of both service-classes and the link utilization.

(f) Calculate the conditional CBP of service-class 2 calls with b_{2c}, given that $j > J_0$.

(a) If $j \le J_0$ i.e., $j = 0$ or 1 at the time of arrival, then the call is accepted in the system with $b_2 = 3$ b.u. Otherwise, if $j > J_0$, the call requests $b_{2c} = 2$ b.u.; then, the call is accepted if $j = 2$ or 3, while it is blocked and lost if $j = 4$ or 5.

(b) There are 16 permissible states, of the form $\mathbf{n} = (n_1, n_2, n_{2c})$. The state space Ω and the state transition diagram are shown in Figure 2.13.

(c) Due to the selected value of J_0, LB is destroyed between adjacent states:

- (0,0,1) and (0,1,1): When a new call of service-class 2 arrives in the system and the state is (0,0,1) (which means $j = 2$) then the call is accepted with $b_{2c} = 2$ b.u. and the new state becomes (0,0,2) and not (0,1,1).
- (2,0,0) and (2,1,0): Similarly, from state (2,0,0) the new state is (2,0,1), not (2,1,0).

(d) Based on the GB, the corresponding 16 GB equations are:

$(0,0,0)$: $\quad P(0,1,0) + P(1,0,0) + 2/3P(0,0,1) - 2P(0,0,0) = 0$

$(0,0,1)$: $\quad P(0,1,1) + P(1,0,1) + 4/3P(0,0,2) - 8/3P(0,0,1) = 0$

$(0,0,2)$: $\quad P(1,0,2) + P(0,0,1) - 7/3P(0,0,2) = 0$

$(0,1,0)$: $\quad P(0,0,0) + 2/3P(0,1,1) + P(1,1,0) - 3P(0,1,0) = 0$

$(0,1,1)$: $\quad P(0,1,0) - 5/3P(0,1,1) = 0$

$(1,0,0)$: $\quad P(0,0,0) + 2/3P(1,0,1) + 2P(2,0,0) + P(1,1,0) - 3P(1,0,0) = 0$

$(1,0,1)$: $\quad P(0,0,1) + 4/3P(1,0,2) + 2P(2,0,1) - 11/3P(1,0,1) = 0$

$(1,0,2)$: $\quad P(0,0,2) + P(1,0,1) - 7/3P(1,0,2) = 0$

$(1,1,0)$: $\quad P(0,1,0) + P(1,0,0) + 2P(2,1,0) - 3P(1,1,0) = 0$

$(2,0,0)$: $\quad P(1,0,0) + 3P(3,0,0) + P(2,1,0) + 2/3P(2,0,1) - 4P(2,0,0) = 0$

$(2,0,1)$: $\quad P(1,0,1) + 3P(3,0,1) + P(2,0,0) - 11/3P(2,0,1) = 0$

$(2,1,0)$: $\quad P(1,1,0) - 3P(2,1,0) = 0$

$(3,0,0)$: $\quad P(2,0,0) + 2/3P(3,0,1) + 4P(4,0,0) - 5P(3,0,0) = 0$

$(3,0,1)$: $\quad P(3,0,0) + P(2,0,1) - 11/3P(3,0,1) = 0$

$(4,0,0)$: $\quad P(3,0,0) + 5P(5,0,0) - 5P(4,0,0) = 0$

$(5,0,0)$: $\quad P(4,0,0) - 5P(5,0,0) = 0$

By replacing the GB equation of $(1,0,0)$ with the equation $\sum_{n\in\Omega} P(n_1, n_2, n_{2c}) = 1$, the solution of this linear system is:

$P(0,0,0) = 0.144192$	$P(0,0,1) = 0.074982$	$P(0,0,2) = 0.055048$
$P(0,1,0) = 0.094754$	$P(0,1,1) = 0.056853$	$P(1,0,0) = 0.143642$
$P(1,0,1) = 0.069701$	$P(1,0,2) = 0.053464$	$P(1,1,0) = 0.10217$
$P(2,0,0) = 0.069048$	$P(2,0,1) = 0.054652$	$P(2,1,0) = 0.034057$
$P(3,0,0) = 0.020686$	$P(3,0,1) = 0.020547$	$P(4,0,0) = 0.005172$
$P(5,0,0) = 0.001034$		

Based on the values of $P(n_1, n_2, n_{2c})$ we have:

$Q(0) = P(0,0,0) = 0.144192$

$Q(1) = P(1,0,0) = 0.143642$

$Q(2) = P(0,0,1) + P(2,0,0) = 0.14403$

$Q(3) = P(0,1,0) + P(1,0,1) + P(3,0,0) = 0.185141$

$Q(4) = P(0,0,2) + P(1,1,0) + P(2,0,1) + P(4,0,0) = 0.217042$

$Q(5) = P(0,1,1) + P(1,0,2) + P(2,1,0) + P(3,0,1) + P(5,0,0) = 0.165955$

(e) The CBP of service-class 1 is given by:

$$B_1 = \sum_{j=C-b_1+1}^{C} Q(j) = Q(5) = 0.165955 \qquad \text{(compare with 0.206923 in the SRM)}$$

The CBP of service-class 2 is given by:

$$B_{2c} = \sum_{j=C-b_{2c}+1}^{C} Q(j) = Q(4) + Q(5) = 0.382997 \qquad \text{(compare with 0.377639 in the SRM)}$$

The link utilization is determined by:

$$U = \sum_{j=1}^{C} jQ(j) = 2.685 \text{ b.u.} \qquad \text{(compare with 2.66 b.u. in the SRM)}$$

(f) The conditional CBP of service-class 2 calls with b_{2c}, given that $j > J_0$ is:

$$B_{2c}^{*} = \text{Prob}\{j > C - b_{2c} | j > J_0\} = \frac{B_{2c}}{\text{Prob}(j > J_0)} = \frac{Q(4) + Q(5)}{Q(2) + Q(3) + Q(4) + Q(5)} = 0.53779$$

2.5.2 The Analytical Model

2.5.2.1 Steady State Probabilities

Aiming at deriving a recursive formula for the calculation of $q(j)$ (the unnormalized link occupancy distribution), we consider a link of capacity C b.u. that accommodates calls of two service-classes, whose initial bandwidth requirements are b_1 and b_2 b.u., respectively. Calls of each service-class arrive in the link according to a Poisson process with means λ_1 and λ_2, and have exponentially distributed service times with means μ_1^{-1} and μ_2^{-1}, respectively. If $j > J_0$ upon the arrival of a service-class 2 call, then this call requests from the system $b_{2c} < b_2$ and $\mu_{2c}^{-1} > \mu_2^{-1}$. No such option is considered for calls of service-class 1.

Although the STM does not have a PFS, we assume that the LB equation (1.51) does hold for calls of service-class 1, for $j = 1, \ldots, C$:

$$\alpha_1 b_1 q(j - b_1) = y_1(j) b_1 q(j) \tag{2.31}$$

For calls of service-class 2, we assume the existence of LB between adjacent states that can be expressed as follows [2]:

$$\alpha_2 b_2 q(j - b_2) = y_2(j) b_2 q(j), \quad \text{when} \quad j - b_2 \leq J_0 \tag{2.32}$$

$$\alpha_{2c} b_{2c} q(j - b_{2c}) = y_{2c}(j) b_{2c} q(j), \quad \text{when} \quad j - b_{2c} > J_0 \tag{2.33}$$

where $y_{2c}(j)$ is the mean number of service-class 2 calls with b_{2c} in state j.

Equations (2.31)–(2.33) lead to the following system of equations [2]:

$$\alpha_1 b_1 q(j - b_1) + \alpha_2 b_2 q(j - b_2) = (y_1(j) b_1 + y_2(j) b_2) q(j) \quad \text{when} \quad 1 \leq j \leq J_0 + b_{2c} \tag{2.34}$$

$$\alpha_1 b_1 q(j - b_1) + \alpha_2 b_2 q(j - b_2) + \alpha_{2c} b_{2c} q(j - b_{2c}) = jq(j) \text{ when } J_0 + b_{2c} < j \leq J_0 + b_2 \tag{2.35}$$

$$\alpha_1 b_1 q(j - b_1) + \alpha_{2c} b_{2c} q(j - b_{2c}) = (y_1(j) b_1 + y_{2c}(j) b_{2c}) q(j) \quad \text{when} \quad J_0 + b_2 < j \leq C \tag{2.36}$$

For (2.34), the following approximation is adopted: the value of $y_{2c}(j)$ in state j is negligible when $1 \le j \le J_0 + b_{2c}$. This approximation is similar to the migration approximation used in the SRM. For (2.36), the following approximation is applied: the value of $y_2(j)$ in state j is negligible when $J_0 + b_2 < j \le C$. This approximation is named the *upward migration approximation* and is different from the migration approximation since it considers negligible the population of calls with their initial bandwidth requirement [2]. The error introduced by the upward migration approximation in the calculation of $q(j)$ can be higher than the corresponding error introduced by the migration approximation of the SRM, especially when the offered traffic-load is light. In that case, it is highly probable that calls are accepted in the system with their initial bandwidth requirement [2].

Based on the above-mentioned approximations, we have (for $1 \le j \le C$):

$$\alpha_1 b_1 q(j - b_1) + \alpha_2 b_2 \delta_2(j) q(j - b_2) + \alpha_{2c} b_{2c} \delta_{2c}(j) q(j - b_{2c}) = jq(j) \tag{2.37}$$

where $\delta_2(j) = \begin{cases} 1 \text{ for } 1 \le j \le J_0 + b_2 \\ 0 \text{ otherwise} \end{cases}$, $\delta_{2c}(j) = \begin{cases} 1 \text{ for } j > J_0 + b_{2c} \\ 0 \text{ otherwise} \end{cases}$, and $\alpha_{2c} = \lambda_2 \mu_{2c}^{-1}$.

Note that in (2.37), $\delta_2(j)$ expresses the upward migration approximation and $\delta_{2c}(j)$ expresses the migration approximation.

In the general case of K service-classes, the approximate but recursive formula for $q(j)$ is the following [2]:

$$q(j) = \begin{cases} 1 & \text{if } j = 0 \\ \dfrac{1}{j}\left(\displaystyle\sum_{k=1}^{K} \alpha_k b_k \delta_k(j) q(j - b_k) + \displaystyle\sum_{k=1}^{K} \alpha_{kc} b_{kc} \delta_{kc}(j) q(j - b_{kc}) \right), & j = 1, \dots, C \\ 0 & \text{otherwise} \end{cases} \tag{2.38}$$

where $\delta_k(j) = \begin{cases} 1 \text{ (if } 1 \le j \le J_0 + b_k \text{ and } b_{kc} > 0) \text{ or (if } 1 \le j \le C \text{ and } b_{kc} = 0) \\ 0 \text{ otherwise} \end{cases}$, $\delta_{kc}(j) =$

$\begin{cases} 1 \text{ if } j > J_0 + b_{kc} \\ 0 \text{ otherwise} \end{cases}$ and $\alpha_{kc} = \lambda_k \mu_{kc}^{-1}$.

2.5.2.2 CBP, Utilization, and Mean Number of In-service Calls

Having determined the unnormalized values of $q(j)$, we can calculate the following performance measures:

- The CBP of service-class k calls with b_{kc} b.u., B_{kc}, via the following formula (if $G = \sum_{j=0}^{C} q(j)$ is the normalization constant) [2]:

$$B_{kc} = \sum_{j=C-b_{kc}+1}^{C} G^{-1} q(j) \tag{2.39}$$

- The CBP of service-class k calls with b_k b.u. (assuming that they have no option for b_{kc}), B_k, via (2.12).

- The conditional CBP of service-class k calls with b_{kc} given that $j > J_0$, B_{kc}^*, via:

$$B_{kc}^* = Prob\{j > C - b_{kc} | j > J_0\} = \frac{B_{kc}}{Prob(j > J_0)} = \frac{\sum\limits_{j=C-b_{kc}+1}^{C} q(j)}{\sum\limits_{j=J_0+1}^{C} q(j)} \qquad (2.40)$$

Note that if $J_0 = C - b_k$, then (2.40) is identical to (2.13) of the SRM.
- The link utilization, U, via (1.54).
- The mean number of service-class k calls with b_k b.u. in state j, $y_k(j)$, via:

$$y_k(j) = \frac{\alpha_k \delta_k(j) q(j - b_k)}{q(j)}, \qquad q(j) > 0 \qquad (2.41)$$

- The mean number of service-class k calls with b_{kc} b.u. in state j, $y_{kc}(j)$, via:

$$y_{kc}(j) = \frac{\alpha_{kc} \delta_{kc}(j) q(j - b_{kc})}{q(j)}, \qquad q(j) > 0 \qquad (2.42)$$

- The mean number of in-service calls of service-class k accepted in the system with b_k, $\bar{n}_k$, via (2.16).
- The mean number of in-service calls of service-class k accepted in the system with b_{kc}, $\bar{n}_{kc}$, via:

$$\bar{n}_{kc} = \sum_{j=1}^{C} y_{kc}(j) \frac{q(j)}{G} \qquad (2.43)$$

Example 2.12 In the system of Example 2.11 ($C = 5, K = 2, b_1 = 1, b_2 = 3, b_{2c} = 2, \lambda_1 = \lambda_2 = \mu_1^{-1} = \mu_2^{-1} = 1, \mu_{2c}^{-1} = 1.5, J_0 = 1$):

(a) Calculate the values of $Q(j)$ (link occupancy distribution) based on (2.38).
(b) Calculate the CBP of both service-classes including the conditional B_{2c}^*.

(a) To determine the values of $Q(j)$ based on (2.38), we recursively calculate $q(j)$ for $j = 1, \ldots, 5$, starting with $q(0) = 1$, while $\alpha_1 = \alpha_2 = 1.0$ erl, $\alpha_{2c} = \frac{b_2}{b_{2c}} \alpha_2 = 1.5$ erl, $\delta_2(j) = 1$ for $1 \le j \le 4$, and $\delta_{2c}(j) = 1$ for $3 < j \le 5$:

$j = 1 : q(1) = \alpha_1 b_1 q(1 - b_1) + 0 = 1.0$ $\Rightarrow q(1) = 1.0$

$j = 2 : 2q(2) = \alpha_1 b_1 q(2 - b_1) + 0 = 1.0$ $\Rightarrow q(2) = 0.5$

$j = 3 : 3q(3) = \alpha_1 b_1 q(3 - b_1) + \alpha_2 b_2 q(3 - b_2) = 3.5$ $\Rightarrow q(3) = 1.16667$

$j = 4 : 4q(4) = \alpha_1 b_1 q(4 - b_1) + \alpha_2 b_2 q(4 - b_2) + \alpha_{2c} b_{2c} q(4 - b_{2c}) = 5.66667 \Rightarrow q(4) = 1.416667$

$j = 5 : 5q(5) = \alpha_1 b_1 q(4 - b_1) + 0 + \alpha_{2c} b_{2c} q(5 - b_{2c}) = 4.916666$ $\Rightarrow q(5) = 0.98333$

The normalization constant is $G = 1 + q(1) + q(2) + q(3) + q(4) + q(5) = 6.066667$. Thus:

$Q(0) = \frac{q(0)}{G} = 0.164835$ $Q(1) = \frac{q(1)}{G} = 0.164835$ $Q(2) = \frac{q(2)}{G} = 0.082417$

$Q(3) = \frac{q(3)}{G} = 0.192308$ $Q(4) = \frac{q(4)}{G} = 0.23352$ $Q(5) = \frac{q(5)}{G} = 0.162087$

(b) CBP and conditional B_{2c}^*

$$B_1 = \sum_{j=C-b_1+1}^{C} Q(j) = Q(5) = 0.162087 \quad \text{(compare with the exact 0.165955)}$$

$$B_{2c} = \sum_{j=C-b_{2c}+1}^{C} Q(j) = Q(4) + Q(5) = 0.3956 \quad \text{(compare with the exact 0.382997)}$$

$$B_{2c}^* = \frac{B_{2c}}{Prob(j > J_0)} = \frac{\sum_{j=C-b_{2c}+1}^{C} Q(j)}{\sum_{j=J_0+1}^{C} Q(j)} = \frac{Q(4) + Q(5)}{Q(2) + Q(3) + Q(4) + Q(5)} = 0.59016$$

(compare with the exact 0.53779)

It is apparent that the error of the results in this small STM example is higher compared to the corresponding SRM example. This is due to the fact that in addition to the LB assumption and the migration approximation, which hold in the SRM, the upward migration approximation is introduced to the STM.

2.6 The Single-Threshold Model under the BR Policy

2.6.1 The Service System

In the *STM under the BR policy (STM/BR)*, t_k b.u. are reserved to benefit calls of all other service-classes apart from service-class k. The application of the BR policy in the STM is similar to that of the SRM/BR as the following example shows.

Example 2.13 Consider Example 2.3 ($C = 5, K = 2, b_1 = 1, b_2 = 3, b_{2r} = 2, t_1 = 2, t_2 = 0, \lambda_1 = \lambda_2 = \mu_1^{-1} = \mu_2^{-1} = 1, \mu_{2r}^{-1} = 1.5$) and let $J_0 = 1$ b.u. This means that calls of service-class 2 are accepted in the system with $b_{2c} = 2$ b.u. whenever $j > J_0$.

(a) Find the total number of permissible states $\mathbf{n} = (n_1, n_2, n_{2c})$ (state space Ω) and draw the state transition diagram. (*Hint*: elaborate on Figure 2.13).
(b) Calculate the state probabilities $P(n_1, n_2, n_{2c})$ and the corresponding values of $Q(j)$ (link occupancy distribution) based on the GB equations.
(c) Calculate the CBP of both service-classes.

(a) Elaborating on Figure 2.13, we find that we have to exclude three states, namely the states (4,0,0), (5,0,0), and (2,1,0). Compared to the SRM/BR in Example 2.3 (Figure 2.4), we see that in this STM/BR example, state (2,1,0) is not a permissible state because it is accessible neither from state (1,1,0) due to the BR policy, nor from state (2,0,0) due to the threshold J_0. States (4,0,0) and (5,0,0) are not permissible due to the BR policy. So, the total number of permissible states, of the form $\mathbf{n} = (n_1, n_2, n_{2c})$, is 13. They are shown in Figure 2.14 together with the state transition diagram.

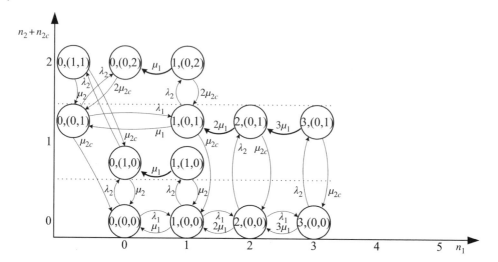

Figure 2.14 The state space Ω (BR policy) and the state transition diagram (Example 2.13).

(b) Based on the GB in each state, we write 13 GB equations:

$(0,0,0)$:	$P(0,1,0) + P(1,0,0) + 2/3P(0,0,1) - 2P(0,0,0) = 0$
$(0,0,1)$:	$P(0,1,1) + P(1,0,1) + 4/3P(0,0,2) - 8/3P(0,0,1) = 0$
$(0,0,2)$:	$P(1,0,2) + P(0,0,1) - 4/3P(0,0,2) = 0$
$(0,1,0)$:	$P(0,0,0) + 2/3P(0,1,1) + P(1,1,0) - 2P(0,1,0) = 0$
$(0,1,1)$:	$P(0,1,0) - 5/3P(0,1,1) = 0$
$(1,0,0)$:	$P(0,0,0) + 2/3P(1,0,1) + 2P(2,0,0) + P(1,1,0) - 3P(1,0,0) = 0$
$(1,0,1)$:	$P(0,0,1) + 4/3P(1,0,2) + 2P(2,0,1) - 8/3P(1,0,1) = 0$
$(1,0,2)$:	$P(1,0,1) - 7/3P(1,0,2) = 0$
$(1,1,0)$:	$P(1,0,0) - 2P(1,1,0) = 0$
$(2,0,0)$:	$P(1,0,0) + 3P(3,0,0) + 2/3P(2,0,1) - 4P(2,0,0) = 0$
$(2,0,1)$:	$P(2,0,0) + 3P(3,0,1) - 8/3P(2,0,1) = 0$
$(3,0,0)$:	$P(2,0,0) + 2/3P(3,0,1) - 4P(3,0,0) = 0$
$(3,0,1)$:	$P(3,0,0) - 11/3P(3,0,1) = 0$

By replacing the GB equation of (1,0,0) with the equation $\sum_{n\in\Omega} P(n_1, n_2, n_{2c}) = 1$, the solution of this linear system is: $P(0,0,0) = 0.173463$

$P(0,0,1) = 0.116024$	$P(0,0,2) = 0.110711$	$P(0,1,0) = 0.146786$	$P(0,1,1) = 0.088072$
$P(1,0,0) = 0.122790$	$P(1,0,1) = 0.073712$	$P(1,0,2) = 0.031591$	$P(1,1,0) = 0.061395$
$P(2,0,0) = 0.042185$	$P(2,0,1) = 0.019209$	$P(3,0,0) = 0.011049$	$P(3,0,1) = 0.003013$

Based on the values of $P(n_1, n_2, n_{2c})$, we have:

$Q(0) = P(0,0,0) = 0.173463$
$Q(1) = P(1,0,0) = 0.122790$
$Q(2) = P(0,0,1) + P(2,0,0) = 0.158209$
$Q(3) = P(0,1,0) + P(1,0,1) + P(3,0,0) = 0.231547$

$$Q(4) = P(0,0,2) + P(1,1,0) + P(2,0,1) = 0.191315$$
$$Q(5) = P(0,1,1) + P(1,0,2) + P(3,0,1) = 0.122676$$

(c) The CBP of service-class 1 is given by:

$$B_1 = \sum_{j=C-b_1-t_1+1}^{C} Q(j) = Q(3) + Q(4) + Q(5) = 0.545538 \text{ (compare with 0.548536 in the SRM/BR)}$$

Finally, the CBP of service-class 2 is given by:

$$B_{2c} = \sum_{j=C-b_{2c}+1}^{C} Q(j) = Q(4) + Q(5) = 0.313991 \qquad \text{(compare with 0.301968 in the SRM/BR)}$$

2.6.2   The Analytical Model

2.6.2.1   Steady State Probabilities

Similar to the SRM/BR, we adopt the Roberts method for the calculation of $q(j)$ in the STM/BR.

Based on the Roberts method, (2.38) takes the form [4]:

$$q(j) = \begin{cases} 1 & \text{if } j = 0 \\ \dfrac{1}{j}\left(\displaystyle\sum_{k=1}^{K} \alpha_k D_k(j-b_k)\delta_k(j)q(j-b_k) + \sum_{k=1}^{K} \alpha_{kc}D_{kc}(j-b_{kc})\delta_{kc}(j)q(j-b_{kc}) \right) \\ \qquad j = 1, \dots, C \\ 0 & \text{otherwise} \end{cases}$$

$$(2.44)$$

where $\qquad \delta_k(j) = \begin{cases} 1 & \text{(if } 1 \le j \le J_0 + b_k \text{ and } b_{kc} > 0) \text{ or (if } 1 \le j \le C \text{ and } b_{kc} = 0) \\ 0 & \text{otherwise} \end{cases}$,

$\delta_{kc}(j) = \begin{cases} 1 \text{ if } j > J_0 + b_{kc} \\ 0 \text{ otherwise} \end{cases}$, $\alpha_{kc} = \lambda_k \mu_{kc}^{-1}$, $D_k(j - b_k)$ is given by (1.65), and

$$D_{kc}(j - b_{kc}) = \begin{cases} b_{kc} & \text{for } j \le C - t_k \\ 0 & \text{for } j > C - t_k \end{cases} \qquad (2.45)$$

2.6.2.2   CBP, Utilization, and Mean Number of In-service Calls

Based on (2.44) and (2.45), we can determine the following performance measures:

- The CBP of service-class k calls with b_{kc} b.u., B_{kc}, via the formula [4]:

$$B_{kc} = \sum_{j=C-b_{kc}-t_k+1}^{C} G^{-1}q(j) \qquad (2.46)$$

where $G = \sum_{j=0}^{C} q(j)$ is the normalization constant.
- The CBP of service-class k calls with b_k b.u., B_k, via (1.66).
- The conditional CBP of service-class k calls with b_{kc} given that $j > J_0$, B_{kc}^*, via (2.40), while subtracting the BR parameter t_k from $C - b_{kc}$.

- The link utilization, U, via (1.54).
- The mean number of service-class k calls with b_k b.u. in state j, $y_k(j)$, via:

$$
y_k(j) = \begin{cases} \dfrac{\alpha_k \delta_k(j) q(j - b_k)}{q(j)}, & \text{for } j \le C - t_k \\ 0, & \text{for } j > C - t_k \end{cases}
\tag{2.47}
$$

$$
\delta_k(j) = \begin{cases} 1 \text{ (if } 1 \le j \le J_0 + b_k \text{ and } b_{kc} > 0) \text{ or (if } 1 \le j \le C \text{ and } b_{kc} = 0) \\ 0 \text{ otherwise} \end{cases}.
$$

- The mean number of service-class k calls with b_{kc} b.u. in state j, $y_{kc}(j)$, via:

$$
y_{kc}(j) = \begin{cases} \dfrac{\alpha_{kc} \delta_{kc}(j) q(j - b_{kc})}{q(j)}, & \text{for } j \le C - t_k \\ 0, & \text{for } j > C - t_k \end{cases}
\tag{2.48}
$$

where $\delta_{kc}(j) = \begin{cases} 1 & \text{if } j > J_0 + b_{kc} \\ 0 & \text{otherwise} \end{cases}$.

- The mean number of in-service calls of service-class k accepted in the system with b_k, $\bar{n}_k$, via (2.16).
- The mean number of in-service calls of service-class k accepted in the system with b_{kc}, $\bar{n}_{kc}$, via (2.43).

Example 2.14 In the system of Example 2.13 ($C = 5, K = 2, b_1 = 1, b_2 = 3, b_{2c} = 2, t_1 = 2, t_2 = 0, \lambda_1 = \lambda_2 = \mu_1^{-1} = \mu_2^{-1} = 1, \mu_{2c}^{-1} = 1.5, J_0 = 1$):

(a) Calculate the values of $Q(j)$ (link occupancy distribution) based on (2.44).
(b) Calculate the CBP of both service-classes including the conditional B_{2c}^*.

(a) To determine the state probability $Q(j)$ based on (2.44) (the unnormalized link occupancy distribution), we recursively calculate $q(j)$ for $j = 1, \dots, 5$, starting with $q(0) = 1$, while $\alpha_1 = \alpha_2 = 1.0$ erl, $\alpha_{2c} = \frac{b_2}{b_{2c}} \alpha_2 = 1.5$ erl, $\delta_2(j) = 1$ for $1 \le j \le 4$, and $\delta_{2c}(j) = 1$ for $3 < j \le 5$:

$j = 1:$ $q(1) = \alpha_1 b_1 q(1 - b_1) + 0 = 1.0$ $\Rightarrow q(1) = 1.0$

$j = 2:$ $2q(2) = \alpha_1 b_1 q(2 - b_1) + 0 = 1.0$ $\Rightarrow q(2) = 0.5$

$j = 3:$ $3q(3) = \alpha_1 b_1 q(3 - b_1) + \alpha_2 b_2 q(3 - b_2) = 3.5$ $\Rightarrow q(3) = 1.16667$

$j = 4:$ $4q(4) = 0 + \alpha_2 b_2 q(4 - b_2) + \alpha_{2c} b_{2c} q(4 - b_{2c}) = 4.5$ $\Rightarrow q(4) = 1.125$

$j = 5:$ $5q(5) = 0 + 0 + \alpha_{2c} b_{2c} q(5 - b_{2c}) = 3.5$ $\Rightarrow q(5) = 0.7$

The normalization constant is $G = 5.491667$. Thus:

$Q(0) = \dfrac{q(0)}{G} = 0.18209$ $Q(1) = \dfrac{q(1)}{G} = 0.18209$ $Q(2) = \dfrac{q(2)}{G} = 0.09105$

$Q(3) = \dfrac{q(3)}{G} = 0.21244$ $Q(4) = \dfrac{q(4)}{G} = 0.20486$ $Q(5) = \dfrac{q(5)}{G} = 0.12746$

$$
B_1 = \sum_{j=C-b_1-t_1+1}^{C} Q(j) = Q(3) + Q(4) + Q(5) = 0.54476 \text{ (compare with the exact 0.545538)}
$$

$$B_{2c} = \sum_{j=C-b_{2c}+1}^{C} Q(j) = Q(4) + Q(5) = 0.33232 \text{ (compare with the exact 0.31399)}$$

$$B_{2c}^* = \frac{B_{2c}}{Prob(j > J_0)} = \frac{\sum\limits_{j=C-b_{2c}+1}^{C} Q(j)}{\sum\limits_{j=J_0+1}^{C} Q(j)} = \frac{Q(4) + Q(5)}{Q(2) + Q(3) + Q(4) + Q(5)} = 0.52267$$

(compare with the exact 0.44617)

It is apparent that in this small STM/BR example the error introduced by the assumption of LB, the migration approximation, the upward migration approximation, and the introduction of the BR policy via the Roberts method is high, especially for B_{2c}^*.

Example 2.15 Consider a single link of capacity $C = 500$ b.u. that accommodates calls of four different service-classes with the following traffic characteristics: $(\lambda_1, \mu_1^{-1}, b_1) = (8, 12, 1)$, $(\lambda_2, \mu_2^{-1}, b_2) = (4, 10, 7)$, $(\lambda_3, \mu_3^{-1}, b_3) = (2, 8, 14)$, $(\lambda_4, \mu_4^{-1}, b_4) = (1, 6, 28)$, $(\mu_{4c}^{-1}, b_{4c}) = (12, 14)$, and $b_4\mu_4^{-1} = b_{4c}\mu_{4c}^{-1}$.

(a) Present graphically the CBP of all service-classes, including the conditional B_{4c}^*, for the STM under the CS policy (no BR parameters), when considering two different values of threshold, $J_0 = C - 2b_4$ and $J_0 = C - 3b_4$. Compare the results with those obtained by the SRM in Example 2.5 (or by the STM when $J_0 = C - b_4$), assuming an increase of C from 500 to 1000 b.u. in steps of 100 b.u. Provide simulation results for evaluation.

(b) Present graphically the equalized CBP of all service-classes, in the STM/BR, for the following BR parameters: $t_1 = 13, t_2 = 7$, and $t_3 = 0$ b.u., which cause CBP equalization (the same increase of C, from 500 to 1000 b.u., is assumed). Consider both threshold values, $J_0 = C - 2b_4$ and $J_0 = C - 3b_4$.

(a) Figure 2.15 presents in descending order the analytical CBP of service-classes 1, 2 and 3, 4 (at the RHS and LHS, respectively). Simulation CBP results for the STM are close to the analytical results, especially when $C = 500$ b.u., and therefore are not included in the figure. As an example, we present in Tables 2.4 and 2.5 the corresponding analytical and simulation CBP results, when $J_0 = C - 2b_4$ and $J_0 = C - 3b_4$, respectively, for $C = 500$ and $C = 1000$ b.u. Simulation results are based on SIMSCRIPT III [6] and are mean values of 12 runs with 95% confidence interval. Note that in the case of $C = 1000$ b.u., the offered traffic-load is light and there is a difference between analytical and simulation results. This is because calls of service-class 4 are mainly accepted in the system with their initial bandwidth requirement, a fact that is not taken into account in (2.38) due to the upward migration approximation.

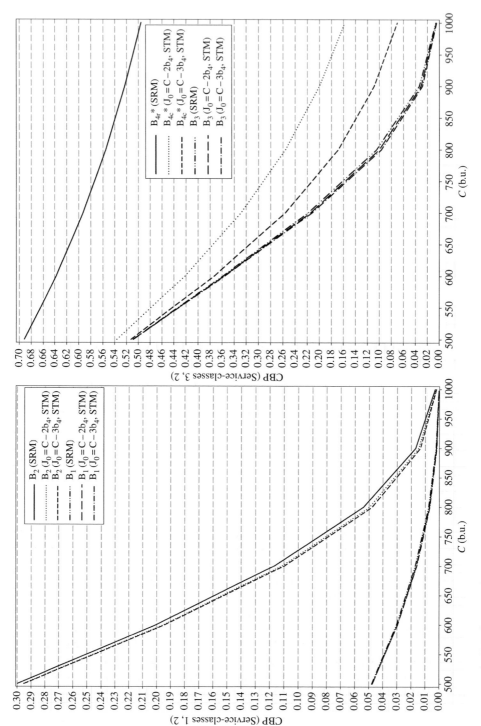

Figure 2.15 Left: CBP of service-classes 1, 2 in the STM and SRM versus various values of C. Right: The corresponding graphs for service-classes 3, 4 (Example 2.15).

Table 2.4 CBP of Example 2.15 (STM, $C = 500$ or $C = 1000$ b.u., and $J_0 = C - 2b_4$).

CBP	$C = 500$ b.u.		$C = 1000$ b.u.	
	Analytical results	Simulation results	Analytical results	Simulation results
B_1	0.0474	$0.0479 \pm 2.9368\text{e-}4$	0.0003	$0.00026 \pm 1.6765\text{e-}5$
B_2	0.2953	$0.2948 \pm 3.3213\text{e-}4$	0.0025	$0.0019 \pm 3.3650\text{e-}5$
B_3	0.5086	$0.5074 \pm 3.6020\text{e-}4$	0.0054	$0.0042 \pm 3.0290\text{e-}5$
B_{4c}^*	0.5361	$0.5302 \pm 3.2453\text{e-}4$	0.1579	$0.1363 \pm 2.3964\text{e-}3$

Table 2.5 CBP of Example 2.15 (STM, $C = 500$ or $C = 1000$ b.u., and $J_0 = C - 3b_4$).

CBP	$C = 500$ b.u.		$C = 1000$ b.u.	
	Analytical results	Simulation results	Analytical results	Simulation results
B_1	0.0475	$0.0480 \pm 1.4185\text{e-}4$	0.0003	$0.00017 \pm 1.2923\text{e-}5$
B_2	0.2949	$0.2948 \pm 5.6484\text{e-}4$	0.0021	$0.00137 \pm 2.9135\text{e-}5$
B_3	0.5082	$0.5074 \pm 6.7936\text{e-}4$	0.0047	$0.00297 \pm 6.4709\text{e-}5$
B_{4c}^*	0.5124	$0.5113 \pm 7.5074\text{e-}4$	0.0702	$0.0511 \pm 8.6489\text{e-}4$

Table 2.6 CBP of Example 2.15 (STM/BR, $C = 500$ or $C = 1000$ b.u., and $J_0 = C - 2b_4$).

CBP	$C = 500$ b.u.		$C = 1000$ b.u.	
	Analytical results	Simulation results	Analytical results	Simulation results
B_1	0.3783	$0.3799 \pm 5.0062\text{e-}4$	0.00410	$0.00332 \pm 2.6103\text{e-}5$
B_2	0.3783	$0.3799 \pm 4.6590\text{e-}4$	0.00410	$0.00333 \pm 4.1082\text{e-}5$
B_3	0.3783	$0.3799 \pm 7.1394\text{e-}4$	0.00410	$0.00332 \pm 3.8769\text{e-}5$
B_{4c}	0.3783	$0.3799 \pm 6.9529\text{e-}4$	0.00410	$0.00333 \pm 3.6205\text{e-}5$

Based on Figure 2.15, we see that the increase of J_0 results in the substantial decrease of B_{4c}^* and a minor decrease in the CBP of the first three service-classes. This was anticipated since calls of service-class 4 use the b_{4c} requirement more frequently compared to the SRM.

(b) Figure 2.16 presents the corresponding equalized CBP of all service-classes for the STM/BR. For comparison we include the corresponding results of the SRM/BR. Simulation and analytical equalized CBP results are presented in Table 2.6 for $C = 500$, or $C = 1000$ b.u., and $J_0 = C - 2b_4$. According to Figure 2.16, we see that (i) the equalized CBP decreases as C increases and (ii) reducing the threshold J_0 results in the decrease (although slight) in the equalized CBP.

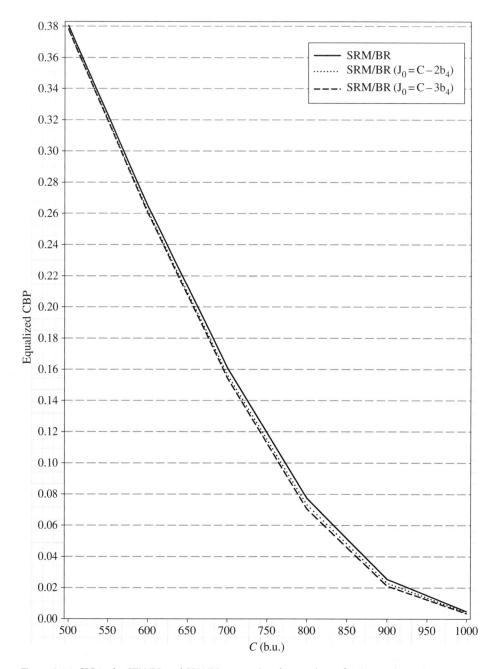

Figure 2.16 CBP in the STM/BR and SRM/BR versus C and two values of J_0 (Example 2.15).

2.7 The Multi-Threshold Model

2.7.1 The Service System

In the *multi-threshold model (MTM)*, there exist S different thresholds which are common to all service-classes [1, 2]. A call of service-class k with initial requirements (b_k, μ_k^{-1}) can use, depending on the occupied link bandwidth, one of the $S + 1$ requirements $(b_{kc_s}, \mu_{kc_s}^{-1})$, $s = 0, \ldots, S$, where the pair $(b_{kc_s}, \mu_{kc_s}^{-1})$ is used when $J_{s-1} < j \le J_s$ (where $J_{-1} = 0$). The maximum possible threshold is $J_{S-1} = C - b_{kc_s}$, while $J_S = C$. As far as the bandwidth requirements of a service-class k call are concerned, we assume that they decrease as j increases, i.e., $b_k > b_{kc_1} > \ldots > b_{kc_S}$, while by definition $b_k = b_{kc_0}$ (see Figure 2.17).

2.7.2 The Analytical Model

2.7.2.1 Steady State Probabilities
To describe the MTM in steady state, the following LB equations are considered:

$$\alpha_k b_k q(j - b_k) = y_k(j) b_k q(j)$$
$$\text{(for } j \le J_0 + b_k \text{ when } b_{kc_s} > 0\text{), or (for } j = 1, \ldots, C, \text{ when } b_{kc_s} = 0)$$

(2.49)

and

$$\alpha_{kc_s} b_{kc_s} q(j - b_{kc_s}) = y_{kc_s}(j) b_{kc_s} q(j)$$
$$\text{for } J_s + b_{kc_s} \ge j > J_{s-1} + b_{kc_s}$$

(2.50)

where $y_{kc_s}(j)$ denotes the mean number of service-class k calls, with b_{kc_s}, in state j.

Similar to the analysis of the STM and based on (2.49) and (2.50), we have the following recursive formula for the calculation of $q(j)$ [1, 2]:

$$q(j) = \begin{cases} 1, & \text{if } j = 0 \\ \dfrac{1}{j}\left(\displaystyle\sum_{k=1}^{K} \alpha_k b_k \delta_k(j) q(j - b_k) + \sum_{k=1}^{K} \sum_{s=1}^{S} \alpha_{kc_s} b_{kc_s} \delta_{kc_s}(j) q(j - b_{kc_s}) \right) & \\ & j = 1, \ldots, C \\ 0, & \text{otherwise} \end{cases}$$

(2.51)

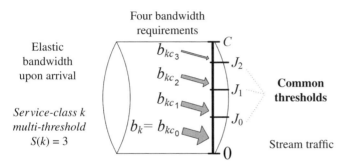

Figure 2.17 The MTM principle of operation.

where
$$\delta_k(j) = \begin{cases} 1 & \text{(if } 1 \leq j \leq J_0 + b_k \text{ and } b_{kc_s} > 0) \text{ or (if } 1 \leq j \leq C \text{ and } b_{kc_s} = 0) \\ 0 & \text{otherwise} \end{cases}$$

$$\delta_{kc_s}(j) = \begin{cases} 1 & \text{if } J_s + b_{kc_s} \geq j > J_{s-1} + b_{kc_s} \text{ and } b_{kc_s} > 0 \\ 0 & \text{otherwise} \end{cases} \quad \text{and } \alpha_{kc_s} = \lambda_k \mu_{kc_s}^{-1}.$$

Note that in (2.51), $\delta_k(j)$ expresses the upward migration approximation, while $\delta_{kc_s}(j)$ expresses the migration approximation.

2.7.2.2 CBP, Utilization, and Mean Number of In-service Calls

Based on (2.51), we can determine the following performance measures:

- The CBP of service-class k calls with b_{kc_s} b.u., B_{kc_s}, via the formula [2]:

$$B_{kc_s} = \sum_{j=C-b_{kc_s}+1}^{C} G^{-1} q(j) \tag{2.52}$$

  where $G = \sum_{j=0}^{C} q(j)$ is the normalization constant.
- The CBP of service-class k calls with b_k b.u., B_k, via (1.66).
- The conditional CBP of service-class k calls with b_{kc_s} given that $j > J_{s-1}$, $B_{kc_s}^*$, via the formula:

$$B_{kc_s}^* = \frac{\sum_{j=C-b_{kc_s}+1}^{C} q(j)}{\sum_{j=J_{s-1}+1}^{C} q(j)} \tag{2.53}$$

- The link utilization, U, via (1.54).
- The mean number of service-class k calls with b_k b.u. in state j, $y_k(j)$, via:

$$y_k(j) = \frac{\alpha_k \delta_k(j) q(j - b_k)}{q(j)}, \quad q(j) > 0 \tag{2.54}$$

  where $\delta_k(j) = \begin{cases} 1 & \text{(if } 1 \leq j \leq J_0 + b_k \text{ and } b_{kc_s} > 0) \text{ or (if } 1 \leq j \leq C \text{ and } b_{kc_s} = 0) \\ 0 & \text{otherwise} \end{cases}$
- The mean number of service-class k calls with b_{kc_s} b.u. in state j, $y_{kc_s}(j)$, via:

$$y_{kc_s}(j) = \frac{\alpha_{kc_s} \delta_{kc_s}(j) q(j - b_{kc_s})}{q(j)}, \quad q(j) > 0 \tag{2.55}$$

  where $\delta_{kc_s}(j) = \begin{cases} 1 & \text{if } J_s + b_{kc_s} \geq j > J_{s-1} + b_{kc_s} \text{ and } b_{kc_s} > 0 \\ 0 & \text{otherwise} \end{cases}$.
- The mean number of in-service calls of service-class k accepted in the system with b_k, $\bar{n}_k$, via (2.16).
- The mean number of in-service calls of service-class k accepted in the system with b_{kc_s}, $\bar{n}_{kc_s}$, via:

$$\bar{n}_{kc_s} = \sum_{j=1}^{C} y_{kc_s}(j) \frac{q(j)}{G} \tag{2.56}$$

2.8 The Multi-Threshold Model under the BR Policy

2.8.1 The Service System

In the *MTM under the BR policy (MTM/BR)*, t_k b.u. are reserved to benefit calls of all other service-classes apart from service-class k. The application of the BR policy in the MTM is similar to that of the MRM/BR.

2.8.2 The Analytical Model

2.8.2.1 Steady State Probabilities

Similar to the MRM/BR, we adopt the Roberts method for the calculation of the unnormalized link occupancy distribution $q(j)$ in the MTM/ BR.

Based on the Roberts method, (2.51) takes the form [4]:

$$q(j) = \begin{cases} 1, & \text{if } j = 0 \\ \frac{1}{j}\left(\sum_{k=1}^{K} \alpha_k D_k(j - b_k)\delta_k(j)q(j - b_k) \right) + \\ \frac{1}{j}\left(\sum_{k=1}^{K}\sum_{s=1}^{S} \alpha_{kc_s} D_{kc_s}(j - b_{kc_s})\delta_{kc_s}(j)q(j - b_{kc_s}) \right) & j = 1, \dots, C \\ 0, & \text{otherwise} \end{cases} \tag{2.57}$$

where
$$\delta_k(j) = \begin{cases} 1 & (\text{if } 1 \le j \le J_0 + b_k \text{ and } b_{kc_s} > 0) \text{ or } (\text{if } 1 \le j \le C \text{ and } b_{kc_s} = 0) \\ 0 & \text{otherwise} \end{cases}$$

$$\delta_{kc_s}(j) = \begin{cases} 1 & (\text{if } J_s + b_{kc_s} \ge j > J_{s-1} + b_{kc_s} \text{ and } b_{kc_s} > 0 \\ 0 & \text{otherwise} \end{cases}, \quad \alpha_{kc_s} = \lambda_k \mu_{kc_s}^{-1}, \text{ and}$$

$$D_{kc_s}(j - b_{kc_s}) = \begin{cases} b_{kc_s} & \text{for } j \le C - t_k \\ 0 & \text{for } j > C - t_k \end{cases} \tag{2.58}$$

2.8.2.2 CBP, Utilization, and Mean Number of In-service Calls

Based on (2.57) and (2.58), we can determine the following performance measures:

- The CBP of service-class k calls with b_{kc_s} b.u., B_{kc_s}, via the formula [4]:

$$B_{kc_s} = \sum_{j=C-b_{kc_s}-t_k+1}^{C} G^{-1}q(j) \tag{2.59}$$

where $G = \sum_{j=0}^{C} q(j)$ is the normalization constant.
- The CBP of service-class k calls with b_k b.u., B_k, via (1.66).
- The conditional CBP of service-class k calls with b_{kc_s} given that $j > J_{S-1}$, $B^*_{kc_s}$, via the formula:

$$B^*_{kc_s} = \frac{\sum\limits_{j=C-b_{kc_s}-t_k+1}^{C} q(j)}{\sum\limits_{j=J_{S-1}+1}^{C} q(j)} \tag{2.60}$$

- The link utilization, U, via (1.54).
- The mean number of service-class k calls with b_k b.u. in state j, $y_k(j)$, via:

$$y_k(j) = \begin{cases} \dfrac{\alpha_k \delta_k(j) q(j - b_k)}{q(j)}, & \text{for } j \leq C - t_k \\ 0, & \text{for } j > C - t_k \end{cases} \tag{2.61}$$

where $\delta_k(j) = \begin{cases} 1 & (\text{if } 1 \leq j \leq J_0 + b_k \text{ and } b_{kc_s} > 0) \text{ or (if } 1 \leq j \leq C \text{ and } b_{kc_s} = 0) \\ 0 & \text{otherwise.} \end{cases}$

- The mean number of service-class k calls with b_{kc_s} b.u. in state j, $y_{kc_s}(j)$, via:

$$y_{kc_s}(j) = \begin{cases} \dfrac{\alpha_{kc_s} \delta_{kc_s}(j) q(j - b_{kc_s})}{q(j)} & \text{for } j \leq C - t_k \\ 0 & \text{for } j > C - t_k \end{cases} \tag{2.62}$$

where $\delta_{kc_s}(j) = \begin{cases} 1 & \text{if } J_s + b_{kc_s} \geq j > J_{s-1} + b_{kc_s} \text{ and } b_{kc_s} > 0 \\ 0 & \text{otherwise} \end{cases}$.

- The mean number of in-service calls of service-class k accepted in the system with b_k, $\overline{n}_k$, via (2.16).
- The mean number of in-service calls of service-class k accepted in the system with b_{kc_s}, $\overline{n}_{kc_s}$, via (2.56).

Example 2.16 Consider again Example 2.10 ($C = 300$, $(\lambda_1, \mu_1^{-1}, b_1) = (8, 6, 1)$, $(\lambda_2, \mu_2^{-1}, b_2) = (6, 4, 4)$, $(\lambda_3, \mu_3^{-1}, b_3) = (4, 3, 6)$, $(\lambda_4, \mu_4^{-1}, b_4) = (1, 1, 24)$, $(b_{4r_1}, b_{4r_2}, b_{4r_3}, b_{4r_4}) = (20, 16, 12, 8)$, and $(\mu_{4r_1}^{-1}, \mu_{4r_2}^{-1}, \mu_{4r_3}^{-1}, \mu_{4r_4}^{-1}) = (1.2, 1.5, 2.0, 3.0)$). Calls of service-class 4 reduce their bandwidth four times according to the following 12 sets of thresholds:

Set 1: $J_0 = 276, J_1 = 280, J_2 = 284, J_3 = 288$

Set 2: $J_0 = 266, J_1 = 270, J_2 = 274, J_3 = 278$

Set 3: $J_0 = 256, J_1 = 260, J_2 = 264, J_3 = 268$

. . .

Set 12: $J_0 = 166, J_1 = 170, J_2 = 174, J_3 = 178$

In the case of Set 1 the same CBP results are anticipated by the MRM and the MTM.

(a) Present graphically the CBP of all service-classes $(B_1, B_2, B_3, B^*_{4c_4})$ for all sets of thresholds and $C = 300$ b.u.
(b) Present graphically the equalized CBP of all service-classes in the MTM/BR for all sets of thresholds and the following set of BR parameters: $t_1 = 7, t_2 = 4, t_3 = 2, t_4 = 0$, which causes CBP equalization. Assume three values of C: 300, 310, and 320 b.u.

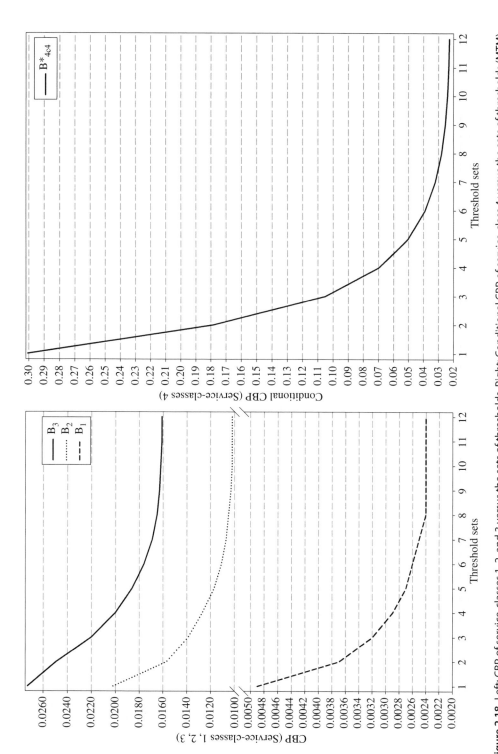

Figure 2.18 Left: CBP of service-classes 1, 2, and 3 versus the sets of thresholds. Right: Conditional CBP of service-class 4 versus the sets of thresholds (MTM) (Example 2.16).

(a) In the LHS of Figure 2.18, we present the CBP of the first three service-classes and in the RHS of the same figure the conditional CBP of service-class 4. There, we see that decreasing the values of the thresholds results in the CBP decrease of all service-classes. This is because calls of service-class 4 use their initial bandwidth requirement less frequently, $b_4 = 24$ b.u.

(b) In Figure 2.19, we present the equalized CBP of all service-classes. We see that decreasing the values of thresholds or increasing the capacity of the system results in the CBP decrease of all service-classes. Note that when $C = 300$ b.u., the MTM/BR results obtained for Set 1 coincide with the MRM/BR (Figure 2.12).

2.9 The Connection Dependent Threshold Model

2.9.1 The Service System

In the *connection dependent threshold model (CDTM)*, bandwidth and service time requests depend on the total number j of occupied b.u. of a link of capacity C, as in the MTM. The only difference with the MTM is that different service-classes may have different sets of thresholds. Specifically, we consider K ($k = 1, 2, \ldots, K$) service-classes of Poisson arriving calls with mean arrival rates λ_k that require b_k b.u. per call and a mean service time μ_k^{-1}, exponentially distributed. Calls compete for the available bandwidth under the CS policy. The offered traffic-load of calls of service-class k is $\alpha_k = \lambda_k \mu_k^{-1}$. Let $\lambda = (\lambda_1, \lambda_2, \ldots, \lambda_K)$, $\mu^{-1} = (\mu_1^{-1}, \mu_2^{-1}, \ldots, \mu_K^{-1})$, $\alpha = (\alpha_1, \alpha_2, \ldots, \alpha_K)$, and $\mathbf{b} = (b_1, b_2, \ldots, b_K)$. Each arriving call of a service-class k may have $S(k) + 1$ bandwidth and service-time requirements, that is, one initial requirement with values (b_k, μ_k^{-1}) and $S(k)$ more requirements with values $(b_{kc_s}, \mu_{kc_s}^{-1})$, where $s = 1, \ldots, S(k)$ and $b_{kc_{S(k)}} < \ldots < b_{kc_1} < b_k$, and $\mu_{kc_{S(k)}}^{-1} > \ldots > \mu_{kc_1}^{-1} > \mu_k^{-1}$. The pair $(b_{kc_s}, \mu_{kc_s}^{-1})$ is used when $J_{k_{s-1}} < j \leq J_{k_s}$, where $J_{k_{s-1}}$ and J_{k_s} are two successive thresholds of service-class k, while $J_{k_{S(k)}} = C$; the highest possible threshold (other than C) is $J_{k_{S(k)-1}} = C - b_{kc_{S(k)}}$ (see Figure 2.20). By convention, $b_k = b_{kc_0}$ and $\mu_k^{-1} = \mu_{kc_0}^{-1}$, while the pair (b_k, μ_k^{-1}) is used when $j \leq J_{k_0}$.

Example 2.17 As an application example of the CDTM, imagine a CPU (server in a LAN) exclusively devoted to video file format conversion (e.g., from AVI to DVD). The CPU collaborates with a CAC, which either accepts or denies conversion requests, depending on the current status and the processing capacity of the CPU (let it be 60 video frames/sec). We consider conversion requests for movies (service-class 1), video clips (service-class 2), and advertisements (short video clips, service-class 3). Requests for movies are processed with a conversion rate of either 40 or 30 frames/sec, while requests for video clips are processed with a conversion rate of either 20 or 10 frames/sec, depending on the current CPU status, as Figure 2.21 shows. In Figure 2.21, the CPU together with the CAC is equivalent to a link of capacity $C = 6$ b.u., considering that 1 b.u.= 10 frames/sec. Requests for advertisements are processed with a fixed conversion rate of 10 frames/sec. In order to

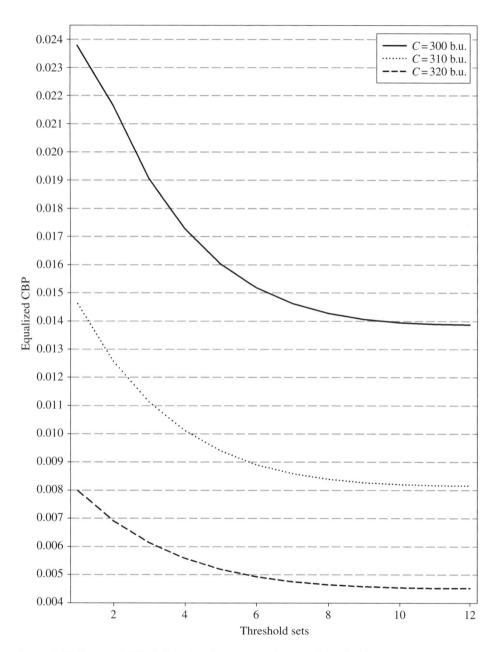

Figure 2.19 Equalized CBP of all service-classes versus the sets of thresholds (MTM/BR) (Example 2.16).

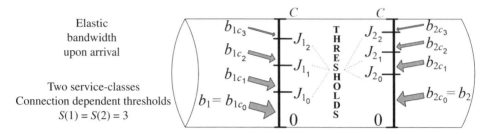

Figure 2.20 The CDTM principle of operation.

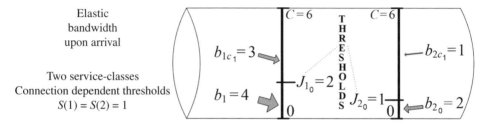

Figure 2.21 The service system (Example 2.17).

determine the percentage of denied conversion requests per service-class, we apply the CDTM with the following traffic and bandwidth requirements for each service-class: $(\lambda_1, \mu_1^{-1}, b_1) = (0.01, 100, 4)$, $(\lambda_2, \mu_2^{-1}, b_2) = (0.05, 20, 2)$, and $(\lambda_3, \mu_3^{-1}, b_3) = (1, 1, 1)$, respectively. Furthermore, $b_{1c_1} = 3$ b.u., $\mu_{1c_1}^{-1} = 133.333$, $b_{2c_1} = 1$, and $\mu_{2c_1}^{-1} = 40$, so that $b_1\mu_1^{-1} = b_{1c_1}\mu_{1c_1}^{-1}$ and $b_2\mu_2^{-1} = b_{2c_1}\mu_{2c_1}^{-1}$.

2.9.2 The Analytical Model

2.9.2.1 Steady State Probabilities
Similar to the MTM, the CDTM has no PFS. To describe the CDTM in steady state, the following LB equations are assumed:

$$\alpha_k b_k q(j - b_k) = y_k(j) b_k q(j)$$

(for $j \le J_{k_0} + b_k$ when $b_{kc_s} > 0$), or (for $j = 1, \dots, C$ when $b_{kc_s} = 0$).

(2.63)

$$\alpha_{kc_s} b_{kc_s} q(j - b_{kc_s}) = y_{kc_s}(j) b_{kc_s} q(j)$$

for $J_{k_s} + b_{kc_s} \ge j > J_{k_{s-1}} + b_{kc_s}$

(2.64)

where $y_{kc_s}(j)$ denotes the mean number of service-class k calls, with b_{kc_s}, in state j.

Formulas (2.63) and (2.64) are graphically presented in Figure 2.22.

Similar to the analysis of the MTM and based on (2.63) and (2.64), we have the following recursive formula for the calculation of $q(j)$ [4]:

$$q(j) = \begin{cases} 1, & \text{if } j = 0 \\ \dfrac{1}{j}\left(\displaystyle\sum_{k=1}^{K} \alpha_k b_k \delta_k(j) q(j - b_k) + \sum_{k=1}^{K} \sum_{s=1}^{S(k)} \alpha_{kc_s} b_{kc_s} \delta_{kc_s}(j) q(j - b_{kc_s}) \right) \\ & j = 1, \dots, C \\ 0, & \text{otherwise} \end{cases}$$

(2.65)

Figure 2.22 Graphical representation of the LB equations (2.63) (left) and (2.64) (right).

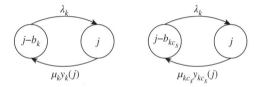

where
$$\delta_k(j) = \begin{cases} 1 & \text{(if } 1 \le j \le J_{k_0} + b_k \text{ and } b_{kc_s} > 0) \text{ or (if } 1 \le j \le C \text{ and } b_{kc_s} = 0) \\ 0 & \text{otherwise} \end{cases}$$

$$\delta_{kc_s}(j) = \begin{cases} 1 & \text{if } J_{k_s} + b_{kc_s} \ge j > J_{k_{s-1}} + b_{kc_s} \text{ and } b_{kc_s} > 0 \\ 0 & \text{otherwise} \end{cases} \quad \text{and } \alpha_{kc_s} = \lambda_k \mu_{kc_s}^{-1}.$$

As a summary, in order to derive (2.65), the following assumptions (approximations) are necessary:

(i) The assumption that the LB equations (2.63) and (2.64) do exist. This is the first source of error in (2.65).

(ii) $y_{kc_s}(j)$ is assumed negligible (i.e., zero) outside $J_{k_s} + b_{kc_s} \ge j > J_{k_{s-1}} + b_{kc_s}$. This assumption is the migration approximation, and we name the state space in which $y_{kc_s}(j) = 0$, the migration space ($j \le J_{k_{s-1}} + b_{kc_s}$ or $j > J_{k_s} + b_{kc_s}$). Let us recall that in the migration space, calls accepted in the system with other than the maximum bandwidth requirement are negligible. This assumption is the second source of error in (2.65) and is represented by the variable $\delta_{kc_s}(j)$.

(iii) $y_k(j)$ is assumed negligible (i.e., zero), if $j > J_{k_0} + b_k$ and $b_{kc_s} > 0$. This is the upward migration approximation, and we name the state space in which $y_k(j) = 0$, the upward migration space. Let us recall that in the upward migration space, calls accepted in the system with their maximum bandwidth are negligible. This assumption is the third source of error in (2.65) and is represented by the variable $\delta_k(j)$.

Note that in both (ii) and (iii), the values of $y_{kc_s}(j)$ and $y_k(j)$ may not be negligible in the corresponding migration and upward migration spaces, respectively (see Example 2.18). The determination of these values can improve the accuracy of the CDTM, compared to simulation, but is beyond the scope of this book. The reader may refer to [7, 8].

Example 2.18 Consider again Example 2.17 ($C = 6, K = 3, b_1 = 4, b_{1c_1} = 3, b_2 = 2, b_{2c_1} = 1, b_3 = 1, J_{1_0} = 2, J_{2_0} = 1$). Calls of service-class 1 behave as in the SRM due to the associated threshold parameter $J_{1_0} = 2$ ($J_{1_0} = C - b_1 \Rightarrow$ SRM). Calls of service-class 2 behave as in the STM due to the associated threshold parameter $J_{2_0} = 1$. A migration space exists for calls of service-class 1, while both migration and upward migration spaces exist for calls of service-class 2. More precisely:

- $y_{1c_1}(j) = 0$ for $j \le J_{1_0} + b_{1c_1} = 5$ (migration space of service-class 1)
- $y_2(j) = 0$ for $j > J_{2_0} + b_2 = 3$ (upward migration space of service-class 2)
- $y_{2c_1}(j) = 0$ for $j \le J_{2_0} + b_{2c_1} = 2$ (migration space of service-class 2).

In reality, however, the values of $y_1(j), y_{1c_1}(j)$ and $y_{2c_1}(j)$ may not be negligible. To illustrate this statement as well as the migration and upward migration spaces for Example 2.17, we present in Figure 2.23 an excerpt from the state transition diagram. In Figure 2.23, we give only the following specific state transitions. Assume that the system

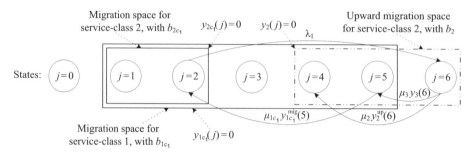

Figure 2.23 Migration and upward migration spaces (Example 2.18).

is in state $j = 2$, servicing a call of service-class 2 with bandwidth $b_2 = 2$, when a new call of service-class 1 arrives. This call is accepted with its initial bandwidth ($b_1 = 4$) and the system passes to state $j = 6$, transferring to that state the call of service-class 2 which is still in service. It is therefore apparent to expect that the average number of service-class 2 calls in state $j = 6$ (which belongs to the upward migration space of service-class 2), denoted as $y_2^{up}(6)$, will not be zero. On the other hand, if the system is in state $j = 6$ and a call of service-class 3 (with $b_3 = 1$) leaves the system, then the system passes to state $j = 5$ and the population of service-class 1 calls with $b_{1c_1} = 3$ (if any) is transferred to $j = 5$. Thus, we also expect that the average number of service-class 1 calls with b_{1c_1} in state $j = 5$ (which belongs to the migration space of service-class 1), denoted as $y_{1c_1}^{mig}(5)$, will not be zero.

2.9.2.2 CBP, Utilization, and Mean Number of In-service Calls
Based on (2.65), we can determine the following performance measures:

- The CBP of service-class k calls with $b_{kc_{S(k)}}$ b.u., $B_{kc_{S(k)}}$, via:

$$B_{kc_{S(k)}} = \sum_{j=C-b_{kc_{S(k)}}+1}^{C} G^{-1}q(j) \tag{2.66}$$

  where $G = \sum_{j=0}^{C} q(j)$ is the normalization constant.
- The CBP of service-class k calls with b_k b.u., B_k, via (1.66).
- The conditional CBP of service-class k calls with $b_{kc_{S(k)}}$ given that $j > J_{k_{S(k)-1}}$, $B^*_{kc_{S(k)}}$, via:

$$B^*_{kc_{S(k)}} = \frac{\sum_{j=C-b_{kc_{S(k)}}+1}^{C} q(j)}{\sum_{j=J_{k_{S(k)-1}+1}}^{C} q(j)} \tag{2.67}$$

- The link utilization, U, via (1.54).
- The mean number of service-class k calls with b_k b.u. in state j, $y_k(j)$, via:

$$y_k(j) = \frac{\alpha_k \delta_k(j)q(j-b_k)}{q(j)}, \quad q(j) > 0 \tag{2.68}$$

where $\delta_k(j) = \begin{cases} 1 & \text{(if } 1 \leq j \leq J_{k_0} + b_k \text{ and } b_{kc_s} > 0) \text{ or (if } 1 \leq j \leq C \text{ and } b_{kc_s} = 0) \\ 0 & \text{otherwise} \end{cases}$

- The mean number of service-class k calls with b_{kc_s} b.u. in state j, $y_{kc_s}(j)$, via:

$$y_{kc_s}(j) = \frac{\alpha_{kc_s}\delta_{kc_s}(j)q(j - b_{kc_s})}{q(j)}, \quad q(j) > 0 \tag{2.69}$$

- The mean number of in-service calls of service-class k accepted in the system with $b_k, \bar{n}_k$, via (2.16).
- The mean number of in-service calls of service-class k accepted in the system with $b_{kc_s}, \bar{n}_{kc_s}$, via (2.56).

Example 2.19 Consider a link of capacity $C = 580$ b.u. in which calls of four service-classes are accommodated. Calls of service-classes 2, 3, and 4 can reduce their bandwidth requirements one, two, and three times, respectively. The traffic and bandwidth requirements of all service-classes are the following:

$\lambda = (20, 12, 28, 6)$, $\mu^{-1} = (1, 1, 1, 1)$, $\mathbf{b} = (1, 6, 12, 20)$, $\mathbf{b}_{2c} = 4$, $\mathbf{b}_{3c} = (8, 4)$, $\mathbf{b}_{4c} = (16, 12, 8)$, $\mu_{2c}^{-1} = 1.5$, $\mu_{3c}^{-1} = (1.5, 3)$, and $\mu_{4c}^{-1} = (1.25, 1.667, 2.5)$,

where $\mathbf{b}_{kc}$ and μ_{kc}^{-1} are the vectors of the reduced bandwidth and increased service-time of service-class k, respectively.

Use the following three sets of threshold parameters for service-classes 2, 3, and 4:

Set 1: $J_{2_0} = 574$ $J_{3_0} = 568$ $J_{3_1} = 572$ $J_{4_0} = 560$ $J_{4_1} = 564$ $J_{4_2} = 568$

Set 2: $J_{2_0} = 574$ $J_{3_0} = 568$ $J_{3_1} = 572$ $J_{4_0} = 500$ $J_{4_1} = 504$ $J_{4_2} = 508$

Set 3: $J_{2_0} = 540$ $J_{3_0} = 520$ $J_{3_1} = 524$ $J_{4_0} = 500$ $J_{4_1} = 504$ $J_{4_2} = 508$

By using Set 1, service-classes 2, 3, and 4 behave according to the MRM. By using Set 2, service-classes 2 and 3 behave according to the MRM, while service-class 4 behaves according to the CDTM. By using Set 3, all service-classes behave as in the CDTM. Provide CBP results of all service-classes and compare them to the corresponding simulation results. Comment on the results.

Table 2.7 Analytical and simulation CBP results for Set 1 (Example 2.19).

	Analytical CBP (%)				Simulation CBP (%)			
P	B_1	B_{2c}	B_{3c_2}	B_{4c_3}	B_1	B_{2c}	B_{3c_2}	B_{4c_3}
1	1.89	7.43	7.43	9.98	1.89 ± 0.06	6.73 ± 0.17	6.79 ± 0.15	9.03 ± 0.22
2	2.41	9.35	9.35	12.54	2.47 ± 0.07	8.63 ± 0.11	8.67 ± 0.14	11.62 ± 0.19
3	2.98	11.40	11.40	15.28	3.06 ± 0.07	10.68 ± 0.27	10.69 ± 0.24	14.53 ± 0.36
4	3.58	13.54	13.54	18.12	3.73 ± 0.07	12.78 ± 0.16	12.75 ± 0.18	17.32 ± 0.33
5	4.21	15.74	15.74	21.03	4.37 ± 0.07	14.94 ± 0.18	14.89 ± 0.19	20.22 ± 0.25
6	4.86	17.96	17.96	23.95	5.06 ± 0.07	17.08 ± 0.22	17.05 ± 0.18	23.36 ± 0.33
7	5.52	20.16	20.16	26.85	5.71 ± 0.08	19.40 ± 0.25	19.32 ± 0.31	26.38 ± 0.42

Table 2.8 Analytical and simulation CBP results for Set 2 (Example 2.19).

	Analytical CBP (%)				Simulation CBP (%)			
P	B_1	B_{2c}	B_{3c_2}	B_{4c_3}	B_1	B_{2c}	B_{3c_2}	B_{4c_3}
1	1.68	6.53	6.53	9.49	1.56 ± 0.007	5.69 ± 0.01	5.70 ± 0.006	7.90 ± 0.04
2	2.19	8.42	8.42	12.17	2.13 ± 0.01	7.62 ± 0.03	7.62 ± 0.03	10.68 ± 0.04
3	2.76	10.47	10.47	15.07	2.75 ± 0.02	9.70 ± 0.04	9.72 ± 0.03	13.68 ± 0.06
4	3.38	12.63	12.63	18.10	3.44 ± 0.02	11.95 ± 0.03	11.96 ± 0.03	16.91 ± 0.02
5	4.03	14.86	14.86	21.20	4.14 ± 0.02	14.23 ± 0.04	14.23 ± 0.03	20.20 ± 0.05
6	4.70	17.12	17.12	24.31	4.90 ± 0.02	16.56 ± 0.05	16.55 ± 0.03	23.47 ± 0.06
7	5.39	19.37	19.37	27.39	5.64 ± 0.01	18.85 ± 0.04	18.86 ± 0.04	26.79 ± 0.07

Table 2.9 Analytical and simulation CBP results for Set 3 (Example 2.19).

	Analytical CBP (%)				Simulation CBP (%)			
P	B_1	B_{2c}	B_{3c_2}	B_{4c_3}	B_1	B_{2c}	B_{3c_2}	B_{4c_3}
1	0.95	4.01	4.01	8.21	0.51 ± 0.05	2.15 ± 0.13	2.12 ± 0.12	4.28 ± 0.24
2	1.35	5.70	5.70	11.47	1.00 ± 0.05	4.11 ± 0.15	4.10 ± 0.14	8.15 ± 0.34
3	1.82	7.66	7.66	15.15	1.61 ± 0.07	6.41 ± 0.24	6.47 ± 0.17	12.64 ± 0.40
4	2.35	9.80	9.80	19.07	2.23 ± 0.04	8.79 ± 0.16	8.87 ± 0.18	17.34 ± 0.21
5	2.91	12.06	12.06	23.11	2.90 ± 0.07	11.49 ± 0.18	11.42 ± 0.17	21.71 ± 0.42
6	3.50	14.39	14.39	27.14	3.42 ± 0.06	13.78 ± 0.21	13.73 ± 0.22	26.00 ± 0.46
7	4.12	16.73	16.73	31.08	4.19 ± 0.10	16.18 ± 0.24	16.13 ± 0.27	30.34 ± 0.51

In Tables 2.7–2.9 we present the analytical and the simulation CBP results for Sets 1–3, respectively, and for seven values of $\lambda = (\lambda_1, \lambda_2, \lambda_3, \lambda_4)$. Needless to say that the CBP of service-classes 2, 3, and 4 are determined based on their last bandwidth requirement. Simulation results are mean values of 12 runs with 95% confidence interval.

Each point P in the first column of Tables 2.7–2.9 corresponds to a vector λ. Point P = 1 corresponds to $\lambda = (20, 12, 28, 6)$. In the successive points the values of λ_1 and λ_2 are increased by 5 and 3, respectively, while λ_3 and λ_4 remain constant. That is, point P = 2 corresponds to $\lambda = (25, 15, 28, 6)$ and point P = 7 to $\lambda = (50, 30, 28, 6)$. The analytical CBP results of service-classes 2 and 3 coincide since both service-classes have the same last bandwidth requirement (i.e., 4). This is validated from the simulation results. Based on Tables 2.7–2.9, we see that:

(i) Set 3 reduces the CBP of service-classes 1, 2, and 3 more than the other two sets. On the contrary, Set 3 results in the CBP increase of service-class 4. This is expected since calls of service-classes 2 and 3 reduce their bandwidth faster by using Set 3. In addition, the arrival rate of service-classes 1 and 2 increases, a fact that also affects negatively the CBP of service-class 4.

(ii) The analytical results of Set 1 are closer to simulation results, compared to the corresponding results of Sets 2 or 3, especially as the offered traffic load increases. This is because in Set 1, calls of service-classes 2, 3, and 4 behave as in the MRM, so only the LB and the migration approximation add error in the analytical results. In Set 2, service-class 4 behaves as in the CDTM, so an upward migration approximation error is added to the analytical results. Finally, in Set 3 calls of service-classes 2, 3, and 4 behave as in the CDTM, a fact that increases the error introduced in the model.

2.10 The Connection Dependent Threshold Model under the BR Policy

2.10.1 The Service System

In the *CDTM under the BR policy (CDTM/BR)*, t_k b.u. are reserved to benefit calls of all other service-classes apart from service-class k. The application of the BR policy in the CDTM is similar to that of the MTM/BR.

2.10.2 The Analytical Model

2.10.2.1 Link Occupancy Distribution

Similar to the MTM/BR, we adopt the Roberts method for the calculation of $q(j)$ in the CDTM/BR. Based on the Roberts method, (2.65) takes the form [4]:

$$q(j) = \begin{cases} 1, & \text{if } j = 0 \\ \dfrac{1}{j}\left(\displaystyle\sum_{k=1}^{K} \alpha_k D_k(j - b_k)\delta_k(j)q(j - b_k)\right) + \\ \dfrac{1}{j}\left(\displaystyle\sum_{k=1}^{K}\sum_{s=1}^{S(k)} \alpha_{kc_s} D_{kc_s}(j - b_{kc_s})\delta_{kc_s}(j)q(j - b_{kc_s})\right) & j = 1, ..., C \\ 0, & \text{otherwise} \end{cases} \tag{2.70}$$

where $\delta_k(j) = \begin{cases} 1 & (\text{if } 1 \le j \le J_{k_0} + b_k \text{ and } b_{kc_s} > 0) \text{ or } (\text{if } 1 \le j \le C \text{ and } b_{kc_s} = 0) \\ 0 & \text{otherwise} \end{cases}$

$\delta_{kc_s}(j) = \begin{cases} 1 & \text{if } J_{k_s} + b_{kc_s} \ge j > J_{k_{s-1}} + b_{kc_s} \text{ and } b_{kc_s} > 0 \\ 0 & \text{otherwise} \end{cases}$ $\quad D_{kc_s}(j - b_{kc_s}) = \begin{cases} b_{kc_s} & \text{for } j \le C - t_k \\ 0 & \text{for } j > C - t_k \end{cases}$

and $\alpha_{kc_s} = \lambda_k \mu_{kc_s}^{-1}$.

2.10.2.2 CBP, Utilization, and Mean Number of In-service Calls

Based on (2.70), we can determine the following performance measures:

- The CBP of service-class k calls with $b_{kc_{S(k)}}$ b.u., $B_{kc_{S(k)}}$, as follows [4]:

$$B_{kc_{S(k)}} = \sum_{j=C-b_{kc_{S(k)}}-t_k+1}^{C} G^{-1} q(j) \qquad (2.71)$$

where $G = \sum_{j=0}^{C} q(j)$ is the normalization constant.

- The CBP of service-class k calls with b_k b.u., B_k, via (1.66).
- The conditional CBP of service-class k calls with $b_{kc_{S(k)}}$ given that $j > J_{k_{S(k)-1}}$, $B^*_{kc_{S(k)}}$, via:

$$B^*_{kc_{S(k)}} = \frac{\displaystyle\sum_{j=C-b_{kc_{S(k)}}-t_k+1}^{C} q(j)}{\displaystyle\sum_{j=J_{k_{S(k)-1}}+1}^{C} q(j)} \qquad (2.72)$$

- The link utilization, U, via (1.54).
- The mean number of service-class k calls with b_k b.u. in state j, $y_k(j)$, via:

$$y_k(j) = \begin{cases} \dfrac{\alpha_k \delta_k(j) q(j-b_k)}{q(j)}, & \text{for } j \le C - t_k \\ 0, & \text{for } j > C - t_k \end{cases} \qquad (2.73)$$

where $\delta_k(j) = \begin{cases} 1 \text{ (if } 1 \le j \le J_{k_0} + b_k \text{ and } b_{kc_s} > 0) \text{ or (if } 1 \le j \le C \text{ and } b_{kc_s} = 0) \\ 0 \text{ otherwise.} \end{cases}$

- The mean number of service-class k calls with b_{kc_s} b.u. in state j, $y_{kc_s}(j)$, via:

$$y_{kc_s}(j) = \begin{cases} \dfrac{\alpha_{kc_s} \delta_{kc_s}(j) q(j-b_{kc_s})}{q(j)} & \text{for } j \le C - t_k \\ 0 & \text{for } j > C - t_k \end{cases} \qquad (2.74)$$

where $\delta_{kc_s}(j) = \begin{cases} 1 \text{ if } J_{k_s} + b_{kc_s} \ge j > J_{k_{s-1}} + b_{kc_s} \text{ and } b_{kc_s} > 0 \\ 0 \text{ otherwise} \end{cases}$.

- The mean number of in-service calls of service-class k accepted in the system with b_k, $\bar{n}_k$, via (2.16).
- The mean number of in-service calls of service-class k accepted in the system with b_{kc_s}, $\bar{n}_{kc_s}$, via (2.56).

Example 2.20 Consider four service-classes of Poisson arriving calls with the following traffic characteristics: $(\alpha_1 = 100, b_1 = 1)$, $(\alpha_2 = 12, b_2 = 6)$, $(\alpha_3 = 12, b_3 = 6)$, and $(\alpha_4 = 1, b_3 = 24)$. Calls are accommodated by a link of capacity $C = 300$ b.u. under the BR policy. Calls of service-classes 3 and 4 may reduce their bandwidth, upon their arrival, according to the thresholds of Figure 2.24. Choose the BR parameters so that CBP are equalized among all service-classes. Calculate the equalized CBP and compare them to the corresponding simulation results when the offered traffic-load increases from the initial value to $\alpha_1 = 160$, $\alpha_2 = 19.2$, $\alpha_3 = 19.2$, and $\alpha_4 = 1.6$ in six equal steps.

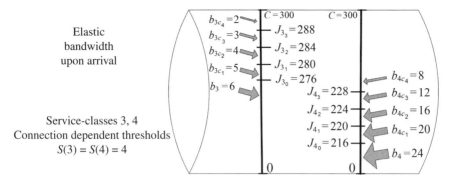

Figure 2.24 Thresholds and bandwidth requirements of service-classes 3 and 4 (Example 2.20).

Table 2.10 Equalized CBP for Example 2.20.

$(\alpha_1, \alpha_2, \alpha_3, \alpha_4)$ (erl)	Equalized CBP (%)	Simulation CBP (%)			
		B_1	B_2	B_{3c_4}	B_{4c_4}
(100, 12.0, 12.0, 1.0)	4.19	3.36 ± 0.11	3.36 ± 0.11	3.35 ± 0.13	3.32 ± 0.20
(110, 13.2, 13.2, 1.1)	8.64	7.61 ± 0.15	7.60 ± 0.15	7.61 ± 0.21	7.63 ± 0.21
(120, 14.4, 14.4, 1.2)	13.85	13.11 ± 0.22	13.11 ± 0.17	13.08 ± 0.23	13.10 ± 0.25
(130, 15.6, 15.6, 1.3)	19.11	18.57 ± 0.26	18.54 ± 0.24	18.56 ± 0.27	18.52 ± 0.22
(140, 16.8, 16.8, 1.4)	24.07	23.68 ± 0.23	23.70 ± 0.22	23.70 ± 0.24	23.71 ± 0.30
(150, 18.0, 18.0, 1.5)	28.62	28.43 ± 0.20	28.43 ± 0.25	28.44 ± 0.21	28.45 ± 0.32
(160, 19.2, 19.2, 1.6)	32.75	32.58 ± 0.31	32.60 ± 0.27	32.57 ± 0.17	32.59 ± 0.40

Since $b_1 = 1, b_2 = 6, b_{3c_4} = 2$, and $b_{4c_4} = 8$ b.u., we choose the BR parameters that achieve CBP equalization as follows: $t_1 = 7$, $t_2 = 2$, $t_3 = 6$, and $t_4 = 0$. Then, $b_1 + t_1 = b_2 + t_2 = b_{3c_4} + t_3 = b_{4c_4} + t_4 = 8$. Table 2.10 shows the analytical and simulation CBPs for the seven different sets of offered traffic-load. Simulation CBP results are very close to the analytical equalized CBP results and validate the CTDM.

2.11 Applications

We concentrate only on the CDTM since it comprises the retry and threshold models. The initial motivation for the CDTM was the available bit rate (ABR) service of asynchronous transfer mode (ATM) networks. The ABR service is a purely elastic service in which the notion of equivalent bandwidth is not well applicable (i.e., the ABR service cannot be considered a stream service having its average bandwidth per call, as constant rate). Therefore, a different model to the EMLM is needed, and this is the CDTM because it sufficiently models an elastic call at its set-up phase (but not during the entire call duration) by adequately setting the threshold parameters. Thus, the CDTM is applicable to any elastic service at the call set-up phase, as long as it is not a bandwidth hungry application wasting all the available bandwidth. For this reason, a threshold scheme must be applied (e.g., Figure 2.20). The logic behind the threshold scheme is that even if the available bandwidth of a link is large enough, a CAC does not always waste it on one call only, but saves a part of it for sharing with the next calls.

The minimum and the maximum bandwidth requirements of an elastic call are important CDTM parameters for the CBP calculation no matter what the thresholds are. The minimum bandwidth requirement is critical for the CBP value. If the minimum required bandwidth is zero, an elastic call should wait for any available bandwidth to start servicing. If the network (CAC) ignores the details of bandwidth requirements (i.e., the threshold scheme) of an elastic call, the assigned bandwidth will not meet the real needs of the call and the CBP calculation will not be accurate. Suppose, for instance, that an elastic call has the following thresholds scheme in a transmission link with bandwidth capacity of 19.2 Mbps: maximum rate of 1.536 Mbps for available link bandwidth at least 6.4 Mbps (first threshold at $19.2 - 6.4 = 12.8$ Mbps), rate of 768 kbps for available link bandwidth at least 3.2 Mbps at least (second threshold at $19.2 - 3.2 = 16.0$ Mbps), and minimum rate of 384 kbps for available link bandwidth less than 3.2 Mbps (third threshold at 19.2 Mbps, or at $19.2 - 0.384 = 18.816$ Mbps). Assume that the CAC knows only the minimum and maximum resource requirements of this elastic call, and offers to it (a) 700 kbps or (b) 1.536 Mbps when the available bandwidth is 4.0 Mbps at least in both cases. In the first case, the holding time will be estimated incorrectly (by taking into account 768 kbps instead of 700 kbps), while in the second case, although the holding time will be estimated correctly, the threshold scheme has been violated, therefore the CBP through the CDTM cannot be accurate. As far as the number of thresholds between the minimum and the maximum bandwidth requirements is concerned, several values exist since bandwidth is quantized and provided as a group of b.u. (trunks). So, in a realistic network environment the number of thresholds is manageable.

In what follows, we concentrate on the applicability of the CDTM to WCDMA networks. We have skipped straightforward applications, albeit some of them are very interesting, such as the application of the CDTM on smart grid, for a fine control of energy consumption [9].

Applicability of the CDTM to WCDMA Networks

The CDTM can be applied to WCDMA networks (in the uplink) in a similar way to the EMLM. A single BS controlling a cell can be modeled as a system of certain bandwidth capacity. The b.u. can be an equivalent bandwidth defined by the load factor introduced, for instance, by a lower rate service-class (e.g., voice). The load factor is determined by the signal-to-noise ratio (SNR), data rate, and activity factor (probability that a call is active – transmits) of the associated service-class. As far as the inter-cell interference is concerned, it is assumed log-normally distributed[1] and independent of the cell load. A call is accepted for service as long as there are enough resources available in the cell. The CAC policy is based on the estimation of the increase in the total interference (intra- and inter-cell interference plus thermal noise) caused by the acceptance of new calls. After call acceptance, the SNR of all in-service calls deteriorates; because of

---

1 The logarithm of a lognormal random variable is normally distributed.

this, WCDMA systems usually have no hard limits on call capacity. A call should not be accepted if it increases the noise of all in-service calls above a tolerable level. Poisson arriving calls to a cell may have several contingency resource/QoS requirements.

Let us consider that the QoS offered to each service-class k ($k = 1, \ldots, K$) belongs to one out of $S(k) + 1$ alternative QoS levels, which depend on the occupied cell resources. In what follows, a service-class k call of QoS level l ($l = 0, \ldots, S(k)$) is referred to as service-class (k, l) call. A service-class (k, l) call is characterized by the following QoS parameters: (i) $TR_{k,l}$, transmission bit rate, (ii) $\mu_{k,l}^{-1}$, mean service time (exponentially distributed), and (iii) $(E_b/N_0)_{k,l}$, BER parameter.

The application of the CDTM for the call-level performance evaluation of WCDMA networks is necessary when assuming that a WCDMA cell accommodates not only stream service-classes but also elastic service-classes, which are associated with individual sets of thresholds (indicating the occupied cell resources). A variation of an elastic service-class is an adaptive service-class, in which calls may reduce their resources/bandwidth, but their service time is kept fixed. We can therefore consider three types of service-classes:

- *Stream type*: service-classes that have only one QoS level ($S(k) = 0$).
- *Elastic type*: service-classes that have more than one QoS level ($S(k) > 0$) and the call's mean service time strongly depends on the QoS level (it holds: $\mu_{k,S(k)}^{-1} > \ldots > \mu_{k,l}^{-1} > \ldots > \mu_{k,1}^{-1} > \mu_{k,0}^{-1}$).
- *Adaptive type*: service-classes that have more than one QoS level ($S(k) > 0$) and the call's mean service time is the same for all QoS levels (it holds: $\mu_{k,S(k)}^{-1} = \ldots = \mu_{k,l}^{-1} = \ldots = \mu_{k,1}^{-1} = \mu_{k,0}^{-1}$).

Upon their arrival, elastic or adaptive calls select one resource requirement according to an associated threshold scheme; a resource requirement is not altered during the service-time. For example, a QoS level can be assigned to an elastic service-class k call at the arrival time and is based on the occupied system resources (cell load c), which is indicated through thresholds. The thresholds of an elastic service-class k are denoted by $T_{k,l}$ ($l = 0, \ldots, S(k)$). The QoS level assignment is performed as follows. If $c \leq T_{k,0}$, then the elastic call is assigned the first QoS level ($l = 0$) and occupies $LF_{k,0}$ system resources for an exponentially distributed service time with mean $\mu_{k,0}^{-1}$. The symbol LF comes from the load factor (see (2.78)). If $T_{k,0} < c \leq T_{k,1}$, then the call is assigned to the second QoS level and occupies $LF_{k,1}$ resources for an exponentially distributed service-time with mean $\mu_{k,1}^{-1}$, and so on. Finally, if $T_{k,S(k)-1} < c \leq c_{\max} \equiv T_{k,S(k)}$, then the call is assigned to the $(1 + S(k))$th QoS level and occupies LF_{k,S_k} resources for an exponentially distributed service time with mean $\mu_{k,S(k)}^{-1}$. We assume that an elastic call has a certain amount of data to transmit. Therefore, a call's service time should be conversely proportional to the allocated resources. For this reason, the mean call service times, $\mu_{k,l}^{-1}$, are chosen so that the product $\mu_{k,l}^{-1} \cdot LF_{k,l}$ remains constant for every QoS level l. As far as the offered traffic-load of service-class (k, l) calls is concerned, it is defined as $\alpha_{k,l} = \lambda_k \mu_{k,l}^{-1}$.

Interference and Call Admission Control We assume perfect power control, i.e., at the BS, the same amount of power, $W_{k,l}$, is received from each service-class (k, l) call. Since in WCDMA systems all users transmit within the same frequency band, a single user sees the signals generated by all other users as interference. Intra-cell interference, I_{intra}, is caused by users of the cell and inter-cell interference, I_{inter}, is caused by users of the neighbouring cells. An amount of power I_N is due to thermal noise in the cell and corresponds to the intra-cell interference when the cell is empty.

The CAC is performed by measuring the noise rise, NR, which is defined as the ratio of the total received power at the BS, I_{total}, to the thermal noise power, I_N:

$$NR = \frac{I_{total}}{I_N} = \frac{I_{intra} + I_{inter} + I_N}{I_N} \tag{2.75}$$

When a new call arrives, the CAC estimates the noise rise and if it exceeds a maximum value, NR_{max}, the new call is blocked and lost.

Load factor and cell load The cell load, c, is defined as the ratio of the received power from all active users to the total received power:

$$c = \frac{I_{intra} + I_{inter}}{I_{intra} + I_{inter} + I_N} < 1 \tag{2.76}$$

From (2.75) and (2.76), the relation between the noise rise and the cell load is:

$$NR = \frac{1}{1-c} \quad \Longleftrightarrow \quad c = \frac{NR - 1}{NR} \tag{2.77}$$

The maximum value of the cell load, c_{max}, is the cell load which corresponds to the maximum noise rise, NR_{max}[2]: $c_{max} = (NR_{max} - 1)/NR_{max}$.

The resource/bandwidth requirement of a service-class (k, l) call is expressed by the load factor, $LF_{k,l}$ [10]:

$$LF_{k,l} = \frac{(E_b/N_0)_{k,l}\, TR_{k,l}}{W + (E_b/N_0)_{k,l}\, TR_{k,l}} \tag{2.78}$$

where W is the chip rate of the WCDMA carrier.

The cell load c can be written as the sum of the intra-cell load, c_{intra} (cell load derived from the active users of the reference cell), and the inter-cell load, c_{inter} (cell load derived from the active users of the neighbouring cells), i.e., $c = c_{intra} + c_{inter}$. The values of c_{intra} and c_{inter} are given by (2.79) and (2.80), respectively:

$$c_{intra} = \sum_{k=1}^{K} \sum_{l=0}^{S(k)} m_{k,l} LF_{k,l} \tag{2.79}$$

where $m_{k,l}$ is the number of active users of service-class (k, l), while

$$c_{inter} = (1 - c_{max}) \frac{I_{inter}}{I_N} \tag{2.80}$$

For a new service-class (k, l) call acceptance, the following condition must hold in the BS:

$$c + LF_{k,l} \le c_{max} \tag{2.81}$$

That is, an arriving call with resource requirement $LF_{k,l}$ is accepted in the cell if and only if, after its acceptance, the cell load remains below c_{max}.

---

2 A typical value of $c_{max} = 0.8$, which is considered as the shared system resource.

Local Blocking Probabilities   Due to (2.81), the probability that a new service-class (k, l) call is blocked when arriving at an instant with intra-cell load, c_{intra}, is called the local blocking probability (LBP), $\beta_{k,l}(c_{intra})$, and can be calculated by (based on (2.78)–(2.80)):

$$\beta_{k,l}(c_{intra}) = Prob \left[c_{intra} + c_{inter} + LF_{k,l} > c_{max} \right] \tag{2.82}$$

In (2.80), the I_{inter} can be modelled as a lognormal random variable (with parameters mean μ_I and variance σ_I), which is independent of the intra-cell interference. Hence, the mean, $E[I_{inter}]$, and the variance, $Var[I_{inter}]$, of I_{inter} are calculated by:

$$E[I_{inter}] = e^{\mu_I + \frac{\sigma_I^2}{2}} \tag{2.83}$$

$$Var[I_{inter}] = (e^{\sigma_I^2} - 1)e^{2\mu_I + \sigma_I^2} \tag{2.84}$$

Consequently, because of (2.80), the inter-cell load, c_{inter}, will also be a lognormal random variable. Its mean, $E[c_{inter}]$, and variance, $Var[c_{inter}]$, are calculated as follows:

$$E[c_{inter}] = e^{\mu_c + \frac{\sigma_c^2}{2}} = \frac{1 - c_{max}}{I_N} E[I_{inter}] \tag{2.85}$$

$$Var[c_{inter}] = (e^{\sigma_c^2} - 1)e^{2\mu_c + \sigma_c^2} = \left(\frac{1 - c_{max}}{I_N} \right) Var[I_{inter}] \tag{2.86}$$

where the parameters μ_c and σ_c can be determined by solving (2.85) and (2.86):

$$\mu_c = \ln(E[I_{inter}]) - \frac{\ln(1 + CV[I_{inter}]^2)}{2} + \ln(1 - c_{max}) - \ln(I_N) \tag{2.87}$$

$$\sigma_c = \sqrt{\ln(1 + CV[I_{inter}]^2)} \tag{2.88}$$

where $CV[I_{inter}] = \frac{\sqrt{Var[I_{inter}]}}{E[I_{inter}]}$ is the coefficient of variation.

Thus, (2.82) can be rewritten as:

$$1 - \beta_{k,l}(c_{intra}) = Prob \left[c_{inter} \leq c_{max} - c_{intra} - LF_{k,l} \right] \tag{2.89}$$

The RHS of (2.89), is the cumulative distribution function (CDF) of c_{inter}. It is denoted by $F_c(x) = P(c_{inter} \leq x)$ and can be calculated from:

$$F_c(x) = \frac{1}{2} \left[1 + erf \left(\frac{\ln x - \mu_c}{\sigma_c \sqrt{2}} \right) \right] \tag{2.90}$$

where $erf(\cdot)$ is the well-known error function.

Hence, if we substitute $x = c_{max} - c_{intra} - LF_{k,l}$ into (2.90), from (2.89) we can calculate the LBP of service-class (k, l) calls as follows:

$$\beta_{k,l}(c_{intra}) = \begin{cases} 1 - F_c(x), & x \geq 0 \\ 1, & x < 0 \end{cases} \tag{2.91}$$

Parameters' Discretization   To apply the CDTM in WCDMA systems, parameters' discretization is required. It is achieved by the introduction of a basic cell load unit g (e.g., granularity of $g = 0.005$, used in Example 2.23). The CDTM parameters of system capacity, the total number of occupied b.u. in the system, the assigned number of b.u. to an in-service call, and a bandwidth threshold are obtained by discretizing the cell load, the maximum cell load, the load factor, and the resource threshold, respectively:

$$j = \left\lfloor \frac{c}{g} \right\rfloor, \quad C = \left\lfloor \frac{c_{max}}{g} \right\rfloor, \quad b_{k,l} = \left\lfloor \frac{LF_{k,l}}{g} \right\rfloor, \quad \text{and} \quad J_{k,l} = \left\lfloor \frac{T_{k,l}}{g} \right\rfloor \tag{2.92}$$

Incorporating the User Activity and LBP The user activity is described by the activity factor, v_k, which represents the fraction of the active period of a service-class k call/user over the entire service time ($0 < v_k \leq 1$). In the CDTM, we consider that calls are active during the entire service time and we do not distinguish active users from passive users. However, in WCDMA systems it is essential to consider such a distinction because passive users do not consume any system resources. Hence, a system state j does not represent the total number of occupied b.u. Instead, it represents the total number of b.u. that would be occupied if all (mobile) users were active. Let n denote the total number of occupied b.u. at an instant. In the CDTM, n is always equal to j, while in WCDMA networks we have $0 \leq n \leq j$. When all users are passive, $n = 0$, while $n = j$ when all users are active.

The bandwidth occupancy, $\Lambda(n|j)$, is defined as the conditional probability that n b.u. are occupied in state j and, for user activity v_k, it can be calculated recursively by:

$$\Lambda(n|j) = \sum_{k=1}^{K} \sum_{l=0}^{S_k} P_{k,l}(j)[v_k \Lambda(n - b_{k,l}|j - b_{k,l}) + (1 - v_k)\Lambda(n|j - b_{k,l})] \tag{2.93}$$

where $j = 1, \ldots, j_{max}$ and $n \leq j$, j_{max} is the highest reachable system state, $\Lambda(0|0) = 1$, $\Lambda(n|j) = 0$ for $n > j$, and $P_{k,l}(j)$ is called resource/bandwidth share and denotes the proportion of the total occupied resources, j, from service-class (k, l) calls (see (2.95)).

In WCDMA systems, due to the intra-/inter-cell interference, blocking of a service-class (k, l) call may occur at any state j with a probability $LB_{k,l}(j)$. This probability, called the local blocking factor (LBF), is calculated by summing over n the LBP multiplied by the corresponding bandwidth occupancies:

$$LB_{k,l}(j) = \sum_{n=0}^{j} \beta_{k,l}(n)\Lambda(n|j) \tag{2.94}$$

where for $\beta_{k,l}(n)$ use (2.91) with $x = c_{max} - n - LF_{k,l}$. Note that when $j = 0$, $LB_{k,l}(0) = \beta_{k,l}(0)$ (since in this case $n = 0$ and $\Lambda(0|0) = 1$).

The service-class (k, l) bandwidth share in state j (requiring $b_{k,l}$ b.u.) is derived assuming LB between adjacent systems states, while incorporating the LBF and the parameter delta (indicating the upward migration and migration approximations):

$$P_{k,l}(j) = \frac{\alpha_k(1 - LB_{k,l}(j - b_{k,l}))b_{k,l}\delta_{k,l}(j)q(j - b_{k,l})}{jq(j)} \tag{2.95}$$

where $l = 0, \ldots, S(k)$, while for $l > 0$:

$$\delta_{k,l}(j) = \begin{cases} 1 & \text{if } J_{k,l} + b_{k,l} \geq j > J_{k,l-1} + b_{k,l} \text{ and } b_{k,l} > 0 \\ 0 & \text{otherwise} \end{cases}$$

$$\delta_{k,0}(j) = \begin{cases} 1 & (\text{if } 1 \leq j \leq J_{k,0} + b_{k,0} \text{ and } b_{k,l} > 0, l \neq 0) \text{ or} \\ & (\text{if } 1 \leq j \leq j_{max} \text{ and } b_{k,l} = 0, l \neq 0) \\ 0 & \text{otherwise} \end{cases} \tag{2.96}$$

Figure 2.25 Recurrent determination
of the resource share (Example 2.21).

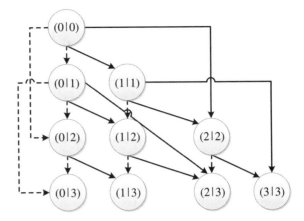

Example 2.21 In Figure 2.25 we show how we can recursively determine the bandwidth occupancy (2.93). Consider a system with $K = 2$ service-classes and a single QoS level per service-class (i.e., $S(k) = 0$, $k = 1, 2$), while $b_1 = 1, b_2 = 2$ b.u. A dashed line shows the arrival of a passive user, while a solid line represents the arrival of an active user. Starting from state (*number of active users | total number of users*) $= (0|0)$, four possibilities exist:

(i) A passive user of service-class 1 is accepted in the system with probability $(1 - v_1)P_1(0)$ and the system passes to state $(0|1)$.
(ii) A passive user of service-class 2 is accepted in the system with probability $(1 - v_2)P_2(0)$ and the system passes to state $(0|2)$.
(iii) An active user of service-class 1 is accepted in the system with probability $v_1 P_1(0)$ and the system passes to state $(1|1)$.
(iv) An active user of service-class 2 is accepted in the system with probability $v_2 P_2(0)$ and the system passes to state $(2|2)$.

Then, $\Lambda(1|2)$ is determined from $\Lambda(0|1)$ and $\Lambda(1|1)$:
$$\Lambda(1|2) = (1 - v_1)P_1(0)\Lambda(0|1) + v_1 P_1(0)\Lambda(1|1).$$

Example 2.22 Thanks to discretization, we can continue presenting a WCDMA cell in terms of the CDTM. Let us consider a link of capacity $C = 5$ b.u. accommodating $K = 3$ service-classes. Calls of service-class 1 require 1 b.u. without any threshold. Service-class 2 has one threshold, $J_{2,1} = 2$, and two contingency bandwidth requirements, $b_{2,0} = 2$ and $b_{2,1} = 1$, while service-class 3 has two thresholds, $J_{3,1} = 2$ and $J_{3,2} = 3$, and three contingency bandwidth requirements, $b_{3,0} = 3, b_{3,1} = 2$, and $b_{3,2} = 1$. In this specific example, a call is blocked and lost whenever the link bandwidth is fully occupied because the minimum bandwidth per call requirement of all three service-classes is 1. If we apply this threshold scheme to a WCDMA system, due to the existence of local blocking, there are no pure blocking and non-blocking states, but blocking of a service-class (k, l) call may occur in any state j with probability $LB_{k,l}(j)$ (LBF). In Figure 2.26 we show the (macro-) state transition diagram of this example for service-class 2. Observe that in the Markov chain of this system, due to the local blocking, the transition rates from lower states to higher are reduced by the factor $1 - LB_{k,l}(j)$. A more important difference is that the system state j can exceed C. The

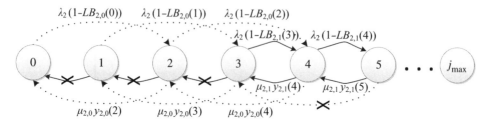

Figure 2.26 Excerpt of the state transition diagram (Example 2.22).

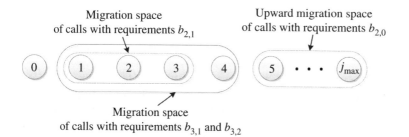

Figure 2.27 Migration and upward migration space (Example 2.22).

maximum value of j is denoted by j_{max} and is the state at which $LB_{k,l}(j)$ approach 1. In other words, the higher states are unreachable due to severe local blocking. This fact shows that WCDMA systems may have no hard limit on the system capacity and therefore we talk about soft capacity. The Markov chain of Figure 2.26 does not have a PFS (all arrows are valid, ignore the Xs on the arrows for the moment) due to the existence of different contingency bandwidth requirements (as in the CDTM) and the local blocking; they both destroy the local balance between adjacent system states.

For LB, the Markov chain must be transformed to a reversible Markov chain (represented in Figure 2.26 when ignoring the arrows bearing an X) by taking into account the migration and upward migration approximation (Figure 2.27).

State Probabilities and CBP The state probabilities are given by:

$$jq(j) = \sum_{k=1}^{K} \sum_{l=0}^{S(k)} \alpha_{k,l}(1 - LB_{k,l}(j - b_{k,l}))b_{k,l}\delta_{k,l}(j)q(j - b_{k,l}) \tag{2.97}$$

for $j = 1, \dots, j_{max}$ and $q(j) = 0$ for $j < 0$, with $\sum_{j=0}^{j_{max}} q(j) = 1$.

The CBP of service-class k can be calculated by adding all the state probabilities multiplied by the corresponding LBFs:

$$B_k = \sum_{j=0}^{j_{max}} q(j) \sum_{l=0}^{S(k)} \gamma_{k,l} LB_{k,l}(j) \tag{2.98}$$

Due to the contingency bandwidth requirements, $b_{k,l}$, we need also to sum over l in specific areas defined by thresholds. This is done with the aid of the parameter gamma:

$$\gamma_{k,0}(j) = \begin{cases} 1, & \text{if } j \le J_{k,0} \\ 0, & \text{otherwise} \end{cases} \qquad \gamma_{k,l}(j) = \begin{cases} 1, & \text{if } J_{k,l} < j \le J_{k,l+1} \\ 0, & \text{otherwise} \end{cases} \tag{2.99}$$

Table 2.11 Various parameters and CBP results of Example 2.23.

	Service-class 1		Service-class 2	
Activity factor	1		0.7	
E_b/N_0	4 dB		3 dB	
Traffic load	4 erl	8 erl	1 erl	2 erl
CBP (EMLM)	0.9052%	5.1663%	1.1131%	6.8848%
CBP (CDTM)	0.9%	4.5441%	1.0978%	5.9980%

Example 2.23   A WCDMA cell of $c_{max} = 0.8$, with $I_N = 3.98 \cdot 10^{-18}$ mW, suffering $E[I_{inter}] = 2 \cdot 10^{-18}$ mW and $CV[I_{inter}] = 1$, supports $K = 2$ elastic service-classes having $S(1) = S(2) = 1$, $T_{1,0} = 0.6$, $T_{2,0} = 0.5$, $(TR_{1,0} = 64, TR_{1,1} = 32, TR_{2,0} = 144, TR_{1,0} = 112)$ kbps, and $(\alpha_1, \alpha_2) = (4, 1)$ or $(8, 2)$ erl. Table 2.11 contains the CBP results.

2.12   Further Reading

Extensions of the retry or thresholds models are categorized in wired [11–18], wireless [19–21], and optical networks [22]. In [11], the threshold models are extended to include BPP traffic. The CBP calculations are based either on recursive formulas or on convolution algorithms. In [12] and [13], the single threshold of the STM is replaced by two thresholds. When a new call finds the occupied link bandwidth above a threshold, it can be accepted in the link with its lower bandwidth requirement (similar to the STM). When the occupied link bandwidth becomes less than the second threshold then an in-service call (accepted with its lower bandwidth requirement) can increase its bandwidth to its peak-bandwidth requirement. In [14] and [15], the CDTM is extended to allow call bandwidth compression/expansion of in-service calls with [15] or without [14] the existence of the BR policy (more on the subject of bandwidth compression/expansion and Poisson arriving calls can be found in Chapters 3 and 4). In [16–18], a variant of the SRM/STM is proposed. Specifically, some service-classes are characterized cooperative and the rest non-cooperative. Users from a cooperative service-class can retry with a certain probability to be connected in the system with reduced bandwidth when blocked with their initial peak-bandwidth and the total occupied bandwidth of the system is below a threshold. This behavior increases the QoS perceived by other users. In [19], the threshold models are extended to include the CBP calculation in the uplink of a UMTS network. To this end, the notion of local (soft) blocking is incorporated in the model. The latter means that a call may be blocked in any state of the system if its acceptance violates the QoS, in terms of noise, of all in-service calls (see also [23–26]). In [20], the threshold models are extended for the call-level analysis of the Iub interface in UMTS networks. In [21], a multi-threshold teletraffic model for heterogeneous CDMA networks is proposed. The model enables QoS differentiation of handover traffic when elastic and adaptive service-classes are present. Furthermore, an applicability framework is proposed that takes into account advances in Cloud-RAN and self-organizing network (SON) technologies. In [22], the CDTM is extended for the calculation of connection failure probabilities (due to unavailability of a wavelength) and

CBP (due to the restricted bandwidth capacity of a wavelength) in hybrid TDM-WDM PONs with DWA.

References

1 J. Kaufman, Blocking in a completely shared resource environment with state dependent resource and residency requirements. *Proceedings of IEEE INFOCOM'92*, Florence, Italy, 4–8 May 1992, pp. 2224–2232.

2 J. Kaufman, Blocking with retrials in a completely shared resource environment. *North-Holland, Performance Evaluation*, 15(2):99–113, June 1992.

3 J. Kaufman, Blocking in a shared resource environment. *IEEE Transactions on Communications*, 29(10):1474–1481, October 1981.

4 I. Moscholios, M. Logothetis and G. Kokkinakis, Connection dependent threshold model: A generalization of the Erlang multiple rate loss model. *Performance Evaluation*, 48(1–4):177–200, May 2002.

5 I. Moscholios, M. Logothetis and T. Liokos, QoS equalization in the connection dependent threshold model. *Proceedings of the Communication Systems, Networks and Digital Signal Processing Conference, CSNDSP 2002*, Staffordshire, UK, 15–17 July 2002, pp. 442–445.

6 SIMSCRIPT III, http://www.simscript.com/.

7 M. Logothetis, I. Moscholios and G. Kokkinakis, Improvement of the connection dependent threshold model with the aid of reverse transition rates. *12th GI/ITG Conference on Measuring, Modelling and Evaluation of Computer and Comummunication Systems (MMB) and 3rd Polish-German Teletraffic Symposium (PGTS), MMB&PGTS 2004*, Dresden, Germany, 12–15 September 2004.

8 M. Logothetis, I. Moscholios and G. Kokkinakis, New connection dependent threshold model – A generalization of the Erlang multirate loss model. *Mediterranean Journal of Electronics and Communications*, 3(4):126–137, October 2007.

9 J. Vardakas, I. Zenginis, and M. Oikonomakou, Peak demand reduction through demand control: A mathematical analysis, *Proceedings of the IEICE ICTF 2016*, Patras, 6–8 July 2016.

10 V. Vassilakis, G. Kallos, I. Moscholios and M. Logothetis, An analytical model for elastic service-classes in W-CDMA networks, in *Heterogenenous Networks, Vol. II - Performance Analysis & Applications*, D.SEA.6.1.6: Part of Final Deliverables of NoE Euro-NGI to EC, River Publishers, pp. 277–299, 2009.

11 M. Glabowski, A. Kaliszan and M. Stasiak, Modeling product-form state dependent systems with BPP traffic. *Performance Evaluation*, 67(3):174–197, March 2010.

12 M. Sobieraj, M. Stasiak, J. Weissenberg and P. Zwierzykowski, Analytical model fo the single threshold mechanism with hysteresis for multi-service networks, *IEICE Transactions on Communications*, E95-B(1):120–132, January 2012.

13 M. Sobieraj, M. Stasiak and P. Zwierzykowski, Model of the threshold mechanism with double hysteresis for multi-service networks, in *Computer Networks, CN 2012*, A. Kwicien, P. Gaj and P. Stera (eds), Communications in Computer and Information Science, Vol. 291, Springer, Berlin, 2012.

14 V. Vassilakis, I. Moscholios and M. Logothetis, Call-level performance modeling of elastic and adaptive service-classes. *Proceedings of the ICC*, Glasgow, UK, June 2007.

15 V. Vassilakis, I. Moscholios and M. Logothetis, The extended connection-dependent threshold model for call-level performance analysis of multi-rate loss systems under the bandwidth reservation policy. *International Journal of Communication Systems*, 25(7):849–873, July 2012.

16 S. Miyata, K. Yamaoka and H. Kinoshita, Optimal threshold characteristics of call admission control by considering cooperative behavior of users (loss model). *Proceedings of the IEEE PACRIM*, Victoria, Canada, August 2013.

17 S. Miyata, K. Yamaoka and H. Kinoshita, Optimal threshold configuration methods for flow admission control with cooperative users. *IEICE Transactions on Communications*, E97-B(12):2706–2719, December 2014.

18 I. Moscholios, M. Logothetis and S. Shioda, Performance evaluation of multirate loss systems supporting cooperative users with a probabilistic behavior. *IEICE Transactions on Communications*, E100-B(10):1778–1788, October 2017.

19 L. Popova and W. Koch, Analytical performance evaluation of mixed services with variable data rates for the uplink of UMTS. *Proceedings of ISWCS'06*, Valencia, Spain, September 2006.

20 D. Parniewicz, M. Stasiak, and P. Zwierzykowski, Multicast connections in mobile networks with embedded threshold mechanism, in *Computer Networks, CN 2011*, A. Kwicien, P. Gaj and P. Stera (eds), Communications in Computer and Information Science, Vol. 160, Springer, Berlin, 2011.

21 V. Vassilakis, I. Moscholios and M. Logothetis, Quality of service differentiation of elastic and adaptive services in CDMA networks: A mathematical modelling approach. *Wireless Networks*, 24(4):1279–1295, May 2018.

22 J. Vardakas, V. Vassilakis and M. Logothetis, Blocking analysis in hybrid TDM-WDM PONs supporting elastic traffic. *Proceedings of AICT*, Athens, Greece, June 2008.

23 D. Staehle and A. Mäder, An analytic approximation of the uplink capacity in a UMTS network with heterogeneous traffic. *Proceedings of the 18th International Teletraffic Congress*, Berlin, September 2003.

24 V. Iversen, V. Benetis, N. Ha, and S. Stepanov, Evaluation of multi-service CDMA networks with soft blocking. *Proceedings of the ITC Specialist Seminar*, pp. 223–227, Antwerp, August/September 2004.

25 V. Iversen, Evaluation of multi-service CDMA networks with soft blocking. *Proceedings of the 3rd Conference on Smart Spaces, ruSMART 2010, and 10th International Conference, NEW2AN 2010*, St. Petersburg, Russia, August 2010.

26 I. Moscholios, G. Kallos, V. Vassilakis, M. Logothetis and M. Koukias, Congestion probabilities in W-CDMA networks supporting calls of finite sources. *Proceedings of HETNETs*, Ilkley, West Yorkshire, UK, November 2013.

3

Multirate Elastic Adaptive Loss Models

We consider multirate loss models of random arriving calls with fixed bandwidth requirements and elastic bandwidth allocation during service. We consider two types of calls, elastic and adaptive. Elastic calls that can reduce their bandwidth, while simultaneously increasing their service time, compose the so-called elastic traffic (e.g., file transfer). Adaptive calls that can tolerate bandwidth compression, but their service time cannot be altered, compose the so-called adaptive traffic (e.g., adaptive video).

3.1 The Elastic Erlang Multirate Loss Model

3.1.1 The Service System

In the *elastic EMLM (E-EMLM)*, we consider a link of capacity C b.u. that accommodates elastic calls of K different service classes. Calls of service class k arrive in the link according to a Poisson process with an arrival rate λ_k and request b_k b.u. (peak-bandwidth requirement). To introduce bandwidth compression, we permit the occupied link bandwidth j to virtually exceed C up to a limit of T b.u. Suppose that a new call of service class k arrives in the link while the link is in (macro-) state j. Then, for call admission, we consider three cases [1]:

(i) If $j + b_k \leq C$, no bandwidth compression takes place and the new call is accepted in the system with its peak-bandwidth requirement for an exponentially distributed service time with mean μ_k^{-1}. In that case, all in-service calls continue to have their peak-bandwidth requirement.

(ii) If $j + b_k > T$, the call is blocked and lost without further affecting the system.

(iii) If $T \geq j + b_k > C$, the call is accepted in the system by compressing its peak-bandwidth requirement, as well as the assigned bandwidth of all in-service calls (of all service classes). After compression, all calls (both in-service and new) share the capacity C in proportion to their peak bandwidth requirement, while the link operates at its full capacity C. This is in fact the so-called *processor sharing* discipline [2].

Efficient Multirate Teletraffic Loss Models Beyond Erlang, First Edition.
Ioannis D. Moscholios and Michael D. Logothetis.
© 2019 John Wiley & Sons Ltd. Published 2019 by John Wiley & Sons Ltd.
Companion website: www.wiley.com/go/logocode

When $T \geq j + b_k > C$, the compressed bandwidth b'_k of the newly accepted call of service-class k, is given by [1]:

$$b'_k = rb_k = \frac{C}{j + b_k} b_k \qquad (3.1)$$

where $r = \frac{C}{j+b_k}$ denotes the compression factor.

Since $j = \mathbf{nb} = \sum_{k=1}^{K} n_k b_k$, where n_k is the number of in-service calls of service-class k (in the steady state), $\mathbf{n} = (n_1, \dots, n_k, \dots, n_K)$, and $\mathbf{b} = (b_1, \dots, b_k, \dots, b_K)$, the values of r can be expressed by:

$$r \equiv r(\mathbf{n}) = \begin{cases} \dfrac{C}{\mathbf{nb} + b_k} & \text{for } \mathbf{nb} + b_k > C \quad \text{(bandwidth compression)} \\ 1 & \text{for } \mathbf{nb} + b_k \leq C \quad \text{(no bandwidth compression)} \end{cases} \qquad (3.2)$$

To keep constant the product *service time* by *bandwidth per call* (when bandwidth compression occurs), the mean service time of the new service-class k call becomes $(\mu'_k)^{-1}$:

$$\frac{1}{\mu'_k} = \frac{b_k}{b'_k} \frac{1}{\mu_k} = \frac{j + b_k}{C} \frac{1}{\mu_k} \qquad (3.3)$$

The compressed bandwidth of all in-service calls changes to $b'_i = \frac{C}{j+b_i} b_i$ for $i = 1, \dots, K$ and $\sum_{i=1}^{K} n_i b'_i = C$. Similarly, their remaining service time increases by a factor of $\frac{j+b_k}{C}$. The minimum bandwidth given to a service-class k call is:

$$b'_{k,\min} = r_{\min} b_k = \frac{C}{T} b_k \qquad (3.4)$$

where $r_{\min} = C/T$ and is common for all service-classes.

Note that increasing T decreases the $r_{\min}$ and increases the delay (service-time) of service-class k calls (compared to the initial service time μ_k^{-1}). Thus, T should be chosen so that this delay remains within acceptable levels.

When an in-service call, with compressed bandwidth b'_k, completes its service and departs from the system, then the remaining in-service calls expand their bandwidth to b''_i ($i = 1, \dots, K$) in proportion to b_i, as follows:

$$b''_i = \min\left(b_i, \; b'_i + \frac{b_i}{\sum_{k=1}^{K} n_k b_k} b'_k \right) \qquad (3.5)$$

In terms of the system's state-space Ω, the CAC is expressed as follows. A new call of service-class k is accepted in the system if the system is in state $\mathbf{n} \in \Omega_{\{k\}}$ upon a new call arrival, where $\Omega_{\{k\}} = \{\mathbf{n} \in \Omega : \mathbf{nb} \leq T - b_k\}$, $k = 1, \dots, K$. Hence, the CBP of service-class k is determined by the state space $\Omega - \Omega_{\{k\}}$:

$$B_k = \sum_{\mathbf{n} \in \{\Omega - \Omega_{\{k\}}\}} P(\mathbf{n}) \quad \Rightarrow \quad B_k = 1 - \sum_{\mathbf{n} \in \Omega_{\{k\}}} P(\mathbf{n}) \qquad (3.6)$$

Unfortunately, the compression/expansion of bandwidth destroys the LB between adjacent states in the E-EMLM, or, equivalently, it destroys the reversibility of the system's Markov chain, and therefore no PFS exists for the values of $P(\mathbf{n})$ (a fact that makes (3.6) inefficient). To show that the Markov chain of the E-EMLM is not reversible, an efficient way is to apply the so called *Kolmogorov's criterion* [3, 4]: A Markov chain is reversible if and only if the product of transition probabilities along any loop of adjacent states is the same as that for the reversed loop.[1]

Example 3.1 This example illustrates the bandwidth compression/expansion mechanism and shows that the system's Markov chain is not reversible. Consider a link of $C = 3$ b.u. and $T = 5$ b.u. The link accommodates calls of $K = 2$ service-classes whose calls require $b_1 = 1$ and $b_2 = 2$ b.u., respectively. For simplicity assume that $\lambda_1 = \lambda_2 = \mu_1 = \mu_2 = 1.0$.

(a) Draw the complete state transition diagram of the system and determine the values of j and $r(\mathbf{n})$ for each state $\mathbf{n} = (n_1, n_2)$.
(b) Consider state $(1, 1)$ and explain the bandwidth compression mechanism when a call of service-class 2 arrives in the link.
(c) Next, consider state $(1, 2)$ and explain the bandwidth expansion that takes place when a call of service-class 2 departs from the system.
(d) Investigate whether the Markov chain of the system is reversible.
(e) Write the GB equations, and determine the values of $P(\mathbf{n})$ and the exact CBP of both service-classes.

(a) Figure 3.1 shows the state space Ω that consists of 12 permissible states $\mathbf{n} = (n_1, n_2)$ and the complete state transition diagram of the system. In addition, Table 3.1 presents the 12 states together with the values of $r(\mathbf{n})$ and the occupied link bandwidth, $j = n_1 b_1 + n_2 b_2$, before and after bandwidth compression. Note that after compression has been applied, we have $j = C$ (bold values of the fourth column of Table 3.1).

(b) When a new call of service-class 2 arrives in the system while the system is in state $(n_1, n_2) = (1, 1)$ and $j = C = 3$ b.u. then, since $j' = j + b_2 = T = 5$ b.u., the new call is accepted in the system after bandwidth compression to all calls (new and in-service calls). The new state of the system is now $(n_1, n_2) = (1, 2)$. In this state, calls of both service-classes compress their bandwidth (according to (3.4)) to the values:

$$b'_{1,min} = r_{min}b_1 = \tfrac{3}{5}b_1 = 0.6 \text{ b.u.}$$

$$b'_{2,min} = r_{min}b_2 = \tfrac{3}{5}b_2 = 1.2 \text{ b.u.}$$

so that $j = n_1 b'_{1,min} + n_2 b'_{2,min} = 0.6 + 2.4 = 3 = C$. Similarly, the values of μ_1^{-1} and μ_2^{-1} become $\frac{\mu_1^{-1}}{r_{min}}$ and $\frac{\mu_2^{-1}}{r_{min}}$, so that $b_1\mu_1^{-1}$ and $b_2\mu_2^{-1}$ remain constant.

(c) If a call of service-class 2 departs from the system then its assigned bandwidth $b'_{2,min} = 1.2$ b.u. is shared to the remaining calls in proportion to their peak-bandwidth requirement. Thus, in the new state $(n_1, n_2) = (1, 1)$ the call of service-class 1 expands

---

its bandwidth to $b_1' = b_1 = 1$ b.u. and the call of service-class 2 to $b_2' = b_2 = 2$ b.u. Thus, $j = n_1 b_1 + n_2 b_2 = C = 3$ b.u. Furthermore, the service times of both calls are decreased to their initial values $\mu_1^{-1} = \mu_2^{-1} = 1$ time unit.

(d) If we apply the Kolmogorov's criterion (*flow clockwise = flow counter-clockwise*) to the four adjacent states (2, 1), (3, 1), (3, 0), and (2, 0), which form a square (see Figure 3.1), then this criterion does not hold because $\lambda_1 \cdot \mu_2 r(3, 1) \cdot 3\mu_1 \cdot \lambda_2 \neq \mu_2 r(2, 1) \cdot \lambda_1 \cdot \lambda_2 \cdot 3\mu_1 r(3, 1)$. This means that the Markov chain is not reversible. (One may select another set of states, in order to show the violation of Kolmogorov's criterion.)

(e) Based on Figure 3.1, we obtain the following 12 GB equations:

$(0,0):$ $P(1,0) + P(0,1) - 2P(0,0) = 0$

$(0,1):$ $P(0,0) + P(1,1) + 1.5P(0,2) - 3P(0,1) = 0$

$(0,2):$ $0.6P(1,2) + P(0,1) - 2.5P(0,2) = 0$

$(1,0):$ $P(0,0) + 2P(2,0) + P(1,1) - 3P(1,0) = 0$

$(1,1):$ $P(0,1) + 1.5P(2,1) + 1.2P(1,2) + P(1,0) - 4P(1,1) = 0$

$(1,2):$ $P(1,1) + P(0,2) - 1.8P(1,2) = 0$

$(2,0):$ $P(1,0) + 3P(3,0) + 0.75P(2,1) - 4P(2,0) = 0$

$(2,1):$ $P(1,1) + 1.8P(3,1) + P(2,0) - 3.25P(2,1) = 0$

$(3,0):$ $P(2,0) + 3P(4,0) + 0.6P(3,1) - 5P(3,0) = 0$

$(3,1):$ $P(2,1) + P(3,0) - 2.4P(3,1) = 0$

$(4,0):$ $P(3,0) + 3P(5,0) - 4P(4,0) = 0$

$(5,0):$ $P(4,0) - 3P(5,0) = 0$

The solution of this linear system is:

$P(0,0) = 0.1360,$	$P(0,1) = 0.1332,$	$P(0,2) = 0.0829,$	$P(1,0) = 0.1388$
$P(1,1) = 0.1393,$	$P(1,2) = 0.1235,$	$P(2,0) = 0.0705,$	$P(2,1) = 0.0914$
$P(3,0) = 0.0249,$	$P(3,1) = 0.0485,$	$P(4,0) = 0.0083,$	$P(5,0) = 0.0028.$

Then, based on $P(n_1, n_2)$ and (3.6), we determine the exact CBP:

$B_1 = P(1,2) + P(3,1) + P(5,0) = 0.1748$

$B_2 = P(0,2) + P(2,1) + P(4,0) + P(1,2) + P(3,1) + P(5,0) = 0.3574$

To circumvent the non-reversibility problem in the E-EMLM, $r(\mathbf{n})$ are replaced by the state-dependent compression factors per service-class k, $\varphi_k(\mathbf{n})$, which not only have a similar role with $r(\mathbf{n})$ but also lead to a reversible Markov chain [5]. Thus, (3.1) becomes:

$$b_k' = \varphi_k(\mathbf{n})b_k \tag{3.7}$$

Reversibility facilitates the recursive calculation of the link occupancy distribution (see Section 3.1.2). To ensure reversibility, $\varphi_k(\mathbf{n})$ must have the form [5]:

$$\varphi_k(\mathbf{n}) = \begin{cases} 1 & \text{for } \mathbf{nb} \leq C \text{ and } \mathbf{n} \in \Omega \\ \frac{x(\mathbf{n}_k^-)}{x(\mathbf{n})} & \text{for } C < \mathbf{nb} \leq T \text{ and } \mathbf{n} \in \Omega \\ 0 & \text{otherwise} \end{cases} \tag{3.8}$$

where $\Omega = \{\mathbf{n} : 0 \leq \mathbf{nb} \leq T\}$ and $\mathbf{nb} = \sum_{k=1}^{K} n_k b_k$.

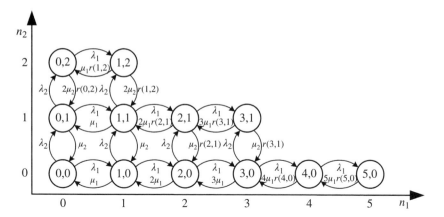

Figure 3.1 The state space Ω and the state transition diagram (Example 3.1).

Table 3.1 The state space and the occupied link bandwidth (Example 3.1).

n_1	n_2	$r(n)$	j $(0 \leq j \leq T)$ (before compression)	j $(0 \leq j \leq C)$ (after compression)
0	0	1.00	0	0
0	1	1.00	2	2
0	2	0.75	4	3
1	0	1.00	1	1
1	1	1.00	3	3
1	2	0.60	5	3
2	0	1.00	2	2
2	1	0.75	4	3
3	0	1.00	3	3
3	1	0.60	5	3
4	0	0.75	4	3
5	0	0.60	5	3

In (3.8), $x(\mathbf{n})$ is a state multiplier associated with state $\mathbf{n}$, whose values are chosen so that $\sum_{k=1}^{K} n_k(b_k \varphi_k(\mathbf{n})) = C$ holds whenever $C < \mathbf{nb} \leq T$, that is, $x(\mathbf{n})$ is given by [5]:

$$x(\mathbf{n}) = \begin{cases} 1 & \text{when } \mathbf{nb} \leq C \text{ and } \mathbf{n} \in \Omega \\ \dfrac{1}{C} \sum_{k=1}^{K} n_k b_k x(\mathbf{n}_k^-) & \text{when } C < \mathbf{nb} \leq T \text{ and } \mathbf{n} \in \Omega \\ 0 & \text{otherwise} \end{cases} \tag{3.9}$$

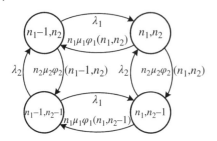

Figure 3.2 State transition diagram of four adjacent states (Example 3.2).

Example 3.2 In order to show that (3.8) ensures reversibility in the E-EMLM, consider a system with two service-classes and the following four adjacent states (depicted in Figure 3.2): $(n_1 - 1, n_2), (n_1, n_2), (n_1, n_2 - 1)$, and $(n_1 - 1, n_2 - 1)$. If we apply the Kolmogorov's criterion *flow clockwise = flow counter-clockwise* to the four adjacent states, we have $\lambda_1 \cdot \varphi_2(n_1, n_2) \cdot n_2 \mu_2 \cdot \varphi_1(n_1, n_2 - 1) \cdot n_1 \mu_1 \cdot \lambda_2 = \varphi_2(n_1 - 1, n_2) \cdot n_2 \mu_2 \cdot \lambda_1 \cdot \lambda_2 \cdot \varphi_1(n_1, n_2) \cdot n_1 \mu_1 \quad \Rightarrow \quad \varphi_2(n_1, n_2) \cdot \varphi_1(n_1, n_2 - 1) = \varphi_2(n_1 - 1, n_2) \cdot \varphi_1(n_1, n_2)$. By substituting the values of φ according to (3.8), we see that the previous equation holds, i.e., $\frac{x(n_1, n_2 - 1)}{x(n_1, n_2)} \frac{x(n_1 - 1, n_2 - 1)}{x(n_1, n_2 - 1)} = \frac{x(n_1 - 1, n_2 - 1)}{x(n_1 - 1, n_2)} \frac{x(n_1 - 1, n_2)}{x(n_1, n_2)}$, and therefore the Markov chain is reversible.

Example 3.3 Consider again Example 3.1 $(C = 3, T = 5, K = 2, b_1 = 1, b_2 = 2, \lambda_1 = \lambda_2 = \mu_1 = \mu_2 = 1.0)$.

(a) Draw the modified state transition diagram based on $\varphi_k(\mathbf{n})$ and determine the values of $\varphi_k(\mathbf{n})$ for each state $\mathbf{n} = (n_1, n_2)$.
(b) Investigate if reversibility holds in the modified system.
(c) Write the GB equations of the modified state transition diagram, and determine the values of $P(\mathbf{n})$ and the CBP of both service-classes.

(a) Figure 3.3 shows the modified state transition diagram of the system, while Table 3.2 presents the 12 states together with the corresponding values of $\varphi_k(\mathbf{n})$, which are calculated through the $x(\mathbf{n})$. (Comparing Figures 3.3 and 3.1, the compression factors $r(\mathbf{n})$ have been replaced by $\varphi_k(\mathbf{n})$, which are different per service-class.)
(b) If we apply the Kolmogorov's criterion (*flow clockwise = flow counter-clockwise*) between the four adjacent states (2, 1), (3, 1), (3, 0), and (2, 0), which form a square, then this criterion now holds (i.e., the Markov chain is reversible) since: $\lambda_1 \cdot \mu_2 \varphi_2(3, 1) \cdot 3\mu_1 \cdot \lambda_2 = \mu_2 \varphi_2(2, 1) \cdot \lambda_1 \cdot \lambda_2 \cdot 3\mu_1 \varphi_1(3, 1) \Rightarrow \varphi_2(3, 1) = \varphi_2(2, 1) \cdot \varphi_1(3, 1)$, which holds according to Table 3.2.
(c) Based on Figure 3.3, we obtain the following 12 GB equations:

$(0, 0):$ $P(1, 0) + P(0, 1) - 2P(0, 0) = 0$

$(0, 1):$ $P(0, 0) + P(1, 1) + 1.5P(0, 2) - 3P(0, 1) = 0$

$(0, 2):$ $0.75P(1, 2) + P(0, 1) - 2.5P(0, 2) = 0$

$(1, 0):$ $P(0, 0) + 2P(2, 0) + P(1, 1) - 3P(1, 0) = 0$

$(1, 1):$ $P(0, 1) + 1.5P(2, 1) + 1.125P(1, 2) + P(1, 0) - 4P(1, 1) = 0$

$(1, 2):$ $P(1, 1) + P(0, 2) - 1.875P(1, 2) = 0$

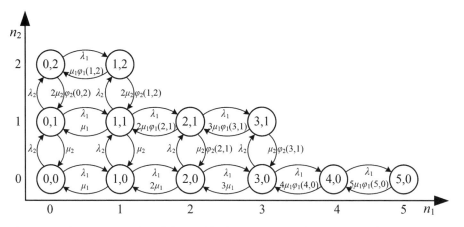

Figure 3.3 The state space Ω and the modified state transition diagram (Example 3.3).

$(2,0):$ $P(1,0) + 3P(3,0) + 0.75P(2,1) - 4P(2,0) = 0$

$(2,1):$ $P(1,1) + 2P(3,1) + P(2,0) - 3.25P(2,1) = 0$

$(3,0):$ $P(2,0) + 3P(4,0) + 0.5P(3,1) - 5P(3,0) = 0$

$(3,1):$ $P(2,1) + P(3,0) - 2.5P(3,1) = 0$

$(4,0):$ $P(3,0) + 3P(5,0) - 4P(4,0) = 0$

$(5,0):$ $P(4,0) - 3P(5,0) = 0$

The solution of this linear system is:

$P(0,0) = 0.1371$	$P(0,1) = 0.1371$	$P(0,2) = 0.0914$	$P(1,0) = 0.1371$
$P(1,1) = 0.1371$	$P(1,2) = 0.1218$	$P(2,0) = 0.0685$	$P(2,1) = 0.0914$
$P(3,0) = 0.0228$	$P(3,1) = 0.0457$	$P(4,0) = 0.0076$	$P(5,0) = 0.0025$

Then, based on $P(n_1, n_2)$ and (3.6), we obtain the approximate values of CBP:

$B_1 = P(1,2) + P(3,1) + P(5,0) = 0.1700$ (compare with the exact 0.1748)

$B_2 = P(0,2) + P(2,1) + P(4,0) + P(1,2) + P(3,1) + P(5,0) = 0.3604$ (compare with the exact 0.3574)

3.1.2 The Analytical Model

3.1.2.1 Steady State Probabilities

The steady state transition rates of the E-EMLM are shown in Figure 3.4. According to this, the GB equation (*rate in = rate out*) for state $\mathbf{n} = (n_1, n_2, \ldots, n_k, \ldots, n_K)$ is given by:

$$\sum_{k=1}^{K} \lambda_k \delta_k^-(\mathbf{n}) P(\mathbf{n}_k^-) + \sum_{k=1}^{K} (n_k + 1) \mu_k \delta_k^+(\mathbf{n}) \varphi_k(\mathbf{n}_k^+) P(\mathbf{n}_k^+) =$$
$$\sum_{k=1}^{K} \lambda_k \delta_k^+(\mathbf{n}) P(\mathbf{n}) + \sum_{k=1}^{K} n_k \mu_k \delta_k^-(\mathbf{n}) \varphi_k(\mathbf{n}) P(\mathbf{n})$$

(3.10)

Table 3.2 The values of the state dependent compression factors $\varphi_k(\mathbf{n})$ (Example 3.3).

n_1	n_2	$x(\mathbf{n})$	$\varphi_1(\mathbf{n})$	$\varphi_2(\mathbf{n})$	n_1	n_2	$x(\mathbf{n})$	$\varphi_1(\mathbf{n})$	$\varphi_2(\mathbf{n})$
0	0	1.0	1.00	1.00	2	0	1.0	1.00	1.00
0	1	1.0	1.00	1.00	2	1	1.3333	0.75	0.75
0	2	1.3333	0.00	0.75	3	0	1.0	1.00	1.00
1	0	1.0	1.00	1.00	3	1	1.9999	0.6667	0.50
1	1	1.0	1.00	1.00	4	0	1.3333	0.75	0.00
1	2	1.7778	0.75	0.5625	5	0	2.2222	0.60	0.00

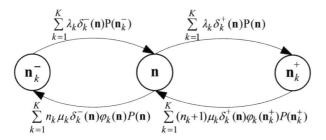

Figure 3.4 State transition diagram of the E-EMLM.

where $\mathbf{n}_k^+ = (n_1, \dots, n_{k-1}, n_k + 1, n_{k+1}, \dots, n_K)$, $\mathbf{n}_k^- = (n_1, \dots, n_{k-1}, n_k - 1, n_{k+1}, \dots, n_K)$

$\delta_k^+(\mathbf{n}) = \begin{cases} 1 & \text{if } \mathbf{n}_k^+ \in \Omega \\ 0 & \text{otherwise} \end{cases}$, $\quad \delta_k^-(\mathbf{n}) = \begin{cases} 1 & \text{if } \mathbf{n}_k^- \in \Omega \\ 0 & \text{otherwise} \end{cases}$, and $P(\mathbf{n})$, $P(\mathbf{n}_k^-)$, $P(\mathbf{n}_k^+)$ are the

probability distributions of the corresponding states $\mathbf{n}$, $\mathbf{n}_k^-$, $\mathbf{n}_k^+$, respectively.

Assume now the existence of LB between adjacent states. Equations (3.11) and (3.12) are the detailed LB equations which exist because the Markov chain of the modified model is reversible. Then, based on Figure 3.4, the following LB equations are extracted:

$$\lambda_k \delta_k^-(\mathbf{n}) P(\mathbf{n}_k^-) = n_k \mu_k \delta_k^-(\mathbf{n}) \varphi_k(\mathbf{n}) P(\mathbf{n}) \tag{3.11}$$

$$\lambda_k \delta_k^+(\mathbf{n}) P(\mathbf{n}) = (n_k + 1) \mu_k \delta_k^+(\mathbf{n}) \varphi_k(\mathbf{n}_k^+) P(\mathbf{n}_k^+) \tag{3.12}$$

for $k = 1, \dots, K$ and $\mathbf{n} \in \Omega$.

Based on the LB assumption, the probability distribution $P(\mathbf{n})$ has the solution:[2]

$$P(\mathbf{n}) = \frac{x(\mathbf{n}) \prod\limits_{k=1}^{K} \dfrac{\alpha_k^{n_k}}{n_k!}}{G} \tag{3.13}$$

where $\alpha_k = \lambda_k / \mu_k$ is the offered traffic-load in erl and G is the normalization constant given by:

$$G \equiv G(\Omega) = \sum_{\mathbf{n} \in \Omega} \left(x(\mathbf{n}) \prod_{k=1}^{K} \frac{\alpha_k^{n_k}}{n_k!} \right) \tag{3.14}$$

---

2 The solution can be verified by substituting (3.13) to (3.11) or (3.12).

Note that although the Markov chain has become reversible, the probability distribution $P(\mathbf{n})$ of (3.13) is not a PFS due to the summation of (3.9) needed for the determination of $x(\mathbf{n})$. We proceed by defining $q(j)$, as:

$$q(j) = \sum_{\mathbf{n} \in \Omega_j} P(\mathbf{n}) \tag{3.15}$$

where Ω_j is the set of states in which exactly j b.u. are occupied by all in-service calls, i.e., $\Omega_j = \{\mathbf{n} \in \Omega : \mathbf{nb} = j\}$.

Consider now two different sets of macro-states: (i) $0 \le j \le C$ and (ii) $C < j \le T$. For the first set, no bandwidth compression takes place and the values of $q(j)$ are determined by the classical Kaufman–Roberts recursion (1.39). For the second set, aiming at deriving a similar recursion, we first substitute (3.8) in (3.11) to obtain:

$$\alpha_k x(\mathbf{n}) P(\mathbf{n}_k^-) = n_k x(\mathbf{n}_k^-) P(\mathbf{n}) \tag{3.16}$$

Multiplying both sides of (3.16) by b_k and summing over k, we have:

$$x(\mathbf{n}) \sum_{k=1}^{K} \alpha_k b_k P(\mathbf{n}_k^-) = P(\mathbf{n}) \sum_{k=1}^{K} n_k b_k x(\mathbf{n}_k^-) \tag{3.17}$$

Equation (3.17), due to (3.9) is written as:

$$P(\mathbf{n})C = \sum_{k=1}^{K} \alpha_k b_k P(\mathbf{n}_k^-) \tag{3.18}$$

Summing both sides of (3.18) over Ω_j and based on (3.15), we have:

$$q(j)C = \sum_{k=1}^{K} \alpha_k b_k \sum_{\mathbf{n} \in \Omega_j} P(\mathbf{n}_k^-) \tag{3.19}$$

or

$$q(j)C = \sum_{k=1}^{K} \alpha_k b_k q(j - b_k) \tag{3.20}$$

The combination of (1.39) and (3.20) results in the recursive formula of the E-EMLM [5]:

$$q(j) = \begin{cases} 1 & \text{if} \quad j = 0 \\ \dfrac{1}{\min(C,j)} \sum_{k=1}^{K} \alpha_k b_k q(j - b_k) & \text{if} \quad j = 1, 2, \ldots, T \\ 0 & \text{otherwise} \end{cases} \tag{3.21}$$

3.1.2.2 CBP, Utilization, and Mean Number of In-service Calls

The following performance measures can be determined based on (3.21):

- The CBP of service-class k, B_k, via:

$$B_k = \sum_{j=T-b_k+1}^{T} G^{-1} q(j) \tag{3.22}$$

where $G = \sum_{j=0}^{T} q(j)$ is the normalization constant.

- The link utilization, U, via:

$$U = G^{-1}\left(\sum_{j=1}^{C} jq(j) + \sum_{j=C+1}^{T} Cq(j)\right) \tag{3.23}$$

- The average number of service-class k calls in the system, $\overline{n}_k$, via:

$$\overline{n}_k = \sum_{j=1}^{T} G^{-1}y_k(j)q(j) \tag{3.24}$$

where $y_k(j)$ is the average number of service-class k calls given that the system (macro-)state is j, and is determined by [6]:

$$y_k(j) = \frac{1}{\min(j, C)q(j)}\alpha_k b_k q(j - b_k)(1 + y_k(j - b_k)) +$$

$$\frac{1}{\min(j, C)q(j)}\sum_{i=1, i\neq k}^{K}\alpha_i b_i q(j - b_i)y_k(j - b_i) \tag{3.25}$$

where $j = 1, \dots, T$, while $y_k(x) = 0$ for $x \leq 0$ and $k = 1, \dots, K$.

Example 3.4 Consider again Example 3.1 ($C = 3, T = 5, K = 2, b_1 = 1, b_2 = 2, \lambda_1 = \lambda_2 = \mu_1 = \mu_2 = 1.0$).

(a) Calculate the (normalized) values of $Q(j)$.
(b) Calculate the CBP of both service-classes.
(c) Calculate the link utilization.
(d) Calculate the mean number of in-service calls of the two service-classes in the system.

(a) State probabilities through the recursion (3.21):

$j = 1$:	$q(1) = q(0) + 0 = 1.0$	$\Rightarrow$	$q(1) = 1.0$
$j = 2$:	$2q(2) = q(1) + 2q(0) = 3$	$\Rightarrow$	$q(2) = 1.5$
$j = 3$:	$3q(3) = q(2) + 2q(1) = 3.5$	$\Rightarrow$	$q(3) = 1.16667$
$j = 4$:	$3q(4) = q(3) + 2q(2) = 4.1667$	$\Rightarrow$	$q(4) = 1.3889$
$j = 5$:	$3q(5) = q(4) + 2q(3) = 3.375$	$\Rightarrow$	$q(5) = 1.2407$

The normalization constant is $G = \sum_{j=0}^{T} q(j) = 7.2963$. The state probabilities are:

$Q(0) = Q(1) = 0.1371 \quad Q(2) = 0.2056 \quad Q(3) = 0.1599 \quad Q(4) = 0.1904 \quad Q(5) = 0.17$

(b) The CBP results of the E-EMLM based on (3.22) are:

$$B_1 = \sum_{j=T-b_1+1}^{T} Q(j) = Q(5) = 0.17 \quad \text{and} \quad B_2 = \sum_{j=T-b_2+1}^{T} Q(j) = Q(4) + Q(5) = 0.3604$$

(For comparison, the CBP results of the EMLM are $B_1 = 0.25$ and $B_2 = 0.5714$, for $C = 3$ b.u.)

(c) The link utilization based on (3.23) is:

$$U = \sum_{j=1}^{C} jQ(j) + \sum_{j=C+1}^{T} CQ(j) = Q(1) + 2Q(2) + 3[Q(3) + Q(4) + Q(5)] = 2.109 \text{ b.u.}$$

(d) We firstly determine the values of $y_k(j)$ for $k = 1, 2$ and $j = 1, \ldots, T$ based on (3.25):

$j = 1$	$y_1(1) = 1.0$	$y_2(1) = 0.0$
$j = 2$	$y_1(2) = 0.6667$	$y_2(2) = 0.6667$
$j = 3$	$y_1(3) = 1.2857$	$y_2(3) = 0.8571$
$j = 4$	$y_1(4) = 1.12$	$y_2(4) = 1.44$
$j = 5$	$y_1(5) = 1.5970$	$y_2(5) = 1.7015$

Then, we determine the mean number of in-service-calls based on (3.24):

$$\bar{n}_1 = 0.9645, \quad \bar{n}_2 = 0.8376.$$

Example 3.5 Consider a link of capacity $C = 32$ b.u. that accommodates calls of $K = 2$ service-classes with the following traffic characteristics: service-class 1 $\alpha_1 = 2$ erl, $b_1 = 4$ b.u., service-class 2 $\alpha_2 = 2$ erl, $b_2 = 1$ b.u. Assuming four different values of $T = 32$, 40, 48, and 56 b.u., calculate the CBP B_1 and B_2 of the two service-classes and the link utilization when α_1 and α_2 increase in steps of 2 erl (up to $\alpha_1 = \alpha_2 = 16$ erl).

Figure 3.5 presents the CBP of both service-classes while Figure 3.6 presents the link utilization for the various values of T. Note that when $T = C = 32$ b.u., the system behaves as in the EMLM. In the x-axis of both figures, point 1 refers to $(\alpha_1, \alpha_2) = (2.0, 2.0)$ while point 8 refers to $(\alpha_1, \alpha_2) = (16.0, 16.0)$. According to Figure 3.5, the CBP of both service-classes decrease as the value of T increases. This is expected due to the bandwidth compression mechanism that let calls enter the system with reduced (compressed) bandwidth. Similarly, the CBP reduction leads to an increase of the link utilization as a result of accepting more calls in the system.

3.1.2.3 Relationship between the E-EMLM and the Balanced Fair Share Model

In the literature, a similar model exists called the *balanced fair share model* [7, 8], which aims to share the capacity of a single link among elastic calls already accepted for service according to a balanced fairness criterion, whereas the E-EMLM focuses on call admission. In what follows, we show that the bandwidth compression mechanism of the E-EMLM and the model of [7, 8] provide the same bandwidth compression.

In [8], a link accommodates Poisson arriving calls of K elastic service-classes. The link capacity C is shared among calls according to the balanced fairness criterion: when $\mathbf{nb} \le C$, all calls use their peak-bandwidth requirement, while when $\mathbf{nb} > C$, all calls share the capacity C in proportion to their peak-bandwidth requirement and the link

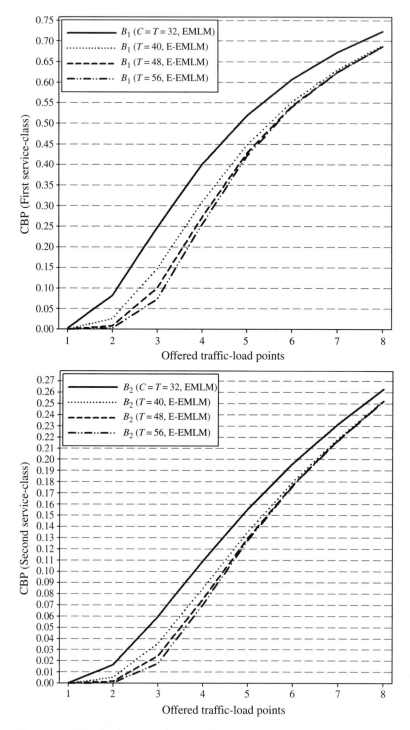

Figure 3.5 CBP of both service-classes in the E-EMLM (Example 3.5).

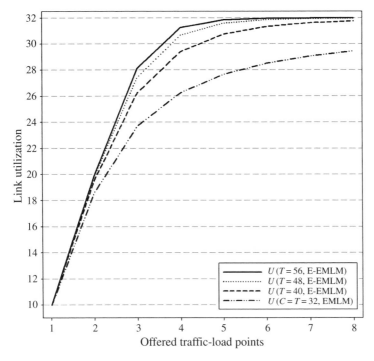

Figure 3.6 Link utilization in the E-EMLM (Example 3.5).

operates at its full capacity C. The main difference between the E-EMLM and the model of [8] lies on the fact that in the E-EMLM, the notion of $T > C$ allows for admission control, whereas there is no such parameter in [8]. The application of balanced fairness in multirate networks and its comparison with other classical bandwidth allocation policies, such as max–min fairness and proportional fairness can be found in [9, 10]. See Example 3.11 for a comparison between the approach of [9] and the compression mechanism of the E-EMLM under a threshold policy.

According to [8], the balanced fair sharing $\phi_k(\mathbf{n})$ of all n_k calls of service-class k in state $\mathbf{n} = (n_1, n_2, \ldots, n_k, \ldots, n_K)$ is given by:

$$\phi_k(\mathbf{n}) = \frac{\Phi(\mathbf{n} - \mathbf{e}_k)}{\Phi(\mathbf{n})}, \qquad n_k > 0 \tag{3.26}$$

where $\Phi(\mathbf{n})$ is a balance function defined by:

$$\Phi(\mathbf{n}) = \begin{cases} 0 & \text{if } n_k < 0 \text{ for some } k \\ \dfrac{1}{\left(\prod\limits_{k=1}^{K} n_k!\right)\left(\prod\limits_{k=1}^{K} b_k^{n_k}\right)} & \text{if } \mathbf{n} \geq 0, \ \mathbf{nb} \leq C \\ \dfrac{1}{C}\sum\limits_{k=1}^{K} \Phi(\mathbf{n} - \mathbf{e}_k) & \text{if } \mathbf{nb} > C \end{cases} \tag{3.27}$$

and $\mathbf{e}_k$ is the unit line vector with 1 in the kth element and 0 elsewhere. According to (3.27), when $C < \mathbf{nb}$, (3.26) is written as [8]:

$$\phi_k(\mathbf{n}) = C \frac{\Phi(\mathbf{n} - \mathbf{e}_k)}{\sum\limits_{k=1}^{K} \Phi(\mathbf{n} - \mathbf{e}_k)} \qquad (3.28)$$

The balance fair share model determines (through (3.28)) the total bandwidth which will be allocated to each service-class, whereas the E-EMLM determines (through (3.8)) the percentage of the peak-bandwidth per call requirement which will be assigned to each call of each service-class. This percentage has a limit which is defined through the T parameter, while the absence of T in the balance fair share model means that there is no limitation in bandwidth compression. The relationship between the $\varphi_k(\mathbf{n})$ of the E-EMLM and the $\phi_k(\mathbf{n})$ of the balance fair share model is $\phi_k(\mathbf{n}) = \varphi_k(\mathbf{n})b_k n_k$. To show this, let $K = 2$ service-classes (for presentation purposes). Assuming that in state $\mathbf{n} - \mathbf{e}_k$, i.e., $(n_1, n_2 - 1)$ or $(n_1 - 1, n_2)$, calls of service-class k use their peak-bandwidth requirements, the balanced fairness allocation gives:

$$\phi_1(n_1, n_2) = C \frac{\frac{1}{(n_1-1)!\, n_2!\, b_1^{n_1-1} b_2^{n_2}}}{\frac{1}{(n_1-1)!n_2!b_1^{n_1-1}b_2^{n_2}} + \frac{1}{n_1!(n_2-1)!b_1^{n_1} b_2^{n_2-1}}} = C \frac{n_1 b_1}{n_1 b_1 + n_2 b_2} \qquad (3.29)$$

Similarly,

$$\phi_2(n_1, n_2) = C \frac{n_2 b_2}{n_1 b_1 + n_2 b_2} \qquad (3.30)$$

So, in state $\mathbf{n} = (n_1, n_2)$, where $C < \mathbf{nb}$, the bandwidth allocated to a service-class k call is:

$$b_k' = \frac{\phi_k(n_1, n_2)}{n_k} = \frac{C}{n_1 b_1 + n_2 b_2} b_k, \qquad k = 1,\ 2 \qquad (3.31)$$

Based on (3.8) and (3.9), the E-EMLM gives:

$$\varphi_k(\mathbf{n}) = \varphi_k(n_1, n_2) = \frac{C}{n_1 b_1 + n_2 b_2}, \qquad k = 1,\ 2 \qquad (3.32)$$

assuming that $x(\mathbf{n}_k^{-1}) = 1$ (i.e., no bandwidth compression takes place in state $\mathbf{n}_k^{-1}$). Combining (3.31) with (3.32), we obtain $\phi_k(\mathbf{n}) = \varphi_k(\mathbf{n})\, b_k\, n_k$.

3.2 The Elastic Erlang Multirate Loss Model under the BR Policy

3.2.1 The Service System

We now consider the multiservice system of the *E-EMLM under the BR policy (E-EMLM/ BR)*: A new service-class k call is accepted in the link, if after its acceptance, the occupied link bandwidth $j \leq T - t_k$, where t_k refers to the BR parameter used to benefit (in CBP) calls of other service-classes apart from k (see also the EMLM/BR in Section 1.3.2).

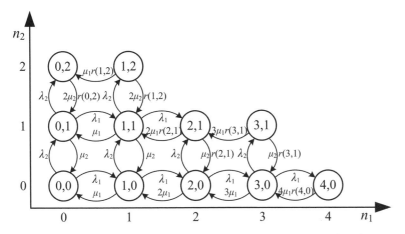

Figure 3.7 The state space Ω and the state transition diagram (Example 3.6).

In terms of the system state-space Ω, the CAC is expressed as follows. A new call of service-class k is accepted in the system if the system is in state $\mathbf{n} \in \Omega_{\{k\}}$ upon a new call arrival, where $\Omega_{\{k\}} = \{\mathbf{n} \in \Omega : \mathbf{nb} \le T - b_k - t_k\}$, $k = 1, \ldots, K$. Hence, the CBP of service-class k is determined by the state space $\Omega - \Omega_{\{k\}}$:

$$B_k = \sum_{\mathbf{n} \in \{\Omega - \Omega_{\{k\}}\}} P(\mathbf{n}) \quad \Rightarrow \quad B_k = 1 - \sum_{\mathbf{n} \in \Omega_{\{k\}}} P(\mathbf{n}) \tag{3.33}$$

As far as the compression factors and the state dependent compression factors per service-class are concerned, they are determined by (3.2) and (3.8), respectively.

Example 3.6 Consider again Example 3.1 ($C = 3, T = 5, K = 2, b_1 = 1, b_2 = 2, \lambda_1 = \lambda_2 = \mu_1 = \mu_2 = 1.0$). Assume that $t_1 = 1$ and $t_2 = 0$ b.u., so that $b_1 + t_1 = b_2 + t_2$.

(a) Draw the complete state transition diagram of the system and determine the values of j and $r(\mathbf{n})$, for each state $\mathbf{n} = (n_1, n_2)$.
(b) Write the GB equations, and determine the values of $P(\mathbf{n})$ and the exact CBP of both service-classes.
(c) Draw the modified state transition diagram based on $\varphi_k(\mathbf{n})$ and determine the values of $\varphi_k(\mathbf{n})$ for each state $\mathbf{n} = (n_1, n_2)$.
(d) Write the GB equations of the modified state transition diagram, and determine the values of $P(\mathbf{n})$ and the CBP of both service-classes.

(a) Figure 3.7 shows the state space Ω that consists of 11 permissible states $\mathbf{n} = (n_1, n_2)$ together with the complete state transition diagram of the system. The corresponding values of $r(\mathbf{n})$ and $j = n_1 b_1 + n_2 b_2$ are exactly the same as those presented in Table 3.1 (ignore the last row); for the same state (n_1, n_2), obviously the same $r(\mathbf{n})$ is determined because it only depends on state $\mathbf{n}$.

(b) Based on Figure 3.7, we obtain the following 11 GB equations:

$(0,0):$ $\quad$ $P(1,0) + P(0,1) - 2P(0,0) = 0$

$(0,1):$ $\quad$ $P(0,0) + P(1,1) + 1.5P(0,2) - 3P(0,1) = 0$

$(0,2):$ $\quad$ $0.6P(1,2) + P(0,1) - 1.5P(0,2) = 0$

$(1,0):$ $\quad$ $P(0,0) + 2P(2,0) + P(1,1) - 3P(1,0) = 0$

$(1,1):$ $\quad$ $P(0,1) + 1.5P(2,1) + 1.2P(1,2) + P(1,0) - 4P(1,1) = 0$

$(1,2):$ $\quad$ $P(1,1) - 1.8P(1,2) = 0$

$(2,0):$ $\quad$ $P(1,0) + 3P(3,0) + 0.75P(2,1) - 4P(2,0) = 0$

$(2,1):$ $\quad$ $P(1,1) + 1.8P(3,1) + P(2,0) - 2.25P(2,1) = 0$

$(3,0):$ $\quad$ $P(2,0) + 3P(4,0) + 0.6P(3,1) - 5P(3,0) = 0$

$(3,1):$ $\quad$ $P(3,0) - 2.4P(3,1) = 0$

$(4,0):$ $\quad$ $P(3,0) - 3P(4,0) = 0$

The solution of this linear system is:

$P(0,0) = 0.1529$	$P(0,1) = 0.1661$	$P(0,2) = 0.1406$	$P(1,0) = 0.1397$
$P(1,1) = 0.1344$	$P(1,2) = 0.0747$	$P(2,0) = 0.0659$	$P(2,1) = 0.0949$
$P(3,0) = 0.0176$	$P(3,1) = 0.0073$	$P(4,0) = 0.0059$	

Then, based on the values of $P(n_1, n_2)$ and (3.33), we obtain the exact value of equalized CBP:

$$B_1 = B_2 = P(0,2) + P(2,1) + P(4,0) + P(1,2) + P(3,1) = 0.3234.$$

(c) Figure 3.8 shows the modified state transition diagram. Similarly to the $r(\mathbf{n})$, the corresponding values of $\varphi_k(\mathbf{n})$ are exactly the same as those presented in Table 3.2 (ignore the last row) for the E-EMLM. Although the E-EMLM/BR differs from the E-EMLM in respect of the state transition diagram (and the state space), they both have the same bandwidth compression parameters.

(d) Based on Figure 3.8, we obtain the following 11 GB equations:

$(0,0):$ $\quad$ $P(1,0) + P(0,1) - 2P(0,0) = 0$

$(0,1):$ $\quad$ $P(0,0) + P(1,1) + 1.5P(0,2) - 3P(0,1) = 0$

$(0,2):$ $\quad$ $0.75P(1,2) + P(0,1) - 1.5P(0,2) = 0$

$(1,0):$ $\quad$ $P(0,0) + 2P(2,0) + P(1,1) - 3P(1,0) = 0$

$(1,1):$ $\quad$ $P(0,1) + 1.5P(2,1) + 1.125P(1,2) + P(1,0) - 4P(1,1) = 0$

$(1,2):$ $\quad$ $P(1,1) - 1.875P(1,2) = 0$

$(2,0):$ $\quad$ $P(1,0) + 3P(3,0) + 0.75P(2,1) - 4P(2,0) = 0$

$(2,1):$ $\quad$ $P(1,1) + 2P(3,1) + P(2,0) - 2.25P(2,1) = 0$

$(3,0):$ $\quad$ $P(2,0) + 3P(4,0) + 0.5P(3,1) - 5P(3,0) = 0$

$(3,1):$ $\quad$ $P(3,0) - 2.5P(3,1) = 0$

$(4,0):$ $\quad$ $P(3,0) - 3P(4,0) = 0$

The solution of this linear system is:

$P(0,0) = 0.1539$	$P(0,1) = 0.1692$	$P(0,2) = 0.1480$	$P(1,0) = 0.1386$
$P(1,1) = 0.1318$	$P(1,2) = 0.0703$	$P(2,0) = 0.0650$	$P(2,1) = 0.0936$
$P(3,0) = 0.0171$	$P(3,1) = 0.0068$	$P(4,0) = 0.0057$	

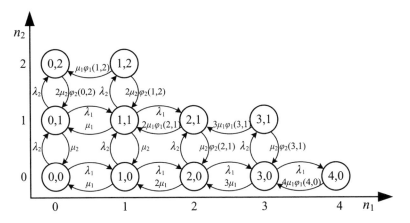

Figure 3.8 The state space Ω and the modified state transition diagram (Example 3.6).

Then, based on the values of $P(n_1, n_2)$ and (3.33), we obtain the value of equalized CBP:

$$B_1 = B_2 = P(0, 2) + P(2, 1) + P(4, 0) + P(1, 2) + P(3, 1) = 0.3244,$$

which is quite close to the exact value of 0.3234.

3.2.2 The Analytical Model

3.2.2.1 Link Occupancy Distribution

In the E-EMLM/BR, the link occupancy distribution, $q(j)$, can be calculated in an approximate way, according to the Roberts method (see Section 1.3.2.2), which leads to the following recursive formula [11]:

$$q(j) = \begin{cases} 1 & \text{if } j = 0 \\ \dfrac{1}{\min(C, j)} \displaystyle\sum_{k=1}^{K} \alpha_k D_k(j - b_k) q(j - b_k) & \text{if } j = 1, 2, \ldots, T \\ 0 & \text{otherwise} \end{cases} \tag{3.34a}$$

$$\text{where} \quad D_k(j - b_k) = \begin{cases} b_k & \text{for } j \leq T - t_k \\ 0 & \text{for } j > T - t_k \end{cases} \tag{3.34b}$$

This formula is similar to (1.64) of the EMLM/BR. If $t_k = 0$ for all k ($k = 1, \ldots, K$) then the E-EMLM results. In addition, if $T = C$ then we have the classical EMLM.

3.2.2.2 CBP, Utilization, and Mean Number of In-service Calls

The following performance measures can be determined based on (3.34):

- The CBP of service-class k, B_k, via:

$$B_k = \sum_{j=T-b_k-t_k+1}^{T} G^{-1} q(j) \tag{3.35}$$

where $G = \sum_{j=0}^{T} q(j)$ is the normalization constant.

- The link utilization, U, via (3.23).
- The average number of service-class k calls in the system, $\bar{n}_k$, via (3.24), where $y_k(j)$ are determined by (3.25) under the following two assumptions: (i) $y_k(j) = 0$ when $j > T - t_k$, and (ii) $\alpha_i b_i q(j - b_i) = 0$ when $j > T - t_i$.

Example 3.7 Consider again Example 3.6 ($C = 3, T = 5, K = 2, b_1 = 1, b_2 = 2, t_1 = 1, t_2 = 0, \lambda_1 = \lambda_2 = \mu_1 = \mu_2 = 1.0$).

(a) Calculate the (normalized) values of $Q(j)$.
(b) Calculate the CBP of both service-classes.
(c) Calculate the link utilization.
(d) Calculate the mean number of in-service calls of the two service-classes in the system.

(a) State probabilities through the recursion (3.34):

$j = 0$: $q(0) = 1$

$j = 1$: $q(1) = q(0) + 0 = 1.0$ $\Rightarrow q(1) = 1.0$

$j = 2$: $2q(2) = q(1) + 2q(0) = 3$ $\Rightarrow q(2) = 1.5$

$j = 3$: $3q(3) = q(2) + 2q(1) = 3.5$ $\Rightarrow q(3) = 1.16667$

$j = 4$: $3q(4) = q(3) + 2q(2) = 4.1667$ $\Rightarrow q(4) = 1.3889$

$j = 5$: $3q(5) = 2q(3) = 2.3333$ $\Rightarrow q(5) = 0.7777$

The normalization constant is:

$$G = \sum_{j=0}^{T} q(j) = 6.8333$$

The state probabilities are:

$Q(0) = 0.1463, Q(1) = 0.1463, Q(2) = 0.2195, Q(3) = 0.1707, Q(4) = 0.2033, Q(5) = 0.1138$

(b) The CBP based on (3.35) are:

$$B_1 = \sum_{j=T-b_1-t_1+1}^{T} Q(j) = Q(4) + Q(5) = 0.3171$$

$$B_2 = \sum_{j=T-b_2-t_2+1}^{T} Q(j) = Q(4) + Q(5) = 0.3171 \quad \text{(compare with the exact value of 0.3234)}$$

(c) The link utilization based on (3.23) is:

$$U = \sum_{j=1}^{C} jQ(j) + \sum_{j=C+1}^{T} CQ(j) = Q(1) + 2Q(2) + 3[Q(3) + Q(4) + Q(5)] = 2.049 \text{ b.u.}$$

(d) We firstly determine the values of $y_k(j)$ for $k = 1, 2$ and $j = 1, \ldots, T$, based on (3.25):

$j = 1$: $y_1(1) = 1.0$ $y_2(1) = 0.0$

$j = 2$: $y_1(2) = 0.6667$ $y_2(2) = 0.6667$

$j = 3$: $y_1(3) = 1.2857$ $y_2(3) = 0.8571$

$j = 4$: $y_1(4) = 1.12$ $y_2(4) = 1.44$

$j = 5$: $y_1(5) = 0.0$ $y_2(5) = 1.8571$

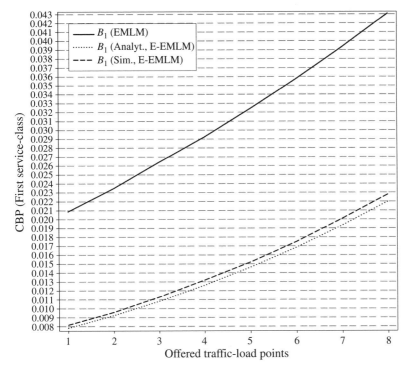

Figure 3.9 CBP of service-class 1 (EMLM, E-EMLM) (Example 3.8).

From (3.24), we obtain the mean values of in-service calls:

$$\bar{n}_1 = 0.7398, \ \bar{n}_2 = 0.7967.$$

Example 3.8 Consider a link of capacity $C = 60$ b.u. that accommodates calls of $K = 2$ service-classes with the following traffic characteristics: service-class 1 $\alpha_1 = 24$ erl, $b_1 = 1$ b.u., service-class 2 $\alpha_2 = 6$ erl, $b_2 = 4$ b.u. The maximum allowed bandwidth compression ratio to all in-service calls is 85.7%. The BR policy is applied in order to achieve CBP equalization between the two service-classes. Compare the CBP B_1 and B_2 of the two service-classes and the link utilization, obtained by the E-EMLM/BR, the E-EMLM, the EMLM/BR, and the EMLM, when α_1 increases in steps of 1 erl (up to $\alpha_1 = 31$ erl). Also provide simulation results for the E-EMLM/BR.

For bandwidth compression, we choose $T = 70$ because the maximum bandwidth compression is achieved for $r_{\min} = C/T \Rightarrow T = 60/70 = 0.857$. For CBP equalization under the BR policy, we choose $t_1 = 3$ and $t_2 = 0$ since $b_1 + t_1 = b_2 + t_2$ (in this way we have an equal number of blocking states for the two service classes). Figures 3.9 and 3.10 present the analytical and the simulation CBP results of service-classes 1 and 2, respectively, in the case of the E-EMLM. For comparison, we give the corresponding analytical CBP results of

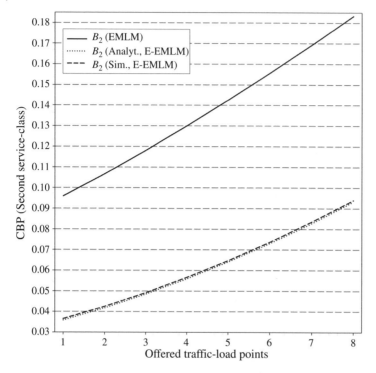

Figure 3.10 CBP of service-class 2 (EMLM, E-EMLM) (Example 3.8).

the EMLM. In Figure 3.11, we present the analytical and simulation CBP results (equalized CBP) in the case of the E-EMLM/BR. Simulation results are based on SIMSCRIPT III and are mean values of 12 runs (no reliability ranges are shown because they are very small). For comparison, we give the corresponding analytical results for the EMLM/BR. In Figure 3.12, we present the link utilization (analytical results only) for all models. In the x-axis of all figures, point 1 refers to $(\alpha_1, \alpha_2) = (24.0, 6.0)$, while point 8 refers to $(\alpha_1, \alpha_2) = (31.0, 6.0)$. From the figures, we observe the following:

(i) Analytical and simulation CBP results are very close.
(ii) The compression/expansion mechanism of the E-EMLM and E-EMLM/BR reduces the CBP compared to those obtained by the EMLM and EMLM/BR, respectively.
(iii) The compression/expansion mechanism increases the link utilization since it decreases CBP.

3.3 The Elastic Erlang Multirate Loss Model under the Threshold Policy

3.3.1 The Service System

We now consider the multi-service system of the *E-EMLM under the TH policy (E-EMLM/ TH)*, as follows. A new call of service-class k is accepted in the system, of C b.u., if [12]:

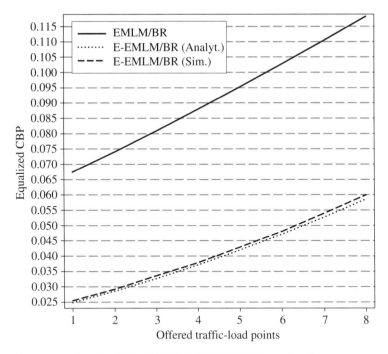

Figure 3.11 Equalized CBP (EMLM/BR, E-EMLM/BR) (Example 3.8).

(i) The number of in-service calls of service-class k, n_k, together with the new call, does not exceed a threshold $n_{k,\max}$, i.e., $n_k + 1 \leq n_{k,\max}$. Otherwise the call is blocked. This constraint expresses the TH policy.

(ii) If constraint (i) is met, then: (a) If $j + b_k \leq C$, the call is accepted in the system with b_k b.u. and remains in the system for an exponentially distributed service time with mean μ_k^{-1}. (b) If $T \geq j + b_k > C$ the call is accepted by compressing its b_k together with the bandwidth of all in-service calls of all service-classes. The bandwidth compression/expansion mechanism is identical to the one described in Section 3.1.

In terms of the system state-space Ω, the CAC is expressed as follows. A new call of service-class k is accepted in the system if the system is in state $\mathbf{n} \in \Omega_{\{k\}}$ upon a new call arrival, where $\Omega_{\{k\}} = \{\mathbf{n} \in \Omega : \mathbf{nb} \leq T - b_k, \ n_k \leq n_{k,\max}\}$, $k = 1, \ldots, K$. Hence, the CBP of service-class k is determined by the state space $\Omega - \Omega_{\{k\}}$:

$$B_k = \sum_{\mathbf{n} \in \{\Omega - \Omega_{\{k\}}\}} P(\mathbf{n}) \quad \Rightarrow \quad B_k = 1 - \sum_{\mathbf{n} \in \Omega_{\{k\}}} P(\mathbf{n}) \tag{3.36}$$

Example 3.9 This example clarifies the bandwidth compression-expansion mechanism in conjunction with the TH policy. Consider a link of $C = 4$ b.u. and let $T = 8$ b.u. The link accommodates calls of $K = 2$ service-classes whose calls require $b_1 = 2$ and $b_2 = 4$ b.u., respectively. The TH policy is applied to calls of both service-classes by assuming that $n_{1,\max} = 3$ and $n_{2,\max} = 1$. For simplicity, assume that $\lambda_1 = \lambda_2 = \mu_1 = \mu_2 = 1.0$.

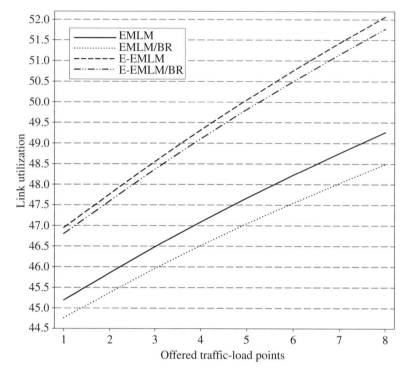

Figure 3.12 Link utilization for all models (Example 3.8).

(a) Draw the complete state transition diagram of the system and determine the values of j and $r(\mathbf{n})$, based on (3.2), for each state $\mathbf{n} = (n_1, n_2)$.

(b) Write the GB equations, determine the values of $P(\mathbf{n})$ and the exact CBP of both service-classes.

(c) Draw the modified state transition diagram based on $\varphi_k(\mathbf{n})$ and determine the values of $\varphi_k(\mathbf{n})$, based on (3.8) and (3.9), for each state $\mathbf{n} = (n_1, n_2)$.

(d) Write the GB equations of the modified state transition diagram, determine the values of $P(\mathbf{n})$ and the CBP of both service-classes.

(a) Figure 3.13 shows the state space Ω which consists of seven permissible states $\mathbf{n} = (n_1, n_2)$ together with the complete state transition diagram of the system. The corresponding values of $r(\mathbf{n})$ and $j = n_1 b_1 + n_2 b_2$ are presented in Table 3.3.

(b) Based on Figure 3.13, we obtain the following seven GB equations:

$(0,0):$ $P(1,0) + P(0,1) - 2P(0,0) = 0$

$(0,1):$ $P(0,0) + 0.6667P(1,1) - 2P(0,1) = 0$

$(1,0):$ $P(0,0) + 2P(2,0) + 0.6667P(1,1) - 3P(1,0) = 0$

$(1,1):$ $P(0,1) + P(2,1) + P(1,0) - 2.3333P(1,1) = 0$

$(2,0):$ $P(1,0) + 2P(3,0) + 0.5P(2,1) - 4P(2,0) = 0$

$(2,1):$ $P(1,1) + P(2,0) - 1.5P(2,1) = 0$

$(3,0):$ $P(2,0) - 2P(3,0) = 0$

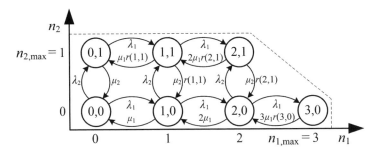

Figure 3.13 The state space Ω and the state transition diagram (Example 3.9).

The solution of this linear system is:

$P(0,0) = 0.1516$	$P(0,1) = 0.1479$	$P(1,0) = 0.1555$	$P(1,1) = 0.2161$
$P(2,0) = 0.0854$	$P(2,1) = 0.2009$	$P(3,0) = 0.0427$	

Then, based on the values of $P(n_1, n_2)$ and (3.36), we determine the exact CBP:

$$B_1 = P(2,1) + P(3,0) = 0.2436 \qquad B_2 = P(1,1) + P(2,1) + P(3,0) + P(0,1) = 0.6076$$

(c) Figure 3.14 shows the modified state transition diagram. The corresponding values of $\varphi_k(\mathbf{n})$ (which are calculated through the $x(\mathbf{n})$), are presented in Table 3.4. (Although the state transition diagrams depend on the applied bandwidth sharing policy, e.g., CS, BR or TH, the bandwidth compression parameters, $r(\mathbf{n})$ and $\varphi_k(\mathbf{n})$, depend only on the number of in-service calls of each service-class.)

(d) Based on Figure 3.14, we obtain the following seven GB equations:

$(0,0)$: $P(1,0) + P(0,1) - 2P(0,0) = 0$

$(0,1)$: $P(0,0) + 0.6667P(1,1) - 2P(0,1) = 0$

$(1,0)$: $P(0,0) + 2P(2,0) + 0.6667P(1,1) - 3P(1,0) = 0$

$(1,1)$: $P(0,1) + 1.2P(2,1) + P(1,0) - 2.3333P(1,1) = 0$

$(2,0)$: $P(1,0) + 2P(3,0) + 0.4P(2,1) - 4P(2,0) = 0$

$(2,1)$: $P(1,1) + P(2,0) - 1.6P(2,1) = 0$

$(3,0)$: $P(2,0) - 2P(3,0) = 0$

The solution of this linear system is:

$P(0,0) = 0.1538$	$P(0,1) = 0.1538$	$P(1,0) = 0.1538$	$P(1,1) = 0.2308$
$P(2,0) = 0.0769$	$P(2,1) = 0.1923$	$P(3,0) = 0.0385$	

Then, based on the values of $P(n_1, n_2)$ and (3.36), we determine the CBP for each service-class:

$$B_1 = P(2,1) + P(3,0) = 0.2308 \quad \text{and} \quad B_2 = P(1,1) + P(2,1) + P(3,0) + P(0,1) = 0.6154,$$

which are close to the exact values of 0.2436 and 0.6076, respectively.

Table 3.3 The state space and the occupied link bandwidth (Example 3.9).

n_1	n_2	$r(n)$	j $(0 \le j \le T)$ (before compression)	j $(0 \le j \le C)$ (after compression)
0	0	1.00	0	0
0	1	1.00	4	4
1	0	1.00	2	2
1	1	0.6667	6	4
2	0	1.00	4	4
2	1	0.5	8	4
3	0	0.6667	6	4

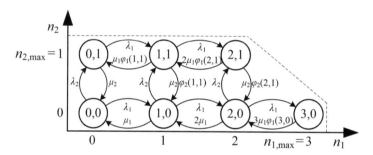

Figure 3.14 The state space Ω and the modified state transition diagram (Example 3.9).

Table 3.4 The values of the state dependent compression factors $\varphi_k(n)$ (Example 3.9).

n_1	n_2	$x(n)$	$\varphi_1(n)$	$\varphi_2(n)$	n_1	n_2	$x(n)$	$\varphi_1(n)$	$\varphi_2(n)$
0	0	1.0	1.00	1.00	2	0	1.0	1.00	1.00
0	1	1.0	1.00	1.00	2	1	2.5	0.6	0.4
1	0	1.0	1.00	1.00	3	0	1.5	0.6667	0.0
1	1	1.5	0.6667	0.6667					

3.3.2 The Analytical Model

3.3.2.1 Steady State Probabilities

The steady state transition rates of the E-EMLM/TH are shown in Figure 3.4. According to this, the GB equation for state $\mathbf{n} = (n_1, n_2, \dots, n_k, \dots, n_K)$ is given by (3.10), while the LB equations are given by (3.11) and (3.12) where: $\Omega = \{\mathbf{n} : 0 \le \mathbf{nb} \le T, n_k \le n_{k,\max}, k = 1, \dots, K\}$.

Based on the LB assumption, the probability distribution $P(\mathbf{n})$ has the solution of (3.13) where the normalization constant is given by (3.14). Since j is the occupied link bandwidth, we consider two different sets of macro-states: (i) $0 \le j \le C$ and (ii) $C < j \le T$. For set (i), no bandwidth compression takes place and $q(j)$ are determined via (1.73). For set (ii), we follow the analysis of the E-EMLM up to (3.19). Since $n_k \le n_{k,\max}$, we have:

$$\sum_{\mathbf{n} \in \Omega_j} P(\mathbf{n}_k^-) = q(j - b_k) - Prob[x = j - b_k, \ n_k = n_{k,\max}] \tag{3.37}$$

Thus, (3.19) can be written as:

$$q(j) = \frac{1}{C} \sum_{k=1}^{K} \alpha_k b_k [q(j - b_k) - \Theta_k(j - b_k)] \tag{3.38}$$

where $\Theta_k(x) = Prob[x, \ n_k = n_{k,\max}]$ is the probability that x b.u. are occupied when the number of service-class k in-service calls is $n_{k,\max}$, and is determined by (1.74). The combination of (1.73) and (3.38) results in the recursive formula of the E-EMLM/TH [12]:

$$q(j) = \begin{cases} 1 & \text{if } j = 0 \\ \frac{1}{\min(C,j)} \sum\limits_{k=1}^{K} \alpha_k b_k [q(j - b_k) - \Theta_k(j - b_k)] & \text{if } j = 1, 2, \dots, T \\ 0 & \text{otherwise} \end{cases} \tag{3.39}$$

3.3.2.2 CBP, Utilization, and Mean Number of In-service Calls
The following performance measures can be determined based on (3.39):

- The CBP of service-class k, B_k, via:

$$B_k = \sum_{j=T-b_k+1}^{T} G^{-1} q(j) + \sum_{j=n_{k,\max} b_k}^{T-b_k} G^{-1} \Theta_k(j) \tag{3.40}$$

  where $G = \sum_{j=0}^{T} q(j)$ is the normalization constant.
- The link utilization, U, according to (3.23).
- The average number of service-class k calls in the system, $\bar{n}_k$, via:

$$\bar{n}_k = \sum_{j=1}^{T} G^{-1} y_k(j) q(j) \tag{3.41}$$

  where $y_k(j)$ is the average number of service-class k calls given that the system state is j, and is given by:

$$y_k(j) = \frac{1}{\min(j, C) q(j)} \alpha_k b_k [q(j - b_k) - \Theta_k(j - b_k)][1 + y_k(j - b_k)] +$$
$$\frac{1}{\min(j, C) q(j)} \sum_{i=1, \ i \ne k}^{K} \alpha_i b_i [q(j - b_i) - \Theta_i(j - b_i)] y_k(j - b_i) \tag{3.42}$$

  where $j = 1, \dots, T$, while $y_k(x) = 0$ for $x \le 0$ and $k = 1, \dots, K$.

In (3.39), knowledge of $\Theta_k(j)$ is required. Since $\Theta_k(j) > 0$ when $j = n_{k,\max}b_k, \dots, T - b_k$, we distinguish two regions of j: (i) $n_{k,\max}b_k \leq j \leq C$ and (ii) $C + 1 \leq j \leq T - b_k$.

For the first region (where no bandwidth compression occurs), consider a system of capacity $F_k = T - b_k - n_{k,\max}b_k$ that accommodates all service-classes but service-class k. For this system, we define $\vartheta_k(j)$ as follows:

$$\vartheta_k(j) = \begin{cases} 1 & \text{if } j = 0 \\ \dfrac{1}{j} \displaystyle\sum_{i=1,i\neq k}^{K} \alpha_i b_i [\vartheta_k(j - b_i) - \Theta_i(j - b_i)] & \text{if } j = 1, \dots, F_k \\ 0 & \text{otherwise} \end{cases} \tag{3.43}$$

Based on $\vartheta_k(j)$, we compute the unnormalized $\Theta_k(j)$, recursively, via the following formula:

$$\Theta_k(j) = \frac{\alpha_k^{n_{k,\max}}}{n_{k,\max}!} \vartheta_k(j - n_{k,\max}b_k) \tag{3.44}$$

For the second region (where bandwidth compression occurs), the values of $\Theta_k(j)$ can be determined (taking into account (3.9)) by:

$$\Theta_k(j) = \frac{\alpha_k^{n_{k,\max}}}{n_{k,\max}!} \sum_{\mathbf{n} \in \Omega'} x(\mathbf{n}) \prod_{i=1,i\neq k}^{K} \frac{\alpha_i^{n_i}}{n_i!} \tag{3.45}$$

where $\Omega' = \left\{ \mathbf{n} \in \Omega' : n_{k,\max}b_k + \sum_{i=1,\, i\neq k}^{K} n_i b_i = j,\ C + 1 \leq j \leq T - b_k \right\}$.

Example 3.10 Consider again Example 3.9 $(C = 4, T = 8, K = 2, b_1 = 2, b_2 = 4, n_{1,\max} = 3, n_{2,\max} = 1, \lambda_1 = \lambda_2 = \mu_1 = \mu_2 = 1.0)$.

(a) Calculate the (normalized) values of $Q(j)$ in the E-EMLM/TH based on (3.39).
(b) Calculate the CBP of both service-classes based on (3.40).

(a) State probabilities through the recursion (3.39): For $j = 1, \dots, T$ (where $T = 8$), given that $q(0) = 1$, we have:

$j = 1:$	$q(1) = 0$	$\Rightarrow q(1) = 0$
$j = 2:$	$2q(2) = 2q(1) = 2.0$	$\Rightarrow q(2) = 1.0$
$j = 3:$	$3q(3) = 0$	$\Rightarrow q(3) = 0$
$j = 4:$	$4q(4) = 2q(2) + 4q(0) = 6.0$	$\Rightarrow q(4) = 1.5$
$j = 5:$	$4q(5) = 0$	$\Rightarrow q(5) = 0$
$j = 6:$	$4q(6) = 2q(4) + 4q(2) = 7.0$	$\Rightarrow q(6) = 1.75$
$j = 7:$	$4q(7) = 0$	$\Rightarrow q(7) = 0$
$j = 8:$	$4q(8) = 2[q(6) - \Theta_1(6)] + 4[q(4) - \Theta_2(4)] = 5.0$	$\Rightarrow q(8) = 1.25$
where	$\Theta_1(6) = 0.25$ calculated via (3.45) while $x(3, 0) = 1.5$	
and	$\Theta_2(4) = 1.0$ calculated via (3.44) while $F_2 = 0$.	

The normalization constant is $G = \sum_{j=0}^{T} q(j) = 6.5$. The state probabilities are:

$Q(0) = Q(2) = 0.1538$ $Q(4) = 0.2308$ $Q(6) = 0.2692$ $Q(8) = 0.1923$

(b) The CBP, B_1 and B_2, are:

$$B_1 = \sum_{j=T-b_1+1}^{T} Q(j) + \sum_{j=n_{1,\max}\cdot b_1}^{T-b_1} G^{-1}\Theta_1(j) = Q(8) + G^{-1}\Theta_1(6) = 0.2308$$

$$B_2 = \sum_{j=T-b_2+1}^{T} Q(j) + \sum_{j=n_{2,\max}\cdot b_2}^{T-b_2} G^{-1}\Theta_2(j) = Q(6) + Q(8) + G^{-1}\Theta_2(4) = 0.6154$$

Example 3.11 Consider again Example 3.9. We show the relationship between the E-EMLM/TH and the balanced fair share model of [9]. In [9], the balanced fair sharing is applied to access tree networks. The loss system of Example 3.9 can be represented as the simple access tree network of Figure 3.15. According to [9], the balanced fair sharing $\phi_k(\mathbf{n})$ of all calls of service-class k in state $\mathbf{n} = (n_1, n_2, \ldots, n_k, \ldots, n_K)$ is given by (3.26), where $\Phi(\mathbf{n})$ is a balance function for a tree network, defined by:

$$\Phi(\mathbf{n}) = \begin{cases} 0 & \text{if } n_k < 0 \text{ for some } k \\ & \text{if } \mathbf{n} \geq 0, \ \mathbf{nb} \leq C \\ \dfrac{1}{\left(\prod_{k=1}^{K} n_k!\right)\left(\prod_{k=1}^{K} b_k^{n_k}\right)} & \\ \max_l \left[\dfrac{1}{C_l} \sum_{i \in K_l} \Phi(\mathbf{n} - \mathbf{e}_k) \text{ if } \mathbf{nb} > C\right] & \end{cases} \quad (3.46)$$

where link l has capacity C_l, K_l is the set of service-classes going through link l, and $\mathbf{e}_k$ is the unit line vector with 1 in component k and 0 elsewhere.

Calculate the values of $\phi_k(\mathbf{n})$ for states $(1, 1)$, $(2, 1)$, and $(3, 0)$ of Example 3.9, through (3.26) and (3.46) (of the balance fair share model), where bandwidth compression occurs, find the allocated bandwidth per service-class call and compare it with that of the E-EMLM/TH. Then, repeat for state $(3,1)$ and comment.

Figure 3.15 The loss system of Example 3.9 as an access tree network (Example 3.11).

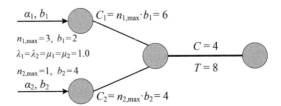

State (1,1):

- $\phi_1(1,1) = \frac{\Phi(0,1)}{\Phi(1,1)}$ where:

$$\Phi(0,1) = \frac{1}{4} \text{ and}$$

$$\Phi(1,1) = \max\left\{ \frac{1}{C_1}\Phi(\mathbf{n} - \mathbf{e}_1), \frac{1}{C_2}\Phi(\mathbf{n} - \mathbf{e}_2), \frac{1}{C}[\Phi(\mathbf{n} - \mathbf{e}_1) + \Phi(\mathbf{n} - \mathbf{e}_2)] \right\} \Rightarrow$$

$$\Phi(1,1) = \max\left\{ \frac{1}{6}\Phi(0,1), \frac{1}{4}\Phi(1,0), \frac{1}{4}[\Phi(0,1) + \Phi(1,0)] \right\} \overset{\Phi(1,0)=0.5}{\Rightarrow}$$

$$\Phi(1,1) = \max\left\{ \frac{1}{24}, \frac{1}{8}, \frac{3}{16} \right\} = \frac{3}{16}$$

Thus $\phi_1(1,1) = \frac{1/4}{3/16} = \frac{4}{3}$. This means that in state (1,1) the call of service-class 1 has an allocated bandwidth of $\phi_1(1,1)/n_1 = 4/3$ b.u. according to [9]. This is the same as the allocated bandwidth provided according to the E-EMLM/TH (see Table 3.4 for the value of $\varphi_1(1,1)$): $b_1' = \varphi_1(1,1) b_1 = \frac{2}{3} \cdot 2 = \frac{4}{3}$.

- $\phi_2(1,1) = \frac{\Phi(1,0)}{\Phi(1,1)} = \frac{1/2}{3/16} = \frac{8}{3}$. This means that in state (1,1) the call of service-class 2 has an allocated bandwidth of 8/3 b.u. This is the same as the allocated bandwidth provided according to the E-EMLM/TH (see Table 3.4 for the value of $\varphi_2(1,1)$): $b_2' = \varphi_2(1,1) b_2 = \frac{2}{3} \cdot 4 = \frac{8}{3}$.

State (2,1):

- $\phi_1(2,1) = \frac{\Phi(1,1)}{\Phi(2,1)}$ where:

$$\Phi(1,1) = \frac{3}{16} \quad \text{and}$$

$$\Phi(2,1) = \max\left\{ \frac{1}{6}\Phi(1,1), \frac{1}{4}\Phi(2,0), \frac{1}{4}[\Phi(1,1) + \Phi(2,0)] \right\} \overset{\Phi(2,0)=1/8}{\Rightarrow}$$

$$\Phi(2,1) = \max\left\{ \frac{1}{32}, \frac{1}{32}, \frac{5}{64} \right\} = \frac{5}{64}$$

Thus $\phi_1(2,1) = \frac{3/16}{5/64} = \frac{12}{5}$. This means that in state (2,1) a call of service-class 1 has an allocated bandwidth of $\phi_1(2,1)/n_1 = 1.2$ b.u. This is the same as the allocated bandwidth provided according to the E-EMLM/TH: $b_1' = \varphi_1(2,1) b_1 = 0.6 \cdot 2 = 1.2$.

- $\phi_2(2,1) = \frac{\Phi(2,0)}{\Phi(2,1)} = \frac{1/8}{5/64} = \frac{8}{5} = 1.6$. This means that in state (2,1) the call of service-class 2 has an allocated bandwidth of 1.6 b.u. This is the same as the allocated bandwidth provided according to the E-EMLM/TH: $b_2' = \varphi_2(2,1) b_2 = 0.4 \cdot 4 = 1.6$.

State (3,0):

- $\phi_1(3,0) = \frac{\Phi(2,0)}{\Phi(3,0)}$ where:

$$\Phi(2,0) = \frac{1}{8} \quad \text{and}$$

$$\Phi(3,0) = \max\left\{ \frac{1}{6}\Phi(2,0), \frac{1}{4} \cdot 0, \frac{1}{4}\Phi(2,0) \right\} = \max\left\{ \frac{1}{48}, 0, \frac{1}{32} \right\} = \frac{1}{32}$$

Thus $\phi_1(3,0) = \frac{1/8}{1/32} = 4$.

This means that in state (3,0) a call of service-class 1 has an allocated bandwidth of $\phi_1(3,0)/n_1 = 4/3$ b.u. This is the same as the allocated bandwidth provided according to the E-EMLM/TH (see Table 3.4): $b_1' = \varphi_1(3,0) b_1 = \frac{2}{3} \cdot 2 = 4/3$.

- $\phi_2(3,0) = 0$ (obviously).

Based on the above, we see that the E-EMLM/TH results in the same bandwidth compression values with those provided by the balanced fair sharing of [9].

State (3,1): In the case of the E-EMLM, the network (Figure 3.15) cannot be in state (3,1) due to the T parameter. The total requested bandwidth (before compression, $3 \cdot 2 + 1 \cdot 4 = 10$ b.u.) would exceed the virtual capacity of $T = 8$ b.u. and therefore the call should be blocked and lost. On the contrary, in the case of the balanced fair share model which does not have the parameter T, (3,1) is a permissible state and the CAC should allocate the following bandwidth per service-class call:

- $\phi_1(3, 1) = \frac{\Phi(2,1)}{\Phi(3,1)}$ where:

$$\Phi(3, 1) = \max\left\{\frac{1}{6}\Phi(2, 1), \frac{1}{4}\Phi(3, 0), \frac{1}{4}[\Phi(2, 1) + \Phi(3, 0)]\right\} \Rightarrow$$

$$\Phi(3, 1) = \max\left\{\frac{1}{6}\frac{5}{64}, \frac{1}{4}\frac{1}{32}, \frac{1}{4}\frac{7}{64}\right\} = \frac{7}{256}$$

Thus $\phi_1(3, 1) = \frac{5/64}{7/256} = \frac{20}{7}$. This means that in state (3,1) a call of service-class 1 has an allocated bandwidth of $\phi_1(3, 1)/n_1 = 0.9524$ b.u. Compare this value with the corresponding maximum compressed values of the E-EMLM, which is $\frac{C}{T} b_1 = 1$ b.u.

- $\phi_2(3, 1) = \frac{\Phi(3,0)}{\Phi(3,1)} = \frac{1/32}{7/256} = 1.1429$. This means that in state (3,1) a call of service-class 2 has an allocated bandwidth of $\phi_2(3, 1)/n_2 = 1.1429$ b.u. Compare this value with the corresponding maximum compressed value of the E-EMLM, which is $\frac{C}{T} b_2 = 2$ b.u.

Example 3.12   Consider a link of capacity $C = 70$ b.u. and three values of T: (i) $T = C = 70$ b.u., (ii) $T = 75$ b.u., and (iii) $T = 80$ b.u. The link accommodates calls of $K = 3$ service-classes with the following traffic characteristics:

α_1	α_2	α_3	b_1	b_2	b_3	$n_{1,max}$	$n_{2,max}$	$n_{3,max}$
5.0 erl	1.5 erl	1.0 erl	2 b.u.	5 b.u.	9 b.u.	25 calls	11 calls	6 calls

(a) Compare the CBP B_1, B_2, and B_3 of the service-classes and the link utilization obtained by the E-EMLM/TH and the EMLM/TH when the offered traffic-loads α_1, α_2, and α_3 increase in steps of 1.0, 0.5, and 0.25 erl, respectively, up to $(\alpha_1, \alpha_2, \alpha_3) = (11.0, 4.5, 2.5)$. Also provide simulation results for the E-EMLM/TH.

(b) Consider the E-EMLM/TH and the E-EMLM and present the analytical CBP of all service-classes for $T = 75$ b.u. and $n_{3,max} = 3, 4$, and 5 calls.

(a) Figures 3.16–3.18 present the analytical and the simulation CBP results of all service-classes, respectively, in the case of the E-EMLM/TH. For comparison, we give the corresponding analytical CBP results of the EMLM/TH. In the x-axis of all figures, point 1 refers to $(\alpha_1, \alpha_2, \alpha_3) = (5.0, 1.5, 1.0)$, while point 7 refers to $(\alpha_1, \alpha_2, \alpha_3) = (11.0, 4.5, 2.5)$. Simulation results are based on SIMSCRIPT III and are

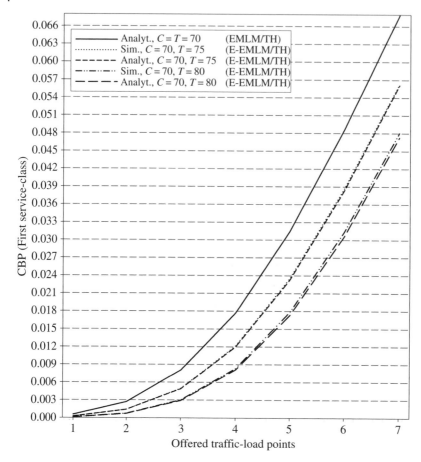

Figure 3.16 CBP of service-class 1, when $n_{3,\text{max}} = 6$ (Example 3.12).

mean values of seven runs (with very small reliability ranges). In Figure 3.19 we present the link utilization for both models. The figures show the following:

- The results obtained by the E-EMLM/TH formulas are close to the simulation results.
- The bandwidth compression mechanism reduces the CBP of all service-classes.
- The analytical results of the EMLM/TH fail to approximate the simulation results of the E-EMLM/TH.
- The link utilization is higher when $T = 80$ b.u., a result that is expected since this value of T achieves the highest CBP reduction (highest bandwidth compression, compared to $T = 70$ or 75 b.u.).

(b) In Figures 3.20–3.22 we consider the E-EMLM/TH together with the E-EMLM and present the analytical CBP results of all service-classes for $T = 75$ b.u. and $n_{3,\text{max}} = 3$, 4, and 5 calls. The E-EMLM fails to approximate the CBP results obtained by the E-EMLM/TH, in the cases of $n_{3,\text{max}} = 3$ and 4 (this proves the necessity of the E-EMLM/TH). The fact that the two models give quite close CBP results for $n_{3,\text{max}} = 5$ is explained as follows. Assuming that only calls of service-class 3 exist in the link

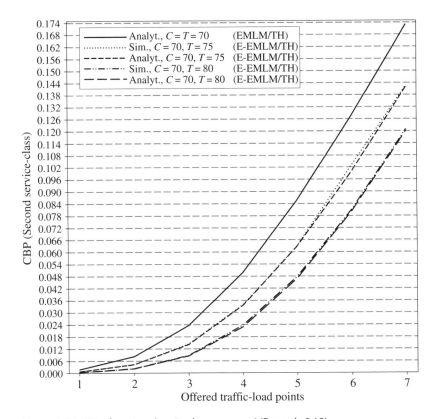

Figure 3.17 CBP of service-class 2, when $n_{3,max} = 6$ (Example 3.12).

then the theoretical maximum number of calls of service-class 3 is 8 (= $\lfloor \frac{75}{9} \rfloor$) (each of which occupies $\frac{70}{75} \cdot 9 = 8.4$ b.u.). Approaching this value makes the E-EMLM/TH behave as the E-EMLM. We also see that the increase of $n_{3,max}$ results in the CBP increase for service-classes 1 and 2 (Figures 3.20 and 3.21, respectively) and the CBP decrease for service-class 3 (Figure 3.22).

3.4 The Elastic Adaptive Erlang Multirate Loss Model

3.4.1 The Service System

In the *elastic adaptive EMLM (EA-EMLM)*, we consider a link of capacity C b.u. that accommodates K service-classes which are distinguished into K_e elastic service-classes and K_a adaptive service-classes, $K = K_e + K_a$. The call arrival process remains Poisson. As already mentioned, adaptive traffic is considered a variant of elastic traffic in the sense that adaptive calls can tolerate bandwidth compression without altering their service time.

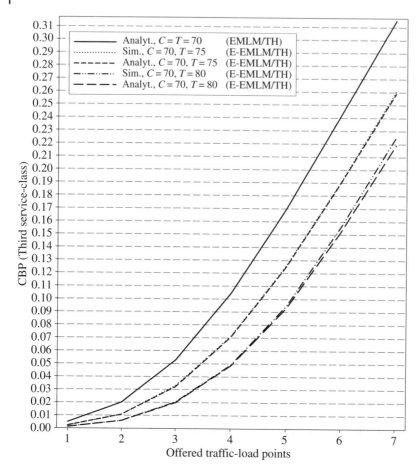

Figure 3.18 CBP of service-class 3, when $n_{3,\max} = 6$ (Example 3.12).

The bandwidth compression/expansion mechanism and the CAC of the EA-EMLM are the same as those of the E-EMLM (Section 3.1.1). The only difference is in (3.3), which is applied only on elastic calls. Similar to the E-EMLM, the corresponding Markov chain in the EA-EMLM does not meet the necessary and sufficient Kolmogorov's criterion for reversibility between four adjacent states.

Example 3.13 Consider Example 3.1 ($C = 3, T = 5, K = 2, b_1 = 1, b_2 = 2, \lambda_1 = \lambda_2 = \mu_1 = \mu_2 = 1.0$) and assume that calls of service-class 2 are adaptive. This example clarifies the differences between the E-EMLM and the EA-EMLM.

(a) Draw the complete state transition diagram of the system and determine the values of j and $r(\mathbf{n})$ for each state $\mathbf{n} = (n_1, n_2)$.
(b) Consider state $(1, 1)$ and explain the bandwidth compression mechanism when an adaptive call of service-class 2 arrives in the link.
(c) Now, consider state $(1, 2)$ and explain the bandwidth expansion that takes place when an adaptive call of service-class 2 departs from the system.

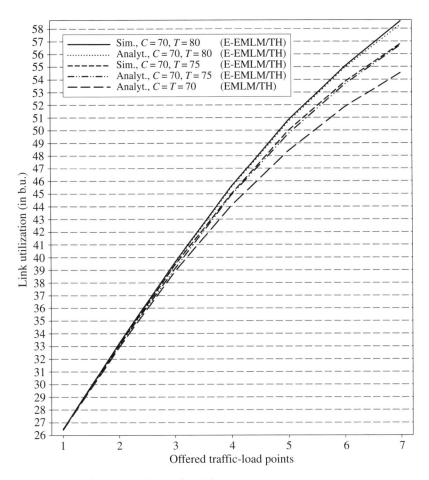

Figure 3.19 Link utilization (Example 3.12).

(d) Write the GB equations, and determine the values of $P(\mathbf{n})$ and the exact CBP of both service-classes.

(a) Figure 3.23 shows the state space Ω that consists of 12 permissible states $\mathbf{n} = (n_1, n_2)$ together with the complete state transition diagram of the system. The values of $r(\mathbf{n})$ and $j = n_1 b_1 + n_2 b_2$, before and after bandwidth compression has been applied, are the same as those presented in Table 3.1.

(b) When a new adaptive call of service-class 2 arrives in the system while the system is in state $(n_1, n_2) = (1, 1)$ where $j = C = 3$ b.u. then, since in the new state it would be $j' = j + b_2 = T = 5$ b.u., the new call is accepted in the system after bandwidth compression to all calls (new and in-service calls). In the new state of the system, (1, 2), based on (3.4), calls of both service-classes compress their bandwidth to $b'_{1,\min} = r_{\min} b_1 = \frac{3}{5} b_1 = 0.6$ b.u., $b'_{2,\min} = r_{\min} b_2 = \frac{3}{5} b_2 = 1.2$ b.u. so that $j = n_1 b'_{1,\min} + n_2 b'_{2,\min} = 0.6 +$

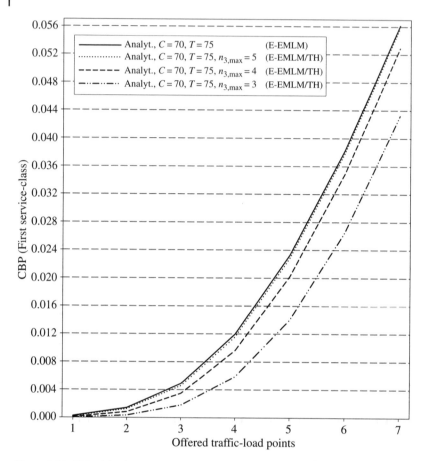

Figure 3.20 CBP of the first service-class, when $n_{3,max} = 3$, 4, and 5 (Example 3.12).

$2.4 = 3 = C$. As far as service-time is concerned, the value of μ_1^{-1} becomes $\frac{\mu_1^{-1}}{r_{min}}$, while the value of μ_2^{-1} does not alter.

(c) If an adaptive call of service-class 2 departs from the system then its assigned bandwidth $b'_{2,min} = 1.2$ b.u. is released to be immediately shared among the remaining calls in proportion to their peak-bandwidth requirement. The system passes to state $(n_1, n_2) = (1, 1)$, the elastic call of service-class 1 expands its bandwidth to $b'_1 = b_1 = 1$ b.u., and the adaptive call of service-class 2 to $b'_2 = b_2 = 2$ b.u. Thus, $j = n_1 b_1 + n_2 b_2 = C = 3$ b.u. As far as the service time of the elastic call is concerned, it decreases to its initial value $\mu_1^{-1} = 1$ time unit.

(d) Based on Figure 3.22, we obtain the following 12 GB equations:

$(0, 0)$:	$P(1, 0) + P(0, 1) - 2P(0, 0) = 0$
$(0, 1)$:	$P(0, 0) + P(1, 1) + 2P(0, 2) - 3P(0, 1) = 0$
$(0, 2)$:	$0.6P(1, 2) + P(0, 1) - 3P(0, 2) = 0$
$(1, 0)$:	$P(0, 0) + 2P(2, 0) + P(1, 1) - 3P(1, 0) = 0$

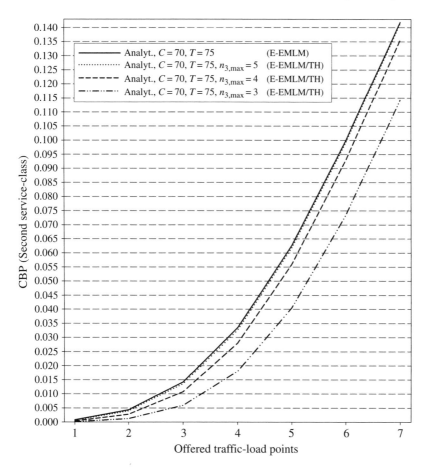

Figure 3.21 CBP of the second service-class, when $n_{3,\max} = 3$, 4, and 5 (Example 3.12).

$(1,1):\quad P(0,1) + 1.5P(2,1) + 2P(1,2) + P(1,0) - 4P(1,1) = 0$

$(1,2):\quad P(1,1) + P(0,2) - 2.6P(1,2) = 0$

$(2,0):\quad P(1,0) + 3P(3,0) + P(2,1) - 4P(2,0) = 0$

$(2,1):\quad P(1,1) + 1.8P(3,1) + P(2,0) - 3.5P(2,1) = 0$

$(3,0):\quad P(2,0) + 3P(4,0) + P(3,1) - 5P(3,0) = 0$

$(3,1):\quad P(2,1) + P(3,0) - 2.8P(3,1) = 0$

$(4,0):\quad P(3,0) + 3P(5,0) - 4P(4,0) = 0$

$(5,0):\quad P(4,0) - 3P(5,0) = 0$

The solution of this linear system is:

$P(0,0) = 0.1481$	$P(0,1) = 0.1408$	$P(0,2) = 0.0632$	$P(1,0) = 0.1554$
$P(1,1) = 0.1479$	$P(1,2) = 0.0812$	$P(2,0) = 0.0851$	$P(2,1) = 0.0888$
$P(3,0) = 0.0321$	$P(3,1) = 0.0432$	$P(4,0) = 0.0107$	$P(5,0) = 0.0036$

Then, based on the values of $P(n_1, n_2)$ and (3.6), we determine the exact CBP:

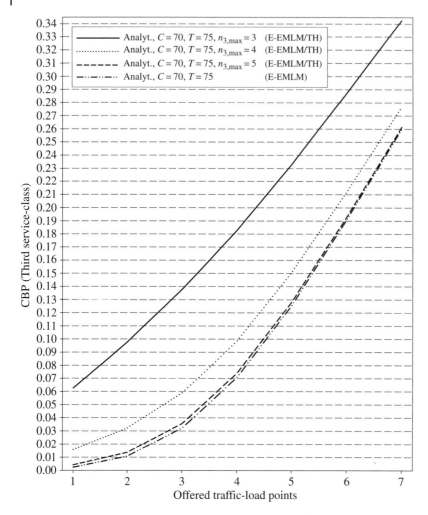

Figure 3.22 CBP of the third service-class, when $n_{3,max} = 3$, 4, and 5 (Example 3.12).

$B_1 = P(1, 2) + P(3, 1) + P(5, 0) = 0.128$

(compare with 0.1748 of the E-EMLM in Example 3.1)

$B_2 = P(0, 2) + P(2, 1) + P(4, 0) + P(1, 2) + P(3, 1) + P(5, 0) = 0.2907$

(compare with 0.3574 of the E-EMLM in Example 3.1)

The comparison between the CBP obtained in the EA-EMLM and the E-EMLM reveals that the E-EMLM does not approximate the EA-EMLM. In addition, the CBP of the EA-EMLM are lower, a fact that it is intuitively expected since, in this example, adaptive calls remain less time in the system than the corresponding elastic calls.

To circumvent the non-reversibility problem in the EA-EMLM, similar to the E-EMLM, $r(\mathbf{n})$ are replaced by the state-dependent factors per service-class k, $\varphi_k(\mathbf{n})$,

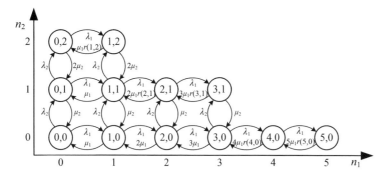

Figure 3.23 The state space Ω and the state transition diagram (Example 3.13).

which individualize the role of $r(\mathbf{n})$ per service-class in order to lead to a reversible Markov chain [6]. Thus the compressed bandwidth of service-class k calls is determined by (3.7), while the values of $\varphi_k(\mathbf{n})$ are given by (3.8). However, due to the adaptive service-classes, in the EA-EMLM the values of the state multipliers $x(\mathbf{n})$ are determined by [6]:

$$
x(\mathbf{n}) = \begin{cases}
1 & \text{when } \mathbf{nb} \leq C, \ \mathbf{n} \in \Omega \\[2mm]
\dfrac{1}{C}\left(\displaystyle\sum_{k \in K_e} n_k b_k x(\mathbf{n}_k^-) + r(\mathbf{n}) \sum_{k \in K_a} n_k b_k x(\mathbf{n}_k^-) \right) & \text{when } C < \mathbf{nb} \leq T, \ \mathbf{n} \in \Omega \\[4mm]
0 & \text{otherwise}
\end{cases}
$$

(3.47)

where $r(\mathbf{n}) = C/(\mathbf{nb}) = C/j$.

The derivation of (3.47) is based on the following assumptions:

(i) The bandwidth of all in-service calls of service-class $k \in K$ (elastic or adaptive) is compressed by a factor $\varphi_k(\mathbf{n})$ to a new value b_k' in state n, where $C < \mathbf{nb} \leq T$, so that:

$$
\sum_{k \in K_e} n_k b_k' + \sum_{k \in K_a} n_k b_k' = C
$$

(3.48)

(ii) The product *service time* by *bandwidth per call* of service-class k calls, $k \in K$, remains the same in state $\mathbf{n}$ regardless of the reversibility of the Markov chain. In other words, it holds that:

$$
\frac{b_k r(\mathbf{n})}{\mu_k r(\mathbf{n})} = \frac{b_k'}{\mu_k \varphi_k(\mathbf{n})} \Rightarrow b_k' = b_k \varphi_k(\mathbf{n}) \qquad \text{for elastic service classes}
$$

(3.49)

$$
\frac{b_k r(\mathbf{n})}{\mu_k} = \frac{b_k'}{\mu_k \varphi_k(\mathbf{n})} \Rightarrow b_k' = b_k \varphi_k(\mathbf{n}) r(\mathbf{n}) \qquad \text{for adaptive service classes}
$$

(3.50)

Now, we can derive (3.47) by substituting (3.49), (3.50), and (3.8) into (3.48).

Table 3.5 The values of the state dependent factors $\varphi_k(\mathbf{n})$ (Example 3.14).

n_1	n_2	$x(n)$	$\varphi_1(n)$	$\varphi_2(n)$	n_1	n_2	$x(n)$	$\varphi_1(n)$	$\varphi_2(n)$
0	0	1.0	1.00	1.00	2	0	1.0	1.00	1.00
0	1	1.0	1.00	1.00	2	1	1.1667	0.8571	0.8571
0	2	1.0	0.00	1.00	3	0	1.0	1.00	1.00
1	0	1.0	1.00	1.00	3	1	1.5667	0.7447	0.6383
1	1	1.0	1.00	1.00	4	0	1.3333	0.75	0.00
1	2	1.1333	0.8824	0.8824	5	0	2.2222	0.60	0.00

Example 3.14 Consider again Example 3.13 ($K = 2, K_e = 1, K_a = 1, C = 3, T = 5$, $\lambda_1 = \lambda_2 = \mu_1 = \mu_2 = 1.0$).

(a) Draw the modified state transition diagram based on $\varphi_k(\mathbf{n})$ and determine the values of $\varphi_k(\mathbf{n})$ for each state $\mathbf{n} = (n_1, n_2)$.
(b) Write the GB equations of the modified state transition diagram, and determine the values of $P(\mathbf{n})$ and the CBP of both service-classes.

(a) The graphical representation of the modified state transition diagram is identical to that of Figure 3.3. Table 3.5 presents the 12 states together with the corresponding values of $\varphi_k(\mathbf{n})$ (calculated through $x(\mathbf{n})$ –(3.47)). Compared to Table 3.2, we see that the existence of adaptive traffic modifies the values of $\varphi_1(\mathbf{n})$ and $\varphi_2(\mathbf{n})$.
(b) Based on Figure 3.3 and Table 3.5, we obtain the following 12 GB equations:

$(0,0)$: $\quad P(1,0) + P(0,1) - 2P(0,0) = 0$
$(0,1)$: $\quad P(0,0) + P(1,1) + 2P(0,2) - 3P(0,1) = 0$
$(0,2)$: $\quad (3/3.4)P(1,2) + P(0,1) - 3P(0,2) = 0$
$(1,0)$: $\quad P(0,0) + 2P(2,0) + P(1,1) - 3P(1,0) = 0$
$(1,1)$: $\quad P(0,1) + (6/3.5)P(2,1) + (6/3.4)P(1,2) + P(1,0) - 4P(1,1) = 0$
$(1,2)$: $\quad P(1,1) + P(0,2) - (9/3.4)P(1,2) = 0$
$(2,0)$: $\quad P(1,0) + 3P(3,0) + (3/3.5)P(2,1) - 4P(2,0) = 0$
$(2,1)$: $\quad P(1,1) + (10.5/4.7)P(3,1) + P(2,0) - (12.5/3.5)P(2,1) = 0$
$(3,0)$: $\quad P(2,0) + 3P(4,0) + (3/4.7)P(3,1) - 5P(3,0) = 0$
$(3,1)$: $\quad P(2,1) + P(3,0) - (13.5/4.7)P(3,1) = 0$
$(4,0)$: $\quad P(3,0) + 3P(5,0) - 4P(4,0) = 0$
$(5,0)$: $\quad P(4,0) - 3P(5,0) = 0$

The solution of this linear system is:

$P(0,0) = 0.1503$	$P(0,1) = 0.1503$	$P(0,2) = 0.0752$	$P(1,0) = 0.1503$
$P(1,1) = 0.1503$	$P(1,2) = 0.0852$	$P(2,0) = 0.0752$	$P(2,1) = 0.0877$
$P(3,0) = 0.0251$	$P(3,1) = 0.0393$	$P(4,0) = 0.0084$	$P(5,0) = 0.0028$

Then, based on the values of $P(n_1, n_2)$ and (3.6), we determine the CBP:

$B_1 = P(1, 2) + P(3, 1) + P(5, 0) = 0.1273$

(compare with the exact 0.128 in Example 3.13)

$B_2 = P(0, 2) + P(2, 1) + P(4, 0) + P(1, 2) + P(3, 1) + P(5, 0) = 0.2986$

(compare with the exact 0.2907 in Example 3.13)

3.4.2 The Analytical Model

3.4.2.1 Steady State Probabilities

The steady state transition rates of the EA-EMLM are shown in Figure 3.4. According to this, the GB equation for state $\mathbf{n} = (n_1, n_2, \ldots, n_k, \ldots, n_K)$ is given by (3.10) and the LB equations by (3.11) and (3.12).

Similar to the E-EMLM, we consider two different sets of macro-states: (i) $0 \leq j \leq C$ and (ii) $C < j \leq T$. For set (i), no bandwidth compression takes place and $q(j)$ are determined by the classical Kaufman–Roberts recursion (1.39). For set (ii), we substitute (3.8) in (3.11) to have:

$$\alpha_k x(\mathbf{n}) P(\mathbf{n}_k^-) = n_k x(\mathbf{n}_k^-) P(\mathbf{n}), \ k \in K_e \qquad \text{for elastic traffic} \qquad (3.51\text{a})$$

$$\alpha_k x(\mathbf{n}) P(\mathbf{n}_k^-) = n_k x(\mathbf{n}_k^-) P(\mathbf{n}), \ k \in K_a \qquad \text{for adaptive traffic} \qquad (3.51\text{b})$$

Multiplying both sides of (3.50) by b_k and summing over $k \in K_e$, we take:

$$x(\mathbf{n}) \sum_{k=1}^{K_e} \alpha_k b_k P(\mathbf{n}_k^-) = P(\mathbf{n}) \sum_{k=1}^{K_e} n_k b_k x(\mathbf{n}_k^-) \qquad (3.52)$$

Similarly, multiplying both sides of (3.50) by b_k and C/j, and summing over $k \in K_a$, we take:

$$(C/j) x(\mathbf{n}) \sum_{k=1}^{K_a} \alpha_k b_k P(\mathbf{n}_k^-) = (C/j) P(\mathbf{n}) \sum_{k=1}^{K_a} n_k b_k x(\mathbf{n}_k^-) \qquad (3.53)$$

By adding (3.52) and (3.53), we have:

$$P(\mathbf{n}) \left(\sum_{k=1}^{K_e} n_k b_k x(\mathbf{n}_k^-) + \frac{C}{j} \sum_{k=1}^{K_a} n_k b_k x(\mathbf{n}_k^-) \right) = \\ x(\mathbf{n}) \left(\sum_{k=1}^{K_e} \alpha_k b_k P(\mathbf{n}_k^-) + \frac{C}{j} \sum_{k=1}^{K_a} \alpha_k b_k P(\mathbf{n}_k^-) \right) \qquad (3.54)$$

Based on (3.47), (3.54) is written as:

$$P(\mathbf{n}) = \frac{1}{C} \sum_{k=1}^{K_e} \alpha_k b_k P(\mathbf{n}_k^-) + \frac{1}{j} \sum_{k=1}^{K_a} \alpha_k b_k P(\mathbf{n}_k^-) \qquad (3.55)$$

Summing both sides of (3.55) over Ω_j and based on the fact that $q(j) = \sum_{\mathbf{n} \in \Omega_j} P(\mathbf{n})$, we have:

$$q(j) = \frac{1}{C} \sum_{k=1}^{K_e} \alpha_k b_k q(j - b_k) + \frac{1}{j} \sum_{k=1}^{K_a} \alpha_k b_k q(j - b_k) \qquad (3.56)$$

The combination of (1.39) and (3.56) leads to the recursive formula of the EA-EMLM [6]:

$$
q(j) = \begin{cases}
1 & \text{if } j = 0 \\
\frac{1}{\min(C,j)} \sum\limits_{k=1}^{K_e} \alpha_k b_k q(j - b_k) + \frac{1}{j} \sum\limits_{k=1}^{K_a} \alpha_k b_k q(j - b_k) & \text{if } j = 1, 2, \ldots, T \\
0 & \text{otherwise}
\end{cases}
\tag{3.57}
$$

3.4.2.2 CBP, Utilization, and Mean Number of In-service Calls

The following performance measures can be determined based on (3.57):

- The CBP of service-class k, B_k, based on (3.22).
- The link utilization, U, based on (3.23).
- The average number of service-class k calls in the system, $\bar{n}_k$, based on (3.24) where the values of $y_k(j)$ are given by (3.58) for elastic traffic and (3.59) for adaptive traffic [6]:

$$
y_k(j) = \frac{1}{\min(j, C)q(j)} \alpha_k b_k q(j - b_k)(1 + y_k(j - b_k)) +
$$

$$
\frac{1}{\min(j, C)q(j)} \sum_{i=1, i \neq k}^{K_e} \alpha_i b_i q(j - b_i) y_k(j - b_i) + \frac{1}{jq(j)} \sum_{i=1}^{K_a} \alpha_i b_i q(j - b_i) y_k(j - b_i)
$$

$$\tag{3.58}$$

$$
y_k(j) = \frac{1}{jq(j)} \alpha_k b_k q(j - b_k)(1 + y_k(j - b_k)) +
$$

$$
\frac{1}{\min(j, C)q(j)} \sum_{i=1}^{K_e} \alpha_i b_i q(j - b_i) y_k(j - b_i) + \frac{1}{jq(j)} \sum_{i=1, i \neq k}^{K_a} \alpha_i b_i q(j - b_i) y_k(j - b_i)
$$

$$\tag{3.59}$$

where $j = 1, \ldots, T$, while $y_k(x) = 0$ for $x \leq 0$ and $k = 1, \ldots, K$.

Example 3.15 Consider Example 3.14 ($C = 3, T = 5, K = 2, \alpha_1 = \alpha_2 = 1, b_1 = 1, b_2 = 2$).

(a) Calculate the (normalized) values of $Q(j)$ based on (3.57).
(b) Calculate the CBP of both service-classes based on (3.22).
(c) Calculate the link utilization based on (3.23).
(d) Calculate the mean number of in-service calls of the two service-classes in the system based on (3.24), (3.58), and (3.59).

(a) State probabilities through the recursion (3.57):

$j = 1$:	$q(1) = q(0) + 0 = 1.0$	$\Rightarrow$	$q(1) = 1.0$
$j = 2$:	$2q(2) = q(1) + 2q(0) = 3$	$\Rightarrow$	$q(2) = 1.5$
$j = 3$:	$3q(3) = q(2) + 2q(1) = 3.5$	$\Rightarrow$	$q(3) = 1.16667$

$j = 4:$ $3q(4) = q(3) + 1.5q(2) = 3.41667$ $\Rightarrow$ $q(4) = 1.13889$

$j = 5:$ $3q(5) = q(4) + 1.2q(3) = 2.53889$ $\Rightarrow$ $q(5) = 0.8463$

The normalization constant is $G = \sum_{j=0}^{T} q(j) = 6.65186$.
The state probabilities are:

$Q(0) = 0.1503, Q(1) = 0.1503, Q(2) = 0.2255, Q(3) = 0.1754, Q(4) = 0.1712, Q(5) = 0.1272$

(b) The CBP are:

$$B_1 = \sum_{j=T-b_1+1}^{T} Q(j) = Q(5) = 0.1272, \quad B_2 = \sum_{j=T-b_2+1}^{T} Q(j) = Q(4) + Q(5) = 0.2984$$

(c) The link utilization is: $U = \sum_{j=1}^{C} jQ(j) + \sum_{j=C+1}^{T} CQ(j) = Q(1) + 2Q(2) + 3(Q(3) + Q(4) +$

$Q(5)) = 2.023$ b.u.

(d) For $\bar{n}_1, \bar{n}_2$, we initially determine the values of $y_k(j)$ for $k = 1, 2$ and $j = 1, \ldots, T$:

$j = 1$ $y_1(1) = 1.0$ $y_2(1) = 0.0$

$j = 2$ $y_1(2) = 0.6667$ $y_2(2) = 0.6667$

$j = 3$ $y_1(3) = 1.2857$ $y_2(3) = 0.8571$

$j = 4$ $y_1(4) = 1.2195$ $y_2(4) = 1.3902$

$j = 5$ $y_1(5) = 1.7046$ $y_2(5) = 1.6477$

Then, based on (3.24), we obtain

$\bar{n}_1 = 0.9518$ and $\bar{n}_2 = 0.7483$.

Example 3.16   Consider Example 3.5 ($C = 32, K = 2, b_1 = 4, b_2 = 1, \alpha_1 = \alpha_2 = 2$) and let calls of service-class 1 be adaptive. Assuming four values of $T = 32, 40, 48$, and 56 b.u., calculate the CBP B_1 and B_2 of the two service-classes and the link utilization when α_1 and α_2 increase in steps of 2 erl (up to $\alpha_1 = \alpha_2 = 16$ erl). Compare the CBP and the link utilization results with those obtained by the E-EMLM in Example 3.5.

Figure 3.24 presents the CBP of both service-classes while Figure 3.25 presents the link utilization for the three values of T. Observe that when $T = C = 32$ b.u., the system behaves as in the EMLM. In the x-axis of both figures, point 1 refers to $(\alpha_1, \alpha_2) = (2.0, 2.0)$, while point 8 refers to $(\alpha_1, \alpha_2) = (16.0, 16.0)$. According to Figure 3.24, the CBP of both service-classes decrease as the value of T increases. Compared to Figure 3.5, we see that (i) the CBP of the EA-EMLM are much lower than the corresponding CBP of the E-EMLM and (ii) the impact of the increase of T on the CBP is higher in the EA-EMLM. Both (i) and (ii) can be explained by the fact that in-service calls of service-class 1 remain less in the system when they are adaptive, thus allowing more calls to be accepted in the system. As far as the link utilization is concerned, the values of U in the EA-EMLM are slightly lower (worse) than those of the E-EMLM because of the adaptive service-class 1 calls.

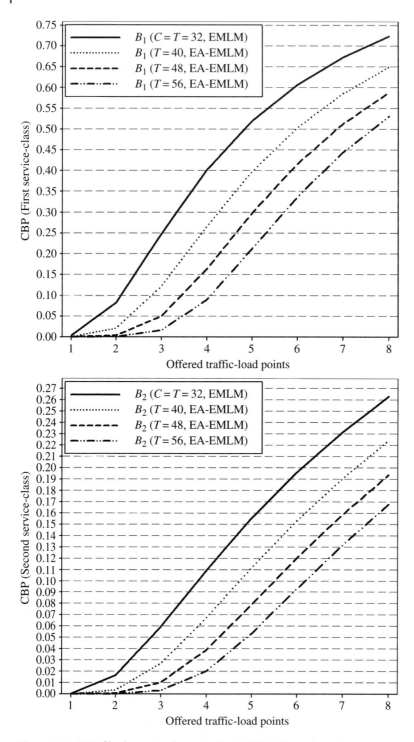

Figure 3.24 CBP of both service-classes in the EA-EMLM (Example 3.16).

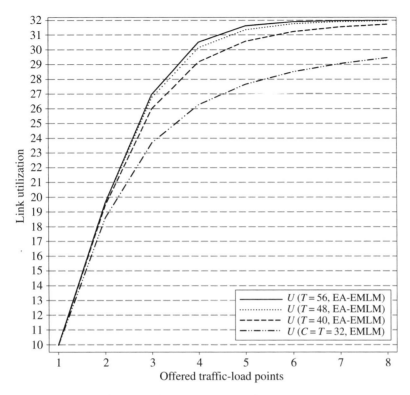

Figure 3.25 Link utilization in the EA-EMLM (Example 3.16).

3.5 The Elastic Adaptive Erlang Multirate Loss Model under the BR Policy

3.5.1 The Service System

We now consider the multiservice system of the *EA-EMLM under the BR policy (EA-EMLM/BR)* [13]. A new service-class k call is accepted in the link if, after its acceptance, the occupied link bandwidth $j \leq T - t_k$, where t_k refers to the BR parameter used to benefit (in CBP) calls of other service-classes apart from k. In terms of the system state-space Ω, the CBP is expressed according to (3.33).

Example 3.17 Consider again Example 3.13 ($K = 2, K_e = 1, K_a = 1, C = 3, T = 5$, $\lambda_1 = \lambda_2 = \mu_1 = \mu_2 = 1.0$). Assume that $t_1 = 1$ and $t_2 = 0$ b.u., so that $b_1 + t_1 = b_2 + t_2$.

(a) Draw the complete state transition diagram of the system and determine the values of j and $r(\mathbf{n})$ for each state $\mathbf{n} = (n_1, n_2)$, $\mathbf{n} \in \Omega$.
(b) Write the GB equations, determine the values of $P(\mathbf{n})$ and the exact CBP of both service-classes.
(c) Draw the modified state transition diagram based on $\varphi_k(\mathbf{n})$ and determine the values of $\varphi_k(\mathbf{n})$ for each state $\mathbf{n} = (n_1, n_2)$.
(d) Write the GB equations of the modified state transition diagram, and determine the values of $P(\mathbf{n})$ and the CBP of both service-classes.

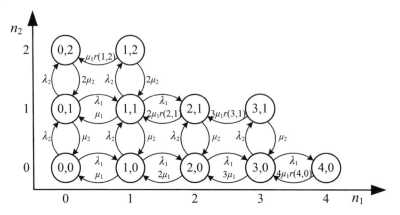

Figure 3.26 The state space Ω and the state transition diagram (Example 3.17).

(a) Figure 3.26 shows the state space Ω that consists of 11 permissible states $\mathbf{n} = (n_1, n_2)$ together with the complete state transition diagram of the system. The corresponding values of $r(\mathbf{n})$ and $j = n_1 b_1 + n_2 b_2$ are exactly the same as those presented in Table 3.1.

(b) Based on Figure 3.26, we obtain the following 11 GB equations:

$(0,0):$	$P(1,0) + P(0,1) - 2P(0,0) = 0$
$(0,1):$	$P(0,0) + P(1,1) + 2P(0,2) - 3P(0,1) = 0$
$(0,2):$	$0.6P(1,2) + P(0,1) - 2P(0,2) = 0$
$(1,0):$	$P(0,0) + 2P(2,0) + P(1,1) - 3P(1,0) = 0$
$(1,1):$	$P(0,1) + 1.5P(2,1) + 2P(1,2) + P(1,0) - 4P(1,1) = 0$
$(1,2):$	$P(1,1) - 2.6P(1,2) = 0$
$(2,0):$	$P(1,0) + 3P(3,0) + P(2,1) - 4P(2,0) = 0$
$(2,1):$	$P(1,1) + 1.8P(3,1) + P(2,0) - 2.5P(2,1) = 0$
$(3,0):$	$P(2,0) + 3P(4,0) + P(3,1) - 5P(3,0) = 0$
$(3,1):$	$P(3,0) - 2.8P(3,1) = 0$
$(4,0):$	$P(3,0) - 3P(4,0) = 0$

The solution of this linear system is:

$P(0,0) = 0.1626$	$P(0,1) = 0.1703$	$P(0,2) = 0.1019$	$P(1,0) = 0.1548$
$P(1,1) = 0.1447$	$P(1,2) = 0.0557$	$P(2,0) = 0.0786$	$P(2,1) = 0.0949$
$P(3,0) = 0.0216$	$P(3,1) = 0.0077$	$P(4,0) = 0.0072$	

Then, based on the $P(n_1, n_2)$ and (3.32), we obtain the exact value of equalized CBP:

$$B_1 = B_2 = P(0,2) + P(2,1) + P(4,0) + P(1,2) + P(3,1) = 0.2674$$

(compare with 0.3234 of the E-EMLM/BR in Example 3.6).

(c) The graphical representation of the modified state transition diagram is identical to that of Figure 3.8. The corresponding values of $\varphi_k(\mathbf{n})$ are exactly the same as those presented in Table 3.5.

(d) Based on Figure 3.8 and Table 3.5, we obtain the following 11 GB equations:

$(0,0)$: $P(1,0) + P(0,1) - 2P(0,0) = 0$

$(0,1)$: $P(0,0) + P(1,1) + 2P(0,2) - 3P(0,1) = 0$

$(0,2)$: $(3/3.4)P(1,2) + P(0,1) - 2P(0,2) = 0$

$(1,0)$: $P(0,0) + 2P(2,0) + P(1,1) - 3P(1,0) = 0$

$(1,1)$: $P(0,1) + (6/3.5)P(2,1) + (6/3.4)P(1,2) + P(1,0) - 4P(1,1) = 0$

$(1,2)$: $P(1,1) - (9/3.4)P(1,2) = 0$

$(2,0)$: $P(1,0) + 3P(3,0) + (3/3.5)P(2,1) - 4P(2,0) = 0$

$(2,1)$: $P(1,1) + (10.5/4.7)P(3,1) + P(2,0) - (9.0/3.5)P(2,1) = 0$

$(3,0)$: $P(2,0) + 3P(4,0) + (3/4.7)P(3,1) - 5P(3,0) = 0$

$(3,1)$: $P(3,0) - (13.5/4.7)P(3,1) = 0$

$(4,0)$: $P(3,0) - 3P(4,0) = 0$

The solution of this linear system is:

$P(0,0) = 0.1648$	$P(0,1) = 0.1791$	$P(0,2) = 0.1137$	$P(1,0) = 0.1505$
$P(1,1) = 0.1450$	$P(1,2) = 0.0548$	$P(2,0) = 0.0709$	$P(2,1) = 0.0896$
$P(3,0) = 0.0188$	$P(3,1) = 0.0065$	$P(4,0) = 0.0063$	

Then, based on $P(n_1, n_2)$ and (3.32), we obtain the value of equalized CBP:

$$B_1 = B_2 = P(0,2) + P(2,1) + P(4,0) + P(1,2) + P(3,1) = 0.2709$$

which is quite close to the exact value of 0.2674.

3.5.2 The Analytical Model

3.5.2.1 Link Occupancy Distribution

In the EA-EMLM/BR, the link occupancy distribution, $q(j)$, is calculated in an approximate way, according to the following recursive formula (Roberts method) [13]:

$$q(j) = \begin{cases} 1 & \text{if } j = 0 \\ \dfrac{1}{\min(C,j)} \displaystyle\sum_{k=1}^{K_e} \alpha_k D_k(j - b_k)q(j - b_k) + \\ \quad + \dfrac{1}{j} \displaystyle\sum_{k=1}^{K_a} \alpha_k D_k(j - b_k)q(j - b_k) & \text{if } j = 1, 2, \ldots, T \\ 0 & \text{otherwise} \end{cases}$$ (3.60a)

$$\text{where} \quad D_k(j - b_k) = \begin{cases} b_k & \text{for } j \le T - t_k \\ 0 & \text{for } j > T - t_k \end{cases}$$ (3.60b)

This formula is similar to (3.34) of the E-EMLM/BR. If $t_k = 0$ for all k ($k = 1, \ldots, K$), then the EA-EMLM results. In addition, if $T = C$, then we have the classical EMLM.

3.5.2.2 CBP, Utilization, and Mean Number of In-service Calls

The following performance measures can be determined via (3.60):

- The CBP of service-class k, B_k, via (3.35).
- The link utilization, U, via (3.23).
- The average number of service-class k calls in the system, $y_k(j)$, is determined by (3.24), where $y_k(j)$ are given by (3.58) and (3.59) for elastic and adaptive service-classes, respectively, under the assumptions that (i) $y_k(j) = 0$ when $j > T - t_k$ and (ii) $\alpha_i b_i q(j - b_i) = 0$ when $j > T - t_i$.

Example 3.18 Consider again Example 3.17 ($C = 3, T = 5, K = 2, \alpha_1 = \alpha_2 = 1, b_1 = 1, b_2 = 2, t_1 = 1, t_2 = 0$).

(a) Calculate the (normalized) values of $Q(j)$ based on (3.60).
(b) Calculate the CBP of both service-classes based on (3.35).
(c) Calculate the link utilization based on (3.23).
(d) Calculate the mean number of in-service calls of the two service-classes in the system based on (3.24), (3.58), and (3.59).

(a) State probabilities through the recursion (3.60):

$j = 1:$	$q(1) = q(0) + 0 = 1.0$	$\Rightarrow q(1) = 1.0$
$j = 2:$	$2q(2) = q(1) + 2q(0) = 3$	$\Rightarrow q(2) = 1.5$
$j = 3:$	$3q(3) = q(2) + 2q(1) = 3.5$	$\Rightarrow q(3) = 1.16667$
$j = 4:$	$3q(4) = q(3) + 1.5q(2) = 3.41667$	$\Rightarrow q(4) = 1.13889$
$j = 5:$	$3q(5) = 1.2q(3) = 1.4$	$\Rightarrow q(5) = 0.46667$

The normalization constant is $G = \sum_{j=0}^{T} q(j) = 6.2722$

(b) The state probabilities are:

$Q(0) = 0.1594$	$Q(1) = 0.1594$	$Q(2) = 0.2392$
$Q(3) = 0.1860$	$Q(4) = 0.1816$	$Q(5) = 0.0744$

(c) The CBP are:

$$B_1 = \sum_{j=T-b_1-t_1+1}^{T} Q(j) = Q(4) + Q(5) = 0.256$$

$$B_2 = \sum_{j=T-b_2-t_2+1}^{T} Q(j) = Q(4) + Q(5) = 0.256$$

(compare with the value of 0.3171 obtained in the E-EMLM/BR of Example 3.7)

(d) The link utilization is:

$$U = \sum_{j=1}^{C} jQ(j) + \sum_{j=C+1}^{T} CQ(j) = Q(1) + 2Q(2) + 3(Q(3) + Q(4) + Q(5)) = 1.964 \text{ b.u.}$$

(e) For $\bar{n}_1, \bar{n}_2$, we initially determine the values of $y_k(j)$ for $k = 1, 2$ and $j = 1, \dots, T$:

$$j = 1: \quad y_1(1) = 1.0 \qquad y_2(1) = 0.0$$
$$j = 2: \quad y_1(2) = 0.6667 \qquad y_2(2) = 0.6667$$
$$j = 3: \quad y_1(3) = 1.2857 \qquad y_2(3) = 0.8571$$
$$j = 4: \quad y_1(4) = 1.2195 \qquad y_2(4) = 1.3902$$
$$j = 5: \quad y_1(5) = 0.0 \qquad y_2(5) = 1.8571$$

Then, based on (3.24), we have

$$\bar{n}_1 = 0.7795 \text{ and } \bar{n}_2 = 0.7095.$$

Example 3.19 Consider a link of capacity $C = 100$, $T = 140$ b.u. that accommodates calls of four service-classes, with the following traffic characteristics:

α_1	α_2	α_3	α_4	b_1	b_2	b_3	b_4	t_1	t_2	t_3	t_4
12 erl	6 erl	3 erl	2 erl	1 b.u.	2 b.u.	4 b.u.	10 b.u.	9 b.u.	8 b.u.	6 b.u.	0 b.u.

Calls of service-classes 1 and 2 are elastic, while calls of service-classes 3 and 4 are adaptive. Compare the CBP of all service-classes obtained by the EA-EMLM/BR and the EA-EMLM when the offered traffic-loads increase in steps of 2, 1, 0.5, and 0.25 erl up to $(\alpha_1, \alpha_2, \alpha_3, \alpha_4) = (24.0, 12.0, 6.0, 3.5)$ erl. Also provide simulation results for the EA-EMLM/BR.

Figure 3.27 presents the analytical and the simulation equalized CBP results of all service-classes, respectively, in the case of the EA-EMLM/BR. For comparison, we include the corresponding analytical CBP results of the EA-EMLM. In the x-axis of Figure 3.27, point 1 refers to $(\alpha_1, \alpha_2, \alpha_3, \alpha_4) = (12.0, 6.0, 3.0, 2.0)$, while point 7 is $(\alpha_1, \alpha_2, \alpha_3, \alpha_4) = (24.0, 12.0, 6.0, 3.5)$. Simulation results are based on SIMSCRIPT III and are mean values of 12 runs (no reliability ranges are shown). From Figure 3.27, we observe that (i) analytical and simulation CBP results are very close and (ii) the EA-EMLM fails to capture the behavior of the EA-EMLM/BR (hence, both models are necessary).

3.6 The Elastic Adaptive Erlang Multirate Loss Model under the Threshold Policy

3.6.1 The Service System

We now consider the *EA-EMLM under the TH policy (EA-EMLM/TH)*, as in the case of the E-EMLM/TH (Section 3.3). That is, the total number of in-service calls per service-class must not exceed a threshold (per service-class). The bandwidth compression/expansion mechanism and the CAC in the EA-EMLM/TH are the same as those of the E-EMLM/TH, but (3.3) is applied only on elastic calls to satisfy their service time requirement.

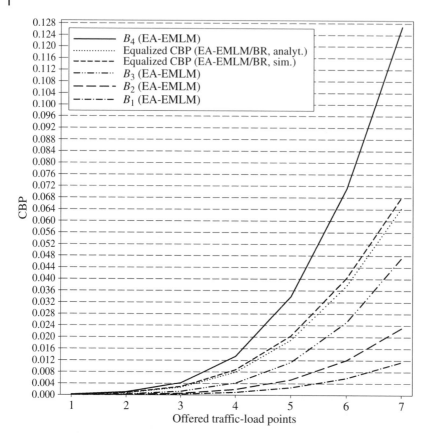

Figure 3.27 Equalized CBP of the EA-EMLM/BR and CBP per service-class of the EA-EMLM (Example 3.19).

Example 3.20 Consider Example 3.9 ($C = 4, T = 8, K = 2, b_1 = 2, b_2 = 4, n_{1,\max} = 3, n_{2,\max} = 1, \lambda_1 = \lambda_2 = \mu_1 = \mu_2 = 1.0$) and assume that calls of service-class 2 are adaptive. This example clarifies the differences between the E-EMLM/TH and the EA-EMLM/TH.

(a) Draw the complete state transition diagram of the system and determine the values of j and $r(\mathbf{n})$, based on (3.2), for each state $\mathbf{n} = (n_1, n_2)$.
(b) Write the GB equations, and determine the values of $P(\mathbf{n})$ and the exact CBP of both service-classes.
(c) Draw the modified state transition diagram based on $\varphi_k(\mathbf{n})$ and determine the values of $\varphi_k(\mathbf{n})$, based on (3.8) and (3.47), for each state $\mathbf{n} = (n_1, n_2)$.
(d) Write the GB equations of the modified state transition diagram, and determine the values of $P(\mathbf{n})$ and the CBP of both service-classes.

(a) Figure 3.28 shows the state space Ω that consists of seven permissible states $\mathbf{n} = (n_1, n_2)$ together with the complete state transition diagram of the system. Compared

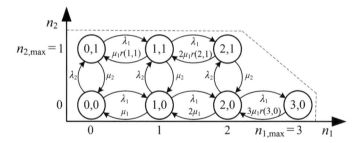

Figure 3.28 The state space Ω and the state transition diagram (Example 3.20).

to Figure 3.13, the differences are in μ_2 whose values do not alter in states (1, 1) and (2, 1). The corresponding values of $r(\mathbf{n})$ and $j = n_1 b_1 + n_2 b_2$ remain the same as in the case of the E-EMLM/TH (Table 3.3).

(b) According to Figure 3.28, we write the following seven GB equations:

$(0, 0)$:	$P(1, 0) + P(0, 1) - 2P(0, 0) = 0$
$(0, 1)$:	$P(0, 0) + 0.6667P(1, 1) - 2P(0, 1) = 0$
$(1, 0)$:	$P(0, 0) + 2P(2, 0) + P(1, 1) - 3P(1, 0) = 0$
$(1, 1)$:	$P(0, 1) + P(2, 1) + P(1, 0) - 2.6666P(1, 1) = 0$
$(2, 0)$:	$P(1, 0) + 2P(3, 0) + P(2, 1) - 4P(2, 0) = 0$
$(2, 1)$:	$P(1, 1) + P(2, 0) - 2P(2, 1) = 0$
$(3, 0)$:	$P(2, 0) - 2P(3, 0) = 0$

The solution of this linear system is:

$P(0, 0) = 0.1677$	$P(0, 1) = 0.1442$	$P(1, 0) = 0.1914$	$P(1, 1) = 0.1809$
$P(2, 0) = 0.1127$	$P(2, 1) = 0.1468$	$P(3, 0) = 0.0563$	

Then, based on the values of $P(n_1, n_2)$ and (3.36), we determine the exact CBP for each service-class:

$$B_1 = P(2, 1) + P(3, 0) = 0.2031 \text{ and } B_2 = P(1, 1) + P(2, 1) + P(3, 0) + P(0, 1) = 0.5282$$

(much lower than 0.2436 and 0.6076, respectively, of the E-EMLM/TH in Example 3.9).

(b) The modified state transition diagram is exactly the same as that of Figure 3.14. As far as the values of $\varphi_k(\mathbf{n})$ are concerned, they are presented in Table 3.6.

(c) Based on Figure 3.14 and Table 3.6, we obtain the following seven GB equations:

$(0, 0)$:	$P(1, 0) + P(0, 1) - 2P(0, 0) = 0$
$(0, 1)$:	$P(0, 0) + 0.8571P(1, 1) - 2P(0, 1) = 0$
$(1, 0)$:	$P(0, 0) + 2P(2, 0) + 0.8571P(1, 1) - 3P(1, 0) = 0$
$(1, 1)$:	$P(0, 1) + 1.4P(2, 1) + P(1, 0) - 2.7143P(1, 1) = 0$
$(2, 0)$:	$P(1, 0) + 2P(3, 0) + 0.6P(2, 1) - 4P(2, 0) = 0$
$(2, 1)$:	$P(1, 1) + P(2, 0) - 2P(2, 1) = 0$
$(3, 0)$:	$P(2, 0) - 2P(3, 0) = 0$

Table 3.6 The values of the state dependent factors $\varphi_k(\mathbf{n})$ (Example 3.20).

n_1	n_2	$x(\mathbf{n})$	$\varphi_1(\mathbf{n})$	$\varphi_2(\mathbf{n})$	n_1	n_2	$x(\mathbf{n})$	$\varphi_1(\mathbf{n})$	$\varphi_2(\mathbf{n})$
0	0	1.0	1.00	1.00	2	0	1.0	1.00	1.00
0	1	1.0	1.00	1.00	2	1	1.6667	0.70	0.60
1	0	1.0	1.00	1.00	3	0	1.5	0.6667	0.0
1	1	1.1667	0.8571	0.8571					

The solution of this linear system is:

$P(0,0) = 0.1739$ $\qquad$ $P(0,1) = 0.1739$ $\qquad$ $P(1,0) = 0.1739$ $\qquad$ $P(1,1) = 0.2029$

$P(2,0) = 0.0869$ $\qquad$ $P(2,1) = 0.1449$ $\qquad$ $P(3,0) = 0.0435$

Then, based on the values of $P(n_1, n_2)$ and (3.36), we determine the CBP for each service-class:

$B_1 = P(2,1) + P(3,0) = 0.1884$ $\qquad\qquad$ (compare with the exact 0.2031)

$B_2 = P(1,1) + P(2,1) + P(3,0) + P(0,1) = 0.5652$ $\qquad$ (compare with the exact 0.5282)

3.6.2 The Analytical Model

3.6.2.1 Steady State Probabilities

The steady state transition rates of the EA-EMLM/TH are shown in Figure 3.4. According to this, the GB equation for state $\mathbf{n} = (n_1, n_2, \dots, n_k, \dots, n_K)$ is given by (3.10), while the LB equations are given by (3.11) and (3.12) where $\Omega = \{\mathbf{n} : 0 \leq nb \leq T, \ n_k \leq n_{k,max}, \ k = 1, \dots, K\}$.

Similar to the EA-EMLM, we consider two different sets of macro-states: (i) $0 \leq j \leq C$ and (ii) $C < j \leq T$. For set (i), no bandwidth compression takes place and $q(j)$ are determined via (1.73). For set (ii), in order to derive a recursive formula, we follow the analysis of the EA-EMLM up to (3.55). Since $n_k \leq n_{k,max}$, we have:

$$\sum_{\mathbf{n} \in \Omega_j} P(\mathbf{n}_k^-) = q(j - b_k) - Prob[x = j - b_k, \ n_k = n_{k,max}] \qquad (3.61)$$

Thus, (3.55) can be written as:

$$P(\mathbf{n}) = \frac{1}{C} \sum_{k=1}^{K_e} \alpha_k b_k [q(j - b_k) - \Theta_k(j - b_k)] + \frac{1}{j} \sum_{k=1}^{K_a} \alpha_k b_k [q(j - b_k) - \Theta_k(j - b_k)]$$

$$(3.62)$$

where $\Theta_k(x)$ expresses the blocking constraint of the TH policy and is given by (1.74).

Summing both sides of (3.62) over Ω_j and based on the fact that $q(j) = \sum_{\mathbf{n} \in \Omega_j} P(\mathbf{n})$, we have:

$$q(j) = \frac{1}{C} \sum_{k=1}^{K_e} \alpha_k b_k [q(j - b_k) - \Theta_k(j - b_k)] + \frac{1}{j} \sum_{k=1}^{K_a} \alpha_k b_k [q(j - b_k) - \Theta_k(j - b_k)]$$

(3.63)

The combination of (1.73) and (3.63) results in the formula of the EA-EMLM/TH [14]:

$$q(j) = \begin{cases} 1 & \text{if } j = 0 \\ \frac{1}{\min(C,j)} \sum_{k=1}^{K_e} \alpha_k b_k [q(j - b_k) - \Theta_k(j - b_k)] + \\ + \frac{1}{j} \sum_{k=1}^{K_a} \alpha_k b_k [q(j - b_k) - \Theta_k(j - b_k)] & \text{if } j = 1, 2, \dots, T \\ 0 & \text{otherwise} \end{cases}$$

(3.64)

3.6.2.2 CBP, Utilization, and Mean Number of In-service Calls

The following performance measures can be determined based on (3.64):

- The CBP of service-class k, B_k, via (3.40).
- The link utilization, U, according to (3.23).
- The average number of service-class k calls in the system, $\bar{n}_k$, via (3.24) where the values of $y_k(j)$ are given by (3.65) for elastic traffic and (3.66) for adaptive traffic:

$$y_k(j) = \frac{1}{\min(j, C)q(j)} \alpha_k b_k [q(j - b_k) - \Theta_k(j - b_k)](1 + y_k(j - b_k)) +$$

$$\frac{1}{\min(j, C)q(j)} \sum_{i=1, i \neq k}^{K_e} \alpha_i b_i [q(j - b_i) - \Theta_i(j - b_i)] y_k(j - b_i) +$$

(3.65)

$$\frac{1}{jq(j)} \sum_{i=1}^{K_a} \alpha_i b_i [q(j - b_i) - \Theta_i(j - b_i)] y_k(j - b_i)$$

$$y_k(j) = \frac{1}{jq(j)} \alpha_k b_k [q(j - b_k) - \Theta_k(j - b_k)](1 + y_k(j - b_k)) +$$

$$\frac{1}{\min(j, C)q(j)} \sum_{i=1}^{K_e} \alpha_i b_i [q(j - b_i) - \Theta_i(j - b_i)] y_k(j - b_i) +$$

(3.66)

$$\frac{1}{jq(j)} \sum_{i=1, i \neq k}^{K_a} \alpha_i b_i [q(j - b_i) - \Theta_i(j - b_i)] y_k(j - b_i)$$

where $j = 1, \dots, T$, while $y_k(x) = 0$ for $x \leq 0$ and $k = 1, \dots, K$.

In (3.64) knowledge of $\Theta_k(j)$ is required. Since $\Theta_k(j) > 0$ when $j = n_{k,\max} b_k, \dots, T - b_k$, we consider two subsets of j: (i) $n_{k,\max} b_k \leq j \leq C$ and (ii) $C + 1 \leq j \leq T - b_k$. In both subsets, we assume that $K = K_e + K_a$.

For the first subset, let a system of capacity $F_k = T - b_k - n_{k,\max} b_k$ that accommodates all service-classes but service-class k. For this system, we define $\vartheta_k(j)$ via (3.43). Based on $\vartheta_k(j)$, we compute $\Theta_k(j)$ through (3.44). For the second subset, $\Theta_k(j)$ can be determined via (3.45).

Example 3.21 Consider again Example 3.20 $(C = 4, T = 8, K = 2, b_1 = 2, b_2 = 4, n_{1,\max} = 3, n_{2,\max} = 1, \alpha_1 = \alpha_2 = 1)$.

(a) Calculate the (normalized) values of $Q(j)$ based on (3.64).
(b) Calculate the CBP of both service-classes based on (3.40).

(a) State probabilities through the recursion (3.64):

$j = 1:$ $\quad q(1) = 0$ $\qquad\qquad\qquad\qquad\qquad\qquad\qquad\qquad \Rightarrow q(1) = 0$

$j = 2:$ $\quad q(2) = \frac{1}{2}2q(1) = 1.0$ $\qquad\qquad\qquad\qquad\qquad\qquad \Rightarrow q(2) = 1.0$

$j = 3:$ $\quad q(3) = 0$ $\qquad\qquad\qquad\qquad\qquad\qquad\qquad\qquad \Rightarrow q(3) = 0$

$j = 4:$ $\quad q(4) = \frac{1}{4}2q(2) + \frac{1}{4}4q(0)$ $\qquad\qquad\qquad\qquad\qquad \Rightarrow q(4) = 1.5$

$j = 5:$ $\quad q(5) = 0$ $\qquad\qquad\qquad\qquad\qquad\qquad\qquad\qquad \Rightarrow q(5) = 0$

$j = 6:$ $\quad q(6) = \frac{1}{4}2q(4) + \frac{1}{6}4q(2) = 1.41667$ $\qquad\qquad\qquad \Rightarrow q(6) = 1.41667$

$j = 7:$ $\quad q(7) = 0$ $\qquad\qquad\qquad\qquad\qquad\qquad\qquad\qquad \Rightarrow q(7) = 0$

$j = 8:$ $\quad q(8) = \frac{1}{4}2[q(6) - \Theta_1(6)] + \frac{1}{8}4[q(4) - \Theta_2(4)] = 0.8333 \quad \Rightarrow q(8) = 0.8333$

where $\quad \Theta_1(6) = 0.25$ and $\Theta_2(4) = 1.0$

The normalization constant is $G = \sum_{j=0}^{T} q(j) = 5.75$.
The state probabilities are:

$Q(0) = 0.1739 \qquad Q(2) = 0.1739 \qquad Q(4) = 0.2609 \qquad Q(6) = 0.2464 \qquad Q(8) = 0.1449$

(b) The CBP are:

$$B_1 = \sum_{j=T-b_1+1}^{T} Q(j) + \sum_{j=n_{1,\max}}^{T-b_1} G^{-1}\Theta_1(j) = Q(8) + G^{-1}\Theta_1(6) = 0.1884$$

$$B_2 = \sum_{j=T-b_2+1}^{T} Q(j) + \sum_{j=n_{2,\max}}^{T-b_2} G^{-1}\Theta_2(j) = Q(6) + Q(8) + G^{-1}\Theta_2(4) = 0.5652.$$

Example 3.22 Consider Example 3.12 and assume that service-class 1 is elastic while the other two service-classes are adaptive. Assuming the EA-EMLM/TH and the EA-EMLM, calculate the CBP of all service-classes for $T = 75$ b.u. and $n_{3,\max} = 3, 4$, and 5 calls.

The results of both the EA-EMLM/TH and EA-EMLM are presented in Figures 3.29, 3.30 and 3.31 for the three service-classes, respectively. Observe that the EA-EMLM fails to approximate the CBP results obtained by the EA-EMLM/TH in the cases of $n_{3,\max} = 3$ and 4. With the same explanation as in the case of Example 3.12, the two models give quite close CBP results for $n_{3,\max} = 5$.

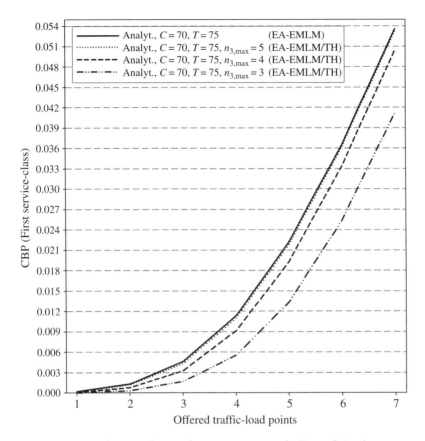

Figure 3.29 CBP of service-class 1, when $n_{3,\max} = 3, 4$, and 5 (Example 3.22).

3.7 Applications

We discuss the applicability of the models in the context of new architectural and functional enhancements of next-generation (5G) cellular networks. It is widely acknowledged that 5G systems will extensively rely on software-defined networking (SDN) and network function virtualization (NFV), which have attracted a lot of research efforts and gained tremendous attention from both academic and industry communities. The SDN technology is the driver towards completely programmable networks, which can be achieved by decoupling the control and data planes [15, 16]. On the other hand, the NFV technology allows executing the software-based network functions on general-purpose hardware via virtualization [17, 18]. SDN and NFV, due to their complementary nature, are traditionally seen as related concepts and implemented together [19]. Some of the expected benefits of SDN/NFV include CAPEX and OPEX reduction for network operators, by reducing the cost of hardware and automating services, flexibility in terms

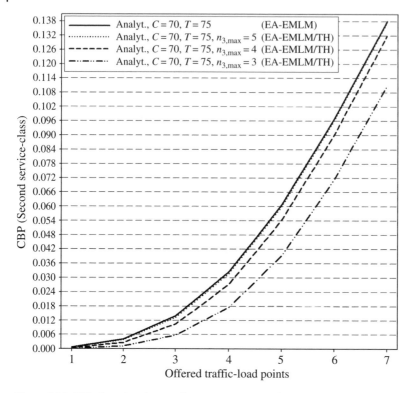

Figure 3.30 CBP of service-class 2, when $n_{3,max} = 3, 4$, and 5 (Example 3.22).

of deployment and operation of new infrastructure and applications, faster innovation cycles due to the creation of enhanced services/applications, and new business models. Due to these benefits, SDN/NFV will play a major role in the emerging 5G systems [20]. In what follows, we briefly describe the considered SDN/NFV based cellular network architecture, shown in Figure 3.32, and its main elements [21].

The realization of an intelligent radio access network (RAN) is greatly facilitated by SDN and NFV technologies [22]. SDN enables abstraction and modularity of the network functions at the RAN level. As a consequence, a hierarchical control architecture can be implemented, in which the high control layer controls lower layers by specifying procedures and without the requirement to have access to the specific implementation details of the lower layers [23]. Such an implementation, however, requires a holistic view of the cellular network at the higher control layer to be designed by taking into account appropriate abstraction of lower layers via well-defined control interfaces. This is essential to enable programmable radio resource management (RRM) functions, such as radio resource allocation (RRA) and CAC. On the other hand, NFV technology allows the execution of control programs on general purpose computing/storage resources [24]. This is contrary to the traditional approach in which the BS consists of a tightly coupled software and hardware platforms. Hence, an NFV-based BS may have some network functions implemented as physical network functions, while other functions are implemented as virtual network functions (VNFs). An advantage of VNFs is that the

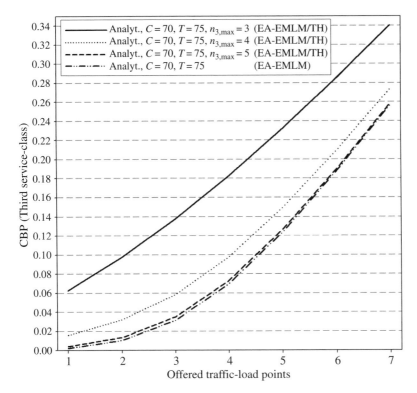

Figure 3.31 CBP of service-class 3, when $n_{3,max} = 3, 4,$ and 5 (Example 3.22).

underlying hardware can be efficiently utilized since VNFs run on shared NFV infrastructure (NFVI).

The architecture of Figure 3.32 relies on the SDN concept, whose different layers are depicted in Figure 3.33. In the control layer, the SDN controller provides a global view of the available underlying resources to one or more network applications that are located at the application layer. This communication is done using the so-called northbound open application programming interface (API). On the other hand, the southbound open API is used to configure the forwarding elements (FEs) that are located at the infrastructure layer. The configuration of FEs is performed by the SDN controller, which sends control messages to the SDN agents located within the FEs.

The main elements at the RAN level are small cell BSs (SBSs), macro BSs (MBSs), WiFi APs, local offload gateways (LO-GWs) [25], and mobile users (MUs). These entities are controlled by the local SDN controller (LSC). The geographical area of the RAN consists of a number of clusters. Each cluster typically consists of many cells and is under the control of a single LSC. For example, in Figure 3.32 the first cluster contains one MBS, one SBS, one WiFi AP, one LO-GW, and four MUs, whereas the second cluster contains one MBS and three MUs. MUs can freely move between clusters or even may belong to more than one cluster at the same time.

When a network entity wishes to establish a connection, it sends the request to the corresponding LSC of the cluster. Upon receiving the request, the LSC will identify the appropriate destination address for the requested connection. In particular, the LSC

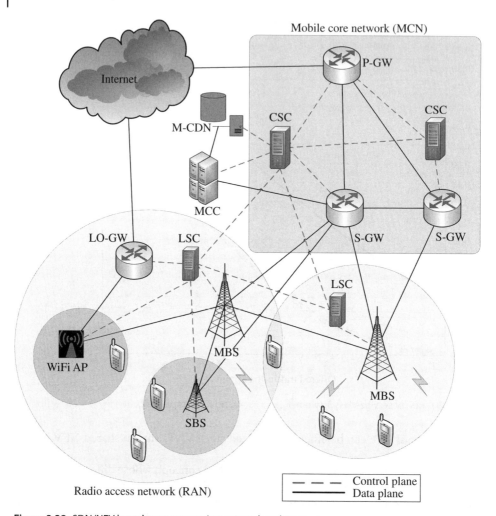

Figure 3.32 SDN/NFV based next-generation network architecture.

will forward the request to either the appropriate in-cluster recipient (e.g. MU or MBS) or the mobile core network (MCN) if the recipient is outside the cluster. To be able to perform this, the LSC maintains the knowledge of the cluster topology as well as the external connections towards the MCN and neighbouring clusters. The LSC is also responsible for multi radio access technologies (RATs) coordination, that is, it takes the RRA decisions in geographical areas where multiple RATs are available (e.g., LTE and WiFi). In the cache-enabled mode [26], the LSC takes caching decisions within the cluster by exploiting the knowledge of content popularity and available in-cluster resources. Another important function of the LSC is in-cluster content routing. Upon receiving the connection request from an MU, the LSC constructs the path from the content source (if the source is within the cluster) or the border entity (if the source is outside the cluster) towards the requesting MU. The LSC then modifies the flow tables at the FEs along the content delivery path. Finally, the LCS is responsible for MU mobility within its cluster. Hence, mobility-related information does not need to be sent over to the MCN.

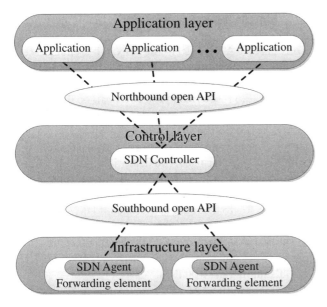

Figure 3.33 Layering concept in SDN.

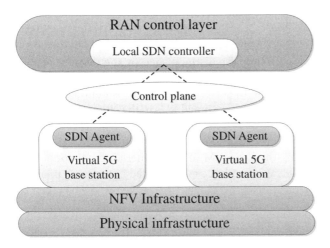

Figure 3.34 SDN/NFV based RAN.

In Figure 3.34, the basic components of a virtualized RAN are shown. Multiple virtual BSs (VBSs) may run on top of the NFVI, essentially sharing the resources of the same physical infrastructure.

The MCN consists of the mobile cloud computing (MCC) infrastructure, mobile content delivery network (M-CDN) servers, packet data network (PDN) GWs and serving GWs (S-GWs). The control is performed by one or more core SDN controllers (CSCs). A CSC receives and handles the connection requests from the RAN via the corresponding LSCs. A CSC is also responsible for storage (e.g., M-CDN), compute (e.g., MCC), spectrum, and energy resources, and for providing QoS support. Finally, the PDN-GW (or simply P-GW) forwards traffic to/from the Internet and other external IP networks, whereas the S-GW receives/sends traffic from/to the RAN.

We continue by describing our considered RAN model in the SDN/NFV-enabled cellular network [21]. We assume a cluster of VBSs controlled by a single LSC at the RAN level (Figure 3.34). The cluster has a fixed number V of VBSs. For the purposes of the analysis it is assumed that the amount of radio resources in the RAN can be discretized and is measured in resource units (RUs). The RU definition depends on the adopted channel access scheme. When schemes based on the FDMA and the TDMA are used, the RU can be defined as an integer number of frequency carriers or time slots. On the other hand, when schemes based on the CDMA are used, the definition of the RU must take into account the multiple access interference [27]. To this end, the notions of the cell load and load factor have been used [28, 29]. In [21], the LTE orthogonal FDMA (OFDMA) scheme is adopted. We define a RU to be equal to a single OFDMA resource block (RB). For example, if the LTE channel bandwidth is 9 MHz and one subcarrier is 15 kHz, then there are in total 600 subcarriers. Since one OFDMA RB corresponds to 12 subcarriers, we have 50 RUs per channel per time slot. Similarly, a 13.5 MHz LTE channel has 75 RUs and a 18 MHz LTE channel has 100 RUs.

Let us denote by C the total number of RUs in the RAN. RUs are dynamically allocated by the LSC to the VBSs such that the VBS v ($v = 1, \ldots, V$) receives r_v RUs. Hence, at any given moment it must hold that:

$$C = \sum_{v=1}^{V} r_v \tag{3.67}$$

Considering K different service-classes, they are distinguished by the number of RUs requested by a single call that originates from a MU. We assume that the calls follow a Poisson distribution. The arrival rate of service-class k calls is denoted as λ_k. A service-class k call requests r_k RUs. Let j be the occupied RUs in the cluster and assume that j can virtually exceed C up to a limit of T RUs. Then the CAC of a service-class k call may follow the one described in Section 3.1.1 for the E-EMLM.

We showed the method of applying the E-EMLM in next-generation networks. It is worth mentioning that almost all teletraffic models can be applied in the same manner, after some necessary adjustments.

3.8 Further Reading

An interesting extension of the E-EMLM includes the co-existence of stream and elastic traffic with or without prioritization of stream traffic [30–32]. In both cases there is no single recursive formula for the calculation of the link occupancy distribution. In the case of stream traffic prioritization, the CBP calculation of stream (not elastic) calls can be based on the Kaufman–Roberts formula. On the other hand, in the case of no prioritization, the CBP determination of stream and elastic calls can only be based on approximate (non-recursive) algorithms [32]. An interesting extension of the E-EMLM is proposed in [33], in which the E-EMLM is described as a multirate loss-queueing model with a finite number of buffers, a fact that provides a springboard for the efficient analysis of multirate queues. A generalization of [33] that provides a framework for the calculation of various queueing characteristics for each elastic service-class is proposed in [34]. The case of adaptive traffic is studied in [35].

Another interesting model (since it is recursive) for elastic traffic in wireless networks has been proposed in [36], where the uplink of a CDMA cell is analysed. Service-class k calls arrive following a Poisson process with rate λ_k ($k = 1, \ldots, K$) and having a peak transmission bit rate requirement, TR_k. The service time is exponentially distributed with mean μ_k^{-1}. When sending with the peak bit rate, the required target ratio of the received power from the mobile terminal to the total interference energy at the BS is given by [36]:

$$\tilde{\Delta}_k = \frac{(E_k/N_0)}{W} TR_k \tag{3.68}$$

where E_k/N_0 is the bit-energy-to-noise ratio and W is the spread spectrum bandwidth.

Let n_k be the number of in-service service-class k calls and P_k the power received at the BS from the user equipment (UE). The power P_k should fulfil the equation [36]:

$$\frac{P_k}{P_N + Y_{own} + Y_{other} - P_k} = \tilde{\Delta}_k \tag{3.69}$$

where $Y_{own} = \sum_{k=1}^{K} n_k P_k$ is the total power received by the BS within its cell, Y_{other} is the total power received from other cells and P_N is the background noise power.

Based on (3.68) we obtain the following equation for P_k [36]:

$$P_k = \frac{P_N \Delta_k}{1 - \Psi}, \quad \Delta_k = \frac{\tilde{\Delta}_k}{1 + \tilde{\Delta}_k}, \quad \Psi = \sum_{k=1}^{K} n_k \Delta_k \tag{3.70}$$

According to the denominator of (3.69), we see that the CAC must prevent Ψ becoming larger than $\overline{\Psi} = 1 - \varepsilon$, $\varepsilon > 0$.

Finally, it can be proved (see [36, 37]) that there exists a recursive formula for the determination of CBP in a CDMA cell of maximum capacity $\overline{\Psi}$ which accommodates Poisson arriving calls of K different service-classes with offered traffic-load $\alpha_k = \lambda_k/\mu_k$ and bandwidth requirement Δ_k ($k = 1, \ldots, K$).

References

1 G. Stamatelos and V. Koukoulidis, Reservation-based bandwidth allocation in a radio ATM network. *IEEE/ACM Transactions on Networking*, 5(3):420–428, June 1997.

2 S. Yashkov and A. Yashkova, Processor sharing: A survey of the mathematical theory. *Automation and Remote Control*, 68(9):1662–1731, September 2007.

3 R. Dobrushin, Yu. Sukhov and J. Fritz, A.N. Kolmogorov – the founder of the theory of reversible Markov processes. *Russian Mathematical Surveys*, 43(6):157–182, 1988.

4 V. Iversen, Reversible fair scheduling: The teletraffic theory revisited. *Proceedings of the 20th International Teletraffic Congress, LNCS 4516*, pp. 1135–1148, Ottawa, Canada, June 2007.

5 V. Koukoulidis, A characterization of reversible Markov processes with applications to shared-resource environments, PhD thesis, Concordia University, Montreal, Canada, April 1993.

6 S. Racz, B. Gero and G. Fodor, Flow level performance analysis of a multi-service system supporting elastic and adaptive services. *Performance Evaluation*, 49(1–4): 451–469, September 2002.

7 T. Bonald, A. Proutiere, J. Roberts and J. Virtamo, Computational aspects of balanced fairness. *Proceedings of the International Teletraffic Congress (ITC) 18*, Berlin, Germany, September 2003.

8 T. Bonald and J. Virtamo, A recursive formula for multirate systems with elastic traffic. *IEEE Communications Letters*, 9(8):753–755, August 2005.

9 T. Bonald and J. Virtamo, Calculating the flow level performance of balanced fairness in tree networks. *Performance Evaluation*, 58(1):1–14, October 2004.

10 T. Bonald, L. Massoulie, A. Proutiere and J. Virtamo, A queueing analysis of max-min fairness, proportional fairness and balanced fairness. *Queueing Systems*, 53(1): 65–84, June 2006.

11 I. Moscholios, V. Vassilakis, M. Logothetis and A. Boucouvalas, Blocking equalization in the Erlang multirate loss model for elastic traffic. *Proceedings of the 2nd International Conference on Emerging Network Intelligence (EMERGING)*, Florence, Italy, October 2010.

12 I. Moscholios, M. Logothetis, A. Boucouvalas and V. Vassilakis, An Erlang multirate loss model supporting elastic traffic under the threshold policy. *Proceedings of the IEEE International Communications Conference (ICC)*, London, UK, June 2015.

13 I. Moscholios, V. Vassilakis, M. Logothetis and J. Vardakas, Bandwidth reservation in the Erlang multirate loss model for elastic and adaptive traffic. *Proceedings of the 9th Advanced International Conference on Telecommunications (AICT)*, Rome, Italy, June 2013.

14 I. Moscholios, M. Logothetis and A. Boucouvalas, Blocking probabilities of elastic and adaptive calls in the Erlang multirate loss model under the threshold policy. *Telecommunication Systems*, 62(1): 245–262, May 2016.

15 B. Nunes, M. Mendonca, X. Nguyen, K. Obraczka and T. Turletti, A survey of software-defined networking: past, present and future of programmable networks. *IEEE Communications Surveys & Tutorials*, 16(3): 1617–1634, third quarter 2014.

16 W. Xia, Y. Wen, C. Foh, D. Niyato and H. Xie, A survey on software-defined networking. *IEEE Communications Surveys & Tutorials*, 17(1):27–51, first quarter 2015.

17 R. Mijumbi, J. Serrat, J. Gorricho, N. Bouten, F. Turck and R. Boutaba, Network function virtualization: state-of-the-art and research challenges. *IEEE Communications Surveys & Tutorials*, 18(1):236–262, first quarter 2016.

18 B. Han, V. Gopalakrishnan, L. Ji and S. Lee, Network function virtualization: challenges and opportunities for innovations. *IEEE Communications Magazine*, 53(2):90–97, February 2015.

19 Q. Duan, N. Ansari and M. Toy, Software-defined network virtualization: an architectural framework for integrating SDN and NFV for service provisioning in future networks. *IEEE Network*, 30(5):10–16, September–October 2016.

20 P. Agyapong, M. Iwamura, D. Staehle, W. Kiess and A. Benjebbour, Design considerations for a 5G network architecture. *IEEE Communications Magazine*, 52(11):65–75, November 2014.

21 V. Vassilakis, I. Moscholios and M. Logothetis, Efficient radio resource allocation in SDN/NFV based mobile cellular networks under the complete sharing policy. *IET Networks*, 7(3):103–108, May 2018.

22 V. Vassilakis, I. Moscholios, B. Alzahrani and M. Logothetis, A software-defined architecture for next-feneration cellular networks. *Proceedings of the IEEE ICC*, Kuala Lumpur, Malaysia, May 2016.

23 T. Chen, M. Matinmikko, X. Chen, X. Zhou and P. Ahokangas, Software defined mobile networks: concept, survey, and research directions. *IEEE Communications Magazine*, 53(11):126–133, November 2015.

24 F. Yousaf, M. Bredel, S. Schaller and F. Schneider, NFV and SDN key technology enablers for 5G networks. *IEEE Journal on Selected Areas in Communications*, 35(11):2468–2478, November 2017.

25 K. Samdanis, T. Taleb and S. Schmid, Traffic offload enhancements for eUTRAN. *IEEE Communications Surveys & Tutorials*, 14(3):884–896, third quarter 2012.

26 K. Poularakis, G. Iosifidis and L. Tassiulas, Approximation algorithms for mobile data caching in small cell networks. *IEEE Transactions on Communications*, 62(10):3665–3677, October 2014.

27 Y. Shen, Y. Wang, Z. Peng and S. Wu, Multiple-access interference mitigation for acquisition of code-division multiple access continuous-wave signals. *IEEE Communications Letters*, 21(1):192–195, January 2017.

28 D. Staehle and A. Mäder, An analytic approximation of the uplink capacity in a UMTS network with heterogeneous traffic. *Proceedings of the 18th International Teletraffic Congress (ITC18)*, Berlin, September 2003.

29 V. Vassilakis, I. Moscholios, A. Bontozoglou and M. Logothetis, Mobility-aware QoS assurance in software – Defined radio access networks: An analytical study. *Proceedings of the IEEE International Workshop on Software Defined 5G Networks*, London, UK, April 2015.

30 M. Ivanovich and P. Fitzpatrick, An accurate performance approximation for beyond 3G wireless broadband systems with QoS. *IEEE Transactions on Vehicular Technology*, 62(5):2230–2238, June 2013.

31 Y. Huang, Z. Rosberg, K. Ko and M. Zukerman, Blocking probability approximations and bounds for best-effort calls in an integrated service system. *IEEE Transactions on Communications*, 63(12):5014–5026, Dec. 2015.

32 B. Geró, P. Palyi, S. Rácz, Flow-level performance analysis of a multi-rate system supporting stream and elastic services. *International Journal of Communication Systems*, 26(8):974–988, August 2013.

33 S. Hanczewski, M. Stasiak and J. Weissenberg, A queueing model of a multi-service system with state-dependent distribution of resources for each class of calls. *IEICE Transactions on Communications*, E97-B(8):1592–1605, August 2014.

34 M. Stasiak, Queuing systems for the Internet. *IEICE Transactions on Communications*, E99-B(6):1234–1242, June 2016.

35 S. Hanczewski, M. Stasiak and J. Weissenberg, The model of the queuing system with adaptive traffic. *Proceedings of the IEEE 19th International Conference on HPCC/Smart City/DSS*, Bangkok, Thailand, December 2017.

36 G. Fodor and M. Telek, A recursive formula to calculate the steady state of CDMA networks. *Proceedings of the ITC*, Beijing, China, September 2005.

37 G. Fodor, Performance analysis of resource sharing policies in CDMA networks. *International Journal of Communication Systems*, 20(2):207–233, February 2007.

4

Multirate Elastic Adaptive Retry Loss Models

In this chapter we consider multirate loss models of random arriving calls not only with elastic bandwidth requirements upon arrival but also elastic bandwidth allocation during service. Calls may retry several times upon arrival, requiring less bandwidth each time, in order to be accepted for service. If call admission is not possible with the last (least) bandwidth requirement then bandwidth compression is attempted.

4.1 The Elastic Single-Retry Model

4.1.1 The Service System

In the *elastic single-retry model (E-SRM)*, we consider a link of capacity C b.u. that accommodates elastic calls of K service-classes. Calls of service-class k follow a Poisson process with mean arrival rate λ_k and have a peak-bandwidth requirement of b_k b.u. and an exponentially distributed service time with mean μ_k^{-1}. To introduce bandwidth compression, we permit the occupied link bandwidth j to virtually exceed C up to a limit of T b.u. Let j be the occupied link bandwidth, $j = 0, 1, \ldots, T$, when a new service-class k call arrives in the link. Then, for call admission we consider the following cases:

(a) If $j + b_k \leq C$, no bandwidth compression takes place and the call is accepted in the link with b_k b.u.
(b) If $j + b_k > C$, then the call is blocked with b_k and retries immediately to be connected in the link with $b_{kr} < b_k$. Now if:
  b1) $j + b_{kr} \leq C$, no bandwidth compression occurs and the retry call is accepted in the system with b_{kr} and $\mu_{kr}^{-1} > \mu_k^{-1}$, so that $b_{kr}\mu_{kr}^{-1} = b_k\mu_k^{-1}$,
  b2) $j + b_{kr} > T$, the retry call is blocked and lost, and
  b3) $T \geq j + b_{kr} > C$, the retry call is accepted in the system by compressing its bandwidth requirement b_{kr} together with the bandwidth of all in-service calls of all service-classes. In that case, the compressed bandwidth of the retry call becomes $b'_{kr} = rb_{kr} = \frac{C}{j+b_{kr}}b_{kr}$, where r is the compression factor, common to all service-classes. Similarly, all in-service calls, which have been accepted in the link with b_k (or b_{kr}), compress their bandwidth to $b'_k = rb_k$ (or $b'_{kr} = rb_{kr}$) for $k = 1, \ldots, K$. After the compression of all calls, the link state is $j = C$. The minimum value of the compression factor is $r_{\min} = C/T$.

Efficient Multirate Teletraffic Loss Models Beyond Erlang, First Edition.
Ioannis D. Moscholios and Michael D. Logothetis.
© 2019 John Wiley & Sons Ltd. Published 2019 by John Wiley & Sons Ltd.
Companion website: www.wiley.com/go/logocode

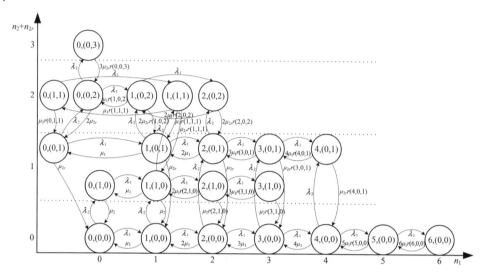

Figure 4.1 The state space Ω and the state transition diagram (Example 4.1).

Similar to the E-EMLM, when a service-class k call, with bandwidth b'_k (or b'_{kr}), departs from the system, the remaining in-service calls of each service-class i ($i = 1, \ldots, K$) expand their bandwidth in proportion to their initially assigned bandwidth b_i (or b_{ir}). After bandwidth compression/expansion, elastic service-class calls increase/decrease their service time so that the product *service time* by *bandwidth* remains constant.

Similar to the SRM, the steady state probabilities in the E-SRM do not have a PFS, since LB is destroyed between adjacent states (see Figure 4.1). Thus, the unnormalized values of $q(j)$ can be determined by an approximate but recursive formula, as presented in Section 4.1.2.

Example 4.1 This example illustrates the bandwidth compression/expansion mechanism together with the notion of retrials. Consider a link of $C = 4$ b.u. and $T = 6$ b.u. The link accommodates calls of $K = 2$ service-classes whose calls require $b_1 = 1$ and $b_2 = 3$ b.u., respectively. Blocked calls of service-class 2 immediately retry with $b_{2r} = 2$ b.u. For simplicity, let $\lambda_1 = \lambda_2 = 1$ call/sec, $\mu_1^{-1} = \mu_2^{-1} = 1$ sec, and $\mu_{2r}^{-1} = \frac{b_2}{b_{2r}}\mu_2^{-1} = 1.5$ sec.

(a) Find the total number of permissible states $\mathbf{n} = (n_1, n_2, n_{2r})$, draw the state transition diagram and determine the values of j and $r(\mathbf{n})$ for each state $\mathbf{n} = (n_1, n_2, n_{2r})$.
(b) Calculate the state probabilities $P(n_1, n_2, n_{2r})$ based on the GB equations. Then determine the values of the link occupancy distribution $Q(j)$ (for $j = 0, \ldots, T$).
(c) Calculate the CBP of both service-classes including the retry probability and the link utilization.

(a) There are 22 permissible states of the form $\mathbf{n} = (n_1, n_2, n_{2r})$. The state space Ω and the state transition diagram are shown in Figure 4.1. Table 4.1 presents the 22 states together with the values of $r(\mathbf{n})$ and the occupied link bandwidth, $j = n_1 b_1 + n_2 b_2 + n_2 r b_{2r}$, before and after compression.

(b) Based on Figure 4.1, we obtain the following 22 GB equations:

$(0,0,0):$ $P(0,1,0) + P(1,0,0) + (2/3)P(0,0,1) - 2P(0,0,0) = 0$

$(0,0,1):$ $0.8P(0,1,1) + (4/3)P(0,0,2) + P(1,0,1) - (8/3)P(0,0,1) = 0$

$(0,0,2):$ $P(0,0,1) + (4/3)P(0,0,3) + 0.8P(1,0,2) - (10/3)P(0,0,2) = 0$

$(0,0,3):$ $P(0,0,2) - (4/3)P(0,0,3) = 0$

$(0,1,0):$ $P(0,0,0) + (8/15)P(0,1,1) + P(1,1,0) - 3P(0,1,0) = 0$

$(0,1,1):$ $P(0,1,0) + (2/3)P(1,1,1) - (7/3)P(0,1,1) = 0$

$(1,0,0):$ $P(0,0,0) + 2P(2,0,0) + (2/3)P(1,0,1) + P(1,1,0) - 3P(1,0,0) = 0$

$(1,0,1):$ $P(0,0,1) + 2P(2,0,1) + (16/15)P(1,0,2) + (2/3)P(1,1,1) - (11/3)P(1,0,1) = 0$

$(1,0,2):$ $P(0,0,2) + (4/3)P(2,0,2) + P(1,0,1) - (43/15)P(1,0,2) = 0$

$(1,1,0):$ $P(0,1,0) + P(1,0,0) + 1.6P(2,1,0) + (4/9)P(1,1,1) - 4P(1,1,0) = 0$

$(1,1,1):$ $P(0,1,1) + P(1,1,0) - (16/9)P(1,1,1) = 0$

$(2,0,0):$ $P(1,0,0) + 3P(3,0,0) + 0.8P(2,1,0) + (2/3)P(2,0,1) - 4P(2,0,0) = 0$

$(2,0,1):$ $P(1,0,1) + P(2,0,0) + 2.4P(3,0,1) + (8/9)P(2,0,2) - (14/3)P(2,0,1) = 0$

$(2,0,2):$ $P(1,0,2) + P(2,0,1) - (20/9)P(2,0,2) = 0$

$(2,1,0):$ $P(1,1,0) + 2P(3,1,0) - 3.4P(2,1,0) = 0$

$(3,0,0):$ $P(2,0,0) + 4P(4,0,0) + (2/3)P(3,1,0) + (8/15)P(3,0,1) - 5P(3,0,0) = 0$

$(3,0,1):$ $P(2,0,1) + (8/3)P(4,0,1) + P(3,0,0) - (59/15)P(3,0,1) = 0$

$(3,1,0):$ $P(2,1,0) - (8/3)P(3,1,0) = 0$

$(4,0,0):$ $P(3,0,0) + 4P(5,0,0) + (4/9)P(4,0,1) - 6P(4,0,0) = 0$

$(4,0,1):$ $P(4,0,0) + P(3,0,1) - (28/9)P(4,0,1) = 0$

$(5,0,0):$ $P(4,0,0) + 4P(6,0,0) - 5P(5,0,0) = 0$

$(6,0,0):$ $P(5,0,0) - 4P(6,0,0) = 0$

The solution of this linear system is:

$P(0,0,0) = 0.1093$	$P(0,0,1) = 0.0695$	$P(0,0,2) = 0.0544$	$P(0,0,3) = 0.0408$
$P(0,1,0) = 0.0636$	$P(0,1,1) = 0.0436$	$P(1,0,0) = 0.1087$	$P(1,0,1) = 0.0779$
$P(1,0,2) = 0.0718$	$P(1,1,0) = 0.0582$	$P(1,1,1) = 0.0573$	$P(2,0,0) = 0.0533$
$P(2,0,1) = 0.0507$	$P(2,0,2) = 0.0551$	$P(2,1,0) = 0.0220$	$P(3,0,0) = 0.0177$
$P(3,0,1) = 0.0234$	$P(3,1,0) = 0.0082$	$P(4,0,0) = 0.0043$	$P(4,0,1) = 0.0089$
$P(5,0,0) = 0.0011$	$P(6,0,0) = 0.0003$		

Based on the values of $P(n_1, n_2, n_{2r})$, we determine the values of $Q(j)$:

$Q(0) = P(0,0,0) = 0.1093$

$Q(1) = P(1,0,0) = 0.1087$

$Q(2) = P(0,0,1) + P(2,0,0) = 0.1228$

$Q(3) = P(0,1,0) + P(1,0,1) + P(3,0,0) = 0.1592$

$Q(4) = P(0,0,2) + P(1,1,0) + P(2,0,1) + P(4,0,0) = 0.1676$

$Q(5) = P(0,1,1) + P(1,0,2) + P(2,1,0) + P(3,0,1) + P(5,0,0) = 0.1619$

$Q(6) = P(0,0,3) + P(1,1,1) + P(2,0,2) + P(3,1,0) + P(4,0,1) + P(6,0,0) = 0.1706$

Table 4.1 The state space Ω and the occupied link bandwidth (Example 4.1).

n_1	n_2	n_{2r}	$r(n)$	j $(0 \leq j \leq T)$ (before compr.)	j $(0 \leq j \leq C)$ (after compr.)	n_1	n_2	n_{2r}	$r(n)$	j $(0 \leq j \leq T)$ (before compr.)	j $(0 \leq j \leq C)$ (after compr.)
0	0	0	1.00	0	0	2	0	0	1.00	2	2
0	0	1	1.00	2	2	2	0	1	1.00	4	4
0	0	2	1.00	4	4	2	0	2	0.67	6	4
0	0	3	0.67	6	4	2	1	0	0.80	5	4
0	1	0	1.00	3	3	3	0	0	1.00	3	3
0	1	1	0.80	5	4	3	0	1	0.80	5	4
1	0	0	1.00	1	1	3	1	0	0.67	6	4
1	0	1	1.00	3	3	4	0	0	1.00	4	4
1	0	2	0.80	5	4	4	0	1	0.67	6	4
1	1	0	1.00	4	4	5	0	0	0.80	5	4
1	1	1	0.67	6	4	6	0	0	0.67	6	4

(c) Based on the values of $Q(j)$, we obtain the exact CBP:

$$B_1 = \sum_{j=T-b_1+1}^{T} Q(j) = Q(6) = 0.1706$$

The $Prob\{retry\}$ of service-class 2 calls is denoted by B_2 in order to use the same subscript with the required b.u. upon arrival, $b_2 = 3$; the $Prob\{retry\}$ refers to the percentage of calls which retry and is given by:

$$B_2 = \sum_{j=C-b_2+1}^{T} Q(j) = Q(2) + Q(3) + Q(4) + Q(5) + Q(6) = 0.7821$$

The CBP of service-class 2 is denoted by B_{2r} and refers to service-class 2 retry calls which require b_{2r} b.u.; B_{2r} is given by:

$$B_{2r} = \sum_{j=T-b_{2r}+1}^{T} Q(j) = Q(5) + Q(6) = 0.3325$$

The link utilization is determined by:

$$U = \sum_{j=1}^{C} jQ(j) + \sum_{j=C+1}^{T} CQ(j) = 2.832 \text{ b.u.}$$

To facilitate the recursive calculation of $q(j)$, we replace $r(\mathbf{n})$ by the state-dependent compression factors per service-class k, $\varphi_k(\mathbf{n})$, which have a similar role to $r(\mathbf{n})$ and have already been described in the E-EMLM. The only difference is that apart from $\varphi_k(\mathbf{n})$, which are given by (3.8), we should also define $\varphi_{kr}(\mathbf{n})$ to account for retry calls of service-class k in state $\mathbf{n}$. The form of $\varphi_{kr}(\mathbf{n})$ is the following [1]:

$$\varphi_{kr}(\mathbf{n}) = \begin{cases} 1 & \text{for } \mathbf{nb} \leq C \text{ and } \mathbf{n} \in \Omega \\ \frac{x(\mathbf{n}_{kr}^-)}{x(\mathbf{n})} & \text{for } C < \mathbf{nb} \leq T \text{ and } \mathbf{n} \in \Omega \\ 0 & \text{otherwise} \end{cases} \quad (4.1)$$

where $\mathbf{n} = (n_1, n_{1r}, n_2, n_{2r}, \dots, n_k, n_{kr}, \dots, n_K, n_{Kr})$, $\mathbf{n}_k^- = (n_1, n_{1r}, n_2, n_{2r}, \dots, n_k - 1,$
$n_{kr}, \dots, n_K, n_{Kr})$, $\mathbf{n}_{kr}^- = (n_1, n_{1r}, n_2, n_{2r}, \dots, n_k, n_{kr} - 1, \dots, n_K, n_{Kr})$, and

$$x(\mathbf{n}) = \begin{cases} 1 & \text{when } \mathbf{nb} \leq C \text{ and } \mathbf{n} \in \Omega \\ \frac{1}{C} \sum_{k=1}^{K} (n_k b_k x(\mathbf{n}_k^-) + n_{kr} b_{kr} x(\mathbf{n}_{kr}^-)) & \text{when } C < \mathbf{nb} \leq T \text{ and } \mathbf{n} \in \Omega \\ 0 & \text{otherwise} \end{cases} \quad (4.2)$$

Example 4.2 Consider again Example 4.1 ($C = 4, T = 6, K = 2, b_1 = 1, b_2 = 3,$
$b_{2r} = 2, \lambda_1 = \lambda_2 = \mu_1 = \mu_2 = 1, \mu_{2r} = 2/3$):

(a) Draw the modified state transition diagram based on $\varphi_k(\mathbf{n})$ and $\varphi_{kr}(\mathbf{n})$ and determine their values for each state $\mathbf{n} = (n_1, n_2, n_{2r})$.
(b) Calculate the state probabilities $P(n_1, n_2, n_{2r})$ based on the GB equations. Then determine the values of the link occupancy distribution $Q(j)$ (for $j = 0, \dots, T$).
(c) Calculate the CBP of both service-classes including the retry probability and the link utilization.

(a) Figure 4.2 shows the modified state transition diagram of the system, while Table 4.2 presents the 22 states together with the corresponding values of $\varphi_k(\mathbf{n})$ and $\varphi_{kr}(\mathbf{n})$, which are calculated through the $x(\mathbf{n})$.
(b) Based on Figure 4.2, we obtain the following 22 GB equations:

$(0,0,0)$: $\quad P(0,1,0) + P(1,0,0) + (2/3)P(0,0,1) - 2P(0,0,0) = 0$

$(0,0,1)$: $\quad 0.8P(0,1,1) + (4/3)P(0,0,2) + P(1,0,1) - (8/3)P(0,0,1) = 0$

$(0,0,2)$: $\quad P(0,0,1) + (4/3)P(0,0,3) + 0.8P(1,0,2) - (10/3)P(0,0,2) = 0$

$(0,0,3)$: $\quad P(0,0,2) - (4/3)P(0,0,3) = 0$

$(0,1,0)$: $\quad P(0,0,0) + (8/15)P(0,1,1) + P(1,1,0) - 3P(0,1,0) = 0$

$(0,1,1)$: $\quad P(0,1,0) + 0.8P(1,1,1) - (7/3)P(0,1,1) = 0$

$(1,0,0)$: $\quad P(0,0,0) + 2P(2,0,0) + (2/3)P(1,0,1) + P(1,1,0) - 3P(1,0,0) = 0$

$(1,0,1)$: $\quad P(0,0,1) + 2P(2,0,1) + (16/15)P(1,0,2) + 0.64P(1,1,1) - (11/3)P(1,0,1) = 0$

$(1,0,2)$: $\quad P(0,0,2) + (20/13)P(2,0,2) + P(1,0,1) - (43/15)P(1,0,2) = 0$

$(1,1,0)$: $\quad P(0,1,0) + P(1,0,0) + 1.6P(2,1,0) + (32/75)P(1,1,1) - 4P(1,1,0) = 0$

$(1,1,1)$: $\quad P(0,1,1) + P(1,1,0) - (28/15)P(1,1,1) = 0$

$(2,0,0)$: $\quad P(1,0,0) + 3P(3,0,0) + 0.8P(2,1,0) + (2/3)P(2,0,1) - 4P(2,0,0) = 0$

$(2,0,1)$: $\quad P(1,0,1) + P(2,0,0) + 2.4P(3,0,1) + (32/39)P(2,0,2) - (14/3)P(2,0,1) = 0$

$(2,0,2)$: $\quad P(1,0,2) + P(2,0,1) - (92/39)P(2,0,2) = 0$

$(2,1,0)$: $\quad P(1,1,0) + (20/9)P(3,1,0) - 3.4P(2,1,0) = 0$

$(3,0,0)$: $P(2,0,0) + 4P(4,0,0) + (16/27)P(3,1,0) + (8/15)P(3,0,1) - 5P(3,0,0) = 0$

$(3,0,1)$: $P(2,0,1) + (20/7)P(4,0,1) + P(3,0,0) - (59/15)P(3,0,1) = 0$

$(3,1,0)$: $P(2,1,0) - (76/27)P(3,1,0) = 0$

$(4,0,0)$: $P(3,0,0) + 4P(5,0,0) + (8/21)P(4,0,1) - 6P(4,0,0) = 0$

$(4,0,1)$: $P(4,0,0) + P(3,0,1) - (68/21)P(4,0,1) = 0$

$(5,0,0)$: $P(4,0,0) + 4P(6,0,0) - 5P(5,0,0) = 0$

$(6,0,0)$: $P(5,0,0) - 4P(6,0,0) = 0$

The solution of this linear system is:

$P(0,0,0) = 0.1097$ $P(0,0,1) = 0.071$ $P(0,0,2) = 0.056$ $P(0,0,3) = 0.042$

$P(0,1,0) = 0.0642$ $P(0,1,1) = 0.0467$ $P(1,0,0) = 0.1079$ $P(1,0,1) = 0.0774$

$P(1,0,2) = 0.0746$ $P(1,1,0) = 0.0579$ $P(1,1,1) = 0.056$ $P(2,0,0) = 0.0523$

$P(2,0,1) = 0.0487$ $P(2,0,2) = 0.0522$ $P(2,1,0) = 0.0222$ $P(3,0,0) = 0.017$

$P(3,0,1) = 0.0227$ $P(3,1,0) = 0.0079$ $P(4,0,0) = 0.004$ $P(4,0,1) = 0.0083$

$P(5,0,0) = 0.001$ $P(6,0,0) = 0.0003$

Based on the values of $P(n_1, n_2, n_{2r})$, we determine the values of $Q(j)$:

$Q(0) = P(0,0,0) = 0.1097$

$Q(1) = P(1,0,0) = 0.1079$

$Q(2) = P(0,0,1) + P(2,0,0) = 0.1233$

$Q(3) = P(0,1,0) + P(1,0,1) + P(3,0,0) = 0.1586$

$Q(4) = P(0,0,2) + P(1,1,0) + P(2,0,1) + P(4,0,0) = 0.1666$

$Q(5) = P(0,1,1) + P(1,0,2) + P(2,1,0) + P(3,0,1) + P(5,0,0) = 0.1672$

$Q(6) = P(0,0,3) + P(1,1,1) + P(2,0,2) + P(3,1,0) + P(4,0,1) + P(6,0,0) = 0.1667$

(c) Based on the values of $Q(j)$, we obtain the approximate CBP:

$$B_1 = \sum_{j=T-b_1+1}^{T} Q(j) = Q(6) = 0.1667 \text{ (compare with the exact 0.1706)}$$

The *Prob*{retry} of service-class 2 calls, B_2, when they require $b_2 = 3$ b.u. upon arrival is given by:

$$B_2 = \sum_{j=C-b_2+1}^{T} Q(j) = Q(2) + Q(3) + Q(4) + Q(5) + Q(6) = 0.7824 \text{ (compare with the exact 0.7821)}$$

The CBP of service-class 2, B_{2r}, is given by:

$$B_{2r} = \sum_{j=T-b_{2r}+1}^{T} Q(j) = Q(5) + Q(6) = 0.3339 \text{ (compare with the exact 0.3325)}$$

The link utilization is determined by:

$$U = \sum_{j=1}^{C} jQ(j) + \sum_{j=C+1}^{T} CQ(j) = 2.832 \text{ b.u. (the same as the exact value).}$$

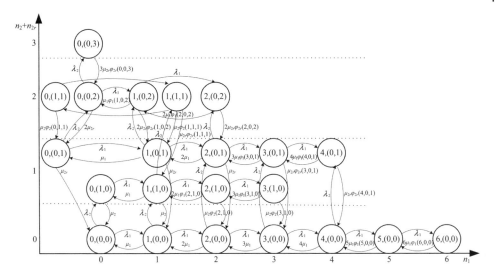

Figure 4.2 The state space Ω and the modified state transition diagram (Example 4.2)

Table 4.2 The values of the state-dependent compression factors $\varphi_k(n)$ and $\varphi_{kr}(n)$ (Example 4.2).

n_1	n_2	n_{2r}	$x(n)$	$\varphi_1(n)$	$\varphi_2(n)$	$\varphi_{2r}(n)$	n_1	n_2	n_{2r}	$x(n)$	$\varphi_1(n)$	$\varphi_2(n)$	$\varphi_{2r}(n)$
0	0	0	1.0	1.00	1.00	1.00	2	0	0	1.0	1.00	1.00	1.00
0	0	1	1.0	1.00	1.00	1.00	2	0	1	1.0	1.00	1.00	1.00
0	0	2	1.0	1.00	1.00	1.00	2	0	2	1.625	0.7692	0.00	0.6154
0	0	3	1.5	0.00	0.00	0.6667	2	1	0	1.25	0.80	0.80	0.00
0	1	0	1.0	1.00	1.00	1.00	3	0	0	1.0	1.00	1.00	1.00
0	1	1	1.25	0.00	0.80	0.80	3	0	1	1.25	0.80	0.00	0.80
1	0	0	1.0	1.00	1.00	1.00	3	1	0	1.6875	0.7407	0.5926	0.00
1	0	1	1.0	1.00	1.00	1.00	4	0	0	1.0	1.00	1.00	1.00
1	0	2	1.25	0.80	0.00	0.80	4	0	1	1.75	0.7143	0.00	0.5714
1	1	0	1.0	1.00	1.00	1.00	5	0	0	1.25	0.80	0.00	0.00
1	1	1	1.5625	0.80	0.64	0.64	6	0	0	1.875	0.6667	0.00	0.00

4.1.2 The Analytical Model

4.1.2.1 Steady State Probabilities

To describe the analytical model in the steady state, we consider a link of capacity C b.u. that accommodates calls of two service-classes with traffic parameters: $(\lambda_1, \mu_1^{-1}, b_1)$ for service-class 1 and $(\lambda_2, \mu_2^{-1}, \mu_{2r}^{-1}, b_2, b_{2r})$ for service-class 2. Calls of service-class 2 have retry parameters with $b_{2r} < b_2$ and $\mu_{2r}^{-1} > \mu_2^{-1}$. Let T be the virtual capacity so that the maximum permitted bandwidth compression is $C/T \cdot 100\%$ for calls of both service-classes.

Although the E-SRM is a non-PFS model, we will use the LB of (3.11), initially for calls of service-class 1:

$$\lambda_1 P(\mathbf{n}_1^-) = n_1 \mu_1 \varphi_1(\mathbf{n})P(\mathbf{n}), \ 1 \leq \mathbf{nb} \leq T \tag{4.3}$$

where $\mathbf{n} = (n_1, n_2, n_{2r})$, $\mathbf{n}_1^- = (n_1 - 1, n_2, n_{2r})$ with $n_1 \geq 1$, $\mathbf{nb} = j = n_1 b_1 + n_2 b_2 + n_{2r} b_{2r}$, and

$$\varphi_1(\mathbf{n}) = \begin{cases} 1 & \text{for } \mathbf{nb} \leq C \text{ and } \mathbf{n} \in \Omega \\ \frac{x(\mathbf{n}_1^-)}{x(\mathbf{n})} & \text{for } C < \mathbf{nb} \leq T \text{ and } \mathbf{n} \in \Omega \\ 0 & \text{otherwise} \end{cases} \tag{4.4}$$

Based on (4.4) and multiplying both sides of (4.3) with b_1, we have:

$$\alpha_1 b_1 x(\mathbf{n})P(\mathbf{n}_1^-) = n_1 b_1 x(\mathbf{n}_1^-)P(\mathbf{n}) \tag{4.5}$$

where $\alpha_1 = \lambda_1 / \mu_1$ and the values of $x(\mathbf{n})$ are given by (4.2).

Based on the CAC of the E-SRM, we consider the following LB equations for calls of service-class 2:

(a) No bandwidth compression

$$\lambda_2 P(\mathbf{n}_2^-) = n_2 \mu_2 \varphi_2(\mathbf{n})P(\mathbf{n}), \quad 1 \leq \mathbf{nb} \leq C \tag{4.6}$$

where $\mathbf{n}_2^- = (n_1, n_2 - 1, n_{2r})$ with $n_2 \geq 1$ and

$$\varphi_2(\mathbf{n}) = \begin{cases} 1 & \text{for } \mathbf{nb} \leq C \text{ and } \mathbf{n} \in \Omega \\ \frac{x(\mathbf{n}_2^-)}{x(\mathbf{n})} & \text{for } C < \mathbf{nb} \leq T \quad \text{and} \quad \mathbf{n} \in \Omega \\ 0 & \text{otherwise} \end{cases} \tag{4.7}$$

Based on (4.7) and multiplying both sides of (4.6) with b_2, we have:

$$\alpha_2 b_2 x(\mathbf{n})P(\mathbf{n}_2^-) = n_2 b_2 x(\mathbf{n}_2^-)P(\mathbf{n}) \tag{4.8}$$

where $\alpha_2 = \lambda_2 / \mu_2$ and the values of $x(\mathbf{n})$ are given by (4.2).

(b) Bandwidth compression

$$\lambda_2 P(\mathbf{n}_{2r}^-) = n_{2r} \mu_{2r} \varphi_{2r}(\mathbf{n})P(\mathbf{n}), \ C - b_2 + b_{2r} < \mathbf{nb} \leq T \tag{4.9}$$

where $n_{2r}^- = (n_1, n_2, n_{2_r} - 1)$ and

$$\varphi_{2r}(\mathbf{n}) = \begin{cases} 1 & \text{for } \mathbf{nb} \leq C \text{ and } \mathbf{n} \in \Omega \\ \frac{x(\mathbf{n}_{2r}^-)}{x(\mathbf{n})} & \text{for } C < \mathbf{nb} \leq T \text{ and } \mathbf{n} \in \Omega \\ 0 & \text{otherwise} \end{cases} \tag{4.10}$$

Based on (4.10) and multiplying both sides of (4.9) with b_{2r}, we have:

$$a_{2r} b_{2r} x(\mathbf{n})P(\mathbf{n}_{2r}^-) = n_{2r} b_{2r} x(\mathbf{n}_{2r}^-)P(\mathbf{n}), \ C - b_2 + b_{2r} < \mathbf{nb} \leq T \tag{4.11}$$

where $\alpha_{2r} = \lambda_2 / \mu_{2r}$ and the values of $x(\mathbf{n})$ are given by (4.2).

Equations (4.5), (4.8), and (4.11) lead to the following system of equations:

$$\alpha_1 b_1 x(\mathbf{n})P(\mathbf{n}_1^-) + \alpha_2 b_2 x(\mathbf{n})P(\mathbf{n}_2^-) = (n_1 b_1 x(\mathbf{n}_1^-) + n_2 b_2 x(\mathbf{n}_2^-))P(\mathbf{n})$$
$$\text{for } 1 < \mathbf{nb} \leq C - b_2 + b_{2r} \tag{4.12}$$

$$a_1 b_1 x(\mathbf{n}) P(\mathbf{n}_1^-) + a_2 b_2 x(\mathbf{n}) P(\mathbf{n}_2^-) + a_{2r} b_{2r} x(\mathbf{n}) P(\mathbf{n}_{2r}^-) =$$
$$(n_1 b_1 x(\mathbf{n}_1^-) + n_2 b_2 x(\mathbf{n}_2^-) + n_{2r} b_{2r} x(\mathbf{n}_{2r}^-)) P(\mathbf{n}) \quad \text{for} \quad C - b_2 + b_{2r} < \mathbf{nb} \leq C$$
$$(4.13)$$

$$a_1 b_1 x(\mathbf{n}) P(\mathbf{n}_1^-) + \alpha_{2r} b_{2r} x(\mathbf{n}) P(\mathbf{n}_{2r}^-) = (n_1 b_1 x(\mathbf{n}_1^-) + n_{2r} b_{2r} x(\mathbf{n}_{2r}^-)) P(\mathbf{n})$$
$$\text{for} \quad C < \mathbf{nb} \leq T$$
$$(4.14)$$

Equations (4.12)–(4.14) can be combined into one equation by assuming that calls with b_{2r} are negligible when $1 \leq \mathbf{nb} \leq C - b_2 + b_{2r}$ and calls with b_2 are negligible when $C < \mathbf{nb} \leq T$:

$$\alpha_1 b_1 x(\mathbf{n}) P(\mathbf{n}_1^-) + \alpha_2 b_2 \gamma_2(\mathbf{nb}) x(\mathbf{n}) P(\mathbf{n}_2^-) + \alpha_{2r} b_{2r} \gamma_{2r}(\mathbf{nb}) x(\mathbf{n}) P(\mathbf{n}_{2r}^-) =$$
$$(n_1 b_1 x(\mathbf{n}_1^-) + n_2 b_2 x(\mathbf{n}_2^-) + n_{2r} b_{2r} x(\mathbf{n}_{2r}^-)) P(\mathbf{n})$$
$$(4.15)$$

where $\gamma_2(\mathbf{nb}) = 1$ for $1 \leq \mathbf{nb} \leq C$, otherwise $\gamma_2(\mathbf{nb}) = 0$ and $\gamma_{2r}(\mathbf{nb}) = 1$ for $C - b_2 + b_{2r} < \mathbf{nb} \leq T$, otherwise $\gamma_{2r}(\mathbf{nb}) = 0$.

Note that the approximations introduced in (4.15) are similar to those introduced in the STM of [2].

Since $x(\mathbf{n}) = 1$, when $0 \leq \mathbf{nb} \leq C$, it is proved in [2] (see also (2.9)) that:

$$\alpha_1 b_1 q(j - b_1) + \alpha_2 b_2 q(j - b_2) + \alpha_{2r} b_{2r} \gamma_{2r}(j) q(j - b_{2r}) = j q(j) \tag{4.16}$$

for $1 \leq j \leq C$ and $\gamma_{2r}(j) = 1$ for $C - b_2 + b_{2r} < j$, otherwise $\gamma_{2r}(j) = 0$.

Reminder: To prove (4.16), the migration approximation is needed, which assumes that the population of retry calls of service-class 2 is negligible in states $j \leq C - b_2 + b_{2r}$.

When $C < \mathbf{nb} \leq T$ and based on (4.2), (4.15) can be written as:

$$\alpha_1 b_1 P(\mathbf{n}_1^-) + \alpha_{2r} b_{2r} \gamma_{2r}(\mathbf{nb}) P(\mathbf{n}_{2r}^-) = C P(\mathbf{n}) \tag{4.17}$$

To introduce the link occupancy distribution $q(j)$ in (4.17), we sum both sides of (4.17) over the set of states $\Omega_j = \{\mathbf{n} \in \Omega : \mathbf{nb} = j\}$:

$$\alpha_1 b_1 \sum_{\mathbf{n} \in \Omega_j} P(\mathbf{n}_1^-) + \alpha_{2r} b_{2r} \gamma_{2r}(\mathbf{nb}) \sum_{\mathbf{n} \in \Omega_j} P(\mathbf{n}_{2r}^-) = C \sum_{\mathbf{n} \in \Omega_j} P(\mathbf{n}) \tag{4.18}$$

Since by definition $\sum_{\mathbf{n} \in \Omega_j} P(\mathbf{n}) = q(j)$, (4.18) is written as:

$$\alpha_1 b_1 q(j - b_1) + \alpha_{2r} b_{2r} \gamma_{2r}(j) q(j - b_{2r}) = C q(j) \tag{4.19}$$

where $\gamma_{2r}(j) = 1$ for $C < j \leq T$.

The combination of (4.16) and (4.19) gives the following approximate recursive formula for the calculation of $q(j)$ in the case of two service-classes, when only calls of service-class 2 have retry parameters (for $1 \leq j \leq T$):

$$q(j) = \frac{1}{\min(j, C)} [\alpha_1 b_1 q(j - b_1) + \alpha_2 b_2 \gamma_2(j) q(j - b_2) + \alpha_{2r} b_{2r} \gamma_{2r}(j) q(j - b_{2r})] \tag{4.20}$$

where $\gamma_2(j) = 1$ for $1 \leq j \leq C$, otherwise $\gamma_2(j) = 0$, and $\gamma_{2r}(j) = 1$ for $C - b_2 + b_{2r} < j \leq T$, otherwise $\gamma_{2r}(j) = 0$.

In the case of K service-classes and assuming that all service-classes may have retry parameters (4.20) takes the general form:

$$q(j) = \begin{cases} 1 & \text{if } j = 0 \\ \dfrac{1}{\min(j,C)} \displaystyle\sum_{k=1}^{K} \alpha_k b_k \gamma_k(j) q(j - b_k) \\ \quad + \dfrac{1}{\min(j,C)} \displaystyle\sum_{k=1}^{K} \alpha_{kr} b_{kr} \gamma_{kr}(j) q(j - b_{kr}) & \text{if } j = 1, 2, \ldots, T \\ 0 & \text{otherwise} \end{cases} \tag{4.21}$$

where $\gamma_k(j) = \begin{cases} 1 & \text{if } 1 \le j \le C \text{ and } b_{kr} > 0 \\ 1 & \text{if } 1 \le j \le T \text{ and } b_{kr} = 0, \\ 0 & \text{otherwise} \end{cases}$ $\gamma_{kr}(j) = \begin{cases} 1 & \text{if } C - b_k + b_{kr} < j \le T \\ 0 & \text{otherwise} \end{cases}$.

4.1.2.2 CBP, Utilization, and Mean Number of In-service Calls

Having determined the unnormalized values of $q(j)$, we can calculate [1]:

- The CBP of service-class k calls with b_{kr} b.u., B_{kr}, via:

$$B_{kr} = \sum_{j=T-b_{kr}+1}^{T} G^{-1} q(j) \tag{4.22}$$

where $G = \sum_{j=0}^{T} q(j)$ is the normalization constant and $b_{kr} > 0$.
- The CBP of service-class k calls with b_k b.u., B_k, when $b_{kr} = 0$, via:

$$B_k = \sum_{j=T-b_k+1}^{T} G^{-1} q(j) \tag{4.23}$$

Note that if $b_{kr} > 0$, then B_k refers to the *Prob{retry}* and the summation in (4.23) should start from $C - b_k + 1$.
- The conditional CBP of service-class k retry calls given that they have been blocked with their initial bandwidth requirement b_k, B_{kr}^*, via:

$$B_{kr}^* = Prob\{j > T - b_{kr} | j > C - b_k\} = \frac{B_{kr}}{B_k} \tag{4.24}$$

- The link utilization, U, by (3.23).
- The mean number of service-class k calls with b_k b.u. in state j, $y_k(j)$, via:

$$y_k(j) = \frac{\alpha_k \gamma_k(j) q(j - b_k)}{q(j)}, \quad q(j) > 0 \tag{4.25}$$

- The mean number of service-class k calls with b_{kr} b.u. in state j, $y_{kr}(j)$, via:

$$y_{kr}(j) = \frac{\alpha_{kr} \gamma_{kr}(j) q(j - b_{kr})}{q(j)}, \quad q(j) > 0 \tag{4.26}$$

where $\gamma_k(j) = 1$ for $1 \le j \le C$, otherwise $\gamma_k(j) = 0$ and $\gamma_{kr}(j) = 1$ for $C - b_k + b_{kr} < j \le T$, otherwise $\gamma_{kr}(j) = 0$.

- The mean number of in-service calls of service-class k accepted with $b_k, \bar{n}_k$, via:

$$\bar{n}_k = \sum_{j=1}^{T} y_k(j) \frac{q(j)}{G} \tag{4.27}$$

- The mean number of in-service calls of service-class k accepted with $b_{kr}, \bar{n}_{kr}$, via:

$$\bar{n}_{kr} = \sum_{j=1}^{T} y_{kr}(j) \frac{q(j)}{G} \tag{4.28}$$

Example 4.3 Consider again Example 4.1 ($C = 4, T = 6, K = 2, b_1 = 1, b_2 = 3, b_{2r} = 2, \lambda_1 = \lambda_2 = \mu_1 = \mu_2 = 1, \mu_{2r} = 2/3$).

(a) Calculate the values of $Q(j)$ based on (4.21).
(b) Calculate the CBP of both service-classes including the retry probability and the conditional B_{2r}^*.

(a) State probabilities through the recursion (4.21):

$j = 1$:	$q(1) = q(0) + 0 = 1.0$	$\Rightarrow q(1) = 1.0$
$j = 2$:	$2q(2) = q(1) + 0 = 1.0$	$\Rightarrow q(2) = 0.5$
$j = 3$:	$3q(3) = q(2) + 3q(0) = 3.5$	$\Rightarrow q(3) = 1.16667$
$j = 4$:	$4q(4) = q(3) + 3q(1) + 3q(2) = 5.66667$	$\Rightarrow q(4) = 1.41667$
$j = 5$:	$4q(5) = q(4) + 0 + 3q(3) = 4.91668$	$\Rightarrow q(5) = 1.22917$
$j = 6$:	$4q(6) = q(5) + 0 + 3q(4) = 5.47918$	$\Rightarrow q(6) = 1.36979$

The normalization constant is: $G = \sum_{j=0}^{T} q(j) = 7.6823$.

The state probabilities are:

$Q(0) = 0.13017$ $Q(1) = 0.13017$ $Q(2) = 0.06508$ $Q(3) = 0.15186$
$Q(4) = 0.18441$ $Q(5) = 0.16$ $Q(6) = 0.1783$

The CBP are as follows:

$$B_1 = \sum_{j=T-b_1+1}^{T} Q(j) = Q(6) = 0.1783 \text{ (compare with the exact 0.1706)}$$

$$B_2 = \sum_{j=C-b_2+1}^{T} Q(j) = Q(2) + Q(3) + Q(4) + Q(5) + Q(6) = 0.73965 \text{ (compare with the exact 0.7821)}$$

$$B_{2r} = \sum_{j=T-b_{2r}+1}^{T} Q(j) = Q(5) + Q(6) = 0.3383 \text{ (compare with the exact 0.3325)}$$

$$B_{2r}^* = \frac{B_{2r}}{B_2} = 0.4574 \text{ (compare with the exact 0.4251)}$$

It is apparent that even in small E-SRM examples the error introduced by the assumption of LB, the introduction of $\varphi_k(\mathbf{n})$ and $\varphi_{kr}(\mathbf{n})$, and the migration approximation is not significant.

4.2 The Elastic Single-Retry Model under the BR Policy

4.2.1 The Service System

We now consider the *E-SRM under the BR policy (E-SRM/BR)* with BR parameter t_k for service-class k calls ($k = 1, \ldots, K$). For CAC in the E-SRM/BR, we consider the following cases:

(a) If $j + b_k \leq C$, no bandwidth compression takes place and the call is accepted in the link with b_k b.u.
(b) If $j + b_k > C$, then the call is blocked with b_k and retries immediately to be connected in the link with $b_{kr} < b_k$. Now if:
   b1) $j + b_{kr} \leq C$, no bandwidth compression occurs and the retry call is accepted in the system with b_{kr} and $\mu_{kr}^{-1} > \mu_k^{-1}$, so that $b_{kr}\mu_{kr}^{-1} = b_k\mu_k^{-1}$,
   b2) $j + b_{kr} > T - t_k$, the retry call is blocked and lost, and
   b3) $T - t_k \geq j + b_{kr} > C$, the retry call is accepted in the system by compressing its bandwidth requirement b_{kr} together with the bandwidth of all in-service calls of all service-classes. In that case, the compressed bandwidth of the retry call becomes $b'_{kr} = rb_{kr} = \frac{C}{j+b_{kr}}b_{kr}$ where r is the compression factor, common to all service-classes. Similarly, all in-service calls, which have been accepted in the link with b_k (or b_{kr}), compress their bandwidth to $b'_k = rb_k$ (or $b'_{kr} = rb_{kr}$) for $k = 1, \ldots, K$. After the compression of all calls the link state is $j = C$. The minimum value of the compression factor is $r_{\min} = C/T$.

As far as the values of $\varphi_k(\mathbf{n})$, $\varphi_{kr}(\mathbf{n})$, and $x(\mathbf{n})$ are concerned they are determined by (3.8), (4.1), and (4.2), respectively.

Example 4.4 Consider again Example 4.1 ($C = 4, T = 6, K = 2, b_1 = 1, b_2 = 3$, $b_{2r} = 2, \lambda_1 = \lambda_2 = \mu_1 = \mu_2 = 1, \mu_{2r} = 2/3$) and apply the BR parameters $t_1 = 1$ b.u. and $t_2 = 0$ b.u. to calls of service-class 1 and 2, respectively.

(a) Find the total number of permissible states $\mathbf{n} = (n_1, n_2, n_{2r})$, draw the state transition diagram, and determine the values of j and $r(\mathbf{n})$ for each state $\mathbf{n} = (n_1, n_2, n_{2r})$.
(b) Calculate the state probabilities $P(n_1, n_2, n_{2r})$ based on the GB equations. Then determine the values of the link occupancy distribution $Q(j)$ (for $j = 0, \ldots, T$).
(c) Calculate the CBP of both service-classes, including the retry probability and the link utilization.
(d) Draw the modified state transition diagram based on $\varphi_k(\mathbf{n})$ and $\varphi_{kr}(\mathbf{n})$, and determine their values for each state $\mathbf{n} = (n_1, n_2, n_{2r})$.
(e) Based on $\varphi_k(\mathbf{n})$ and $\varphi_{kr}(\mathbf{n})$, calculate the values of $P(n_1, n_2, n_{2r})$, $Q(j)$, CBP, and link utilization.

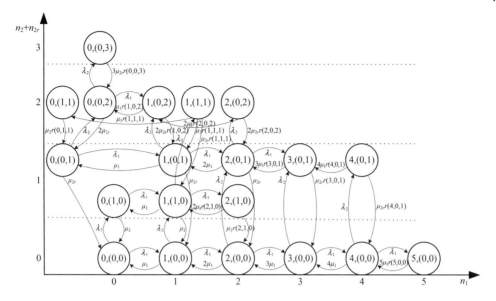

Figure 4.3 The state space Ω and the state transition diagram (Example 4.4)

(a) There are 20 permissible states of the form $\mathbf{n} = (n_1, n_2, n_{2r})$. The state space Ω and the state transition diagram are shown in Figure 4.3. Compared to Figure 4.1, there are two states that do not exist: (3,1,0) and (6,0,0). The $r(\mathbf{n})$ (for the 20 states) are the same as those presented in Table 4.1 (the BR policy does not affect $r(\mathbf{n})$).

(b) Based on Figure 4.3, we obtain the following 20 GB equations:

$(0,0,0):$ $P(0,1,0) + P(1,0,0) + (2/3)P(0,0,1) - 2P(0,0,0) = 0$

$(0,0,1):$ $0.8P(0,1,1) + (4/3)P(0,0,2) + P(1,0,1) - (8/3)P(0,0,1) = 0$

$(0,0,2):$ $P(0,0,1) + (4/3)P(0,0,3) + 0.8P(1,0,2) - (10/3)P(0,0,2) = 0$

$(0,0,3):$ $P(0,0,2) - (4/3)P(0,0,3) = 0$

$(0,1,0):$ $P(0,0,0) + (8/15)P(0,1,1) + P(1,1,0) - 3P(0,1,0) = 0$

$(0,1,1):$ $P(0,1,0) + (2/3)P(1,1,1) - (4/3)P(0,1,1) = 0$

$(1,0,0):$ $P(0,0,0) + 2P(2,0,0) + (2/3)P(1,0,1) + P(1,1,0) - 3P(1,0,0) = 0$

$(1,0,1):$ $P(0,0,1) + 2P(2,0,1) + (16/15)P(1,0,2) + (2/3)P(1,1,1) - (11/3)P(1,0,1) = 0$

$(1,0,2):$ $P(0,0,2) + (4/3)P(2,0,2) + P(1,0,1) - (28/15)P(1,0,2) = 0$

$(1,1,0):$ $P(0,1,0) + P(1,0,0) + 1.6P(2,1,0) + (4/9)P(1,1,1) - 4P(1,1,0) = 0$

$(1,1,1):$ $P(1,1,0) - (16/9)P(1,1,1) = 0$

$(2,0,0):$ $P(1,0,0) + 3P(3,0,0) + 0.8P(2,1,0) + (2/3)P(2,0,1) - 4P(2,0,0) = 0$

$(2,0,1):$ $P(1,0,1) + P(2,0,0) + 2.4P(3,0,1) + (8/9)P(2,0,2) - (14/3)P(2,0,1) = 0$

$(2,0,2):$ $P(2,0,1) - (20/9)P(2,0,2) = 0$

$(2,1,0):$ $P(1,1,0) - 2.4P(2,1,0) = 0$

$(3,0,0):$ $P(2,0,0) + 4P(4,0,0) + (8/15)P(3,0,1) - 5P(3,0,0) = 0$

$(3,0,1):$ $P(2,0,1) + (8/3)P(4,0,1) + P(3,0,0) - (44/15)P(3,0,1) = 0$

$(4,0,0)$: $P(3,0,0) + 4P(5,0,0) + (4/9)P(4,0,1) - 6P(4,0,0) = 0$

$(4,0,1)$: $P(4,0,0) - (28/9)P(4,0,1) = 0$

$(5,0,0)$: $P(4,0,0) - 4P(5,0,0) = 0$

The solution of this linear system is:

$P(0,0,0) = 0.118066$ $P(0,0,1) = 0.083274$ $P(0,0,2) = 0.066624$ $P(0,0,3) = 0.049968$

$P(0,1,0) = 0.07132$ $P(0,1,1) = 0.069965$ $P(1,0,0) = 0.109296$ $P(1,0,1) = 0.077261$

$P(1,0,2) = 0.090228$ $P(1,1,0) = 0.058578$ $P(1,1,1) = 0.03295$ $P(2,0,0) = 0.049869$

$P(2,0,1) = 0.040902$ $P(2,0,2) = 0.018406$ $P(2,1,0) = 0.024408$ $P(3,0,0) = 0.014462$

$P(3,0,1) = 0.019744$ $P(4,0,0) = 0.002977$ $P(4,0,1) = 0.000957$ $P(5,0,0) = 0.000744$

Based on the values of $P(n_1, n_2, n_{2r})$, we determine the values of $Q(j)$:

$Q(0) = P(0,0,0) = 0.118066$

$Q(1) = P(1,0,0) = 0.109296$

$Q(2) = P(0,0,1) + P(2,0,0) = 0.133143$

$Q(3) = P(0,1,0) + P(1,0,1) + P(3,0,0) = 0.163043$

$Q(4) = P(0,0,2) + P(1,1,0) + P(2,0,1) + P(4,0,0) = 0.169081$

$Q(5) = P(0,1,1) + P(1,0,2) + P(2,1,0) + P(3,0,1) + P(5,0,0) = 0.205089$

$Q(6) = P(0,0,3) + P(1,1,1) + P(2,0,2) + P(4,0,1) = 0.102281$

(c) Based on the values of $Q(j)$, we obtain the exact CBP:

$$B_1 = \sum_{j=T-b_1-t_1+1}^{T} Q(j) = Q(5) + Q(6) = 0.30737 \text{ (compare with 0.1706 in the E-SRM)}$$

The $Prob\{retry\}$ of service-class 2 calls, B_2, is given by:

$$B_2 = \sum_{j=C-b_2+1}^{T} Q(j) = Q(2) + Q(3) + Q(4) + Q(5) + Q(6) = 0.77264$$

(compare with 0.7821 in the E-SRM)

Due to the selection of the BR parameters, the CBP of service-class 2, B_{2r} equals B_1:

$$B_{2r} = \sum_{j=T-b_{2r}+1}^{T} Q(j) = Q(5) + Q(6) = 0.30737 \text{ (compare with 0.3325 in the E-SRM)}$$

The link utilization is determined by:

$$U = \sum_{j=1}^{C} jQ(j) + \sum_{j=C+1}^{T} CQ(j) = 2.771 \text{ b.u. (compare with 2.832 in the E-SRM)}$$

(d) Figure 4.4 shows the modified state transition diagram of the system. The values of $\varphi_k(\mathbf{n})$ and $\varphi_{kr}(\mathbf{n})$ (for the 20 states) are exactly the same as those of Table 4.2.

(e) Based on Figure 4.4, we obtain the following 20 GB equations:

$(0,0,0):\quad P(0,1,0)+P(1,0,0)+(2/3)P(0,0,1)-2P(0,0,0)=0$

$(0,0,1):\quad 0.8P(0,1,1)+(4/3)P(0,0,2)+P(1,0,1)-(8/3)P(0,0,1)=0$

$(0,0,2):\quad P(0,0,1)+(4/3)P(0,0,3)+0.8P(1,0,2)-(10/3)P(0,0,2)=0$

$(0,0,3):\quad P(0,0,2)-(4/3)P(0,0,3)=0$

$(0,1,0):\quad P(0,0,0)+(8/15)P(0,1,1)+P(1,1,0)-3P(0,1,0)=0$

$(0,1,1):\quad P(0,1,0)+0.8P(1,1,1)-(4/3)P(0,1,1)=0$

$(1,0,0):\quad P(0,0,0)+2P(2,0,0)+(2/3)P(1,0,1)+P(1,1,0)-3P(1,0,0)=0$

$(1,0,1):\quad P(0,0,1)+2P(2,0,1)+(16/15)P(1,0,2)+(16/25)P(1,1,1)-(11/3)P(1,0,1)=0$

$(1,0,2):\quad P(0,0,2)+(20/13)P(2,0,2)+P(1,0,1)-(28/15)P(1,0,2)=0$

$(1,1,0):\quad P(0,1,0)+P(1,0,0)+1.6P(2,1,0)+(32/75)P(1,1,1)-4P(1,1,0)=0$

$(1,1,1):\quad P(1,1,0)-(28/15)P(1,1,1)=0$

$(2,0,0):\quad P(1,0,0)+3P(3,0,0)+0.8P(2,1,0)+(2/3)P(2,0,1)-4P(2,0,0)=0$

$(2,0,1):\quad P(1,0,1)+P(2,0,0)+2.4P(3,0,1)+(32/39)P(2,0,2)-(14/3)P(2,0,1)=0$

$(2,0,2):\quad P(2,0,1)-(92/39)P(2,0,2)=0$

$(2,1,0):\quad P(1,1,0)-2.4P(2,1,0)=0$

$(3,0,0):\quad P(2,0,0)+4P(4,0,0)+(8/15)P(3,0,1)-5P(3,0,0)=0$

$(3,0,1):\quad P(2,0,1)+(20/7)P(4,0,1)+P(3,0,0)-(44/15)P(3,0,1)=0$

$(4,0,0):\quad P(3,0,0)+4P(5,0,0)+(8/21)P(4,0,1)-6P(4,0,0)=0$

$(4,0,1):\quad P(4,0,0)-(68/21)P(4,0,1)=0$

$(5,0,0):\quad P(4,0,0)-4P(5,0,0)=0$

The solution of this linear system is:

$P(0,0,0)=0.11841\quad P(0,0,1)=0.084224\quad P(0,0,2)=0.06736\quad P(0,0,3)=0.05052$

$P(0,1,0)=0.071761\quad P(0,1,1)=0.072525\quad P(1,0,0)=0.108911\quad P(1,0,1)=0.076763$

$P(1,0,2)=0.091188\quad P(1,1,0)=0.058192\quad P(1,1,1)=0.031174\quad P(2,0,0)=0.049478$

$P(2,0,1)=0.040011\quad P(2,0,2)=0.016961\quad P(2,1,0)=0.024247\quad P(3,0,0)=0.01431$

$P(3,0,1)=0.0194\quad P(4,0,0)=0.002931\quad P(4,0,1)=0.000905\quad P(5,0,0)=0.000733$

Based on the values of $P(n_1,n_2,n_{2r})$, we determine the values of $Q(j)$:

$Q(0)=P(0,0,0)=0.11841$

$Q(1)=P(1,0,0)=0.108911$

$Q(2)=P(0,0,1)+P(2,0,0)=0.133702$

$Q(3)=P(0,1,0)+P(1,0,1)+P(3,0,0)=0.162834$

$Q(4)=P(0,0,2)+P(1,1,0)+P(2,0,1)+P(4,0,0)=0.168494$

$Q(5)=P(0,1,1)+P(1,0,2)+P(2,1,0)+P(3,0,1)+P(5,0,0)=0.208093$

$Q(6)=P(0,0,3)+P(1,1,1)+P(2,0,2)+P(4,0,1)=0.09956$

Based on the values of $Q(j)$, we obtain the following CBP:

$$B_1=\sum_{j=T-b_1-t_1+1}^{T}Q(j)=Q(5)+Q(6)=0.30765\text{ (compare with the exact 0.30737)}$$

The $Prob\{\text{retry}\}$ of service-class 2 calls, B_2, is given by:

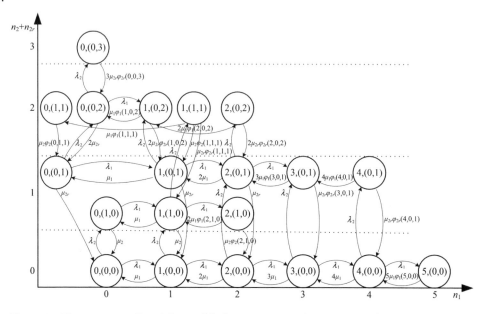

Figure 4.4 The state space Ω and the modified state transition diagram (Example 4.4).

$$B_2 = \sum_{j=C-b_2+1}^{T} Q(j) = Q(2) + Q(3) + Q(4) + Q(5) + Q(6) = 0.7727$$

(compare with the exact 0.77264)

The CBP of service-class 2, B_{2r}, equals B_1:

$$B_{2r} = \sum_{j=T-b_{2r}+1}^{T} Q(j) = Q(5) + Q(6) = 0.30765$$

The link utilization is determined by:

$$U = \sum_{j=1}^{C} jQ(j) + \sum_{j=C+1}^{T} CQ(j) = 2.769 \text{ b.u. (compare with the exact 2.771)}$$

4.2.2 The Analytical Model

4.2.2.1 Link Occupancy Distribution
In the E-SRM/BR, the recursive calculation of $q(j)$ is based on the Roberts method (see Section 1.3.2.2), which leads to the formula [4]:

$$q(j) = \begin{cases} 1 & \text{if } j = 0 \\ \dfrac{1}{\min(C,j)} \left[\displaystyle\sum_{k=1}^{K} \alpha_k D_k(j - b_k)\gamma_k(j)q(j - b_k) + \sum_{k=1}^{K} \alpha_{kr} D_{kr}(j - b_{kr})\gamma_{kr}(j)q(j - b_{kr}) \right] & \\ & \text{if } j = 1, 2, \ldots, T \\ 0 & \text{otherwise} \end{cases}$$

$$(4.29)$$

where $D_k(j - b_k) = \begin{cases} b_k & \text{for } j \le T - t_k \\ 0 & \text{for } j > T - t_k \end{cases}$ and $D_{kr}(j - b_{kr}) = \begin{cases} b_{kr} & \text{for } j \le T - t_k \\ 0 & \text{for } j > T - t_k \end{cases}$.

4.2.2.2 CBP, Utilization, and Mean Number of In-service Calls

Based on (4.29), the following performance measures can be calculated:

- The CBP of service-class k calls with b_{kr} b.u., B_{kr}, via:

$$B_{kr} = \sum_{j=T-b_{kr}-t_k+1}^{T} G^{-1}q(j) \tag{4.30}$$

where $G = \sum_{j=0}^{T} q(j)$ is the normalization constant and $b_{kr} > 0$.
- The CBP of service-class k calls with b_k b.u., B_k, when $b_{kr} = 0$, via:

$$B_k = \sum_{j=T-b_k-t_k+1}^{T} G^{-1}q(j) \tag{4.31}$$

Note that if $b_{kr} > 0$, then B_k refers to the *Prob{retry}* and the summation in (4.31) should start from $C - b_k + 1$.
- The conditional CBP of service-class k retry calls given that they have been blocked with their initial bandwidth requirement b_k, B_{kr}^*, via:

$$B_{kr}^* = Prob\{j > T - b_{kr} - t_k | j > C - b_k\} = \frac{B_{kr}}{B_k} \tag{4.32}$$

- The link utilization, U, via (3.23).
- The mean number of service-class k calls with b_k b.u. in state j, $y_k(j)$, via (4.25), and the mean number of service-class k calls with b_{kr} b.u. in state j, $y_{kr}(j)$, via (4.26).
- The mean number of in-service calls of service-class k accepted in the system with b_k, $\bar{n}_k$, via (4.27), and the mean number of in-service calls of service-class k accepted in the system with b_{kr}, $\bar{n}_{kr}$, via (4.28).

Example 4.5 Consider again Example 4.4 ($C = 4, T = 6, K = 2, b_1 = 1, b_2 = 3$, $b_{2r} = 2, t_1 = 1, t_2 = 0, \lambda_1 = \lambda_2 = \mu_1 = \mu_2 = 1, \mu_{2r} = 2/3$).

(a) Calculate the values of $Q(j)$ based on (4.29).
(b) Calculate the CBP of both service-classes including the retry probability and the conditional B_{2r}^*.

(a) State probabilities through the recursion (4.29):

$j = 1:$	$q(1) = q(0) + 0 = 1.0$	$\Rightarrow q(1) = 1.0$
$j = 2:$	$2q(2) = q(1) + 0 = 1.0$	$\Rightarrow q(2) = 0.5$
$j = 3:$	$3q(3) = q(2) + 3q(0) = 3.5$	$\Rightarrow q(3) = 1.16667$
$j = 4:$	$4q(4) = q(3) + 3q(1) + 3q(2) = 5.66667$	$\Rightarrow q(4) = 1.41667$
$j = 5:$	$4q(5) = q(4) + 0 + 3q(3) = 4.91668$	$\Rightarrow q(5) = 1.22917$
$j = 6:$	$4q(6) = 0 + 0 + 3q(4) = 4.25$	$\Rightarrow q(6) = 1.0625$

The normalization constant is:

$$G = \sum_{j=0}^{T} q(j) = 7.375.$$

The state probabilities are:

$Q(0) = 0.13559$ $\quad$ $Q(1) = 0.13559$ $\quad$ $Q(2) = 0.06780$ $\quad$ $Q(3) = 0.15819$

$Q(4) = 0.19209$ $\quad$ $Q(5) = 0.16667$ $\quad$ $Q(6) = 0.14407$

(b) The CBP are as follows:

$$B_1 = \sum_{j=T-b_1-t_1+1}^{T} Q(j) = Q(5) + Q(6) = 0.31074 \text{ (compare with the exact 0.30737)}$$

$$B_2 = \sum_{j=C-b_2+1}^{T} Q(j) = Q(2) + Q(3) + Q(4) + Q(5) + Q(6) = 0.72882 \text{ (compare with the exact 0.77264)}$$

$$B_{2r} = \sum_{j=T-b_{2r}+1}^{T} Q(j) = Q(5) + Q(6) = 0.31074 \text{ (compare with the exact 0.30737)}$$

$$B_{2r}^* = \frac{B_{2r}}{B_2} = 0.42636 \text{ (compare with the exact 0.39782)}$$

It is apparent that even in small E-SRM/BR examples the error introduced by the assumption of LB, the introduction of $\varphi_k(\mathbf{n})$ and $\varphi_{kr}(\mathbf{n})$, the migration approximation, and the application of the BR policy remains acceptable.

4.3 The Elastic Multi-Retry Model

4.3.1 The Service System

Similar to the MRM, in the *elastic multi-retry model (E-MRM)* a blocked call of service-class k can have more than one retry parameter $(b_{kr_s}, \mu_{kr_s}^{-1})$ for $s = 1, \ldots, S(k)$, where $b_{kr_{S(k)}} < \ldots < b_{kr_1} < b_k$ and $\mu_{kr_{S(k)}}^{-1} > \ldots > \mu_{kr_1}^{-1} > \mu_k^{-1}$.

To simply describe the CAC, we assume that a service-class k call has a peak-bandwidth requirement of b_k b.u. and may retry twice to be connected in the system, the first time with $b_{kr_1} < b_k$ and the second time (if blocked with b_{kr_1}) with $b_{kr_2} < b_{kr_1}$. Then, for call admission, we consider the following cases:

(a) If $j + b_k \le C$, no bandwidth compression takes place and the call is accepted in the link with b_k b.u.

(b) If $j + b_k > C$, then the call is blocked with b_k and retries immediately to be connected in the link with $b_{kr_1} < b_k$. If $j + b_{kr_1} \le C$, the retry call is accepted in the system with b_{kr_1} and $\mu_{kr_1}^{-1} > \mu_k^{-1}$ (no bandwidth compression occurs).

(c) If $j + b_{kr_1} > C$, the retry call is blocked with b_{kr_1} and immediately retries with $b_{kr_2} < b_{kr_1}$. Now if:

c1) $j + b_{kr_2} \le C$, the retry call is accepted in the system with b_{kr_2} and $\mu_{kr_2}^{-1} > \mu_{kr_1}^{-1} > \mu_k^{-1}$ (no bandwidth compression occurs).

c2) $j + b_{kr_2} > T$, the retry call is blocked and lost, and c3) $T \geq j + b_{kr_2} > C$, the retry call is accepted in the system by compressing its bandwidth requirement b_{kr_2} together with the bandwidth of all in-service calls of all service-classes. In that case, the compressed bandwidth of the retry call becomes $b'_{kr_2} = r b_{kr_2} = \frac{C}{j + b_{kr_2}} b_{kr_2}$, where r is the compression factor, common to all service-classes. Similarly, all in-service calls, which have been accepted in the link with b_k (or b_{kr_1} or b_{kr_2}), compress their bandwidth to $b'_k = r b_k$ (or $b'_{kr_1} = r b_{kr_1}$ or $b'_{kr_2} = r b_{kr_2}$) for $k = 1, \dots, K$. After the compression of all calls the link state is $j = C$. The minimum value of the compression factor is $r_{min} = C/T$.

Similar to the E-SRM, when a service-class k call, with bandwidth b'_k (or b'_{kr_1} or b'_{kr_2}), departs from the system, the remaining in-service calls of each service-class i ($i = 1, \dots, K$) expand their bandwidth in proportion to their initially assigned bandwidth b_i (or b_{ir_1} or b_{ir_2}). After bandwidth compression/expansion, elastic service-class calls increase/decrease their service time so that the product *service time* by *bandwidth* remains constant.

Similar to the E-SRM, the steady state probabilities in the E-MRM do not have a PFS. Thus, the unnormalized values of $q(j)$ can be determined by an approximate but recursive formula, as presented in Section 4.3.2.

Example 4.6 Consider again Example 2.6 ($C = 3, K = 2, b_1 = 1, b_2 = 3, b_{2r_1} = 2, b_{2r_2} = 1, \lambda_1 = \lambda_2 = 1, \mu_1^{-1} = \mu_2^{-1} = 1, \mu_{2r_1}^{-1} = 2.0, \mu_{2r_2}^{-1} = 4.0$) and let $T = 4$ b.u.

(a) Describe the CAC of a new call of service-class 2 that arrives in the system and has a peak-bandwidth requirement of $b_2 = 3$ b.u.
(b) Find the total number of permissible states $\mathbf{n} = (n_1, n_2, n_{2r_1}, n_{2r_2})$ and determine the values of j and $r(\mathbf{n})$ for each state $\mathbf{n} = (n_1, n_2, n_{2r_1}, n_{2r_2})$.
(c) Calculate the state probabilities $P(n_1, n_2, n_{2r_1}, n_{2r_2})$ based on the GB equations. Then determine the values of the link occupancy distribution $Q(j)$ (for $j = 0, \dots, T$).
(d) Calculate the CBP of both service-classes, including the retry probabilities and the link utilization.
(e) Calculate the conditional CBP of service-class 2 retry calls with b_{2r_2}, given that they have been blocked with their initial bandwidth requirement, b_2.

(a) Let j be the occupied link bandwidth at the time of arrival of a service-class 2 call. Then:
- If $j \leq C - b_2$, that is, $j = 0$, then the call is accepted in the link with $b_2 = 3$ b.u.
- If $j > C - b_2$, that is, $j > 0$, then the call is blocked with b_2 and retries immediately with $b_{2r_1} = 2$ b.u. Now if $j \leq C - b_{2r_1}$, which means $j = 1$, then the retry call is accepted in the system with $b_{2r_1} = 2$ b.u.
- If $j > C - b_{2r_1}$, that is, $j > 1$, then the retry call is blocked with b_{2r_1} and immediately retries with $b_{2r_2} = 1$ b.u. Now we consider three sub-cases:
  - If $j \leq C - b_{2r_2} \to j = 2$, then the retry call is accepted in the system with b_{2r_2},
  - If $j > T - b_{2r_2} \to j > 3$, then the retry call is blocked and lost, and
  - If $T - b_{2r_2} \geq j > C - b_{2r_2} \to 3 \geq j > 2$, that is, $j = 3$, then the retry call is accepted in the system by compressing its bandwidth requirement b_{2r_2} together with the bandwidth of all in-service calls of all service-classes.

(b) There are 24 permissible states of the form $\mathbf{n} = (n_1, n_2, n_{2r_1}, n_{2r_2})$. Table 4.3 presents the 24 states together with the values of $r(\mathbf{n})$ and the occupied link bandwidth, $j = n_1 b_1 + n_2 b_2 + n_{2r_1} b_{2r_1} + n_{2r_2} b_{2r_2}$, before and after compression.

(c) In what follows, we present the 24 GB equations:

$(0,0,0,0)$: $\quad 0.5P(0,0,1,0) + 0.25P(0,0,0,1) + P(0,1,0,0) + P(1,0,0,0) - 2P(0,0,0,0) = 0$

$(0,0,0,1)$: $\quad 0.5P(0,0,0,2) + 0.75P(0,1,0,1) + 0.5P(0,0,1,1) + P(1,0,0,1)$
$\qquad\qquad -2.25P(0,0,0,1) = 0$

$(0,0,0,2)$: $\quad P(1,0,0,2) + 0.75P(0,0,0,3) + 0.375P(0,0,1,2) - 2.5P(0,0,0,2) = 0$

$(0,0,0,3)$: $\quad P(0,0,0,2) + 0.75P(0,0,0,4) + 0.75P(1,0,0,3) - 2.75P(0,0,0,3) = 0$

$(0,0,0,4)$: $\quad P(0,0,0,3) - 0.75P(0,0,0,4) = 0$

$(0,0,1,0)$: $\quad 0.25P(0,0,1,1) + P(1,0,1,0) - 2.5P(0,0,1,0) = 0$

$(0,0,1,1)$: $\quad P(0,0,0,1) + P(0,0,1,0) + 0.75P(1,0,1,1) + 0.375P(0,0,1,2)$
$\qquad\qquad -2.75P(0,0,1,1) = 0$

$(0,0,1,2)$: $\quad P(0,0,1,1) - 0.75P(0,0,1,2) = 0$

$(0,1,0,0)$: $\quad P(0,0,0,0) + 0.1875P(0,1,0,1) + 0.75P(1,1,0,0) - 3P(0,1,0,0) = 0$

$(0,1,0,1)$: $\quad P(0,1,0,0) - 0.9375P(0,1,0,1) = 0$

$(1,0,0,0)$: $\quad 0.25P(1,0,0,1) + 2P(2,0,0,0) + 0.75P(1,1,0,0) + 0.5P(1,0,1,0) + P(0,0,0,0)$
$\qquad\qquad -3P(1,0,0,0) = 0$

$(1,0,0,1)$: $\quad 2P(2,0,0,1) + 0.5P(1,0,0,2) + P(0,0,0,1) + 0.375P(1,0,1,1)$
$\qquad\qquad -3.25P(1,0,0,1) = 0$

$(1,0,0,2)$: $\quad P(0,0,0,2) + P(1,0,0,1) + 0.5625P(1,0,0,3) + 1.5P(2,0,0,2)$
$\qquad\qquad -3.5P(1,0,0,2) = 0$

$(1,0,0,3)$: $\quad P(0,0,0,3) + P(1,0,0,2) - 1.3125P(1,0,0,3) = 0$

$(1,0,1,0)$: $\quad P(0,0,1,0) + 0.1875P(1,0,1,1) + 1.5P(2,0,1,0) + P(1,0,0,0)$
$\qquad\qquad -3.5P(1,0,1,0) = 0$

$(1,0,1,1)$: $\quad P(0,0,1,1) + P(1,0,1,0) - 1.3125P(1,0,1,1) = 0$

$(1,1,0,0)$: $\quad P(0,1,0,0) - 1.5P(1,1,0,0) = 0$

$(2,0,0,0)$: $\quad P(1,0,0,0) + 0.375P(2,0,1,0) + 3P(3,0,0,0) + 0.25P(2,0,0,1)$
$\qquad\qquad -4P(2,0,0,0) = 0$

$(2,0,0,1)$: $\quad P(1,0,0,1) + 0.375P(2,0,0,2) + 2.25P(3,0,0,1) + P(2,0,0,0)$
$\qquad\qquad -4.25P(2,0,0,1) = 0$

$(2,0,0,2)$: $\quad P(1,0,0,2) + P(2,0,0,1) - 1.875P(2,0,0,2) = 0$

$(2,0,1,0)$: $\quad P(1,0,1,0) - 1.875P(2,0,1,0) = 0$

$(3,0,0,0)$: $\quad P(2,0,0,0) + 0.1875P(3,0,0,1) + 3P(4,0,0,0) - 5P(3,0,0,0) = 0$

$(3,0,0,1)$: $\quad P(2,0,0,1) + P(3,0,0,0) - 2.4375P(3,0,0,1) = 0$

$(4,0,0,0)$: $\quad P(3,0,0,0) - 3P(4,0,0,0) = 0$

The solution of this linear system is:

$P(0,0,0,0) = 0.028575 \quad P(0,0,0,1) = 0.051495 \quad P(0,0,0,2) = 0.070265 \quad P(0,0,0,3)$
$\qquad\qquad\qquad\qquad\qquad\qquad\qquad\qquad\qquad\qquad\qquad\qquad\qquad\qquad = 0.098514$

$P(0,0,0,4) = 0.131353 \quad P(0,0,1,0) = 0.011127 \quad P(0,0,1,1) = 0.043108 \quad P(0,0,1,2)$
$\qquad\qquad\qquad\qquad\qquad\qquad\qquad\qquad\qquad\qquad\qquad\qquad\qquad\qquad = 0.057477$

$P(0, 1, 0, 0) = 0.012424$ $P(0, 1, 0, 1) = 0.013252$ $P(1, 0, 0, 0) = 0.026288$ $P(1, 0, 0, 1)$
$= 0.04924$

$P(1, 0, 0, 2) = 0.080223$ $P(1, 0, 0, 3) = 0.136181$ $P(1, 0, 1, 0) = 0.01704$ $P(1, 0, 1, 1)$
$= 0.045827$

$P(1, 1, 0, 0) = 0.008282$ $P(2, 0, 0, 0) = 0.011624$ $P(2, 0, 0, 1) = 0.025619$ $P(2, 0, 0, 2)$
$= 0.056449$

$P(2, 0, 1, 0) = 0.009088$ $P(3, 0, 0, 0) = 0.003465$ $P(3, 0, 0, 1) = 0.011932$ $P(4, 0, 0, 0)$
$= 0.001155$

Based on the values of $P(n_1, n_2, n_{2r})$, we determine the values of $Q(j)$:

$Q(0) = P(0, 0, 0, 0) = 0.028575$

$Q(1) = P(0, 0, 0, 1) + P(1, 0, 0, 0) = 0.077783$

$Q(2) = P(0, 0, 0, 2) + P(0, 0, 1, 0) + P(1, 0, 0, 1) + P(2, 0, 0, 0) = 0.142256$

$Q(3) = P(0, 0, 0, 3) + P(0, 0, 1, 1) + P(0, 1, 0, 0) + P(1, 0, 0, 2) + P(1, 0, 1, 0)$
$\quad + P(2, 0, 0, 1) + P(3, 0, 0, 0) = 0.280393$

$Q(4) = P(0, 0, 0, 4) + P(0, 0, 1, 2) + P(0, 1, 0, 1) + P(1, 0, 0, 3) + P(1, 0, 1, 1)$
$\quad + P(1, 1, 0, 0) + P(2, 0, 0, 2) + P(2, 0, 1, 0) + P(3, 0, 0, 1) + P(4, 0, 0, 0) = 0.470996$

(d) Based on the values of $Q(j)$, we obtain the exact CBP:

$$B_1 = \sum_{j=T-b_1+1}^{T} Q(j) = Q(4) = 0.470996 \text{ (compare with 0.545687 in the MRM)}$$

The *Prob{1st* retry} of service-class 2 calls, B_2, when they require $b_2 = 3$ b.u. upon arrival, is given by:

$$B_2 = \sum_{j=C-b_2+1}^{T} Q(j) = Q(1) + Q(2) + Q(3) + Q(4) = 0.971428 \text{ (compare with 0.876443 in the MRM)}$$

The *Prob{2nd* retry} of service-class 2 calls, B_{2r_1}, when they require $b_{2r_1} = 2$ b.u. upon arrival, is given by:

$$B_{2r_1} = \sum_{j=C-b_{2r_1}+1}^{T} Q(j) = Q(2) + Q(3) + Q(4) = 0.893645 \text{ (compare with 0.725882 in the MRM)}$$

The CBP of service-class 2, B_{2r_2}, refers to service-class 2 retry calls which require $b_{2r_2} = 1$ b.u. and is given by:

$$B_{2r_2} = \sum_{j=T-b_{2r_2}+1}^{T} Q(j) = Q(4) = 0.470996 \text{ (compare with 0.545687 in the MRM)}$$

The link utilization is determined by:

$$U = \sum_{j=1}^{C} jQ(j) + \sum_{j=C+1}^{T} CQ(j) = 2.616 \text{ b.u. (compare with 2.148 in the MRM)}$$

(e) $B_{2r_2}^* = Prob\{j > T - b_{2r_2} | j > C - b_2\} = \dfrac{B_{2r_2}}{B_2} = 0.48485$ (compare with 0.62262 in the MRM)

Table 4.3 The state space Ω and the occupied link bandwidth (Example 4.6).

n_1	n_2	n_{2r_1}	n_{2r_2}	$r(n)$	j $(0 \le j \le T)$ (before compr.)	j $(0 \le j \le C)$ (after compr.)	n_1	n_2	n_{2r_1}	n_{2r_2}	$r(n)$	j $(0 \le j \le T)$ (before compr.)	j $(0 \le j \le C)$ (after compr.)
0	0	0	0	1.00	0	0	1	0	0	2	1.00	3	3
0	0	0	1	1.00	1	1	1	0	0	3	0.75	4	3
0	0	0	2	1.00	2	2	1	0	1	0	1.00	3	3
0	0	0	3	1.00	3	3	1	0	1	1	0.75	4	3
0	0	0	4	0.75	4	3	1	1	0	0	0.75	4	3
0	0	1	0	1.00	2	2	2	0	0	0	1.00	2	2
0	0	1	1	1.00	3	3	2	0	0	1	1.00	3	3
0	0	1	2	0.75	4	3	2	0	0	2	0.75	4	3
0	1	0	0	1.00	3	3	2	0	1	0	0.75	4	3
0	1	0	1	0.75	4	3	3	0	0	0	1.00	3	3
1	0	0	0	1.00	1	1	3	0	0	1	0.75	4	3
1	0	0	1	1.00	2	2	4	0	0	0	0.75	4	3

To facilitate the recursive calculation of $q(j)$, we replace $r(\mathbf{n})$ by the state-dependent compression factors per service-class k, $\varphi_k(\mathbf{n})$, and $\varphi_{kr_s}(\mathbf{n})$, $s = 1, \ldots, S(k)$. The values of $\varphi_k(\mathbf{n})$ are given by (3.8), while those of $\varphi_{kr_s}(\mathbf{n})$ are determined by:

$$
\varphi_{kr_s}(\mathbf{n}) = \begin{cases} 1 & \text{for } \mathbf{nb} \le C \text{ and } \mathbf{n} \in \Omega \\ \dfrac{x(\mathbf{n}_{kr_s}^-)}{x(\mathbf{n})} & \text{for } C < \mathbf{nb} \le T \text{ and } \mathbf{n} \in \Omega \\ 0 & \text{otherwise} \end{cases} \tag{4.33}
$$

where $\mathbf{n} = (n_1, n_{1r_1}, \ldots, n_{1r_s}, \ldots, n_{1r_{S(1)}}, n_2, n_{2r_1}, \ldots, n_{2r_s}, \ldots, n_{2r_{S(2)}}, \ldots, n_k, n_{kr_1}, \ldots, n_{kr_s},$
$\ldots, n_{kr_{S(k)}}, \ldots, n_K, n_{Kr_1}, \ldots, n_{Kr_s}, \ldots, n_{Kr_{S(K)}}), \mathbf{n}_k^- = (n_1, n_{1r_1}, \ldots, n_{1r_s}, \ldots, n_{1r_{S(1)}}, n_2, n_{2r_1}, \ldots,$
$n_{2r_s}, \ldots, n_{2r_{S(2)}}, \ldots, n_k - 1, n_{kr_1}, \ldots, n_{kr_s}, \ldots, n_{kr_{S(k)}}, \ldots, n_K, n_{Kr_1}, \ldots, n_{Kr_s}, \ldots, n_{Kr_{S(K)}}),$
$\mathbf{n}_{kr_s}^- = (n_1, n_{1r_1}, \ldots, n_{1r_s}, \ldots, n_{1r_{S(1)}}, n_2, n_{2r_1}, \ldots, n_{2r_s}, \ldots, n_{2r_{S(2)}}, \ldots, n_k, n_{kr_1}, \ldots, n_{kr_s}, \ldots, n_{kr_s} - 1,$
$\ldots, n_{kr_{S(k)}}, \ldots, n_K, n_{Kr_1}, \ldots, n_{Kr_s}, \ldots, n_{Kr_{S(K)}}),$ and

$$
x(\mathbf{n}) = \begin{cases} 1 & \text{if } \mathbf{nb} \le C \text{ and } \mathbf{n} \in \Omega \\ \dfrac{1}{C}\left[\displaystyle\sum_{k=1}^{K} n_k b_k x(\mathbf{n}_k^-) + \sum_{k=1}^{K} \sum_{s=1}^{S(k)} n_{kr_s} b_{kr_s} x(\mathbf{n}_{kr_s}^-) \right] & \text{if } C < \mathbf{nb} \le T \text{ and } \mathbf{n} \in \Omega \\ 0 & \text{otherwise} \end{cases} \tag{4.34}
$$

Example 4.7 Consider again Example 4.6 ($C = 3$, $T = 4$, $K = 2$, $b_1 = 1$, $b_2 = 3$, $b_{2r_1} = 2$, $b_{2r_2} = 1$, $\lambda_1 = \lambda_2 = 1$, $\mu_1^{-1} = \mu_2^{-1} = 1$, $\mu_{2r_1}^{-1} = 2.0$, $\mu_{2r_2}^{-1} = 4.0$).

(a) Determine the values of $\varphi_k(\mathbf{n})$ and $\varphi_{kr_s}(\mathbf{n})$ for each state $\mathbf{n} = (n_1, n_2, n_{2r_1}, n_{2r_2})$.
(b) Calculate the state probabilities $P(n_1, n_2, n_{2r_1}, n_{2r_2})$ based on the GB equations. Then determine the values of the link occupancy distribution $Q(j)$ (for $j = 0, \ldots, T$).

Table 4.4 The values of the state-dependent compression factors $\varphi_k(n)$ and $\varphi_{kr_s}(n)$ (Example 4.7).

n_1	n_2	n_{2r_1}	n_{2r_2}	$x(n)$	$\varphi_1(n)$	$\varphi_2(n)$	$\varphi_{2r_1}(n)$	$\varphi_{2r_2}(n)$
0	0	0	0	1.00	1.00	1.00	1.00	1.00
0	0	0	1	1.00	1.00	1.00	1.00	1.00
0	0	0	2	1.00	1.00	1.00	1.00	1.00
0	0	0	3	1.00	1.00	1.00	1.00	1.00
0	0	0	4	1.3333	0.00	0.00	0.00	0.75
0	0	1	0	1.00	1.00	1.00	1.00	1.00
0	0	1	1	1.00	1.00	1.00	1.00	1.00
0	0	1	2	1.3333	0.00	0.00	0.75	0.75
0	1	0	0	1.00	1.00	1.00	1.00	1.00
0	1	0	1	1.3333	0.00	0.75	0.00	0.75
1	0	0	0	1.00	1.00	1.00	1.00	1.00
1	0	0	1	1.00	1.00	1.00	1.00	1.00
1	0	0	2	1.00	1.00	1.00	1.00	1.00
1	0	0	3	1.3333	0.75	0.00	0.00	0.75
1	0	1	0	1.00	1.00	1.00	1.00	1.00
1	0	1	1	1.3333	0.75	0.00	0.75	0.75
1	1	0	0	1.3333	0.75	0.75	0.00	0.00
2	0	0	0	1.00	1.00	1.00	1.00	1.00
2	0	0	1	1.00	1.00	1.00	1.00	1.00
2	0	0	2	1.3333	0.75	0.00	0.00	0.75
2	0	1	0	1.3333	0.75	0.00	0.75	0.00
3	0	0	0	1.00	1.00	1.00	1.00	1.00
3	0	0	1	1.3333	0.75	0.00	0.00	0.75
4	0	0	0	1.3333	0.75	0.00	0.00	0.00

(c) Calculate the CBP of both service-classes, including the retry probabilities and the link utilization.

(d) Calculate the conditional CBP of service-class 2 retry calls with b_{2r_2}, given that they have been blocked with their initial bandwidth requirement, b_2.

(a) Table 4.4 presents the 24 states together with the corresponding values of $\varphi_k(n)$ and $\varphi_{kr_s}(n)$, which are calculated through the $x(n)$.

(b–d) Based on Tables 4.3 and 4.4, we see that the values of $\varphi_k(n)$, $\varphi_{kr_s}(n)$, and $r(n)$ are always equal to 0.75 when $j > C$, i.e., when $j = 4$. This means that for this particular example the GB equations and consequently all CBP are identical to those presented in Example 4.6. This behavior can be explained by the fact that C and T differ only by 1 b.u. For higher values of T, the values of $\varphi_k(n)$ and $\varphi_{kr_s}(n)$ may be different from the values of $r(n)$.

4.3.2 The Analytical Model

4.3.2.1 Steady State Probabilities

Following the analysis of Section 4.1.2.1, the calculation of the unnormalized values of $q(j)$ is based on an approximate but recursive formula whose proof is similar to that of (4.21) [1]:

$$q(j) = \begin{cases} 1 & \text{if } j = 0 \\ \frac{1}{\min(j,C)} \sum_{k=1}^{K} \alpha_k b_k \gamma_k(j) q(j - b_k) + \\ \frac{1}{\min(j,C)} \sum_{k=1}^{K} \sum_{s=1}^{S(k)} \alpha_{kr_s} b_{kr_s} \gamma_{kr_s}(j) q(j - b_{kr_s}) & \text{if } j = 1, 2, \ldots, T \\ 0 & \text{otherwise} \end{cases} \tag{4.35}$$

where $\alpha_{kr_s} = \lambda_k \mu_{kr_s}^{-1}$, $\gamma_k(j) = \begin{cases} 1 & \text{if } 1 \leq j \leq C \quad \text{and} \quad b_{kr_s} > 0 \\ 1 & \text{if } 1 \leq j \leq T \quad \text{and} \quad b_{kr_s} = 0 \\ 0 & \text{otherwise} \end{cases}$

and $\gamma_{kr_s}(j) = \begin{cases} 1 & \text{if } C - b_{kr_{s-1}} + b_{kr_s} < j \leq C \quad \text{and} \quad s \neq S(k) \\ 1 & \text{if } C - b_{kr_{s-1}} + b_{kr_s} < j \leq T \quad \text{and} \quad s = S(k). \\ 0 & \text{otherwise} \end{cases}$

4.3.2.2 CBP, Utilization, and Mean Number of In-service Calls

Having determined the unnormalized values of $q(j)$ via (4.35) we can calculate [1]:

- The final CBP of service-class k calls with their last bandwidth requirement $b_{kr_{S(k)}}$ b.u., $B_{kr_{S(k)}}$, via:

$$B_{kr_{S(k)}} = \sum_{j=T-b_{kr_{S(k)}}+1}^{T} G^{-1} q(j) \tag{4.36}$$

  where $G = \sum_{j=0}^{T} q(j)$ is the normalization constant.
- The CBP of service-class k calls with b_k b.u., B_k, via (4.23).
- The conditional CBP of service-class k retry calls with $b_{kr_{S(k)}}$ given that they have been blocked with their initial bandwidth requirement b_k, $B^*_{kr_{S(k)}}$, via:

$$B^*_{kr_{S(k)}} = Prob\{j > T - b_{kr_{S(k)}} \mid j > C - b_k\} = \frac{B_{kr_{S(k)}}}{B_k} \tag{4.37}$$

- The link utilization, U, by (3.23).
- The mean number of service-class k calls with b_k b.u. in state j, $y_k(j)$, via (4.25).
- The mean number of service-class k calls with b_{kr_s} b.u. in state j, $y_{kr_s}(j)$, via:

$$y_{kr_s}(j) = \frac{\alpha_{kr_s} \gamma_{kr_s}(j) q(j - b_{kr_s})}{q(j)}, \quad q(j) > 0 \tag{4.38}$$

- The mean number of in-service calls of service-class k accepted with b_k, $\bar{n}_k$, via (4.27).
- The mean number of in-service calls of service-class k accepted with b_{kr_s}, $\bar{n}_{kr_s}$, via:

$$\bar{n}_{kr_s} = \sum_{j=1}^{T} y_{kr_s}(j) \frac{q(j)}{G} \tag{4.39}$$

Example 4.8 Consider again Example 4.6 $(C = 3, T = 4, K = 2, b_1 = 1, b_2 = 3, b_{2r_1} = 2, b_{2r_2} = 1, \lambda_1 = \lambda_2 = 1, \mu_1^{-1} = \mu_2^{-1} = 1, \mu_{2r_1}^{-1} = 2.0, \mu_{2r_2}^{-1} = 4.0)$:

(a) Calculate the values of $Q(j)$ based on (4.35).
(b) Calculate the CBP of both service-classes, including the retry probabilities and the conditional $B_{2r_2}^*$.

(a) State probabilities through the recursion (4.35):

$j = 1:$ $q(1) = q(0) + 0 = 1.0$ $\Rightarrow q(1) = 1.0$

$j = 2:$ $2q(2) = q(1) + 0 = 1.0$ $\Rightarrow q(2) = 0.5$

$j = 3:$ $3q(3) = q(2) + 3q(0) + 4q(1) + 4q(2) = 9.5$ $\Rightarrow q(3) = 3.16667$

$j = 4:$ $3q(4) = q(3) + 0 + 0 + 4q(3) = 15.83335$ $\Rightarrow q(4) = 5.27778$

The normalization constant is:

$$G = \sum_{j=0}^{T} q(j) = 10.94445.$$

The state probabilities are:

$$Q(0) = Q(1) = 0.09137 \quad Q(2) = 0.04568 \quad Q(3) = 0.28934 \quad Q(4) = 0.48223$$

(b) The CBP are as follows:

$$B_1 = \sum_{j=T-b_1+1}^{T} Q(j) = Q(4) = 0.48223 \text{ (compare with the exact 0.470996)}$$

$$B_2 = \sum_{j=C-b_2+1}^{T} Q(j) = Q(1) + Q(2) + Q(3) + Q(4) = 0.90862 \text{ (compare with the exact 0.971428)}$$

$$B_{2r_1} = \sum_{j=C-b_{2r_1}+1}^{T} Q(j) = Q(2) + Q(3) + Q(4) = 0.81725 \text{ (compare with the exact 0.893645)}$$

$$B_{2r_2} = \sum_{j=T-b_{2r_2}+1}^{T} Q(j) = Q(4) = 0.48223 \text{ (compare with the exact 0.470996)}$$

$$B_{2r_2}^* = \frac{B_{2r_2}}{B_2} = 0.5307 \text{ (compare with the exact 0.48485)}$$

It is apparent that even in small E-MRM examples the error introduced by the assumption of LB, the introduction of $\varphi_k(\mathbf{n})$, $\varphi_{kr_s}(\mathbf{n})$, and the migration approximation is not significant.

Table 4.5 The state space Ω and the occupied link bandwidth (Example 4.9).

n_1	n_2	n_{2r_1}	n_{2r_2}	$r(\mathbf{n})$	$j\ (0 \leq j \leq T)$ (before compr.)	$j\ (0 \leq j \leq C)$ (after compr.)	n_1	n_2	n_{2r_1}	n_{2r_2}	$r(\mathbf{n})$	$j\ (0 \leq j \leq T)$ (before compr.)	$j\ (0 \leq j \leq C)$ (after compr.)
0	0	0	0	1.00	0	0	1	0	0	0	1.00	1	1
0	0	0	1	1.00	1	1	1	0	0	1	1.00	2	2
0	0	0	2	1.00	2	2	1	0	0	2	1.00	3	3
0	0	0	3	1.00	3	3	1	0	0	3	0.75	4	3
0	0	0	4	0.75	4	3	1	0	1	0	1.00	3	3
0	0	1	0	1.00	2	2	1	0	1	1	0.75	4	3
0	0	1	1	1.00	3	3	2	0	0	0	1.00	2	2
0	0	1	2	0.75	4	3	2	0	0	1	1.00	3	3
0	1	0	0	1.00	3	3	2	0	0	2	0.75	4	3
0	1	0	1	0.75	4	3							

4.4 The Elastic Multi-Retry Model under the BR Policy

4.4.1 The Service System

Compared to the E-SRM/BR, in the *elastic multi-retry model under the BR policy* (E-MRM/BR) with BR parameter t_k for service-class k calls ($k = 1, \ldots, K$), blocked calls of service-class k can retry more than once to be connected in the system.

Example 4.9 Consider again Example 4.6 ($C = 3, T = 4, K = 2, b_1 = 1, b_2 = 3,$ $b_{2r_1} = 2, b_{2r_2} = 1, \lambda_1 = \lambda_2 = 1, \mu_1^{-1} = \mu_2^{-1} = 1, \mu_{2r_1}^{-1} = 2.0, \mu_{2r_2}^{-1} = 4.0$) and let the BR parameters $t_1 = 2$ and $t_2 = 0$, so that $b_1 + t_1 = b_2 + t_2$.

(a) Find the total number of permissible states $\mathbf{n} = (n_1, n_2, n_{2r_1}, n_{2r_2})$ and determine the values of j and $r(\mathbf{n})$ for each state $\mathbf{n} = (n_1, n_2, n_{2r_1}, n_{2r_2})$.
(b) Calculate the state probabilities $P(n_1, n_2, n_{2r_1}, n_{2r_2})$ based on the GB equations. Then determine the values of the link occupancy distribution $Q(j)$ (for $j = 0, \ldots, T$).
(c) Calculate the CBP of both service-classes, including the retry probabilities and the link utilization.
(d) Calculate the conditional CBP of service-class 2 retry calls with b_{2r_2}, given that they have been blocked with their initial bandwidth requirement, b_2.

(a) There are 19 permissible states of the form $\mathbf{n} = (n_1, n_2, n_{2r_1}, n_{2r_2})$. Table 4.5 presents the 19 states together with the values of $r(\mathbf{n})$ and the occupied link bandwidth, $j = n_1 b_1 + n_2 b_2 + n_{2r_1} b_{2r_1} + n_{2r_2} b_{2r_2}$, before and after compression.
(b) In what follows, we present the 19 GB equations:

$(0, 0, 0, 0) : 0.5P(0, 0, 1, 0) + 0.25P(0, 0, 0, 1) + P(0, 1, 0, 0) + P(1, 0, 0, 0) - 2P(0, 0, 0, 0) = 0$

$(0, 0, 0, 1) : 0.5P(0, 0, 0, 2) + 0.75P(0, 1, 0, 1) + 0.5P(0, 0, 1, 1) + P(1, 0, 0, 1) - 2.25P(0, 0, 0, 1) = 0$

$(0, 0, 0, 2) : P(1, 0, 0, 2) + 0.75P(0, 0, 0, 3) + 0.375P(0, 0, 1, 2) - 1.5P(0, 0, 0, 2) = 0$

$(0, 0, 0, 3) : P(0, 0, 0, 2) + 0.75P(0, 0, 0, 4) + 0.75P(1, 0, 0, 3) - 1.75P(0, 0, 0, 3) = 0$

$(0, 0, 0, 4) : P(0, 0, 0, 3) - 0.75P(0, 0, 0, 4) = 0$

$(0, 0, 1, 0) : 0.25P(0, 0, 1, 1) + P(1, 0, 1, 0) - 1.5P(0, 0, 1, 0) = 0$

$(0, 0, 1, 1) : P(0, 0, 0, 1) + P(0, 0, 1, 0) + 0.75P(1, 0, 1, 1) + 0.375P(0, 0, 1, 2) - 1.75P(0, 0, 1, 1) = 0$

$(0, 0, 1, 2) : P(0, 0, 1, 1) - 0.75P(0, 0, 1, 2) = 0$

$(0, 1, 0, 0) : P(0, 0, 0, 0) + 0.1875P(0, 1, 0, 1) - 2P(0, 1, 0, 0) = 0$

$(0, 1, 0, 1) : P(0, 1, 0, 0) - 0.9375P(0, 1, 0, 1) = 0$

$(1, 0, 0, 0) : 0.25P(1, 0, 0, 1) + 2P(2, 0, 0, 0) + 0.5P(1, 0, 1, 0) + P(0, 0, 0, 0) - 3P(1, 0, 0, 0) = 0$

$(1, 0, 0, 1) : 2P(2, 0, 0, 1) + 0.5P(1, 0, 0, 2) + P(0, 0, 0, 1) + 0.375P(1, 0, 1, 1) - 2.25P(1, 0, 0, 1) = 0$

$(1, 0, 0, 2) : P(1, 0, 0, 1) + 0.5625P(1, 0, 0, 3) + 1.5P(2, 0, 0, 2) - 2.5P(1, 0, 0, 2) = 0$

$(1, 0, 0, 3) : P(1, 0, 0, 2) - 1.3125P(1, 0, 0, 3) = 0$

$(1, 0, 1, 0) : 0.1875P(1, 0, 1, 1) + P(1, 0, 0, 0) - 2.5P(1, 0, 1, 0) = 0$

$(1, 0, 1, 1) : P(1, 0, 1, 0) - 1.3125P(1, 0, 1, 1) = 0$

$(2, 0, 0, 0) : P(1, 0, 0, 0) + 0.25P(2, 0, 0, 1) - 3P(2, 0, 0, 0) = 0$

$(2, 0, 0, 1) : 0.375P(2, 0, 0, 2) + P(2, 0, 0, 0) - 3.25P(2, 0, 0, 1) = 0$

$(2, 0, 0, 2) : P(2, 0, 0, 1) - 1.875P(2, 0, 0, 2) = 0$

The solution of this linear system is:

$P(0, 0, 0, 0) = 0.030877 \quad P(0, 0, 0, 1) = 0.067406 \quad P(0, 0, 0, 2) = 0.1303 \quad P(0, 0, 0, 3) = 0.187993$

$P(0, 0, 0, 4) = 0.250657 \quad P(0, 0, 1, 0) = 0.017313 \quad P(0, 0, 1, 1) = 0.071478 \quad P(0, 0, 1, 2) = 0.095304$

$P(0, 1, 0, 0) = 0.017154 \quad P(0, 1, 0, 1) = 0.018297 \quad P(1, 0, 0, 0) = 0.019092 \quad P(1, 0, 0, 1) = 0.037053$

$P(1, 0, 0, 2) = 0.018716 \quad P(1, 0, 0, 3) = 0.01426 \quad P(1, 0, 1, 0) = 0.008099 \quad P(1, 0, 1, 1) = 0.006171$

$P(2, 0, 0, 0) = 0.006543 \quad P(2, 0, 0, 1) = 0.002145 \quad P(2, 0, 0, 2) = 0.001144$

Based on the values of $P(n_1, n_2, n_{2r_1}, n_{2r_2})$, we determine the values of $Q(j)$:

$Q(0) = P(0, 0, 0, 0) = 0.030877$

$Q(1) = P(0, 0, 0, 1) + P(1, 0, 0, 0) = 0.086498$

$Q(2) = P(0, 0, 0, 2) + P(0, 0, 1, 0) + P(1, 0, 0, 1) + P(2, 0, 0, 0) = 0.191209$

$Q(3) = P(0, 0, 0, 3) + P(0, 0, 1, 1) + P(0, 1, 0, 0) + P(1, 0, 0, 2) + P(1, 0, 1, 0) + P(2, 0, 0, 1)$
$= 0.305585$

$Q(4) = P(0, 0, 0, 4) + P(0, 0, 1, 2) + P(0, 1, 0, 1) + P(1, 0, 0, 3) + P(1, 0, 1, 1) + P(2, 0, 0, 2)$
$= 0.385833$

(c) Based on the values of $Q(j)$, we obtain the exact CBP:

$$B_1 = \sum_{j=T-b_1-t_1+1}^{T} Q(j) = Q(2) + Q(3) + Q(4) = 0.882627 \text{ (compare with 0.819672 in the MRM/BR)}$$

The *Prob*{1st retry} of service-class 2 calls, B_2, when they require $b_2 = 3$ b.u. upon arrival, is given by:

$$B_2 = \sum_{j=C-b_2+1}^{T} Q(j) = Q(1) + Q(2) + Q(3) + Q(4) = 0.969125.$$

The $Prob\{2nd\ retry\}$ of service-class 2 calls, B_{2r_1}, when they require $b_{2r_1} = 2$ b.u. upon arrival, is given by:

$$B_{2r_1} = \sum_{j=C-b_{2r_1}+1}^{T} Q(j) = Q(2) + Q(3) + Q(4) = 0.882627 \text{ (compare with 0.606557 in the MRM/BR)}$$

The CBP of service-class 2, B_{2r_2}, refers to service-class 2 retry calls which require $b_{2r_2} = 1$ b.u. and is given by:

$$B_{2r_2} = \sum_{j=T-b_{2r_2}+1}^{T} Q(j) = Q(4) = 0.385833 \text{ (compare with 0.514754 in the MRM/BR)}$$

The link utilization is determined by:

$$U = \sum_{j=1}^{C} jQ(j) + \sum_{j=C+1}^{T} CQ(j) = 2.543 \text{ b.u. (compare with 1.941 in the MRM/BR)}$$

(d) $B_{2r_2}^* = Prob\{j > C - b_{2r_2} | j > C - b_2\} = \dfrac{B_{2r_2}}{B_2} = 0.39813$ (compare with 0.628 in the MRM/BR)

To facilitate the recursive calculation of $q(j)$ in the E-MRM/BR, we replace $r(\mathbf{n})$ by the state-dependent compression factors per service-class k, $\varphi_k(\mathbf{n})$, and $\varphi_{kr_s}(\mathbf{n})$, $s = 1, \ldots, S(k)$. The values of $\varphi_k(\mathbf{n})$ and $\varphi_{kr_s}(\mathbf{n})$ are given by (3.8) and (4.33), respectively.

Example 4.10 Consider again Example 4.9 ($C = 3, T = 4, K = 2, b_1 = 1, b_2 = 3, b_{2r_1} = 2, b_{2r_2} = 1, t_1 = 2, t_2 = 0, \lambda_1 = \lambda_2 = 1, \mu_1^{-1} = \mu_2^{-1} = 1, \mu_{2r_1}^{-1} = 2.0, \mu_{2r_2}^{-1} = 4.0$):

(a) Determine the values of $\varphi_k(n)$ and $\varphi_{kr_s}(n)$ for each state $\mathbf{n} = (n_1, n_2, n_{2r_1}, n_{2r_2})$.
(b) Calculate the state probabilities $P(n_1, n_2, n_{2r_1}, n_{2r_2})$ based on the GB equations. Then determine the values of the link occupancy distribution $Q(j)$ (for $j = 0, \ldots, T$).
(c) Calculate the CBP of both service-classes, including the retry probabilities and the link utilization.
(d) Calculate the conditional CBP of service-class 2 retry calls with b_{2r_2}, given that they have been blocked with their initial bandwidth requirement, b_2.

(a) Table 4.6 presents the 19 states together with the corresponding values of $\varphi_k(\mathbf{n})$ and $\varphi_{kr_s}(\mathbf{n})$, which are calculated through the $x(\mathbf{n})$.
(b–d) Based on Tables 4.5 and 4.6, we see that the values of $\varphi_k(\mathbf{n})$, $\varphi_{kr_s}(\mathbf{n})$, and $r(\mathbf{n})$ are always equal to 0.75 when $j = 4$. This means that for this particular example the GB equations and consequently all CBP are identical to those presented in Example 4.9.

Table 4.6 The values of the state-dependent compression factors $\varphi_k(\mathbf{n})$ and $\varphi_{kr_s}(\mathbf{n})$ (Example 4.10).

n_1	n_2	n_{2r_1}	n_{2r_2}	$x(\mathbf{n})$	$\varphi_1(\mathbf{n})$	$\varphi_2(\mathbf{n})$	$\varphi_{2r_1}(\mathbf{n})$	$\varphi_{2r_2}(\mathbf{n})$
0	0	0	0	1.00	1.00	1.00	1.00	1.00
0	0	0	1	1.00	1.00	1.00	1.00	1.00
0	0	0	2	1.00	1.00	1.00	1.00	1.00
0	0	0	3	1.00	1.00	1.00	1.00	1.00
0	0	0	4	1.3333	0.00	0.00	0.00	0.75
0	0	1	0	1.00	1.00	1.00	1.00	1.00
0	0	1	1	1.00	1.00	1.00	1.00	1.00
0	0	1	2	1.3333	0.00	0.00	0.75	0.75
0	1	0	0	1.00	1.00	1.00	1.00	1.00
0	1	0	1	1.3333	0.00	0.75	0.00	0.75
1	0	0	0	1.00	1.00	1.00	1.00	1.00
1	0	0	1	1.00	1.00	1.00	1.00	1.00
1	0	0	2	1.00	1.00	1.00	1.00	1.00
1	0	0	3	1.3333	0.75	0.00	0.00	0.75
1	0	1	0	1.00	1.00	1.00	1.00	1.00
1	0	1	1	1.3333	0.75	0.00	0.75	0.75
2	0	0	0	1.00	1.00	1.00	1.00	1.00
2	0	0	1	1.00	1.00	1.00	1.00	1.00
2	0	0	2	1.3333	0.75	0.00	0.00	0.75

This behavior can be explained by the fact that C and T differ only by one b.u. For higher values of T the values of $\varphi_k(\mathbf{n})$, $\varphi_{kr_s}(\mathbf{n})$, and $r(\mathbf{n})$ will not be always the same.

4.4.2 The Analytical Model

4.4.2.1 Steady State Probabilities
Following the analysis of Section 4.2.2.1, the calculation of the unnormalized values of $q(j)$ is based on an approximate but recursive formula whose proof is similar to that of (4.29) [4]:

$$q(j) = \begin{cases} 1 & \text{if } j = 0 \\ \dfrac{1}{\min(j,C)} \displaystyle\sum_{k=1}^{K} \alpha_k D_k(j - b_k)\gamma_k(j)q(j - b_k) + \\ \dfrac{1}{\min(j,C)} \displaystyle\sum_{k=1}^{K}\sum_{s=1}^{S(k)} \alpha_{kr_s} D_{kr_s}(j - b_{kr_s})\gamma_{kr_s}(j)q(j - b_{kr_s}) & \text{if } j = 1, 2, \ldots, T \\ 0 & \text{otherwise} \end{cases} \tag{4.40}$$

where $\alpha_{kr_s} = \lambda_k \mu_{kr_s}^{-1}$, $D_k(j - b_k) = \begin{cases} b_k & \text{for } j \le T - t_k \\ 0 & \text{for } j > T - t_k \end{cases}$, $D_{kr_s}(j - b_{kr_s})$

$= \begin{cases} b_{kr_s} & \text{for } j \le T - t_k \\ 0 & \text{for } j > T - t_k \end{cases}$, $\gamma_k(j) = \begin{cases} 1 & \text{if } 1 \le j \le C \text{ and } b_{kr_s} > 0 \\ 1 & \text{if } 1 \le j \le T \text{ and } b_{kr_s} = 0, \\ 0 & \text{otherwise} \end{cases}$

$\gamma_{kr_s}(j) = \begin{cases} 1 & \text{if } C - b_{kr_{s-1}} + b_{kr_s} < j \le C \text{ and } s \ne S(k) \\ 1 & \text{if } C - b_{kr_{s-1}} + b_{kr_s} < j \le T \text{ and } s = S(k) \\ 0 & \text{otherwise} \end{cases}$.

4.4.2.2 CBP, Utilization, and Mean Number of In-service Calls

Having determined the unnormalized values of $q(j)$ via (4.40) we can calculate:

- The final CBP of service-class k calls with their last bandwidth requirement $b_{kr_{S(k)}}$ b.u., $B_{kr_{S(k)}}$, via:

$$B_{kr_{S(k)}} = \sum_{j=T-b_{kr_{S(k)}}-t_k+1}^{T} G^{-1}q(j) \tag{4.41}$$

where $G = \sum_{j=0}^{T} q(j)$ is the normalization constant.

- The CBP of service-class k calls with b_k b.u., B_k, via (4.31).
- The conditional CBP of service-class k retry calls with $b_{kr_{S(k)}}$ given that they have been blocked with their initial bandwidth requirement b_k, $B_{kr_{S(k)}}^*$, via:

$$B_{kr_{S(k)}}^* = Prob\{j > T - b_{kr_{S(k)}} - t_k \mid j > C - b_k\} = \frac{B_{kr_{S(k)}}}{B_k} \tag{4.42}$$

- The link utilization, U, by (3.23).
- The mean number of service-class k calls with b_k b.u. in state j, $y_k(j)$, via (4.25).
- The mean number of service-class k calls with b_{kr_s} b.u. in state j, $y_{kr_s}(j)$, via (4.38).
- The mean number of in-service calls of service-class k accepted with b_k, $\bar{n}_k$, via (4.27).
- The mean number of in-service calls of service-class k accepted with b_{kr_s}, $\bar{n}_{kr_s}$, via (4.39).

Example 4.11 Consider again Example 4.9 ($C = 3, T = 4, K = 2, b_1 = 1, b_2 = 3$, $b_{2r_1} = 2, b_{2r_2} = 1, t_1 = 2, t_2 = 0, \lambda_1 = \lambda_2 = 1, \mu_1^{-1} = \mu_2^{-1} = 1, \mu_{2r_1}^{-1} = 2.0, \mu_{2r_2}^{-1} = 4.0$):

(a) Calculate the values of $Q(j)$ based on (4.40).
(b) Calculate the CBP of both service-classes, including the retry probabilities and the conditional $B_{2r_2}^*$.

(a) State probabilities through the recursion (4.40):

$j = 1 : q(1) = q(0) + 0 = 1 \Rightarrow q(1) = 1$ $j = 3 : 3q(3) = 0 + 3q(0) + 4q(1) + 4q(2)$
$= 9 \Rightarrow q(3) = 3$

$j = 2 : 2q(2) = q(1) + 0 = 1 \Rightarrow q(2) = 0.5$ $j = 4 : 3q(4) = 0 + 0 + 0 + 4q(3)$
$= 12 \Rightarrow q(4) = 4$

The normalization constant is:

$$G = \sum_{j=0}^{T} q(j) = 9.5.$$

The state probabilities are:

$Q(0) = Q(1) = 0.10526$ $Q(2) = 0.05263$ $Q(3) = 0.31579$ $Q(4) = 0.42105$

(b) The CBP are as follows:

$$B_1 = \sum_{j=T-b_1-t_1+1}^{T} Q(j) = Q(2) + Q(3) + Q(4) = 0.78947 \text{ (compare with the exact 0.882627)}$$

$$B_2 = \sum_{j=C-b_2+1}^{T} Q(j) = Q(1) + Q(2) + Q(3) + Q(4) = 0.89473 \text{ (compare with the exact 0.969125)}$$

$$B_{2r_1} = \sum_{j=C-b_{2r_1}+1}^{T} Q(j) = Q(2) + Q(3) + Q(4) = 0.78947 \text{ (compare with the exact 0.882627)}$$

$$B_{2r_2} = \sum_{j=T-b_{2r_2}+1}^{T} Q(j) = Q(4) = 0.42105 \text{ (compare with the exact 0.385833)}$$

$$B_{2r_2}^* = \frac{B_{2r_2}}{B_2} = 0.47059 \text{ (compare with the exact 0.39813)}$$

It is apparent that in small E-MRM/BR examples the error introduced by the assumption of LB, the introduction of $\varphi_k(\mathbf{n})$ and $\varphi_{kr_s}(\mathbf{n})$, the migration approximation, and the application of the BR policy can be acceptable.

Example 4.12   Consider a single link of capacity $C = 80$ b.u. that accommodates three service-classes of elastic calls which require $b_1 = 1$ b.u., $b_2 = 2$ b.u., and $b_3 = 6$ b.u., respectively. All calls arrive in the system according to a Poisson process. The call holding time is exponentially distributed with mean value $\mu_1^{-1} = \mu_2^{-1} = \mu_3^{-1} = 1$. The initial values of the offered traffic-load are $\alpha_1 = 20$ erl, $\alpha_2 = 6$ erl, and $\alpha_3 = 2$ erl. Calls of service-class 3 may retry twice with reduced bandwidth requirement $b_{3r_1} = 5$ b.u. and $b_{3r_2} = 4$ b.u., and increased service time so that $\alpha_3 b_3 = \alpha_{3r_1} b_{3r_1} = \alpha_{3r_2} b_{3r_2}$. In the case of the E-MRM/BR, we consider the following BR parameters: $t_1 = 3$, $t_2 = 2$ and $t_3 = 0$ so that $b_1 + t_1 = b_2 + t_2 = b_{3r_2} + t_3$. We also consider three different values of T: (i) $T = C = 80$ b.u., where no bandwidth compression takes place, in which case the E-MRM and the E-MRM/BR give exactly the same CBP results with the MRM and the MRM/BR, respectively, (ii) $T = 82$ b.u. where bandwidth compression takes place and $r_{min} = C/T = 80/82$, and (iii) $T = 84$ b.u. where bandwidth compression takes place and $r_{min} = C/T = 80/84$. Present graphically the analytical CBP of all service-classes for the E-MRM, the E-MRM/BR, the MRM, and the MRM/BR by assuming that α_3 remains constant while α_1, α_2 increase in steps of 1.0 and 0.5 erl, respectively (up to $\alpha_1 = 26$ erl and $\alpha_2 = 9$ erl). Also provide simulation CBP results for the E-MRM and the E-MRM/BR.

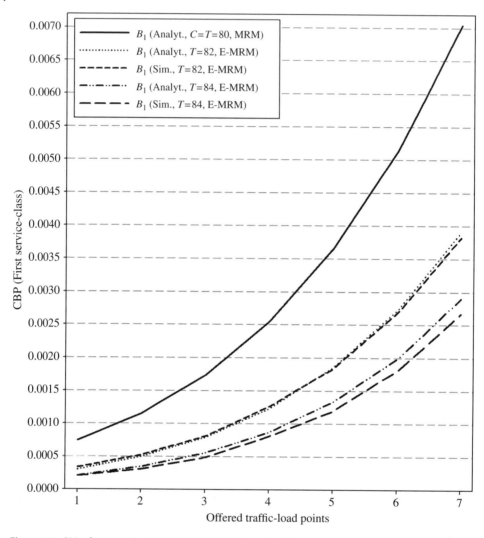

Figure 4.5 CBP of service-class 1 (MRM, E-MRM) (Example 4.12).

Figures 4.5–4.8 present, for all values of T, the analytical and simulation CBP results of service-classes 1, 2, and 3 (CBP of calls with b_{3r_2}), respectively. All figures show that (i) the accuracy of the analytical models is absolutely satisfactory compared to simulation and (ii) the increase of T above C results in a CBP decrease due to the existence of the compression mechanism.

4.5 The Elastic Adaptive Single-Retry Model

4.5.1 The Service System

In the *elastic adaptive single-retry model (EA-SRM)*, we consider a link of capacity C b.u. that accommodates K service-classes which are distinguished into K_e elastic

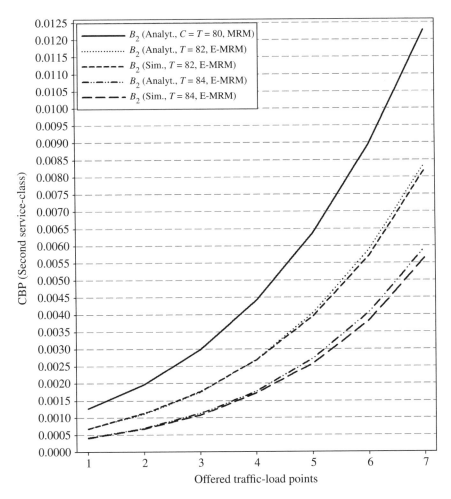

Figure 4.6 CBP of service-class 2 (MRM, E-MRM) (Example 4.12).

service-classes and K_a adaptive service-classes. Calls of service-class k follow a Poisson process with an arrival rate λ_k and have a peak-bandwidth requirement of b_k b.u. and an exponentially distributed service time with mean μ_k^{-1}. The bandwidth compression/expansion mechanism and the CAC of the EA-SRM are the same as those of the E-SRM (Section 4.1.1). The only difference is that adaptive calls do not alter their service time after bandwidth compression/expansion.

Similar to the E-SRM, the steady state probabilities in the EA-SRM do not have a PFS, since LB is destroyed between adjacent states (see Figure 4.9). Thus, the unnormalized values of $q(j)$ can be determined by an approximate but recursive formula, as presented in Section 4.5.2.

Example 4.13 Consider again Example 4.1 ($C = 4, T = 6, K = 2, b_1 = 1, b_2 = 3,$ $b_{2r} = 2, \lambda_1 = \lambda_2 = \mu_1 = \mu_2 = 1,$ $\mu_{2r} = 2/3$) but now service-class 1 is adaptive. This example clarifies the differences between the E-SRM and the EA-SRM.

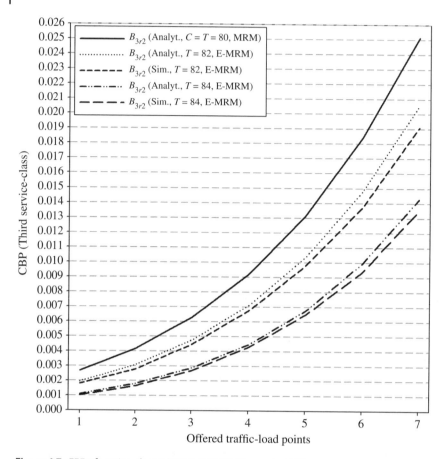

Figure 4.7 CBP of service-class 3 (MRM, E-MRM) (Example 4.12).

(a) Find the total number of permissible states $\mathbf{n} = (n_1, n_2, n_{2r})$, draw the state transition diagram, and determine the values of j and $r(\mathbf{n})$ for each state $\mathbf{n} = (n_1, n_2, n_{2r})$.

(b) Calculate the state probabilities $P(n_1, n_2, n_{2r})$ based on the GB equations. Then determine the values of the link occupancy distribution $Q(j)$ (for $j = 0, \dots, T$).

(c) Calculate the CBP of both service-classes, including the retry probability and the link utilization.

(a) There are 22 permissible states of the form $\mathbf{n} = (n_1, n_2, n_{2r})$. The state space Ω and the state transition diagram are shown in Figure 4.9. The values of $r(\mathbf{n})$ and $j = n_1 b_1 + n_2 b_2 + n_{2r} b_{2r}$, before and after compression has been applied, are the same as those presented in Table 4.1.

(b) Based on Figure 4.9, we obtain the following 22 GB equations:

$(0, 0, 0):$ $P(0, 1, 0) + P(1, 0, 0) + (2/3)P(0, 0, 1) - 2P(0, 0, 0) = 0$

$(0, 0, 1):$ $0.8P(0, 1, 1) + (4/3)P(0, 0, 2) + P(1, 0, 1) - (8/3)P(0, 0, 1) = 0$

$(0, 0, 2):$ $P(0, 0, 1) + (4/3)P(0, 0, 3) + P(1, 0, 2) - (10/3)P(0, 0, 2) = 0$

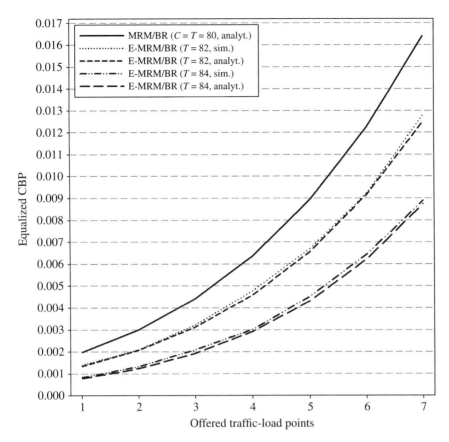

Figure 4.8 Equalized CBP (MRM/BR, E-MRM/BR) (Example 4.12).

$(0,0,3)$: $P(0,0,2) - (4/3)P(0,0,3) = 0$

$(0,1,0)$: $P(0,0,0) + (8/15)P(0,1,1) + P(1,1,0) - 3P(0,1,0) = 0$

$(0,1,1)$: $P(0,1,0) + P(1,1,1) - (7/3)P(0,1,1) = 0$

$(1,0,0)$: $P(0,0,0) + 2P(2,0,0) + (2/3)P(1,0,1) + P(1,1,0) - 3P(1,0,0) = 0$

$(1,0,1)$: $P(0,0,1) + 2P(2,0,1) + (16/15)P(1,0,2) + (2/3)P(1,1,1) - (11/3)P(1,0,1) = 0$

$(1,0,2)$: $P(0,0,2) + 2P(2,0,2) + P(1,0,1) - (46/15)P(1,0,2) = 0$

$(1,1,0)$: $P(0,1,0) + P(1,0,0) + 2P(2,1,0) + (4/9)P(1,1,1) - 4P(1,1,0) = 0$

$(1,1,1)$: $P(0,1,1) + P(1,1,0) - (19/9)P(1,1,1) = 0$

$(2,0,0)$: $P(1,0,0) + 3P(3,0,0) + 0.8P(2,1,0) + (2/3)P(2,0,1) - 4P(2,0,0) = 0$

$(2,0,1)$: $P(1,0,1) + P(2,0,0) + 3P(3,0,1) + (8/9)P(2,0,2) - (14/3)P(2,0,1) = 0$

$(2,0,2)$: $P(1,0,2) + P(2,0,1) - (26/9)P(2,0,2) = 0$

$(2,1,0)$: $P(1,1,0) + 3P(3,1,0) - 3.8P(2,1,0) = 0$

$(3,0,0)$: $P(2,0,0) + 4P(4,0,0) + (2/3)P(3,1,0) + (8/15)P(3,0,1) - 5P(3,0,0) = 0$

$(3,0,1)$: $P(2,0,1) + 4P(4,0,1) + P(3,0,0) - (68/15)P(3,0,1) = 0$

$(3,1,0)$: $P(2,1,0) - (11/3)P(3,1,0) = 0$

$(4,0,0)$: $P(3,0,0) + 5P(5,0,0) + (4/9)P(4,0,1) - 6P(4,0,0) = 0$

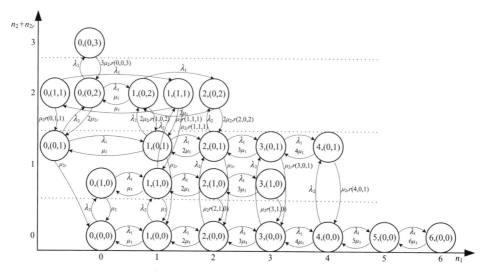

Figure 4.9 The state space Ω and the state transition diagram (Example 4.13).

$(4, 0, 1):$ $P(4, 0, 0) + P(3, 0, 1) - (40/9)P(4, 0, 1) = 0$

$(5, 0, 0):$ $P(4, 0, 0) + 6P(6, 0, 0) - 6P(5, 0, 0) = 0$

$(6, 0, 0):$ $P(5, 0, 0) - 6P(6, 0, 0) = 0$

The solution of this linear system is:

$P(0, 0, 0) = 0.11322$	$P(0, 0, 1) = 0.076499$	$P(0, 0, 2) = 0.064251$	$P(0, 0, 3) = 0.048188$
$P(0, 1, 0) = 0.066723$	$P(0, 1, 1) = 0.051087$	$P(1, 0, 0) = 0.108718$	$P(1, 0, 1) = 0.077459$
$P(1, 0, 2) = 0.07342$	$P(1, 1, 0) = 0.059702$	$P(1, 1, 1) = 0.052479$	$P(2, 0, 0) = 0.050797$
$P(2, 0, 1) = 0.047109$	$P(2, 0, 2) = 0.041722$	$P(2, 1, 0) = 0.020022$	$P(3, 0, 0) = 0.015682$
$P(3, 0, 1) = 0.018167$	$P(3, 1, 0) = 0.005461$	$P(4, 0, 0) = 0.003571$	$P(4, 0, 1) = 0.004891$
$P(5, 0, 0) = 0.000714$	$P(6, 0, 0) = 0.000119$		

Based on the values of $P(n_1, n_2, n_{2r})$, we determine the values of $Q(j)$:

$Q(0) = P(0, 0, 0) = 0.11322$

$Q(1) = P(1, 0, 0) = 0.108718$

$Q(2) = P(0, 0, 1) + P(2, 0, 0) = 0.127296$

$Q(3) = P(0, 1, 0) + P(1, 0, 1) + P(3, 0, 0) = 0.159864$

$Q(4) = P(0, 0, 2) + P(1, 1, 0) + P(2, 0, 1) + P(4, 0, 0) = 0.174633$

$Q(5) = P(0, 1, 1) + P(1, 0, 2) + P(2, 1, 0) + P(3, 0, 1) + P(5, 0, 0) = 0.16341$

$Q(6) = P(0, 0, 3) + P(1, 1, 1) + P(2, 0, 2) + P(3, 1, 0) + P(4, 0, 1) + P(6, 0, 0) = 0.15286$

(c) Based on the values of $Q(j)$, we obtain the exact CBP:

$$B_1 = \sum_{T - b_1 + 1}^{T} Q(j) = Q(6) = 0.15286 \text{ (compare with 0.1706 in the E-SRM)}$$

The *Prob{retry}* of service-class 2 calls, B_2, when they require $b_2 = 3$ b.u. upon arrival, refers to the percentage of calls which retry and is given by:

$$B_2 = \sum_{C-b_2+1}^{T} Q(j) = Q(2) + Q(3) + Q(4) + Q(5) + Q(6) = 0.77806 \text{ (compare with 0.7821}$$

in the E-SRM)

The CBP of service-class 2, B_{2r}, refers to service-class 2 retry calls which require b_{2r} b.u. and is given by:

$$B_{2r} = \sum_{T-b_{2r}+1}^{T} Q(j) = Q(5) + Q(6) = 0.31627 \text{ (compare with 0.3325 in the E-SRM)}$$

The link utilization is determined by:

$$U = \sum_{j=1}^{C} jQ(j) + \sum_{j=C+1}^{T} CQ(j) = 2.777 \text{ b.u. (compare with 2.832 in the E-SRM)}$$

The comparison between the CBP obtained in the E-SRM and the EA-SRM shows that the E-SRM cannot approximate the EA-SRM. Furthermore, the CBP of the EA-SRM are lower, a fact that it is expected since, in this example, adaptive calls of service-class 1 remain in the system for less time than the corresponding elastic calls.

To facilitate the recursive calculation of $q(j)$, we replace $r(\mathbf{n})$ by the state-dependent compression factors per service-class k, $\varphi_k(\mathbf{n})$ and $\varphi_{kr}(\mathbf{n})$ which have already been described in the E-SRM. The only difference compared to the E-SRM has to do with the determination of $x(\mathbf{n})$ which is now given by [5]:

$$x(\mathbf{n}) = \begin{cases} 1 & \text{when} \quad \mathbf{nb} \le C \text{ and } \mathbf{n} \in \Omega \\ \dfrac{1}{C} \sum_{k \in K_e} (n_k b_k x(\mathbf{n}_k^-) + n_{kr} b_{kr} x(\mathbf{n}_{kr}^-)) + \\ \dfrac{r(\mathbf{n})}{C} \sum_{k \in K_a} (n_k b_k x(\mathbf{n}_k^-) + n_{kr} b_{kr} x(\mathbf{n}_{kr}^-)) & \text{when} \quad C < \mathbf{nb} \le T \text{ and } \mathbf{n} \in \Omega \\ 0 & \text{otherwise} \end{cases}$$

(4.43)

where $\mathbf{n} = (n_1, n_{1r}, n_2, n_{2r}, \dots, n_k, n_{kr}, \dots, n_K, n_{Kr})$, $\mathbf{n}_k^- = (n_1, n_{1r}, n_2, n_{2r}, \dots, n_k - 1, n_{kr}, \dots, n_K, n_{Kr})$ and $\mathbf{n}_{kr}^- = (n_1, n_{1r}, n_2, n_{2r}, \dots, n_k, n_{kr} - 1, \dots, n_K, n_{Kr})$.

Example 4.14 Consider again Example 4.13 ($C = 4, T = 6, K = 2, b_1 = 1, b_2 = 3, b_{2r} = 2, \lambda_1 = \lambda_2 = \mu_1 = \mu_2 = 1, \mu_{2r} = 2/3$, calls of service-class 1 are adaptive):

(a) Draw the modified state transition diagram based on $\varphi_k(\mathbf{n})$ and $\varphi_{kr}(\mathbf{n})$, and determine their values for each state $\mathbf{n} = (n_1, n_2, n_{2r})$.
(b) Calculate the state probabilities $P(n_1, n_2, n_{2r})$ based on the GB equations. Then determine the values of the link occupancy distribution $Q(j)$ (for $j = 0, \dots, T$).
(c) Calculate the CBP of both service-classes, including the retry probability and the link utilization.

Table 4.7 The values of the state-dependent compression factors $\varphi_k(\mathbf{n})$ and $\varphi_{kr}(\mathbf{n})$ (Example 4.14).

n_1	n_2	n_{2r}	$x(\mathbf{n})$	$\varphi_1(\mathbf{n})$	$\varphi_2(\mathbf{n})$	$\varphi_{2r}(\mathbf{n})$	n_1	n_2	n_{2r}	$x(\mathbf{n})$	$\varphi_1(\mathbf{n})$	$\varphi_2(\mathbf{n})$	$\varphi_{2r}(\mathbf{n})$
0	0	0	1.00	1.00	1.00	1.00	2	0	0	1.00	1.00	1.00	1.00
0	0	1	1.00	1.00	1.00	1.00	2	0	1	1.00	1.00	1.00	1.00
0	0	2	1.00	1.00	1.00	1.00	2	0	2	1.40	0.8571	0.00	0.7143
0	0	3	1.5	0.00	0.00	0.6667	2	1	0	1.15	0.8696	0.8696	0.00
0	1	0	1.00	1.00	1.00	1.00	3	0	0	1.00	1.00	1.00	1.00
0	1	1	1.25	0.00	0.80	0.80	3	0	1	1.10	0.9090	0.00	0.9090
1	0	0	1.00	1.00	1.00	1.00	3	1	0	1.3250	0.8679	0.7547	0.00
1	0	1	1.00	1.00	1.00	1.00	4	0	0	1.00	1.00	1.00	1.00
1	0	2	1.20	0.8333	0.00	0.8333	4	0	1	1.2333	0.8919	0.00	0.8108
1	1	0	1.00	1.00	1.00	1.00	5	0	0	1.00	1.00	0.00	0.00
1	1	1	1.4583	0.8571	0.6857	0.6857	6	0	0	1.00	1.00	0.00	0.00

(a) The graphical representation of the modified state transition diagram is identical to that of Figure 4.2. Table 4.7 presents the 22 states together with the corresponding values of $\varphi_k(\mathbf{n})$ and $\varphi_{kr}(\mathbf{n})$ (determined through $x(\mathbf{n})$, (4.43)). Compared to Table 4.2, we see that the existence of adaptive traffic modifies the values of $\varphi_1(\mathbf{n})$, $\varphi_2(\mathbf{n})$, and $\varphi_{2r}(\mathbf{n})$.

(b) Based on Figure 4.2, we obtain the following 22 GB equations:

$(0,0,0):$ $P(0,1,0) + P(1,0,0) + (2/3)P(0,0,1) - 2P(0,0,0) = 0$

$(0,0,1):$ $0.8P(0,1,1) + (4/3)P(0,0,2) + P(1,0,1) - (8/3)P(0,0,1) = 0$

$(0,0,2):$ $P(0,0,1) + (4/3)P(0,0,3) + (5/6)P(1,0,2) - (10/3)P(0,0,2) = 0$

$(0,0,3):$ $P(0,0,2) - (4/3)P(0,0,3) = 0$

$(0,1,0):$ $P(0,0,0) + (8/15)P(0,1,1) + P(1,1,0) - 3P(0,1,0) = 0$

$(0,1,1):$ $P(0,1,0) + (6/7)P(1,1,1) - (7/3)P(0,1,1) = 0$

$(1,0,0):$ $P(0,0,0) + 2P(2,0,0) + (2/3)P(1,0,1) + P(1,1,0) - 3P(1,0,0) = 0$

$(1,0,1):$ $P(0,0,1) + 2P(2,0,1) + (10/9)P(1,0,2) + (24/35)P(1,1,1) - (11/3)P(1,0,1) = 0$

$(1,0,2):$ $P(0,0,2) + (12/7)P(2,0,2) + P(1,0,1) - (53/18)P(1,0,2) = 0$

$(1,1,0):$ $P(0,1,0) + P(1,0,0) + (40/23)P(2,1,0) + (48/105)P(1,1,1) - 4P(1,1,0) = 0$

$(1,1,1):$ $P(0,1,1) + P(1,1,0) - 2P(1,1,1) = 0$

$(2,0,0):$ $P(1,0,0) + 3P(3,0,0) + (20/23)P(2,1,0) + (2/3)P(2,0,1) - 4P(2,0,0) = 0$

$(2,0,1):$ $P(1,0,1) + P(2,0,0) + (30/11)P(3,0,1) + (20/21)P(2,0,2) - (14/3)P(2,0,1) = 0$

$(2,0,2):$ $P(1,0,2) + P(2,0,1) - (56/21)P(2,0,2) = 0$

$(2,1,0):$ $P(1,1,0) + (138/53)P(3,1,0) - (83/23)P(2,1,0) = 0$

$(3,0,0):$ $P(2,0,0) + 4P(4,0,0) + (40/53)P(3,1,0) + (20/33)P(3,0,1) - 5P(3,0,0) = 0$

$(3,0,1):$ $P(2,0,1) + (132/37)P(4,0,1) + P(3,0,0) - (143/33)P(3,0,1) = 0$

$(3,1,0):$ $P(2,1,0) - (178/53)P(3,1,0) = 0$

$(4,0,0):$ $P(3,0,0) + 5P(5,0,0) + (20/37)P(4,0,1) - 6P(4,0,0) = 0$

$(4, 0, 1):$ $P(4, 0, 0) + P(3, 0, 1) - (152/37)P(4, 0, 1) = 0$

$(5, 0, 0):$ $P(4, 0, 0) + 6P(6, 0, 0) - 6P(5, 0, 0) = 0$

$(6, 0, 0):$ $P(5, 0, 0) - 6P(6, 0, 0) = 0$

The solution of this linear system is:

$P(0, 0, 0) = 0.112313$ $P(0, 0, 1) = 0.072689$ $P(0, 0, 2) = 0.057299$ $P(0, 0, 3) = 0.042974$

$P(0, 1, 0) = 0.06569$ $P(0, 1, 1) = 0.047819$ $P(1, 0, 0) = 0.110478$ $P(1, 0, 1) = 0.079185$

$P(1, 0, 2) = 0.07321$ $P(1, 1, 0) = 0.059702$ $P(1, 1, 1) = 0.053536$ $P(2, 0, 0) = 0.053539$

$P(2, 0, 1) = 0.0498$ $P(2, 0, 2) = 0.046129$ $P(2, 1, 0) = 0.020912$ $P(3, 0, 0) = 0.017432$

$P(3, 0, 1) = 0.020439$ $P(3, 1, 0) = 0.006227$ $P(4, 0, 0) = 0.004133$ $P(4, 0, 1) = 0.005981$

$P(5, 0, 0) = 0.000827$ $P(6, 0, 0) = 0.000138$

Based on the values of $P(n_1, n_2, n_{2r})$, we determine the values of $Q(j)$:

$Q(0) = P(0, 0, 0) = 0.112313$

$Q(1) = P(1, 0, 0) = 0.110478$

$Q(2) = P(0, 0, 1) + P(2, 0, 0) = 0.126228$

$Q(3) = P(0, 1, 0) + P(1, 0, 1) + P(3, 0, 0) = 0.162307$

$Q(4) = P(0, 0, 2) + P(1, 1, 0) + P(2, 0, 1) + P(4, 0, 0) = 0.170484$

$Q(5) = P(0, 1, 1) + P(1, 0, 2) + P(2, 1, 0) + P(3, 0, 1) + P(5, 0, 0) = 0.163207$

$Q(6) = P(0, 0, 3) + P(1, 1, 1) + P(2, 0, 2) + P(3, 1, 0) + P(4, 0, 1) + P(6, 0, 0) = 0.154985$

(c) Based on the values of $Q(j)$, we obtain the approximate CBP:

$$B_1 = \sum_{T-b_1+1}^{T} Q(j) = Q(6) = 0.154985 \text{ (compare with the exact 0.15286)}$$

$$B_2 = \sum_{C-b_2+1}^{T} Q(j) = Q(2) + Q(3) + Q(4) + Q(5) + Q(6) = 0.77721 \text{ (compare with the exact 0.77806)}$$

$$B_{2r} = \sum_{T-b_{2r}+1}^{T} Q(j) = Q(5) + Q(6) = 0.31819 \text{ (compare with the exact 0.31627)}$$

The link utilization is determined by:

$$U = \sum_{j=1}^{C} jQ(j) + \sum_{j=C+1}^{T} CQ(j) = 2.805 \text{ b.u. (compare with the exact 2.777)}$$

4.5.2 The Analytical Model

4.5.2.1 Steady State Probabilities

To describe the analytical model in the steady state, we consider a link of capacity C b.u. that accommodates calls of two service-classes with traffic parameters: $(\lambda_1, \mu_1^{-1}, b_1)$ for service-class 1 and $(\lambda_2, \mu_2^{-1}, \mu_{2r}^{-1}, b_2, b_{2r})$ for service-class 2. Service-class 1 is adaptive while service-class 2 is elastic. Only calls of service-class 2 have retry parameters with $b_{2r} < b_2$ and $\mu_{2r}^{-1} > \mu_2^{-1}$. Let T be the limit up to which bandwidth compression is permitted for calls of both service-classes.

Although the EA-SRM is a non-PFS model we will use the LB of (4.3), initially for calls of service-class 1. As far as $\varphi_1(\mathbf{n})$ is concerned it is determined by (4.4). Based on (4.4) and multiplying both sides of (4.3) with b_1 and $r(\mathbf{n})$, we have:

$$\alpha_1 b_1 x(\mathbf{n}) r(\mathbf{n}) P(\mathbf{n}_1^-) = n_1 b_1 x(\mathbf{n}_1^-) r(\mathbf{n}) P(\mathbf{n}) \tag{4.44}$$

where $\alpha_1 = \lambda_1 / \mu_1$, $r(\mathbf{n}) = \min(1, C/j)$ and the values of $x(\mathbf{n})$ are given by (4.43).

Based on the CAC of the EA-SRM, we consider the following LB equations for calls of service-class 2:

- No bandwidth compression: in this case, we use (4.8) of the E-SRM.
- Bandwidth compression: in this case, we use (4.11) of the E-SRM.

Equations (4.44), (4.8) and (4.11) lead to the following system of equations:

$$\alpha_1 b_1 x(\mathbf{n}) r(\mathbf{n}) P(\mathbf{n}_1^-) + \alpha_2 b_2 x(\mathbf{n}) P(\mathbf{n}_2^-)$$
$$= (n_1 b_1 x(\mathbf{n}_1^-) r(\mathbf{n}) + n_2 b_2 x(\mathbf{n}_2^-)) P(\mathbf{n}) \ 1 < \mathbf{nb} \le C - b_2 + b_{2r} \tag{4.45}$$

$$\alpha_1 b_1 x(\mathbf{n}) r(\mathbf{n}) P(\mathbf{n}_1^-) + \alpha_2 b_2 x(\mathbf{n}) P(\mathbf{n}_2^-) + \alpha_{2r} b_{2r} x(\mathbf{n}) P(\mathbf{n}_{2r}^-)$$
$$= (n_1 b_1 x(\mathbf{n}_1^-) r(\mathbf{n}) + n_2 b_2 x(\mathbf{n}_2^-) + n_{2r} b_{2r} x(\mathbf{n}_{2r}^-)) P(\mathbf{n}) \tag{4.46}$$
$$C - b_2 + b_{2r} < \mathbf{nb} \le C$$

$$\alpha_1 b_1 x(\mathbf{n}) r(\mathbf{n}) P(\mathbf{n}_1^-) + \alpha_{2r} b_{2r} x(\mathbf{n}) P(\mathbf{n}_{2r}^-)$$
$$= (n_1 b_1 x(\mathbf{n}_1^-) r(\mathbf{n}) + n_{2r} b_{2r} x(\mathbf{n}_{2r}^-)) P(\mathbf{n}) \tag{4.47}$$
$$C < \mathbf{nb} \le T$$

Equations (4.45)–(4.47) can be combined into one equation by assuming that calls with b_{2r} are negligible when $1 \le \mathbf{nb} \le C - b_2 + b_{2r}$ and calls with b_2 are negligible when $C < \mathbf{nb} \le T$:

$$\alpha_1 b_1 x(\mathbf{n}) r(\mathbf{n}) P(\mathbf{n}_1^-) + \alpha_2 b_2 \gamma_2(\mathbf{nb}) x(\mathbf{n}) P(\mathbf{n}_2^-) + \alpha_{2r} b_{2r} \gamma_{2r}(\mathbf{nb}) x(\mathbf{n}) P(\mathbf{n}_{2r}^-) =$$
$$(n_1 b_1 x(\mathbf{n}_1^-) r(\mathbf{n}) + n_2 b_2 x(\mathbf{n}_2^-) + n_{2r} b_{2r} x(\mathbf{n}_{2r}^-)) P(\mathbf{n}) \tag{4.48}$$

where $\gamma_2(\mathbf{nb}) = 1$ for $1 \le \mathbf{nb} \le C$, otherwise $\gamma_2(\mathbf{nb}) = 0$ and $\gamma_{2r}(\mathbf{nb}) = 1$ for $C - b_2 + b_{2r} < \mathbf{nb} \le T$, otherwise $\gamma_{2r}(\mathbf{nb}) = 0$.

At this point, we derive a formula for $x(\mathbf{n})$ (which is a simplified version of (4.43)) by making the following assumptions:

- When $C < \mathbf{nb} \le T$, the bandwidth of all in-service calls should be compressed by $\phi_k(\mathbf{n})$, $k = 1, 2$, so that:

$$n_1 b_1' + n_2 b_2' + n_{2r} b_{2r}' = C \tag{4.49}$$

- We keep the product *service time* by *bandwidth* of service-class k calls (elastic or adaptive) in state n of the initial Markov chain (with $r(\mathbf{n})$) equal to the corresponding product in the same state $\mathbf{n}$ of the modified Markov chain (with $\varphi_k(\mathbf{n})$ and $\varphi_{kr}(\mathbf{n})$):

$$
\frac{b_1 r(\mathbf{n})}{\mu_1} = \frac{b_1'}{\mu_1 \varphi_1(\mathbf{n})} \quad \Rightarrow \quad b_1' = b_1 \varphi_1(\mathbf{n}) r(\mathbf{n})
$$

$$
\frac{b_2 r(\mathbf{n})}{\mu_2 r(\mathbf{n})} = \frac{b_2'}{\mu_2 \varphi_2(\mathbf{n})} \quad \Rightarrow \quad b_2' = b_2 \phi_2(\mathbf{n}) \tag{4.50}
$$

$$
\frac{b_{2r} r(\mathbf{n})}{\mu_{2r} r(\mathbf{n})} = \frac{b_{2r}'}{\mu_{2r} \varphi_{2r}(\mathbf{n})} \quad \Rightarrow \quad b_{2r}' = b_{2r} \varphi_{2r}(\mathbf{n})
$$

By substituting (4.50) in (4.49) we obtain:

$$
n_1 b_1 \varphi_1(\mathbf{n}) r(\mathbf{n}) + n_2 b_2 \varphi_2(\mathbf{n}) + n_{2r} b_{2r} \varphi_{2r}(\mathbf{n}) = C \tag{4.51}
$$

where $\varphi_1(\mathbf{n})$ and $\varphi_2(\mathbf{n})$ are given by (3.8), and $\varphi_{2r}(\mathbf{n})$ by (4.1).

Equation (4.51), due to (3.8) and (4.1), is written as:

$$
x(\mathbf{n}) = \begin{cases} 1 & \text{when } \mathbf{nb} \leq C \text{ and } \mathbf{n} \in \Omega \\ \frac{1}{C}(n_1 b_1 x(\mathbf{n}_1^-) r(\mathbf{n}) + n_2 b_2 x(\mathbf{n}_2^-) + n_{2r} b_{2r} x(\mathbf{n}_{2r}^-)) \\ & \text{when } C < \mathbf{nb} \leq T \text{ and } \mathbf{n} \in \Omega \\ 0 & \text{otherwise} \end{cases} \tag{4.52}
$$

Based on (4.52), we consider again (4.48). Since $x(\mathbf{n}) = 1$, when $0 \leq \mathbf{nb} \leq C$, we have (4.16).

When $C < \mathbf{nb} \leq T$ and based on (4.52), (4.48) can be written as:

$$
(C/j)\alpha_1 b_1 P(\mathbf{n}_1^-) + \alpha_{2r} b_{2r} \gamma_{2r}(\mathbf{nb}) P(\mathbf{n}_{2r}^-) = CP(\mathbf{n}) \tag{4.53}
$$

since $r(\mathbf{n}) = C/j$, when $C < \mathbf{nb} \leq T$.

To introduce the link occupancy distribution $q(j)$ in (4.53), we sum both sides of (4.53) over the set of states $\Omega_j = \{\mathbf{n} \in \Omega : \mathbf{nb} = j\}$:

$$
(C/j)\alpha_1 b_1 \sum_{\mathbf{n} \in \Omega_j} P(\mathbf{n}_1^-) + \alpha_{2r} b_{2r} \gamma_{2r}(\mathbf{nb}) \sum_{\mathbf{n} \in \Omega_j} P(\mathbf{n}_{2r}^-) = C \sum_{\mathbf{n} \in \Omega_j} P(\mathbf{n}) \tag{4.54}
$$

Since by definition $\sum_{\mathbf{n} \in \Omega_j} P(\mathbf{n}) = q(j)$, (4.54) is written as:

$$
(C/j)\alpha_1 b_1 q(j - b_1) + \alpha_{2r} b_{2r} \gamma_{2r}(j) q(j - b_{2r}) = Cq(j) \tag{4.55}
$$

where $\gamma_{2r}(j) = 1$ for $C < j \leq T$.

The combination of (4.16) and (4.55) gives the following approximate recursive formula for the calculation of $q(j)$ in the case of two service-classes when service-class 1 is adaptive, service-class 2 is elastic, and only calls of service-class 2 have retry parameters:

$$
q(j) = \frac{1}{j}\alpha_1 b_1 q(j - b_1) + \frac{1}{\min(j, C)}[\alpha_2 b_2 \gamma_2(j) q(j - b_2) + \alpha_{2r} b_{2r} \gamma_{2r}(j) q(j - b_{2r})] \tag{4.56}
$$

where $1 \leq j \leq T$, and $\gamma_2(j) = 1$ for $1 \leq j \leq C$, otherwise $\gamma_2(j) = 0$, while $\gamma_{2r}(j) = 1$ for $C - b_2 + b_{2r} < j \leq T$, otherwise $\gamma_{2r}(j) = 0$.

In the case of K service-classes and assuming that all service-classes may have retry parameters, (4.56) takes the general form [5]:

$$q(j) = \begin{cases} 1 & \text{if } j = 0 \\ \dfrac{1}{\min(j,C)} \left[\sum_{k \in K_e} \alpha_k b_k \gamma_k(j) q(j - b_k) + \sum_{k \in K_e} \alpha_{kr} b_{kr} \gamma_{kr}(j) q(j - b_{kr}) \right] \\ \quad + \dfrac{1}{j} \left[\sum_{k \in K_a} \alpha_k b_k \gamma_k(j) q(j - b_k) + \sum_{k \in K_a} \alpha_{kr} b_{kr} \gamma_{kr}(j) q(j - b_{kr}) \right] & \text{if } j = 1, \dots, T \\ 0 & \text{otherwise} \end{cases}$$

(4.57)

where $\gamma_k(j) = \begin{cases} 1 & \text{if } 1 \le j \le C \text{ and } b_{kr} > 0 \\ 1 & \text{if } 1 \le j \le T \text{ and } b_{kr} = 0 \\ 0 & \text{otherwise} \end{cases}$, $\gamma_{kr}(j) = \begin{cases} 1 & \text{if } C - b_k + b_{kr} < j \le T \\ 0 & \text{otherwise} \end{cases}$.

4.5.2.2 CBP, Utilization, and Mean Number of In-service Calls

Having determined the unnormalized values of $q(j)$, we can calculate:

- The CBP of service-class k calls with b_{kr} b.u., B_{kr}, via (4.22).
- The CBP of service-class k calls with b_k b.u., B_k, via (4.23).
- The conditional CBP of service-class k retry calls given that they have been blocked with their initial bandwidth requirement b_k, B_{kr}^*, via (4.24).
- The link utilization, U, via (3.23).
- The mean number of elastic service-class k calls with b_k b.u. in state j, $y_k(j)$, via (4.25).
- The mean number of elastic service-class k calls with b_{kr} b.u. in state j, $y_{kr}(j)$, via (4.26).
- The mean number of adaptive service-class k calls with b_k b.u. in state j, $y_k(j)$, via:

$$y_k(j) = \frac{C}{j} \frac{\alpha_k \gamma_k(j) q(j - b_k)}{q(j)}, \quad q(j) > 0 \tag{4.58}$$

- The mean number of adaptive service-class k calls with b_{kr} b.u. in state j, $y_{kr}(j)$, via:

$$y_{kr}(j) = \frac{C}{j} \frac{\alpha_{kr} \gamma_{kr}(j) q(j - b_{kr})}{q(j)}, \quad q(j) > 0 \tag{4.59}$$

- The mean number of in-service calls of service-class k accepted with b_k, $\bar{n}_k$, via (4.27).
- The mean number of in-service calls of service-class k accepted with b_{kr}, $\bar{n}_{kr}$, via (4.28).

Example 4.15 Consider again Example 4.13 ($C = 4, T = 6, K = 2, b_1 = 1, b_2 = 3, b_{2r} = 2, \lambda_1 = \lambda_2 = \mu_1 = \mu_2 = 1, \mu_{2r} = 2/3$, calls of service-class 1 are adaptive):

(a) Calculate the values of $Q(j)$ based on (4.57).
(b) Calculate the CBP of both service-classes, including the retry probability and the conditional B_{2r}^*.

(a) State probabilities through the recursion (4.57):

$j = 1:$ $q(1) = q(0) + 0 = 1.0$ $\Rightarrow q(1) = 1.0$
$j = 2:$ $2q(2) = q(1) + 0 = 1.0$ $\Rightarrow q(2) = 0.5$

$j = 3:$ $3q(3) = q(2) + 3q(0) = 3.5$ $\Rightarrow q(3) = 1.16667$

$j = 4:$ $4q(4) = q(3) + 3q(1) + 3q(2) = 5.66667$ $\Rightarrow q(4) = 1.41667$

$j = 5:$ $q(5) = \frac{1}{5}q(4) + 0 + \frac{1}{4}3q(3) = 1.15833$ $\Rightarrow q(5) = 1.15833$

$j = 6:$ $q(6) = \frac{1}{6}q(5) + 0 + \frac{1}{4}3q(4) = 1.25555$ $\Rightarrow q(6) = 1.25555$

The normalization constant is:

$$G = \sum_{j=0}^{T} q(j) = 7.4972.$$

The state probabilities are:

$Q(0) = 0.13338$ $Q(1) = 0.13338$ $Q(2) = 0.06669$ $Q(3) = 0.15561$ $Q(4) = 0.18896$

$Q(5) = 0.15450$ $Q(6) = 0.16747$

(b) The CBP are as follows:

$$B_1 = \sum_{T-b_1+1}^{T} Q(j) = Q(6) = 0.16747 \text{ (compare with the exact 0.15286)}$$

$$B_2 = \sum_{C-b_2+1}^{T} Q(j) = Q(2) + Q(3) + Q(4) + Q(5) + Q(6) = 0.73323 \text{ (compare with the exact 0.77806)}$$

$$B_{2r} = \sum_{T-b_{2r}+1}^{T} Q(j) = Q(5) + Q(6) = 0.32197 \text{ (compare with the exact 0.31627)}$$

$$B_{2r}^* = \frac{B_{2r}}{B_2} = 0.4065 \text{ (compare with the exact 0.4065(!))}$$

It is apparent that even in small EA-SRM examples the error introduced by the assumption of LB, the introduction of $\varphi_k(\mathbf{n})$ and $\varphi_{kr}(\mathbf{n})$, and the migration approximation is not significant.

4.6 The Elastic Adaptive Single-Retry Model under the BR Policy

4.6.1 The Service System

We now consider the *EA-SRM under the BR policy (EA-SRM/BR)* with BR parameter t_k for service-class k calls ($k = 1, \ldots, K$). The CAC in the EA-SRM/BR is the same as that of the E-SRM/BR. As far as the values of $\varphi_k(\mathbf{n})$, $\varphi_{kr}(\mathbf{n})$, and $x(\mathbf{n})$ are concerned they are determined by (3.8), (4.1), and (4.43), respectively.

Example 4.16   Consider again Example 4.13 ($C = 4, T = 6, K = 2, b_1 = 1, b_2 = 3$, $b_{2r} = 2, \lambda_1 = \lambda_2 = \mu_1 = \mu_2 = 1, \mu_{2r} = 2/3$, calls of service-class 1 are adaptive) and apply the BR parameters $t_1 = 1$ b.u. and $t_2 = 0$ b.u. to calls of service-class 1 and 2, respectively.

(a) Find the total number of permissible states $\mathbf{n} = (n_1, n_2, n_{2r})$, draw the state transition diagram, and determine the values of j and $r(\mathbf{n})$ for each state $\mathbf{n} = (n_1, n_2, n_{2r})$.

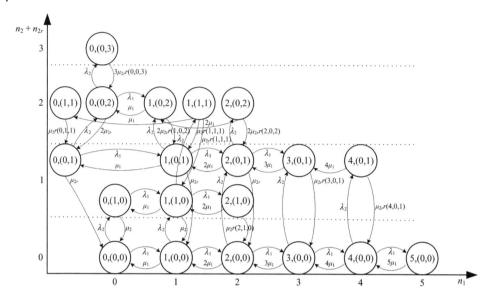

Figure 4.10 The state space Ω and the state transition diagram (Example 4.16).

(b) Calculate the state probabilities $P(n_1, n_2, n_{2r})$ based on the GB equations. Then determine the values of the link occupancy distribution $Q(j)$ (for $j = 0, 1, \ldots, T$).

(c) Calculate the CBP of both service-classes, including the retry probability and the link utilization.

(d) Draw the modified state transition diagram based on $\varphi_k(\mathbf{n})$ and $\varphi_{kr}(\mathbf{n})$, and determine their values for each state $\mathbf{n} = (n_1, n_2, n_{2r})$.

(e) Based on $\varphi_k(\mathbf{n})$ and $\varphi_{kr}(\mathbf{n})$, calculate the values of $P(n_1, n_2, n_{2r})$, $Q(j)$, CBP, and link utilization.

(a) There are 20 permissible states of the form $\mathbf{n} = (n_1, n_2, n_{2r})$. The state space Ω and the state transition diagram are shown in Figure 4.10. Compared to Figure 4.9, there are two states that do not exist: (3,1,0) and (6,0,0). The values of $r(\mathbf{n})$ are exactly the same as those presented in Table 4.1 (the BR policy does not affect $r(\mathbf{n})$).

(b) Based on Figure 4.10, we obtain the following 20 GB equations:

$(0, 0, 0):$ $P(0, 1, 0) + P(1, 0, 0) + (2/3)P(0, 0, 1) - 2P(0, 0, 0) = 0$

$(0, 0, 1):$ $0.8P(0, 1, 1) + (4/3)P(0, 0, 2) + P(1, 0, 1) - (8/3)P(0, 0, 1) = 0$

$(0, 0, 2):$ $P(0, 0, 1) + (4/3)P(0, 0, 3) + P(1, 0, 2) - (10/3)P(0, 0, 2) = 0$

$(0, 0, 3):$ $P(0, 0, 2) - (4/3)P(0, 0, 3) = 0$

$(0, 1, 0):$ $P(0, 0, 0) + (8/15)P(0, 1, 1) + P(1, 1, 0) - 3P(0, 1, 0) = 0$

$(0, 1, 1):$ $P(0, 1, 0) + P(1, 1, 1) - (4/3)P(0, 1, 1) = 0$

$(1, 0, 0):$ $P(0, 0, 0) + 2P(2, 0, 0) + (2/3)P(1, 0, 1) + P(1, 1, 0) - 3P(1, 0, 0) = 0$

$(1, 0, 1):$ $P(0, 0, 1) + 2P(2, 0, 1) + (16/15)P(1, 0, 2) + (2/3)P(1, 1, 1) - (11/3)P(1, 0, 1) = 0$

$(1, 0, 2):$ $P(0, 0, 2) + 2P(2, 0, 2) + P(1, 0, 1) - (31/15)P(1, 0, 2) = 0$

$(1, 1, 0):$ $P(0, 1, 0) + P(1, 0, 0) + 2P(2, 1, 0) + (4/9)P(1, 1, 1) - 4P(1, 1, 0) = 0$

$(1, 1, 1)$: $P(1, 1, 0) - (19/9)P(1, 1, 1) = 0$

$(2, 0, 0)$: $P(1, 0, 0) + 3P(3, 0, 0) + 0.8P(2, 1, 0) + (2/3)P(2, 0, 1) - 4P(2, 0, 0) = 0$

$(2, 0, 1)$: $P(1, 0, 1) + P(2, 0, 0) + 3P(3, 0, 1) + (8/9)P(2, 0, 2) - (14/3)P(2, 0, 1) = 0$

$(2, 0, 2)$: $P(2, 0, 1) - (26/9)P(2, 0, 2) = 0$

$(2, 1, 0)$: $P(1, 1, 0) - 2.8P(2, 1, 0) = 0$

$(3, 0, 0)$: $P(2, 0, 0) + 4P(4, 0, 0) + (8/15)P(3, 0, 1) - 5P(3, 0, 0) = 0$

$(3, 0, 1)$: $P(2, 0, 1) + 4P(4, 0, 1) + P(3, 0, 0) - (53/15)P(3, 0, 1) = 0$

$(4, 0, 0)$: $P(3, 0, 0) + 5P(5, 0, 0) + (4/9)P(4, 0, 1) - 6P(4, 0, 0) = 0$

$(4, 0, 1)$: $P(4, 0, 0) - (40/9)P(4, 0, 1) = 0$

$(5, 0, 0)$: $P(4, 0, 0) - 5P(5, 0, 0) = 0$

The solution of this linear system is:

$P(0, 0, 0) = 0.120454$	$P(0, 0, 1) = 0.088361$	$P(0, 0, 2) = 0.074554$	$P(0, 0, 3) = 0.055915$
$P(0, 1, 0) = 0.073405$	$P(0, 1, 1) = 0.076079$	$P(1, 0, 0) = 0.108597$	$P(1, 0, 1) = 0.07536$
$P(1, 0, 2) = 0.085598$	$P(1, 1, 0) = 0.059184$	$P(1, 1, 1) = 0.028034$	$P(2, 0, 0) = 0.047956$
$P(2, 0, 1) = 0.038983$	$P(2, 0, 2) = 0.013494$	$P(2, 1, 0) = 0.021137$	$P(3, 0, 0) = 0.013443$
$P(3, 0, 1) = 0.015536$	$P(4, 0, 0) = 0.002744$	$P(4, 0, 1) = 0.000617$	$P(5, 0, 0) = 0.000549$

Based on the values of $P(n_1, n_2, n_{2r})$, we determine the values of $Q(j)$:

$Q(0) = P(0, 0, 0) = 0.120454$

$Q(1) = P(1, 0, 0) = 0.108597$

$Q(2) = P(0, 0, 1) + P(2, 0, 0) = 0.136317$

$Q(3) = P(0, 1, 0) + P(1, 0, 1) + P(3, 0, 0) = 0.162208$

$Q(4) = P(0, 0, 2) + P(1, 1, 0) + P(2, 0, 1) + P(4, 0, 0) = 0.175465$

$Q(5) = P(0, 1, 1) + P(1, 0, 2) + P(2, 1, 0) + P(3, 0, 1) + P(5, 0, 0) = 0.198899$

$Q(6) = P(0, 0, 3) + P(1, 1, 1) + P(2, 0, 2) + P(4, 0, 1) = 0.09806$

(c) Based on the values of $Q(j)$, we obtain the exact CBP:

$$B_1 = \sum_{T-b_1-t_1+1}^{T} Q(j) = Q(5) + Q(6) = 0.29696 \text{ (compare with 0.30737 in the E-SRM/BR)}$$

The $Prob\{retry\}$ of service-class 2 calls, B_2, is given by:

$$B_2 = \sum_{C-b_2+1}^{T} Q(j) = Q(2) + Q(3) + \ldots + Q(6) = 0.77095 \text{ (compare with 0.77264 in the E-SRM/BR)}$$

Due to the selection of the BR parameters, the CBP of service-class 2, B_{2r}, equals B_1:

$$B_{2r} = \sum_{T-b_{2r}+1}^{T} Q(j) = Q(5) + Q(6) = 0.29696 \text{ (compare with 0.30737 in the E-SRM/BR)}$$

The link utilization is determined by:

$$U = \sum_{j=1}^{C} jQ(j) + \sum_{j=C+1}^{T} CQ(j) = 2.757 \text{ b.u. (compare with 2.771 in the E-SRM/BR)}$$

(d) The graphical representation of the modified state transition diagram is identical to that of Figure 4.4. The values of $\varphi_k(\mathbf{n})$ and $\varphi_{kr}(\mathbf{n})$ (for the 20 states) are exactly the same as those of Table 4.7.

(e) Based on Figure 4.4, we obtain the following 20 GB equations:

$(0,0,0)$: $P(0,1,0) + P(1,0,0) + (2/3)P(0,0,1) - 2P(0,0,0) = 0$

$(0,0,1)$: $0.8P(0,1,1) + (4/3)P(0,0,2) + P(1,0,1) - (8/3)P(0,0,1) = 0$

$(0,0,2)$: $P(0,0,1) + (4/3)P(0,0,3) + P(1,0,2) - (10/3)P(0,0,2) = 0$

$(0,0,3)$: $P(0,0,2) - (4/3)P(0,0,3) = 0$

$(0,1,0)$: $P(0,0,0) + (8/15)P(0,1,1) + P(1,1,0) - 3P(0,1,0) = 0$

$(0,1,1)$: $P(0,1,0) + (6/7)P(1,1,1) - (4/3)P(0,1,1) = 0$

$(1,0,0)$: $P(0,0,0) + 2P(2,0,0) + (2/3)P(1,0,1) + P(1,1,0) - 3P(1,0,0) = 0$

$(1,0,1)$: $P(0,0,1) + 2P(2,0,1) + (10/9)P(1,0,2) + (24/35)P(1,1,1) - (11/3)P(1,0,1) = 0$

$(1,0,2)$: $P(0,0,2) + (12/7)P(2,0,2) + P(1,0,1) - (35/18)P(1,0,2) = 0$

$(1,1,0)$: $P(0,1,0) + P(1,0,0) + (40/23)P(2,1,0) + (48/105)P(1,1,1) - 4P(1,1,0) = 0$

$(1,1,1)$: $P(1,1,0) - 2P(1,1,1) = 0$

$(2,0,0)$: $P(1,0,0) + 3P(3,0,0) + (20/23)P(2,1,0) + (2/3)P(2,0,1) - 4P(2,0,0) = 0$

$(2,0,1)$: $P(1,0,1) + P(2,0,0) + (30/11)P(3,0,1) + (20/21)P(2,0,2) - (14/3)P(2,0,1) = 0$

$(2,0,2)$: $P(2,0,1) - (56/21)P(2,0,2) = 0$

$(2,1,0)$: $P(1,1,0) - (60/23)P(2,1,0) = 0$

$(3,0,0)$: $P(2,0,0) + 4P(4,0,0) + (20/33)P(3,0,1) - 5P(3,0,0) = 0$

$(3,0,1)$: $P(2,0,1) + (132/37)P(4,0,1) + P(3,0,0) - (110/33)P(3,0,1) = 0$

$(4,0,0)$: $P(3,0,0) + 5P(5,0,0) + (20/37)P(4,0,1) - 6P(4,0,0) = 0$

$(4,0,1)$: $P(4,0,0) - (152/37)P(4,0,1) = 0$

$(5,0,0)$: $P(4,0,0) - 5P(5,0,0) = 0$

The solution of this linear system is:

$P(0,0,0) = 0.119897$ $P(0,0,1) = 0.085227$ $P(0,0,2) = 0.068106$ $P(0,0,3) = 0.051079$

$P(0,1,0) = 0.072667$ $P(0,1,1) = 0.073443$ $P(1,0,0) = 0.110309$ $P(1,0,1) = 0.077711$

$P(1,0,2) = 0.088424$ $P(1,1,0) = 0.058934$ $P(1,1,1) = 0.029467$ $P(2,0,0) = 0.050145$

$P(2,0,1) = 0.040628$ $P(2,0,2) = 0.015236$ $P(2,1,0) = 0.022591$ $P(3,0,0) = 0.014513$

$P(3,0,1) = 0.017319$ $P(4,0,0) = 0.002981$ $P(4,0,1) = 0.000726$ $P(5,0,0) = 0.000596$

Based on the values of $P(n_1, n_2, n_{2r})$, we determine the values of $Q(j)$:

$Q(0) = P(0,0,0) = 0.119897$

$Q(1) = P(1,0,0) = 0.110309$

$Q(2) = P(0,0,1) + P(2,0,0) = 0.135372$

$Q(3) = P(0,1,0) + P(1,0,1) + P(3,0,0) = 0.164891$

$Q(4) = P(0,0,2) + P(1,1,0) + P(2,0,1) + P(4,0,0) = 0.170649$

$Q(5) = P(0,1,1) + P(1,0,2) + P(2,1,0) + P(3,0,1) + P(5,0,0) = 0.202373$

$Q(6) = P(0,0,3) + P(1,1,1) + P(2,0,2) + P(4,0,1) = 0.096508$

Based on the values of $Q(j)$, we obtain the following CBP:

$$B_1 = \sum_{T-b_1-t_1+1}^{T} Q(j) = Q(5) + Q(6) = 0.29888 \text{ (compare with the exact 0.29696)}$$

$$B_2 = \sum_{C-b_2+1}^{T} Q(j) = Q(2) + Q(3) + Q(4) + Q(5) + Q(6) = 0.76979$$

(compare with the exact 0.77095)

$$B_{2r} = \sum_{T-b_{2r}+1}^{T} Q(j) = Q(5) + Q(6) = 0.29888 \text{ (compare with the exact 0.29696)}$$

The link utilization is determined by:

$$U = \sum_{j=1}^{C} jQ(j) + \sum_{j=C+1}^{T} CQ(j) = 2.754 \text{ b.u. (compare with the exact 2.757)}$$

4.6.2 The Analytical Model

4.6.2.1 Link Occupancy Distribution

In the EA-SRM/BR, the recursive calculation of $q(j)$ is based on the Roberts method (see Section 1.3.2.2), which leads to the formula [4]:

$$q(j) = \begin{cases} 1 & \text{if } j = 0 \\[2mm] \dfrac{1}{\min(j,C)} \left[\sum_{k \in K_e} \alpha_k D_k(j - b_k) \gamma_k(j) q(j - b_k) + \right. \\ \left. \sum_{k \in K_e} \alpha_{kr} D_{kr}(j - b_{kr}) \gamma_{kr}(j) q(j - b_{kr}) \right] + \\[2mm] \dfrac{1}{j} \left[\sum_{k \in K_a} \alpha_k D_k(j - b_k) \gamma_k(j) q(j - b_k) + \right. \\ \left. \sum_{k \in K_a} \alpha_{kr} D_{kr}(j - b_{kr}) \gamma_{kr}(j) q(j - b_{kr}) \right] & \text{if } j = 1, \dots, T \\[2mm] 0 & \text{otherwise} \end{cases} \tag{4.60}$$

where $D_k(j - b_k) = \begin{cases} b_k & \text{for } j \le T - t_k \\ 0 & \text{for } j > T - t_k \end{cases}$, $\quad D_{kr}(j - b_{kr}) = \begin{cases} b_{kr} & \text{for } j \le T - t_k \\ 0 & \text{for } j > T - t_k \end{cases}$.

4.6.2.2 CBP, Utilization, and Mean Number of In-service Calls

Based on (4.60), the following performance measures can be calculated:

- The CBP of service-class k calls with b_{kr} b.u., B_{kr}, via (4.30).
- The CBP of service-class k calls with b_k b.u., B_k, via (4.31).
- The conditional CBP of service-class k retry calls given that they have been blocked with their initial bandwidth requirement b_k, B_{kr}^* via (4.32).
- The link utilization, U, via (3.23).
- The mean number of service-class k calls with b_k b.u. in state j, $y_k(j)$, via (4.58), and the mean number of service-class k calls with b_{kr} b.u. in state j, $y_{kr}(j)$, via (4.59).

- The mean number of in-service calls of service-class k accepted in the system with $b_k, \bar{n}_k$, via (4.27), and the mean number of in-service calls of service-class k accepted in the system with $b_{kr}, \bar{n}_{kr}$, via (4.28).

Example 4.17 Consider again Example 4.16 ($C = 4, T = 6, K = 2, b_1 = 1, b_2 = 3, b_{2r} = 2, t_1 = 1, t_2 = 0, \lambda_1 = \lambda_2 = \mu_1 = \mu_2 = 1, \mu_{2r} = 2/3$, calls of service-class 1 are adaptive).

(a) Calculate the values of $Q(j)$ based on (4.60).
(b) Calculate the CBP of both service-classes, including the retry probability and the conditional B_{2r}^*.

(a) State probabilities through the recursion (4.60):

$j = 1:$ $q(1) = q(0) + 0 = 1.0$ $\Rightarrow q(1) = 1.0$

$j = 2:$ $2q(2) = q(1) + 0 = 1.0$ $\Rightarrow q(2) = 0.5$

$j = 3:$ $3q(3) = q(2) + 3q(0) = 3.5$ $\Rightarrow q(3) = 1.16667$

$j = 4:$ $4q(4) = q(3) + 3q(1) + 3q(2) = 5.66667$ $\Rightarrow q(4) = 1.41667$

$j = 5:$ $q(5) = \frac{1}{5}q(4) + 0 + \frac{1}{4}3q(3) = 1.15833$ $\Rightarrow q(5) = 1.15833$

$j = 6:$ $q(6) = 0 + 0 + \frac{1}{4}3q(4) = 1.0625$ $\Rightarrow q(6) = 1.0625$

The normalization constant is:

$$G = \sum_{j=0}^{T} q(j) = 7.30417.$$

The state probabilities are:

$Q(0) = 0.13691$ $Q(1) = 0.13691$ $Q(2) = 0.06845$ $Q(3) = 0.15973$

$Q(4) = 0.19395$ $Q(5) = 0.15858$ $Q(6) = 0.14546$

(b) The CBP are as follows:

$$B_1 = \sum_{T-b_1-t_1+1}^{T} Q(j) = Q(5) + Q(6) = 0.30404 \text{ (compare with the exact 0.29696)}$$

$$B_2 = \sum_{C-b_2+1}^{T} Q(j) = Q(2) + Q(3) + Q(4) + Q(5) + Q(6) = 0.72617$$

(compare with the exact 0.77095)

$$B_{2r} = \sum_{T-b_{2r}+1}^{T} Q(j) = Q(5) + Q(6) = 0.30404 \text{ (compare with the exact 0.29696)}$$

$$B_{2r}^* = \frac{B_{2r}}{B_2} = 0.41869 \text{ (compare with the exact 0.38519)}$$

It is apparent that even in small EA-SRM/BR examples, the error introduced by the assumption of LB, the introduction of $\varphi_k(\mathbf{n})$ and $\varphi_{kr}(\mathbf{n})$, the migration approximation, and the application of the BR policy remains acceptable.

4.7 The Elastic Adaptive Multi-Retry Model

4.7.1 The Service System

Similar to the E-MRM, in the *elastic adaptive multi-retry model (EA-MRM)* a blocked call of service-class k can have more than one retry parameter $(b_{kr_s}, \mu_{kr_s}^{-1})$ for $s = 1, \dots, S(k)$, where $b_{kr_{S(k)}} < \dots < b_{kr_1} < b_k$ and $\mu_{kr_{S(k)}}^{-1} > \dots > \mu_{kr_1}^{-1} > \mu_k^{-1}$. The call admission in the EA-MRM is the same as the E-MRM with the exception that adaptive calls do not alter their service time when their bandwidth is compressed/expanded.

Similar to the EA-SRM, the steady state probabilities in the EA-MRM do not have a PFS. Thus, the unnormalized values of $q(j)$ can be determined by an approximate but recursive formula, as presented in Section 4.7.2.

Example 4.18 Consider again Example 4.6 ($C = 3, T = 4, K = 2, b_1 = 1, b_2 = 3,$ $b_{2r_1} = 2, b_{2r_2} = 1, \lambda_1 = \lambda_2 = 1, \mu_1^{-1} = \mu_2^{-1} = 1, \mu_{2r_1}^{-1} = 2.0, \ \mu_{2r_2}^{-1} = 4.0$), and let calls of service-class 1 be adaptive.

(a) Find the total number of permissible states $\mathbf{n} = (n_1, n_2, n_{2r_1}, n_{2r_2})$ and determine the values of j and $r(\mathbf{n})$ for each state $\mathbf{n} = (n_1, n_2, n_{2r_1}, n_{2r_2})$.
(b) Calculate the state probabilities $P(n_1, n_2, n_{2r_1}, n_{2r_2})$ based on the GB equations. Then determine the values of the link occupancy distribution $Q(j)$ (for $j = 0, \dots, T$).
(c) Calculate the CBP of both service-classes, including the retry probabilities and the link utilization.
(d) Calculate the conditional CBP of service-class 2 retry calls with b_{2r_2}, given that they have been blocked with their initial bandwidth requirement, b_2.

(a) There are 24 permissible states of the form $\mathbf{n} = (n_1, n_2, n_{2r_1}, n_{2r_2})$. The values of $r(\mathbf{n})$ and $j = n_1 b_1 + n_2 b_2 + n_{2r_1} b_{2r_1} + n_{2r_2} b_{2r_2}$, before and after compression has been applied, are the same as those presented in Table 4.3.

(b) In what follows, we present the 24 GB equations:

$(0,0,0,0): 0.5P(0,0,1,0) + 0.25P(0,0,0,1) + P(0,1,0,0) + P(1,0,0,0) - 2P(0,0,0,0) = 0$

$(0,0,0,1): 0.5P(0,0,0,2) + 0.75P(0,1,0,1) + 0.5P(0,0,1,1) + P(1,0,0,1)$
$\qquad - 2.25P(0,0,0,1) = 0$

$(0,0,0,2): P(1,0,0,2) + 0.75P(0,0,0,3) + 0.375P(0,0,1,2) - 2.5P(0,0,0,2) = 0$

$(0,0,0,3): P(0,0,0,2) + 0.75P(0,0,0,4) + P(1,0,0,3) - 2.75P(0,0,0,3) = 0$

$(0,0,0,4): P(0,0,0,3) - 0.75P(0,0,0,4) = 0$

$(0,0,1,0): 0.25P(0,0,1,1) + P(1,0,1,0) - 2.5P(0,0,1,0) = 0$

$(0,0,1,1): P(0,0,0,1) + P(0,0,1,0) + P(1,0,1,1) + 0.375P(0,0,1,2) - 2.75P(0,0,1,1) = 0$

$(0,0,1,2): P(0,0,1,1) - 0.75P(0,0,1,2) = 0$

$(0,1,0,0): P(0,0,0,0) + 0.1875P(0,1,0,1) + P(1,1,0,0) - 3P(0,1,0,0) = 0$

$(0,1,0,1): P(0,1,0,0) - 0.9375P(0,1,0,1) = 0$

$(1,0,0,0): 0.25P(1,0,0,1) + 2P(2,0,0,0) + 0.75P(1,1,0,0) + 0.5P(1,0,1,0) + P(0,0,0,0)$
$\qquad - 3P(1,0,0,0) = 0$

$(1, 0, 0, 1) : 2P(2, 0, 0, 1) + 0.5P(1, 0, 0, 2) + P(0, 0, 0, 1) + 0.375P(1, 0, 1, 1)$
$\qquad - 3.25P(1, 0, 0, 1) = 0$

$(1, 0, 0, 2) : P(0, 0, 0, 2) + P(1, 0, 0, 1) + 0.5625P(1, 0, 0, 3) + 2P(2, 0, 0, 2) - 3.5P(1, 0, 0, 2) = 0$

$(1, 0, 0, 3) : P(0, 0, 0, 3) + P(1, 0, 0, 2) - 1.5625P(1, 0, 0, 3) = 0$

$(1, 0, 1, 0) : P(0, 0, 1, 0) + 0.1875P(1, 0, 1, 1) + 2P(2, 0, 1, 0) + P(1, 0, 0, 0) - 3.5P(1, 0, 1, 0) = 0$

$(1, 0, 1, 1) : P(0, 0, 1, 1) + P(1, 0, 1, 0) - 1.5625P(1, 0, 1, 1) = 0$

$(1, 1, 0, 0) : P(0, 1, 0, 0) - 1.75P(1, 1, 0, 0) = 0$

$(2, 0, 0, 0) : P(1, 0, 0, 0) + 0.375P(2, 0, 1, 0) + 3P(3, 0, 0, 0) + 0.25P(2, 0, 0, 1) - 4P(2, 0, 0, 0) = 0$

$(2, 0, 0, 1) : P(1, 0, 0, 1) + 0.375P(2, 0, 0, 2) + 3P(3, 0, 0, 1) + P(2, 0, 0, 0) - 4.25P(2, 0, 0, 1) = 0$

$(2, 0, 0, 2) : P(1, 0, 0, 2) + P(2, 0, 0, 1) - 2.375P(2, 0, 0, 2) = 0$

$(2, 0, 1, 0) : P(1, 0, 1, 0) - 2.375P(2, 0, 1, 0) = 0$

$(3, 0, 0, 0) : P(2, 0, 0, 0) + 0.1875P(3, 0, 0, 1) + 4P(4, 0, 0, 0) - 5P(3, 0, 0, 0) = 0$

$(3, 0, 0, 1) : P(2, 0, 0, 1) + P(3, 0, 0, 0) - 3.1875P(3, 0, 0, 1) = 0$

$(4, 0, 0, 0) : P(3, 0, 0, 0) - 4P(4, 0, 0, 0) = 0$

The solution of this linear system is:

$P(0, 0, 0, 0) = 0.028101$	$P(0, 0, 0, 1) = 0.052409$	$P(0, 0, 0, 2) = 0.075082$
$P(0, 0, 0, 3) = 0.113519$	$P(0, 0, 0, 4) = 0.151358$	$P(0, 0, 1, 0) = 0.011154$
$P(0, 0, 1, 1) = 0.045994$	$P(0, 0, 1, 2) = 0.061325$	$P(0, 1, 0, 0) = 0.012609$
$P(0, 1, 0, 1) = 0.01345$	$P(1, 0, 0, 0) = 0.024913$	$P(1, 0, 0, 1) = 0.047295$
$P(1, 0, 0, 2) = 0.079569$	$P(1, 0, 0, 3) = 0.123576$	$P(1, 0, 1, 0) = 0.016386$
$P(1, 0, 1, 1) = 0.039923$	$P(1, 1, 0, 0) = 0.007205$	$P(2, 0, 0, 0) = 0.010609$
$P(2, 0, 0, 1) = 0.023272$	$P(2, 0, 0, 2) = 0.043301$	$P(2, 0, 1, 0) = 0.006899$
$P(3, 0, 0, 0) = 0.003039$	$P(3, 0, 0, 1) = 0.008254$	$P(4, 0, 0, 0) = 0.00076$

Based on the values of $P(n_1, n_2, n_{2r_1}, n_{2r_2})$, we determine the values of $Q(j)$:

$Q(0) = P(0, 0, 0, 0) = 0.028101$

$Q(1) = P(0, 0, 0, 1) + P(1, 0, 0, 0) = 0.077322$

$Q(2) = P(0, 0, 0, 2) + P(0, 0, 1, 0) + P(1, 0, 0, 1) + P(2, 0, 0, 0) = 0.14414$

$Q(3) = P(0, 0, 0, 3) + P(0, 0, 1, 1) + P(0, 1, 0, 0) + P(1, 0, 0, 2) + P(1, 0, 1, 0) + P(2, 0, 0, 1)$
$\qquad + P(3, 0, 0, 0) = 0.294388$

$Q(4) = P(0, 0, 0, 4) + P(0, 0, 1, 2) + P(0, 1, 0, 1) + P(1, 0, 0, 3) + P(1, 0, 1, 1) + P(1, 1, 0, 0)$
$\qquad + P(2, 0, 0, 2) + P(2, 0, 1, 0) + P(3, 0, 0, 1) + P(4, 0, 0, 0) = 0.456051$

(c) Based on the values of $Q(j)$, we obtain the exact CBP:

$$B_1 = \sum_{T-b_1+1}^{T} Q(j) = Q(4) = 0.456051 \text{ (compare with 0.470996 in the E-MRM)}$$

The *Prob*{1st retry} of service-class 2 calls, B_2, when they require $b_2 = 3$ b.u. upon arrival, is given by:

$$B_2 = \sum_{C-b_2+1}^{T} Q(j) = Q(1) + Q(2) + Q(3) + Q(4) = 0.9719$$

(compare with 0.971428 in the E-MRM)

The $Prob\{$2nd retry$\}$ of service-class 2 calls, B_{2r_1}, when they require $b_{2r_1} = 2$ b.u. upon arrival, is given by:

$$B_{2r_1} = \sum_{C-b_{2r_1}+1}^{T} Q(j) = Q(2) + Q(3) + Q(4) = 0.894579 \text{ (compare with 0.893645 in the E-MRM)}$$

The CBP of service-class 2, B_{2r_2}, refers to service-class 2 retry calls which require $b_{2r_2} = 1$ b.u. and is given by:

$$B_{2r_2} = \sum_{T-b_{2r_2}+1}^{T} Q(j) = Q(4) = 0.456051 \text{ (compare with 0.470996 in the E-MRM)}$$

The link utilization is determined by:

$$U = \sum_{j=1}^{C} jQ(j) + \sum_{j=C+1}^{T} CQ(j) = 2.617 \text{ b.u. (compare with 2.616 in the E-MRM)}$$

(d) $B^*_{2r_2} = Prob\{j > T - b_{2r_2}|j > C - b_2\} = \dfrac{B_{2r_2}}{B_2} = 0.46924$ (compare with 0.48485 in the E-MRM)

To facilitate the recursive calculation of $q(j)$, we replace $r(\mathbf{n})$ by the state-dependent compression factors per service-class k, $\varphi_k(\mathbf{n})$ and $\varphi_{kr_s}(\mathbf{n})$, $s = 1, \ldots, S(k)$ whose values are given by (3.8) and (4.33), respectively. Due to the existence of adaptive traffic, the values of $x(\mathbf{n})$ are given by the following formula:

$$x(\mathbf{n}) = \begin{cases} 1 & \text{when } \mathbf{nb} \leq C \text{ and } \mathbf{n} \in \Omega \\ \dfrac{1}{C} \sum_{k \in K_e} n_k b_k x(\mathbf{n}_k^-) + \dfrac{1}{C} \sum_{k \in K_e} \sum_{s=1}^{S(k)} n_{kr_s} b_{kr_s} x(\mathbf{n}_{kr_s}^-) + \\ \dfrac{r(\mathbf{n})}{C} \left(\sum_{k \in K_a} n_k b_k x(\mathbf{n}_k^-) + \sum_{k \in K_a} \sum_{s=1}^{S(k)} n_{kr_s} b_{kr_s} x(\mathbf{n}_{kr_s}^-) \right) \\ \qquad \text{when } C < \mathbf{nb} \leq T \text{ and } \mathbf{n} \in \Omega \\ 0 & \text{otherwise} \end{cases} \qquad (4.61)$$

where $\mathbf{n} = (n_1, n_{1r_1}, \ldots, n_{1r_s}, \ldots, n_{1r_{S(1)}}, \ldots, n_k, n_{kr_1}, \ldots, n_{kr_s}, \ldots, n_{kr_{S(k)}}, \ldots, n_K, n_{Kr_1}, \ldots, n_{Kr_s}, \ldots, n_{Kr_{S(K)}})$, $\mathbf{n}_k^- = (n_1, n_{1r_1}, \ldots, n_{1r_s}, \ldots, n_{1r_{S(1)}}, \ldots, n_k - 1, n_{kr_1}, \ldots, n_{kr_s}, \ldots, n_{kr_{S(k)}}, \ldots, n_K, n_{Kr_1}, \ldots, n_{Kr_s}, \ldots, n_{Kr_{S(K)}})$ and $\mathbf{n}_{kr_s}^- = (n_1, n_{1r_1}, \ldots, n_{1r_s}, \ldots, n_{1r_{S(1)}}, \ldots, n_k, n_{kr_1}, \ldots, n_{kr_s} - 1, \ldots, n_{kr_{S(k)}}, \ldots, n_K, n_{Kr_1}, \ldots, n_{Kr_s}, \ldots, n_{Kr_{S(K)}})$.

Example 4.19 Consider again Example 4.18 ($C = 3, T = 4, K = 2, b_1 = 1, b_2 = 3, b_{2r_1} = 2, b_{2r_2} = 1, \lambda_1 = \lambda_2 = 1, \mu_1^{-1} = \mu_2^{-1} = 1, \mu_{2r_1}^{-1} = 2.0, \mu_{2r_2}^{-1} = 4.0$, service-class 1 is adaptive):

1. Determine the values of $\varphi_k(\mathbf{n})$ and $\varphi_{kr_s}(\mathbf{n})$ for each state $\mathbf{n} = (n_1, n_2, n_{2r_1}, n_{2r_2})$.
2. Calculate the state probabilities $P(n_1, n_2, n_{2r_1}, n_{2r_2})$ based on the GB equations. Then determine the values of the link occupancy distribution $Q(j)$ (for $j = 0, \ldots, T$).
3. Calculate the CBP of both service-classes, including the retry probabilities and the link utilization.

Table 4.8 The values of the state-dependent compression factors $\varphi_k(\mathbf{n})$ and $\varphi_{kr_s}(\mathbf{n})$ (Example 4.19).

n_1	n_2	n_{2r_1}	n_{2r_2}	$x(\mathbf{n})$	$\varphi_1(\mathbf{n})$	$\varphi_2(\mathbf{n})$	$\varphi_{2r_1}(\mathbf{n})$	$\varphi_{2r_2}(\mathbf{n})$
0	0	0	0	1.00	1.00	1.00	1.00	1.00
0	0	0	1	1.00	1.00	1.00	1.00	1.00
0	0	0	2	1.00	1.00	1.00	1.00	1.00
0	0	0	3	1.00	1.00	1.00	1.00	1.00
0	0	0	4	1.33333	0.00	0.00	0.00	0.75
0	0	1	0	1.00	1.00	1.00	1.00	1.00
0	0	1	1	1.00	1.00	1.00	1.00	1.00
0	0	1	2	1.33333	0.00	0.00	0.75	0.75
0	1	0	0	1.00	1.00	1.00	1.00	1.00
0	1	0	1	1.33333	0.00	0.75	0.00	0.75
1	0	0	0	1.00	1.00	1.00	1.00	1.00
1	0	0	1	1.00	1.00	1.00	1.00	1.00
1	0	0	2	1.00	1.00	1.00	1.00	1.00
1	0	0	3	1.25	0.80	0.00	0.00	0.80
1	0	1	0	1.00	1.00	1.00	1.00	1.00
1	0	1	1	1.25	0.80	0.00	0.80	0.80
1	1	0	0	1.25	0.80	0.80	0.00	0.00
2	0	0	0	1.00	1.00	1.00	1.00	1.00
2	0	0	1	1.00	1.00	1.00	1.00	1.00
2	0	0	2	1.16667	0.8571	0.00	0.00	0.8571
2	0	1	0	1.16667	0.8571	0.00	0.8571	0.00
3	0	0	0	1.00	1.00	1.00	1.00	1.00
3	0	0	1	1.08333	0.9231	0.00	0.00	0.9231
4	0	0	0	1.00	1.00	0.00	0.00	0.00

4. Calculate the conditional CBP of service-class 2 retry calls with b_{2r_2}, given that they have been blocked with their initial bandwidth requirement, b_2.

(a) Table 4.8 presents the 24 states together with the corresponding values of $\varphi_k(\mathbf{n})$ and $\varphi_{kr_s}(\mathbf{n})$, which are calculated through the $x(\mathbf{n})$.

(b) In what follows, we present the 24 GB equations:

$(0,0,0,0):$ $0.5P(0,0,1,0) + 0.25P(0,0,0,1) + P(0,1,0,0) + P(1,0,0,0) - 2P(0,0,0,0) = 0$

$(0,0,0,1):$ $0.5P(0,0,0,2) + 0.75P(0,1,0,1) + 0.5P(0,0,1,1) + P(1,0,0,1)$
$- 2.25P(0,0,0,1) = 0$

$(0,0,0,2):$ $P(1,0,0,2) + 0.75P(0,0,0,3) + 0.375P(0,0,1,2) - 2.5P(0,0,0,2) = 0$

$(0,0,0,3):$ $P(0,0,0,2) + 0.75P(0,0,0,4) + 0.8P(1,0,0,3) - 2.75P(0,0,0,3) = 0$

$(0,0,0,4):$ $P(0,0,0,3) - 0.75P(0,0,0,4) = 0$

$(0, 0, 1, 0) : 0.25P(0, 0, 1, 1) + P(1, 0, 1, 0) - 2.5P(0, 0, 1, 0) = 0$

$(0, 0, 1, 1) : P(0, 0, 0, 1) + P(0, 0, 1, 0) + 0.8P(1, 0, 1, 1) + 0.375P(0, 0, 1, 2) - 2.75P(0, 0, 1, 1) = 0$

$(0, 0, 1, 2) : P(0, 0, 1, 1) - 0.75P(0, 0, 1, 2) = 0$

$(0, 1, 0, 0) : P(0, 0, 0, 0) + 0.1875P(0, 1, 0, 1) + 0.8P(1, 1, 0, 0) - 3P(0, 1, 0, 0) = 0$

$(0, 1, 0, 1) : P(0, 1, 0, 0) - 0.9375P(0, 1, 0, 1) = 0$

$(1, 0, 0, 0) : 0.25P(1, 0, 0, 1) + 2P(2, 0, 0, 0) + 0.8P(1, 1, 0, 0) + 0.5P(1, 0, 1, 0) + P(0, 0, 0, 0)$
$\qquad\qquad - 3P(1, 0, 0, 0) = 0$

$(1, 0, 0, 1) : 2P(2, 0, 0, 1) + 0.5P(1, 0, 0, 2) + P(0, 0, 0, 1) + 0.4P(1, 0, 1, 1) - 3.25P(1, 0, 0, 1) = 0$

$(1, 0, 0, 2) : P(0, 0, 0, 2) + P(1, 0, 0, 1) + 0.6P(1, 0, 0, 3) + (12/7)P(2, 0, 0, 2) - 3.5P(1, 0, 0, 2) = 0$

$(1, 0, 0, 3) : P(0, 0, 0, 3) + P(1, 0, 0, 2) - 1.4P(1, 0, 0, 3) = 0$

$(1, 0, 1, 0) : P(0, 0, 1, 0) + 0.2P(1, 0, 1, 1) + (12/7)P(2, 0, 1, 0) + P(1, 0, 0, 0) - 3.5P(1, 0, 1, 0) = 0$

$(1, 0, 1, 1) : P(0, 0, 1, 1) + P(1, 0, 1, 0) - 1.4P(1, 0, 1, 1) = 0$

$(1, 1, 0, 0) : P(0, 1, 0, 0) - 1.6P(1, 1, 0, 0) = 0$

$(2, 0, 0, 0) : P(1, 0, 0, 0) + (3/7)P(2, 0, 1, 0) + 3P(3, 0, 0, 0) + 0.25P(2, 0, 0, 1) - 4P(2, 0, 0, 0) = 0$

$(2, 0, 0, 1) : P(1, 0, 0, 1) + (3/7)P(2, 0, 0, 2) + (36/13)P(3, 0, 0, 1) + P(2, 0, 0, 0)$
$\qquad\qquad - 4.25P(2, 0, 0, 1) = 0$

$(2, 0, 0, 2) : P(1, 0, 0, 2) + P(2, 0, 0, 1) - (15/7)P(2, 0, 0, 2) = 0$

$(2, 0, 1, 0) : P(1, 0, 1, 0) - (15/7)P(2, 0, 1, 0) = 0$

$(3, 0, 0, 0) : P(2, 0, 0, 0) + (3/13)P(3, 0, 0, 1) + 4P(4, 0, 0, 0) - 5P(3, 0, 0, 0) = 0$

$(3, 0, 0, 1) : P(2, 0, 0, 1) + P(3, 0, 0, 0) - 3P(3, 0, 0, 1) = 0$

$(4, 0, 0, 0) : P(3, 0, 0, 0) - 4P(4, 0, 0, 0) = 0$

The solution of this linear system is:

$P(0, 0, 0, 0) = 0.029236$	$P(0, 0, 0, 1) = 0.052687$	$P(0, 0, 0, 2) = 0.07189$
$P(0, 0, 0, 3) = 0.100794$	$P(0, 0, 0, 4) = 0.134391$	$P(0, 0, 1, 0) = 0.011384$
$P(0, 0, 1, 1) = 0.044105$	$P(0, 0, 1, 2) = 0.058806$	$P(0, 1, 0, 0) = 0.012711$
$P(0, 1, 0, 1) = 0.013559$	$P(1, 0, 0, 0) = 0.026896$	$P(1, 0, 0, 1) = 0.050379$
$P(1, 0, 0, 2) = 0.082078$	$P(1, 0, 0, 3) = 0.130623$	$P(1, 0, 1, 0) = 0.017434$
$P(1, 0, 1, 1) = 0.043956$	$P(1, 1, 0, 0) = 0.007944$	$P(2, 0, 0, 0) = 0.011893$
$P(2, 0, 0, 1) = 0.026211$	$P(2, 0, 0, 2) = 0.050535$	$P(2, 0, 1, 0) = 0.008136$
$P(3, 0, 0, 0) = 0.003546$	$P(3, 0, 0, 1) = 0.009919$	$P(4, 0, 0, 0) = 0.000886$

Based on the values of $P(n_1, n_2, n_{2r_1}, n_{2r_2})$, we determine the values of $Q(j)$:

$Q(0) = P(0, 0, 0, 0) = 0.029236$

$Q(1) = P(0, 0, 0, 1) + P(1, 0, 0, 0) = 0.079583$

$Q(2) = P(0, 0, 0, 2) + P(0, 0, 1, 0) + P(1, 0, 0, 1) + P(2, 0, 0, 0) = 0.145546$

$Q(3) = P(0, 0, 0, 3) + P(0, 0, 1, 1) + P(0, 1, 0, 0) + P(1, 0, 0, 2) + P(1, 0, 1, 0) + P(2, 0, 0, 1)$
$\qquad + P(3, 0, 0, 0) = 0.286879$

$Q(4) = P(0, 0, 0, 4) + P(0, 0, 1, 2) + P(0, 1, 0, 1) + P(1, 0, 0, 3) + P(1, 0, 1, 1) + P(1, 1, 0, 0)$
$\qquad + P(2, 0, 0, 2) + P(2, 0, 1, 0) + P(3, 0, 0, 1) + P(4, 0, 0, 0) = 0.458755$

(c) Based on the values of $Q(j)$, we obtain the approximate CBP:

$$B_1 = \sum_{T-b_1+1}^{T} Q(j) = Q(4) = 0.458755 \text{ (compare with the exact 0.456051)}$$

$$B_2 = \sum_{C-b_2+1}^{T} Q(j) = Q(1) + Q(2) + Q(3) + Q(4) = 0.9708 \text{ (compare with the exact 0.9719)}$$

$$B_{2r_1} = \sum_{C-b_{2r_1}+1}^{T} Q(j) = Q(2) + Q(3) + Q(4) = 0.89118 \text{ (compare with the exact 0.894579)}$$

$$B_{2r_2} = \sum_{T-b_{2r_2}+1}^{T} Q(j) = Q(4) = 0.458755 \text{ (compare with the exact 0.456051)}$$

The link utilization is determined by:

$$U = \sum_{j=1}^{C} jQ(j) + \sum_{j=C+1}^{T} CQ(j) = 2.607 \text{ b.u. (compare with the exact 2.617)}$$

(d) $B_{2r_2}^* = Prob\{j > C - b_{2r_2} | j > C - b_2\} = \dfrac{B_{2r_2}}{B_2} = 0.47255$ (compare with the exact 0.46924)

4.7.2 The Analytical Model

4.7.2.1 Steady State Probabilities
Following the analysis of Section 4.5.2.1, the calculation of the unnormalized values of $q(j)$ is based on an approximate but recursive formula whose proof is similar to that of (4.57) [5]:

$$q(j) = \begin{cases} 1 & \text{if } j = 0 \\ \dfrac{1}{\min(j,C)} \left[\displaystyle\sum_{k \in K_e} \alpha_k b_k \gamma_k(j)q(j-b_k) + \sum_{k \in K_e} \sum_{s=1}^{S(k)} \alpha_{kr_s} b_{kr_s} \gamma_{kr_s}(j)q(j-b_{kr_s}) \right] + \\ \dfrac{1}{j} \left[\displaystyle\sum_{k \in K_a} \alpha_k b_k \gamma_k(j)q(j-b_k) + \sum_{k \in K_a} \sum_{s=1}^{S(k)} \alpha_{kr_s} b_{kr_s} \gamma_{kr_s}(j)q(j-b_{kr_s}) \right] & \text{if } j = 1, ..., T \\ 0 & \text{otherwise} \end{cases}$$

(4.62)

where $\alpha_{kr_s} = \lambda_k \mu_{kr_s}^{-1}$, $\quad \gamma_k(j) = \begin{cases} 1 & \text{if } 1 \le j \le C \text{ and } b_{kr_s} > 0 \\ 1 & \text{if } 1 \le j \le T \text{ and } b_{kr_s} = 0, \text{ and} \\ 0 & \text{otherwise} \end{cases}$

$$\gamma_{kr_s}(j) = \begin{cases} 1 & \text{if } C - b_{kr_{s-1}} + b_{kr_s} < j \le C \text{ and } s \ne S(k) \\ 1 & \text{if } C - b_{kr_{s-1}} + b_{kr_s} < j \le T \text{ and } s = S(k) \\ 0 & \text{otherwise} \end{cases} .$$

4.7.2.2 CBP, Utilization, and Mean Number of In-service Calls

Having determined the unnormalized values of $q(j)$ via (4.62) we can calculate [5]:

- The final CBP of service-class k calls with their last bandwidth requirement $b_{kr_{S(k)}}$ b.u., $B_{kr_{S(k)}}$, via (4.36).
- The CBP of service-class k calls with b_k b.u., B_k, via (4.23).
- The conditional CBP of service-class k retry calls with $b_{kr_{S(k)}}$ given that they have been blocked with their initial bandwidth requirement b_k, $B^*_{kr_{S(k)}}$, via (4.37).
- The link utilization, U, by (3.23).
- The mean number of elastic service-class k calls with b_k b.u. in state j, $y_k(j)$, via (4.25).
- The mean number of elastic service-class k calls with b_{kr_s} b.u. in state j, $y_{kr_s}(j)$, via (4.38).
- The mean number of adaptive service-class k calls with b_k b.u. in state j, $y_k(j)$, via (4.58).
- The mean number of adaptive service-class k calls with b_{kr_s} b.u. in state j, $y_{kr_s}(j)$:

$$y_{kr_s}(j) = \frac{C}{j} \cdot \frac{\alpha_{kr_s} \gamma_{kr_s}(j) q(j - b_{kr_s})}{q(j)}, \qquad q(j) > 0 \tag{4.63}$$

- The mean number of in-service calls of service-class k accepted with b_k, $\bar{n}_k$, via (4.27).
- The mean number of in-service calls of service-class k accepted with b_{kr_s}, $\bar{n}_{kr_s}$, via (4.39).

Example 4.20 Consider again Example 4.18 ($C = 3, T = 4, K = 2, b_1 = 1, b_2 = 3$, $b_{2r_1} = 2, b_{2r_2} = 1, \lambda_1 = \lambda_2 = 1, \mu_1^{-1} = \mu_2^{-1} = 1, \mu_{2r_1}^{-1} = 2.0, \mu_{2r_2}^{-1} = 4.0$, service-class 1 is adaptive):

(a) Calculate the values of $Q(j)$ based on (4.62).
(b) Calculate the CBP of both service-classes, including the retry probabilities and the conditional $B^*_{2r_2}$.

(a) State probabilities through the recursion (4.62):

$j = 1$:	$q(1) = q(0) + 0 = 1.0$	$\Rightarrow q(1) = 1.0$
$j = 2$:	$2q(2) = q(1) + 0 = 1.0$	$\Rightarrow q(2) = 0.5$
$j = 3$:	$q(3) = q(2) + 3q(0) + 4q(1) + 4q(2) = 9.5$	$\Rightarrow q(3) = 3.16667$
$j = 4$:	$q(4) = \frac{1}{4}q(3) + 0 + 0 + \frac{1}{3}4q(3) = 15.83335$	$\Rightarrow q(4) = 5.01388$

The normalization constant is:

$$G = \sum_{j=0}^{T} q(j) = 10.68055.$$

The state probabilities are:

$$Q(0) = Q(1) = 0.093628 \qquad Q(2) = 0.046814 \qquad Q(3) = 0.296489 \qquad Q(4) = 0.46944$$

(b) The CBP are as follows:

$$B_1 = \sum_{j=T-b_1+1}^{T} Q(j) = Q(4) = 0.46944 \text{ (compare with the exact 0.456051)}$$

$$B_2 = \sum_{j=C-b_2+1}^{T} Q(j) = Q(1) + Q(2) + Q(3) + Q(4) = 0.90637 \text{ (compare with the exact 0.9719)}$$

$$B_{2r_1} = \sum_{j=C-b_{2r_1}+1}^{T} Q(j) = Q(2) + Q(3) + Q(4) = 0.812743 \text{ (compare with the exact 0.894579)}$$

$$B_{2r_2} = \sum_{j=T-b_{2r_2}+1}^{T} Q(j) = Q(4) = 0.46944 \text{ (compare with the exact 0.456051)}$$

$$B_{2r_2}^* = \frac{B_{2r_2}}{B_2} = 0.51793 \text{ (compare with the exact 0.46924)}$$

It is apparent that even in small EA-MRM examples the error introduced by the assumption of LB, the introduction of $\varphi_k(\mathbf{n})$ and $\varphi_{kr_s}(\mathbf{n})$, and the migration approximation is not significant.

4.8 The Elastic Adaptive Multi-Retry Model under the BR Policy

4.8.1 The Service System

Compared to the EA-SRM/BR, in the *elastic adaptive multi-retry model under the BR policy (EA-MRM/BR)* with BR parameter t_k for service-class k calls ($k = 1, \ldots, K$), blocked calls of service-class k can retry more than once to be connected in the system.

Example 4.21 Consider again Example 4.18 ($C = 3, T = 4, K = 2, b_1 = 1, b_2 = 3,$ $b_{2r_1} = 2, b_{2r_2} = 1, \lambda_1 = \lambda_2 = 1, \mu_1^{-1} = \mu_2^{-1} = 1, \mu_{2r_1}^{-1} = 2.0, \mu_{2r_2}^{-1} = 4.0,$ service-class 1 is adaptive) and let the BR parameters $t_1 = 2$ and $t_2 = 0$ so that $b_1 + t_1 = b_2 + t_2$ and $B_1 = B_2$.

(a) Find the total number of permissible states $\mathbf{n} = (n_1, n_2, n_{2r_1}, n_{2r_2})$ and determine the values of j and $r(\mathbf{n})$ for each state $\mathbf{n} = (n_1, n_2, n_{2r_1}, n_{2r_2})$.
(b) Calculate the state probabilities $P(n_1, n_2, n_{2r_1}, n_{2r_2})$ based on the GB equations. Then determine the values of the link occupancy distribution $Q(j)$ (for $j = 0, \ldots, T$).
(c) Calculate the CBP of both service-classes, including the retry probabilities and the link utilization, as well as the conditional CBP of service-class 2 retry calls with b_{2r_2}, given that they have been blocked with their initial bandwidth requirement, b_2.

(a) There are 19 permissible states, $\mathbf{n} = (n_1, n_2, n_{2r_1}, n_{2r_2})$. The values of $r(\mathbf{n})$ and $j = n_1 b_1 + n_2 b_2 + n_{2r_1} b_{2r_1} + n_{2r_2} b_{2r_2}$ are the same as those presented in Table 4.5.
(b) In what follows, we present the 19 GB equations:

$(0, 0, 0, 0) : 0.5P(0, 0, 1, 0) + 0.25P(0, 0, 0, 1) + P(0, 1, 0, 0) + P(1, 0, 0, 0) - 2P(0, 0, 0, 0) = 0$

$(0, 0, 0, 1) : 0.5P(0, 0, 0, 2) + 0.75P(0, 1, 0, 1) + 0.5P(0, 0, 1, 1) + P(1, 0, 0, 1) - 2.25P(0, 0, 0, 1) = 0$

$(0, 0, 0, 2) : P(1, 0, 0, 2) + 0.75P(0, 0, 0, 3) + 0.375P(0, 0, 1, 2) - 1.5P(0, 0, 0, 2) = 0$

$(0, 0, 0, 3) : P(0, 0, 0, 2) + 0.75P(0, 0, 0, 4) + P(1, 0, 0, 3) - 1.75P(0, 0, 0, 3) = 0$

$(0, 0, 0, 4) : P(0, 0, 0, 3) - 0.75P(0, 0, 0, 4) = 0$

$(0, 0, 1, 0) : 0.25P(0, 0, 1, 1) + P(1, 0, 1, 0) - 1.5P(0, 0, 1, 0) = 0$

$(0, 0, 1, 1) : P(0, 0, 0, 1) + P(0, 0, 1, 0) + P(1, 0, 1, 1) + 0.375P(0, 0, 1, 2) - 1.75P(0, 0, 1, 1) = 0$

$(0, 0, 1, 2) : P(0, 0, 1, 1) - 0.75P(0, 0, 1, 2) = 0$

$(0, 1, 0, 0) : P(0, 0, 0, 0) + 0.1875P(0, 1, 0, 1) - 2P(0, 1, 0, 0) = 0$

$(0, 1, 0, 1) : P(0, 1, 0, 0) - 0.9375P(0, 1, 0, 1) = 0$

$(1, 0, 0, 0) : 0.25P(1, 0, 0, 1) + 2P(2, 0, 0, 0) + 0.5P(1, 0, 1, 0) + P(0, 0, 0, 0) - 3P(1, 0, 0, 0) = 0$

$(1, 0, 0, 1) : 2P(2, 0, 0, 1) + 0.5P(1, 0, 0, 2) + P(0, 0, 0, 1) + 0.375P(1, 0, 1, 1) - 2.25P(1, 0, 0, 1) = 0$

$(1, 0, 0, 2) : P(1, 0, 0, 1) + 0.5625P(1, 0, 0, 3) + 2P(2, 0, 0, 2) - 2.5P(1, 0, 0, 2) = 0$

$(1, 0, 0, 3) : P(1, 0, 0, 2) - 1.5625P(1, 0, 0, 3) = 0$

$(1, 0, 1, 0) : 0.1875P(1, 0, 1, 1) + P(1, 0, 0, 0) - 2.5P(1, 0, 1, 0) = 0$

$(1, 0, 1, 1) : P(1, 0, 1, 0) - 1.5625P(1, 0, 1, 1) = 0$

$(2, 0, 0, 0) : P(1, 0, 0, 0) + 0.25P(2, 0, 0, 1) - 3P(2, 0, 0, 0) = 0$

$(2, 0, 0, 1) : 0.375P(2, 0, 0, 2) + P(2, 0, 0, 0) - 3.25P(2, 0, 0, 1) = 0$

$(2, 0, 0, 2) : P(2, 0, 0, 1) - 2.375P(2, 0, 0, 2) = 0$

The solution of this linear system is:

$P(0, 0, 0, 0) = 0.030812$	$P(0, 0, 0, 1) = 0.067436$	$P(0, 0, 0, 2) = 0.130824$
$P(0, 0, 0, 3) = 0.189768$	$P(0, 0, 0, 4) = 0.253024$	$P(0, 0, 1, 0) = 0.017301$
$P(0, 0, 1, 1) = 0.071876$	$P(0, 0, 1, 2) = 0.095835$	$P(0, 1, 0, 0) = 0.017118$
$P(0, 1, 0, 1) = 0.018259$	$P(1, 0, 0, 0) = 0.018997$	$P(1, 0, 0, 1) = 0.036688$
$P(1, 0, 0, 2) = 0.017972$	$P(1, 0, 0, 3) = 0.011502$	$P(1, 0, 1, 0) = 0.007982$
$P(1, 0, 1, 1) = 0.005108$	$P(2, 0, 0, 0) = 0.006508$	$P(2, 0, 0, 1) = 0.002105$
$P(2, 0, 0, 2) = 0.000886$		

Based on the values of $P(n_1, n_2, n_{2r_1}, n_{2r_2})$, we determine the values of $Q(j)$:

$Q(0) = P(0, 0, 0, 0) = 0.030812$

$Q(1) = P(0, 0, 0, 1) + P(1, 0, 0, 0) = 0.086433$

$Q(2) = P(0, 0, 0, 2) + P(0, 0, 1, 0) + P(1, 0, 0, 1) + P(2, 0, 0, 0) = 0.191321$

$Q(3) = P(0, 0, 0, 3) + P(0, 0, 1, 1) + P(0, 1, 0, 0) + P(1, 0, 0, 2) + P(1, 0, 1, 0) + P(2, 0, 0, 1)$
$\qquad = 0.306821$

$Q(4) = P(0, 0, 0, 4) + P(0, 0, 1, 2) + P(0, 1, 0, 1) + P(1, 0, 0, 3) + P(1, 0, 1, 1) + P(2, 0, 0, 2)$
$\qquad = 0.384614$

(c) Based on the values of $Q(j)$, we obtain the exact CBP:

$$B_1 = \sum_{T-b_1-t_1+1}^{T} Q(j) = Q(2) + Q(3) + Q(4) = 0.882756$$

(compare with the exact 0.882627 in the E-MRM/BR)

The *Prob*{1st retry} of service-class 2 calls, B_2, when they require $b_2 = 3$ b.u. upon arrival, is given by:

$$B_2 = \sum_{j=C-b_2+1}^{T} Qj = Q(1) + Q(2) + Q(3) + Q(4) = 0.9692$$

The *Prob*{2nd retry} of service-class 2 calls, B_{2r_1}, when they require $b_{2r_1} = 2$ b.u. upon arrival, is given by:

$$B_{2r_1} = \sum_{C-b_{2r_1}+1}^{T} Q(j) = Q(2) + Q(3) + Q(4) = 0.8828$$

(compare with the exact 0.882627 in the E-MRM/BR)

The CBP of service-class 2, B_{2r_2}, refers to service-class 2 retry calls which require $b_{2r_2} = 1$ b.u. and is given by:

$$B_{2r_2} = \sum_{T-b_{2r_2}+1}^{T} Q(j) = Q(4) = 0.384614 \text{ (compare with the exact 0.385833 in the E-MRM/BR)}$$

The link utilization is determined by:

$$U = \sum_{j=1}^{C} jQ(j) + \sum_{j=C+1}^{T} CQ(j) = 2.543 \text{ b.u. (the same as the E-MRM/BR).}$$

$$B_{2r_2}^{*} = Prob\{j > T - b_{2r_2} \mid j > C - b_2\} = \frac{B_{2r_2}}{B_2} = 0.39684$$

(compare with the exact 0.39813 in the E-MRM/BR)

To facilitate the recursive calculation of $q(j)$ in the EA-MRM/BR, we replace $r(\mathbf{n})$ by the state-dependent compression factors per service-class k, $\varphi_k(\mathbf{n})$ and $\varphi_{kr_s}(\mathbf{n})$, $s = 1, \ldots, S(k)$. The values of $\varphi_k(\mathbf{n})$ and $\varphi_{kr_s}(\mathbf{n})$ are given by (3.8) and (4.33), respectively.

Example 4.22 Consider again Example 4.21 ($C = 3, T = 4, K = 2, b_1 = 1, b_2 = 3$, $b_{2r_1} = 2, b_{2r_2} = 1, t_1 = 2, t_2 = 0, \lambda_1 = \lambda_2 = 1, \mu_1^{-1} = \mu_2^{-1} = 1, \mu_{2r_1}^{-1} = 2.0, \mu_{2r_2}^{-1} = 4.0$, calls of service-class 1 are adaptive):

(a) Determine the values of $\varphi_k(\mathbf{n})$ and $\varphi_{kr_s}(\mathbf{n})$ for each state $\mathbf{n} = (n_1, n_2, n_{2r_1}, n_{2r_2})$.
(b) Calculate the state probabilities $P(n_1, n_2, n_{2r_1}, n_{2r_2})$ based on the GB equations. Then determine the values of the link occupancy distribution $Q(j)$ (for $j = 0, \ldots, T$).
(c) Calculate the CBP of both service-classes, including the retry probabilities and the link utilization, as well as the conditional CBP of service-class 2 retry calls with b_{2r_2}, given that they have been blocked with their initial bandwidth requirement, b_2.

(a) Table 4.9 presents the 19 states together with the corresponding values of $\varphi_k(\mathbf{n})$ and $\varphi_{kr_s}(\mathbf{n})$, which are calculated through the $x(\mathbf{n})$.
(b) In what follows, we present the 19 GB equations:

$(0,0,0,0)$: $0.5P(0,0,1,0) + 0.25P(0,0,0,1) + P(0,1,0,0) + P(1,0,0,0) - 2P(0,0,0,0) = 0$

$(0,0,0,1)$: $0.5P(0,0,0,2) + 0.75P(0,1,0,1) + 0.5P(0,0,1,1) + P(1,0,0,1) - 2.25P(0,0,0,1) = 0$

Table 4.9 The values of the state-dependent compression factors $\varphi_k(\mathbf{n})$ and $\varphi_{kr_s}(\mathbf{n})$ (Example 4.21).

n_1	n_2	n_{2r_1}	n_{2r_2}	$x(\mathbf{n})$	$\varphi_1(\mathbf{n})$	$\varphi_2(\mathbf{n})$	$\varphi_{2r_1}(\mathbf{n})$	$\varphi_{2r_2}(\mathbf{n})$
0	0	0	0	1.00	1.00	1.00	1.00	1.00
0	0	0	1	1.00	1.00	1.00	1.00	1.00
0	0	0	2	1.00	1.00	1.00	1.00	1.00
0	0	0	3	1.00	1.00	1.00	1.00	1.00
0	0	0	4	1.33333	0.00	0.00	0.00	0.75
0	0	1	0	1.00	1.00	1.00	1.00	1.00
0	0	1	1	1.00	1.00	1.00	1.00	1.00
0	0	1	2	1.33333	0.00	0.00	0.75	0.75
0	1	0	0	1.00	1.00	1.00	1.00	1.00
0	1	0	1	1.33333	0.00	0.75	0.00	0.75
1	0	0	0	1.00	1.00	1.00	1.00	1.00
1	0	0	1	1.00	1.00	1.00	1.00	1.00
1	0	0	2	1.00	1.00	1.00	1.00	1.00
1	0	0	3	1.25	0.80	0.00	0.00	0.80
1	0	1	0	1.00	1.00	1.00	1.00	1.00
1	0	1	1	1.25	0.80	0.00	0.80	0.80
2	0	0	0	1.00	1.00	1.00	1.00	1.00
2	0	0	1	1.00	1.00	1.00	1.00	1.00
2	0	0	2	1.16667	0.8571	0.00	0.00	0.8571

$(0,0,0,2) : P(1,0,0,2) + 0.75P(0,0,0,3) + 0.375P(0,0,1,2) - 1.5P(0,0,0,2) = 0$

$(0,0,0,3) : P(0,0,0,2) + 0.75P(0,0,0,4) + 0.8P(1,0,0,3) - 1.75P(0,0,0,3) = 0$

$(0,0,0,4) : P(0,0,0,3) - 0.75P(0,0,0,4) = 0$

$(0,0,1,0) : 0.25P(0,0,1,1) + P(1,0,1,0) - 1.5P(0,0,1,0) = 0$

$(0,0,1,1) : P(0,0,0,1) + P(0,0,1,0) + 0.8P(1,0,1,1) + 0.375P(0,0,1,2) - 1.75P(0,0,1,1) = 0$

$(0,0,1,2) : P(0,0,1,1) - 0.75P(0,0,1,2) = 0$

$(0,1,0,0) : P(0,0,0,0) + 0.1875P(0,1,0,1) - 2P(0,1,0,0) = 0$

$(0,1,0,1) : P(0,1,0,0) - 0.9375P(0,1,0,1) = 0$

$(1,0,0,0) : 0.25P(1,0,0,1) + 2P(2,0,0,0) + 0.5P(1,0,1,0) + P(0,0,0,0) - 3P(1,0,0,0) = 0$

$(1,0,0,1) : 2P(2,0,0,1) + 0.5P(1,0,0,2) + P(0,0,0,1) + 0.4P(1,0,1,1) - 2.25P(1,0,0,1) = 0$

$(1,0,0,2) : P(1,0,0,1) + 0.6P(1,0,0,3) + (12/7)P(2,0,0,2) - 2.5P(1,0,0,2) = 0$

$(1,0,0,3) : P(1,0,0,2) - 1.4P(1,0,0,3) = 0$

$(1,0,1,0) : 0.2P(1,0,1,1) + P(1,0,0,0) - 2.5P(1,0,1,0) = 0$

$(1,0,1,1) : P(1,0,1,0) - 1.4P(1,0,1,1) = 0$

$(2,0,0,0) : P(1,0,0,0) + 0.25P(2,0,0,1) - 3P(2,0,0,0) = 0$

$(2,0,0,1) : (3/7)P(2,0,0,2) + P(2,0,0,0) - 3.25P(2,0,0,1) = 0$

$(2,0,0,2) : P(2,0,0,1) - (15/7)P(2,0,0,2) = 0$

The solution of this linear system is:

$P(0,0,0,0) = 0.03092$ $P(0,0,0,1) = 0.067502$ $P(0,0,0,2) = 0.130485$

$P(0,0,0,3) = 0.18826$ $P(0,0,0,4) = 0.251013$ $P(0,0,1,0) = 0.017337$

$P(0,0,1,1) = 0.071579$ $P(0,0,1,2) = 0.095439$ $P(0,1,0,0) = 0.017178$

$P(0,1,0,1) = 0.018323$ $P(1,0,0,0) = 0.019119$ $P(1,0,0,1) = 0.037105$

$P(1,0,0,2) = 0.018743$ $P(1,0,0,3) = 0.013388$ $P(1,0,1,0) = 0.008111$

$P(1,0,1,1) = 0.005794$ $P(2,0,0,0) = 0.006552$ $P(2,0,0,1) = 0.002148$

$P(2,0,0,2) = 0.001002$

Based on the values of $P(n_1, n_2, n_{2r_1}, n_{2r_2})$, we determine the values of $Q(j)$:

$Q(0) = P(0,0,0,0) = 0.03092$

$Q(1) = P(0,0,0,1) + P(1,0,0,0) = 0.086621$

$Q(2) = P(0,0,0,2) + P(0,0,1,0) + P(1,0,0,1) + P(2,0,0,0) = 0.191479$

$Q(3) = P(0,0,0,3) + P(0,0,1,1) + P(0,1,0,0) + P(1,0,0,2) + P(1,0,1,0) + P(2,0,0,1)$
$\quad\quad = 0.306019$

$Q(4) = P(0,0,0,4) + P(0,0,1,2) + P(0,1,0,1) + P(1,0,0,3) + P(1,0,1,1) + P(2,0,0,2)$
$\quad\quad = 0.384959$

(c) Based on the values of $Q(j)$, we obtain the exact CBP:

$$B_1 = \sum_{j=T-b_1-t_1+1}^{T} Q(j) = Q(2) + Q(3) + Q(4) = 0.882457 \text{ (compare with the exact 0.882756)}$$

$$B_2 = \sum_{j=C-b_2+1}^{T} Q(j) = Q(1) + Q(2) + Q(3) + Q(4) = 0.96908$$

(compare with the exact 0.9692)

$$B_{2r_1} = \sum_{j=C-b_{2r_1}+1}^{T} Q(j) = Q(2) + Q(3) + Q(4) = 0.882457 \text{ (compare with the exact 0.8828)}$$

$$B_{2r_2} = \sum_{j=T-b_{2r_2}+1}^{T} Q(j) = Q(4) = 0.384959 \text{ (compare with the exact 0.384614)}$$

The link utilization is determined by:

$$U = \sum_{j=1}^{C} jQ(j) + \sum_{j=C+1}^{T} CQ(j) = 2.543 \text{ b.u. (same as the exact)}$$

$$B_{2r_2}^* = \text{Prob}\{j > T - b_{2r_2} \mid j > C - b_2\} = \frac{B_{2r_2}}{B_2} = 0.39724 \text{ (compare with the exact 0.39684)}$$

4.8.2 The Analytical Model

4.8.2.1 Steady State Probabilities

Following the analysis of Section 4.6.2.1, the calculation of the unnormalized values of $q(j)$ is based on an approximate but recursive formula whose proof is similar to that of

(4.60) [3]:

$$q(j) = \begin{cases} 1 & \text{if } j = 0 \\[2mm] \dfrac{1}{\min(j,C)} \left[\displaystyle\sum_{k \in K_e} \alpha_k D_k \ (j - b_k)\gamma_k \ (j)q(j - b_k) + \right. \\[4mm] \left. \displaystyle\sum_{k \in K_e} \sum_{s=1}^{S(k)} \alpha_{kr_s} D_{kr_s} \ (j - b_{kr_s})\gamma_{kr_s} \ (j)q(j - b_{kr_s}) \right] \\[4mm] + \dfrac{1}{j} \left[\displaystyle\sum_{k \in K_a} \alpha_k D_k (j - b_k)\gamma_k(j)q(j - b_k) + \right. \\[4mm] \left. \displaystyle\sum_{k \in K_a} \sum_{s=1}^{S(k)} \alpha_{kr_s} D_{kr_s} (j - b_{kr_s})\gamma_{kr_s}(j)q(j - b_{kr_s}) \right] \\[2mm] \quad\quad \text{if } j = 1, 2, \ldots, T \\[2mm] 0 & \text{otherwise} \end{cases} \tag{4.64}$$

where $\alpha_{kr_s} = \lambda_k \mu_{kr_s}^{-1}$, $D_k(j - b_k) = \begin{cases} b_k & \text{for } j \le T - t_k \\ 0 & \text{for } j > T - t_k \end{cases}$, $D_{kr_s} \ (j - b_{kr_s})$

$= \begin{cases} b_{kr_s} & \text{for } j \le T - t_k \\ 0 & \text{for } j > T - t_k \end{cases}$, $\gamma_k \ (j) = \begin{cases} 1 \text{ if } 1 \le j \le C \text{ and } b_{kr_s} > 0 \\ 1 \text{ if } 1 \le j \le T \text{ and } b_{kr_s} = 0 \\ 0 \text{ otherwise} \end{cases}$,

$\gamma_{kr_s} \ (j) = \begin{cases} 1 \text{ if } C - b_{kr_{s-1}} + b_{kr_s} < j \le C \text{ and } s \ne S(k) \\ 1 \text{ if } C - b_{kr_{s-1}} + b_{kr_s} < j \le T \text{ and } s = S(k) \\ 0 \text{ otherwise} \end{cases}$

4.8.2.2 CBP, Utilization, and Mean Number of In-service Calls

Having determined the unnormalized values of $q(j)$ via (4.64) we can calculate:

- The final CBP of service-class k calls with their last bandwidth requirement $b_{kr_{S(k)}}$ b.u., $B_{kr_{S(k)}}$, via (4.41).
- The CBP of service-class k calls with b_k b.u., B_k, via (4.31).
- The conditional CBP of service-class k retry calls with $b_{kr_{S(k)}}$ given that they have been blocked with their initial bandwidth requirement b_k, $B^*_{kr_{S(k)}}$, via (4.42).
- The link utilization, U, by (3.23).
- The mean number of elastic service-class k calls with b_k b.u. in state j, $y_k(j)$, via (4.25).
- The mean number of elastic service-class k calls with b_{kr_s} b.u. in state j, $y_{kr_s}(j)$, via (4.38).
- The mean number of adaptive service-class k calls with b_k b.u. in state j, $y_k(j)$, via (4.58).
- The mean number of adaptive service-class k calls with b_{kr_s} b.u. in state j, $y_{kr_s}(j)$, via (4.63).
- The mean number of in-service calls of service-class k accepted in the system with b_k, $\bar{n}_k$, via (4.27).
- The mean number of in-service calls of service-class k accepted in the system with b_{kr_s}, $\bar{n}_{kr_s}$, via (4.39).

Example 4.23 Consider again Example 4.21 ($C = 3, T = 4, K = 2, b_1 = 1, b_2 = 3$, $b_{2r_1} = 2, b_{2r_2} = 1, t_1 = 2, t_2 = 0, \lambda_1 = \lambda_2 = 1, \mu_1^{-1} = \mu_2^{-1} = 1, \mu_{2r_1}^{-1} = 2.0, \mu_{2r_2}^{-1} = 4.0$, calls of service-class 1 are adaptive):

(a) Calculate the values of $Q(j)$ based on (4.64).
(b) Calculate the CBP of both service-classes, including the retry probabilities and the conditional $B_{2r_2}^*$.

(a) State probabilities through the recursion (4.64):

$j = 1$:	$q(1) = q(0) + 0 = 1.0$	$\Rightarrow q(1) = 1.0$
$j = 2$:	$2q(2) = q(1) + 0 = 1.0$	$\Rightarrow q(2) = 0.5$
$j = 3$:	$3q(3) = 0 + 3q(0) + 4q(1) + 4q(2) = 9.0$	$\Rightarrow q(3) = 3.0$
$j = 4$:	$q(4) = 0 + 0 + 0 + \frac{1}{3}4q(3) = 4.0$	$\Rightarrow q(4) = 4.0$

The normalization constant is: $G = \sum_{j=0}^{T} q(j) = 9.5$.
The state probabilities are:

$Q(0) = Q(1) = 0.10526$ $\quad$ $Q(2) = 0.05263$ $\quad$ $Q(3) = 0.31579$ $\quad$ $Q(4) = 0.42105$

(b) The CBP are as follows:

$$B_1 = \sum_{j=T-b_1-t_1+1}^{T} Q(j) = Q(2) + Q(3) + Q(4) = 0.78947 \text{ (compare with the exact } 0.882756)$$

$$B_2 = \sum_{j=C-b_2+1}^{T} Q(j) = Q(1) + Q(2) + Q(3) + Q(4) = 0.89473 \text{ (compare with the exact } 0.9692)$$

$$B_{2r_1} = \sum_{j=C-b_{2r_1}+1}^{T} Q(j) = Q(2) + Q(3) + Q(4) = 0.78947 \text{ (compare with the exact } 0.8828)$$

$$B_{2r_2} = \sum_{j=T-b_{2r_2}+1}^{T} Q(j) = Q(4) = 0.42105 \text{ (compare with the exact } 0.384614)$$

$$B_{2r_2}^* = \frac{B_{2r_2}}{B_2} = 0.47059 \text{ (compare with the exact } 0.39684)$$

It is apparent that in small EA-MRM/BR examples the error introduced by the assumption of LB, the introduction of $\varphi_k(\mathbf{n})$ and $\varphi_{kr_s}(\mathbf{n})$, the migration approximation, and the application of the BR policy can be acceptable (with the exception of B_1 and B_2 in our example).

Example 4.24 Consider again Example 4.12 ($C = 80$, $T = 80, 82, 84$, $K = 3$, $b_1 = 1$, $b_2 = 2$, $b_3 = 6$, $b_{3r_1} = 5$, $b_{3r_2} = 4$, $\alpha_1 = 20, \alpha_2 = 6$, $\alpha_3 = 2$, $\alpha_3 b_3 = \alpha_{3r_1} b_{3r_1} = \alpha_{3r_2} b_{3r_2}$, $t_1 = 3$, $t_2 = 2$, $t_3 = 0$) and assume that service-classes 1, 2 are adaptive while service-class 3 is elastic. Present graphically the analytical CBP of all service-classes for the EA-MRM, the EA-MRM/BR, the MRM, and the MRM/BR by assuming that α_3 remains constant while α_1, α_2 increase in steps of 1.0 and 0.5 erl, respectively (up to $\alpha_1 = 28$ erl and $\alpha_2 = 10$ erl). In addition, present graphically the link utilization for the EA-MRM/BR and the MRM/BR. Finally, provide simulation CBP and link utilization results for the EA-MRM/BR.

Figures 4.11–4.13 present, for all values of T, the analytical and simulation CBP results of service-classes 1, 2, and 3 (CBP of calls with b_{3r_2}), respectively, while Figure 4.14 presents the analytical and simulation results for the link utilization. All figures show that the analytical results obtained by the EA-MRM/BR are of absolutely satisfactory accuracy, compared to simulation, and that the MRM/BR fails to approximate the behavior of the EA-MRM/BR. This is expected since in the MRM/BR the bandwidth compression/expansion mechanism is not incorporated. Similarly, the results obtained by the MRM and the EA-MRM fail to approximate the behavior of the EA-MRM/BR since the BR policy is not applied in these models. Furthermore, Figures 4.11–4.13 show that the existence of the bandwidth compression/expansion mechanism in the EA-MRM/BR reduces CBP even for small values of T. This decrease results in the increase of link utilization in the EA-MRM/BR compared to the MRM/BR (Figure 4.14).

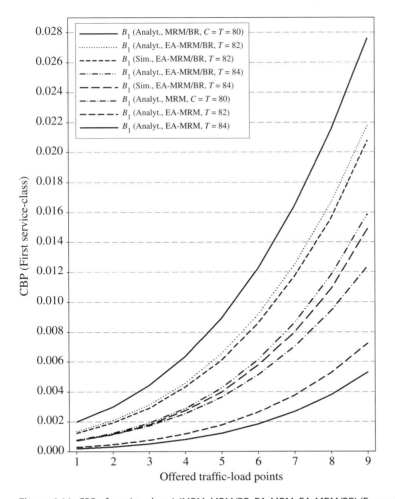

Figure 4.11 CBP of service-class 1 (MRM, MRM/BR, EA-MRM, EA-MRM/BR) (Example 4.24).

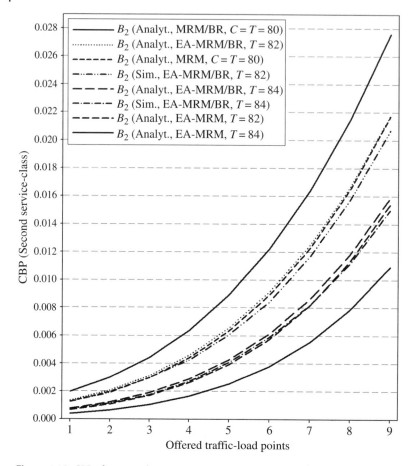

Figure 4.12 CBP of service-class 2 (MRM, MRM/BR, EA-MRM, EA-MRM/BR) (Example 4.24).

4.9 Applications

Since the multirate elastic adaptive retry loss models are a combination of the retry loss models (see Chapter 2) and the elastic adaptive loss models (see Chapter 3), the interested reader may refer to Sections 2.11 and 3.7 for possible applications.

4.10 Further Reading

Similar to the previous section, the interested reader may refer to the corresponding sections of Chapter 2 (Section 2.12) and Chapter 3 (Section 3.8). In addition to these sections, interesting extensions of the models presented in this chapter have been proposed in [6]. More precisely, in [6] the case of finite sources is considered as well as the application of the BR and TH policies.

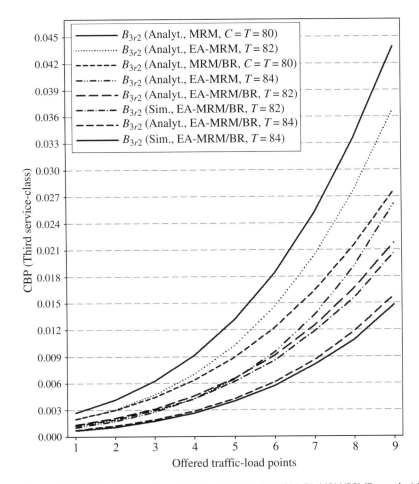

Figure 4.13 CBP of service-class 3 (MRM, MRM/BR, EA-MRM, EA-MRM/BR) (Example 4.24).

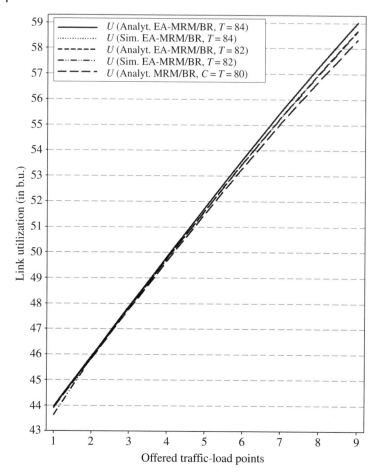

Figure 4.14 Link utilization (MRM/BR, EA-MRM/BR) (Example 4.24).

References

1 I. Moscholios, V. Vassilakis, J. Vardakas and M. Logothetis, Retry loss models supporting elastic traffic. *Advances in Electronics and Telecommunications*, Poznan University
of Technology, Poland, 2,(3):8–13, September 2011.

2 J. Kaufman, Blocking with retrials in a completely shared resource environment.
Performance Evaluation, 15(2):99–113, June 1992.

3 I. Moscholios, V. Vassilakis, M. Logothetis and J. Vardakas, Erlang–Engset multirate
retry loss models for elastic and adaptive traffic under the bandwidth reservation policy. *International Journal on Advances in Networks and Services*, 7(1&2):12–24, July
2014.

4 I. Moscholios, V. Vassilakis, M. Logothetis and M. Koukias, QoS equalization in a
multirate loss model of elastic and adaptive traffic with retrials. *5th International
Conference on Emerging Network Intelligence, EMERGING*, Porto, Portugal, October
2013.

5 I. Moscholios, V. Vassilakis, J. Vardakas and M. Logothetis, Call blocking probabilities of elastic and adaptive traffic with retrials. *Proceedings of the 8th Advanced International Conference on Telecommunications, AICT*, Stuttgart, Germany, 27 May–1 June 2012.

6 I. Moscholios, M. Logothetis, J. Vardakas and A. Boucouvalas, Congestion probabilities of elastic and adaptive calls in Erlang–Engset multirate loss models under the threshold and bandwidth reservation policies. *Computer Networks*, 92(Part 1):1–23, December 2015.

5

On–Off Multirate Loss Models

We consider ON–OFF multirate loss models of random arriving calls with fixed bandwidth requirements. Contrary to the models described in all previous chapters, in the ON–OFF loss models of this chapter in-service calls do not constantly keep their assigned bandwidth but alternate between transmission periods (ON) and idle periods (OFF). The basic characteristics of these ON–OFF loss models are: (i) they can be used for the analysis of the call-level behavior of bursty traffic (the ON–OFF model is a simple representation of bursty traffic) and (ii) their analysis is based on the classical EMLM (a fact that facilitates their computer implementation).

5.1 The ON–OFF Multirate Loss Model

5.1.1 The Service System

In the *ON–OFF multirate loss model* (*ON–OFF*), we consider a link of capacity C b.u. that accommodates K service-classes of ON–OFF-type calls. Each call of a service-class k ($k = 1, \ldots, K$) follows a Poisson process with arrival rate λ_k, requires b_k b.u., and competes for the available bandwidth of the system under the CS policy. If the b_k b.u. are available then the call enters the system in state ON, otherwise the call is blocked and lost, and the occupied link bandwidth is characterized as real. The capacity C, named real (real link), corresponds to state ON.

At the end of an ON-period a call of service-class k releases the b_k b.u. and may begin an OFF-period with probability σ_k, or depart from the system with probability $1 - \sigma_k$. While the call is in state OFF, it is assumed that it seizes fictitious bandwidth (b_k b.u.) of a fictitious link of capacity C^*. The capacity C^*, named fictitious, corresponds to state OFF. The call holding time of a service-class k call in state ON or OFF is exponentially distributed with mean μ_{ik}^{-1}, where $i = 1$ refers to state ON and $i = 2$ to state OFF.

At the end of an OFF-period the call returns to state ON with probability 1 (i.e., the call cannot leave the system from state OFF) (Figure 5.1), while re-requesting b_k b.u. When $C = C^*$, b_k b.u. are always available for that call in state ON, i.e., no blocking occurs while returning to state ON. When $C < C^*$, and there is available bandwidth in the link, i.e., if $j_1 + b_k \leq C$ (where j_1 is the occupied real link bandwidth), the call returns to state ON and a new *burst* begins; otherwise burst blocking occurs (no return to state ON) and the call remains in state OFF for another period (Figure 5.2).

Efficient Multirate Teletraffic Loss Models Beyond Erlang, First Edition.
Ioannis D. Moscholios and Michael D. Logothetis.
© 2019 John Wiley & Sons Ltd. Published 2019 by John Wiley & Sons Ltd.
Companion website: www.wiley.com/go/logocode

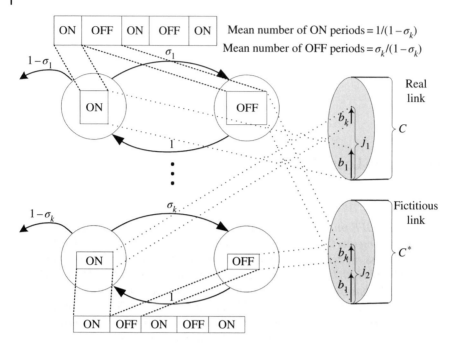

Figure 5.1 The service model of ON–OFF calls.

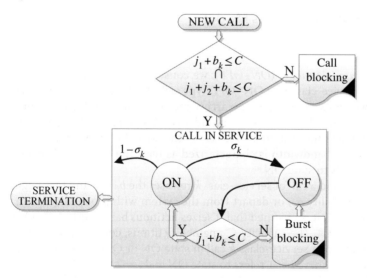

Figure 5.2 The mechanisms of call and burst blocking in the ON–OFF model.

A new service-class k call is accepted in the system with b_k b.u. if it meets the following constraints:

$$j_1 + b_k \leq C \tag{5.1}$$

$$j_1 + j_2 + b_k \leq C^* \tag{5.2}$$

where j_2 is the occupied bandwidth of the fictitious link.

The first constraint ensures that the occupied bandwidth of all existing ON calls together with the new call does not exceed the real link capacity. The second constraint prevents the system from accepting new calls when most of the system calls are in state OFF, i.e., this constraint ensures that the *burst blocking probability* (*BBP*) of OFF calls remains at an acceptable level. Note that, when $C = C^*$, a service-class k call is accepted in the system only if it meets (5.2).

Based on (5.1) and (5.2), the state space Ω of all possible states $\mathbf{j} = (j_1, j_2)$ is given by:

$$\mathbf{j} \in \Omega \Leftrightarrow \left\{ \left(j_1 \leq C \cap \left(\sum_{s=1}^{2} j_s \leq C^* \right) \right) \right\} \tag{5.3}$$

5.1.2 The Analytical Model

5.1.2.1 Steady State Probabilities

To describe the analytical model in the steady state we initially define by n_k^i the number of in-service calls of service-class k in state i ($i = 1$ and 2 refers to states ON and OFF, respectively). Additionally, we present the following notations [1]:

$\mathbf{n}^i = (n_1^i, \ldots, n_k^i, \ldots, n_K^i)$: the vector of the number of in-service calls of service-class k in state i ($i = 1 \Rightarrow$ state ON, $i = 2 \Rightarrow$ state OFF).

$\mathbf{n} = (\mathbf{n}^1, \mathbf{n}^2)$, $\mathbf{n}_{k+}^i = (n_1^i, \ldots, n_k^i + 1, \ldots, n_K^i)$, $\mathbf{n}_{k-}^i = (n_1^i, \ldots, n_k^i - 1, \ldots, n_K^i)$, $\mathbf{n}_{k+}^1 = (\mathbf{n}_{k+}^1, \mathbf{n}^2)$, $\mathbf{n}_{k+}^2 = (\mathbf{n}^1, \mathbf{n}_{k+}^2)$, $\mathbf{n}_{k-}^1 = (\mathbf{n}_{k-}^1, \mathbf{n}^2)$, $\mathbf{n}_{k-}^2 = (\mathbf{n}^1, \mathbf{n}_{k-}^2)$.

$\mathbf{n}_{k+-} = (\mathbf{n}_{k+}^1, \mathbf{n}_{k-}^2)$: a vector that shows a service-class k call transition from state OFF to ON.

$\mathbf{n}_{k-+} = (\mathbf{n}_{k-}^1, \mathbf{n}_{k+}^2)$: a vector that shows a service-class k call transition from state ON to OFF.

λ_{ik} is the external arrival rate of service-class k calls to state i. Since external arrivals enter the system only in state ON, we have:

$$\lambda_{ik} = \begin{cases} \lambda_k & \text{for } i = 1 \\ 0 & \text{for } i = 2 \end{cases} \tag{5.4}$$

$r_{ij}(k)$ is the *Prob*{next state is j | current state is i and the service-class is k} and is determined by:

$$r_{1j}(k) = \begin{cases} 0 & \text{for } j = 1 \\ \sigma_k & \text{for } j = 2 \end{cases} \tag{5.5a}$$

$$r_{2j}(k) = \begin{cases} 1 & \text{for } j = 1 \\ 0 & \text{for } j = 2 \end{cases} \tag{5.5b}$$

e_{ik} is the total arrival rate of service-class k calls to state i and is given by:

$$e_{ik} = \lambda_{ik} + \sum_{j=1}^{2} e_{jk} r_{ji}(k) = \begin{cases} \lambda_k/(1 - \sigma_k) & \text{for } i = 1 \\ \lambda_k \sigma_k/(1 - \sigma_k) & \text{for } i = 2 \end{cases} \tag{5.6}$$

p_{ik} is the offered traffic-load to state i from service-class k and is determined by:

$$p_{ik} = \frac{e_{ik}}{\mu_{ik}} = \begin{cases} \dfrac{\lambda_k}{(1 - \sigma_k)\mu_{1k}} & \text{for } i = 1 \\ \dfrac{\lambda_k \sigma_k}{(1 - \sigma_k)\mu_{2k}} & \text{for } i = 2 \end{cases} \tag{5.7}$$

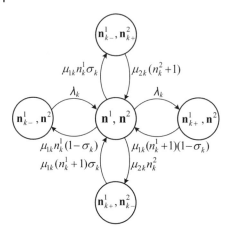

Figure 5.3 The state transition diagram of the ON–OFF model.

Figure 5.3 shows the state transition rates of the ON–OFF model (in equilibrium).

Example 5.1 Consider a link of $C = 3$ b.u. and $C^* = 4$ b.u. The link accommodates calls of $K = 2$ service-classes whose calls require $b_1 = 3$ and $b_2 = 1$ b.u., respectively. Let $\lambda_1 = \lambda_2 = 1$ call/s, $\mu_{11}^{-1} = \mu_{12}^{-1} = \mu_{21}^{-1} = \mu_{22}^{-1} = 1$ sec, and $\sigma_1 = \sigma_2 = 0.9$.

(a) Find the total number of permissible states $\mathbf{n} = (\mathbf{n}^1, \mathbf{n}^2) = (n_1^1, n_2^1, n_1^2, n_2^2)$ and determine the values of j_1, j_2 for each state $\mathbf{n}$.

(b) Calculate the state probabilities $P(\mathbf{n})$ based on the GB equations. Then determine the values of the occupancy distribution $Q(j_1, j_2)$ (for $j_1 = 0, \ldots, C$ and $j_2 = 0, \ldots, C^*$).

(c) Based on the constraints (5.1) and (5.2) and the values of $Q(j_1, j_2)$ determine the CBP of both service-classes.

(a) There are 19 permissible states of the form $\mathbf{n} = (\mathbf{n}^1, \mathbf{n}^2) = (n_1^1, n_2^1, n_1^2, n_2^2)$. Table 5.1 presents the 19 states together with the corresponding values of j_1 and j_2.

Table 5.1 State space and occupied real and fictitious link bandwidth (Example 5.1)

n_1^1	n_2^1	n_1^2	n_2^2	j_1 $(0 \leq j_1 \leq C)$	j_2 $(0 \leq j_2 \leq C^*)$	n_1^1	n_2^1	n_1^2	n_2^2	j_1 $(0 \leq j_1 \leq C)$	j_2 $(0 \leq j_2 \leq C^*)$
0	0	0	0	0		0	1	0	3	1	3
0	0	0	1	0	1	0	1	1	0	1	3
0	0	0	2	0	2	0	2	0	0	2	0
0	0	0	3	0	3	0	2	0	1	2	1
0	0	0	4	0	4	0	2	0	2	2	2
0	0	1	0	0	3	0	3	0	0	3	0
0	0	1	1	0	4	0	3	0	1	3	1
0	1	0	0	1	0	1	0	0	0	3	0
0	1	0	1	1	1	1	0	0	1	3	1
0	1	0	2	1	2						

(b) Based on Figure 5.3 and Table 5.1, we obtain the following 19 GB equations:

$(0, 0, 0, 0)$: $0.1P(0, 1, 0, 0) + 0.1P(1, 0, 0, 0) - 2P(0, 0, 0, 0) = 0$

$(0, 0, 0, 1)$: $0.1P(0, 1, 0, 1) + 0.9P(0, 1, 0, 0) + 0.1P(1, 0, 0, 1) - 3P(0, 0, 0, 1) = 0$

$(0, 0, 0, 2)$: $0.9P(0, 1, 0, 1) + 0.1P(0, 1, 0, 2) - 3P(0, 0, 0, 2) = 0$

$(0, 0, 0, 3)$: $0.9P(0, 1, 0, 2) + 0.1P(0, 1, 0, 3) - 4P(0, 0, 0, 3) = 0$

$(0, 0, 0, 4)$: $0.9P(0, 1, 0, 3) - 4P(0, 0, 0, 4) = 0$

$(0, 0, 1, 0)$: $0.9P(1, 0, 0, 0) + 0.1P(0, 1, 1, 0) - 2P(0, 0, 1, 0) = 0$

$(0, 0, 1, 1)$: $0.9P(1, 0, 0, 1) + 0.9P(0, 1, 1, 0) - 2P(0, 0, 1, 1) = 0$

$(0, 1, 0, 0)$: $P(0, 0, 0, 0) + 0.2P(0, 2, 0, 0) + P(0, 0, 0, 1) - 2P(0, 1, 0, 0) = 0$

$(0, 1, 0, 1)$: $P(0, 0, 0, 1) + 1.8P(0, 2, 0, 0) + 0.2P(0, 2, 0, 1) + 2P(0, 0, 0, 2) - 3P(0, 1, 0, 1) = 0$

$(0, 1, 0, 2)$: $P(0, 0, 0, 2) + 3P(0, 0, 0, 3) + 0.2P(0, 2, 0, 2) + 1.8P(0, 2, 0, 1) - 4P(0, 1, 0, 2) = 0$

$(0, 1, 0, 3)$: $P(0, 0, 0, 3) + 4P(0, 0, 0, 4) + 1.8P(0, 2, 0, 2) - 4P(0, 1, 0, 3) = 0$

$(0, 1, 1, 0)$: $P(0, 0, 1, 0) + P(0, 0, 1, 1) - P(0, 1, 1, 0) = 0$

$(0, 2, 0, 0)$: $P(0, 1, 0, 0) + P(0, 1, 0, 1) + 0.3P(0, 3, 0, 0) - 3P(0, 2, 0, 0) = 0$

$(0, 2, 0, 1)$: $P(0, 1, 0, 1) + 2P(0, 1, 0, 2) + 0.3P(0, 3, 0, 1) + 2.7P(0, 3, 0, 0) - 4P(0, 2, 0, 1) = 0$

$(0, 2, 0, 2)$: $P(0, 1, 0, 2) + 3P(0, 1, 0, 3) + 2.7P(0, 3, 0, 1) - 4P(0, 2, 0, 2) = 0$

$(0, 3, 0, 0)$: $P(0, 2, 0, 0) + P(0, 2, 0, 1) - 3P(0, 3, 0, 0) = 0$

$(0, 3, 0, 1)$: $P(0, 2, 0, 1) + 2P(0, 2, 0, 2) - 3P(0, 3, 0, 1) = 0$

$(1, 0, 0, 0)$: $P(0, 0, 0, 0) + P(0, 0, 1, 0) - P(1, 0, 0, 0) = 0$

$(1, 0, 0, 1)$: $P(0, 0, 0, 1) + P(0, 0, 1, 1) - P(1, 0, 0, 1) = 0$

The solution of this linear system is:

$P(0, 0, 0, 0) = 0.0001507$ $\quad P(0, 0, 0, 1) = 0.001356$ $\quad P(0, 0, 0, 2) = 0.0061021$

$P(0, 0, 0, 3) = 0.0183063$ $\quad P(0, 0, 0, 4) = 0.0411893$ $\quad P(0, 0, 1, 0) = 0.001356$

$P(0, 0, 1, 1) = 0.0122042$ $\quad P(0, 1, 0, 0) = 0.0015067$ $\quad P(0, 1, 0, 1) = 0.0135603$

$P(0, 1, 0, 2) = 0.0610212$ $\quad P(0, 1, 0, 3) = 0.1830635$ $\quad P(0, 1, 1, 0) = 0.0135603$

$P(0, 2, 0, 0) = 0.0075335$ $\quad P(0, 2, 0, 1) = 0.0678013$ $\quad P(0, 2, 0, 2) = 0.3051058$

$P(0, 3, 0, 0) = 0.0251116$ $\quad P(0, 3, 0, 1) = 0.2260043$ $\quad P(1, 0, 0, 0) = 0.0015067$

$P(1, 0, 0, 1) = 0.0135603$

Based on the values of $P(n_1^1, n_2^1, n_1^2, n_2^2)$, we determine the values of $Q(j_1, j_2)$:

$Q(0, 0) = P(0, 0, 0, 0) = 0.0001507,$ $\quad Q(1, 2) = P(0, 1, 0, 2) = 0.0610212$

$Q(0, 1) = P(0, 0, 0, 1) = 0.001356,$ $\quad Q(1, 3) = P(0, 1, 0, 3) + P(0, 1, 1, 0) = 0.1966238$

$Q(0, 2) = P(0, 0, 0, 2) = 0.0061021,$ $\quad Q(2, 0) = P(0, 2, 0, 0) = 0.0075335$

$Q(0, 3) = P(0, 0, 0, 3) + P(0, 0, 1, 0) = 0.0196623,$ $\quad Q(2, 1) = P(0, 2, 0, 1) = 0.0678013$

$Q(0, 4) = P(0, 0, 0, 4) + P(0, 0, 1, 1) = 0.0533935,$ $\quad Q(2, 2) = P(0, 2, 0, 2) = 0.3051058$

$Q(1, 0) = P(0, 1, 0, 0) = 0.0015067,$ $\quad Q(3, 0) = P(0, 3, 0, 0) + P(1, 0, 0, 0) = 0.0266183$

$Q(1, 1) = P(0, 1, 0, 1) = 0.0135603,$ $\quad Q(3, 1) = P(0, 3, 0, 1) + P(1, 0, 0, 1) = 0.2395646$

(c) Based on the values of $Q(j)$ and the constraints of (5.1) and (5.2) we obtain the exact CBP:

$$B_1 = \sum_{(j_1>C-b_1)\cup(j_1+j_2>C^*-b_1)} Q(j_1,j_2) = \sum_{(j_1>0)\cup(j_1+j_2>1)} Q(j_1,j_2) = 1 - Q(0,0) - Q(0,1) = 0.9987947$$

$$B_2 = \sum_{(j_1>C-b_2)\cup(j_1+j_2>C^*-b_2)} Q(j_1,j_2) = \sum_{(j_1>2)\cup(j_1+j_2>3)} Q(j_1,j_2) =$$

$$= Q(0,4) + Q(1,3) + Q(2,2) + Q(3,1) + Q(3,0) = 0.821306$$

Assuming the existence of LB between adjacent states, the following LB equations are extracted from the state transition diagram of Figure 5.3:

$$n_k^1 \mu_{1k} \sigma_k P(\mathbf{n}) = \mu_{2k}(n_k^2 + 1)P(\mathbf{n}_{k-+}) \tag{5.8a}$$

$$\lambda_k P(\mathbf{n}_{k-}^1) = \mu_{1k} n_k^1 (1 - \sigma_k) P(\mathbf{n}) \tag{5.8b}$$

$$\lambda_k P(\mathbf{n}) = \mu_{1k}(n_k^1 + 1)(1 - \sigma_k)P(\mathbf{n}_{k+}^1) \tag{5.8c}$$

$$\mu_{1k}(n_k^1 + 1)\sigma_k P(\mathbf{n}_{k+-}) = \mu_{2k} n_k^2 P(\mathbf{n}) \tag{5.8d}$$

where $P(\mathbf{n})$, $P(\mathbf{n}_{k-+})$, $P(\mathbf{n}_{k-}^1)$, $P(\mathbf{n}_{k+}^1)$, and $P(\mathbf{n}_{k+-})$ are the probability distributions of the corresponding states: $\mathbf{n} = (\mathbf{n}^1, \mathbf{n}^2)$, $\mathbf{n}_{k-+} = (\mathbf{n}_{k-}^1, \mathbf{n}_{k+}^2)$, $\mathbf{n}_{k-}^1 = (n_1^i, \ldots, n_k^i - 1, \ldots, n_K^i)$, $\mathbf{n}_{k+}^i = (n_1^i, \ldots, n_k^i + 1, \ldots, n_K^i)$, $\mathbf{n}_{k+-} = (\mathbf{n}_{k+}^1, \mathbf{n}_{k-}^2)$.

Equations (5.8b) and (5.8c) describe the balance between the rates of a new call arrival of service-class k and the corresponding departure from the system, while (5.8a) and (5.8d) refer to the ON-OFF alternations of a service-class k call. Based on the LB assumption, it can be shown that the probability distribution $P(\mathbf{n})$ has a PFS which satisfies (5.8a)–(5.8d) and has the form [1]:

$$P(\mathbf{n}) = \frac{1}{G} \prod_{i=1}^{2} \prod_{k=1}^{K} \frac{p_{ik}^{n_k^i}}{n_k^i!} \tag{5.9}$$

where $G \equiv G(\Omega)$ is the normalization constant chosen so that the sum of the probabilities of all states is unity.

We now define by $b_{i,k,s}$ the b.u. held by a service-class k call in state i:

$$b_{i,k,s} = \begin{cases} b_k & \text{if } s = i \\ 0 & \text{if } s \neq i \end{cases} \tag{5.10}$$

where $i = 1 \Rightarrow$ state ON, $i = 2 \Rightarrow$ state OFF, $s = 1 \Rightarrow$ real link, and $s = 2 \Rightarrow$ fictitious link.

We also define a $(2K \times 2)$ matrix B whose elements are the values of $b_{i,k,s}$ and let $\mathbf{B}_{i,k}$ be the (i,k) row of $\mathbf{B}$, where $\mathbf{B}_{i,k} = (b_{i,k,1}, b_{i,k,2})$. For example, when $K = 2$ service-classes with bandwidth requirements b_1 and b_2, respectively, the form of $\mathbf{B}$ is:

$$\mathbf{B} = \begin{bmatrix} b_{1,1,1} & b_{1,1,2} \\ b_{2,1,1} & b_{2,1,2} \\ b_{1,2,1} & b_{1,2,2} \\ b_{2,2,1} & b_{2,2,2} \end{bmatrix} = \begin{bmatrix} b_1 & 0 \\ 0 & b_1 \\ b_2 & 0 \\ 0 & b_2 \end{bmatrix}.$$

In addition, let $\mathbf{j} = \mathbf{n} \cdot \mathbf{B}$ with $\mathbf{j} = (j_1, j_2)$, where the occupied bandwidth j_s of link s ($s = 1, 2$) is given by:

$$j_s = \sum_{i=1}^{2} \sum_{k=1}^{K} n_k^i b_{i,k,s} \tag{5.11}$$

Having found an expression for $P(\mathbf{n})$ and since the CS policy is a coordinate convex policy (see Section I.12, Example I.30), the probability $P(\mathbf{n}_{k-}^i)$ can be expressed by [2]:

$$n_k^i P(\mathbf{n}) = p_{ik} P(\mathbf{n}_{k-}^i) \tag{5.12}$$

Consider now the set of states $\Omega_j = \{\mathbf{n} \in \Omega_j : \mathbf{n} \cdot \mathbf{B} = \mathbf{j}, \; n_k^i \geq 0, \; k = 1, \ldots, K, \; i = 1, 2\}$ where the occupied real and fictitious link bandwidths are exactly j_1 and j_2, respectively. The probability $q(\mathbf{j})$ (links occupancy distribution) is denoted as:

$$q(\mathbf{j}) = Prob\{\mathbf{j} = \mathbf{n} \cdot \mathbf{B}\} = \sum_{\mathbf{n} \in \Omega_j} P(\mathbf{n}) \tag{5.13}$$

To derive a recursive formula for the unnormalized values of $q(\mathbf{j})$, we start by multiplying both sides of (5.12) by $b_{i,k,s}$ and summing over i and k, we have [2]:

$$P(\mathbf{n}) \sum_{i=1}^{2} \sum_{k=1}^{K} n_k^i b_{i,k,s} = \sum_{i=1}^{2} \sum_{k=1}^{K} b_{i,k,s} p_{ik} P(\mathbf{n}_{k-}^i) \tag{5.14}$$

or according to (5.11):

$$P(\mathbf{n}) j_s = \sum_{i=1}^{2} \sum_{k=1}^{K} b_{i,k,s} p_{ik} P(\mathbf{n}_{k-}^i) \tag{5.15}$$

Summing both sides of (5.15) over the set Ω_j we have:

$$j_s \sum_{\mathbf{n} \in \Omega_j} P(\mathbf{n}) = \sum_{i=1}^{2} \sum_{k=1}^{K} b_{i,k,s} p_{ik} \sum_{\mathbf{n} \in \Omega_j} P(\mathbf{n}_{k-}^i) \tag{5.16}$$

In the RHS of (5.16), the term $\sum_{\mathbf{n} \in \Omega_j} P(\mathbf{n}_{k-}^i) = q(\mathbf{j} - \mathbf{B}_{i,k})$ and therefore by substituting (5.13) in (5.16), we have the following accurate and recursive formula for the calculation of the unnormalized values of $q(\mathbf{j})$ [1]:

$$q(\mathbf{j}) = \begin{cases} 1 & \text{for } \mathbf{j} = 0 \\ \dfrac{1}{j_s} \displaystyle\sum_{i=1}^{2} \sum_{k=1}^{K} b_{i,k,s} p_{ik} q(\mathbf{j} - \mathbf{B}_{i,k}) & \\ \quad \text{for } j_1 = 1, \ldots, C \;\; (\text{if } s = 1), \quad \text{or for } j_2 = 1, \ldots, C^* - j_1 \;\; (\text{if } s = 2) \\ 0 & \text{otherwise} \end{cases} \tag{5.17}$$

5.1.2.2 CBP and Utilization
The following performance measures can be determined based on (5.17):

- The CBP of service-class k, B_k, via the formula [1]:

$$B_k = \sum_{\{\mathbf{j} \,|\, [(b_{1,k,1}+j_1)>C] \,\cup\, [(b_{1,k,1}+j_1+j_2)>C^*]\}} G^{-1} q(\mathbf{j}) \tag{5.18}$$

where $G = \sum_{\mathbf{j} \in \Omega} q(\mathbf{j})$.
- The link utilization, U_s, via the formula [1]:

$$U_s = \sum_{\tau=0}^{C_s} \tau Q_s(\tau) \tag{5.19}$$

where $Q_s(\tau) = \sum_{\{\mathbf{j} \,|\, j_s = \tau\}} G^{-1} q(\mathbf{j})$.

Example 5.2 Consider again Example 5.1 ($C = 3, C^* = 4, K = 2, b_1 = 3, b_2 = 1$, $\lambda_1 = \lambda_2 = 1, \mu_{11}^{-1} = \mu_{12}^{-1} = \mu_{21}^{-1} = \mu_{22}^{-1} = 1, \; \sigma_1 = \sigma_2 = 0.9$). Calculate the CBP of both service-classes via (5.18).

According to (5.17) we have $\mathbf{j} = (j_1, j_2)$, with $j_1 = 0, \ldots, 3$ and $j_2 = 0, \ldots, 4$. Starting with $q(0,0) = 1$ and considering the real link first, we recursively calculate $q(j_1, 0)$ for $j_1 = 1, 2, 3$:

$1q(1,0) = 0 + b_{1,2,1}P_{12}q(0,0) = 10q(0,0) = 10$ $\Rightarrow q(1,0) = 1.0$

$2q(2,0) = 0 + b_{1,2,1}P_{12}q(1,0) = 10q(1,0) = 100$ $\Rightarrow q(2,0) = 50.0$

$3q(3,0) = b_{1,1,1}P_{11}q(0,0) + b_{1,2,1}P_{12}q(2,0) = 30q(0,0) + 10q(2,0) = 530$ $\Rightarrow q(3,0) = 176.667$

We continue by recursively calculating $q(0, j_2)$ for $j_2 = 1, \ldots, 4$:

$1q(0,1) = 0 + b_{2,2,2}P_{22}q(0,0) = 9q(0,0) = 9$ $\Rightarrow q(0,1) = 9.0$

$2q(0,2) = 0 + b_{2,2,2}P_{22}q(0,1) = 9q(0,1) = 81$ $\Rightarrow q(0,2) = 40.5$

$3q(0,3) = b_{2,1,2}P_{21}q(0,0) + b_{2,2,2}P_{22}q(0,2) = 27q(0,0) + 9q(0,2) = 391.5$ $\Rightarrow q(0,3) = 130.5$

$4q(0,4) = b_{2,1,2}P_{21}q(0,1) + b_{2,2,2}P_{22}q(0,3) = 27q(0,1) + 9q(0,3) = 1417.5$ $\Rightarrow q(0,4) = 354.375$

Finally, we determine the values of $q(j_1, j_2)$ for $j_1 = 1, 2, 3$ and $j_2 = 1, \ldots, 4$:

$1q(1,1) = 0 + b_{1,2,1}P_{12}q(0,1) = 10q(0,1) = 90$ $\Rightarrow q(1,1) = 90.0$

$1q(1,2) = 0 + b_{1,2,1}P_{12}q(0,2) = 10q(0,2) = 405$ $\Rightarrow q(1,2) = 405.0$

$1q(1,3) = 0 + b_{1,2,1}P_{12}q(0,3) = 10q(0,3) = 1305$ $\Rightarrow q(1,3) = 1305.0$

$2q(2,1) = 0 + b_{1,2,1}P_{12}q(1,1) = 10q(1,1) = 900$ $\Rightarrow q(2,1) = 450.0$

$2q(2,2) = 0 + b_{1,2,1}P_{12}q(1,2) = 10q(1,2) = 4050$ $\Rightarrow q(2,2) = 2025.0$

$3q(3,1) = b_{1,1,1}P_{11}q(0,1) + b_{1,2,1}P_{12}q(2,1) = 30q(0,1) + 10q(2,1) = 4770$ $\Rightarrow q(3,1) = 1590.0$

The normalization constant is $G = \sum_{\mathbf{j} \in \Omega} q(\mathbf{j}) = 6637.0416$. Thus, the values of $Q(j_1, j_2)$ and CBP are identical to those presented in Example 5.1.

Before we proceed with the BBP determination, we show the relationship between the ON–OFF model and the EMLM. Both models are equivalent, in the sense that they provide the same CBP, when:

(i) $\sigma_k = 0$ (i.e., when state OFF does not exist) for each service-class k ($k = 1, \ldots, K$). In that case the calculation of $q(j)$ can be done by (1.39).

(ii) $\sigma_k > 0$ and $C = C^*$. Then we can determine the mean holding time, μ_k^{-1}, of a service-class k call of the ON-OFF model by the following formula [1]:

$$\mu_k^{-1} = \frac{\sigma_k}{(1 - \sigma_k)}(\mu_{1k}^{-1} + \mu_{2k}^{-1}) + \mu_{1k}^{-1} \tag{5.20}$$

The summation $(\mu_{1k}^{-1} + \mu_{2k}^{-1})$ is possible, since the mean holding time in state i, μ_{ik}^{-1}, is exponentially distributed. The ratio $\frac{\sigma_k}{(1-\sigma_k)}$ shows the average number of times that a service-class k call visits state OFF during its lifetime. The ON–OFF model is equivalent to the EMLM with traffic parameters λ_k, b_k and μ_k^{-1} determined by (5.20).

5.1.2.3 BBP

Two different approximations exist in the literature for the determination of BBP in the ON–OFF model. The first one is proposed in [1] and the second one is proposed in [2, 3].

■ To describe the first approximation, the following notation is required:

$\overline{n}_k^i$ is the mean number of service-class k calls in state i.

$\overline{d}_k^i$ is the mean time that a service-class k call spends in state i.

v_{ik} is the internal arrival of a service-class k call in state i.

Since a service-class k call does not encounter burst blocking during its transition from state ON to state OFF, it is clear that the average time that the call spends in state ON is $\overline{d}_{1k} = \mu_{1k}^{-1}$. On the other hand, since a call may encounter burst blocking during its transition from state OFF to state ON, it is expected that the average time that the call spends in state OFF is $\overline{d}_{2k} \geq \mu_{2k}^{-1}$. To simplify the proposed formula for the BBP determination, it is assumed in [1] that a service-class k call does not spend more than two consecutive periods in state OFF (Figure 5.4). This assumption (approximation) relies on the fact that a call should not experience repeated burst blocking in a system of an acceptable performance.

Based on the previous assumption, the average time that a service-class k call spends in state OFF is calculated by [1]:

$$\overline{d}_{2k} = B_k^* \frac{2}{\mu_{2k}} + (1 - B_k^*)\frac{1}{\mu_{2k}} \tag{5.21}$$

where B_k^* is the BBP of service-class k calls.

According to (5.21), we write:

$$B_k^* = \mu_{2k}\overline{d}_{2k} - 1 \tag{5.22}$$

To determine the values of $\overline{d}_{2k}$ in (5.22) we need the mean number of service-class k calls in states ON and OFF, which is given by:

$$\overline{n}_k^i = \sum_{\mathbf{n}\in\Omega} n_k^i P(\mathbf{n}) \tag{5.23}$$

The RHS of (5.23) can be written as:

$$\sum_{\mathbf{n}\in\Omega} n_k^i P(\mathbf{n}) = \sum_{\mathbf{j}\in\Omega} \sum_{\mathbf{n}\in\Omega_\mathbf{j}} n_k^i P(\mathbf{n}) = \sum_{\mathbf{j}\in\Omega} G^{-1} p_{ik} q(\mathbf{j} - \mathbf{B}_{i,k}) \tag{5.24}$$

Equation (5.23) due to (5.24) takes the form:

$$\overline{n}_k^i = \sum_{\mathbf{j}\in\Omega} G^{-1} p_{ik} q(\mathbf{j} - \mathbf{B}_{i,k}) \tag{5.25}$$

By applying Little's law (see Section I.9) to service-class k calls in state i, we have:

$$\overline{d}_{ik} = \frac{\overline{n}_k^i}{e_{ik}} \tag{5.26}$$

Figure 5.4 Basic assumption (approximation) for the determination of BBP.

Burst blocking
(Inability to pass from state OFF to state ON)

| ON | OFF | ON | OFF | OFF | ON |

Assumption:
(Only two consecutive periods in state OFF)

and since $\overline{d}_{1k} = \mu_{1k}^{-1}$, (5.26) takes the following form for state ON:

$$e_{1k} = \overline{n}_k^{-1} \mu_{1k} \tag{5.27}$$

Based on (5.27), we can define the internal arrival rate of service-class k calls in state ON as follows:

$$\upsilon_{1k} = e_{1k} - \lambda_k(1 - B_k) = \overline{n}_k^{-1} \mu_{1k} - \lambda_k(1 - B_k) \tag{5.28}$$

Since the internal arrival rates in states ON and OFF should be equal, we have:

$$\upsilon_{1k} = \upsilon_{2k} = e_{2k} \tag{5.29}$$

where the second equality holds since there is no external call arrival rate towards state OFF.

Based on (5.26), (5.28), and (5.29), the average time that a service-class k call spends in state OFF is determined by:

$$\overline{d}_{2k} = \frac{\overline{n}_k^2}{\overline{n}_k^{-1} \mu_{1k} - \lambda_k(1 - B_k)} \tag{5.30}$$

By substituting (5.30) in (5.22), we have an approximate formula for the BBP of service-class k calls [1]:

$$B_k^* = \frac{\overline{n}_k^2 \mu_{2k}}{\overline{n}_k^{-1} \mu_{1k} - \lambda_k(1 - B_k)} - 1 \tag{5.31}$$

where the values of $\overline{n}_k^i$, $i = 1, 2$, are determined via (5.25).

Generally speaking, BBP in a system of well-acceptable QoS should be less than 10^{-4} [4]. For values of practical interest, the BBP formula of (5.31) provides quite satisfactory results compared to simulation results. However, (5.31) fails in cases where the BBP are extremely high or extremely low.

Example 5.3 To give an example in which (5.31) fails, consider a link of real and fictitious capacity of $C = 10$ b.u. and $C^* = 14$, respectively, accommodating two service-classes whose traffic requirements are the following:

For service-class 1: $b_1 = 4$ b.u., $\lambda_1 = 0.1$, $\mu_{11}^{-1} = 0.8$, $\mu_{21}^{-1} = 0.4$, $\sigma_1 = 0.95$.
For service-class 2: $b_2 = 1$ b.u., $\lambda_1 = 1.0$, $\mu_{12}^{-1} = 0.9$, $\mu_{22}^{-1} = 0.3$, $\sigma_2 = 0.95$.

✓ Simulation results: $B_1^* = 68.21\%$, $B_2^* = 28.02\%$
✓ Analytical results: (5.31) fails for B_1^* ($B_1^* = 214.71\%$!!!), $B_2^* = 39.03\%$

This example shows that (5.31) is not robust and fails under extremely heavy traffic-load conditions because it is based on the assumption that a call remains in the OFF-period for two consecutive times at most; one can intuitively understand that this assumption cannot be valid under heavy traffic-load conditions. Moreover, (5.31) is based on the PFS of the ON–OFF model and therefore it fails when applied to non-PFS models such as the ON–OFF model under the BR policy (see Section 5.2). This discussion shows the necessity of another robust formula for the BBP calculation.

■ According to [2, 3], the derivation of the BBP formula requires a different proof of (5.17) compared to the one proposed in [1]. Equation (5.17) can be interpreted as a multi-dimensional birth–death balance equation. We assume that $\hat{n}_k^i(\mathbf{j})$ is the number of service-class k calls in state i given that the occupied bandwidth is $\mathbf{j}$. Intuitively (due to LB) we expect that $p_{ik}q(\mathbf{j} - \mathbf{B}_{i,k}) = \hat{n}_k^i(\mathbf{j})q(\mathbf{j})$. In what follows, we prove that $p_{ik}q(\mathbf{j} - \mathbf{B}_{i,k}) = y_{ik}(\mathbf{j})q(\mathbf{j})$, where $y_{ik}(\mathbf{j})$ is the mean number of service-class k calls in state i given that the system state is $\mathbf{j}$, and then prove (5.17).

Proof: The springboard of the proof is (5.12). Since the CS policy is a coordinate convex policy, (5.12) can be written as:

$$p_{ik}\gamma_{ik}(\mathbf{n})P(\mathbf{n}_{k-}^i) = n_k^i P(\mathbf{n}) \tag{5.32}$$

Summing (5.32) over the set $\mathbf{\Omega}_{\mathbf{j}}$ we have:

$$p_{ik}\sum_{\mathbf{n}\in\mathbf{\Omega}_{\mathbf{j}}}\gamma_{ik}(\mathbf{n})P(\mathbf{n}_{k-}^i) = \sum_{\mathbf{n}\in\mathbf{\Omega}_{\mathbf{j}}} n_k^i P(\mathbf{n}) \tag{5.33}$$

Since $\mathbf{\Omega}_{\mathbf{j}} \cap \{n_k^i \geq 1\} = \{\mathbf{n} : \mathbf{n}_{k-}^i\mathbf{B} = \mathbf{j} - \mathbf{B}_{i,k}\}$, the LHS of (5.33) is written as:

$$p_{ik}\sum_{\mathbf{n}\in\mathbf{\Omega}_{\mathbf{j}}}\gamma_{ik}(\mathbf{n})P(\mathbf{n}_{k-}^i) = p_{ik}\sum_{\mathbf{n}\in\mathbf{\Omega}_{\mathbf{j}}\cap\{n_k^i\geq 1\}} P(\mathbf{n}_{k-}^i) = p_{ik}\sum_{\mathbf{n}\in\mathbf{\Omega}_{\mathbf{j}-B_{i,k}}} P(\mathbf{n}_{k-}^i) \tag{5.34}$$

Now we continue by using the change of variables $n_m^{*i} = \begin{cases} n_m^i & \text{for } m \neq k \\ n_m^i - 1 & \text{for } m = k \end{cases}$ whereby (5.34) can be written as:

$$p_{ik}\sum_{\mathbf{n}\in\mathbf{\Omega}_{\mathbf{j}-B_{i,k}}} P(\mathbf{n}_{k-}^i) = p_{ik}\sum_{\vec{\mathbf{n}}^{*i}\in\mathbf{\Omega}_{\mathbf{j}-B_{i,k}}} P(\vec{\mathbf{n}}^{*i}) = p_{ik}q(\mathbf{j} - \mathbf{B}_{i,k}) \tag{5.35}$$

where $\vec{\mathbf{n}}^{*1} = (\mathbf{n}^{*1}, \mathbf{n}^2)$, $\vec{\mathbf{n}}^{*2} = (\mathbf{n}^1, \mathbf{n}^{*2})$, $\mathbf{n}^{*1} = (n_1^{*1}, \ldots, n_k^{*1}, \ldots, n_K^{*1})$, and $\mathbf{n}^{*2} = (n_1^{*2}, \ldots, n_k^{*2}, \ldots, n_K^{*2})$.

The RHS of (5.33) can be written as (for $\mathbf{j} \in \mathbf{\Omega}$ and $k = 1, \ldots, K$):

$$\sum_{\mathbf{n}\in\mathbf{\Omega}_{\mathbf{j}}} n_k^i P(\mathbf{n}) = \sum_{\mathbf{n}\in\mathbf{\Omega}_{\mathbf{j}}} \frac{n_k^i P(\mathbf{n})q(\mathbf{j})}{q(\mathbf{j})} = \sum_{\mathbf{n}\in\mathbf{\Omega}_{\mathbf{j}}} n_k^i P(\mathbf{n}|\mathbf{j})q(\mathbf{j}) = y_{ik}(\mathbf{j})q(\mathbf{j}) \tag{5.36}$$

Combining (5.35) and (5.36), it is proved that:

$$p_{ik}q(\mathbf{j} - \mathbf{B}_{i,k}) = y_{ik}(\mathbf{j})q(\mathbf{j}) \tag{5.37}$$

In order to derive (5.17) from (5.37), one should multiply both sides of (5.37) by $b_{i,k,s}$ and sum over $k = 1, \ldots, K$ and $i = 1, 2$:

$$\sum_{i=1}^{2}\sum_{k=1}^{K} b_{i,k,s}p_{ik}q(\mathbf{j} - \mathbf{B}_{i,k}) = \sum_{i=1}^{2}\sum_{k=1}^{K} b_{i,k,s}y_{ik}(\mathbf{j})q(\mathbf{j}) = j_s q(\mathbf{j}).$$

Q.E.D.

Based on (5.37), we can determine the values of $y_{ik}(\mathbf{j})$ via:

$$y_{ik}(\mathbf{j}) = p_{ik}q(\mathbf{j} - \mathbf{B}_{i,k})/q(\mathbf{j}) \tag{5.38}$$

We now approximate the BBP of a service-class k by the proportion of the rate whereby OFF calls of service-class k would depart from a burst blocking state, if it were possible, to the total rate of all OFF calls of service-class k in the system.

Specifically, we are interested in $y_{2k}(\mathbf{j})$, i.e., the mean number of service-class k calls in state OFF, when the system is in a burst blocking state $\mathbf{j}$. Multiplying $y_{2k}(\mathbf{j})$ by the corresponding $q(\mathbf{j})$ and the service rate in state OFF μ_{2k}, we obtain the rate whereby service-class k OFF-calls would depart from the burst blocking state if it were possible. By summing up these rates over the burst blocking state-space

$$\Omega^*, \ \mathbf{j} \in \Omega^* \Leftrightarrow \left\{ C - b_k + 1 \leq j_1 \leq C \cap \left(\sum_{s=1}^{2} j_s \leq C^* \right) \right\}, \quad \text{we obtain the following}$$

summation $\sum_{(\mathbf{j} \in \Omega^*)} y_{2k}(\mathbf{j}) q(\mathbf{j}) \mu_{2k}$.

By normalizing it (taking into account the whole state space Ω), we obtain the following formula for the BBP calculation:

$$B_k^* = \frac{\sum\limits_{\mathbf{j} \in \Omega^*} y_{2k}(\mathbf{j}) q(\mathbf{j}) \mu_{2k}}{\sum\limits_{\mathbf{j} \in \Omega} y_{2k}(\mathbf{j}) q(\mathbf{j}) \mu_{2k}} \tag{5.39}$$

where $\mathbf{j} \in \Omega \Leftrightarrow \left\{ j_1 \leq C \cap \left(\sum\limits_{s=1}^{2} j_s \leq C^* \right) \right\}$ and $q(\mathbf{j})$ are calculated by (5.17).

The BBP calculation via (5.39) is quite satisfactory, even under extremely low or extremely high traffic-load conditions.

Example 5.4 Consider again Example 5.1 ($C = 3, C^* = 4, K = 2, b_1 = 3, b_2 = 1$, $\lambda_1 = \lambda_2 = 1, \mu_{11}^{-1} = \mu_{12}^{-1} = \mu_{21}^{-1} = \mu_{22}^{-1} = 1, \ \sigma_1 = \sigma_2 = 0.9$). Calculate the BBP of both service-classes via (5.31) and (5.39). Compare them with simulation results.

- **BBP calculation based on (5.31).** We initially determine $\overline{n}_k^i$ according to (5.25):

$$\overline{n}_1^1 = \sum_{\mathbf{j} \in \Omega} G^{-1} p_{11} q(\mathbf{j} - \mathbf{B}_{1,1}) = p_{11}(Q(0,0) + Q(0,1)) \stackrel{p_{11}=10.0}{=} 0.015067$$

$$\overline{n}_1^2 = \sum_{\mathbf{j} \in \Omega} G^{-1} p_{21} q(\mathbf{j} - \mathbf{B}_{2,1}) = p_{21}(Q(0,0) + Q(0,1) + Q(1,0)) \stackrel{p_{21}=9.0}{=} 0.0271206$$

$$\overline{n}_2^1 = \sum_{\mathbf{j} \in \Omega} G^{-1} p_{12} q(\mathbf{j} - \mathbf{B}_{1,2}) = p_{12}(Q(0,0) + Q(0,1) + Q(0,2) + Q(0,3) + Q(1,0)$$

$$+ Q(1,1) + Q(1,2) + Q(2,0) + Q(2,1)) \stackrel{p_{12}=10.0}{=} 1.786941$$

$$\overline{n}_2^2 = \sum_{\mathbf{j} \in \Omega} G^{-1} p_{22} q(\mathbf{j} - \mathbf{B}_{2,2}) = p_{22}(Q(0,0) + Q(0,1) + Q(0,2) + Q(0,3) + Q(1,0)$$

$$+ Q(1,1) + Q(1,2) + Q(2,0) + Q(2,1) + Q(3,0)) \stackrel{p_{22}=9.0}{=} 1.847812$$

Thus, $B_1^* = \dfrac{\overline{n}_1^2 \mu_{21}}{\overline{n}_1^1 \mu_{11} - \lambda_1(1 - B_1)} - 1 \cong 0.9565$ and $B_2^* = \dfrac{\overline{n}_2^2 \mu_{22}}{\overline{n}_2^1 \mu_{12} - \lambda_2(1 - B_2)} - 1 \cong 0.14896$.

- **BBP calculation based on (5.39).** We initially determine $y_{2k}(\mathbf{j})$ according to (5.38):

$\mathbf{j} = (j_1, j_2) = (0, 1)$	$\Rightarrow \ y_{2,1}(0,1) = 0.0$	$y_{2,2}(0,1) = 1.0$
$\mathbf{j} = (j_1, j_2) = (0, 2)$	$\Rightarrow \ y_{2,1}(0,2) = 0.0$	$y_{2,2}(0,2) = 2.0$
$\mathbf{j} = (j_1, j_2) = (0, 3)$	$\Rightarrow \ y_{2,1}(0,3) = 0.0689655$	$y_{2,2}(0,3) = 2.793103$
$\mathbf{j} = (j_1, j_2) = (0, 4)$	$\Rightarrow \ y_{2,1}(0,4) = 0.2285715$	$y_{2,2}(0,4) = 3.314286$
$\mathbf{j} = (j_1, j_2) = (1, 1)$	$\Rightarrow \ y_{2,1}(1,1) = 0.0$	$y_{2,2}(1,1) = 1.0$
$\mathbf{j} = (j_1, j_2) = (1, 2)$	$\Rightarrow \ y_{2,1}(1,2) = 0.0$	$y_{2,2}(1,2) = 2.0$
$\mathbf{j} = (j_1, j_2) = (1, 3)$	$\Rightarrow \ y_{2,1}(1,3) = 0.0689655$	$y_{2,2}(1,3) = 2.793103$
$\mathbf{j} = (j_1, j_2) = (2, 1)$	$\Rightarrow \ y_{2,1}(2,1) = 0.0$	$y_{2,2}(2,1) = 1.0$
$\mathbf{j} = (j_1, j_2) = (2, 2)$	$\Rightarrow \ y_{2,1}(2,2) = 0.0$	$y_{2,2}(2,2) = 2.0$
$\mathbf{j} = (j_1, j_2) = (3, 1)$	$\Rightarrow \ y_{2,1}(3,1) = 0.0$	$y_{2,2}(3,1) = 1.0$

Table 5.2 Analytical and simulation BBP results (Example 5.5)

Arrival rate case	BBP	Analyt. (5.31)	BBP	Analyt. (5.39)	BBP	(Simul.)
	B_1^*	B_2^*	B_1^*	B_2^*	B_1^*	B_2^*
(i)	$8.05 \cdot 10^{-5}$	fails	$8.12 \cdot 10^{-5}$	$2.01 \cdot 10^{-8}$	$8.13 \cdot 10^{-5}$	$2.39 \cdot 10^{-8}$
					$\pm 1.62 \cdot 10^{-6}$	$\pm 3.12 \cdot 10^{-9}$
(ii)	$1.91 \cdot 10^{-3}$	$2.53 \cdot 10^{-5}$	$1.91 \cdot 10^{-3}$	$2.52 \cdot 10^{-5}$	$1.83 \cdot 10^{-3}$	$2.17 \cdot 10^{-5}$
					$\pm 2.52 \cdot 10^{-4}$	$\pm 7.01 \cdot 10^{-6}$
(iii)	$8.11 \cdot 10^{-2}$	$1.04 \cdot 10^{-2}$	$7.50 \cdot 10^{-2}$	$1.03 \cdot 10^{-2}$	$7.43 \cdot 10^{-2}$	$1.04 \cdot 10^{-2}$
					$\pm 2.06 \cdot 10^{-3}$	$\pm 2.50 \cdot 10^{-4}$
(iv)	fails	$39.03 \cdot 10^{-2}$	$68.22 \cdot 10^{-2}$	$28.07 \cdot 10^{-2}$	$68.21 \cdot 10^{-2}$	$28.02 \cdot 10^{-2}$
					$\pm 5.93 \cdot 10^{-3}$	$\pm 9.21 \cdot 10^{-4}$

Note that we do not present the values of $y_{2k}(j)$ for $(j_1, j_2) = (1, 0)$, $(2, 0)$, and $(3, 0)$, since $j_2 = 0$ and therefore $y_{21}(j) = y_{22}(j) = 0$ for these states. Based on the values of $y_{2k}(j)$, we can determine the BBP as follows:

$$B_1^* = \frac{y_{2,1}(1,3)q(1,3)}{y_{2,1}(0,3)q(0,3) + y_{2,1}(0,4)q(0,4) + y_{2,1}(1,3)q(1,3)} \Rightarrow B_1^* = 0.5$$

$$B_2^* = \frac{y_{2,2}(3,1)q(3,1)}{Y} \Rightarrow B_2^* = 0.12965$$

where $Y = y_{2,2}(0,1)q(0,1) + y_{2,2}(0,2)q(0,2) + y_{2,2}(1,1)q(1,1) + y_{2,2}(1,2)q(1,2) + y_{2,2}(0,3)q(0,3) + y_{2,2}(1,3)q(1,3) + y_{2,2}(0,4)q(0,4) + y_{2,2}(2,1)q(2,1) + y_{2,2}(2,2)q(2,2) + y_{2,2}(3,1)q(3,1)$.

Simulation results give $B_1^* = 0.502$ and $B_2^* = 0.128$, which show that (5.39) provides better accuracy compared to (5.31) even in small (tutorial) examples.

Example 5.5 Consider again Example 5.3 ($C = 10$, $C^* = 14$, $K = 2$, $b_1 = 4$, $b_2 = 1$, $\mu_{11}^{-1} = 0.8$, $\mu_{21}^{-1} = 0.4$, $\mu_{12}^{-1} = 0.9$, $\mu_{22}^{-1} = 0.3$, $\sigma_1 = \sigma_2 = 0.95$). Calculate the BBP according to (5.31) and (5.39) and compare the analytical results with simulation results for the following cases of λ_1, λ_2: (i) $\lambda_1 = 0.0008$, $\lambda_2 = 0.001$, (ii) $\lambda_1 = 0.004$, $\lambda_2 = 0.01$, (iii) $\lambda_1 = 0.02$, $\lambda_2 = 0.1$, and (iv) $\lambda_1 = 0.1$, $\lambda_2 = 1.0$.

Table 5.2 shows the analytical BBP results obtained by using (5.31) and (5.39) and the corresponding simulation results (with 95% confidence interval), for various values of arrival rates. It is obvious that (5.31) may fail under extremely low or high values of traffic-load.

5.2 The ON–OFF Multirate Loss Model under the BR Policy

5.2.1 The Service System

By incorporating the BR policy in the ON–OFF model (*ON–OFF/BR*), a new service-class k call is accepted in the system with b_k b.u. if it meets the following constraints:

$$j_1 + b_k \leq C - t_k \tag{5.40}$$

$$j_1 + j_2 + b_k \leq C^* - t_k \tag{5.41}$$

where t_k is the BR parameter of service-class k calls.

Thus, in Figure 5.2 the first decision block on call admission must now contain (5.40) and (5.41), instead of (5.1) and (5.2).

5.2.2 The Analytical Model

5.2.2.1 Steady State Probabilities
The new model does not have a PFS. Therefore, $q(\mathbf{j})$ can be determined in an approximate way, according to the following recursive formula [3]:

$$q(\mathbf{j}) = \begin{cases} 1 & \text{for } \mathbf{j} = 0 \\ \dfrac{1}{j_s} \displaystyle\sum_{i=1}^{2} \sum_{k=1}^{K} D_{i,k,s}(\mathbf{j} - \mathbf{B}_{i,k}) p_{ik} q(\mathbf{j} - \mathbf{B}_{i,k}) & \text{for } j_1 = 1, \dots, C \text{ (if } s = 1) \text{ or,} \\ & \text{for } j_2 = 1, \dots, C^* - j_1 \text{ (if } s = 2) \\ 0 & \text{otherwise} \end{cases}$$

(5.42)

where $D_{i,k,s}(\mathbf{j} - \mathbf{B}_{i,k}) = \begin{cases} b_{i,k,s} & \text{for } j_1 \le C - t_k \quad \text{and } j_1 + j_2 \le C^* - t_k \\ 0 & \text{otherwise} \end{cases}$, where $i = 1 \Rightarrow$ state ON, $i = 2 \Rightarrow$ state OFF, and $s = 1 \Rightarrow$ real link, $s = 2 \Rightarrow$ fictitious link.

5.2.2.2 CBP, Utilization, and Mean Number of In-service Calls
The following performance measures can be determined based on (5.42):

- The CBP of service-class k, B_k, via the formula [3]:

$$B_k = \sum_{\{\mathbf{j} \ | \ [(b_{1,k,1}+j_1)>C-t_k]\cup[(b_{1,k,1}+j_1+j_2)>C^*-t_k]\}} G^{-1} q(\mathbf{j}) \tag{5.43}$$

where $G = \sum_{(\mathbf{j} \in \Omega)} q(\mathbf{j})$.
- The link utilization, U_s ($s = 1 \Rightarrow$ real link, $s = 2 \Rightarrow$ fictitious link), via (5.19).
- The mean number of service-class k calls in state i given that the system state is $\mathbf{j}$, $y_{ik}(\mathbf{j})$, via (5.38).
- The mean number of service-class k calls in state i, $\overline{n}_k^i$, via (5.25).

5.2.2.3 BBP
The BBP calculation can be based on (5.39), which is independent of the fact that the ON–OFF/BR model does not have a PFS. The determination of the average population of calls of service-class k in state OFF, $y_{2k}(\mathbf{j})$, is based on (5.38), while the corresponding values of $q(\mathbf{j})$ are given by (5.42).

The analytical BBP results obtained by the aforementioned procedure may significantly diverge from simulation BBP results when the BR parameters have high values (e.g., when CBP equalization is required) due to the following case which is not taken into account. Consider two service-classes whose calls require b_1, b_2 b.u. with $b_2 > b_1$. Calls of service-class 1 have a BR parameter equal to $t_1 = b_2 - b_1$ so that the CBP of both service-classes are the same. The BR parameter for calls of service-class 2 is $t_2 = 0$. Due to the application of the BR policy, the population of calls of service-class 1 is restricted to the region denoted by the constraints $j_1 \le C - t_1$ and $j_2 \le C^* - j_1 - t_1$. When

$j_1 > C - t_1$ or $j_2 > C^* - j_1 - t_1$ then the population of calls of service-class 1 is considered to be zero (these states belong to the so-called reservation space). Assume now that a call of service-class 1 is in the system (in either state ON or state OFF), whereas the system state is $\mathbf{j} = (j_1, j_2)$ where $j_1 \leq C - t_1$ and $j_2 \leq C^* - j_1 - t_1$ when an external (new) call of service-class 2 arrives in state ON. This arrival may transfer the system to a new state $\mathbf{j} = (j_1, j_2)$ such that $j_1 > C - t_1$. In that new state, the call of service-class 1 is still in the system. It is therefore apparent that in a more realistic model calls of service-class 1 may also appear in their reservation space due to the arrival of calls of service-class 2.

To improve the analytical BBP, the method of Stasiak–Glabowski ([5]) (already presented in Section 1.3.2.3 for the CBP calculation in the EMLM/BR) can be applied in (5.39) according to the following algorithm [3]:

Algorithm 5.1 Calculation of BBP of a service-class k with $t_k > 0$

For the system state $\mathbf{j} = (j_1, j_2)$
if $j_1 \leq C - t_k$ *and* $j_2 \leq C^* - j_1 - t_k$ **then**
    Determine $y_{2k}(\mathbf{j})$ according to (5.38) and (5.42)
end if
if $j_1 > C - t_k$ **then**
    For all service-classes x ($x = 1, \dots, K$ but $x \neq k$)
    if $j_1 \leq C - t_x$ *and* $j_2 \leq C^* - j_1 - t_x$ **then**
    $y_{2k}(\mathbf{j}) \leftarrow y_{2k}(\mathbf{j}) + y_{2k}(j_1 - b_x, j_2)$
    end if
end if
Determine the BBP according to (5.39)

Example 5.6 Consider a link of (real) capacity $C = 80$ b.u. that accommodates three service-classes and let the fictitious capacity take two values: (i) $C^* = 80$ b.u. (no burst blocking) and (ii) $C^* = 100$ b.u. The traffic description parameters of the service-classes for the ON–OFF model are $(\lambda_1, \lambda_2, \lambda_3) = (0.05, 0.06, 0.09)$, $(\mu_{11}^{-1}, \mu_{12}^{-1}, \mu_{13}^{-1}) = (0.5, 1.0, 1.2)$, $(\mu_{21}^{-1}, \mu_{22}^{-1}, \mu_{23}^{-1}) = (0.8, 1.9, 0.9)$, and $(b_1, b_2, b_3) = (10, 8, 6)$, $(\sigma_1, \sigma_2, \sigma_3) = (0.85, 0.9, 0.95)$. CBP equalization is achieved in the ON–OFF/BR model by using the BR parameters $(t_1, t_2, t_3) = (0, 2, 4)$. Compare the CBP and BBP of all service-classes by assuming that λ_1, λ_2 remain constant, while λ_3 increases in steps of 0.03 (up to $(\lambda_1, \lambda_2, \lambda_3) = (0.05, 0.06, 0.24)$). Also provide simulation results, with 95% confidence interval, for the CBP and BBP for the ON–OFF/BR model and for both models, respectively.

Figures 5.5 and 5.6 present the analytical and the simulation CBP results of all service-classes for $C^* = 80$ and $C^* = 100$, respectively. In the horizontal axis of both figures, point 1 refers to $(\lambda_1, \lambda_2, \lambda_3) = (0.05, 0.06, 0.09)$, point 2 to $(\lambda_1, \lambda_2, \lambda_3) = (0.05, 0.06, 0.12)$, while point 6 refers to $(\lambda_1, \lambda_2, \lambda_3) = (0.05, 0.06, 0.24)$. Simulation results are not presented for the ON–OFF model since it is a PFS model (i.e., accurate). Both figures show that (i) the application of the BR policy reduces the CBP of service-class 1 at the cost of increasing the CBP of service-classes 2 and 3 and (ii) the analytical

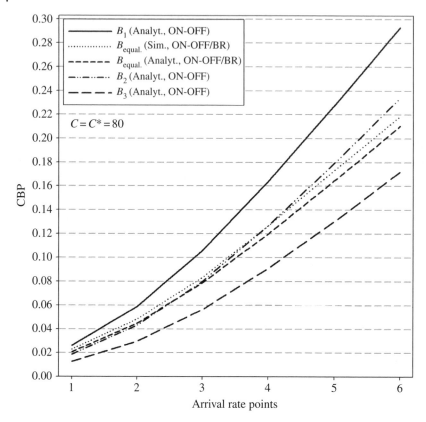

Figure 5.5 Analytical CBP when $C = C^* = 80$ b.u. (Example 5.6).

and simulation CBP results are quite close in the case of the ON–OFF/BR model. In addition, Figure 5.6 shows that the increase in the fictitious capacity from 80 to 100 b.u. substantially reduces CBP. This increase, however, causes the appearance of BBP for all service-classes (Tables 5.3–5.4).

In Table 5.3, we present the analytical and simulation BBP of the three service-classes under the CS policy (ON–OFF model). In Table 5.4, we give the analytical and simulation BBP of all service-classes under the BR policy. In the case of the BR policy, the analytical BBP results of service-classes 2 and 3 are obtained by applying or not the Stasiak–Glabowski (S&G) method. For service-class 1, however, the application or not of the S&G method in the BBP formula does not affect the BBP results, since there is no reservation space for service-class 1 ($t_1 = 0$). For service-class 2, the S&G method results in slightly better BBP results compared to the corresponding results when the S&G method is not applied (columns 5 and 4, respectively, of Table 5.4). For service-class 3, the S&G method results in much better BBP results compared to the corresponding results when the S&G method is not applied (columns 8 and 7, respectively, of Table 5.4).

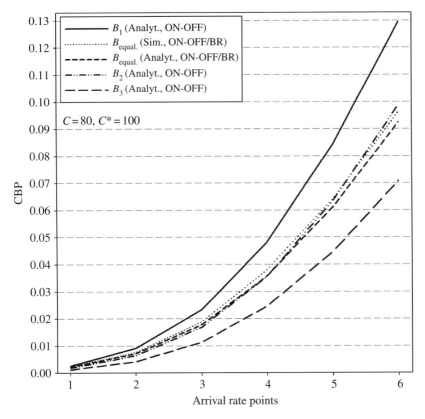

Figure 5.6 Analytical CBP when $C = 80$, $C^* = 100$ b.u. (Example 5.6).

Table 5.3 Analytical and simulation BBP of the ON–OFF model (Example 5.6)

Arrival rate points	BBP B_1^*		BBP B_2^*		BBP B_3^*	
	Analyt.	Simul.	Analyt.	Simul.	Analyt.	Simul.
1	$9.85 \cdot 10^{-5}$	$1.11 \cdot 10^{-4}$ $\pm 4.41 \cdot 10^{-5}$	$6.34 \cdot 10^{-5}$	$5.93 \cdot 10^{-5}$ $\pm 1.71 \cdot 10^{-6}$	$3.88 \cdot 10^{-5}$	$3.63 \cdot 10^{-5}$ $\pm 6.60 \cdot 10^{-6}$
2	$3.16 \cdot 10^{-4}$	$3.51 \cdot 10^{-4}$ $\pm 6.12 \cdot 10^{-5}$	$2.13 \cdot 10^{-4}$	$2.30 \cdot 10^{-4}$ $\pm 1.63 \cdot 10^{-5}$	$1.35 \cdot 10^{-4}$	$1.13 \cdot 10^{-4}$ $\pm 9.41 \cdot 10^{-6}$
3	$7.65 \cdot 10^{-4}$	$8.02 \cdot 10^{-4}$ $\pm 9.00 \cdot 10^{-5}$	$5.38 \cdot 10^{-4}$	$5.42 \cdot 10^{-4}$ $\pm 6.77 \cdot 10^{-5}$	$3.52 \cdot 10^{-4}$	$3.50 \cdot 10^{-4}$ $\pm 1.69 \cdot 10^{-5}$
4	$1.51 \cdot 10^{-3}$	$1.51 \cdot 10^{-3}$ $\pm 1.19 \cdot 10^{-4}$	$1.09 \cdot 10^{-3}$	$1.07 \cdot 10^{-3}$ $\pm 9.00 \cdot 10^{-5}$	$7.31 \cdot 10^{-4}$	$7.09 \cdot 10^{-4}$ $\pm 2.26 \cdot 10^{-5}$
5	$2.56 \cdot 10^{-3}$	$2.63 \cdot 10^{-3}$ $\pm 2.23 \cdot 10^{-4}$	$1.90 \cdot 10^{-3}$	$1.97 \cdot 10^{-3}$ $\pm 1.05 \cdot 10^{-4}$	$1.28 \cdot 10^{-3}$	$1.27 \cdot 10^{-3}$ $\pm 4.80 \cdot 10^{-5}$
6	$3.88 \cdot 10^{-3}$	$3.92 \cdot 10^{-3}$ $\pm 1.93 \cdot 10^{-4}$	$2.92 \cdot 10^{-3}$	$2.94 \cdot 10^{-3}$ $\pm 1.85 \cdot 10^{-5}$	$1.96 \cdot 10^{-3}$	$1.97 \cdot 10^{-3}$ $\pm 4.70 \cdot 10^{-5}$

Table 5.4 Analytical and simulation BBP of the ON–OFF/BR model (Example 5.6)

Arrival rate points	BBP B_1^*		BBP B_2^*		BBP B_3^*	
	Analyt.	Simul.	Analyt., S&G	Simul.	Analyt., S&G	Simul.
1	$9.06 \cdot 10^{-5}$	$9.59 \cdot 10^{-5}$ $\pm 1.45 \cdot 10^{-5}$	$4.67 \cdot 10^{-5}, 4.69 \cdot 10^{-5}$	$5.62 \cdot 10^{-5}$ $\pm 8.90 \cdot 10^{-6}$	$2.00 \cdot 10^{-5}, 2.66 \cdot 10^{-5}$	$3.06 \cdot 10^{-5}$ $\pm 7.05 \cdot 10^{-6}$
2	$2.87 \cdot 10^{-4}$	$2.77 \cdot 10^{-4}$ $\pm 4.90 \cdot 10^{-5}$	$1.48 \cdot 10^{-4}, 1.49 \cdot 10^{-4}$	$1.58 \cdot 10^{-4}$ $\pm 3.22 \cdot 10^{-5}$	$6.44 \cdot 10^{-5}, 8.33 \cdot 10^{-5}$	$9.24 \cdot 10^{-5}$ $\pm 9.05 \cdot 10^{-6}$
3	$6.86 \cdot 10^{-4}$	$6.35 \cdot 10^{-4}$ $\pm 8.51 \cdot 10^{-5}$	$3.54 \cdot 10^{-4}, 3.56 \cdot 10^{-4}$	$3.71 \cdot 10^{-4}$ $\pm 3.80 \cdot 10^{-5}$	$1.56 \cdot 10^{-4}, 1.96 \cdot 10^{-4}$	$2.14 \cdot 10^{-4}$ $\pm 1.35 \cdot 10^{-5}$
4	$1.34 \cdot 10^{-3}$	$1.15 \cdot 10^{-3}$ $\pm 1.32 \cdot 10^{-4}$	$6.83 \cdot 10^{-4}, 6.87 \cdot 10^{-4}$	$7.48 \cdot 10^{-4}$ $\pm 6.10 \cdot 10^{-5}$	$3.01 \cdot 10^{-4}, 3.71 \cdot 10^{-4}$	$4.35 \cdot 10^{-4}$ $\pm 1.89 \cdot 10^{-5}$
5	$2.25 \cdot 10^{-3}$	$2.07 \cdot 10^{-3}$ $\pm 1.16 \cdot 10^{-4}$	$1.12 \cdot 10^{-3}, 1.12 \cdot 10^{-3}$	$1.27 \cdot 10^{-3}$ $\pm 9.00 \cdot 10^{-5}$	$4.87 \cdot 10^{-4}, 5.91 \cdot 10^{-4}$	$7.68 \cdot 10^{-4}$ $\pm 3.46 \cdot 10^{-5}$
6	$3.38 \cdot 10^{-3}$	$2.98 \cdot 10^{-3}$ $\pm 1.52 \cdot 10^{-4}$	$1.61 \cdot 10^{-3}, 1.62 \cdot 10^{-3}$	$1.77 \cdot 10^{-3}$ $\pm 8.61 \cdot 10^{-5}$	$6.91 \cdot 10^{-4}, 8.25 \cdot 10^{-4}$	$9.58 \cdot 10^{-4}$ $\pm 4.40 \cdot 10^{-5}$

5.3 The ON–OFF Multirate Loss Model in a Fixed Routing Network

5.3.1 The Service System

Let us consider that a fixed routing network consists of L links. Each link l ($l = 1, \ldots, L$) has a (real) capacity of C_l b.u. and a fictitious capacity of C_l^* b.u. The network accommodates calls of K service-classes under the CS policy. Calls of service-class k follow a Poisson process with arrival rate λ_k, require b_k b.u., and have an exponentially distributed service-time in state i, μ_{ik}^{-1}. Let R_k be the fixed route of service-class k calls in the network, where $R_k \subseteq \{1, \ldots, L\}$. A call of service-class k is accepted in the network if and only if its b_k b.u. are available in every link $l \in R_k$, in both states ON and OFF. In other words, the CAC of a service-class k call still relies on the constraints (5.1) and (5.2), which should be fulfilled for every link $l \in R_k$. If a call is accepted in the network, then its behavior is exactly the same as that of Section 5.1.1. Otherwise, the call is blocked and lost.

5.3.2 The Analytical Model

5.3.2.1 Steady State Probabilities
By defining the occupied real and fictitious b.u. of link l as j_{1l} and j_{2l}, respectively, the unnormalized values of $q(\mathbf{j})$, where $\mathbf{j} = (j_{11}, \ldots, j_{1l}, \ldots, j_{1L}, j_{21}, \ldots, j_{2l}, \ldots, j_{2L})$ can be determined by the following accurate and recursive formula [1]:

$$q(\mathbf{j}) = \begin{cases} 1 & \text{for } \mathbf{j} = 0 \\ \dfrac{1}{j_{sl}} \sum_{i=1}^{2} \sum_{k=1}^{K} b_{i,k,s,l} P_{ik} q(\mathbf{j} - \mathbf{B}_{i,k}) & \text{for } j_{1l} = 1, \ldots, C_l \text{ (if } s = 1) \text{ or,} \\ & \text{for } j_{2l} = 1, \ldots, C^* - j_{11} \text{ (if } s = 2) \\ 0 & \text{otherwise} \end{cases} \quad (5.44)$$

where $\mathbf{j} \in \Omega \Leftrightarrow \left\{ \left(j_{1l} \le C_l \cap \left(\sum_{s=1}^{2} j_{sl} \le C_l^* \right) \right), l = 1, \dots, L \right\}$, $i = 1 \Rightarrow$ state ON,

$i = 2 \Rightarrow$ state OFF, $s = 1 \Rightarrow$ real link, $s = 2 \Rightarrow$ fictitious link,

$b_{i,k,s,l} = \begin{cases} b_k & \text{if } s = i \text{ and } l \in R_k \\ 0 & \text{if } s \ne i \end{cases}$, and $\mathbf{B}_{ik}$ is the (i,k) row of a $(2K \times 2L)$ matrix

$\mathbf{B}$ with:

$\mathbf{B}_{i,k} = (b_{i,k,1,1}, \dots, b_{i,k,1,l}, \dots, b_{i,k,1,L}, b_{i,k,2,1}, \dots, b_{i,k,2,l}, \dots, b_{i,k,2,L})$.

Before we proceed with the determination of the various performance measures, we show the relationship between the ON–OFF in a fixed routing network model and the EMLM in a fixed routing network [6]. Both models are equivalent, in the sense that they provide the same CBP, when:

(i) $\sigma_k = 0$ (i.e., when no state OFF exists) for each service-class k $(k = 1, \dots, K)$. In that case the calculation of $q(\mathbf{j})$ can be done by (1.83).

(ii) $\sigma_k > 0$ and $C = C^*$. Then we can determine the mean holding time, μ_k^{-1}, of a service-class k call of the ON–OFF model by (5.20) and the values of $q(\mathbf{j})$ by (1.83).

5.3.2.2 CBP, Utilization, Mean Number of In-service Calls, and BBP

The following performance measures can be determined based on (5.44):

- The CBP of service-class k, B_k, via the formula [1]:

$$B_k = \sum_{\left\{ \mathbf{j} \mid \bigcup_{l=1}^{L} ([(b_{1,k,1,l}+j_{1l}) > C_l] \cup [(b_{1,k,1,l}+j_{1l}+j_{2l}) > C_l^*]) \right\}} G^{-1} q(\mathbf{j}) \tag{5.45}$$

where $G = \sum_{\mathbf{j} \in \Omega} q(\mathbf{j})$.

- The link utilization of link l, U_{sl} ($s = 1 \Rightarrow$ real link, $s = 2 \Rightarrow$ fictitious link), via the formula [1]:

$$U_{sl} = \sum_{\tau=0}^{C_{sl}} \tau Q_{sl}(\tau) \tag{5.46}$$

where $Q_{sl}(\tau) = \sum_{(\mathbf{j} \mid j_{sl}=\tau)} G^{-1} q(\mathbf{j})$ and $C_{sl} = C_l$ for $s = 1$ while $C_{sl} = C_l^*$ for $s = 2$.

- The mean number of service-class k calls in state i given that the system state is $\mathbf{j}$, $y_{ik}(\mathbf{j})$, via (5.38).

- The mean number of service-class k calls in state i, $\bar{n}_k^i$, via (5.25).

- The BBP of service-class k, B_k^*, via (5.31) or (5.39).

Example 5.7 Consider a network of two links with (real) capacities $C_1 = 50$ and $C_2 = 40$ b.u. The network accommodates calls of $K = 3$ service-classes with bandwidth requirements $b_1 = 2, b_2 = 4$, and $b_3 = 6$ b.u., respectively [1]. Figure 5.7 shows the routes of all service-classes. Calls of service-class 1 traverse the first link, calls of service-class 2 traverse the second link while calls of service-class 3 traverse both links.

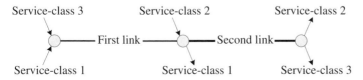

Figure 5.7 The fixed routing network with two links and three service-classes (Example 5.7).

The traffic description parameters of the service-classes for the ON–OFF model are $(\lambda_1, \lambda_2, \lambda_3) = (0.4\lambda, 0.35\lambda, 0.25\lambda), (\mu_{11}^{-1}, \mu_{12}^{-1}, \mu_{13}^{-1}) = (1.32, 1.32, 2.0), (\mu_{21}^{-1}, \mu_{22}^{-1}, \mu_{23}^{-1}) = (1.82, 1.82, 0.5),$ and $(\sigma_1, \sigma_2, \sigma_3) = (0.975, 0.975, 0.9),$ where λ is the total call arrival rate in calls/s. Based on (5.20), we can determine the equivalent service time for each service-class when the EMLM in a fixed routing network is considered [6]: $(\mu_1^{-1}, \mu_2^{-1}, \mu_3^{-1}) = (123.78, 123.78, 24.5)$. Calculate the CBP and the link utilizations for six different values of $\lambda = 0.1, 0.2, \ldots, 0.6$ and three different sets of fictitious capacities: (i) $C_1^* = 50, C_2^* = 40$, (ii) $C_1^* = 60, C_2^* = 50$, and (iii) $C_1^* = 70, C_2^* = 60$. Furthermore, provide analytical BBP results (based on (5.31)) for the third set of fictitious capacities. Also provide simulation results, with 95% confidence interval, for all performance measures.

The first set of fictitious capacities leads to the same CBP as the model of [6] (and zero BBP). The next two sets are studied in order to show the effect of the increase in fictitious capacities on CBP, BBP, and link utilization.

Figure 5.8 presents the analytical CBP results for all service-classes and all sets of fictitious capacities. Tables 5.5–5.7 present the corresponding simulation CBP results for each set, respectively. In Table 5.8, we present the analytical utilization results for the first link (real and fictitious). The corresponding results for the second link are presented in Table 5.9. Figure 5.9 shows the analytical and simulation of the total utilization of the first link. By the term "total utilization", we mean the sum of the utilizations of the real and fictitious b.u. The corresponding results for the second link are presented in Figure 5.10.

Based on Figure 5.8, we see that the increase in the fictitious capacities results in a significant decrease in the CBP and an increase in the utilization of both links (see

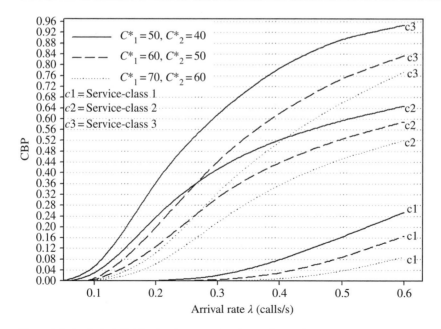

Figure 5.8 Analytical CBP for the three service-classes (Example 5.7).

Table 5.5 Simulation CBP results when $C_1^* = 50$ and $C_2^* = 40$ b.u. (Example 5.7)

λ (calls/s)	B_1	B_2	B_3
0.1	0.00000	$3.11 \cdot 10^{-2} \pm 6.83 \cdot 10^{-4}$	$5.59 \cdot 10^{-2} \pm 1.09 \cdot 10^{-3}$
0.2	$1.45 \cdot 10^{-3} \pm 2.88 \cdot 10^{-4}$	$23.70 \cdot 10^{-2} \pm 3.33 \cdot 10^{-3}$	$36.41 \cdot 10^{-2} \pm 5.10 \cdot 10^{-3}$
0.3	$2.09 \cdot 10^{-2} \pm 1.43 \cdot 10^{-3}$	$41.32 \cdot 10^{-2} \pm 2.46 \cdot 10^{-3}$	$61.92 \cdot 10^{-2} \pm 5.89 \cdot 10^{-3}$
0.4	$8.03 \cdot 10^{-2} \pm 1.89 \cdot 10^{-3}$	$52.24 \cdot 10^{-2} \pm 2.37 \cdot 10^{-3}$	$79.19 \cdot 10^{-2} \pm 2.64 \cdot 10^{-3}$
0.5	$16.52 \cdot 10^{-2} \pm 2.05 \cdot 10^{-3}$	$59.43 \cdot 10^{-2} \pm 2.83 \cdot 10^{-3}$	$89.61 \cdot 10^{-2} \pm 3.82 \cdot 10^{-3}$
0.6	$25.60 \cdot 10^{-2} \pm 2.40 \cdot 10^{-3}$	$64.82 \cdot 10^{-2} \pm 2.55 \cdot 10^{-3}$	$94.99 \cdot 10^{-2} \pm 2.42 \cdot 10^{-3}$

Table 5.6 Simulation CBP results when $C_1^* = 60$ and $C_2^* = 50$ b.u. (Example 5.7)

λ (calls/s)	B_1	B_2	B_3
0.1	0.000000	$5.43 \cdot 10^{-3} \pm 5.42 \cdot 10^{-4}$	$1.07 \cdot 10^{-2} \pm 6.04 \cdot 10^{-4}$
0.2	$1.54 \cdot 10^{-4} \pm 7.09 \cdot 10^{-5}$	$12.84 \cdot 10^{-2} \pm 2.24 \cdot 10^{-3}$	$19.82 \cdot 10^{-2} \pm 3.46 \cdot 10^{-3}$
0.3	$4.89 \cdot 10^{-3} \pm 6.99 \cdot 10^{-4}$	$30.74 \cdot 10^{-2} \pm 3.52 \cdot 10^{-3}$	$44.17 \cdot 10^{-2} \pm 4.69 \cdot 10^{-3}$
0.4	$3.05 \cdot 10^{-2} \pm 1.48 \cdot 10^{-3}$	$43.91 \cdot 10^{-2} \pm 3.47 \cdot 10^{-3}$	$62.25 \cdot 10^{-2} \pm 3.31 \cdot 10^{-3}$
0.5	$8.91 \cdot 10^{-2} \pm 3.27 \cdot 10^{-3}$	$52.64 \cdot 10^{-2} \pm 4.09 \cdot 10^{-3}$	$75.14 \cdot 10^{-2} \pm 3.52 \cdot 10^{-3}$
0.6	$16.94 \cdot 10^{-2} \pm 3.18 \cdot 10^{-3}$	$58.83 \cdot 10^{-2} \pm 2.07 \cdot 10^{-3}$	$83.62 \cdot 10^{-2} \pm 2.09 \cdot 10^{-3}$

Table 5.7 Simulation CBP results when $C_1^* = 70$ and $C_2^* = 60$ b.u. (Example 5.7)

λ (calls/s)	B_1	B_2	B_3
0.1	0.000000	$1.36 \cdot 10^{-3} \pm 1.65 \cdot 10^{-4}$	$2.70 \cdot 10^{-3} \pm 1.60 \cdot 10^{-4}$
0.2	$2.50 \cdot 10^{-5} \pm 1.92 \cdot 10^{-6}$	$6.29 \cdot 10^{-2} \pm 1.69 \cdot 10^{-3}$	$10.50 \cdot 10^{-2} \pm 2.39 \cdot 10^{-3}$
0.3	$8.80 \cdot 10^{-4} \pm 3.34 \cdot 10^{-5}$	$21.59 \cdot 10^{-2} \pm 2.89 \cdot 10^{-3}$	$32.57 \cdot 10^{-2} \pm 2.32 \cdot 10^{-3}$
0.4	$8.70 \cdot 10^{-3} \pm 7.61 \cdot 10^{-4}$	$35.51 \cdot 10^{-2} \pm 3.89 \cdot 10^{-3}$	$51.36 \cdot 10^{-2} \pm 2.75 \cdot 10^{-3}$
0.5	$3.91 \cdot 10^{-2} \pm 1.25 \cdot 10^{-3}$	$45.04 \cdot 10^{-2} \pm 3.28 \cdot 10^{-3}$	$66.24 \cdot 10^{-2} \pm 3.48 \cdot 10^{-3}$
0.6	$8.96 \cdot 10^{-2} \pm 2.52 \cdot 10^{-3}$	$52.13 \cdot 10^{-2} \pm 3.56 \cdot 10^{-3}$	$77.71 \cdot 10^{-2} \pm 2.30 \cdot 10^{-3}$

Figures 5.9–5.10). However, the increase in the fictitious capacities increases the BBP of all service-classes since many calls may enter state OFF but cannot easily be transferred to state ON. In Figure 5.11, we present the analytical and simulation BBP results for the worst case scenario ($C_1^* = 70, C_2^* = 60$). Based on Figure 5.11, we deduce that (5.31) provides quite good BBP results compared to simulation. Note that similar accuracy can be obtained from (5.39) as well.

Table 5.8 Analytical utilization results for the first link (real and fictitious) (Example 5.7)

ᵛ	$C_1^* = 50$ U_{11}	$C_2^* = 40$ U_{21}	$C_1^* = 60$ U_{11}	$C_2^* = 50$ U_{21}	$C_1^* = 70$ U_{11}	$C_2^* = 60$ U_{21}
0.1	7.06	6.32	7.19	6.34	7.22	6.35
0.2	12.24	12.20	13.25	12.44	13.82	12.59
0.3	15.86	17.46	17.63	18.09	18.73	18.45
0.4	18.09	21.49	20.93	23.06	22.58	23.90
0.5	19.23	24.08	22.99	26.72	25.43	28.54
0.6	19.81	25.60	24.08	29.05	27.14	31.99

Table 5.9 Analytical utilization results for the second link (real and fictitious) (Example 5.7)

λ	$C_1^* = 50$ U_{11}	$C_2^* = 40$ U_{21}	$C_1^* = 60$ U_{11}	$C_2^* = 50$ U_{21}	$C_1^* = 70$ U_{11}	$C_2^* = 60$ U_{21}
0.1	10.00	10.27	10.32	10.56	10.37	10.61
0.2	15.08	16.01	17.69	18.47	19.23	20.12
0.3	16.44	18.23	20.37	21.88	23.43	25.43
0.4	16.64	19.53	21.15	23.49	24.90	27.92
0.5	16.57	20.50	21.26	24.52	25.33	29.36
0.6	16.52	21.17	21.14	25.23	25.29	30.45

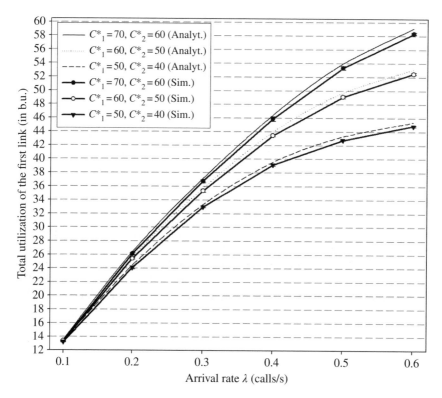

Figure 5.9 Total utilization for the first link (Example 5.7.)

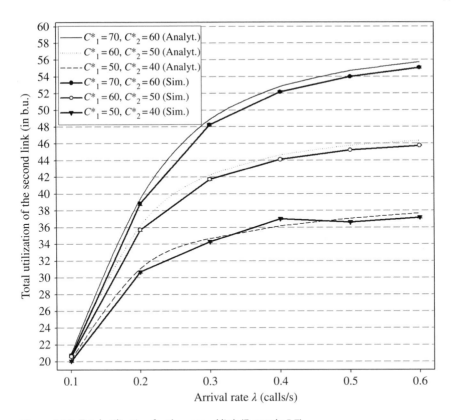

Figure 5.10 Total utilization for the second link (Example 5.7).

5.4 Applications

An interesting application of the ON–OFF model has been proposed in [7]. In [7], a WDM-TDMA passive optical network (PON) is considered (Figure 5.12), which is connected to a wide area or metropolitan network through the optical line terminal (OLT).

In the upstream direction, the PON supports W wavelengths[1]. N optical network units (ONUs) are connected to the OLT through the array waveguide grating (AWG). In the case where $W < N$, DWA is needed; otherwise, an ONU could allocate a wavelength statically. Each ONU accommodates K service-classes; the calls of each service-class are of ON–OFF type when they are in service. Service-class k ($k = 1, \ldots, K$) calls arrive to an ONU according to a Poisson process with mean arrival rate λ_k. They are conveyed through a connection established between the ONU and the OLT that is realized through one (only) wavelength in the PON. The service of a service-class k call is realized by allocating a specific number of time-slots, b_k, within a frame for the entire duration of the call (TDMA scheme). The total number of time-slots in a frame defines the fixed bandwidth capacity, C, of the wavelength (static bandwidth allocation inside the wavelength).

---

1 Typically in the 1310 nm switching window.

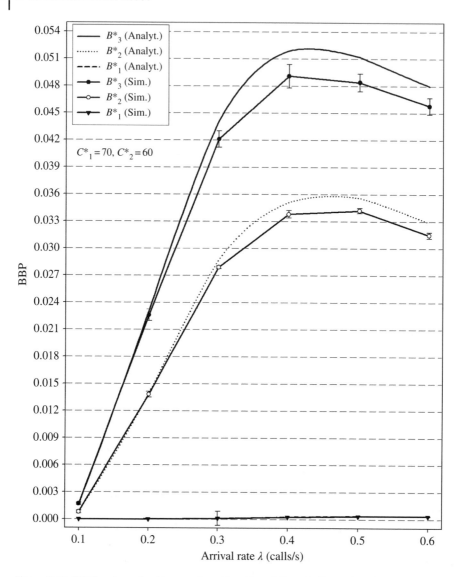

Figure 5.11 BBP for all service-classes when $C^* = 70$ and $C^* = 60$ (Example 5.7).

When no other calls from this ONU are in service, the connection establishment of the ONU to the OLT is realized by the first arriving call from any service-class. If the OLT finds a free wavelength, it is assigned to the ONU; the ONUs are assumed to be color-free (i.e., any PON wavelength can be assigned to an ONU). Thus, a connection is established and the call is conveyed; otherwise, the call is blocked and lost (both connection and call failure occur). After the establishment of the connection, all calls from the same ONU seize the same wavelength. However, given that the bandwidth capacity of the wavelength is restricted, call blocking occurs. Specifically, each time a service-class k call arrives and a wavelength is already assigned to an ONU, a control packet is sent to the OLT to inform it that this call requires b_k time-slots within a frame. The OLT responds

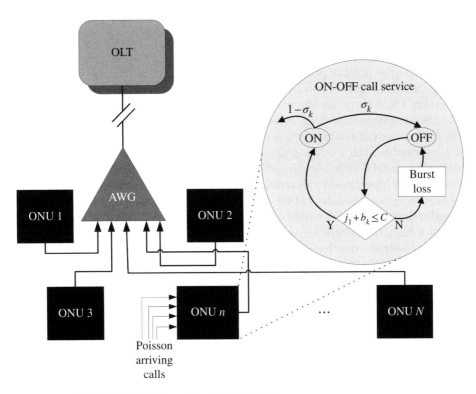

Figure 5.12 A WDM-TDMA PON servicing ON–OFF traffic.

to this request with another control packet: if more than b_k time-slots are available, the OLT informs the ONU that the call is accepted; otherwise the call is blocked and lost. If a wavelength is not assigned to an ONU upon a service-class k call arrival, the ONU firstly sends to the OLT a control packet to request a free wavelength. If a free wavelength is found, the OLT responds with a control packet which contains the frequency of the assigned wavelength and adjusts a receiver to this frequency. At the reception of this control packet, the ONU adjusts a transmitter to this frequency.

The connection between an ONU and the OLT through one wavelength is considered as a single link of C b.u., which accommodates the K service-classes. A b.u. corresponds to a time-slot. Service-class k calls are accepted for service according to the CAC of the ON–OFF multirate loss model. In view of the fact that $W < N$, a DWA algorithm/scenario should be adopted in order to provide connectivity to all ONUs and service all users.

Three basic DWA scenarios and corresponding analytical models are proposed in [7]. Each DWA scenario introduces an alternative wavelength release procedure based on the bandwidth occupancy of the wavelength that is assigned to an ONU. In the primary wavelength release (P-WR) scenario, a wavelength is released when all calls (either in state ON or OFF) have terminated. The connection failure probability (CFP) performance of this scenario could be improved by accelerating the wavelength release procedure/rate. This is achieved by the delay wavelength release (D-WR) scenario: a wavelength is released when no calls in state ON exist in the system, but they do exist in state OFF, when the occupied fictitious bandwidth is up to a percentage of the fictitious capacity; this percentage is defined as an increase or a constant function of the number of occupied wavelengths in the PON, e.g., if one out of four wavelengths is seized in the PON at the time-point of possible wavelength release, this percentage could be 3%, arbitrarily chosen, if there are two seized wavelengths, out of four, this percentage could be higher, say 5%, if there are three seized wavelengths, out of four, this percentage could be 8%, while if there are four seized wavelengths out of four, this percentage could be 12%. Alternatively, it could be 4%, arbitrarily chosen, irrespective of the number of seized wavelengths. Such a relation allows greater ONU connectivity by delaying the servicing of some OFF calls; they are obliged to postpone their service until the next ONU connection (upon a new call arrival). Under a constant function, the wavelength release procedure is independent of the number of occupied wavelengths; the desirable wavelength release procedure would have a low rate when the wavelength occupancy is low and a high rate when the wavelength occupancy is high. Under an increase function, the lower the number of occupied wavelengths, the lower the mean service rate of the wavelength; they both result in a smaller number of calls that suffer delay. This number is further reduced by the primary delay wavelength release (PD-WR) scenario (at the expense of CFP). According to this scenario, the number of occupied wavelengths in the PON defines the applicability of the P-WR or the D-WR scenario. If this number is less than a predefined threshold, the P-WR scenario is applied; otherwise (i.e., heavy load is indicated) the D-WR scenario is preferable. In all cases, the authors of [7] calculate the CFP, which occurs due to the unavailability of a free wavelength in the link between the AWG and the OLT. In addition, the authors calculate:

- the delay that OFF calls suffer from the time instant the wavelength is released until the re-connection of the ONU to the OLT, for the D-WR and PD-WR scenarios, and
- the BBP and the CBP that occur after the establishment of the OLT–ONU connection due to the restricted bandwidth capacity of a wavelength.

5.5 Further Reading

Due to the relationship between the ON–OFF model and the EMLM (see Section 5.1.2.2), the ON–OFF model can be extended to include various characteristics of the EMLM extensions (see e.g., Chapter 2). Thus, the interested reader may actually study extensions of the EMLM and consider as a candidate model the ON–OFF model, especially when the combination of call blocking and burst blocking is necessary. As an example, in [2, 8], the SRM and MRM (which are extensions of the EMLM) have been studied under the framework of the ON–OFF model. In [9], the model of [2] has been applied for the determination of blocking probabilities in an Optical CDMA (OCDMA) PON.

Another notable extension of the ON–OFF model is proposed in [10], in which online and offline scheduling models are proposed for the determination of the total power consumption in a smart grid environment. The proposed load models consider that each consumer's residence is equipped with a certain number of appliances of different power demands and different operational times, while the appliances' feature of alternating between ON and OFF states is also incorporated according to the ON–OFF model.

In [11], an analytical model is proposed that resembles the ON–OFF/BR model for the determination of blocking probabilities in an OCDMA PON that accommodates multiple service-classes, under a code reservation policy. The analysis considers fixed-length and fixed-weight codewords, while the provision of multirate differentiation is realized through the application of the parallel mapping technique.

References

1 M. Mehmet-Ali Asrin, Call-burst blocking and call admission control in a broadband network with bursty sources. *Performance Evaluation*, 38(1):1–19, September 1999.

2 I. Moscholios, M. Logothetis and G. Kokkinakis, Call-burst blocking of ON–OFF traffic sources with retrials under the complete sharing policy. *Performance Evaluation*, 59(4):279–312, March 2005.

3 I. Moscholios and M. Logothetis, An ON–OFF multirate loss model of Poisson traffic under the bandwidth reservation policy. *12th GI/ITG Conference on Measuring, Modelling and Evaluation of Computer and Comummunication Systems (MMB) and 3rd Polish-German Teletraffic Symposium (PGTS), MMB&PGTS 2004*, Dresden, Germany, September 2004.

4 K. Ross, *Multiservice Loss Models for Broadband Telecommunications Networks*, Springer, Berlin, 1995.

5 M. Stasiak and M. Glabowski, A simple approximation of the link model with reservation by a one-dimensional Markov chain. *Performance Evaluation*, 41(2–3):195–208, July 2000.

6 Z. Dziong and J. Roberts, Congestion probabilities in a circuit switched integrated services network. *Performance Evaluation*, 7(4):267–284, November 1987.

7 J. Vardakas, I. Moscholios, M. Logothetis and V. Stylianakis, An analytical approach for dynamic wavelength allocation in WDM-TDMA PONs servicing ON–OFF traffic. *IEEE/OSA Journal of Optical Communications and Networking*, 3(4):347–358, April 2011.

8 I. Moscholios, P. Nikolaropoulos and M. Logothetis. Call level blocking of ON–OFF traffic sources with retrials under the complete sharing policy. *Proceedings of the 18th International Teletraffic Congress (ITC)*, Berlin, Germany, 31 August to 5 September 2003.

9 J. Vardakas, I. Moscholios, M. Logothetis and V. Stylianakis, Performance analysis of OCDMA PON configuration supporting multirate bursty traffic with retrials and QoS differentiation. *Optical Switching and Networking*, 13:112–123, July 2014.

10 J. Vardakas, N. Zorba and C. Verikoukis, Scheduling policies for two-state smart-home appliances in dynamic electricity pricing environments. *Energy*, 69:455–469, May 2014.

11 J. Vardakas, I. Moscholios, M. Logothetis and V. Stylianakis, On code reservation in multi-rate OCDMA passive optical networks. *Proceedings of the 8th IEEE CSNDSP*, Poznan, Poland, July 2012.

Part II

Teletraffic Models of Quasi-Random Input

Part II, includes teletraffic loss models of:

(A) Quasi-random arriving calls with fixed or elastic bandwidth requirements and fixed bandwidth allocation during service.
(B) Quasi-random arriving calls with fixed bandwidth requirements and elastic bandwidth during service.
(C) Quasi-random arriving calls with fixed bandwidth requirements and ON–OFF traffic behavior during service.

6

The Engset Multirate Loss Model

We start with quasi-random arriving calls of fixed bandwidth requirements and fixed bandwidth allocation during service. Before the study of multirate teletraffic loss models, we begin with the simple case of a loss system that accommodates calls of a single service-class.

6.1 The Engset Loss Model

6.1.1 The Service System

Consider a loss system of capacity C b.u. which accommodates calls of a single service-class. A call requires 1 b.u. to be connected in the system. If this bandwidth is available, then the call is accepted in the system and remains for an exponentially distributed service time, with mean value $h = \mu^{-1}$. Otherwise (when all b.u. are occupied), the call is blocked and lost without further affecting the system. What is important is that a call comes from a finite source population N, then the arrival process is smoother than the Poisson process and is known as quasi-random [1]. The mean arrival rate of the idle sources is given by:

$$\lambda_{\text{fin}}(n) = \begin{cases} (N-n)\upsilon & \text{for } 0 \leq n < N \\ 0 & \text{for } n = N \end{cases} \tag{6.1}$$

where n is the number of in-service calls, $N - n$ is the number of idle sources in state n, while υ is the arrival rate per idle source (constant).

6.1.2 The Analytical Model

6.1.2.1 Steady State Probabilities
We are interested in determining the steady state probability P_n. To this end and similar to (1.4) we have the following steady state equation (which is the GB equation of state n):

$$((N-n)\upsilon + n\mu)P_n = (N-n+1)\upsilon P_{n-1} + (n+1)\mu P_{n+1} \tag{6.2}$$

where $n = 0, 1, \ldots, C$ and $P_{-1} = P_{C+1} = 0$.

Efficient Multirate Teletraffic Loss Models Beyond Erlang, First Edition.
Ioannis D. Moscholios and Michael D. Logothetis.
© 2019 John Wiley & Sons Ltd. Published 2019 by John Wiley & Sons Ltd.
Companion website: www.wiley.com/go/logocode

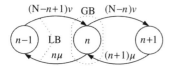

$(N-n+1)v$ GB $(N-n)v$

$n\mu$ $(n+1)\mu$

Figure 6.1 State transition diagram for the Engset loss model $(M(n)/M/C/0)$.

To determine P_n, we solve (6.2) by applying the ladder method and hence we have:

$$P_n = \frac{(N-n+1)vh}{n}P_{n-1} \quad \text{for } n = 1, \dots, C \tag{6.3}$$

which is the LB equation between the adjacent states n and $n-1$.

The graphical representation of (6.2) and (6.3) is given in Figure 6.1.

From (6.3), by successive substitutions, we relate P_n to the probability that the system is empty, P_0:

$$P_n = \binom{N}{n} \alpha_{\text{idle}}^n P_0 \tag{6.4}$$

where $\alpha_{\text{idle}} = vh$ is the offered traffic-load per idle source in erl.

To determine P_0, we know that:

$$\sum_{i=0}^{C} P_i = 1 \Rightarrow \sum_{i=0}^{C} \binom{N}{i} \alpha_{\text{idle}}^i P_0 = 1 \Rightarrow P_0 \sum_{i=0}^{C} \binom{N}{i} \alpha_{\text{idle}}^i = 1 \tag{6.5}$$

That is,

$$P_0 = \left[\sum_{i=0}^{C} \binom{N}{i} \alpha_{\text{idle}}^i \right]^{-1} \tag{6.6}$$

By substituting (6.6) to (6.4), we determine P_n:

$$P_n \equiv P_n(N) = \frac{\binom{N}{n} \alpha_{\text{idle}}^n}{\sum_{i=0}^{C} \binom{N}{i} \alpha_{\text{idle}}^i} \tag{6.7}$$

which is known as the *Engset distribution*.

Assuming that $N \to \infty$ and the total offered traffic-load is constant (i.e., $Nvh = \alpha, v \to 0$), then: $\lim_{N \to \infty} \binom{N}{n}(vh)^n = \lim_{N \to \infty} \frac{N(N-1)(N-2)\dots(N-n+1)}{n!} \frac{(Nvh)^n}{N^n} = \lim_{N \to \infty} \frac{N(N-1)(N-2)\dots(N-n+1)}{N^n} \frac{(Nvh)^n}{n!}$

$= \lim_{N \to \infty} \frac{(Nvh)^n}{n!} \to \frac{a^n}{n!}$, which means that the arrival process becomes Poisson, and (6.7) results in (1.9) (the Erlang distribution).

Example 6.1 Consider an Engset loss system with $C = 3$ b.u., $N = 4$ traffic sources, $v = \mu = 1$ call per idle source, $\alpha_{\text{idle}} = 1$ erl, and $\alpha = N\alpha_{\text{idle}} = 4$ erl. Calculate the steady state probabilities P_n for $N = 4, 8, 16$ and 32 sources, as well as for an infinite number of traffic sources (use the Erlang distribution) by keeping constant the total offered traffic-load α. Comment on the results.

Table 6.1 summarizes the results for the steady state probabilities P_n (derived from (6.7)). It is obvious that as N increases (and α remains constant) the values of P_n tend to reach the values obtained by the Erlang distribution.

Table 6.1 Steady state probabilities P_n (Example 6.1).

P_n	$N = 4, v = 1,$ $\alpha = 4$	$N = 8, v = 0.5,$ $\alpha = 4$	$N = 16, v = 0.25,$ $\alpha = 4$	$N = 32, v = 0.125,$ $\alpha = 4$	$N = \infty, \alpha = 4$
P_0	0.066666	0.052632	0.047059	0.044568	0.042254
P_1	0.266666	0.210526	0.188235	0.178273	0.169014
P_2	0.4	0.368421	0.352941	0.345404	0.338028
P_3	0.266666	0.368421	0.411765	0.431755	0.450704

As $N \to C$, the denominator of (6.7) becomes $(1 + vh)^N$ and (6.7) is simplified to the *binomial distribution*:

$$P_n = \binom{N}{n} \alpha_x^n (1 - \alpha_x)^{N-n} \tag{6.8}$$

where $\alpha_x = \alpha_{\text{idle}}/(1 + \alpha_{\text{idle}}) = vh/(1 + vh)$.

Since (1.9) and (6.8) can result from (6.7), one can consider (6.7) as a unified formula for the determination of the steady state probabilities in single rate loss systems.

6.1.2.2 CBP

To determine CBP in the Engset loss model, we initially need to derive a formula for the probability Π_n that n calls exist in the system just prior to a new call arrival. Based on the Bayes and total probability theorems we have:

$$\Pi_n = P(n \text{ users}|\text{an arrival}) = \frac{P(n \text{ users})P(\text{an arrival}|n \text{ users})}{\sum\limits_{i=0}^{C} P(i \text{ users})P(\text{an arrival}|i \text{ users})}$$

$$= \frac{P_n(N - n)v\Delta t}{\sum\limits_{i=0}^{C} P_i(N - i)v\Delta t} \tag{6.9}$$

Based on (6.4) and since $\binom{N}{n}(N - n) = \binom{N-1}{n}N$, (6.9) is written as:

$$\Pi_n = \frac{\binom{N}{n}\alpha_{\text{idle}}^n P_0(N - n)}{\sum\limits_{i=0}^{C}\binom{N}{i}\alpha_{\text{idle}}^i P_0(N - i)} \Rightarrow \Pi_n = \frac{\binom{N-1}{n}\alpha_{\text{idle}}^n}{\sum\limits_{i=0}^{C}\binom{N-1}{i}\alpha_{\text{idle}}^i}, \qquad \alpha_{\text{idle}} = vh \tag{6.10}$$

By comparing (6.10) with (6.7) we see that:

$$\Pi_n(N) = P_n(N - 1) \tag{6.11}$$

The probabilities $\Pi_n(N)$ express how an internal observer perceives the system (as an internal observer we mean the call just accepted in the system), while the probabilities $P_n(N)$ express how an external observer perceives the system. According to (6.11), $\Pi_n(N)$ coincides with $P_n(N)$ if we subtract one source (i.e., the internal observer). If $N \to \infty$, then we have Poisson arrivals and (6.11) becomes (1.23) (PASTA).

Based on (I.4), we have for the CBP:

$$B = \frac{\alpha - \alpha_c}{\alpha} \tag{6.12}$$

Let n be the number of in-service calls in the steady state of the system. Since an in-service call occupies 1 b.u., then from the fourth traffic-load property (Section I.5) we have:

$$\alpha_c = \bar{n} = \sum_{i=0}^{C} i P_i \overset{(6.4)}{=} \sum_{i=0}^{C} i \binom{N}{i} \alpha_{idle}^i P_0 = N \alpha_{idle} P_0 \sum_{i=0}^{C-1} \binom{N-1}{i} \alpha_{idle}^i \tag{6.13}$$

The offered traffic-load α is determined by:

$$\alpha = \sum_{i=0}^{C} (N-i) \upsilon h P_i \overset{\alpha_{idle}=\upsilon h}{=} \alpha_{idle} \sum_{i=0}^{C} (N-i) \binom{N}{i} \alpha_{idle}^i P_0$$

$$= N \alpha_{idle} P_0 \sum_{i=0}^{C} \binom{N-1}{i} \alpha_{idle}^i \tag{6.14}$$

By substituting (6.13) and (6.14) in (6.12) we have the Engset loss formula for the CBP determination:

$$B = \frac{\binom{N-1}{C} \alpha_{idle}^C}{\sum_{i=0}^{C} \binom{N-1}{i} \alpha_{idle}^i} \tag{6.15}$$

Note that (6.15) is equivalent to Π_C of (6.10), in which a new call arrival finds all b.u. occupied. In the literature, (6.15) is also called the CC probability.

Based on (6.15), we have the following recursive form for the Engset loss formula:

$$B(C,N,\alpha_{idle}) = \frac{(N-C)\alpha_{idle} B(C-1,N,\alpha_{idle})}{C+(N-C)\alpha_{idle} B(C-1,N,\alpha_{idle})}, \qquad C \geq 1 \tag{6.16}$$

where $\alpha_{idle} = \upsilon h$ and $B(0,N,\alpha_{idle}) = 1$.

The proof of (6.16) is similar to the proof of (I.8). From (6.15), we determine the probability $B(C-1,N,\alpha_{idle}) = \frac{\binom{N-1}{C-1}\alpha_{idle}^{C-1}}{\sum_{n=0}^{C-1}\binom{N-1}{n}\alpha_{idle}^n}$ and then the ratio $\frac{B(C,N,\alpha_{idle})}{B(C-1,N,\alpha_{idle})} = \frac{\alpha_{idle}(N-C)}{C}(1-B(C,N,\alpha_{idle}))$, based on which we obtain (6.16).

A basic characteristic of (6.16) is that the CBP are not influenced by the service time distribution but only by its mean value [2]. In that sense, (6.16) is applicable to any system of the form $M(N)/G/C/C$.

For the values of α_{idle} and α, we have the formulas (6.17) and (6.18), respectively:

$$\alpha_{idle} = \frac{\alpha}{N - \alpha(1-B)} \tag{6.17}$$

$$\alpha = \frac{N\alpha_{idle}}{1 + \alpha_{idle}(1-B)} \tag{6.18}$$

Proof of (6.17) *and* (6.18):   Since $\alpha = (N - n)\alpha_{idle} \Rightarrow n = (N\alpha_{idle} - \alpha)/\alpha_{idle}$. However, the number of busy trunks n, due to the fourth traffic-load property, equals the carried traffic: $n = \alpha_c = \alpha(1 - B)$. That is, $(N\alpha_{idle} - \alpha)/\alpha_{idle} = \alpha(1 - B)$, from which (6.17) or (6.18) results by solving for α_{idle} or α, respectively.

Q.E.D.

Example 6.2   This example illustrates how to use (6.16)–(6.18) in order to determine CC probabilities in an Engset loss system. Consider a system of $C = 2$ b.u. which accommodates calls from $N = 4$ traffic sources. The total offered traffic-load is $\alpha = 1$ erl. Determine the CC probabilities in this system.

To determine the CC probabilities via (6.16), we need the value of α_{idle}, which is unknown. Initially, α_{idle} is determined approximately via (6.17) by assuming that $B = 0$. Having determined α_{idle}, we apply (6.16) to obtain B. Then we calculate the total offered-traffic load α via (6.18). If the calculated value of α equals 1.0 erl or approximates to 1 erl with a high accuracy, the obtained B is the correct CC probability. Otherwise, we repeat this procedure until the value of α highly approximates 1 erl, by determining again α_{idle} from the newly obtained B. More precisely, we have:

- *Step* 1: $B(C, N, \alpha_{idle}) = 0 \Rightarrow \alpha_{idle} = \frac{1}{4 - 1 \times (1-0)} = 0.33333$

  $B(0, 4, 0.33333) = 1$

  $B(1, 4, 0.33333) = \dfrac{(4 - 1) \times 0.33333}{1 + (4 - 1) \times 0.33333} = 0.5$

  $B(2, 4, 0.33333) = \dfrac{(4 - 2) \times 0.33333 \times 0.5}{2 + (4 - 2) \times 0.33333 \times 0.5} = 0.14286$

  In order to check if the value $B = 0.14286$ is correct, we calculate α via (6.18):
  $\alpha = \frac{N\alpha_{idle}}{1 + \alpha_{idle}(1-B)} = \frac{4 \times 0.33333}{1 + 0.33333 \times (1 - 0.14286)} = 1.03703 > 1$ and thus we repeat this procedure.

- *Step* 2: $B(C, N, \alpha_{idle}) = 0.14286 \Rightarrow \alpha_{idle} = \frac{1}{4 - 1 \times (1 - 0.14286)} = 0.31818$

  $B(0, 4, 0.31818) = 1$

  $B(1, 4, 0.31818) = \dfrac{(4 - 1) \times 0.31818}{1 + (4 - 1) \times 0.31818} = 0.48837$

  $B(2, 4, 0.31818) = \dfrac{(4 - 2) \times 0.31818 \times 0.48837}{2 + (4 - 2) \times 0.31818 \times 0.48837} = 0.13449$

  The value of α is $\alpha = \frac{4 \times 0.31818}{1 + 0.31818 \times (1 - 0.13449)} = 0.99791 < 1$ and thus we repeat again this procedure (proceeding to step 3).

- *Step* 3: $B(C, N, \alpha_{idle}) = 0.13449 \Rightarrow \alpha_{idle} = \frac{1}{4 - 1 \times (1 - 0.13449)} = 0.31903$

  $B(0, 4, 0.31903) = 1$

  $B(1, 4, 0.31903) = \dfrac{(4 - 1) \times 0.31903}{1 + (4 - 1) \times 0.31903} = 0.48904$

  $B(2, 4, 0.31903) = \dfrac{(4 - 2) \times 0.31903 \times 0.48904}{2 + (4 - 2) \times 0.31903 \times 0.48904} = 0.13496$

The value of α is $\alpha = \dfrac{4 \times 0.31903}{1 + 0.31903 \times (1 - 0.13496)} = 1.0001 \cong 1$ and thus $B = 0.13496$ is the correct CC probability.

The probability that an external observer finds no available b.u. refers to the TC probabilities, P_C, and is determined via (6.7):

$$P_C \equiv P_C(N) = \frac{\dbinom{N}{C} \alpha_{\text{idle}}^C}{\displaystyle\sum_{i=0}^{C} \dbinom{N}{i} \alpha_{\text{idle}}^i} \tag{6.19}$$

Assuming that $N \to \infty$ and the total offered traffic-load is constant then (6.19) results in the Erlang-B formula (1.22).

6.1.2.3 Other Performance Metrics

- Utilization: the utilization, U, can be expressed by the carried traffic of the system:

$$U = \alpha_c = \alpha(1 - B) \tag{6.20}$$

- Trunk efficiency: the trunk efficiency, η, can be determined via (I.35).

Example 6.3 Consider an Engset loss system with $C = 2$ b.u. that accommodates $N = 4$ users. The arrival rate per idle user is $v = 2$ calls/h, while the mean service time is $h = 3$ min.

(a) Determine the CC probabilities via (6.15).
(b) Determine the trunk efficiency via (I.35).

(a) Based on (6.15) and the input of the example, we have $B = 0.0226$.
(b) The trunk efficiency is determined by $\eta = \dfrac{U}{C} = \dfrac{\alpha(1-B)}{C}$, where $\alpha = \dfrac{N\alpha_{\text{idle}}}{1 + \alpha_{\text{idle}}(1-B)} \overset{\alpha_{\text{idle}} = vh = 0.1}{=} 0.3644$ erl. Thus, $\eta = 0.1781$.

6.2 The Engset Multirate Loss Model

6.2.1 The Service System

In the *Engset multirate loss model* (*EnMLM*), a single link of capacity C b.u. accommodates calls of K service-classes under the CS policy. Calls of service class k ($k = 1, \ldots, K$) come from a finite source population N_k. The mean arrival rate of service-class k idle sources is $\lambda_{k,\text{fin}} = (N_k - n_k)v_k$, where n_k is the number of in-service calls and v_k is the arrival rate per idle source. The offered traffic-load per idle source of service-class k is given by $\alpha_{k,\text{idle}} = v_k / \mu_k$ (in erl). Note that if $N_k \to \infty$ for $k = 1, \ldots, K$, and the total offered traffic-load remains constant, then the call arrival process becomes Poisson.

Table 6.2 State space and occupied link bandwidth (Example 6.4).

n_1	n_2	j	n_1	n_2	j	n_1	n_2	j	n_1	n_2	j
0	0	0	0	5	5	1	2	4	2	1	5
0	1	1	0	6	6	1	3	5	2	2	6
0	2	2	0	7	7	1	4	6	2	3	7
0	3	3	1	0	2	1	5	7	3	0	6
0	4	4	1	1	3	2	0	4	3	1	7

Calls of service-class k require b_k b.u. to be serviced. If the requested bandwidth is available, a call is accepted in the system and remains under service for an exponentially distributed service time, with mean μ_k^{-1}. Otherwise, the call is blocked and lost, without further affecting the system. Due to the CS policy, the set Ω of the state space is given by (I.36). In terms of Ω, the CAC is identical to that of the EMLM (see Section 1.2.1).

In order to determine the TC probabilities of service-class k, B_{Tk}, we denote by $\Omega_{\{k\}}$ the admissible state space of service-class k : $\Omega_{\{k\}} = \{\mathbf{n} \in \Omega \; : \; \mathbf{nb} \leq C - b_k\}, k = 1, \dots, K$, where $\mathbf{n} = (n_1, \dots, n_k, \dots, n_K)$ and $\mathbf{b} = (b_1, \dots, b_k, \dots, b_K)$. A new service-class k call is accepted in the system if the system is in a state $\mathbf{n} \in \Omega_{\{k\}}$ at the time point of its arrival. Hence, the TC probabilities of service-class k are determined by the state space $\Omega - \Omega_{\{k\}}$, as follows:

$$B_{Tk} = \sum_{\mathbf{n}\in(\Omega - \Omega_{\{k\}})} P(\mathbf{n}) \Rightarrow B_{Tk} = 1 - \sum_{\mathbf{n}\in\Omega_{\{k\}}} P(\mathbf{n}) \tag{6.21}$$

where $P(\mathbf{n})$ is the probability distribution of state $\mathbf{n}$.

Example 6.4 Consider a single link with $C = 7$ b.u. The link accommodates $K = 2$ service-classes with $b_1 = 2$ b.u and $b_2 = 1$ b.u. Let the number of sources be $N_1 = N_2 = 10$, the arrival rates per idle source be $v_1 = 0.1$ and $v_2 = 0.2$, and the service rates $\mu_1 = \mu_2 = 1$.

(a) Draw the complete state transition diagram of the system and determine the values of j for each state $\mathbf{n} = (n_1, n_2)$.
(b) Write the GB equations, and determine the values of $P(\mathbf{n})$ and the exact TC probabilities of both service-classes.
(c) Discuss the required modifications for the calculation of the CC probabilities of both service-classes.

(a) Figure 6.2 shows the state space that consists of 20 permissible states $\mathbf{n} = (n_1, n_2)$ and the complete state transition diagram of the system. In addition, Table 6.2 presents the 20 states together with the occupied link bandwidth, $j = n_1 b_1 + n_2 b_2$.
(b) Based on Figure 6.2, we obtain the following 20 GB equations:

(0,0): $P(1,0) + P(0,1) - 3P(0,0) = 0$

(0,1): $2P(0,0) + 2P(0,2) + P(1,1) - 3.8P(0,1) = 0$

(0,2): $1.8P(0,1) + 3P(0,3) + P(1,2) - 4.6P(0,2) = 0$

(0,3): $1.6P(0,2) + 4P(0,4) + P(1,3) - 5.4P(0,3) = 0$

(0,4): $1.4P(0,3) + 5P(0,5) + P(1,4) - 6.2P(0,4) = 0$

(0,5): $1.2P(0,4) + 6P(0,6) + P(1,5) - 7P(0,5) = 0$

(0,6): $P(0,5) + 7P(0,7) - 6.8P(0,6) = 0$

(0,7): $0.8P(0,6) - 7P(0,7) = 0$

(1,0): $P(0,0) + 2P(2,0) + P(1,1) - 3.9P(1,0) = 0$

(1,1): $P(0,1) + 2P(2,1) + 2P(1,2) + 2P(1,0) - 4.7P(1,1) = 0$

(1,2): $P(0,2) + 2P(2,2) + 3P(1,3) + 1.8P(1,1) - 5.5P(1,2) = 0$

(1,3): $P(0,3) + 2P(2,3) + 4P(1,4) + 1.6P(1,2) - 6.3P(1,3) = 0$

(1,4): $P(0,4) + 5P(1,5) + 1.4P(1,3) - 6.2P(1,4) = 0$

(1,5): $P(0,5) + 1.2P(1,4) - 6P(1,5) = 0$

(2,0): $0.9P(1,0) + 3P(3,0) + P(2,1) - 4.8P(2,0) = 0$

(2,1): $0.9P(1,1) + 3P(3,1) + 2P(2,2) + 2P(2,0) - 5.6P(2,1) = 0$

(2,2): $0.9P(1,2) + 1.8P(2,1) + 3P(2,3) - 5.6P(2,2) = 0$

(2,3): $0.9P(1,3) + 1.6P(2,2) - 5P(2,3) = 0$

(3,0): $0.8P(2,0) + P(3,1) - 5P(3,0) = 0$

(3,1): $2P(3,0) + 0.8P(2,1) - 4P(3,1) = 0$

The solution of this linear system is:

$P(0,0) = 0.065273$	$P(0,1) = 0.130546$	$P(0,2) = 0.117492$	$P(0,3) = 0.062662$
$P(0,4) = 0.021932$	$P(0,5) = 0.005264$	$P(0,6) = 0.000877$	$P(0,7) = 0.0001$
$P(1,0) = 0.065273$	$P(1,1) = 0.130546$	$P(1,2) = 0.117492$	$P(1,3) = 0.062662$
$P(1,4) = 0.021932$	$P(1,5) = 0.005264$	$P(2,0) = 0.029373$	$P(2,1) = 0.058746$
$P(2,2) = 0.052871$	$P(2,3) = 0.028198$	$P(3,0) = 0.007833$	$P(3,1) = 0.015666$

Then based on the values of $P(n_1, n_2)$ and (6.21) we obtain the values of the TC probabilities:

$B_{T1} = P(0,6) + P(1,4) + P(2,2) + P(3,0) + P(0,7) + P(1,5) + P(2,3) + P(3,1) = 0.132741$

$B_{T2} = P(0,7) + P(1,5) + P(2,3) + P(3,1) = 0.049228$

(c) To calculate the CC probabilities of service-class 1, B_1, we can repeat (b) by assuming that $N_1 = 9$ and $N_2 = 10$ sources. In the case of B_2, we repeat (b) by assuming that $N_1 = 10$ and $N_2 = 9$ sources. The results obtained are $B_1 = 0.11619$ and $B_2 = 0.04348$, slightly lower than the corresponding TC probabilities.

6.2.2   The Analytical Model

6.2.2.1   Steady State Probabilities

The steady state transition rates of the EnMLM are shown in Figure 6.3. According to this, if $\mathbf{n}_k^+ = (n_1, \ldots, n_{k-1}, n_k + 1, n_{k+1}, \ldots, n_K)$ and $\mathbf{n}_k^- = (n_1, \ldots, n_{k-1}, n_k - 1,$

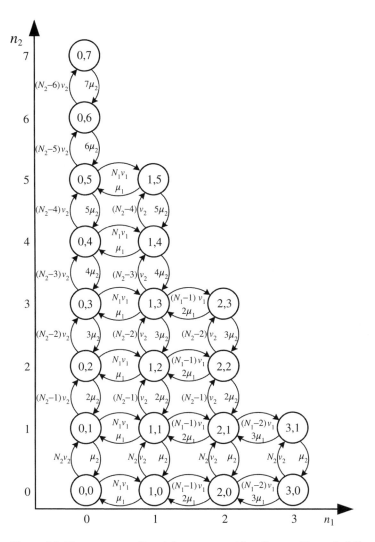

Figure 6.2 The state space Ω and the state transition diagram (Example 6.4).

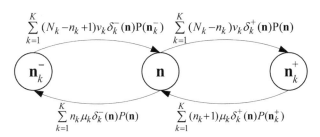

Figure 6.3 State transition diagram of the EnMLM.

$n_{k+1}, \dots, n_K)$, the GB equation (*rate in = rate out*) for state $\mathbf{n} = (n_1, \dots, n_k, \dots, n_K)$ is given by:

$$\sum_{k=1}^{K}(N_k - n_k + 1)v_k \delta_k^-(\mathbf{n})P(\mathbf{n}_k^-) + \sum_{k=1}^{K}(n_k + 1)\mu_k \delta_k^+(\mathbf{n})P(\mathbf{n}_k^+) =$$
$$\sum_{k=1}^{K}(N_k - n_k)v_k \delta_k^+(\mathbf{n})P(\mathbf{n}) + \sum_{k=1}^{K}n_k\mu_k \delta_k^-(\mathbf{n})P(\mathbf{n}) \tag{6.22}$$

where $\delta_k^+(\mathbf{n}) = \begin{cases} 1 \text{ if } \mathbf{n}_k^+ \in \Omega \\ 0 \text{ otherwise} \end{cases}$, $\delta_k^-(\mathbf{n}) = \begin{cases} 1 \text{ if } \mathbf{n}_k^- \in \Omega \\ 0 \text{ otherwise} \end{cases}$ and $P(\mathbf{n}), P(\mathbf{n}_k^-), P(\mathbf{n}_k^+)$ are the probability distributions of the corresponding states $\mathbf{n}$, $\mathbf{n}_k^-$, and $\mathbf{n}_k^+$, respectively.

Assume now the existence of LB between adjacent states. Equations (6.23) and (6.24) are the detailed LB equations which hold (for $k = 1, \dots, K$ and $\mathbf{n} \in \Omega$) because the Markov chain of the EnMLM is reversible:

$$(N_k - n_k + 1)v_k \delta_k^-(\mathbf{n})P(\mathbf{n}_k^-) = n_k\mu_k \delta_k^-(\mathbf{n})P(\mathbf{n}) \tag{6.23}$$

$$(N_k - n_k)v_k \delta_k^+(\mathbf{n})P(\mathbf{n}) = (n_k + 1)\mu_k \delta_k^+(\mathbf{n})P(\mathbf{n}_k^+) \tag{6.24}$$

Based on the LB assumption, the probability distribution $P(\mathbf{n})$ has the following PFS [3]:

$$P(\mathbf{n}) = G^{-1}\left(\prod_{k=1}^{K}\binom{N_k}{n_k}\alpha_{k,\text{idle}}^{n_k}\right) \tag{6.25}$$

where $\alpha_{k,\text{idle}} = v_k/\mu_k$ is the offered traffic-load per idle source of service-class k, G is the normalization constant given by $G \equiv G(\Omega) = \sum_{\mathbf{n}\in\Omega}\left(\prod_{k=1}^{K}\binom{N_k}{n_k}\alpha_{k,\text{idle}}^{n_k}\right)$, and $\Omega = \{\mathbf{n} : 0 \le \mathbf{nb} \le C,\ k = 1, \dots, K\}$.

If we denote by j the occupied link bandwidth $(j = 0, \dots, C)$ then the link occupancy distribution, $q_{\text{fin}}(j)$, is defined as:

$$q_{\text{fin}}(j) = \sum_{\mathbf{n}\in\Omega_j}P(\mathbf{n}) \tag{6.26}$$

where Ω_j is the set of states whereby exactly j b.u. are occupied by all in-service calls, i.e., $\Omega_j = \{\mathbf{n} \in \Omega : \mathbf{nb} = j\}$.

The unnormalized values of $q_{\text{fin}}(j)$ can be recursively determined by [3]:

$$q_{\text{fin}}(j) = \begin{cases} 1 & \text{if } j = 0 \\ \dfrac{1}{j}\sum_{k=1}^{K}(N_k - n_k + 1)\alpha_{k,\text{idle}}b_k q_{\text{fin}}(j - b_k) & j = 1, \dots, C \\ 0 & \text{otherwise} \end{cases} \tag{6.27}$$

Note that if $N_k \to \infty$ for $k = 1, \dots, K$, and the total offered traffic-load remains constant, then we have the Kaufman–Roberts recursion (1.39) of the EMLM.

Proof of (6.27): Based on (6.23) and similar to (1.43), we have the following equation between $P(\mathbf{n}_k^-)$ and $P(\mathbf{n})$ [3]:

$$(N_k - n_k + 1)\alpha_{k,\text{idle}}\gamma_k(\mathbf{n})P(\mathbf{n}_k^-) = n_k P(\mathbf{n}) \tag{6.28}$$

where $\gamma_k(\mathbf{n}) = \begin{cases} 1 & \text{if } n_k \geq 1 \\ 0 & \text{if } n_k = 0 \end{cases}$.

Summing both sides of (6.28) over Ω_j we have:

$$N_k \alpha_{k,\text{idle}} \sum_{\mathbf{n}\in\Omega_j} \gamma_k(\mathbf{n})P(\mathbf{n}_k^-) - \alpha_{k,\text{idle}} \sum_{\mathbf{n}\in\Omega_j} (n_k - 1)\gamma_k(\mathbf{n})P(\mathbf{n}_k^-) = \sum_{\mathbf{n}\in\Omega_j} n_k P(\mathbf{n}) \qquad (6.29)$$

The LHS of (6.29) is written as $N_k \alpha_{k,\text{idle}} \sum_{\mathbf{n}\in\Omega_j\cap\{n_k\geq1\}} P(\mathbf{n}_k^-) - \alpha_{k,\text{idle}} \sum_{\mathbf{n}\in\Omega_j\cap\{n_k\geq1\}} (n_k - 1)$

$P(\mathbf{n}_k^-)$. Since $\Omega_j \cap \{n_k \geq 1\} = \left\{ \mathbf{n} : \sum_{l\neq k} n_l b_l + (n_k - 1)b_k = j - b_k, n_k \geq 1, n_l \geq 0, \ k = 1, \ldots, K \right\}$ and based on (1.47), we may write the LHS of (6.29) as follows [3]:

$$\begin{aligned} &N_k \alpha_{k,\text{idle}} \sum_{\mathbf{n}\in\Omega_j\cap\{n_k\geq1\}} P(\mathbf{n}_k^-) - \alpha_{k,\text{idle}} \sum_{\mathbf{n}\in\Omega_j\cap\{n_k\geq1\}} (n_k - 1)P(\mathbf{n}_k^-) = \\ &N_k \alpha_{k,\text{idle}} \sum_{\hat{\mathbf{n}}\in\Omega_{j-b_k}} P(\hat{\mathbf{n}}) - \alpha_{k,\text{idle}} \sum_{\hat{\mathbf{n}}\in\Omega_{j-b_k}} \hat{n}_k P(\hat{\mathbf{n}}) \end{aligned} \qquad (6.30)$$

The term $N_k \alpha_{k,\text{idle}} \sum_{\hat{\mathbf{n}}\in\Omega_{j-b_k}} P(\hat{\mathbf{n}})$ is written as $N_k \alpha_{k,\text{idle}} q_{\text{fin}}(j - b_k)$, while the term $\alpha_{k,\text{idle}} \sum_{\hat{\mathbf{n}}\in\Omega_{j-b_k}} \hat{n}_k P(\hat{\mathbf{n}})$ is written as $\alpha_{k,\text{idle}} \sum_{\hat{\mathbf{n}}\in\Omega_{j-b_k}} \hat{n}_k \frac{P(\hat{\mathbf{n}})}{q_{\text{fin}}(j-b_k)} q_{\text{fin}}(j - b_k) = \alpha_{k,\text{idle}} y_{k,\text{fin}}(j - b_k)q_{\text{fin}}(j - b_k)$, where $y_{k,\text{fin}}(j - b_k)$ is the mean number of service-class k calls in state $j - b_k$. Then, (6.30) (i.e., the LHS of (6.29)) can be written as:

$$\begin{aligned} &N_k \alpha_{k,\text{idle}} \sum_{\hat{\mathbf{n}}\in\Omega_{j-b_k}} P(\hat{\mathbf{n}}) - \alpha_{k,\text{idle}} \sum_{\hat{\mathbf{n}}\in\Omega_{j-b_k}} \hat{n}_k P(\hat{\mathbf{n}}) = \\ &N_k \alpha_{k,\text{idle}} q_{\text{fin}}(j - b_k) - \alpha_{k,\text{idle}} y_{k,\text{fin}}(j - b_k)q_{\text{fin}}(j - b_k) \end{aligned} \qquad (6.31)$$

The RHS of (6.29) is written as:

$$\sum_{\mathbf{n}\in\Omega_j} n_k P(\mathbf{n}) = \sum_{\mathbf{n}\in\Omega_j} n_k \frac{P(\mathbf{n})}{q_{\text{fin}}(j)} q_{\text{fin}}(j) = y_{k,\text{fin}}(j)q_{\text{fin}}(j) \qquad (6.32)$$

By equating (6.31) and (6.32) (because of (6.29)), we have:

$$(N_k - y_{k,\text{fin}}(j - b_k))\alpha_{k,\text{idle}} q_{\text{fin}}(j - b_k) = y_{k,\text{fin}}(j)q_{\text{fin}}(j) \qquad (6.33)$$

Multiplying both sides of (6.33) by b_k and summing over k we have:

$$\sum_{k=1}^{K} (N_k - y_{k,\text{fin}}(j - b_k))\alpha_{k,\text{idle}} b_k q_{\text{fin}}(j - b_k) = j q_{\text{fin}}(j) \qquad (6.34)$$

The value of $y_{k,\text{fin}}(j - b_k)$ in (6.34) is not known. To determine it, we use a lemma proposed in [3]. According to the lemma, two stochastic systems are equivalent and result in the same CBP if they have: (a) the same traffic description parameters $(K, N_k, \alpha_{k,\text{idle}})$ where $k = 1, \ldots, K$, and (b) exactly the same set of states.

The purpose is therefore to find a new stochastic system in which we can determine the value $y_{k,\text{fin}}(j - b_k)$. The bandwidth requirements of calls of all service-classes and the capacity C in the new stochastic system are chosen according to the following two criteria:

(i) conditions (a) and (b) are valid, and (ii) each state has a unique occupancy j.

Now, state j is reached only via the previous state $j - b_k$. Thus, $y_{k,\text{fin}}(j - b_k) = n_k - 1$. Based on the above, (6.34) can be written as (6.27).

Q.E.D.

6.2.2.2 TC Probabilities, CBP, Utilization, and Mean Number of In-service Calls

The following performance measures can be determined based on (6.27):

- The TC probabilities of service-class k, B_{Tk}, via:

$$B_{Tk} = \sum_{j=C-b_k+1}^{C} G^{-1} q_{\text{fin}}(j) \tag{6.35}$$

where $G = \sum_{j=0}^{C} q_{\text{fin}}(j)$ is the normalization constant.
- The CBP (or CC probabilities) of service-class k, B_k, via (6.35) but for a system with $N_k - 1$ traffic sources.
- The link utilization, U, via:

$$U = G^{-1} \sum_{j=1}^{C} j q_{\text{fin}}(j) \tag{6.36}$$

- The average number of service-class k calls in the system, $\bar{n}_k$, via:

$$\bar{n}_k = \sum_{j=1}^{C} G^{-1} y_{k,\text{fin}}(j) q_{\text{fin}}(j) \tag{6.37}$$

where $y_{k,\text{fin}}(j)$ is the average number of service-class k calls given that the system state is j, and is given by:

$$y_{k,\text{fin}}(j) = \frac{(N_k - n_k + 1)\alpha_{k,\text{idle}} q_{\text{fin}}(j - b_k)}{q_{\text{fin}}(j)} \tag{6.38}$$

where $j = 1, \ldots, C$, while $y_k(x) = 0$ for $x \leq 0$ and $k = 1, \ldots, K$.

The determination of $q_{\text{fin}}(j)$ via (6.27), and consequently of all performance measures, requires the value of n_k, which is unknown. In [3], there exists a method for the determination of n_k in each state j via an equivalent stochastic system, with the same traffic parameters and the same set of states as already described for the proof of (6.27). This method results in the accurate calculation of $q_{\text{fin}}(j)$. However, the state space determination of the equivalent system is complex, especially for large capacity systems that serve many service-classes.

Example 6.5 Consider again Example 6.4 ($C = 7, K = 2, b_1 = 2, b_2 = 1, N_1 = N_2 = 10, v_1 = 0.1, v_2 = 0.2, \mu_1 = \mu_2 = 1$).

(a) Based on Table 6.2 and (6.27), discuss the difficulties in calculating the unnormalized value of $q_{\text{fin}}(2)$.
(b) Find an equivalent stochastic system for this loss system with the same traffic parameters and the same set of states.
(c) Based on (b), determine the TC probabilities via (6.35).
(d) Determine the CC probabilities via (6.35).

Table 6.3 State space, j, j_{eq} and blocking states (Example 6.5).

n_1	n_2	j	j_{eq}	B_{T_1}	B_{T_2}	n_1	n_2	j	j_{eq}	B_{T_1}	B_{T_2}
0	0	0	0			1	2	4	21		
0	1	1	5			1	3	5	26		
0	2	2	10			1	4	6	31	*	
0	3	3	15			1	5	7	36	*	*
0	4	4	20			2	0	4	22		
0	5	5	25			2	1	5	27		
0	6	6	30	*		2	2	6	32	*	
0	7	7	35	*	*	2	3	7	37	*	*
1	0	2	11			3	0	6	33	*	
1	1	3	16			3	1	7	38	*	*

(a) According to Table 6.2, the state $j = 2$ refers either to $(n_1, n_2) = (0, 2)$ or to $(n_1, n_2) = (1, 0)$. This means that the immediate application of (6.27) is impossible for the determination of $q_{fin}(2)$ since there is no criterion on how to choose (n_1, n_2). We can circumvent this problem by matching each pair (n_1, n_2) with a unique value of j.

(b) By state space enumeration and processing (a computer-based task even for small systems) we have the following equivalent stochastic system (other equivalent systems are also possible): $b_1 = 11, b_2 = 5, C = 38$. This system consists of 20 states of the form (n_1, n_2). Each state (n_1, n_2) has a unique value of j, named j_{eq} in Table 6.3. In addition, the equivalent system has the same blocking states with the initial system (depicted in columns 5 and 6 of Table 6.3 for calls of service-classes 1 and 2, respectively).

(c) Unnormalized probabilities through the recursion (6.27). For $C = 38, K = 2, N_1 = N_2 = 10, \alpha_{1,idle} = 0.1, \alpha_{2,idle} = 0.2, b_1 = 11, b_2 = 5$, we have:

$j = 5$: $\quad 5q_{fin}(5) = 0 + 10q_{fin}(0) = 10 \quad\quad\quad\quad\quad \Rightarrow q_{fin}(5) = 2.0$

$j = 10$: $\quad 10q_{fin}(10) = 0 + 9q_{fin}(5) = 18 \quad\quad\quad\quad \Rightarrow q_{fin}(10) = 1.8$

$j = 15$: $\quad 15q_{fin}(15) = 0 + 8q_{fin}(10) = 14.4 \quad\quad\quad \Rightarrow q_{fin}(15) = 0.96$

$j = 20$: $\quad 20q_{fin}(20) = 0 + 7q_{fin}(15) = 6.72 \quad\quad\quad \Rightarrow q_{fin}(20) = 0.336$

$j = 25$: $\quad 25q_{fin}(25) = 0 + 6q_{fin}(20) = 6.72 \quad\quad\quad \Rightarrow q_{fin}(25) = 0.08064$

$j = 30$: $\quad 30q_{fin}(30) = 0 + 5q_{fin}(25) = 0.4032 \quad\quad \Rightarrow q_{fin}(30) = 0.01344$

$j = 35$: $\quad 35q_{fin}(35) = 0 + 4q_{fin}(30) = 0.05376 \quad\quad \Rightarrow q_{fin}(35) = 0.001536$

$j = 11$: $\quad 11q_{fin}(11) = 11q_{fin}(0) + 0 = 11 \quad\quad\quad\quad \Rightarrow q_{fin}(11) = 1.0$

$j = 16$: $\quad 16q_{fin}(16) = 11q_{fin}(5) + 10q_{fin}(11) = 32 \quad\quad \Rightarrow q_{fin}(16) = 2.0$

$j = 21$: $\quad 21q_{fin}(21) = 11q_{fin}(10) + 9q_{fin}(16) = 37.8 \quad \Rightarrow q_{fin}(21) = 1.8$

$j = 26$: $\quad 26q_{fin}(26) = 11q_{fin}(15) + 8q_{fin}(21) = 24.96 \quad \Rightarrow q_{fin}(26) = 0.96$

$j = 31$: $\quad 31q_{fin}(31) = 11q_{fin}(20) + 7q_{fin}(26) = 10.416 \quad \Rightarrow q_{fin}(31) = 0.336$

$j = 36$: $\quad 36q_{fin}(36) = 11q_{fin}(25) + 6q_{fin}(31) = 2.90304 \quad \Rightarrow q_{fin}(36) = 0.08064$

$j = 22$: $\quad 22q_{fin}(22) = 9.9q_{fin}(11) + 0 = 9.9 \quad\quad\quad \Rightarrow q_{fin}(22) = 0.45$

$j = 27$: $\quad 27q_{fin}(27) = 9.9q_{fin}(16) + 10q_{fin}(22) = 24.3 \quad \Rightarrow q_{fin}(27) = 0.9$

$j = 32$:	$32q_{\text{fin}}(32) = 9.9q_{\text{fin}}(21) + 9q_{\text{fin}}(27) = 25.92$	$\Rightarrow q_{\text{fin}}(32) = 0.81$
$j = 37$:	$37q_{\text{fin}}(37) = 9.9q_{\text{fin}}(26) + 8q_{\text{fin}}(32) = 15.984$	$\Rightarrow q_{\text{fin}}(37) = 0.432$
$j = 33$:	$33q_{\text{fin}}(33) = 8.8q_{\text{fin}}(22) + 0 = 3.96$	$\Rightarrow q_{\text{fin}}(33) = 0.12$
$j = 38$:	$38q_{\text{fin}}(38) = 8.8q_{\text{fin}}(27) + 10q_{\text{fin}}(22) = 9.12$	$\Rightarrow q_{\text{fin}}(38) = 0.24$

The normalization constant is: $G = \sum_{j=0}^{C} q_{\text{fin}}(j) = 15.320256$
The TC probabilities are:

$$B_{T1} = \sum_{j=C-b_1+1}^{C} G^{-1} q_{\text{fin}}(j) = 0.13274 \text{ (same as the exact solution)}$$

$$B_{T2} = \sum_{j=C-b_2+1}^{C} G^{-1} q_{\text{fin}}(j) = 0.049227 \text{ (same as the exact solution)}$$

(d) To determine the CBP of service-class 1, we consider the system with $N_1 = 9$ sources (while $N_2 = 10$ sources). Then, the unnormalized probabilities through the recursion (6.27) are:

$j = 5$:	$5q_{\text{fin}}(5) = 0 + 10q_{\text{fin}}(0) = 10$	$\Rightarrow q_{\text{fin}}(5) = 2.0$
$j = 10$:	$10q_{\text{fin}}(10) = 0 + 9q_{\text{fin}}(5) = 18$	$\Rightarrow q_{\text{fin}}(10) = 1.8$
$j = 15$:	$15q_{\text{fin}}(15) = 0 + 8q_{\text{fin}}(10) = 14.4$	$\Rightarrow q_{\text{fin}}(15) = 0.96$
$j = 20$:	$20q_{\text{fin}}(20) = 0 + 7q_{\text{fin}}(15) = 6.72$	$\Rightarrow q_{\text{fin}}(20) = 0.336$
$j = 25$:	$25q_{\text{fin}}(25) = 0 + 6q_{\text{fin}}(20) = 6.72$	$\Rightarrow q_{\text{fin}}(25) = 0.08064$
$j = 30$:	$30q_{\text{fin}}(30) = 0 + 5q_{\text{fin}}(25) = 0.4032$	$\Rightarrow q_{\text{fin}}(30) = 0.01344$
$j = 35$:	$35q_{\text{fin}}(35) = 0 + 4q_{\text{fin}}(30) = 0.05376$	$\Rightarrow q_{\text{fin}}(35) = 0.001536$
$j = 11$:	$11q_{\text{fin}}(11) = 9.9q_{\text{fin}}(0) + 0 = 9.9$	$\Rightarrow q_{\text{fin}}(11) = 0.9$
$j = 16$:	$16q_{\text{fin}}(16) = 9.9q_{\text{fin}}(5) + 10q_{\text{fin}}(11) = 28.8$	$\Rightarrow q_{\text{fin}}(16) = 1.8$
$j = 21$:	$21q_{\text{fin}}(21) = 9.9q_{\text{fin}}(10) + 9q_{\text{fin}}(16) = 34.02$	$\Rightarrow q_{\text{fin}}(21) = 1.62$
$j = 26$:	$26q_{\text{fin}}(26) = 9.9q_{\text{fin}}(15) + 8q_{\text{fin}}(21) = 22.464$	$\Rightarrow q_{\text{fin}}(26) = 0.864$
$j = 31$:	$31q_{\text{fin}}(31) = 9.9q_{\text{fin}}(20) + 7q_{\text{fin}}(26) = 9.3744$	$\Rightarrow q_{\text{fin}}(31) = 0.3024$
$j = 36$:	$36q_{\text{fin}}(36) = 9.9q_{\text{fin}}(25) + 6q_{\text{fin}}(31) = 2.612736$	$\Rightarrow q_{\text{fin}}(36) = 0.072576$
$j = 22$:	$22q_{\text{fin}}(22) = 8.8q_{\text{fin}}(11) + 0 = 7.92$	$\Rightarrow q_{\text{fin}}(22) = 0.36$
$j = 27$:	$27q_{\text{fin}}(27) = 8.8q_{\text{fin}}(16) + 10q_{\text{fin}}(22) = 19.44$	$\Rightarrow q_{\text{fin}}(27) = 0.72$
$j = 32$:	$32q_{\text{fin}}(32) = 8.8q_{\text{fin}}(21) + 9q_{\text{fin}}(27) = 20.736$	$\Rightarrow q_{\text{fin}}(32) = 0.648$
$j = 37$:	$37q_{\text{fin}}(37) = 8.8q_{\text{fin}}(26) + 8q_{\text{fin}}(32) = 12.7872$	$\Rightarrow q_{\text{fin}}(37) = 0.3456$
$j = 33$:	$33q_{\text{fin}}(33) = 7.7q_{\text{fin}}(22) + 0 = 2.772$	$\Rightarrow q_{\text{fin}}(33) = 0.084$
$j = 38$:	$38q_{\text{fin}}(38) = 7.7q_{\text{fin}}(27) + 10q_{\text{fin}}(22) = 6.384$	$\Rightarrow q_{\text{fin}}(38) = 0.168$

The normalization constant is: $G = \sum_{j=0}^{C} q_{\text{fin}}(j) = 14.076192$

$$B_1 = \sum_{j=C-b_1+1}^{C} G^{-1} q_{\text{fin}}(j) = 0.11619 \text{ (same as the exact solution)}.$$

To determine the CBP of service-class 2, we repeat the calculations considering the system with $N_2 = 9$ sources (while $N_1 = 10$ sources).

The new normalization constant is calculated, $G = \sum_{j=0}^{C} q_{\mathrm{fin}}(j) = 12.8600768$, which leads to:

$$B_2 = \sum_{j=C-b_2+1}^{C} G^{-1} q_{\mathrm{fin}}(j) = 0.04348 \text{ (same as the exact solution)}.$$

6.2.2.3 An Approximate Algorithm for the Determination of $q_{\mathrm{fin}}(j)$

Contrary to (6.27), which provides the exact values of the various performance measures, at the cost of state space enumeration and processing, the algorithm presented herein provides approximate values but is much simpler and easy to implement, therefore it is adopted in the forthcoming finite multirate loss models presented in this chapter and the following chapters.

The algorithm comprises the following steps [4]:

Algorithm Approximate calculation of $q_{\mathrm{fin}}(j)$ in the EnMLM

Step 1: Define the corresponding infinite loss model (EMLM) and calculate $q(j)$ via the Kaufman–Roberts recursion (1.39).

Step 2: Determine the values of $y_k(j)$ in the EMLM based on (1.51).

Step 3: Modify (6.27) to the following approximate but recursive formula, where the values of $y_k(j)$ have been determined in step 2 from the corresponding infinite model:

$$q_{\mathrm{fin}}(j) = \begin{cases} 1 & \text{if } j = 0 \\ \dfrac{1}{j} \sum_{k=1}^{K} (N_k - y_k(j-b_k)) \alpha_{k,\mathrm{idle}}\, b_k\, q_{\mathrm{fin}}(j-b_k) & j = 1, \ldots, C \\ 0 & \text{otherwise} \end{cases} \qquad (6.39)$$

Step 4: Determine the various performance measures as follows:

- The TC probabilities of service-class k, B_{Tk}, via (6.35).
- The CC probabilities of service-class k, B_k, via (6.35) but for a system with $N_k - 1$ traffic sources.
- The link utilization, U, via (6.36).
- The average number of service-class k calls in the system, $\bar{n}_k$, via (6.37) where the values of $y_{k,\mathrm{fin}}(j)$ are given by:

$$y_{k,\mathrm{fin}}(j) = \frac{(N_k - y_k(j-b_k)) \alpha_{k,\mathrm{idle}}\, q_{\mathrm{fin}}(j-b_k)}{q_{\mathrm{fin}}(j)} \qquad (6.40)$$

Example 6.6 Consider again Example 6.4 ($C = 7, K = 2, b_1 = 2, b_2 = 1, N_1 = N_2 = 10, v_1 = 0.1, v_2 = 0.2, \mu_1 = \mu_2 = 1$). Apply the algorithm of Section 6.2.2.3 for the determination of TC and CC probabilities.

Step 1: The corresponding infinite loss model (EMLM) has the following parameters:
$C = 7, K = 2, b_1 = 2, b_2 = 1, \alpha_1 = 1$ erl, and $\alpha_2 = 2$ erl.
Based on (1.39), we have the following normalized values of $Q(j)$:

$Q(0) = 0.05460$	$Q(1) = 0.109204$	$Q(2) = 0.163806$	$Q(3) = 0.182007$
$Q(4) = 0.172906$	$Q(5) = 0.141965$	$Q(6) = 0.104957$	$Q(7) = 0.070549$

Step 2: Based on (1.51), we have:

$j = 1 \Rightarrow y_1(1) = 0, y_2(1) = 1$ \qquad $j = 5 \Rightarrow y_1(5) = 1.28205, y_2(5) = 2.435897$

$j = 2 \Rightarrow y_1(2) = 0.333333, y_2(2) = 1.333333$ \quad $j = 6 \Rightarrow y_1(6) = 1.647398, y_2(6) = 2.70520$

$j = 3 \Rightarrow y_1(3) = 0.6, y_2(3) = 1.8$ \qquad $j = 7 \Rightarrow y_1(7) = 2.01228, y_2(7) = 2.97542$

$j = 4 \Rightarrow y_1(4) = 0.947368, y_2(4) = 2.10526$

Step 3: Based on (6.39), we have the following normalized values of $Q_{fin}(j)$:

$Q_{fin}(0) = 0.065656$	$Q_{fin}(1) = 0.131312$	$Q_{fin}(2) = 0.183837$	$Q_{fin}(3) = 0.193758$
$Q_{fin}(4) = 0.168295$	$Q_{fin}(5) = 0.125998$	$Q_{fin}(6) = 0.082553$	$Q_{fin}(7) = 0.048590$

Step 4: The approximate TC probabilities are:

$$B_{T1} = \sum_{j=C-b_1+1}^{C} Q_{fin}(j) = 0.131143 \text{ (compare with the exact 0.13274), and}$$

$$B_{T2} = \sum_{j=C-b_2+1}^{C} Q_{fin}(j) = 0.04859 \text{ (compare with the exact 0.049227).}$$

In order to determine the CC probabilities of service-class 1, we repeat the above steps 1 to 4, but now in step 1 we have $\alpha_1 = (N_1 - 1)v_1 = 0.9$ erl and $\alpha_2 = 2$ erl. Similarly, in order to determine the CC probabilities of service-class 2, we repeat the previous steps, but now in step 1 we have $\alpha_1 = 1$ erl and $\alpha_2 = (N_2 - 1)v_2 = 1.8$ erl. Thus, the approximate CC probabilities are:

$$B_1 = \sum_{j=C-b_1+1}^{C} Q_{fin}(j) = 0.114665 \text{ (compare with the exact 0.11619), and}$$

$$B_2 = \sum_{j=C-b_2+1}^{C} Q_{fin}(j) = 0.042952 \text{ (compare with the exact 0.04348)}$$

6.3 The Engset Multirate Loss Model under the BR Policy

6.3.1 The Service System

We consider again the system of the EnMLM and apply the BR policy (*EnMLM/BR*): A new service-class k call is accepted in the link if, after its acceptance, the occupied link bandwidth $j \le C - t_k$, where t_k refers to the BR parameter used to benefit calls of all other service-classes apart from k (see also the EMLM/BR in Section 1.3.1).

In terms of the system state-space Ω, the CAC is expressed as follows. A new call of service-class k is accepted in the system if the system is in state $\mathbf{n} \in \Omega_{\{k\}}$ upon a

Table 6.4 State space and occupied link bandwidth (Example 6.7).

n_1	n_2	j	n_1	n_2	j	n_1	n_2	j	n_1	n_2	j
0	0	0	0	5	5	1	3	5	2	2	6
0	1	1	0	6	6	1	4	6	2	3	7
0	2	2	1	0	2	1	5	7	3	0	6
0	3	3	1	1	3	2	0	4	3	1	7
0	4	4	1	2	4	2	1	5			

new call arrival, where $\Omega_{\{k\}} = \{\mathbf{n} \in \Omega : \mathbf{nb} \le C - b_k - t_k\}$, $k = 1, \dots, K$. Hence, the TC probabilities of service-class k are determined by the state space $\Omega - \Omega_{\{k\}}$ (see (6.21)).

As far as the CC probabilities, B_k, are concerned, they can be determined by (6.21) as well but for a system with $N_k - 1$ traffic sources.

Example 6.7 Consider again Example 6.4 ($C = 7, K = 2, b_1 = 2, b_2 = 1, N_1 = N_2 = 10, v_1 = 0.1, v_2 = 0.2, \mu_1 = \mu_2 = 1$) and let $t_1 = 0$ and $t_2 = 1$, so that $b_1 + t_1 = b_2 + t_2$.

(a) Draw the complete state transition diagram of the system and determine the values of j for each state $\mathbf{n} = (n_1, n_2)$.
(b) Write the GB equations, and determine the values of $P(\mathbf{n})$ and the exact TC probabilities of both service-classes.

(a) The state space consisting of 19 permissible states $\mathbf{n} = (n_1, n_2)$ and the complete state transition diagram of the system are shown in Figure 6.2 (Example 6.4), if we exclude the following state transitions (due to the BR policy): from (3,0) to (3,1), from (2,2) to (2,3), and from (1,4) to (1,5). Table 6.4 presents the 19 states together with the occupied link bandwidth, $j = n_1 b_1 + n_2 b_2$.

(b) Based on Figure 6.2, according to the aforementioned exclusions, we obtain the following 19 GB equations:

$(0,0):$ $P(1,0) + P(0,1) - 3P(0,0) = 0$

$(0,1):$ $2P(0,0) + 2P(0,2) + P(1,1) - 3.8P(0,1) = 0$

$(0,2):$ $1.8P(0,1) + 3P(0,3) + P(1,2) - 4.6P(0,2) = 0$

$(0,3):$ $1.6P(0,2) + 4P(0,4) + P(1,3) - 5.4P(0,3) = 0$

$(0,4):$ $1.4P(0,3) + 5P(0,5) + P(1,4) - 6.2P(0,4) = 0$

$(0,5):$ $1.2P(0,4) + 6P(0,6) + P(1,5) - 7P(0,5) = 0$

$(0,6):$ $P(0,5) - 6P(0,6) = 0$

$(1,0):$ $P(0,0) + 2P(2,0) + P(1,1) - 3.9P(1,0) = 0$

$(1,1):$ $P(0,1) + 2P(2,1) + 2P(1,2) + 2P(1,0) - 4.7P(1,1) = 0$

$(1,2):$ $P(0,2) + 2P(2,2) + 3P(1,3) + 1.8P(1,1) - 5.5P(1,2) = 0$

$(1,3):$ $P(0,3) + 2P(2,3) + 4P(1,4) + 1.6P(1,2) - 6.3P(1,3) = 0$

$(1,4):$ $P(0,4) + 5P(1,5) + 1.4P(1,3) - 5P(1,4) = 0$

$(1,5):$ $P(0,5) - 6P(1,5) = 0$

$(2,0):$ $0.9P(1,0) + 3P(3,0) + P(2,1) - 4.8P(2,0) = 0$

$(2,1):$ $0.9P(1,1) + 3P(3,1) + 2P(2,2) + 2P(2,0) - 5.6P(2,1) = 0$

$(2,2):$ $0.9P(1,2) + 1.8P(2,1) + 3P(2,3) - 4P(2,2) = 0$

$(2,3):$ $0.9P(1,3) - 5P(2,3) = 0$

$(3,0):$ $0.8P(2,0) + P(3,1) - 3P(3,0) = 0$

$(3,1):$ $0.8P(2,1) - 4P(3,1) = 0$

The solution of this linear system is:

$P(0,0) = 0.067512$	$P(0,1) = 0.132656$	$P(0,2) = 0.116774$	$P(0,3) = 0.059843$
$P(0,4) = 0.020133$	$P(0,5) = 0.004142$	$P(0,6) = 0.00069$	$P(1,0) = 0.069879$
$P(1,1) = 0.135521$	$P(1,2) = 0.11885$	$P(1,3) = 0.055782$	$P(1,4) = 0.020336$
$P(1,5) = 0.00069$	$P(2,0) = 0.034748$	$P(2,1) = 0.063417$	$P(2,2) = 0.062809$
$P(2,3) = 0.010041$	$P(3,0) = 0.013494$	$P(3,1) = 0.012683$	

Then, based on the values of $P(n_1, n_2)$, we obtain the values of the TC probabilities:

$$B_{T1} = B_{T2} = P(0,6) + P(1,4) + P(2,2) + P(3,0) + P(1,5) + P(2,3) + P(3,1) = 0.120743$$

6.3.2 The Analytical Model

6.3.2.1 Link Occupancy Distribution

In the EnMLM/BR, the unnormalized values of $q_{\text{fin}}(j)$ can be calculated in an approximate way according to the Roberts method (see Section 1.3.2.2). Based on this method, we can either find an equivalent stochastic system (which requires enumeration and processing of the state space) [5] or apply an algorithm similar to that presented in Section 6.2.2.3 [6]. Due to its simplicity, we adopt the algorithm of [6], which is described by the following steps:

Algorithm Approximate calculation of $q_{\text{fin}}(j)$ in the EnMLM/BR

Step 1: Define the corresponding infinite loss model (EMLM/BR) and calculate $q(j)$ via the Roberts recursion (1.64).

Step 2: Determine the values of $y_k(j)$ in the EMLM/BR based on (1.67).

Step 3: Modify (6.39) to the following approximate but recursive formula, where the values of $y_k(j)$ have been determined in step 2 from the corresponding infinite model:

$$q_{\text{fin}}(j) = \begin{cases} 1 & \text{if } j = 0 \\ \dfrac{1}{j} \displaystyle\sum_{k=1}^{K} (N_k - y_k(j - b_k)) \alpha_{k,\text{idle}} D_k(j - b_k) q_{\text{fin}}(j - b_k) & j = 1, \dots, C \\ 0 & \text{otherwise} \end{cases} \quad (6.41)$$

where $D_k(j - b_k)$ is determined via (1.65).

6.3.2.2 TC Probabilities, CBP, Utilization, and Mean Number of In-service Calls

The following performance measures can be determined based on (6.41):

- The TC probabilities of service-class k, B_{Tk}, via:

$$B_{Tk} = \sum_{j=C-b_k-t_k+1}^{C} G^{-1} q_{\text{fin}}(j) \tag{6.42}$$

  where $G = \sum_{j=0}^{C} q_{\text{fin}}(j)$ is the normalization constant.
- The CBP (or CC probabilities) of service-class k, B_k, via (6.42) but for a system with $N_k - 1$ traffic sources.
- The link utilization, U, via (6.36).
- The average number of service-class k calls in the system, $\bar{n}_k$, via (6.37), while:

$$y_{k,\text{fin}}(j) = \begin{cases} \dfrac{(N_k - y_k(j - b_k))\alpha_{k,\text{idle}} q_{\text{fin}}(j - b_k)}{q_{\text{fin}}(j)} & \text{for } j \leq C - t_k \\ 0 & \text{for } j > C - t_k \end{cases} \tag{6.43}$$

Example 6.8 Consider again Example 6.7 ($C = 7, K = 2, b_1 = 2, b_2 = 1, t_1 = 0, t_2 = 1, N_1 = N_2 = 10, \upsilon_1 = 0.1, \upsilon_2 = 0.2, \mu_1 = \mu_2 = 1$). Apply the algorithm of Section 6.3.2.1 for the determination of TC and CC probabilities.

Step 1: The corresponding infinite loss model (EMLM/BR) is $C = 7, K = 2, b_1 = 2, b_2 = 1, t_1 = 0, t_2 = 1, \alpha_1 = 1$ erl, and $\alpha_2 = 2$ erl.
Based on (1.64), we have the following normalized values of $Q(j)$:

$Q(0) = 0.05629$ $Q(1) = 0.11258$ $Q(2) = 0.168871$ $Q(3) = 0.187634$
$Q(4) = 0.178252$ $Q(5) = 0.146355$ $Q(6) = 0.108202$ $Q(7) = 0.0418156$

Step 2: Based on (1.67), we have:

$j = 1 \Rightarrow y_1(1) = 0, y_2(1) = 1$

$j = 2 \Rightarrow y_1(2) = 0.333333, y_2(2) = 1.333333$ $j = 3 \Rightarrow y_1(3) = 0.6, y_2(3) = 1.8$
$j = 4 \Rightarrow y_1(4) = 0.947368, y_2(4) = 2.10526$ $j = 5 \Rightarrow y_1(5) = 1.28205, y_2(5) = 2.435897$
$j = 6 \Rightarrow y_1(6) = 1.647398, y_2(6) = 2.70520$ $j = 7 \Rightarrow y_1(7) = 3.5, y_2(7) = 0$

Step 3: Based on (6.41), we have the following normalized values of $Q_{\text{fin}}(j)$:

$Q_{\text{fin}}(0) = 0.066805$ $Q_{\text{fin}}(1) = 0.133611$ $Q_{\text{fin}}(2) = 0.187055$ $Q_{\text{fin}}(3) = 0.197150$
$Q_{\text{fin}}(4) = 0.171242$ $Q_{\text{fin}}(5) = 0.128205$ $Q_{\text{fin}}(6) = 0.083998$ $Q_{\text{fin}}(7) = 0.031934$

Step 4: The approximate TC probabilities are:

$$B_{T1} = B_{T2} = \sum_{j=C-b_2-t_2+1}^{C} Q_{\text{fin}}(j) = 0.115932$$

(compare with the exact 0.120743 and with the value of 0.15 given by the EMLM/BR)

In order to determine the CC probabilities of service-class 1, we repeat the above steps 1 to 3, but now in step 1 we have $\alpha_1 = (N_1 - 1)v_1 = 0.9$ erl and $\alpha_2 = 2$ erl. Similarly, for service-class 2, we repeat steps 1 to 3, but now in step 1 we have $\alpha_1 = 1$ erl and $\alpha_2 = (N_2 - 1)v_2 = 1.8$ erl. Thus, the approximate CC probabilities are:

$$B_1 = \sum_{j=C-b_1-t_1+1}^{C} Q_{\text{fin}}(j) = 0.10109 \text{ and } B_2 = \sum_{j=C-b_2-t_2+1}^{C} Q_{\text{fin}}(j) = 0.105408.$$

Example 6.9 Consider a link of capacity $C = 80$ b.u. that accommodates quasi-random arriving calls of $K = 3$ service-classes under the CS policy with the following traffic characteristics: $(N_1, \alpha_{1,\text{idle}}, b_1) = (60, 0.15, 1), (N_2, \alpha_{2,\text{idle}}, b_2) = (60, 0.05, 5), (N_3, \alpha_{3,\text{idle}}, b_3) = (60, 0.025, 12)$. In the case of the BR policy, let $t_1 = 11, t_2 = 7$ and $t_3 = 0$ b.u. The corresponding offered traffic values for the Poisson arriving calls are $\alpha_1 = 9, \alpha_2 = 3$, and $\alpha_3 = 1.5$ erl. Calculate the TC probabilities in the EnMLM, the EnMLM/BR, the EMLM, and the EMLM/BR assuming that the offered traffic-load of the Poisson arriving calls increases in steps of 1, 0.5, and 0.25 erl for each service-class, respectively, up to $\alpha_1 = 15, \alpha_2 = 6$ and $\alpha_3 = 3$ erl.

Figure 6.4 shows the TC probabilities for all service-classes and all different models (EnMLM, EnMLM/BR, EMLM, and EMLM/BR). In the x-axis of Figure 6.4, point 1 refers to $(\alpha_1, \alpha_2, \alpha_3) = (9, 3, 1.5)$ while point 7 refers to $(\alpha_1, \alpha_2, \alpha_3) = (15, 6, 3)$. According to Figure 6.4, we observe that (i) the EMLM and the EMLM/BR cannot capture the behavior of the corresponding finite models and (ii) the BR policy achieves TC equalization at the expense of increasing the TC probabilities of service-classes 1 and 2.

6.4 The Engset Multirate Loss Model under the TH Policy

6.4.1 The Service System

We consider the multiservice system of the EnMLM under the TH policy (*EnMLM/TH*). The call admission is exactly the same as that of the EMLM/TH (see Section 1.4.1).

6.4.2 The Analytical Model

6.4.2.1 Steady State Probabilities

Since the TH policy is a coordinate convex policy the steady state probabilities in the EnMLM/TH have a PFS whose form is exactly the same as that of the EnMLM (the only change is in the definition of Ω):

$$P(\mathbf{n}) = G^{-1} \left(\prod_{k=1}^{K} \binom{N_k}{n_k} \alpha_{k,\text{idle}}^{n_k} \right) \tag{6.44}$$

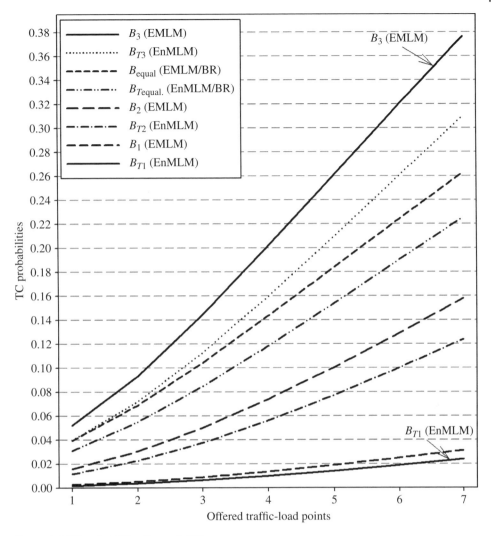

Figure 6.4 TC probabilities (Example 6.9).

where $\alpha_{k,\text{idle}} = \upsilon_k/\mu_k$ is the offered traffic-load per idle source of service-class k, G is the normalization constant given by $G \equiv G(\Omega) = \sum\limits_{\mathbf{n} \in \Omega} \left(\prod\limits_{k=1}^{K} \binom{N_k}{n_k} \alpha_{k,\text{idle}}^{n_k} \right)$, and $\Omega = \{\mathbf{n} : 0 \leq \mathbf{nb} \leq C, n_k \leq n_{k,\text{max}}, \ k = 1, \dots, K\}$.

Equation (6.44) satisfies the GB equation of (6.22) and the LB equations of (6.23) and (6.24), while the state transition diagram of the EnMLM/TH is the same as in Figure 6.3.

In order to determine the TC probabilities of service-class k, B_{Tk}, we denote by $\Omega_{\{k\}}$ the admissible state space of service-class k: $\Omega_{\{k\}} = \{\mathbf{n} \in \Omega : \mathbf{nb} \leq C - b_k, n_k < n_{k,\text{max}}\}$ $k = 1, \dots, K$, where $\mathbf{n} = (n_1, \dots, n_k, \dots, n_K)$ and $\mathbf{b} = (b_1, \dots, b_k, \dots, b_K)$. A new service-class k

Table 6.5 State space and occupied link bandwidth (Example 6.10).

n_1	n_2	n_3	j	n_1	n_2	n_3	j	n_1	n_2	n_3	j
0	0	0	0	1	0	0	1	2	0	0	2
0	0	1	2	1	0	1	3	2	0	1	4
0	1	0	3	1	1	0	4	2	0	0	3

call is accepted in the system if, at the time point of its arrival, the system is in a state $\mathbf{n} \in \Omega_{\{k\}}$. Hence, the TC probabilities of service-class k are determined by the state space $\Omega - \Omega_{\{k\}}$ and according to (6.21).

Example 6.10 Consider a link of capacity $C = 4$ b.u. that accommodates calls of $K = 3$ service-classes with the following traffic characteristics: $b_1 = 1, b_2 = 3, b_3 = 2, N_1 = N_2 = N_3 = 10, v_1 = 0.1, v_2 = v_3 = 0.05, \mu_1 = \mu_2 = 1, \mu_3 = 2/3$. Assume that the TH policy is applied to calls of service-classes 1 and 3, and let $n_{1,\max} = 3$ and $n_{3,\max} = 1$.

(a) Find the state space Ω and determine the values of j for each state $\mathbf{n} = (n_1, n_2, n_3)$.
(b) Write the GB equations, and determine the values of $P(\mathbf{n})$ and the exact TC probabilities of all service-classes.
(c) Determine the exact CC probabilities of all service-classes.

(a) The state space Ω consists of nine states. Table 6.5 presents these states together with the occupied link bandwidth, $j = n_1 b_1 + n_2 b_2 + n_3 b_3$.
(b) Based on Table 6.5 and the GB equation of (6.22), we obtain 9 GB equations:

$(0,0,0):$	$P(0,1,0) + 2/3P(0,0,1) + P(1,0,0) - 2P(0,0,0) = 0$
$(0,0,1):$	$0.5P(0,0,0) + P(1,0,1) - 5/3P(0,0,1) = 0$
$(0,1,0):$	$0.5P(0,0,0) + P(1,1,0) - 2P(0,1,0) = 0$
$(1,0,0):$	$P(0,0,0) + 2/3P(1,0,1) + 2P(2,0,0) + P(1,1,0) - 2.9P(1,0,0) = 0$
$(1,0,1):$	$P(0,0,1) + 2P(2,0,1) + 0.5P(1,0,0) - (8/3 - 0.1)P(1,0,1) = 0$
$(1,1,0):$	$P(0,1,0) + 0.5P(1,0,0) - 2P(1,1,0) = 0$
$(2,0,0):$	$0.9P(1,0,0) + 2/3P(2,0,1) + 3P(3,0,0) - 3.3P(2,0,0) = 0$
$(2,0,1):$	$0.9P(1,0,1) + 0.5P(2,0,0) - 8/3P(2,0,1) = 0$
$(3,0,0):$	$0.8P(2,0,0) - 3P(3,0,0) = 0$

The solution of this linear system is:

$P(0,0,0) = 0.184928 \quad P(0,0,1) = 0.138696 \quad P(0,1,0) = 0.092464 \quad P(1,0,0) = 0.184928$
$P(1,0,1) = 0.138696 \quad P(1,1,0) = 0.092464 \quad P(2,0,0) = 0.083218 \quad P(2,0,1) = 0.062413$
$P(3,0,0) = 0.022191$

Then based on the values of $P(n_1, n_2)$ and (6.21) we calculate the TC probabilities:

$B_{T1} = P(1,1,0) + P(2,0,1) + P(3,0,0) = 0.177068$

(compare with the exact 0.187971 of the EMLM/TH)

$B_{T2} = 1 - P(0,0,0) - P(1,0,0) = 0.630144$

(compare with the exact 0.63911 of the EMLM/TH)

$B_{T3} = P(0,1,0) + P(1,0,1) + P(1,1,0) + P(2,0,1) + P(3,0,0) + P(0,0,1) = 0.546924$

(compare with the exact 0.54888 of the EMLM/TH).

(c) In order to determine the CC probabilities of service-class k, we repeat (b) but decrease the number of sources N_k by 1 (the number of sources for the remaining service-classes does not alter). The values of the exact CC probabilities are:

$B_1 = P(1,1,0) + P(2,0,1) + P(3,0,0) = 0.161154$

$B_2 = 1 - P(0,0,0) - P(1,0,0) = 0.623174$

$B_3 = P(0,1,0) + P(1,0,1) + P(1,1,0) + P(2,0,1) + P(3,0,0) + P(0,0,1) = 0.53099$

Following the analysis of the EnMLM for the determination of $q_{\text{fin}}(j)$ and the analysis of the EMLM/TH it can be proved that the values of $q_{\text{fin}}(j)$ are given by [7]:

$$q_{\text{fin}}(j) = \begin{cases} 1 & \text{if } j = 0 \\ \dfrac{1}{j} \sum_{k=1}^{K} (N_k - n_k + 1)\alpha_{k,\text{idle}} b_k [q_{\text{fin}}(j - b_k) - \Theta_{k,\text{fin}}(j - b_k)] & j = 1, \dots, C \\ 0 & \text{otherwise} \end{cases}$$

(6.45)

where $\Theta_{k,\text{fin}}(x)$ is the probability that x b.u. are occupied, while the number of service-class k calls is $n_{k,\text{max}}$ or:

$$\Theta_{k,\text{fin}}(x) := Prob[j = x, n_k = n_{k,\text{max}}]$$

(6.46)

Equation (6.45) requires knowledge of $\Theta_{k,\text{fin}}(j)$. The latter takes positive values when $j = n_{k,\text{max}} b_k, \dots, C - b_k$. Thus, we consider a subsystem of capacity $F_k = C - b_k - n_{k,\text{max}} b_k$ that accommodates all service-classes but service-class k. For this subsystem, we define $\vartheta_{k,\text{fin}}(j)$, $(j = 0, \dots, F_k)$, which is analogous to $q_{\text{fin}}(j)$ of (6.45):

$$\vartheta_{k,\text{fin}}(j) = \begin{cases} 1 & \text{if } j = 0 \\ \dfrac{1}{j} \sum_{i=1,i\neq k}^{K} (N_i - n_i + 1)\alpha_{i,\text{idle}} b_i [\vartheta_{k,\text{fin}}(j - b_i) - \vartheta_{i,\text{fin}}(j - b_i)] & j = 1, \dots, C \\ 0 & \text{otherwise} \end{cases}$$

(6.47)

We can now compute $\Theta_{k,\text{fin}}(j)$ when $j = n_{k,\text{max}} b_k, \dots, C - b_k$, as follows:

$$\Theta_{k,\text{fin}}(j) = \binom{N_k}{n_{k,\text{max}}} \alpha_{k,\text{idle}}^{n_{k,\text{max}}} \vartheta_{k,\text{fin}}(j - n_{k,\text{max}} b_k)$$

(6.48)

In (6.48), the term $\binom{N_k}{n_{k,\max}} \alpha_{k,\mathrm{idle}}^{n_{k,\max}}$ is expected, since for states $j = n_{k,\max} b_k, \ldots, C - b_k$, the number of in-service calls of service-class k is always $n_{k,\max}$.

If $N_k \to \infty$ for $k = 1, \ldots, K$ and the total offered traffic-load remains constant, then (6.45), (6.47), and (6.48) become (1.73), (1.78), and (1.79), respectively, of the EMLM/TH.

Equations (6.45) and (6.47) require an equivalent stochastic system in order for the various performance measures to be determined, given that the values of n_k are unknown. An alternative procedure is an algorithm similar to that presented in Section 6.2.2.3 [7]:

Algorithm Approximate calculation of $q_{\mathrm{fin}}(j)$ in the EnMLM/TH

Step 1: Define the corresponding infinite loss model (EMLM/TH); calculate $q(j)$, $\vartheta_k(j)$, and $\Theta_k(j)$ via (1.73), (1.78), and (1.79), respectively.

Step 2: Determine the values of $y_k(j)$ in the EMLM/TH based on (1.77).

Step 3: Modify (6.45) and (6.47) to the following approximate but recursive formulas, where the values of $y_k(j)$ have been determined in step 2 from the corresponding infinite model:

$$q_{\mathrm{fin}}(j) = \begin{cases} 1 & \text{if } j = 0 \\ \dfrac{1}{j} \sum_{k=1}^{K} (N_k - y_k(j - b_k)) \alpha_{k,\mathrm{idle}} b_k \left[q_{\mathrm{fin}}(j - b_k) - \Theta_{k,\mathrm{fin}}(j - b_k) \right] & j = 1, \ldots, C \\ 0 & \text{otherwise} \end{cases} \tag{6.49}$$

$$\vartheta_{k,\mathrm{fin}}(j) = \begin{cases} 1 & \text{if } j = 0 \\ \dfrac{1}{j} \sum_{i=1, i \neq k}^{K} (N_i - y_{i,k}(j - b_i)) \alpha_{i,\mathrm{idle}} b_i \left[\vartheta_{k,\mathrm{fin}}(j - b_i) - \Theta_{i,\mathrm{fin}}(j - b_i) \right] & j = 1, \ldots, C \\ 0 & \text{otherwise} \end{cases} \tag{6.50}$$

where $\Theta_{k,\mathrm{fin}}(j)$ is given by (6.48), while $y_{i,k}(j)$ refers to the corresponding infinite model (EMLM/TH) and is given by:

$$y_{i,k}(j) = \frac{\alpha_i \left[\vartheta_k(j - b_i) - \Theta_i(j - b_i) \right]}{\vartheta_k(j)} \tag{6.51}$$

6.4.2.2 CBP, Utilization and Mean Number of In-service Calls

The following performance measures can be determined based on (6.49):

- The TC probabilities of service-class k, B_{Tk}, via:

$$B_{Tk} = \sum_{j=C-b_k+1}^{C} G^{-1} q_{\mathrm{fin}}(j) + \sum_{j=n_{k,\max} b_k+1}^{C-b_k} G^{-1} \Theta_{k,\mathrm{fin}}(j) \tag{6.52}$$

where $G = \sum_{j=0}^{C} q_{\mathrm{fin}}(j)$ is the normalization constant.
- The CBP (or CC probabilities) of service-class k, B_k, via (6.52) but for a system with $N_k - 1$ traffic sources.
- The link utilization, U, via (6.36).

- The average number of service-class k calls in the system, $\bar{n}_k$, via (6.37) where $y_{k,\text{fin}}(j)$ are given by:

$$y_{k,\text{fin}}(j) = \frac{(N_k - y_k(j - b_k))\alpha_{k,\text{idle}}[q_{\text{fin}}(j - b_k) - \Theta_{k,\text{fin}}(j - b_k)]}{q_{\text{fin}}(j)} \tag{6.53}$$

Example 6.11 Consider again Example 6.10 ($C = 4, K = 3, b_1 = 1, b_2 = 3, b_3 = 2, N_1 = N_2 = N_3 = 10, v_1 = 0.1, v_2 = v_3 = 0.05, \mu_1 = \mu_2 = 1, \mu_3 = 2/3, n_{1,\text{max}} = 3, n_{3,\text{max}} = 1$). Apply the three-step algorithm of Section 6.4.2.1 in order to determine the TC probabilities of all service-classes.

Step 1: The corresponding EMLM/TH system is $C = 4, K = 3, b_1 = 1, b_2 = 3, b_3 = 2, \lambda_1 = 1, \lambda_2 = \lambda_3 = 0.5, \mu_1 = \mu_2 = 1, \mu_3 = 2/3, n_{1,\text{max}} = 3$, and $n_{3,\text{max}} = 1$.
Based on (1.73), (1.78), and (1.79), we have the following normalized values of $Q(j)$:

$Q(0) = 0.180451 \quad Q(1) = 0.180451 \quad Q(2) = 0.225564 \quad Q(3) = 0.255639 \quad Q(4) = 0.157895$

Step 2: Based on (1.77), the values of $y_k(j)$ are:

$j = 1 \Rightarrow$	$y_1(1) = 1$	$y_2(1) = 0$	$y_3(1) = 0$
$j = 2 \Rightarrow$	$y_1(2) = 0.8$	$y_2(2) = 0$	$y_3(2) = 0.6$
$j = 3 \Rightarrow$	$y_1(3) = 0.882357$	$y_2(3) = 0.352941$	$y_3(3) = 0.529414$
$j = 4 \Rightarrow$	$y_1(4) = 1.42857$	$y_2(4) = 0.571428$	$y_3(4) = 0.4285714$

Step 3: Based on (6.49), we have the following normalized values of $Q_{\text{fin}}(j)$:

$Q_{\text{fin}}(0) = 0.185663 \qquad Q_{\text{fin}}(1) = 0.185663 \qquad Q_{\text{fin}}(2) = 0.222796$
$Q_{\text{fin}}(3) = 0.253987 \qquad Q_{\text{fin}}(4) = 0.151890$

The approximate TC probabilities are determined via (6.52):

$B_{T1} = Q_{\text{fin}}(4) + \Theta_{1,\text{fin}}(3)/G \overset{G=5.386096}{=} 0.17417$ (compare with the exact 0.177068)
$B_{T2} = Q_{\text{fin}}(2) + Q_{\text{fin}}(3) + Q_{\text{fin}}(4) = 0.62867$ (compare with the exact 0.630144)
$B_{T3} = Q_{\text{fin}}(3) + Q_{\text{fin}}(4) + \Theta_{3,\text{fin}}(2)/G \overset{G=5.386096}{=} 0.545125$ (compare with the exact 0.546924)

Example 6.12 Consider again Example 6.9 ($C = 80$ b.u., $K = 3, (N_1, \alpha_{1,\text{idle}}, b_1) = (60, 0.15, 1), (N_2, \alpha_{2,\text{idle}}, b_2) = (60, 0.05, 5), (N_3, \alpha_{3,\text{idle}}, b_3) = (60, 0.025, 12)$) and assume that $n_{1,\text{max}} = 48, n_{2,\text{max}} = 13$, and $n_{3,\text{max}} = 5$ for the EnMLM/TH and the EMLM/TH. The corresponding offered traffic values for the EMLM/TH are $\alpha_1 = 9, \alpha_2 = 3$ and $\alpha_3 = 1.5$ erl. Assume that the offered traffic-load in the EMLM/TH increases in steps of 1, 0.5, and 0.25 erl for each service-class, respectively, up to $\alpha_1 = 15, \alpha_2 = 6$ and $\alpha_3 = 3$ erl.

(a) Calculate the TC probabilities and the link utilization for both models and provide simulation results for the EnMLM/TH.

(b) Compare the analytical TC probabilities for both models when the number of sources $N = N_1 = N_2 = N_3$ increases from 60 to 150 sources in steps of 30 sources.

(a) In the x-axis of Figures 6.5–6.11, point 1 refers to $(\alpha_1, \alpha_2, \alpha_3) = (9, 3, 1.5)$ while point 7 refers to $(\alpha_1, \alpha_2, \alpha_3) = (15, 6, 3)$.

In Figures 6.5–6.7 we present the analytical and simulation results of the TC probabilities for the EnMLM/TH and the analytical results for the EMLM/TH. The simulation results are presented as mean values of seven runs; since the reliability ranges are found to be very small, they are not presented. All simulation runs are based on the generation of five million calls/run. To account for a warm-up period, the blocking events of the first 5% of these generated calls are not considered in the TC probabilities results.

In Figure 6.8 we present the corresponding results for the link utilization (in b.u.) for both models. Based on Figures 6.5–6.8, we observe that (i) the analytical results are quite close to the simulation results and (ii) the EMLM/TH fails to capture the behavior of the EnMLM/TH.

(b) In Figures 6.9–6.11 we present the analytical results for the TC probabilities, in the case of the EnMLM/TH, versus the increase of the number of traffic sources. As a comparison reference, we present the corresponding results of the EMLM/TH. The results of Figures 6.9–6.11 show that by increasing the number of sources, we approach the results of the infinite model. This fact reveals the consistency of the EnMLM/TH.

6.5 Applications

In order to remember a typical application example of a simple Engset system, it is worth mentioning that Example 6.2 could correspond to an office (in a company) accommodating four clerks with a telephone set dedicated to each clerk, while the four telephone sets equally share two telephone lines.

A recent application of the EnMLM has been proposed in [8] for the calculation of TC and CC probabilities in the X2 link of LTE networks. The main components of an LTE network are the evolved packet core (EPC) and the evolved terrestrial radio access network (E-UTRAN). The EPC is responsible for the management of the core network components and the communication with the external network. The E-UTRAN provides air interface, via evolved NodeBs (eNBs), to user equipment (UE) and acts as an intermediate node handling the radio communication between the UE and the EPC. Each eNB covers a specific cell and exchanges traffic with the core network through the S1 interface. An active UE is quite likely to cross the boundary of the source cell, causing a handover. A handover is the process of a seamless transition of the UE's radio link from the source eNB to one of its neighbors. During this transition, the direct logical interface (link) between two neighboring eNBs – the X2 link – is used for the user data arriving to the source eNB via the S1 link to be transferred to the target eNB (Figure 6.12).

The determination of congestion probabilities in the X2 link can be based on the following multirate teletraffic loss model. Consider the X2 link of fixed capacity C_{X2} that accommodates K different service-classes. Calls of service class k $(k = 1, \ldots, K)$ require

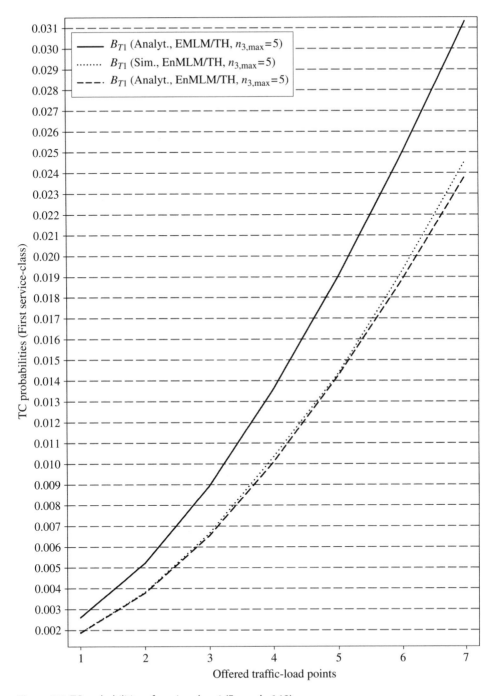

Figure 6.5 TC probabilities of service-class 1 (Example 6.12).

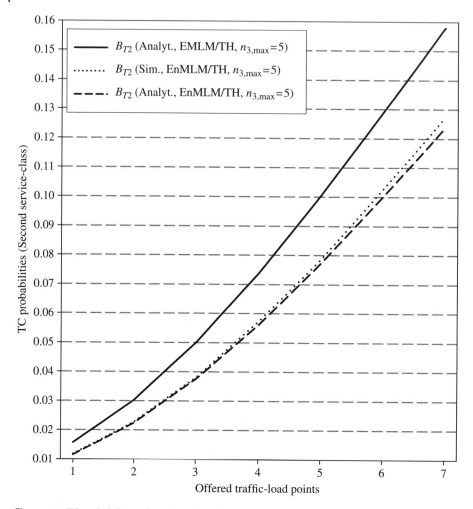

Figure 6.6 TC probabilities of service-class 2 (Example 6.12).

b_k channels and come from a finite source population N_k, while the mean arrival rate of service-class k idle sources is $\lambda_{k,\text{fin}} = (N_k - n_k)\upsilon_k$, where n_k is the number of in-service calls and υ_k is the arrival rate per idle source. To determine the offered traffic-load in the X2 link, the fluid mobility model of [9] is adopted in which traffic flow is considered as the flow of a fluid. Such a model can be used to model the behavior of macroscopic movement (i.e., the movement of an individual UE is considered of little significance) [10]. This fluid mobility model formulates the amount of traffic flowing out of a circular region of a source cell to be proportional to the population density within that region, the average velocity, and the length of the region boundary. More precisely, assuming a population density[1] of $\rho_k = N_k/(\pi R^2)$ for a circular source cell of radius R and that the

---

1 UEs of service-class k per km^2.

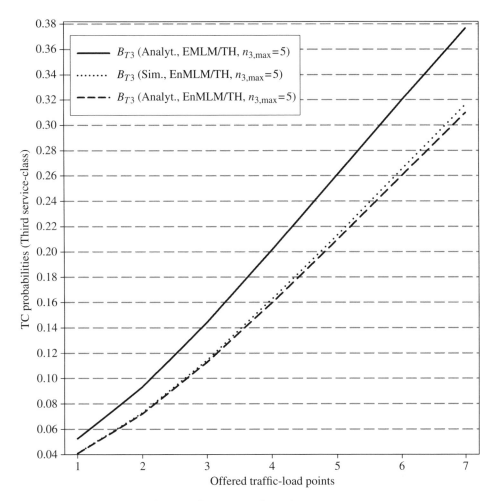

Figure 6.7 TC probabilities of service-class 3 (Example 6.12).

UEs are always active, then the total offered traffic load of service-class k is $2N_k u_k \delta/(\pi R)$, where u_k is the average velocity of service-class k UEs and δ is the interruption time (in the order of 50 ms) of the radio link between the source eNB and the UE. Then, the offered traffic-load per idle source of service-class k is given by $\alpha_{k,\text{idle}} = 2u_k\delta/(\pi R)$ (in erl). Now, the determination of CC and TC probabilities of service-class k in the X2 link can be based on the EnMLM [8].

Another interesting application of the EnMLM on smart grid is proposed in [11]. The authors of [11] propose four power demand control scenarios that correspond to different approaches on the control of power customers' power demands. All scenarios assume that in each residence a specific number of appliances is installed, with diverse power requirements, different operational times, and different power requests arrival

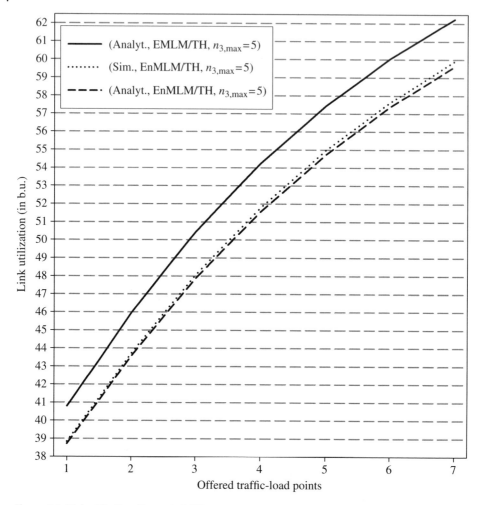

Figure 6.8 Link utilization (Example 6.12).

rates. Of course, a finite number of appliances in the whole residential area is considered. This consideration is expressed by a quasi-random process for the procedure of
arrivals of power requests, which is more realistic compared to the Poisson process (infinite number of power-request sources). A short description of the four scenarios is as
follows:

(i) The default scenario defines the upper bound of the total power consumption, since
it does not consider any scheduling mechanism.
(ii) The compressed demand scenario takes into account the ability of some appliances
to compress their power demands and at the same time expand their operational
times.

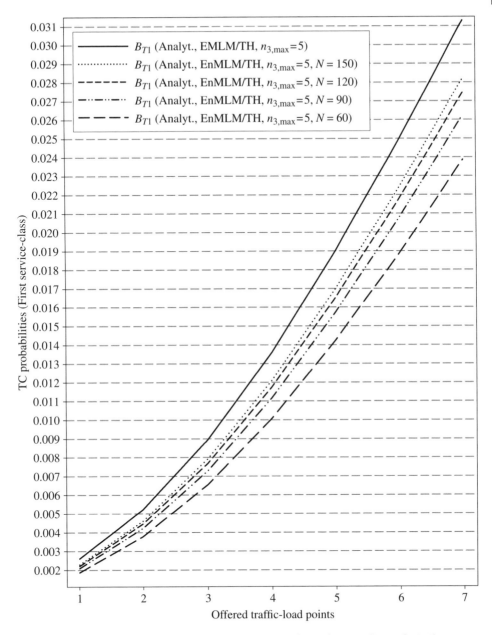

Figure 6.9 TC probabilities of service-class 1 for various numbers of sources (Example 6.12).

(iii) In the delay request scenario, power requests are delayed in buffers for a specific time period, when the total power consumption exceeds a predefined threshold.

(iv) In the postponement request scenario, a similar threshold is used where power requests are postponed not for a specific time period, but until the total power consumption drops below a second threshold.

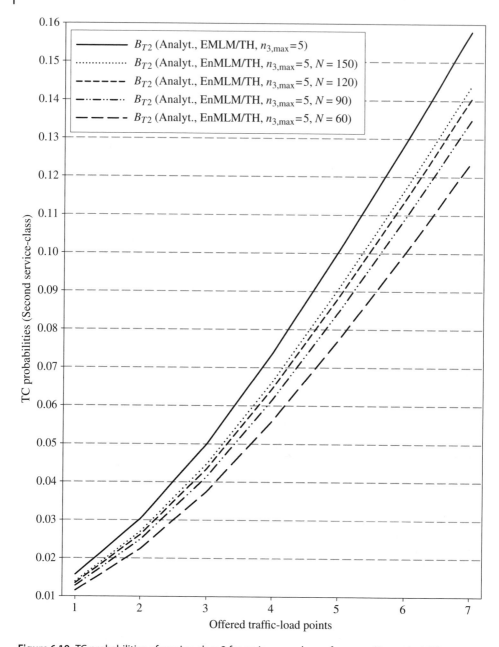

Figure 6.10 TC probabilities of service-class 2 for various numbers of sources (Example 6.12).

6.6 Further Reading

Regarding an in-depth theoretical analysis of the Engset loss model, the interested reader may refer to [12, 13]. In [12], recursive formulas for the determination of CC and TC probabilities are proposed which resemble the recurrent form of the Erlang-B formula.

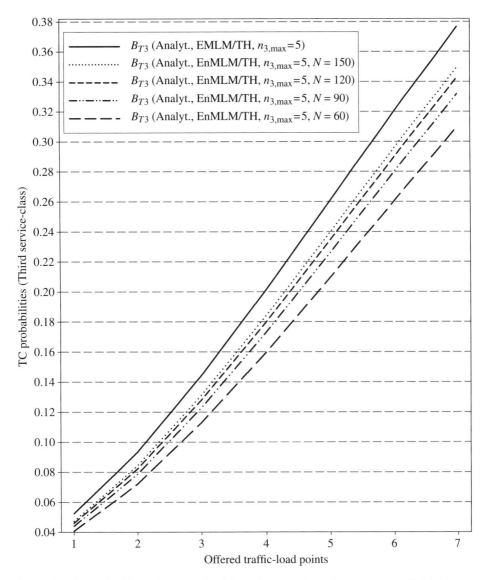

Figure 6.11 TC probabilities of service-class 3 for various numbers of sources (Example 6.12).

In [13], the Engset loss model is extended to include a fractional number of sources and servers.

A quite interesting work whose springboard is the Engset loss model is [14], which is known in the literature as the generalized Engset model. In [14], two generalizations are considered: (i) the distributions of the service (holding) time and interarrival time may differ from source to source and (ii) the idle time distribution may depend on whether or not the previous call was accepted in the system. For applications of the generalized Engset model or extensions of [14], the interested reader may refer to [15–20].

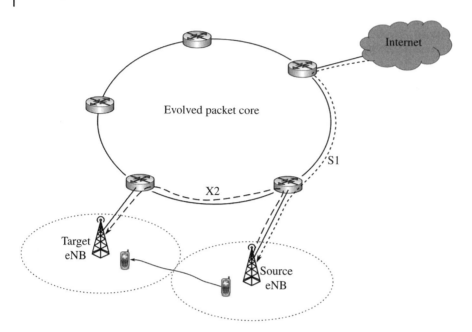

Figure 6.12 The S1 interface and the X2 interface between source and target eNBs.

Regarding the EnMLM, several extensions appear in the literature covering wired [21–24], wireless [25–31], and optical [32, 33] networks. In [21], an analytical method is proposed for the CBP calculation in switching networks accommodating multirate random and quasi-random traffic. In [22], an analytical model is proposed for the determination of TC and CC probabilities in a single link accommodating multirate quasi-random traffic under a reservation policy in which the reserved b.u. can have a real (not integer) value. In [23], an analytical model is proposed for the point-to-point blocking probability calculation in switching networks with multicast connections. In [24], an analytical model is proposed for the determination of blocking probabilities in a switching network carrying Erlang, Engset, and Pascal multirate traffic under different resource allocation control mechanisms. In [25–27], the EnMLM is extended to become suitable for the analysis of WCDMA networks. In [25], the authors incorporate in the model the notion of intra- and inter-cell interference as well as the noise rise and user's activity. A generalization of [25] appears in [26] where handover traffic is explicitly distinguished from new traffic. In [27], a different model is proposed that takes into account not only the uplink (as in [25, 26]) but also the downlink direction. In [28], a time division multiple access/frequency division duplexing (TDMA/FDD) based medium access control (MAC) protocol is proposed for broadband wireless networks that accommodate real-time multimedia applications. The CAC in the proposed MAC is based on the CS policy while the CBP determination is achieved via the EnMLM. In [29], the benefits of software-defined networking (SDN) on the radio resource management (RRM) of future-generation cellular networks are studied. The aim of the proposed RRM scheme is to enable the macro BS to efficiently allocate radio resources for small cell BSs in order to assure QoS of moving users/vehicles during handoffs. To this end, an approximate, but very time- and space-efficient, algorithm for radio resource allocation within a heterogeneous network is proposed based on the EnMLM. In [30], a teletraffic model is proposed for the call-level analysis of priority-based cellular CDMA networks that accommodate multiple service-classes with finite source population. In [31], various state-dependent bandwidth sharing policies are presented and efficient formulas for the CBP determination are proposed for wireless multirate loss networks. In [32], teletraffic loss models are proposed for the calculation of connection failure probabilities (due to unavailability of a wavelength) and CBP (due to the restricted bandwidth capacity of a wavelength) in hybrid TDM-WDM PONs with dynamic wavelength allocation. EMLM and the EnMLM form the springboard of the analysis. Finally, in [33], the EnMLM is used for the determination of blocking probabilities in WDM dynamic networks operating with alternate routing.

References

1 H. Akimaru and K. Kawashima, *Teletraffic – Theory and Applications*, 2nd edn, Springer, Berlin, 1999.

2 E. Pinsky, A. Conway and W. Liu, Blocking formulae for the Engset model. *IEEE Transactions on Communications*, 42(6):2213–2214, June 1994.

3 G. Stamatelos and J. Hayes, Admission control techniques with application to broadband networks. *Computer Communications*, 17(9):663–673, September 1994.

4 M. Glabowski and M. Stasiak, An approximate model of the full-availability group with multi-rate traffic and a finite source population. *Proceedings of the 12th MMB&PGTS*, Dresden, Germany, September 2004.

5 I. Moscholios and M. Logothetis, Engset multirate state-dependent loss models with QoS guarantee. *International Journal of Communications Systems*, 19(1):67–93, February 2006.

6 M. Glabowski, Modelling of state-dependent multirate systems carrying BPP traffic. *Annals of Telecommunications*, 63(7–8):393–407, August 2008.

7 I. Moscholios, M. Logothetis, J. Vardakas and A. Boucouvalas, Performance metrics of a multirate resource sharing teletraffic model with finite sources under both the threshold and bandwidth reservation policies. *IET Networks*, 4(3):195–208, May 2015.

8 P. Panagoulias, I. Moscholios, M. Koukias and M. Logothetis, A multirate loss model of quasi-random input for the X2 link of LTE networks. *Proceedings of the 17th International Conference on Networks (ICN)*, Athens, Greece, April 2018.

9 I. Widjaja and H. La Roche, Sizing X2 bandwidth for inter-connected eNBs. *Proceedings of the IEEE VTC Fall*, Anchorage, Alaska, USA, pp. 1–5, September 2009.

10 D. Lam, D. Cox and J. Widom, Teletraffic modeling for personal communications services. *IEEE Communications Magazine*, 35(2):79–87, February 1997.

11 J. Vardakas, N. Zorba and C. Verikoukis, Power demand control scenarios for smart grid applications with finite number of appliances. *Applied Energy*, 162, 83–98, January 2016.

12 E. Pinsky, A. Conway and W. Liu, Blocking formulae for the Engset model. *IEEE Transactions on Communications*, 42(6): 2213–2214, June 1994.

13 V. Iversen and B. Sanders, Engset formulae with continuous parameters: theory and applications. *International Journal of Electronics and Communications*, 55(1): 3–9, 2001.

14 J.W. Cohen, The generalized Engset formulae. *Philips Telecommunication Review*, 18(4): 158–170, 1957.

15 J. Karvo, O. Martikainen, J. Virtamo and S. Aalto, Blocking of dynamic multicast connections. *Telecommunication Systems*, 16(3–4):467–481, March 2001.

16 H. Kobayashi and B. Mark, Generalized loss models and queueing loss networks. *International Transactions in Operational Research*, 9(1):97–112, January 2002.

17 E. Wong, A. Zalesky and M. Zukerman, A state-dependent approximation for the generalized Engset model. *IEEE Communications Letters*, 13(2):962–964, December 2009.

18 Y. Deng and P. Prucnal, Performance analysis of heterogeneous optical CDMA networks with bursty traffic and variable power control. *IEEE/OSA Journal of Optical Communications and Networking*, 3(6):487–492, June 2011.

19 J. Zhang, Y. Peng, E. Wong and M. Zukerman, Sensitivity of blocking probability in the generalized Engset model for OBS. *IEEE Communications Letters*, 15(11):1243–1245, November 2011.

20 J. Zhang and L. Andrew, Efficient generalized Engset blocking calculation. *IEEE Communications Letters*, 18(9):1535–1538, September 2014.

21 M. Glabowski and M. Stasiak, Internal blocking probability calculation in switching networks with additional inter-stage links and mixture of Erlang and Engset traffic. *Image Processing & Communications*, 17(1–2):67–80, June 2012.

22 I. Moscholios, Congestion probabilities in Erlang–Engset multirate loss models under the multiple fractional channel reservation policy. *Image Processing & Communications*, 21(1):35–46, 2016.

23 M. Sobieraj and P. Zwierzykowski, Blocking probability in switching networks with multi-service sources and multicast traffic. *Proceedings of the IEEE CSNDSP*, Prague, Czech Republic, July 2016.

24 M. Glabowski and M. Sobieraj, Analytical modelling of multiservice switching networks with multiservice sources and resource management mechanisms. *Telecommunication Systems*, 66(3):559–578, November 2017.

25 V. Vassilakis, G. Kallos, I. Moscholios and M. Logothetis, The wireless Engset multi-rate loss model for the call-level analysis of W-CDMA networks. *Proceedings of the 18th Annual IEEE International Symposium on Personal, Indoor and Mobile Radio Communications, PIMRC 07*, Athens, Greece, September 2007.

26 V. Vassilakis, G. Kallos, I. Moscholios and M. Logothetis, On call admission control in W-CDMA networks supporting handoff traffic. *Ubiquitous Computing and Communication Journal*, Special Issue on IEEE CSNDSP 2008, September 2009.

27 M. Glabowski, M. Stasiak, A. Wisniewski and P. Zwierzykowski, Blocking probability calculation for cellular systems with WCDMA radio interface servicing PCT1 and PCT2 multirate traffic. *IEICE Transactions on Communications*, E92-B(4):1156–1165, April 2009.

28 S. Atmaca, A. Karahan, C. Ceken and I. Erturk, A new MAC protocol for broadband wireless communications and its performance evaluation. *Telecommunication Systems*, 57(1):13–23, September 2014.

29 V. Vassilakis, I. Moscholios, A. Bontozoglou and M. Logothetis, Mobility-aware QoS assurance in software-defined radio access networks: An analytical study. *Proceedings of the IEEE International Workshop on Software Defined 5G Networks*, London, UK, April 2015.

30 V. Vassilakis, I. Moscholios and M. Logothetis, Uplink blocking probabilities in priority-based cellular CDMA networks with finite source population. *IEICE Transactions on Communications*, E99-B(6):1302–1309, June 2016.

31 I. Moscholios, V. Vassilakis, M. Logothetis and A. Boucouvalas, State-dependent bandwidth sharing policies for wireless multirate loss networks. *IEEE Transactions on Wireless Communications*, 16(8):5481–5497, August 2017.

32 J. Vardakas, V. Vassilakis and M. Logothetis, Blocking analysis in hybrid TDM-WDM passive optical networks, in *Performance Modelling and Analysis of Heterogeneous Networks*, D. Kouvatsos (ed.), River Publishers, pp. 441–465, 2009.

33 N. Jara and A. Beghelli, Blocking probability evaluation of end-to-end dynamic WDM networks. *Photonic Network Communications*, 24(1):29–38, August 2012.

7

Finite Multirate Retry Threshold Loss Models

We consider multirate loss models of quasi-random arriving calls with elastic bandwidth requirements and fixed bandwidth allocation during service. Calls may retry several times upon arrival (requiring less bandwidth each time) in order to be accepted for service. Alternatively, new calls may request less bandwidth according to the occupied link bandwidth indicated by threshold(s).

7.1 The Finite Single-Retry Model

7.1.1 The Service System

In the *finite single-retry model* (f-SRM), a single link of capacity C b.u. accommodates calls of K service-classes under the CS policy. Calls of service class k ($k = 1, \ldots, K$) come from a finite source population N_k. The mean arrival rate of service-class k idle sources is given by $\lambda_{k,\text{fin}} = (N_k - n_k)v_k$, where n_k is the number of in-service calls and v_k is the arrival rate per idle source. The offered traffic-load per idle source of service-class k is given by $\alpha_{k,\text{idle}} = v_k/\mu_k$ (in erl). Note that if $N_k \to \infty$ for $k = 1, \ldots, K$, and the total offered traffic-load remains constant, then the call arrival process is Poisson. A new call of service-class k ($k = 1, \ldots, K$) has a peak-bandwidth requirement of b_k b.u. and an exponentially distributed service time with mean μ_k^{-1}. If the initially required b.u. are not available in the link, the call is blocked and immediately retries to be connected in the system with $b_{kr} < b_k$ b.u. while the mean of the new service time increases to $\mu_{kr}^{-1} = \frac{b_k}{b_{kr}}\mu_k^{-1}$ so that the product bandwidth requirement by service time remains constant [1]. If the b_{kr} b.u. are not available the call is blocked and lost. The CAC mechanism of a call of service-class k is identical to that of Figure 2.2 of the SRM, i.e., a new call of service-class k is blocked with b_k b.u. if $j > C - b_k$ and is accepted with b_{kr} if $C - b_{kr} \geq j > C - b_k$, where $j = \sum_{k=1}^{K}(n_k b_k + n_{kr}b_{kr})$ and n_k, n_{kr} are the in-service calls of service-class k accepted with b_k, b_{kr} b.u., respectively.

The comparison of the f-SRM with the EnMLM reveals similar differences to those described in Section 2.1.1 for the SRM and the EMLM.

Example 7.1 Consider a link of $C = 5$ b.u. The link accommodates quasi-random arriving calls of two service-classes. Calls of service-class 1 require $b_1 = 1$ b.u. while calls of service-class 2 require $b_2 = 3$ b.u. Blocked calls of service-class 2 can immediately

Efficient Multirate Teletraffic Loss Models Beyond Erlang, First Edition.
Ioannis D. Moscholios and Michael D. Logothetis.
© 2019 John Wiley & Sons Ltd. Published 2019 by John Wiley & Sons Ltd.
Companion website: www.wiley.com/go/logocode

retry with $b_{2r} = 2$ b.u. Let the number of sources be $N_1 = N_2 = 10$, the arrival rate per idle source $v_1 = 0.1$ and $v_2 = 0.1$, and the service rate $\mu_1 = \mu_2 = 1$ sec^{-1}. In addition $\mu_{2r}^{-1} = \frac{b_2}{b_{2r}} \mu_2^{-1} = 1.5$ sec.

(a) Find the total number of permissible states $\mathbf{n} = (n_1, n_2, n_{2r})$ and draw the state transition diagram.
(b) Calculate the state probabilities $P(n_1, n_2, n_{2r})$ and the corresponding values of $Q_{fin}(j)$.
(c) Calculate the TC probabilities of both service-classes, including the retry probability and the link utilization.
(d) Calculate the conditional TC probabilities of service-class 2 retry calls, given that they have been blocked with their initial bandwidth requirement, b_2 b.u.

(a) There are 16 permissible states of the form $\mathbf{n} = (n_1, n_2, n_{2r})$. The state space Ω and the state transition diagram are shown in Figure 7.1.

(b) Based on Figure 7.1, we obtain the following 16 GB equations:

$(0,0,0)$: $\quad P(0,1,0) + P(1,0,0) + 2/3P(0,0,1) - 2P(0,0,0) = 0$

$(0,0,1)$: $\quad P(0,1,1) + P(1,0,1) + 4/3P(0,0,2) - (8/3 - 0.1)P(0,0,1) = 0$

$(0,0,2)$: $\quad P(1,0,2) - 7/3P(0,0,2) = 0$

$(0,1,0)$: $\quad P(0,0,0) + 2/3P(0,1,1) + P(1,1,0) - 2.9P(0,1,0) = 0$

$(0,1,1)$: $\quad 0.9P(0,1,0) + 0.9P(0,0,1) - 5/3P(0,1,1) = 0$

$(1,0,0)$: $\quad P(0,0,0) + 2/3P(1,0,1) + 2P(2,0,0) + P(1,1,0) - 2.9P(1,0,0) = 0$

$(1,0,1)$: $\quad P(0,0,1) + 4/3P(1,0,2) + 2P(2,0,1) - (11/3 - 0.2)P(1,0,1) = 0$

$(1,0,2)$: $\quad P(0,0,2) + 0.9P(1,0,1) - 7/3P(1,0,2) = 0$

$(1,1,0)$: $\quad P(0,1,0) + P(1,0,0) + 2P(2,1,0) - 2.9P(1,1,0) = 0$

$(2,0,0)$: $\quad 0.9P(1,0,0) + 3P(3,0,0) + P(2,1,0) + 2/3P(2,0,1) - 3.8P(2,0,0) = 0$

$(2,0,1)$: $\quad 0.9P(1,0,1) + 3P(3,0,1) - (11/3 - 0.2)P(2,0,1) = 0$

$(2,1,0)$: $\quad 0.9P(1,1,0) + P(2,0,0) - 3P(2,1,0) = 0$

$(3,0,0)$: $\quad 0.8P(2,0,0) + 2/3P(3,0,1) + 4P(4,0,0) - 4.7P(3,0,0) = 0$

$(3,0,1)$: $\quad P(3,0,0) + 0.8P(2,0,1) - 11/3P(3,0,1) = 0$

$(4,0,0)$: $\quad 0.7P(3,0,0) + 5P(5,0,0) - 4.6P(4,0,0) = 0$

$(5,0,0)$: $\quad 0.6P(4,0,0) - 5P(5,0,0) = 0$

The solution of this linear system is:

$P(0,0,0) = 0.167252 \quad P(0,0,1) = 0.053168 \quad P(0,0,2) = 0.005743 \quad P(0,1,0) = 0.132839$

$P(0,1,1) = 0.100444 \quad P(1,0,0) = 0.16622 \quad P(1,0,1) = 0.028363 \quad P(1,0,2) = 0.013401$

$P(1,1,0) = 0.151019 \quad P(2,0,0) = 0.072428 \quad P(2,0,1) = 0.013644 \quad P(2,1,0) = 0.069449$

$P(3,0,0) = 0.015695 \quad P(3,0,1) = 0.007257 \quad P(4,0,0) = 0.002747 \quad P(5,0,0) = 0.00033$

Then based on the values of $P(n_1, n_2, n_{2r})$, we obtain the values of $Q_{fin}(j)$:

$Q_{fin}(0) = P(0,0,0) = 0.167252$

$Q_{fin}(1) = P(1,0,0) = 0.16622$

$Q_{fin}(2) = P(0,0,1) + P(2,0,0) = 0.125596$

$Q_{fin}(3) = P(0,1,0) + P(1,0,1) + P(3,0,0) = 0.176897$

$Q_{fin}(4) = P(0,0,2) + P(1,1,0) + P(2,0,1) + P(4,0,0) = 0.173153$

$Q_{fin}(5) = P(0,1,1) + P(1,0,2) + P(2,1,0) + P(3,0,1) + P(5,0,0) = 0.190881$

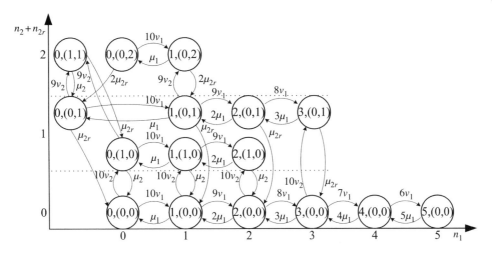

Figure 7.1 The state space Ω and the state transition diagram (Example 7.1).

(c) The TC probabilities of service-class 1, B_{T1}, are given by:

$$B_{T1} = \sum_{j=C-b_1+1}^{C} Q_{\text{fin}}(j) = Q_{\text{fin}}(5) = 0.190881 \ (0.206923 \text{ in the SRM, see Example 2.1})$$

The $Prob\{\text{retry}\}$ of service-class 2 calls, B_{T2}, when they require b_2 b.u. is:

$$B_{T2} = \sum_{j=C-b_2+1}^{C} Q_{\text{fin}}(j) = Q_{\text{fin}}(3) + Q_{\text{fin}}(4) + Q_{\text{fin}}(5) = 0.540931 \ (0.552262 \text{ in the SRM})$$

The TC probabilities of service-class 2 calls, B_{T2r}, when they require b_{2r} b.u. are:

$$B_{T2r} = \sum_{j=C-b_{2r}+1}^{C} Q_{\text{fin}}(j) = Q_{\text{fin}}(4) + Q_{\text{fin}}(5) = 0.364034 \ (0.377639 \text{ in the SRM})$$

(d) The link utilization is determined by $U = \sum_{j=1}^{C} jQ_{\text{fin}}(j) = 2.595$ b.u. (2.66 in the SRM).
(e) The conditional TC probabilities of service-class 2 retry calls are given by:

$$B^*_{T2r} = Prob\{j > C - b_{2r} | j > C - b_2\} = \tfrac{B_{T2r}}{B_{T2}} = 0.672977 \ (0.68380 \text{ in the SRM}).$$

7.1.2 The Analytical Model

7.1.2.1 Steady State Probabilities

To describe the analytical model in the steady state, let us concentrate on a single link of capacity C b.u. that accommodates only two service-classes with the following traffic characteristics: (N_1, N_2, v_1, v_2), (μ_1^{-1}, μ_2^{-1}), (b_1, b_2). Blocked calls of service-class 2 may retry with parameters (b_{2r}, μ_{2r}^{-1}) while blocked calls of service-class 1 do not retry. Although the f-SRM does not have a PFS, we assume that the LB equation (6.33), proposed in the EnMLM, does hold, that is [1]:

$$(N_k - y_{k,\text{fin}}(j - b_k))\alpha_{k,\text{idle}}q_{\text{fin}}(j - b_k) = y_{k,\text{fin}}(j)q_{\text{fin}}(j) \tag{7.1}$$

or, due to the fact that $y_{k,\text{fin}}(j - b_k) = n_k - 1$ in the equivalent stochastic system:

$$(N_k - n_k + 1)\alpha_{k,\text{idle}}q_{\text{fin}}(j - b_k) = y_{k,\text{fin}}(j)q_{\text{fin}}(j), \quad \text{for } j = 1, \dots, C \text{ and } k = 1, 2$$
$$(7.2)$$

This assumption is important for the derivation of an approximate but recursive formula for the $q_{\text{fin}}(j)$. If $j > C - b_2$, when a new call of service-class 2 arrives in the system this call is blocked and retries to be connected with b_{2r} b.u. If $j \le C - b_{2r}$, the retry call will be accepted in the system. To describe this situation we need an additional LB equation [1]:

$$(N_2 - (n_2 + n_{2r}) + 1)\alpha_{2r,\text{idle}}q_{\text{fin}}(j - b_{2r}) = y_{2r,\text{fin}}(j)q_{\text{fin}}(j), \quad \text{for } C \ge j > C - (b_2 - b_{2r})$$
$$(7.3)$$

where $\alpha_{2r,\text{idle}} = v_2\mu_{2r}^{-1}$ is the offered traffic-load per idle source of service-class 2 with b_{2r}, and $y_{2r,\text{fin}}(j)$ is the mean number of service-class 2 calls accepted in state j with b_{2r}.

Multiplying (7.3) with b_{2r}, we have for $C \ge j > C - (b_2 - b_{2r})$:

$$(N_2 - (n_2 + n_{2r}) + 1)\alpha_{2r,\text{idle}}b_{2r}q_{\text{fin}}(j - b_{2r}) = y_{2r,\text{fin}}(j)b_{2r}q_{\text{fin}}(j) \qquad (7.4)$$

Multiplying both sides of (7.2) with b_k, we have for $j = 1, \dots, C$:

$$(N_1 - n_1 + 1)\alpha_{1,\text{idle}}b_1q_{\text{fin}}(j - b_1) + \\ (N_2 - n_2 + 1)\alpha_{2,\text{idle}}b_2q_{\text{fin}}(j - b_2) = (y_{1,\text{fin}}(j)b_1 + y_{2,\text{fin}}(j)b_2)q_{\text{fin}}(j) \qquad (7.5)$$

Adding (7.4) to (7.5), and since $y_{1,\text{fin}}(j)b_1 + y_{2,\text{fin}}(j)b_2 + y_{2r,\text{fin}}(j)b_{2r} = j$, we obtain:

$$(N_1 - n_1 + 1)\alpha_{1,\text{idle}}b_1q_{\text{fin}}(j - b_1) + (N_2 - n_2 + 1)\alpha_{2,\text{idle}}b_2q_{\text{fin}}(j - b_2) + \\ (N_2 - (n_2 + n_{2r}) + 1)\alpha_{2r,\text{idle}}b_{2r}q_{\text{fin}}(j - b_{2r}) = jq_{\text{fin}}(j), \quad \text{for } C \ge j > C - (b_2 - b_{2r})$$
$$(7.6)$$

Apart from the assumption of the LB equation (7.3), another approximation is necessary for the recursive calculation of $q_{\text{fin}}(j)$:

$$y_{1,\text{fin}}(j)b_1 + y_{2,\text{fin}}(j)b_2 \approx j \quad \text{for} \quad j = 1, \dots, C - (b_2 - b_{2r}) \qquad (7.7)$$

In (7.7), the value of $y_{2r,\text{fin}}(j)b_{2r}$ is considered negligible compared to $y_{1,\text{fin}}(j)b_1 + y_{2,\text{fin}}(j)b_2$ when $1 \le j \le C - (b_2 - b_{2r})$. This is the migration approximation (see Section 2.1.2.1). Due to (7.7), equation (7.5) is written as (for $j = 1, \dots, C - (b_2 - b_{2r})$):

$$(N_1 - n_1 + 1)\alpha_{1,\text{idle}}b_1q_{\text{fin}}(j - b_1) + (N_2 - n_2 + 1)\alpha_{2,\text{idle}}b_2q_{\text{fin}}(j - b_2) = jq_{\text{fin}}(j) \quad (7.8)$$

The combination of (7.6) and (7.8) gives an approximate formula for the determination of $q_{\text{fin}}(j)$ in the f-SRM, assuming that only calls of service-class 2 can retry [1]:

$$(N_1 - n_1 + 1)\alpha_{1,\text{idle}}b_1q_{\text{fin}}(j - b_1) + (N_2 - n_2 + 1)\alpha_{2,\text{idle}}b_2q_{\text{fin}}(j - b_2) + \\ (N_2 - (n_2 + n_{2r}) + 1)\alpha_{2r,\text{idle}}b_{2r}\gamma_2(j)q_{\text{fin}}(j - b_{2r}) = jq_{\text{fin}}(j)$$
$$(7.9)$$

where $j = 1, \dots, C$, and $\gamma_2(j) = 1$ when $j > C - (b_2 - b_{2r})$ (otherwise $\gamma_2(j) = 0$).

The generalization of (7.9) in the case of K service-classes, where all service-classes may retry, is as follows [1]:

$$q_{\text{fin}}(j) = \begin{cases} 1 & \text{if } j = 0 \\ \dfrac{1}{j}\sum_{k=1}^{K}(N_k - n_k + 1)\alpha_{k,\text{idle}}b_k q_{\text{fin}}(j - b_k) + \\ \dfrac{1}{j}\sum_{k=1}^{K}(N_k - (n_k + n_{kr}) + 1)\alpha_{kr,\text{idle}}b_{kr}\gamma_k(j)q_{\text{fin}}(j - b_{kr}) & j = 1, \dots, C \\ 0 & \text{otherwise} \end{cases}$$

(7.10)

where $\alpha_{kr,\text{idle}} = \upsilon_k \mu_{kr}^{-1}$, $\gamma_k(j) = 1$ when $j > C - (b_k - b_{kr})$ (otherwise $\gamma_k(j) = 0$).

Note that if $N_k \to \infty$, for $k = 1, \dots, K$, and the total offered traffic-load remains constant, then we have the recursion (2.10) of the SRM.

7.1.2.2 TC Probabilities, CBP, Utilization, and Mean Number of In-service Calls

The following performance measures can be determined based on (7.10):

- The TC probabilities of service-class k calls with b_k b.u., B_{Tk}, via (6.35).
- The TC probabilities of service-class k calls with b_{kr} b.u., B_{Tkr}, via:

$$B_{Tkr} = \sum_{j=C-b_{kr}+1}^{C} G^{-1}q_{\text{fin}}(j)$$

(7.11)

where $G = \sum_{j=0}^{C} q_{\text{fin}}(j)$ is the normalization constant.

- The CBP (or CC probabilities) of service-class k calls with b_k (without retrial), B_k, via (6.35) but for a system with $N_k - 1$ traffic sources.
- The CBP (or CC probabilities) of service-class k calls with b_{kr}, B_{kr}, via (7.11) but for a system with $N_k - 1$ traffic sources.
- The conditional TC probabilities of service-class k retry calls given that they have been blocked with their initial bandwidth requirement b_k, B_{Tkr}^*, via:

$$B_{Tkr}^* = Prob\{j > C - b_{kr}|j > C - b_k\} = \frac{B_{Tkr}}{B_{Tk}}$$

(7.12)

- The link utilization, U, via (6.36).
- The average number of service-class k calls in the system accepted with b_k b.u., $\bar{n}_k$, via (6.37), while the mean number of service-class k calls with b_k given that the system state is j, $y_{k,\text{fin}}(j)$, via (6.38).
- The average number of service-class k calls in the system accepted with b_{kr}, $\bar{n}_{kr}$, via:

$$\bar{n}_{kr} = \sum_{j=1}^{C} G^{-1}y_{kr,\text{fin}}(j)q_{\text{fin}}(j)$$

(7.13)

where $y_{kr,\text{fin}}(j)$ is the average number of service-class k calls with b_{kr} given that the system state is j, and is determined by:

$$y_{kr,\text{fin}}(j) = \frac{(N_k - (n_k + n_{kr}) + 1)\alpha_{kr,\text{idle}}\gamma_k(j)q_{\text{fin}}(j - b_{kr})}{q_{\text{fin}}(j)}$$ (7.14)

where $\alpha_{kr,\text{idle}} = v_k\mu_{kr}^{-1}$ and $\gamma_k(j) = 1$ when $j > C - (b_k - b_{kr})$.

The determination of $q_{\text{fin}}(j)$ via (7.10), and consequently of all performance measures, requires the values of n_k and n_{kr}, which are unknown. In [1–3] give a method for the determination of n_k and n_{kr} in each state j via an equivalent stochastic system, with the same traffic parameters and the same set of states, as already described for the proof of (6.27) in the EnMLM. However, the state space determination of the equivalent system is complex, even for small capacity systems that serve many service-classes with the ability to retry.

Example 7.2   Consider a link of capacity $C = 5$ b.u. and two service-classes whose calls require $b_1 = 3$ and $b_2 = 2$ b.u., respectively. The offered traffic load per idle source is $\alpha_{1,\text{idle}} = \alpha_{2,\text{idle}} = 0.01$ erl, while the number of sources is $N_1 = N_2 = 6$. Blocked calls of service-class 1 retry with reduced bandwidth, $b_{1r} = 1$ b.u., and increased offered traffic $\alpha_{1r,\text{idle}} = 0.03$ erl, so that the total offered traffic load per idle source remains the same $(\alpha_{1,\text{idle}}b_1 = \alpha_{1r,\text{idle}}b_{1r})$. Due to the migration approximation, retry calls of service-class 1 are assumed to be negligible when the occupied link bandwidth $j \le C - (b_1 - b_{1r}) \Rightarrow j \le 3$. Taking into account the migration approximation assumption, the state space consists of eight states (n_1, n_2, n_{1r}), presented in Table 7.1 together with the respective occupied link bandwidth j and the blocking states $(B_{T1}, B_{T2}, B_{T1r})$. According to Table 7.1, the values of $j = 4, 5$ appear more than once, and therefore it is impossible to use (7.10) directly for the calculation of $q_{\text{fin}}(j)$, e.g., the value $j = 4$ corresponds to both $(n_1, n_2, n_{1r}) = (0, 2, 0)$ and $(1, 0, 1)$. To overcome this, an equivalent stochastic system should be determined with the following three characteristics:

(1) The states (n_1, n_2, n_{1r}) are the same as the initial system.
(2) Each state (n_1, n_2, n_{1r}) has a unique occupied link-bandwidth value.
(3) The chosen values of b_1, b_2, and b_{1r} of the equivalent system keep constant (as much as possible) the initial ratios of $b_1 : b_2 : b_{1r} : C = 3 : 2 : 1 : 5$.

In this example, an approximate solution to the initial system is $b_1 = 3000, b_2 = 2000, b_{1r} = 1001$, and $C = 5002$; for these values we present in the last column of Table 7.1 the unique values of the equivalent occupied link bandwidth, j_{eq}. The resultant TC probabilities are $B_{T1} = 5.98\%, B_{T2} = 0.66\%$, and $B_{T1r} = 0.33\%$. Note that

Table 7.1 State space, j, j_{eq}, and blocking states (Example 7.2).

n_1	n_2	n_{1r}	j	j_{eq}	B_{T1}	B_{T2}	B_{T2r}	n_1	n_2	n_{1r}	j	j_{eq}	B_{T1}	B_{T2}	B_{T2r}
0	0	0	0	0				1	0	0	3	3000	*		
0	1	0	2	2000				1	0	1	4	4001	*	*	
0	2	0	4	4000	*	*		1	0	2	5	5002	*	*	*
0	2	1	5	5001	*	*	*	1	1	0	5	5000	*	*	*

every system that is a multiple of $b_1 = 3000, b_2 = 2000, b_{1r} = 1001$, and $C = 5002$ (e.g., $b_1 = 6000, b_2 = 4000, b_{1r} = 2002$, and $C = 10004$) gives exactly the same TC probabilities.

As already mentioned, the determination of an equivalent system is complex, especially when calls retry many times. To circumvent this problem we present, in the next section, the algorithm of Section 6.2.2.3 (initially proposed for the EnMLM) for the f-SRM.

7.1.2.3 An Approximate Algorithm for the Determination of $q_{fin}(j)$ in the f-SRM
Contrary to (7.10), which requires enumeration and processing of the state space, the algorithm presented herein is much simpler and easy to implement [4, 5].

Algorithm Approximate calculation of $q_{fin}(j)$ in the f-SRM

Step 1: Define the corresponding infinite loss model SRM and calculate $q(j)$ via (2.10).
Step 2: Determine the values of $y_k(j)$, $y_{kr}(j)$ in the SRM via (2.14) and (2.15), respectively.
Step 3: Modify (7.10) to the following approximate formula, where the values of $y_k(j)$ and $y_{kr}(j)$ have been determined in step 2 from the corresponding infinite model:

$$q_{fin}(j) = \begin{cases} 1 & \text{if } j = 0 \\ \dfrac{1}{j}\sum_{k=1}^{K}(N_k - y_k(j-b_k))\alpha_{k,idle}b_k\, q_{fin}(j-b_k) + \\ \dfrac{1}{j}\sum_{k=1}^{K}(N_k - (y_k(j-b_{kr}) + y_{kr}(j-b_{kr})))\alpha_{kr,idle}b_{kr}\gamma_k(j)q_{fin}(j-b_{kr}) \\ \qquad \text{if } j = 1, \ldots, C \\ 0 & \text{otherwise} \end{cases}$$

(7.15)

Step 4: Determine the various performance measures as follows:
- The TC probabilities of service-class k calls with b_k b.u., B_{Tk}, via (6.35).
- The TC probabilities of service-class k calls with b_{kr}, B_{Tkr}, via (7.11).
- The CC probabilities of service-class k calls with b_k (without retrial), B_k, via (6.35) but for a system with $N_k - 1$ traffic sources.
- The CC probabilities of service-class k calls with b_{kr}, B_{kr}, via (7.11) but for a system with $N_k - 1$ traffic sources.
- The conditional TC probabilities of service-class k retry calls given that they have been blocked with their initial bandwidth requirement b_k, B^*_{Tkr}, via (7.12).
- The link utilization, U, via (6.36).
- The average number of service-class k calls in the system accepted with b_k b.u., $\overline{n}_k$, via (6.37) where $y_{k,fin}(j)$ is determined by (6.40).
- The average number of service-class k calls in the system accepted with b_{kr} b.u., $\overline{n}_{kr}$, via (7.13) where $y_{kr,fin}(j)$ is determined by:

$$y_{kr,fin}(j) = \frac{[N_k - (y_k(j-b_{kr}) + y_{kr}(j-b_{kr}))]\alpha_{kr,idle}\gamma_k(j)q_{fin}(j-b_{kr})}{q_{fin}(j)}$$

(7.16)

Example 7.3 Consider again Example 7.1 ($C = 5, K = 2, b_1 = 1, b_2 = 3, b_{2r} = 2, N_1 = N_2 = 10, v_1 = 0.1, v_2 = 0.1, \mu_1 = \mu_2 = 1, \mu_{2r}^{-1} = 1.5$). Apply the algorithm of Section 7.1.2.3 for the determination of TC probabilities.

Step 1: The corresponding infinite loss model (SRM) is $C = 5, K = 2, b_1 = 1, b_2 = 3, b_{2r} = 2, \alpha_1 = \alpha_2 = 1$ erl and $\alpha_{2r} = 1.5$ erl.
Based on (2.10), we have the following normalized values of $Q(j)$:

$Q(0) = 0.16901$ $Q(1) = 0.16901$ $Q(2) = 0.08451$
$Q(3) = 0.19718$ $Q(4) = 0.17606$ $Q(5) = 0.20423$

Step 2: Based on (2.14) and (2.15), we have:

$j = 1 \Rightarrow$	$y_1(1) = 1$	$y_2(1) = 0$	$y_{2r}(1) = 0$
$j = 2 \Rightarrow$	$y_1(2) = 2$	$y_2(2) = 0$	$y_{2r}(2) = 0$
$j = 3 \Rightarrow$	$y_1(3) = 0.428571$	$y_2(3) = 0.857143$	$y_{2r}(3) = 0$
$j = 4 \Rightarrow$	$y_1(4) = 1.12$	$y_2(4) = 0.96$	$y_{2r}(4) = 0$
$j = 5 \Rightarrow$	$y_1(5) = 0.86207$	$y_2(5) = 0.41379$	$y_{2r}(5) = 1.44828$

Step 3: Based on (7.15), we have the following normalized values of $Q_{\text{fin}}(j)$:

$Q_{\text{fin}}(0) = 0.176891$ $Q_{\text{fin}}(1) = 0.176891$ $Q_{\text{fin}}(2) = 0.0796$
$Q_{\text{fin}}(3) = 0.198118$ $Q_{\text{fin}}(4) = 0.180075$ $Q_{\text{fin}}(5) = 0.188424$

Step 4: The approximate TC probabilities are:

$$B_{T1} = \sum_{j=C-b_1+1}^{C} Q_{\text{fin}}(j) = 0.188424 \text{ (compare with the exact 0.190881)}$$

$$B_{T2} = \sum_{j=C-b_2+1}^{C} Q_{\text{fin}}(j) = 0.566617 \text{ (compare with the exact 0.540931)}$$

$$B_{T2r} = \sum_{j=C-b_{2r}+1}^{C} Q_{\text{fin}}(j) = 0.368499 \text{ (compare with the exact 0.364034)}$$

7.2 The Finite Single-Retry Model under the BR Policy

7.2.1 The Service System

In the *f-SRM under the BR policy* (*f-SRM/BR*), t_k b.u. are reserved to benefit calls of all other service-classes apart from service-class k. The application of the BR policy in the f-SRM is similar to that of the SRM/BR as the following example shows.

Example 7.4 Consider again Example 7.1 ($C = 5, K = 2, b_1 = 1, b_2 = 3, b_{2r} = 2, N_1 = N_2 = 10, v_1 = v_2 = 0.1, \mu_1 = \mu_2 = 1, \mu_{2r}^{-1} = 1.5$) and let the BR parameters $t_1 = 2$ b.u. and $t_2 = 0$ b.u. so that $b_1 + t_1 = b_2 + t_2$. In that case, equalization of TC probabilities is achieved between new calls of service-class 1 and new (not retry) calls of service-class 2.

(a) Find the total number of permissible states $\mathbf{n} = (n_1, n_2, n_{2r})$ and draw the state transition diagram.

(b) Calculate the state probabilities $P(n_1, n_2, n_{2r})$ and the corresponding values of $Q_{fin}(j)$.
(c) Calculate the TC probabilities of both service-classes, including the retry probability.

(a) There are 14 permissible states of the form $\mathbf{n} = (n_1, n_2, n_{2r})$. The state space Ω and the state transition diagram are shown in Figure 7.2.
(b) Based on Figure 7.2, we obtain the following 14 GB equations:

$(0,0,0):$ $P(0,1,0) + P(1,0,0) + 2/3P(0,0,1) - 2P(0,0,0) = 0$

$(0,0,1):$ $P(0,1,1) + P(1,0,1) + 4/3P(0,0,2) - (8/3 - 0.1)P(0,0,1) = 0$

$(0,0,2):$ $P(1,0,2) - 4/3P(0,0,2) = 0$

$(0,1,0):$ $P(0,0,0) + 2/3P(0,1,1) + P(1,1,0) - 1.9P(0,1,0) = 0$

$(0,1,1):$ $0.9P(0,1,0) + 0.9P(0,0,1) - 5/3P(0,1,1) = 0$

$(1,0,0):$ $P(0,0,0) + 2/3P(1,0,1) + 2P(2,0,0) + P(1,1,0) - 2.9P(1,0,0) = 0$

$(1,0,1):$ $P(0,0,1) + 4/3P(1,0,2) + 2P(2,0,1) - (5/3 + 0.9)P(1,0,1) = 0$

$(1,0,2):$ $0.9P(1,0,1) - 7/3P(1,0,2) = 0$

$(1,1,0):$ $P(1,0,0) + 2P(2,1,0) - 2P(1,1,0) = 0$

$(2,0,0):$ $0.9P(1,0,0) + 3P(3,0,0) + P(2,1,0) + 2/3P(2,0,1) - 3.8P(2,0,0) = 0$

$(2,0,1):$ $3P(3,0,1) - 8/3P(2,0,1) = 0$

$(2,1,0):$ $P(2,0,0) - 3P(2,1,0) = 0$

$(3,0,0):$ $0.8P(2,0,0) + 2/3P(3,0,1) - 4P(3,0,0) = 0$

$(3,0,1):$ $P(3,0,0) - 11/3P(3,0,1) = 0$

The solution of this linear system is:

$P(0,0,0) = 0.196645$ $P(0,0,1) = 0.083169$ $P(0,0,2) = 0.012521$ $P(0,1,0) = 0.201072$

$P(0,1,1) = 0.15349$ $P(1,0,0) = 0.136772$ $P(1,0,1) = 0.043282$ $P(1,0,2) = 0.016694$

$P(1,1,0) = 0.083065$ $P(2,0,0) = 0.044037$ $P(2,0,1) = 0.002831$ $P(2,1,0) = 0.014679$

$P(3,0,0) = 0.009227$ $P(3,0,1) = 0.002516$

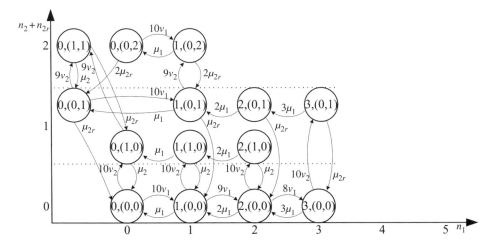

Figure 7.2 The state space Ω and the state transition diagram (Example 7.4).

Then, based on the values of $P(n_1, n_2, n_{2r})$, we obtain the values of $Q_{\text{fin}}(j)$:

$Q_{\text{fin}}(0) = P(0,0,0) = 0.196645$

$Q_{\text{fin}}(1) = P(1,0,0) = 0.136772$

$Q_{\text{fin}}(2) = P(0,0,1) + P(2,0,0) = 0.127206$

$Q_{\text{fin}}(3) = P(0,1,0) + P(1,0,1) + P(3,0,0) = 0.253581$

$Q_{\text{fin}}(4) = P(0,0,2) + P(1,1,0) + P(2,0,1) = 0.098417$

$Q_{\text{fin}}(5) = P(0,1,1) + P(1,0,2) + P(2,1,0) + P(3,0,1) = 0.187379$

(c) The TC probabilities of service-class 1, B_{T1}, are given by:

$$B_{T1} = \sum_{j=C-b_1-t_1+1}^{C} Q_{\text{fin}}(j) = Q_{\text{fin}}(3) + Q_{\text{fin}}(4) + Q_{\text{fin}}(5) = 0.539377$$

(0.548536 in the SRM/BR, see Example 2.3)

The *Prob*{retry} of service-class 2 calls, B_{T2}, when they require b_2 b.u., is:

$$B_{T2} = \sum_{j=C-b_2-t_2+1}^{C} Q_{\text{fin}}(j) = Q_{\text{fin}}(3) + Q_{\text{fin}}(4) + Q_{\text{fin}}(5) = 0.539377 \text{ (0.548536 in the SRM/BR)}$$

The TC probabilities of service-class 2 calls, B_{T2r}, when they require b_{2r} b.u., are:

$$B_{T2r} = \sum_{j=C-b_{2r}+1}^{C} Q_{\text{fin}}(j) = Q_{\text{fin}}(4) + Q_{\text{fin}}(5) = 0.285796 \text{ (0.301968 in the SRM/BR)}$$

7.2.2 The Analytical Model

7.2.2.1 Link Occupancy Distribution

In the f-SRM/BR, the unnormalized values of $q_{\text{fin}}(j)$ can be calculated in an approximate way according to the Roberts method (see Section 1.3.2.2). Based on that method, we can either find an equivalent stochastic system (which is complex) [3] or apply an algorithm similar to the one presented in Section 7.1.2.3. Due to its simplicity, the latter is adopted herein with the following modifications.

7.2.2.2 TC Probabilities, CBP, Utilization, and Mean Number of In-service Calls

The following performance measures can be determined based on (7.17):

- The TC probabilities of service-class k calls with b_k b.u., B_{Tk}, via (6.42).
- The TC probabilities of service-class k calls with b_{kr}, B_{Tkr}, via:

$$B_{Tkr} = \sum_{j=C-b_{kr}-t_k+1}^{C} G^{-1} q_{\text{fin}}(j) \tag{7.18}$$

- The CC probabilities of service-class k calls with b_k (without retrial), B_k, via (6.42) but for a system with $N_k - 1$ traffic sources.
- The CC probabilities of service-class k calls with b_{kr}, B_{Tkr}, via (7.18) but for a system with $N_k - 1$ traffic sources.

Algorithm Approximate calculation of $q_{\text{fin}}(j)$ in the f-SRM/BR

Step 1: Define the corresponding infinite loss model SRM/BR and calculate $q(j)$ via (2.18).

Step 2: Determine $y_k(j)$ and $y_{kr}(j)$ in the SRM/BR from (1.67) and (2.21), respectively.

Step 3: Modify (7.15) to the following approximate formula, where the values of $y_k(j)$ and $y_{kr}(j)$ have been determined in step 2 from the corresponding infinite model:

$$
q_{\text{fin}}(j)=\begin{cases}
1 & \text{if } j=0 \\[2mm]
\dfrac{1}{j}\displaystyle\sum_{k=1}^{K}(N_k-y_k(j-b_k))\alpha_{k,\text{idle}}D_k(j-b_k)q_{\text{fin}}(j-b_k)+ \\
\dfrac{1}{j}\displaystyle\sum_{k=1}^{K}[N_k-(y_k(j-b_{kr})+y_{kr}(j-b_{kr}))]\alpha_{kr,\text{idle}}D_{kr}(j-b_{kr})\gamma_k(j)q_{\text{fin}}(j-b_{kr}) \\[2mm]
& \text{if } j=1,\dots,C \\[2mm]
0 & \text{otherwise}
\end{cases}
\tag{7.17}
$$

where $D_k(j-b_k)$ and $D_{kr}(j-b_{kr})$ are determined via (1.65) and (2.19), respectively.

- The conditional TC probabilities of service-class k retry calls given that they have been blocked with their initial bandwidth requirement b_k, B^*_{Tkr}, via (7.12), while subtracting the BR parameter t_k from both $C-b_{kr}$ and $C-b_k$.
- The link utilization, U, via (6.36).
- The average number of service-class k calls in the system accepted with b_k b.u., $\bar{n}_k$, via (6.37) where $y_{k,\text{fin}}(j)$ is determined by:

$$
y_{k,\text{fin}}(j) = \begin{cases}
\dfrac{(N_k-y_k(j-b_k))\alpha_{k,\text{idle}}q_{\text{fin}}(j-b_k)}{q_{\text{fin}}(j)} & \text{for } j \le C-t_k \\[2mm]
0 & \text{for } j > C-t_k
\end{cases}
\tag{7.19}
$$

- The average number of service-class k calls in the system accepted with b_{kr} b.u., $\bar{n}_{kr}$, via (7.13) where $y_{kr,\text{fin}}(j)$ is determined by:

$$
y_{kr,\text{fin}}(j) = \begin{cases}
\dfrac{[N_k-(y_k(j-b_{kr})+y_{kr}(j-b_{kr}))]\alpha_{kr,\text{idle}}\gamma_k(j)q_{\text{fin}}(j-b_{kr})}{q_{\text{fin}}(j)} & \text{for } j \le C-t_k \\[2mm]
0 & \text{for } j > C-t_k
\end{cases}
\tag{7.20}
$$

where $\alpha_{kr,\text{idle}} = v_k\mu_{kr}^{-1}$, and $\gamma_k(j) = 1$ when $j > C-(b_k-b_{kr})$.

Example 7.5 Consider again Example 7.4 ($C=5, K=2, b_1=1, b_2=3, b_{2r}=2$, $t_1=2, t_2=0, N_1=N_2=10, v_1=v_2=0.1, \mu_1=\mu_2=1, \mu_{2r}^{-1}=1.5$). Apply the algorithm of Section 7.2.2.1 for the determination of TC probabilities.

Step 1: The corresponding infinite loss model (SRM/BR) is $C=5, K=2, b_1=1, b_2=3$, $b_{2r}=2, t_1=2, t_2=0, \alpha_1=\alpha_2=1$ erl and $\alpha_{2r}=1.5$ erl. Based on (2.18), we have the following normalized values of $Q(j)$:

$Q(0)=0.18462 \quad Q(1)=0.18462 \quad Q(2)=0.09231$
$Q(3)=0.21538 \quad Q(4)=0.13846 \quad Q(5)=0.18462$

Step 2: Based on (1.67) and (2.21), we have:

$$j = 1 \Rightarrow y_1(1) = 1 \qquad y_2(1) = 0 \qquad y_{2r}(1) = 0$$
$$j = 2 \Rightarrow y_1(2) = 2 \qquad y_2(2) = 0 \qquad y_{2r}(2) = 0$$
$$j = 3 \Rightarrow y_1(3) = 0.428571 \quad y_2(3) = 0.857143 \quad y_{2r}(3) = 0$$
$$j = 4 \Rightarrow y_1(4) = 0 \qquad y_2(4) = 1.33333 \qquad y_{2r}(4) = 0$$
$$j = 5 \Rightarrow y_1(5) = 0 \qquad y_2(5) = 0.5 \qquad y_{2r}(5) = 1.75$$

Step 3: Based on (7.17), we have the following normalized values of $Q_{\text{fin}}(j)$:

$$Q_{\text{fin}}(0) = 0.192145 \quad Q_{\text{fin}}(1) = 0.192145 \quad Q_{\text{fin}}(2) = 0.086465$$
$$Q_{\text{fin}}(3) = 0.215203 \quad Q_{\text{fin}}(4) = 0.144109 \quad Q_{\text{fin}}(5) = 0.169933$$

The approximate TC probabilities are:

$$B_{T1} = \sum_{j=C-b_1-t_1+1}^{C} Q_{\text{fin}}(j) = 0.529245 \quad \text{(compare with the exact 0.539377)}$$

$$B_{T2} = \sum_{j=C-b_2-t_2+1}^{C} Q_{\text{fin}}(j) = 0.529245 \quad \text{(compare with the exact 0.539377)}$$

$$B_{T2r} = \sum_{j=C-b_{2r}+1}^{C} Q_{\text{fin}}(j) = 0.314042 \quad \text{(compare with the exact 0.285796)}$$

7.3 The Finite Multi-Retry Model

7.3.1 The Service System

In the *finite multi-retry model* (*f-MRM*), calls of service-class k can retry more than once to be connected in the system [2–5]. Let $S(k)$ be the number of retrials for calls of service-class k and assume that $b_k > b_{kr_1} > \ldots > b_{kr_s} > \ldots > b_{kr_{S(k)}}$, where b_{kr_s} is the required bandwidth of a service-class k call in the sth retry, $s = 1, \ldots, S(k)$. Then a service-class k call is accepted in the system with b_{kr_s} b.u. if $C - b_{kr_{s-1}} < j \le C - b_{kr_s}$.

Example 7.6 Consider a link of $C = 3$ b.u. The link accommodates quasi-random arriving calls of two service-classes. Calls of service-class 1 require $b_1 = 1$ b.u. while calls of service-class 2 require $b_2 = 3$. Blocked calls of service-class 2 can retry two times with $b_{2r_1} = 2$ b.u. and $b_{2r_2} = 1$ b.u. Let the number of sources be $N_1 = N_2 = 10$, the arrival rate per idle source be $v_1 = v_2 = 0.1$ and $\mu_1^{-1} = \mu_2^{-1} = 1$ sec, $\mu_{2r_1}^{-1} = 2.0$ sec, and $\mu_{2r_2}^{-1} = 4.0$ sec (in this example we do not assume that $b_2 \mu_2^{-1} = b_{2r_1} \mu_{2r_1}^{-1} = b_{2r_2} \mu_{2r_2}^{-1}$).

(a) Find the total number of permissible states $\mathbf{n} = (n_1, n_2, n_{2r_1}, n_{2r_2})$ and draw the state transition diagram.
(b) Calculate the state probabilities $P(n_1, n_2, n_{2r_1}, n_{2r_2})$ and the corresponding values of $Q_{\text{fin}}(j)$ based on the GB equations.
(c) Calculate the TC probabilities of both service-classes, including the retry probabilities and the link utilization.
(d) Calculate the conditional TC probabilities of service-class 2 retry calls with b_{2r_2}, given that they have been blocked with their initial bandwidth requirement, b_2.

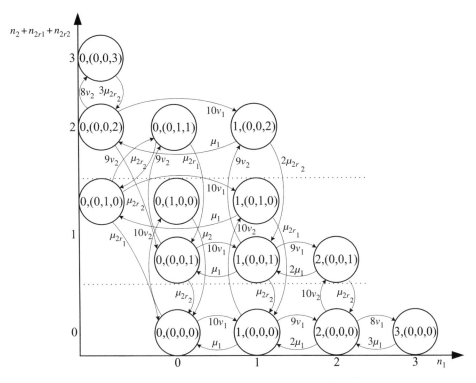

Figure 7.3 The state space Ω and the state transition diagram (Example 7.6).

(a) The total number of permissible states of the form $\mathbf{n} = (n_1, n_2, n_{2r_1}, n_{2r_2})$, is 14. They are shown in Figure 7.3 together with the state transition diagram.

(b) Based on Figure 7.3, the corresponding 14 GB equations are:

$(0, 0, 0, 0)$: $0.5P(0, 0, 1, 0) + 0.25P(0, 0, 0, 1) + P(0, 1, 0, 0) + P(1, 0, 0, 0) - 2P(0, 0, 0, 0) = 0$

$(0, 0, 0, 1)$: $0.5P(0, 0, 0, 2) + 0.5P(0, 0, 1, 1) + P(1, 0, 0, 1) - 2.15P(0, 0, 0, 1) = 0$

$(0, 0, 0, 2)$: $P(1, 0, 0, 2) + 0.75P(0, 0, 0, 3) - 2.3P(0, 0, 0, 2) = 0$

$(0, 0, 0, 3)$: $0.8P(0, 0, 0, 2) - 0.75P(0, 0, 0, 3) = 0$

$(0, 0, 1, 0)$: $0.25P(0, 0, 1, 1) + P(1, 0, 1, 0) - 2.4P(0, 0, 1, 0) = 0$

$(0, 0, 1, 1)$: $0.9P(0, 0, 0, 1) + 0.9P(0, 0, 1, 0) - 0.75P(0, 0, 1, 1) = 0$

$(0, 1, 0, 0)$: $P(0, 0, 0, 0) - P(0, 1, 0, 0) = 0$

$(1, 0, 0, 0)$: $0.25P(1, 0, 0, 1) + 2P(2, 0, 0, 0) + 0.5P(1, 0, 1, 0) + P(0, 0, 0, 0) -$
$2.9P(1, 0, 0, 0) = 0$

$(1, 0, 0, 1)$: $2P(2, 0, 0, 1) + 0.5P(1, 0, 0, 2) + P(0, 0, 0, 1) - 3.05P(1, 0, 0, 1) = 0$

$(1, 0, 0, 2)$: $P(0, 0, 0, 2) + 0.9P(1, 0, 0, 1) - 1.5P(1, 0, 0, 2) = 0$

$(1, 0, 1, 0)$: $P(0, 0, 1, 0) + P(1, 0, 0, 0) - 1.5P(1, 0, 1, 0) = 0$

$(2, 0, 0, 0)$: $0.9P(1, 0, 0, 0) + 3P(3, 0, 0, 0) + 0.25P(2, 0, 0, 1) - 3.8P(2, 0, 0, 0) = 0$

$(2, 0, 0, 1)$: $0.9P(1, 0, 0, 1) + P(2, 0, 0, 0) - 2.25P(2, 0, 0, 1) = 0$

$(3, 0, 0, 0)$: $0.8P(2, 0, 0, 0) - 3P(3, 0, 0, 0) = 0$

The solution of this linear system is:

$P(0,0,0,0) = 0.132426$ $P(0,0,0,1) = 0.071218$ $P(0,0,0,2) = 0.04086$

$P(0,0,0,3) = 0.043584$ $P(0,0,1,0) = 0.055347$ $P(0,0,1,1) = 0.151878$

$P(0,1,0,0) = 0.132426$ $P(1,0,0,0) = 0.086948$ $P(1,0,0,1) = 0.05675$

$P(1,0,0,2) = 0.06129$ $P(1,0,1,0) = 0.094863$ $P(2,0,0,0) = 0.029052$

$P(2,0,0,1) = 0.035612$ $P(3,0,0,0) = 0.007747$

Based on the values of $P(n_1, n_2, n_{2r_1}, n_{2r_2})$, we have:

$Q_{\text{fin}}(0) =$ $P(0,0,0,0) = 0.132426$

$Q_{\text{fin}}(1) =$ $P(0,0,0,1) + P(1,0,0,0) = 0.158166$

$Q_{\text{fin}}(2) =$ $P(0,0,0,2) + P(0,0,1,0) + P(1,0,0,1) + P(2,0,0,0) = 0.182009$

$Q_{\text{fin}}(3) =$ $P(0,0,0,3) + P(0,0,1,1) + P(0,1,0,0) + P(1,0,0,2) +$
      $P(1,0,1,0) + P(2,0,0,1) + P(3,0,0,0) = 0.5274$

(c) The TC probabilities of service-class 1 are given by:

$$B_{T1} = \sum_{j=C-b_1+1}^{C} Q_{\text{fin}}(j) = Q_{\text{fin}}(3) = 0.5274 \ (0.545687 \text{ in the MRM, see Example 2.6)}$$

The TC probability of the first retry of service-class 2 is given by:

$$B_{T2} = \sum_{j=C-b_2+1}^{C} Q_{\text{fin}}(j) = 1 - Q_{\text{fin}}(0) = 0.867574 \ (0.876443 \text{ in the MRM})$$

The TC probability of the second retry of service-class 2, with b_{2r_1} b.u., is given by:

$$B_{T2r_1} = \sum_{j=C-b_{2r_1}+1}^{C} Q_{\text{fin}}(j) = Q_{\text{fin}}(2) + Q_{\text{fin}}(3) = 0.709409 \ (0.725882 \text{ in the MRM})$$

The TC probability of service-class 2, with b_{2r_2} b.u., is given by:

$$B_{T2r_2} = \sum_{j=C-b_{2r_2}+1}^{C} Q_{\text{fin}}(j) = Q_{\text{fin}}(3) = 0.5274 \ (0.545687 \text{ in the MRM})$$

The link utilization is determined by:

$$U = \sum_{j=1}^{C} j Q_{\text{fin}}(j) = 2.104 \text{ b.u. } (2.148 \text{ in the MRM})$$

(d) The conditional TC probabilities of service-class 2 retry calls with b_{2r_2} are given by:

$$B^*_{T2r_2} = Prob\{j > C - b_{2r_2} | j > C - b_2\} = \frac{B_{T2r_2}}{B_{T2}} = 0.6079 \ (0.62262 \text{ in the MRM}).$$

7.3.2 The Analytical Model

7.3.2.1 Steady State Probabilities

Following the analysis of Section 7.1.2.1, in the f-MRM not only LB is assumed but also the migration approximation, that is, the mean number of service-class k calls in state j, $y_{kr_s,\text{fin}}(j)$, accepted with b_{kr_s} b.u., is negligible when $j \le C - (b_{kr_{s-1}} - b_{kr_s})$,

$(s = 1, \ldots , S(k))$. This means that service-class k calls with b_{kr_s} are limited in the area $j > C - (b_{kr_{s-1}} - b_{kr_s})$. The $q_{\text{fin}}(j)$ are determined by [2]:

$$
q_{\text{fin}}(j) = \begin{cases} 1 & \text{if} \quad j = 0 \\ \begin{aligned} &\frac{1}{j} \sum_{k=1}^{K} (N_k - n_k + 1) \alpha_{k,\text{idle}} b_k q_{\text{fin}}(j - b_k) + \frac{1}{j} \sum_{k=1}^{K} \sum_{s=1}^{S(k)} [N_k - (n_k + n_{kr_1} + \ldots + \\ &n_{kr_s} + \ldots + n_{kr_{S(k)}}) + 1] \alpha_{kr_s,\text{idle}} b_{kr_s} \gamma_{k_s}(j) q_{\text{fin}}(j - b_{kr_s}) \quad j = 1, \ldots , C \end{aligned} \\ 0 & \text{otherwise} \end{cases}
$$

(7.21)

where $\alpha_{kr_s,\text{idle}} = v_k \mu_{kr_s}^{-1}$, and $\gamma_{k_s}(j) = 1$ when $j > C - (b_{kr_{s-1}} - b_{kr_s})$ (otherwise $\gamma_{k_s}(j) = 0$).

Note that if $N_k \to \infty$ for $k = 1, \ldots, K$, and the total offered traffic-load remains constant, then we have the recursion (2.22) of the MRM [6]. In addition, if calls may retry only once, then the SRM results [6].

7.3.2.2 TC Probabilities, CBP, Utilization, and Mean Number of In-service Calls

The following performance measures can be determined based on (7.21):

- The TC probabilities of service-class k calls with b_k b.u., B_{Tk}, via (6.35).
- The TC probabilities of service-class k calls with their last bandwidth requirement $b_{kr_{S(k)}}$ b.u., $B_{Tkr_{S(k)}}$, via:

$$
B_{Tkr_{S(k)}} = \sum_{j=C-b_{kr_{S(k)}}+1}^{C} G^{-1} q_{\text{fin}}(j)
$$

(7.22)

where $G = \sum_{j=0}^{C} q_{\text{fin}}(j)$ is the normalization constant.

- The CC probabilities of service-class k calls with b_k (without retrial), B_k, via (6.35) but for a system with $N_k - 1$ traffic sources.
- The CC probabilities of service-class k calls with $b_{kr_{S(k)}}$, $B_{kr_{S(k)}}$, via (7.22) but for a system with $N_k - 1$ traffic sources.
- The conditional TC probabilities of service-class k retry calls, while requesting $b_{kr_{S(k)}}$ b.u. given that they have been blocked with their initial bandwidth requirement b_k, $B^*_{Tkr_{S(k)}}$, via:

$$
B^*_{Tkr_{S(k)}} = Prob\{j > C - b_{kr_{S(k)}} | j > C - b_k\} = \frac{B_{Tkr_{S(k)}}}{B_{Tk}}
$$

(7.23)

- The link utilization, U, via (6.36).
- The average number of service-class k calls in the system accepted with b_k b.u., $\bar{n}_k$, via (6.37), while the mean number of service-class k calls with b_k given that the system state is j, $y_{k,\text{fin}}(j)$, via (6.38).
- The average number of service-class k calls in the system accepted with b_{kr_s} b.u., $\bar{n}_{kr_s}$, via:

$$
\bar{n}_{kr_s} = \sum_{j=1}^{C} G^{-1} y_{kr_s,\text{fin}}(j) q_{\text{fin}}(j)
$$

(7.24)

where $y_{kr_s,\mathrm{fin}}(j)$ is the average number of service-class k calls with b_{kr_s} given that the system state is j, and is determined by:

$$y_{kr_s,\mathrm{fin}}(j) = \frac{(N_k - (n_k + n_{kr_1} + \ldots + n_{kr_s} + \ldots + n_{kr_{S(k)}}) + 1)\alpha_{kr_s,\mathrm{idle}}\gamma_{k_s}(j)q_{\mathrm{fin}}(j - b_{kr_s})}{q_{\mathrm{fin}}(j)}$$

$$(7.25)$$

where $\alpha_{kr,\mathrm{idle}} = v_k \mu_{kr}^{-1}$, and $\gamma_{k_s}(j) = 1$ when $j > C - (b_{kr_{s-1}} - b_{kr_s})$ (otherwise $\gamma_{k_s}(j) = 0$).

The determination of $q_{\mathrm{fin}}(j)$ via (7.21), and consequently of all performance measures, requires the values of n_k and n_{kr_s}, $s = 1, \ldots, S(k)$, which are unknown. In [2], there is a method for the determination of n_k and n_{kr_s} in each state j via an equivalent stochastic system, with the same traffic parameters and the same set of states. However, since this method is complex, we adopt the algorithm of Section 7.3.2.3 (see below), which is similar to the algorithm of Section 7.1.2.3 of the f-SRM.

7.3.2.3 An Approximate Algorithm for the Determination of $q_{\mathrm{fin}}(j)$ in the f-MRM

The algorithm for the calculation of $q_{\mathrm{fin}}(j)$ in the f-MRM can be described as follows [4, 5]:

Algorithm Approximate calculation of $q_{\mathrm{fin}}(j)$ in the f-MRM

Step 1: Define the corresponding infinite loss model MRM and calculate $q(j)$ via (2.22).

Step 2: Determine the values of $y_k(j)$ and $y_{kr_s}(j)$ ($s = 1, \ldots, S(k)$) in the MRM based on (2.14) and (2.25), respectively.

Step 3: Modify (7.21) to the following approximate formula, where the $y_k(j)$ and $y_{kr_s}(j)$ have been determined in step 2 from the corresponding infinite model:

$$q_{\mathrm{fin}}(j) = \begin{cases} 1 & \text{if } j = 0 \\ \begin{aligned} & \frac{1}{j}\sum_{k=1}^{K}(N_k - y_k(j - b_k))\alpha_{k,\mathrm{idle}}b_k q_{\mathrm{fin}}(j - b_k) + \frac{1}{j}\sum_{k=1}^{K}\sum_{s=1}^{S(k)}[N_k - (y_k(j - b_{kr_s}) \\ & + y_{kr_1}(j - b_{kr_s}) + \ldots + y_{kr_{S(k)}}(j - b_{kr_s}))]\alpha_{kr_s,\mathrm{idle}}b_{kr_s}\gamma_{k_s}(j)q_{\mathrm{fin}}(j - b_{kr_s}) \end{aligned} & j = 1, \ldots, C \\ 0 & \text{otherwise} \end{cases}$$

$$(7.26)$$

Step 4: Determine the various performance measures as follows:
- The TC probabilities of service-class k calls with b_k b.u., B_{Tk}, via (6.35).
- The TC probabilities of service-class k calls with their last bandwidth requirement $b_{kr_{S(k)}}$ b.u., $B_{Tkr_{S(k)}}$, via (7.22).
- The CC probabilities of service-class k calls with b_k (without retrial), B_k, via (6.35) but for a system with $N_k - 1$ traffic sources.
- The CC probabilities of service-class k calls with $b_{kr_{S(k)}}$, $B_{kr_{S(k)}}$, via (7.22) but for a system with $N_k - 1$ traffic sources.
- The conditional TC probabilities of service-class k retry calls, while requesting $b_{kr_{S(k)}}$ b.u. given that they have been blocked with their initial bandwidth requirement b_k, $B_{Tkr_{S(k)}}^*$, via (7.23).

- The link utilization, U, via (6.36).
- The average number of service-class k calls in the system accepted with b_k b.u., $\bar{n}_k$, via (6.37) where $y_{k,\mathrm{fin}}(j)$ is determined by (6.38).
- The average number of service-class k calls in the system accepted with b_{kr_s} b.u., $\bar{n}_{kr_s}$, via (7.24) where $y_{kr_s,\mathrm{fin}}(j)$ is determined by:

$$y_{kr_s,\mathrm{fin}}(j) = \frac{(N_k - y_k(j-b_{kr_s}) - y_{kr_1}(j-b_{kr_s}) - \dots - y_{kr_{s(k)}}(j-b_{kr_s})\alpha_{kr_s,\mathrm{idle}})\gamma_k(j)q_{\mathrm{fin}}(j-b_{kr_s})}{q_{\mathrm{fin}}(j)}$$

(7.27)

- where $\alpha_{kr_s,\mathrm{idle}} = v_k \mu_{kr_s}^{-1}$, and $\gamma_{k_s}(j) = 1$ when $j > C - (b_{kr_{s-1}} - b_{kr_s})$ (otherwise $\gamma_{k_s}(j) = 0$).

Example 7.7 Consider again Example 7.6 ($C = 3, K = 2, b_1 = 1, b_2 = 3, b_{2r_1} = 2, b_{2r_2} = 1, N_1 = N_2 = 10, v_1 = v_2 = 0.1, \mu_1 = \mu_2 = 1, \mu_{2r_1}^{-1} = 2.0, \mu_{2r_2}^{-1} = 4.0$). Apply the algorithm of Section 7.3.2.3 for the determination of TC probabilities, including the retry probabilities and the link utilization.

Step 1: The corresponding infinite loss model (MRM) is $C = 3, K = 2, b_1 = 1, b_2 = 3, b_{2r_1} = 2, b_{2r_2} = 1, \alpha_1 = 1$ erl, $\alpha_2 = 1$ erl, $\alpha_{2r_1} = 2$ erl, $\alpha_{2r_2} = 4$ erl. Based on (2.22), we have the following normalized values of $Q(j)$:

$Q(0) = 0.17647 \quad Q(1) = 0.17647 \quad Q(2) = 0.088235 \quad Q(3) = 0.55882$

Step 2: Based on (2.14) and (2.25), we have:

$j = 1 \Rightarrow y_1(1) = 1$	$y_2(1) = 0$	$y_{2r_1}(1) = 0$	$y_{2r_2}(1) = 0$
$j = 2 \Rightarrow y_1(2) = 2$	$y_2(2) = 0$	$y_{2r_1}(2) = 0$	$y_{2r_2}(2) = 0$
$j = 3 \Rightarrow y_1(3) = 0.157895$	$y_2(3) = 0.31579$	$y_{2r_1}(3) = 0.63158$	$y_{2r_2}(3) = 0.63158$

Step 3: Based on (7.26), we have the following normalized values of $Q_{\mathrm{fin}}(j)$:

$Q_{\mathrm{fin}}(0) = 0.181708 \quad Q_{\mathrm{fin}}(1) = 0.181708 \quad Q_{\mathrm{fin}}(2) = 0.081769 \quad Q_{\mathrm{fin}}(3) = 0.554815$

Step 4: The approximate TC probabilities and retry probabilities are:

$$B_{T1} = \sum_{j=C-b_1+1}^{C} Q_{\mathrm{fin}}(j) = Q_{\mathrm{fin}}(3) = 0.554815 \text{ (compare with the exact 0.5274)}$$

$$B_{T2} = \sum_{j=C-b_2+1}^{C} Q_{\mathrm{fin}}(j) = 1 - Q_{\mathrm{fin}}(0) = 0.818292 \text{ (compare with the exact 0.867574)}$$

$$B_{T2r_1} = \sum_{j=C-b_{2r_1}+1}^{C} Q_{\mathrm{fin}}(j) = Q_{\mathrm{fin}}(2) + Q_{\mathrm{fin}}(3) = 0.636584 \text{ (compare with the exact 0.709409)}$$

$$B_{T2r_2} = \sum_{j=C-b_{2r_2}+1}^{C} Q_{\mathrm{fin}}(j) = Q_{\mathrm{fin}}(3) = 0.554815 \text{ (compare with the exact 0.5274)}$$

The link utilization is determined by:

$$U = \sum_{j=1}^{C} j Q_{\mathrm{fin}}(j) = 2.01 \text{ b.u. (compare with the exact 2.104)}$$

7.4 The Finite Multi-Retry Model under the BR Policy

7.4.1 The Service System

Compared to the f-SRM/BR, in the *f-MRM under the BR policy* (*f-MRM/BR*), blocked calls of service-class k can retry more than once to be connected in the system.

Example 7.8 Consider again Example 7.6 ($C = 3, K = 2, b_1 = 1, b_2 = 3, b_{2r_1} = 2$, $b_{2r_2} = 1, N_1 = N_2 = 10, v_1 = v_2 = 0.1, \mu_1 = \mu_2 = 1, \mu_{2r_1}^{-1} = 2.0, \mu_{2r_2}^{-1} = 4.0$) and let the BR parameters $t_1 = 2$ b.u. and $t_2 = 0$ b.u. so that $b_1 + t_1 = b_2 + t_2$.

(a) Find the total number of permissible states $\mathbf{n} = (n_1, n_2, n_{2r_1}, n_{2r_2})$ and draw the state transition diagram.
(b) Calculate the state probabilities $P(n_1, n_2, n_{2r_1}, n_{2r_2})$ and the corresponding values of $Q_{\text{fin}}(j)$ based on the GB equations.
(c) Calculate the TC probabilities of both service-classes, including the retry probabilities and the link utilization.

(a) The total number of permissible states of the form $\mathbf{n} = (n_1, n_2, n_{2r_1}, n_{2r_2})$ is 7. They are shown in Figure 7.4 together with the state transition diagram.

(b) Based on Figure 7.4, the corresponding 7 GB equations are:

$(0,0,0,0)$: $0.5P(0,0,1,0) + 0.25P(0,0,0,1) + P(0,1,0,0) + P(1,0,0,0) - 2P(0,0,0,0) = 0$

$(0,0,0,1)$: $0.5P(0,0,1,1) - 1.15P(0,0,0,1) = 0$

$(0,0,1,0)$: $0.25P(0,0,1,1) + P(1,0,1,0) - 1.4P(0,0,1,0) = 0$

$(0,0,1,1)$: $0.9P(0,0,0,1) + 0.9P(0,0,1,0) - 0.75P(0,0,1,1) = 0$

$(0,1,0,0)$: $P(0,0,0,0) - P(0,1,0,0) = 0$

$(1,0,0,0)$: $0.5P(1,0,1,0) + P(0,0,0,0) - 2P(1,0,0,0) = 0$

$(1,0,1,0)$: $P(1,0,0,0) - 1.5P(1,0,1,0) = 0$

The solution of this linear system is:

$P(0,0,0,0) = 0.185833$ $P(0,0,0,1) = 0.104941$ $P(0,0,1,0) = 0.096196$ $P(0,0,1,1) = 0.241364$
$P(0,1,0,0) = 0.185833$ $P(1,0,0,0) = 0.1115$ $P(1,0,1,0) = 0.074333$

Based on the values of $P(n_1, n_2, n_{2r_1}, n_{2r_2})$, we have:

$Q_{\text{fin}}(0) = P(0,0,0,0) = 0.185833$ $Q_{\text{fin}}(1) = P(0,0,0,1) + P(1,0,0,0) = 0.216441$
$Q_{\text{fin}}(2) = P(0,0,1,0) = 0.096196$ $Q_{\text{fin}}(3) = P(0,0,1,1) + P(0,1,0,0) + P(1,0,1,0) = 0.50153$

(c) The TC probabilities of service-class 1 are given by the formula:

$$B_{T1} = \sum_{j=C-b_1-t_1+1}^{C} Q_{\text{fin}}(j) = 1 - Q_{\text{fin}}(0) = 0.814167$$

(compare with the exact 0.819672 in the MRM/BR, see Example 2.8)

The TC probabilities of service-class 2, with b_2, are given by:

$$B_{T2} = \sum_{j=C-b_2-t_2+1}^{C} Q_{\text{fin}}(j) = B_{T1} = 0.814167$$

(compare with the exact 0.819672 in the MRM/BR)

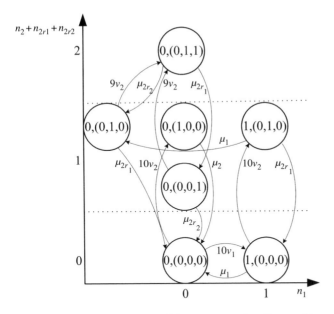

Figure 7.4 The state space Ω and the state transition diagram (Example 7.8).

The TC probabilities of service-class 2, with b_{2r_1} b.u., are given by:

$$B_{T2r_1} = \sum_{j=C-b_{2r_1}+1}^{C} Q_{\text{fin}}(j) = Q_{\text{fin}}(2) + Q_{\text{fin}}(3) = 0.597726$$

(compare with the exact 0.606557 in the MRM/BR)

The TC probabilities of service-class 2, with b_{2r_2} b.u., are given by:

$$B_{T2r_2} = \sum_{j=C-b_{2r_2}+1}^{C} Q_{\text{fin}}(j) = Q_{\text{fin}}(3) = 0.50153$$

(compare with the exact 0.514754 in the MRM/BR)

The link utilization is determined by:

$$U = \sum_{j=1}^{C} jQ_{\text{fin}}(j) = 1.913 \text{ b.u. (compare with the exact 1.941 b.u. in the MRM/BR)}$$

7.4.2 The Analytical Model

7.4.2.1 Link Occupancy Distribution

Based on the Roberts method and the algorithm of Section 7.2.2.1 of the f-SRM/BR, the unnormalized values of the link occupancy distribution, $q_{\text{fin}}(j)$, in the f-MRM/BR can be determined by the following algorithm:

Algorithm Approximate calculation of $q_{\mathrm{fin}}(j)$ in the f-MRM/BR

Step 1: Define the corresponding infinite loss model MRM/BR and calculate $q(j)$ via (2.27).

Step 2: Determine the values of $y_k(j)$ and $y_{kr_s}(j)$ $(s=1,\dots,S(k))$ in the MRM/BR based on (1.67) and (2.30), respectively.

Step 3: Modify (7.26) to the following approximate formula, where the $y_k(j)$ and $y_{kr_s}(j)$ have been determined in step 2 from the corresponding infinite model:

$$
q_{\mathrm{fin}}(j)=\begin{cases}
1 & \text{if } j = 0\\[4pt]
\dfrac{1}{j}\sum\limits_{k=1}^{K}(N_k-y_k(j-b_k))\alpha_{k,\mathrm{idle}}D_k(j-b_k)q_{\mathrm{fin}}(j-b_k)+\dfrac{1}{j}\sum\limits_{k=1}^{K}\sum\limits_{s=1}^{S(k)}[N_k-(y_k(j-b_{kr_s})\\[4pt]
\quad+y_{kr_1}(j-b_{kr_s})+\dots+y_{kr_{S(k)}}(j-b_{kr_s}))]\alpha_{kr_s,\mathrm{idle}}D_{kr_s}(j-b_{kr_s})\gamma_{k_s}(j)q_{\mathrm{fin}}(j-b_{kr_s}) & \\[4pt]
& j = 1,\dots,C\\[4pt]
0 & \text{otherwise}
\end{cases}
\tag{7.28}
$$

where $D_k(j-b_k)$ and $D_{kr_s}(j-b_{kr_s})$ are determined via (1.65) and (2.28), respectively.

7.4.2.2 TC Probabilities, CBP, Utilization, and Mean Number of In-service Calls

The following performance measures can be determined based on (7.28):

- The TC probabilities of service-class k calls with b_k b.u., B_{Tk}, via (6.42).
- The TC probabilities of service-class k calls with $b_{kr_{S(k)}}$, $B_{Tkr_{S(k)}}$, via:

$$
B_{Tkr_{S(k)}} = \sum_{j=C-b_{kr_{S(k)}}-t_k+1}^{C} G^{-1}q_{\mathrm{fin}}(j)
\tag{7.29}
$$

- The CC probabilities of service-class k calls with b_k (without retrial), B_k, via (6.42) but for a system with $N_k - 1$ traffic sources.
- The CC probabilities of service-class k calls with $b_{kr_{S(k)}}$, $B_{Tkr_{S(k)}}$, via (7.29) but for a system with $N_k - 1$ traffic sources.
- The conditional TC probabilities of service-class k retry calls, while requesting $b_{kr_{S(k)}}$ b.u. given that they have been blocked with their initial bandwidth requirement b_k, $B^*_{Tkr_{S(k)}}$, via (7.23), while subtracting t_k from both $C - b_{kr_{S(k)}}$ and $C - b_k$.
- The link utilization, U, via (6.36).
- The average number of service-class k calls in the system accepted with b_k b.u., $\bar{n}_k$, via (6.37) where $y_{k,\mathrm{fin}}(j)$ is determined via (6.43).
- The average number of service-class k calls in the system accepted with b_{kr_s} b.u., $\bar{n}_{kr_s}$, via (7.24) where $y_{kr_s,\mathrm{fin}}(j)$ is determined by:

$$
y_{kr_s,\mathrm{fin}}(j) = \begin{cases}
\dfrac{(N_k-y_k(j-b_{kr_s})-y_{kr_1}(j-b_{kr_s})-\dots-y_{kr_{S(k)}}(j-b_{kr_s}))\alpha_{kr_s,\mathrm{idle}}\gamma_{k_s}(j)q_{\mathrm{fin}}(j-b_{kr_s})}{q_{\mathrm{fin}}(j)} & \text{for}\quad j \le C - t_k\\[6pt]
0 & \text{for}\quad j > C - t_k
\end{cases}
\tag{7.30}
$$

- where $\alpha_{kr_s,\mathrm{idle}} = v_k\mu_{kr_s}^{-1}$, and $\gamma_{k_s}(j) = 1$ when $j > C - (b_{kr_{s-1}} - b_{kr_s})$.

Example 7.9 Consider again Example 7.8 ($C = 3, K = 2, b_1 = 1, b_2 = 3, b_{2r_1} = 2,$ $b_{2r_2} = 1, t_1 = 2, t_2 = 0, N_1 = N_2 = 10, v_1 = v_2 = 0.1, \mu_1 = \mu_2 = 1, \mu_{2r_1}^{-1} = 2.0, \mu_{2r_2}^{-1} = 4.0$). Apply the algorithm of Section 7.4.2.1 for the determination of TC and retry probabilities.

Step 1: The corresponding infinite loss model (MRM/BR) is the following: $C = 3, K = 2,$ $b_1 = 1, b_2 = 3, b_{2r_1} = 2, b_{2r_2} = 1, t_1 = 2, t_2 = 0, \alpha_1 = \alpha_2 = 1$ erl, $\alpha_{2r_1} = 2$ erl, $\alpha_{2r_2} = 4$ erl. Based on (2.27) and since $\gamma_{k_1}(j) = 1$ and $\gamma_{k_2}(j) = 1$ for $j = 3$, we have the following normalized values of $Q(j)$:

$$Q(0) = 0.23077 \quad Q(1) = 0.23077 \quad Q(2) = 0 \quad Q(3) = 0.53846$$

Step 2: Based on (1.67) and (2.30), we have:

$$j = 1 \Rightarrow y_1(1) = 1 \quad y_2(1) = 0 \qquad y_{2r_1}(1) = 0 \qquad y_{2r_2}(1) = 0$$
$$j = 2 \Rightarrow y_1(2) = 0 \quad y_2(2) = 0 \qquad y_{2r_1}(2) = 0 \qquad y_{2r_2}(2) = 0$$
$$j = 3 \Rightarrow y_1(3) = 0 \quad y_2(3) = 0.42857 \quad y_{2r_1}(3) = 0.85714 \quad y_{2r_2}(3) = 0$$

Step 3: Based on (7.28), we have the following normalized values of $Q_{fin}(j)$:

$$Q_{fin}(0) = 0.23077 \quad Q_{fin}(1) = 0.23077 \quad Q_{fin}(2) = 0.0 \quad Q_{fin}(3) = 0.53846$$

The approximate TC probabilities and retry probabilities are:

$$B_{T1} = \sum_{j=C-b_1+1}^{C} Q_{fin}(j) = Q_{fin}(3) = 0.76923 \text{ (compare with the exact 0.814167)}$$

$$B_{T2} = \sum_{j=C-b_2+1}^{C} Q_{fin}(j) = 1 - Q_{fin}(0) = 0.76923 \text{ (compare with the exact 0.814167)}$$

$$B_{T2r_1} = \sum_{j=C-b_{2r_1}+1}^{C} Q_{fin}(j) = Q_{fin}(2) + Q_{fin}(3) = 0.538461 \text{ (compare with the exact 0.597726)}$$

$$B_{T2r_2} = \sum_{j=C-b_{2r_2}+1}^{C} Q_{fin}(j) = Q_{fin}(3) = 0.538461 \text{ (compare with the exact 0.50153)}$$

Example 7.10 Consider a link of capacity $C = 50$ b.u. and $K = 2$ service-classes with $b_1 = 10$ and $b_2 = 7$ b.u. The offered traffic-loads are $\alpha_{1,idle} = 0.06$ and $\alpha_{2,idle} = 0.2$ erl. Blocked calls of service-class 1 reduce their bandwidth requirement twice, from 10 to 8 and finally to 6 b.u. The corresponding retry offered traffic-loads are $\alpha_{1r_1,idle} = 0.075$ and $\alpha_{1r_2,idle} = 0.1$ erl. Blocked calls of service-class 2 reduce their bandwidth once, from 7 to 4 b.u. The retry offered traffic-load of service-class 2 is $\alpha_{2r_1,idle} = 0.35$ erl. The number of sources for both service-classes is $N_1 = N_2 = 12$. Based on the above, we have a f-MRM system. The equivalent stochastic system used for the TC probabilities calculation is $C = 50006, b_1 = 10000, b_2 = 7001, b_{1r_1} = 8000, b_{1r_2} = 6000,$ and $b_{2r_1} = 4000$. Table 7.2 shows the state space, which consists of 30 states.

The corresponding MRM system used for the calculation of $y_k(j)$ and $y_{kr_s}(j)$ and consequently of TC probabilities (according to Section 7.3.2.3) is $C = 50, b_1 = 10,$ $b_{1r_1} = 8, b_{1r_2} = 6, b_2 = 7, b_{2r_1} = 4, \alpha_1 = 0.72, \alpha_2 = 2.4, \alpha_{1r_1} = 0.9, \alpha_{1r_2} = 1.2, \alpha_{2r_1} = 4.2$. In Table 7.3, we present the analytical TC probabilities obtained from the equivalent

Table 7.2 The state space, j, j_{eq}, and the blocking states (Example 7.10).

n_1	n_2	n_{1r_1}	n_{1r_2}	n_{2r_1}	j	j_{eq}	B_{T1r_2}	B_{T2r_1}
0	0	0	0	0	0	0		
0	1	0	0	0	7	7001		
0	2	0	0	0	14	14002		
0	3	0	0	0	21	21003		
0	4	0	0	0	28	28004		
0	5	0	0	0	35	35005		
0	6	0	0	0	42	42006		
0	6	1	0	0	50	50006	*	*
0	7	0	0	0	49	49007	*	*
1	0	0	0	0	10	10000		
1	1	0	0	0	17	17001		
1	2	0	0	0	24	24002		
1	3	0	0	0	31	31003		
1	4	0	0	0	38	38004		
1	5	0	0	0	45	45005	*	
1	5	0	0	1	49	49005	*	*
2	0	0	0	0	20	20000		
2	1	0	0	0	27	27001		
2	2	0	0	0	34	34002		
2	3	0	0	0	41	41003		
2	3	1	0	0	49	49003	*	*
2	4	0	0	0	48	48004	*	*
3	0	0	0	0	30	30000		
3	1	0	0	0	37	37001		
3	2	0	0	0	44	44002		
3	2	0	0	1	48	48002	*	*
3	2	0	1	0	50	50002	*	*
4	0	0	0	0	40	40000		
4	1	0	0	0	47	47001	*	*
5	0	0	0	0	50	50000	*	*

stochastic system and the algorithm of Section 7.3.2.3 together with the corresponding simulation results. The latter are mean values of seven runs with 95% confidence interval. At each point (P) of Table 7.3 the values of $\alpha_{1,idle}$, $\alpha_{1r_1,idle}$, and $\alpha_{1r_2,idle}$ are constant while those of $\alpha_{2,idle}$ and $\alpha_{2r_1,idle}$ are increased by 0.4/12 and 0.7/12, respectively (for $P = 1$: $\alpha_{2,idle} = 0.2$ and $\alpha_{2r_1,idle} = 0.35$ erl). Based on Table 7.3, one observes that the algorithm of Section 7.3.2.3 gives almost the same results as the equivalent stochastic system method and satisfactory results compared to simulation.

Table 7.3 Analytical and simulation results of TC probabilities (Example 7.10).

P	Equivalent stochastic system		Algorithm (Section 7.3.2.3)		Simulation	
	B_{T1r_2} (%)	B_{T2r_1} (%)	B_{T1r_2} (%)	B_{T2r_1} (%)	B_{T1r_2} (%)	B_{T2r_1} (%)
1	3.05	2.03	3.05	2.03	3.23 ± 0.49	1.83 ± 0.13
2	4.32	2.72	4.32	2.72	4.02 ± 0.32	2.44 ± 0.12
3	5.78	3.50	5.78	3.50	5.19 ± 0.32	3.20 ± 0.24
4	7.39	4.36	7.39	4.36	7.01 ± 0.30	3.76 ± 0.29
5	9.12	5.30	9.13	5.30	8.16 ± 0.49	4.71 ± 0.35
6	10.94	6.31	10.94	6.31	9.58 ± 0.44	5.67 ± 0.22

7.5 The Finite Single-Threshold Model

7.5.1 The Service System

In the *finite single-threshold model* (*f-STM*), the requested b.u. and the corresponding service time of a new call are related to the occupied link bandwidth j and a threshold J_0. Specifically, the following CAC is applied. When $j \leq J_0$, then a new call of service-class k is accepted in the system with its initial requirements (b_k, μ_k^{-1}). Otherwise, if $j > J_0$, the call tries to be connected in the system with (b_{kc}, μ_{kc}^{-1}), where $b_{kc} < b_k$ and $\mu_{kc}^{-1} = \frac{b_k}{b_{kc}} \mu_k^{-1}$, so that the product bandwidth requirement by service time remains constant. If the b_{kc} b.u. are not available the call is blocked and lost. The call arrival process is the quasi-random, i.e., calls of service class k ($k = 1, \ldots, K$) come from a finite source population N_k. By denoting as v_k the arrival rate per idle source of service-class k, the offered traffic-load per idle source is given by $\alpha_{k,\text{idle}} = v_k / \mu_k$ (in erl).

The comparison of the f-STM with the f-SRM reveals similar differences to those described in Section 2.5.1 for the STM and the SRM.

Example 7.11 Consider again Example 7.1 ($C = 5, K = 2, b_1 = 1, b_2 = 3, b_{2r} = b_{2c} = 2, N_1 = N_2 = 10, v_1 = v_2 = 0.1, \mu_1 = \mu_2 = 1, \mu_{2r}^{-1} = \mu_{2c}^{-1} = 1.5$) and let $J_0 = 1$ b.u.

(a) Find the total number of permissible states $\mathbf{n} = (n_1, n_2, n_{2c})$, where n_{2c} is the number of service-class 2 calls accepted in the system with b_{2c} b.u. Draw the state transition diagram.

(b) Calculate the state probabilities $P(n_1, n_2, n_{2c})$ and the corresponding values of $Q_{\text{fin}}(j)$ based on the GB equations.

(c) Calculate the TC probabilities of both service-classes and the link utilization.

(a) There are 16 permissible states of the form $\mathbf{n} = (n_1, n_2, n_{2c})$. The state space Ω and the state transition diagram are shown in Figure 7.5.

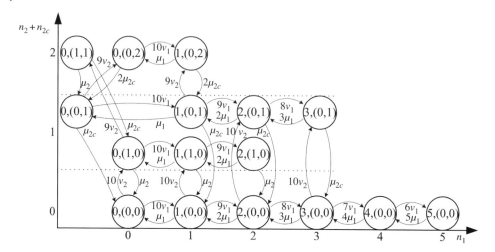

Figure 7.5 The state space Ω and the state transition diagram (Example 7.11).

(b) Based on Figure 7.5, we obtain the following 16 GB equations:

$(0,0,0):$ $P(0,1,0) + P(1,0,0) + (2/3)P(0,0,1) - 2P(0,0,0) = 0$

$(0,0,1):$ $P(0,1,1) + P(1,0,1) + (4/3)P(0,0,2) - (5/3 + 0.9)P(0,0,1) = 0$

$(0,0,2):$ $P(1,0,2) + 0.9P(0,0,1) - (7/3)P(0,0,2) = 0$

$(0,1,0):$ $P(0,0,0) + (2/3)P(0,1,1) + P(1,1,0) - 2.9P(0,1,0) = 0$

$(0,1,1):$ $0.9P(0,1,0) - 5/3P(0,1,1) = 0$

$(1,0,0):$ $P(0,0,0) + (2/3)P(1,0,1) + 2P(2,0,0) + P(1,1,0) - 2.9P(1,0,0) = 0$

$(1,0,1):$ $P(0,0,1) + (4/3)P(1,0,2) + 2P(2,0,1) - (5/3 + 1.8)P(1,0,1) = 0$

$(1,0,2):$ $P(0,0,2) + 0.9P(1,0,1) - (7/3)P(1,0,2) = 0$

$(1,1,0):$ $P(0,1,0) + P(1,0,0) + 2P(2,1,0) - 2.9P(1,1,0) = 0$

$(2,0,0):$ $0.9P(1,0,0) + 3P(3,0,0) + P(2,1,0) + (2/3)P(2,0,1) - 3.8P(2,0,0) = 0$

$(2,0,1):$ $0.9P(1,0,1) + 3P(3,0,1) + P(2,0,0) - (8/3 + 0.8)P(2,0,1) = 0$

$(2,1,0):$ $0.9P(1,1,0) - 3P(2,1,0) = 0$

$(3,0,0):$ $0.8P(2,0,0) + (2/3)P(3,0,1) + 4P(4,0,0) - 4.7P(3,0,0) = 0$

$(3,0,1):$ $P(3,0,0) + 0.8P(2,0,1) - (11/3)P(3,0,1) = 0$

$(4,0,0):$ $0.7P(3,0,0) + 5P(5,0,0) - 4.6P(4,0,0) = 0$

$(5,0,0):$ $0.6P(4,0,0) - 5P(5,0,0) = 0$

The solution of this linear system is:

$P(0,0,0) = 0.153087$ $P(0,0,1) = 0.073875$ $P(0,0,2) = 0.048742$ $P(0,1,0) = 0.104249$

$P(0,1,1) = 0.056295$ $P(1,0,0) = 0.152675$ $P(1,0,1) = 0.068328$ $P(1,0,2) = 0.047244$

$P(1,1,0) = 0.111706$ $P(2,0,0) = 0.066206$ $P(2,0,1) = 0.050001$ $P(2,1,0) = 0.033512$

$P(3,0,0) = 0.015777$ $P(3,0,1) = 0.015212$ $P(4,0,0) = 0.002761$ $P(5,0,0) = 0.000331$

Then, based on the values of $P(n_1, n_2, n_{2c})$, we obtain the values of $Q_{fin}(j)$:

$Q_{\text{fin}}(0) = P(0,0,0) = 0.153087$

$Q_{\text{fin}}(1) = P(1,0,0) = 0.152675$

$Q_{\text{fin}}(2) = P(0,0,1) + P(2,0,0) = 0.140081$

$Q_{\text{fin}}(3) = P(0,1,0) + P(1,0,1) + P(3,0,0) = 0.188354$

$Q_{\text{fin}}(4) = P(0,0,2) + P(1,1,0) + P(2,0,1) + P(4,0,0) = 0.21321$

$Q_{\text{fin}}(5) = P(0,1,1) + P(1,0,2) + P(2,1,0) + P(3,0,1) + P(5,0,0) = 0.152594$

(c) The TC probabilities of service-class 1, B_{T1}, are given by:

$$B_{T1} = \sum_{j=C-b_1+1}^{C} Q_{\text{fin}}(j) = Q_{\text{fin}}(5) = 0.152594 \ (0.165955 \text{ in the STM, see Example 2.11})$$

The TC probabilities of service-class 2 calls, B_{T2c}, when they require b_{2c} b.u., are:

$$B_{T2c} = \sum_{j=C-b_{2c}+1}^{C} Q_{\text{fin}}(j) = Q_{\text{fin}}(4) + Q_{\text{fin}}(5) = 0.365804 \ (0.382997 \text{ in the STM})$$

The link utilization is determined by:

$$U = \sum_{j=1}^{C} jQ_{\text{fin}}(j) = 2.614 \text{ b.u. } (2.685 \text{ in the STM})$$

7.5.2 The Analytical Model

7.5.2.1 Steady State Probabilities

To derive a recursive formula for the calculation of $q_{\text{fin}}(j)$, we concentrate on a single link of capacity C b.u. that accommodates two service-classes with the following traffic characteristics: $(N_1, N_2, v_1, v_2), (\mu_1^{-1}, \mu_2^{-1}), (b_1, b_2)$. If $j > J_0$ upon the arrival of a service-class 2 call, then this call requests $b_{2c} < b_2$ b.u. and $\mu_{2c}^{-1} > \mu_2^{-1}$. No such option is considered for calls of service-class 1.

Although the f-STM does not have a PFS, we assume that the LB equation (6.33) does hold for calls of service-class 1, for $j = 1, \dots, C$:

$$(N_1 - y_{1,\text{fin}}(j - b_1))\alpha_{1,\text{idle}} b_1 q_{\text{fin}}(j - b_1) = y_{1,\text{fin}}(j) b_1 q_{\text{fin}}(j) \tag{7.31}$$

or, due to the fact that in the equivalent stochastic system, $y_{1,\text{fin}}(j - b_1) = n_1 - 1$:

$$(N_1 - n_1 + 1)\alpha_{1,\text{idle}} b_1 q_{\text{fin}}(j - b_1) = y_{1,\text{fin}}(j) b_1 q_{\text{fin}}(j) \quad \text{for } j = 1, \dots, C \tag{7.32}$$

For calls of service-class 2, we assume the existence of LB between adjacent states:

$$(N_2 - n_2 + 1)\alpha_{2,\text{idle}} b_2 q_{\text{fin}}(j - b_2) = y_{2,\text{fin}}(j) b_2 q_{\text{fin}}(j) \quad \text{for } j - b_2 \leq J_0 \tag{7.33}$$

$$(N_2 - (n_2 + n_{2c}) + 1)\alpha_{2c,\text{idle}} b_{2c} q_{\text{fin}}(j - b_{2c}) = y_{2c,\text{fin}}(j) b_{2c} q_{\text{fin}}(j) \quad \text{for } j - b_{2c} > J_0 \tag{7.34}$$

where $\alpha_{2c,\text{idle}} = v_2 \mu_{2c}^{-1}$ is the offered traffic-load per idle source of service-class 2 with b_{2c} and $y_{2c,\text{fin}}(j)$ is the mean number of service-class 2 calls accepted in the system with b_{2c} in state j.

Equations (7.32)–(7.34) lead to the following system of equations:

$$(N_1 - n_1 + 1)\alpha_{1,\text{idle}}b_1 q_{\text{fin}}(j - b_1) + (N_2 - n_2 + 1)\alpha_{2,\text{idle}}b_2 q_{\text{fin}}(j - b_2)$$
$$= (y_{1,\text{fin}}(j)b_1 + y_{2,\text{fin}}(j)b_2)q_{\text{fin}}(j) \quad \text{for } 1 \le j \le J_0 + b_{2c} \tag{7.35}$$

$$(N_1 - n_1 + 1)\alpha_{1,\text{idle}}b_1 q_{\text{fin}}(j - b_1) + (N_2 - n_2 + 1)\alpha_{2,\text{idle}}b_2 q_{\text{fin}}(j - b_2)$$
$$+ (N_2 - (n_2 + n_{2c}) + 1)\alpha_{2c,\text{idle}}b_{2c}q_{\text{fin}}(j - b_{2c}) = jq_{\text{fin}}(j) \quad \text{for } J_0 + b_{2c} < j \le J_0 + b_2 \tag{7.36}$$

$$(N_1 - n_1 + 1)\alpha_{1,\text{idle}}b_1 q_{\text{fin}}(j - b_1) + (N_2 - (n_2 + n_{2c}) + 1)\alpha_{2c,\text{idle}}b_{2c}q_{\text{fin}}(j - b_{2c})$$
$$= (y_{1,\text{fin}}(j)b_1 + y_{2c,\text{fin}}(j)b_{2c})q_{\text{fin}}(j) \text{ for } J_0 + b_2 < j \le C \tag{7.37}$$

For (7.35), we adopt the (migration) approximation that the value of $y_{2c,\text{fin}}(j)$ in state j is negligible when $1 \le j \le J_0 + b_{2c}$. For (7.37), we adopt the (upward migration) approximation that the value of $y_{2,\text{fin}}(j)$ in state j is negligible when $J_0 + b_2 < j \le C$. Based on these approximations, we have (for $1 \le j \le C$):

$$(N_1 - n_1 + 1)\alpha_{1,\text{idle}}b_1 q_{\text{fin}}(j - b_1) + (N_2 - n_2 + 1)\alpha_{2,\text{idle}}b_2 \delta_2(j)q_{\text{fin}}(j - b_2)$$
$$+ (N_2 - (n_2 + n_{2c}) + 1)\alpha_{2c,\text{idle}}b_{2c}\delta_{2c}(j)q_{\text{fin}}(j - b_{2c}) = jq_{\text{fin}}(j) \tag{7.38}$$

where $\delta_2(j) = \begin{cases} 1 \text{ for } 1 \le j \le J_0 + b_2 \\ 0 \text{ otherwise} \end{cases}$, $\delta_{2c}(j) = \begin{cases} 1 \text{ for } j > J_0 + b_{2c} \\ 0 \text{ otherwise} \end{cases}$, and $\alpha_{2c,\text{idle}} = v_2\mu_{2c}^{-1}$.

In the general case of K service-classes, the formula for $q_{\text{fin}}(j)$ is the following [2]:

$$q_{\text{fin}}(j) = \begin{cases} 1 & \text{if } j = 0 \\ \frac{1}{j}\sum_{k=1}^{K}(N_k - n_k + 1)\alpha_{k,\text{idle}}b_k\delta_k(j)q_{\text{fin}}(j - b_k) + \\ \frac{1}{j}\sum_{k=1}^{K}(N_k - (n_k + n_{kc}) + 1)\alpha_{kc,\text{idle}}b_{kc}\delta_{kc}(j)q_{\text{fin}}(j - b_{kc}) & j = 1, \dots, C \\ 0 & \text{otherwise} \end{cases} \tag{7.39}$$

where $\alpha_{kc,\text{idle}} = v_k\mu_{kc}^{-1}$, $\delta_k(j) = \begin{cases} 1 \text{ (if } 1 \le j \le J_0 + b_k \text{ and } b_{kc} > 0) \\ \text{or (if } 1 \le j \le C \text{ and } b_{kc} = 0) \\ 0 \text{ otherwise} \end{cases}$, $\delta_{kc}(j) = \begin{cases} 1 \text{ if } j > J_0 + b_{kc} \\ 0 \text{ otherwise} \end{cases}$

Note that if $N_k \to \infty$ for $k = 1, \dots, K$, and the total offered traffic-load remains constant, then we have the recursion (2.38) of the STM.

7.5.2.2 TC Probabilities, CBP, Utilization, and Mean Number of In-service Calls
The following performance measures can be determined based on (7.39):

- The TC probabilities of service-class k calls with b_k b.u., B_{Tk}, via (6.35) (assuming that calls have no option for b_{kc}).
- The TC probabilities of service-class k calls with b_{kc} b.u., B_{Tkc}, via:

$$B_{Tkc} = \sum_{j=C-b_{kc}+1}^{C} G^{-1}q_{\text{fin}}(j) \tag{7.40}$$

where $G = \sum_{j=0}^{C} q_{\text{fin}}(j)$ is the normalization constant.

- The CBP (or CC probabilities) of service-class k calls with b_k (without the option of b_{kc}), B_k, via (6.35) but for a system with $N_k - 1$ traffic sources.
- The CBP (or CC probabilities) of service-class k calls with b_{kc}, B_{kc}, via (7.40) but for a system with $N_k - 1$ traffic sources.
- The conditional TC probabilities of service-class k calls with b_{kc} given that $j > J_0$, B^*_{Tkc}, via:

$$
B^*_{Tkc} = Prob\{j > C - b_{kc} | j > J_0\} = \frac{B_{Tkc}}{Prob(j > J_0)} = \frac{\sum\limits_{j=C-b_{kc}+1}^{C} q_{fin}(j)}{\sum\limits_{j=J_0+1}^{C} q_{fin}(j)} \tag{7.41}
$$

- The link utilization, U, via (6.36).
- The average number of service-class k calls in the system accepted with b_k b.u., $\bar{n}_k$, via (6.37), while the mean number of service-class k calls with b_k given that the system state is j, $y_{k,fin}(j)$, via:

$$
y_{k,fin}(j) = \frac{(N_k - n_k + 1)\alpha_{k,idle}\delta_k(j)q_{fin}(j - b_k)}{q_{fin}(j)}, q_{fin}(j) > 0 \tag{7.42}
$$

- The average number of service-class k calls in the system accepted with b_{kc} b.u., $\bar{n}_{kc}$, via:

$$
\bar{n}_{kc} = \sum_{j=1}^{C} G^{-1} y_{kc,fin}(j)q_{fin}(j) \tag{7.43}
$$

where $y_{kc,fin}(j)$ is the average number of service-class k calls with b_{kc} given that the system state is j, and is determined by:

$$
y_{kc,fin}(j) = \frac{(N_k - (n_k + n_{kc}) + 1)\alpha_{kc,idle}\delta_{kc}(j)q_{fin}(j - b_{kc})}{q_{fin}(j)}, \quad q_{fin}(j) > 0 \tag{7.44}
$$

The determination of $q_{fin}(j)$ via (7.39), and consequently of all performance measures, requires the value of n_k and n_{kc}, which are unknown. In [2, 3], there is a method for the determination of n_k and n_{kc} in state j via an equivalent stochastic system. However, the state space determination of the equivalent system can be complex (as in the case of the EnMLM and the f-SRM) even for small capacity systems that serve many service-classes.

Example 7.12 Consider Example 7.2 ($C = 5, K = 2, b_1 = 3, b_2 = 2, b_{1r} = b_{1c} = 1$, $N_1 = N_2 = 6, \alpha_{1,idle} = \alpha_{2,idle} = 0.01, \alpha_{1r,idle} = \alpha_{1c,idle} = 0.03$) and let $J_0 = 1$. Due to the migration approximation, calls of service-class 1 with $b_{1c} = 1$ are assumed to be negligible when $j \leq J_0 + b_{1c} \Rightarrow j \leq 2$. In addition, due to the upward migration approximation, calls of service-class 1 with b_1 are assumed to be negligible when $j > J_0 + b_1 \Rightarrow j > 4$. Taking into account these approximations, the state space consists of 11 states (n_1, n_2, n_{1c}), presented in Table 7.4 together with the respective occupied link bandwidth j and the blocking states (B_{T2}, B_{T1c}). According to Table 7.4, the values of $j = 3, 4, 5$ appear more than once, and therefore it is impossible to use directly (7.39) for the calculation of $q_{fin}(j)$. To overcome this, an equivalent stochastic system should be determined with the following three characteristics:

Table 7.4 The state space, j, j_{eq}, and the blocking states (Example 7.12).

n_1	n_2	n_{1c}	j	j_{eq}	B_{T2}	B_{T1c}
0	0	0	0	0		
0	1	0	2	2000		
0	1	1	3	3001		
0	1	2	4	4002	*	
0	1	3	5	**5003**	*	*
0	2	0	4	4000	*	
0	2	1	5	5001	*	*
1	0	0	3	3000		
1	0	1	4	4001	*	
1	0	2	5	5002	*	*
1	1	0	5	5000	*	*

(i) The states (n_1, n_2, n_{1c}) of the equivalent system are the same as the initial one.

(ii) Each state (n_1, n_2, n_{1c}) of the equivalent system has a unique value for the occupied link bandwidth.

(iii) The chosen values of b_1, b_2, and b_{1c} of the equivalent system keep constant (as much as possible) the initial ratios of $b_1 : b_2 : b_{1c} : J_0 : C = 3 : 2 : 1 : 1 : 5$.

In this example, the values $b_1 = 3000, b_2 = 2000, b_{1c} = 1001, J_0 = 1000$, and $C = 5003$ are an approximate solution to the initial system; for these values we present in the last column of Table 7.4 the unique values of the equivalent occupied link bandwidth, j_{eq}. The resultant TC probabilities are $B_{T1c} = 0.14\%$ and $B_{T2} = 0.49\%$.

To circumvent the determination of an equivalent system, in the next section we modify the algorithm of Section 6.2.2.3 (initially proposed for the EnMLM) to fit to the f-STM.

7.5.2.3 An Approximate Algorithm for the Determination of $q_{fin}(j)$ in the f-STM

Contrary to (7.39), which requires enumeration and processing of the state space, the algorithm presented herein is much simpler and easy to implement [5].

Algorithm Approximate calculation of q_{fin} in the f-STM

Step 1: Define the corresponding infinite loss model STM and calculate $q(j)$ via (2.38).

Step 2: Determine the values of $y_k(j)$ and $y_{kc}(j)$ in the STM based on (2.41) and (2.42), respectively.

Step 3: Modify (7.39) to the following approximate formula, where the values of $y_k(j)$ and $y_{kc}(j)$ have been determined in step 2 from the corresponding infinite model:

$$q_{\text{fin}}(j) = \begin{cases} 1 & \text{if } j = 0 \\ \dfrac{1}{j}\displaystyle\sum_{k=1}^{K}(N_k - y_k(j-b_k))\alpha_{k,\text{idle}}b_k\delta_k(j)q_{\text{fin}}(j-b_k) + \dfrac{1}{j}\displaystyle\sum_{k=1}^{K}(N_k - y_k(j-b_{kc}) \\ \quad - y_{kc}(j-b_{kc}))\alpha_{kc,\text{idle}}b_{kc}\delta_{kc}(j)q_{\text{fin}}(j-b_{kc}) & j = 1, \ldots, C \\ 0 & \text{otherwise} \end{cases} \tag{7.45}$$

Step 4: Determine the various performance measures as follows:

- The TC probabilities of service-class k calls with b_k b.u., B_{Tk}, via (6.35).
- The TC probabilities of service-class k calls with b_{kc}, B_{Tkc}, via (7.40).
- The CC probabilities of service-class k calls with b_k (without retrial), B_k, via (6.35) but for a system with $N_k - 1$ traffic sources.
- The CC probabilities of service-class k calls with b_{kc}, B_{kc}, via (7.40) but for a system with $N_k - 1$ traffic sources.
- The conditional TC probabilities of service-class k calls with b_{kc} given that $j > J_0$, B^*_{Tkc}, via (7.41).
- The link utilization, U, via (6.36).
- The average number of service-class k calls in the system accepted with b_k b.u., $\bar{n}_k$, via (6.37) where $y_{k,\text{fin}}(j)$ is determined by:

$$y_{k,\text{fin}}(j) = \frac{\left(N_k - y_k(j-b_k)\right)\alpha_{k,\text{idle}}\delta_k(j)q_{\text{fin}}(j-b_k)}{q_{\text{fin}}(j)}, \quad q_{\text{fin}}(j) > 0 \tag{7.46}$$

- The average number of service-class k calls in the system accepted with b_{kr} b.u., $\bar{n}_{kc}$, via (7.43) where $y_{kc,\text{fin}}(j)$ is determined by (for $q_{\text{fin}}(j) > 0$):

$$y_{kc,\text{fin}}(j) = \frac{(N_k - y_k(j-b_{kc}) - y_{kc}(j-b_{kc}))\alpha_{kc,\text{idle}}\delta_{kc}(j)q_{\text{fin}}(j-b_{kc})}{q_{\text{fin}}(j)} \tag{7.47}$$

Example 7.13 Consider again Example 7.11 ($C = 5, K = 2, b_1 = 1, b_2 = 3, b_{2r} = b_{2c} = 2, N_1 = N_2 = 10, v_1 = v_2 = 0.1, \mu_1 = \mu_2 = 1, \mu_{2r}^{-1} = \mu_{2c}^{-1} = 1.5, J_0 = 1$). Apply the algorithm of Section 7.5.2.3 for the determination of TC probabilities.

Step 1: The corresponding infinite loss model (STM) is $C = 5, K = 2, b_1 = 1, b_2 = 3, b_{2c} = 2, \alpha_1 = \alpha_2 = 1, \alpha_{2c} = 1.5, J_0 = 1$. Based on (2.38), we have the following normalized values of $Q(j)$:

$Q(0) = 0.164835 \quad Q(1) = 0.164835 \quad Q(2) = 0.082417$
$Q(3) = 0.192308 \quad Q(4) = 0.23352 \quad Q(5) = 0.162087$

Step 2: Based on (2.41) and (2.42), we have:

$j = 1 \Rightarrow y_1(1) = 1 \qquad\qquad y_2(1) = 0 \qquad\qquad y_{2c}(1) = 0$
$j = 2 \Rightarrow y_1(2) = 2 \qquad\qquad y_2(2) = 0 \qquad\qquad y_{2c}(2) = 0$
$j = 3 \Rightarrow y_1(3) = 0.428571 \quad y_2(3) = 0.857143 \quad y_{2c}(3) = 0$
$j = 4 \Rightarrow y_1(4) = 0.823529 \quad y_2(4) = 0.705883 \quad y_{2c}(4) = 0.529412$
$j = 5 \Rightarrow y_1(5) = 1.440678 \quad y_2(5) = 0 \qquad\qquad y_{2c}(5) = 1.779661$

Step 3: Based on (7.45), we have the following normalized values of $Q_{fin}(j)$:

$$Q_{fin}(0) = 0.172751 \quad Q_{fin}(1) = 0.172751 \quad Q_{fin}(2) = 0.077738$$
$$Q_{fin}(3) = 0.193481 \quad Q_{fin}(4) = 0.234164 \quad Q_{fin}(5) = 0.149114$$

Step 4: The approximate TC probabilities are:

$$B_{T1} = \sum_{j=C-b_1+1}^{C} Q_{fin}(j) = 0.149114 \text{ (compare with the exact 0.152594)}$$

$$B_{T2c} = \sum_{j=C-b_{2c}+1}^{C} Q_{fin}(j) = 0.383278 \text{ (compare with the exact 0.365804)}$$

7.6 The Finite Single-Threshold Model under the BR Policy

7.6.1 The Service System

In the *f-STM under the BR policy* (*f-STM/BR*), t_k b.u. are reserved to benefit calls of all other service-classes apart from service-class k. The application of the BR policy in the f-STM is similar to that of the STM/BR as the following example shows.

Example 7.14 Consider again Example 7.11 ($C = 5, K = 2, b_1 = 1, b_2 = 3, b_{2r} = b_{2c} = 2, N_1 = N_2 = 10, v_1 = v_2 = 0.1, \mu_1 = \mu_2 = 1, \mu_{2r}^{-1} = \mu_{2c}^{-1} = 1.5, J_0 = 1$) and let the BR parameters be $t_1 = 2$ b.u. and $t_2 = 0$ b.u. so that $b_1 + t_1 = b_2 + t_2$.

(a) Find the total number of permissible states $\mathbf{n} = (n_1, n_2, n_{2c})$, where n_{2c} is the number of service-class 2 calls accepted in the system with b_{2c} b.u. Draw the state transition diagram.
(b) Calculate the state probabilities $P(n_1, n_2, n_{2c})$ and the corresponding values of $Q_{fin}(j)$ based on the GB equations.
(c) Calculate the TC probabilities of both service-classes and the link utilization.

(a) There are 13 permissible states of the form $\mathbf{n} = (n_1, n_2, n_{2c})$. The state space Ω and the state transition diagram are shown in Figure 7.6.
(b) Based on Figure 7.6, we obtain the following 13 GB equations:

$(0,0,0):$ $P(0,1,0) + P(1,0,0) + 2/3P(0,0,1) - 2P(0,0,0) = 0$
$(0,0,1):$ $P(0,1,1) + P(1,0,1) + 4/3P(0,0,2) - (5/3 + 0.9)P(0,0,1) = 0$
$(0,0,2):$ $P(1,0,2) + 0.9P(0,0,1) - 4/3P(0,0,2) = 0$
$(0,1,0):$ $P(0,0,0) + 2/3P(0,1,1) + P(1,1,0) - 1.9P(0,1,0) = 0$
$(0,1,1):$ $0.9P(0,1,0) - 5/3P(0,1,1) = 0$
$(1,0,0):$ $P(0,0,0) + 2/3P(1,0,1) + 2P(2,0,0) + P(1,1,0) - 2.9P(1,0,0) = 0$
$(1,0,1):$ $P(0,0,1) + 4/3P(1,0,2) + 2P(2,0,1) - (5/3 + 0.9)P(1,0,1) = 0$
$(1,0,2):$ $0.9P(1,0,1) - 7/3P(1,0,2) = 0$
$(1,1,0):$ $P(1,0,0) - 2.0P(1,1,0) = 0$
$(2,0,0):$ $0.9P(1,0,0) + 3P(3,0,0) + 2/3P(2,0,1) - 3.8P(2,0,0) = 0$
$(2,0,1):$ $3P(3,0,1) + P(2,0,0) - 8/3P(2,0,1) = 0$
$(3,0,0):$ $0.8P(2,0,0) + 2/3P(3,0,1) - 4.0P(3,0,0) = 0$
$(3,0,1):$ $P(3,0,0) - 11/3P(3,0,1) = 0$

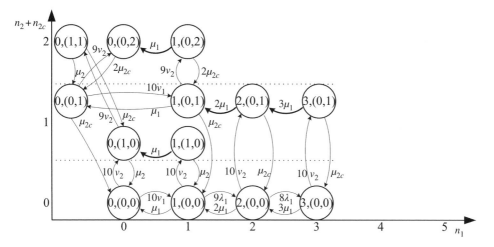

Figure 7.6 The state space Ω and the state transition diagram (Example 7.14).

The solution of this linear system is: $P(0, 0, 0) = 0.182235$

$P(0, 0, 1) = 0.11162$	$P(0, 0, 2) = 0.096096$	$P(0, 1, 0) = 0.160423$	$P(0, 1, 1) = 0.086628$
$P(1, 0, 0) = 0.129633$	$P(1, 0, 1) = 0.071736$	$P(1, 0, 2) = 0.02767$	$P(1, 1, 0) = 0.064817$
$P(2, 0, 0) = 0.04053$	$P(2, 0, 1) = 0.017804$	$P(3, 0, 0) = 0.008492$	$P(3, 0, 1) = 0.002316$

Then, based on the values of $P(n_1, n_2, n_{2c})$, we obtain the values of $Q_{\mathrm{fin}}(j)$:

$Q_{\mathrm{fin}}(0) = P(0, 0, 0) = 0.182235$

$Q_{\mathrm{fin}}(1) = P(1, 0, 0) = 0.129633$

$Q_{\mathrm{fin}}(2) = P(0, 0, 1) + P(2, 0, 0) = 0.15215$

$Q_{\mathrm{fin}}(3) = P(0, 1, 0) + P(1, 0, 1) + P(3, 0, 0) = 0.240651$

$Q_{\mathrm{fin}}(4) = P(0, 0, 2) + P(1, 1, 0) + P(2, 0, 1) = 0.178717$

$Q_{\mathrm{fin}}(5) = P(0, 1, 1) + P(1, 0, 2) + P(3, 0, 1) = 0.116614$

(c) The TC probabilities of service-class 1, B_{T1}, are given by:

$$B_{T1} = \sum_{j=C-b_1-t_1+1}^{C} Q_{\mathrm{fin}}(j) = Q_{\mathrm{fin}}(3) + Q_{\mathrm{fin}}(4) + Q_{\mathrm{fin}}(5) = 0.535982$$

(0.545538 in the STM/BR, see Example 2.13)

The TC probabilities of service-class 2 calls, B_{T2c}, when they require b_{2c} b.u., are:

$$B_{T2c} = \sum_{j=C-b_{2c}+1}^{C} Q_{\mathrm{fin}}(j) = Q_{\mathrm{fin}}(4) + Q_{\mathrm{fin}}(5) = 0.295331 \ (0.313991 \text{ in the STM/BR})$$

The link utilization is determined by:

$$U = \sum_{j=1}^{C} j Q_{\mathrm{fin}}(j) = 2.454 \text{ b.u. } (2.512 \text{ in the STM/BR})$$

7.6.2 The Analytical Model

7.6.2.1 Link Occupancy Distribution

In the f-STM/BR, the unnormalized values of $q_{\text{fin}}(j)$ can be calculated in an approximate way according to the Roberts method. Based on that method, we apply an algorithm similar to the one presented in Section 7.5.2.3, which is modified as follows:

Algorithm Approximate calculation of q_{fin} in the f-STM/BR

Step 1: Define the corresponding infinite loss model STM/BR and calculate $q(j)$ via (2.44).

Step 2: Determine the values of $y_k(j)$ and $y_{kc}(j)$ in the STM/BR based on (2.47) and (2.48), respectively.

Step 3: Modify (7.45) to the following approximate formula, where the values of $y_k(j)$ and $y_{kc}(j)$ have been determined in step 2 from the corresponding infinite model:

$$
q_{\text{fin}}(j) = \begin{cases}
1 & \text{if } j = 0 \\
\frac{1}{j}\sum_{k=1}^{K}N_k - y_k(j-b_k))\alpha_{k,\text{idle}}D_k(j-b_k)\delta_k(j)q_{\text{fin}}(j-b_k) + \frac{1}{j}\sum_{k=1}^{K}N_k - \\
\quad y_k(j-b_{kc}) - y_{kc}(j-b_{kc}))\alpha_{kc,\text{idle}}D_{kc}(j-b_{kc})\delta_{kc}(j)q_{\text{fin}}(j-b_{kc}) \\
\quad j = 1, \dots, C \\
0 & \text{otherwise}
\end{cases}
\tag{7.48}
$$

where $D_k(j-b_k)$ and $D_{kc}(j-b_{kc})$ are determined via (1.65) and (2.45), respectively.

7.6.2.2 TC Probabilities, CBP, Utilization, and Mean Number of In-service Calls

The following performance measures can be determined based on (7.48):

- The TC probabilities of service-class k calls with b_k b.u., B_{Tk}, via (6.42).
- The TC probabilities of service-class k calls with b_{kc}, B_{Tkc}, via:

$$
B_{Tkc} = \sum_{j=C-b_{kc}-t_k+1}^{C} G^{-1}q_{\text{fin}}(j)
\tag{7.49}
$$

- The CC probabilities of service-class k calls with b_k (without the option of b_{kc}), B_k, via (6.42) but for a system with $N_k - 1$ traffic sources.
- The CC probabilities of service-class k calls with b_{kc}, B_{kc}, via (7.49) but for a system with $N_k - 1$ traffic sources.
- The conditional TC probabilities of service-class k calls with b_{kc} given that $j > J_0$, B_{Tkc}^*, via (7.41), while subtracting the BR parameter t_k from $C - b_{kc}$.
- The link utilization, U, via (6.36).
- The average number of service-class k calls in the system accepted with b_k b.u., $\overline{n}_k$, via (6.37) where $y_{k,\text{fin}}(j)$ is determined by:

$$
y_{k,\text{fin}}(j) = \begin{cases}
\frac{(N_k - y_k(j-b_k))\alpha_{k,\text{idle}}\delta_k(j)q_{\text{fin}}(j-b_k)}{q_{\text{fin}}(j)} & \text{for } j \leq C - t_k \\
0 & \text{for } j > C - t_k
\end{cases}
\tag{7.50}
$$

- The average number of service-class k calls in the system accepted with b_{kc} b.u., $\bar{n}_{kc}$, via (7.43) where $y_{kc,\text{fin}}(j)$ is determined by:

$$
y_{kc,\text{fin}}(j) = \begin{cases} \dfrac{(N_k - y_k(j-b_{kc}) - y_{kc}(j-b_{kc})) \alpha_{kc,\text{idle}} \delta_{kc}(j) q_{\text{fin}}(j-b_{kc})}{q_{\text{fin}}(j)} & \text{for } j \le C - t_k \\ 0 & \text{for } j > C - t_k \end{cases} \tag{7.51}
$$

Example 7.15 Consider again Example 7.14 ($C = 5, K = 2, b_1 = 1, b_2 = 3, b_{2c} = 2$, $t_1 = 2, t_2 = 0, N_1 = N_2 = 10, v_1 = 0.1, v_2 = 0.1, \mu_1 = \mu_2 = 1, \mu_{2c}^{-1} = 1.5, J_0 = 1$). Apply the algorithm of Section 7.6.2.1 for the determination of TC probabilities.

Step 1: The corresponding infinite loss model (STM/BR) is $C = 5, K = 2, b_1 = 1$, $b_2 = 3, b_{2c} = 2, t_1 = 2, t_2 = 0, \alpha_1 = \alpha_2 = 1$, and $\alpha_{2c} = 1.5$ erl.
Based on (2.44), we have the following normalized values of $Q(j)$:

$Q(0) = 0.18209 \quad Q(1) = 0.18209 \quad Q(2) = 0.09105$
$Q(3) = 0.21244 \quad Q(4) = 0.20486 \quad Q(5) = 0.12746$

Step 2: Based on (2.47) and (2.48), we have:

$j = 1 \Rightarrow y_1(1) = 1 \qquad\qquad y_2(1) = 0 \qquad\qquad y_{2c}(1) = 0$
$j = 2 \Rightarrow y_1(2) = 2 \qquad\qquad y_2(2) = 0 \qquad\qquad y_{2c}(2) = 0$
$j = 3 \Rightarrow y_1(3) = 0.428571 \quad y_2(3) = 0.857143 \quad y_{2c}(3) = 0$
$j = 4 \Rightarrow y_1(4) = 0 \qquad\qquad y_2(4) = 0.888889 \quad y_{2c}(4) = 0.666667$
$j = 5 \rightarrow y_1(5) = 0 \qquad\qquad y_2(5) = 0 \qquad\qquad y_{2c}(5) = 2.5$

Step 3: Based on (7.48), we have the following normalized values of $Q_{\text{fin}}(j)$:

$Q_{\text{fin}}(0) = 0.18968 \quad Q_{\text{fin}}(1) = 0.18968 \quad Q_{\text{fin}}(2) = 0.08536$
$Q_{\text{fin}}(3) = 0.21245 \quad Q_{\text{fin}}(4) = 0.20628 \quad Q_{\text{fin}}(5) = 0.11654$

The approximate TC probabilities are:

$$B_{T1} = \sum_{j=C-b_1-t_1+1}^{C} Q_{\text{fin}}(j) = 0.53527 \text{ (compare with the exact 0.535982)}$$

$$B_{T2c} = \sum_{j=C-b_{2c}+1}^{C} Q_{\text{fin}}(j) = 0.322825 \text{ (compare with the exact 0.295331)}$$

7.7 The Finite Multi-Threshold Model

7.7.1 The Service System

In the *finite multi-threshold model* (f-MTM), there exist S different thresholds which are common to all service-classes. A call of service-class k with initial requirements (b_k, μ_k^{-1}) can use, depending on the occupied link bandwidth j, one of the $S + 1$ require-ments $(b_{kc_s}, \mu_{kc_s}^{-1}), s = 0, 1, \ldots, S$, where the pair $(b_{kc_s}, \mu_{kc_s}^{-1})$ is used when $J_{s-1} < j \le J_s$, while

$J_{-1} = 0$). The maximum possible threshold is $J_{S-1} = C - b_{kc_s}$, while $J_S = C$. As far as the bandwidth requirements of a service-class k call are concerned, we assume that they decrease as j increases, i.e., $b_k > b_{kc_1} > \dots > b_{kc_S}$, while by definition $b_k = b_{kc_0}$.

7.7.2 The Analytical Model

7.7.2.1 Steady State Probabilities

To derive a recursive formula for the calculation of $q_{\text{fin}}(j)$, the following LB equations are considered:

$$(N_k - n_k + 1)\alpha_{k,\text{idle}}b_k q_{\text{fin}}(j - b_k) = y_{k,\text{fin}}(j)b_k q_{\text{fin}}(j)$$
$$(\text{for} \quad j \leq J_0 + b_k \quad \text{when} \quad b_{kc_s} > 0) \quad \text{or} \quad (\text{for} \quad j = 1, \dots, C \quad \text{when} \quad b_{kc_s} = 0)$$
(7.52)

and

$$(N_k - (n_k + n_{kc_1} + \dots + n_{kc_s} + \dots + n_{kc_S}) + 1)\alpha_{kc_s,\text{idle}}b_{kc_s}q_{\text{fin}}(j - b_{kc_s})$$
$$= y_{kc_s,\text{fin}}(j)b_{kc_s}q_{\text{fin}}(j) \qquad \text{for} \quad J_s + b_{kc_s} \geq j > J_{s-1} + b_{kc_s}$$
(7.53)

where n_{kc_s} is the number of in-service calls of service-class k accepted in the system with b_{kc_s} b.u., $s = 1, \dots, S$ and $\alpha_{kc_s,\text{idle}} = v_k \mu_{kc_s}^{-1}$.

Similar to the analysis of the f-STM and based on (7.52) and (7.53), we have the following recursive formula for the calculation of $q_{\text{fin}}(j)$ [5]:

$$q_{\text{fin}}(j) = \begin{cases} 1 & \text{if} \quad j = 0 \\ \dfrac{1}{j} \sum\limits_{k=1}^{K} (N_k - n_k + 1)\alpha_{k,\text{idle}}b_k \delta_k(j)q_{\text{fin}}(j - b_k) + \sum\limits_{k=1}^{K} \sum\limits_{s=1}^{S} (N_k - n_k - & \\ \quad n_{kc_1} - \dots - n_{kc_S} + 1)\alpha_{kc_s,\text{idle}}b_{kc_s}\delta_{kc_s}(j)q_{\text{fin}}(j - b_{kc_s}) \quad j = 1, \dots, C & \\ 0 & \text{otherwise} \end{cases}$$
(7.54)

where $\delta_k(j) = \begin{cases} 1 & (\text{if} \quad 1 \leq j \leq J_0 + b_k \quad \text{and} \quad b_{kc_s} > 0) \text{ or } (\text{if } 1 \leq j \leq C \text{ and } b_{kc_s} = 0) \\ 0 & \text{otherwise} \end{cases}$

$\delta_{kc_s}(j) = \begin{cases} 1 & \text{if} \quad J_s + b_{kc_s} \geq j > J_{s-1} + b_{kc_s} \quad \text{and} \quad b_{kc_s} > 0 \\ 0 & \text{otherwise} \end{cases}$, and $a_{kc_s,\text{idle}} = v_k \mu_{kc_s}^{-1}$.

Note that if $N_k \to \infty$ for $k = 1, \dots, K$, and the total offered traffic-load remains constant, then we have the recursion (2.51) of the MTM.

7.7.2.2 TC Probabilities, CBP, Utilization, and Mean Number of In-service Calls

The following performance measures can be determined based on (7.54):

- The TC probabilities of service-class k calls with b_k b.u., B_{Tk}, via (6.35).
- The TC probabilities of service-class k calls with their last bandwidth requirement b_{kc_S} b.u., B_{Tkc_S}, via:

$$B_{Tkc_S} = \sum_{j=C-b_{kc_S}+1}^{C} G^{-1}q_{\text{fin}}(j)$$
(7.55)

where $G = \sum_{j=0}^{C} q_{\text{fin}}(j)$ is the normalization constant.

- The CC probabilities of service-class k calls with b_k (without retrial), B_k, via (6.35) but for a system with $N_k - 1$ traffic sources.

- The CC probabilities of service-class k calls with b_{kc_s}, B_{kc_s}, via (7.55) but for a system with $N_k - 1$ traffic sources.
- The conditional TC probabilities of service-class k calls with b_{kc_s} b.u. given that $j > J_{S-1}$, $B^*_{Tkc_s}$, via:

$$B^*_{Tkc_s} = Prob\{j > C - b_{kc_s} | j > J_{S-1}\} = \frac{B_{Tkc_s}}{Prob(j > J_{S-1})} = \frac{\sum\limits_{j=C-b_{kc_{S-1}}+1}^{C} q_{\text{fin}}(j)}{\sum\limits_{j=J_{S-1}+1}^{C} q_{\text{fin}}(j)}$$

(7.56)

- The link utilization, U, via (6.36).
- The average number of service-class k calls in the system accepted with b_k b.u., $\bar{n}_k$, via (6.37), while the mean number of service-class k calls with b_k given that the system state is j, $y_{k,\text{fin}}(j)$, via (7.42).
- The average number of service-class k calls in the system accepted with b_{kc_s} b.u., $\bar{n}_{kc_s}$, via:

$$\bar{n}_{kc_s} = \sum_{j=1}^{C} G^{-1} y_{kc_s,\text{fin}}(j) q_{\text{fin}}(j)$$

(7.57)

where $y_{kc_s,\text{fin}}(j)$ is the average number of service-class k calls with b_{kc_s} given that the system state is j, and is determined by:

$$y_{kc_s,\text{fin}}(j) = \frac{(N_k - n_k - n_{kc_1} - \ldots - n_{kc_s} - \ldots - n_{kc_S} + 1)\alpha_{kc_s,\text{idle}}\delta_{kc_s}(j)q_{\text{fin}}(j - b_{kc_s})}{q_{\text{fin}}(j)}$$

(7.58)

The determination of $q_{\text{fin}}(j)$ via (7.54), and consequently of all performance measures, requires the values of n_k and n_{kc_s}, $s = 1, \ldots, S$, which are unknown. To avoid the determination of an equivalent stochastic system we adopt the algorithm of Section 7.7.2.3 (see below), which is similar to the algorithm of Section 7.5.2.3 of the f-STM.

7.7.2.3 An Approximate Algorithm for the Determination of $q_{\text{fin}}(j)$ in the f-MTM

The algorithm can be described by the following steps [5].

Algorithm Approximate calculation of $q_{\text{fin}}(j)$ in the f-MTM

Step 1: Define the corresponding infinite loss model MTM and calculate $q(j)$ via (2.51).
Step 2: Determine the values of $y_k(j)$ and $y_{kc_s}(j)$ in the MTM based on (2.54) and (2.55), respectively.
Step 3: Modify (7.54) to the following approximate formula, where the $y_k(j)$ and $y_{kc_s}(j)$ have been determined in step 2 from the corresponding infinite model:

$$
q_{\text{fin}}(j)=\begin{cases}
1 & \text{if } j=0 \\[2mm]
\dfrac{1}{j}\sum_{k=1}^{K}N_k-y_k(j-b_k))\alpha_{k,\text{idle}}b_k\delta_k(j)q_{\text{fin}}(j-b_k)+\dfrac{1}{j}\sum_{k=1}^{K}\sum_{s=1}^{S}(N_k-y_k(j-b_{kc_s}) \\[1mm]
-y_{kc_1}(j-b_{kc_s})-\dots-y_{kc_s}(j-b_{kc_s}))\alpha_{kc_s,\text{idle}}b_{kc_s}\delta_{kc_s}(j)q_{\text{fin}}(j-b_{kc_s}), \\[1mm]
\qquad\qquad j=1,\dots,C \\[2mm]
0 & \text{otherwise}
\end{cases}
\tag{7.59}
$$

Step 4: Determine the various performance measures as follows:

- The TC probabilities of service-class k calls with b_k b.u., B_{Tk}, via (6.35).
- The TC probabilities of service-class k calls with b_{kc_s}, B_{Tkc_s}, via (7.55).
- The CC probabilities of service-class k calls with b_k (without retrial), B_k, via (6.35) but for a system with N_k-1 traffic sources.
- The CC probabilities of service-class k calls with with b_{kc_s}, B_{kc_s}, via (7.55) but for a system with N_k-1 traffic sources.
- The conditional TC probabilities of service-class k calls with b_{kc_s} b.u. given that $j>J_{S-1}$, $B^*_{Tkc_s}$, via (7.56).
- The link utilization, U, via (6.36).
- The average number of service-class k calls in the system accepted with b_k b.u., $\bar{n}_k$, via (6.37) where $y_{k,\text{fin}}(j)$ is determined by (7.46).
- The average number of service-class k calls in the system accepted with b_{kc_s} b.u., $\bar{n}_{kc_s}$, via (7.57) where $y_{kc_s,\text{fin}}(j)$ is determined by:

$$
y_{kc_s,\text{fin}}(j)=\frac{(N_k-y_k(j-b_{kc_s})-y_{kc_1}(j-b_{kc_s})-\dots-y_{kc_s}(j-b_{kc_s}))\alpha_{kc_s,\text{idle}}\delta_{kc_s}(j)q_{\text{fin}}(j-b_{kc_s})}{q_{\text{fin}}(j)}
\tag{7.60}
$$

7.8 The Finite Multi-Threshold Model under the BR Policy

7.8.1 The Service System

In the *f-MTM under the BR policy* (*f-MTM/BR*), t_k b.u. are reserved to benefit calls of all other service-classes apart from service-class k. The application of the BR policy in the f-MTM/BR is similar to that of the f-MRM/BR.

7.8.2 The Analytical Model

7.8.2.1 Link Occupancy Distribution
Based on the Roberts method and the algorithm of Section 7.6.2.1 of the f-STM/BR, the unnormalized values of the link occupancy distribution, $q_{\text{fin}}(j)$, in the f-MTM/BR can be determined as follows:

Algorithm Approximate calculation of $q_{\text{fin}}(j)$ in the f-MTM/BR

Step 1: Define the corresponding infinite loss model MTM/BR and calculate $q(j)$ via (2.57).

Step 2: Determine the values of $y_k(j)$ and $y_{kc_s}(j)$ ($s=1,\dots,S$) in the MTM/BR based on (2.61) and (2.62), respectively.

Step 3: Modify (7.59) to the following recursive formula, where the $y_k(j)$ and $y_{kc_s}(j)$ have been determined in step 2 from the corresponding infinite model:

$$
q_{\mathrm{fin}}(j)=
\begin{cases}
1 & \text{if } j=0 \\[4pt]
\begin{aligned}
&\frac{1}{j}\sum_{k=1}^{K}(N_k-y_k(j-b_k))\alpha_{k,\mathrm{idle}}D_k(j-b_k)\delta_k(j)q_{\mathrm{fin}}(j-b_k)+\frac{1}{j}\sum_{k=1}^{K}\sum_{s=1}^{S}(N_k-y_k(j-b_{kc_s}))\\
&-y_{kc_1}(j-b_{kc_s})-\ldots-y_{kc_s}(j-b_{kc_s}))\alpha_{kc_s,\mathrm{idle}}D_{kc_s}(j-b_{kc_s})\delta_{kc_s}(j)q_{\mathrm{fin}}(j-b_{kc_s})\\
&\qquad j=1,\ldots,C
\end{aligned} \\[4pt]
0 & \text{otherwise}
\end{cases}
$$

$$\tag{7.61}$$

where $D_k(j-b_k)$ and $D_{kc_s}(j-b_{kc_s})$ are determined via (1.65) and (2.58), respectively.

7.8.2.2 TC Probabilities, CBP, Utilization and Mean Number of In-service Calls

Based on (7.61) and (2.58), we can determine the following performance measures:

- The TC probabilities of service-class k calls with b_k b.u., B_{Tk}, via (6.42).
- The TC probabilities of service-class k calls with b_{kc_s}, B_{Tkc_s}, via:

$$
B_{Tkc_s} = \sum_{j=C-b_{kc_s}-t_k+1}^{C} G^{-1}q_{\mathrm{fin}}(j) \tag{7.62}
$$

- The CC probabilities of service-class k calls with b_k (without the option of b_{kc_s}), B_k, via (6.42) but for a system with N_k-1 traffic sources.
- The CC probabilities of service-class k calls with with b_{kc_s}, B_{kc_s}, via (7.62) but for a system with N_k-1 traffic sources.
- The conditional TC probabilities of service-class k calls with b_{kc_s} b.u. given that $j > J_{S-1}$, $B^*_{Tkc_s}$, via (7.56), while subtracting the BR parameter t_k from $C-b_{kc_s}$.
- The link utilization, U, via (6.36).
- The average number of service-class k calls in the system accepted with b_k b.u., $\bar{n}_k$, via (6.37) where $y_{k,\mathrm{fin}}(j)$ is determined by (7.50).
- The average number of service-class k calls in the system accepted with b_{kc_s} b.u., $\bar{n}_{kc_s}$, via (7.57) where $y_{kc_s,\mathrm{fin}}(j)$ is determined by:

$$
y_{kc_s,\mathrm{fin}}(j) =
\begin{cases}
\dfrac{(N_k-y_k(j-b_{kc_s})-y_{kc_1}(j-b_{kc_s})-\ldots-y_{kc_s}(j-b_{kc_s}))\alpha_{kc_s,\mathrm{idle}}\delta_{kc_s}(j)q_{\mathrm{fin}}(j-b_{kc_s})}{q_{\mathrm{fin}}(j)} & \text{for } j\le C-t_k \\[10pt]
0 & \text{for } j>C-t_k
\end{cases}
$$

$$\tag{7.63}$$

7.9 The Finite Connection Dependent Threshold Model

7.9.1 The Service System

In the *finite CDTM* (f-*CDTM*), the difference compared to the f-MTM is that different service-classes may have different sets of thresholds. Each arriving call of a service-class k may have $S(k)+1$ bandwidth and service-time requirements, that is, one initial requirement with values (b_k,μ_k^{-1}) and $S(k)$ more requirements with values $(b_{kc_s},\mu_{kc_s}^{-1})$, where $s=1,\ldots,S(k)$, $b_{kc_{S(k)}}<\ldots<b_{kc_1}<b_k$ and $\mu_{kc_{S(k)}}^{-1}>\ldots>\mu_{kc_1}^{-1}>\mu_k^{-1}$. The pair $(b_{kc_s},\mu_{kc_s}^{-1})$ is used when $J_{k_{s-1}}<j\le J_{k_s}$, where $J_{k_{s-1}}$ and J_{k_s} are two successive thresholds

of service-class k, while $J_{k_{S(k)}} = C$; the highest possible threshold (other than C) is $J_{k_{S(k)-1}} = C - b_{kc_{S(k)}}$. By convention, $b_k = b_{kc_0}$ and $\mu_k^{-1} = \mu_{kc_0}^{-1}$, while the pair (b_k, μ_k^{-1}) is used when $j \le J_{k_0}$.

7.9.2 The Analytical Model

7.9.2.1 Steady State Probabilities
Similar to the analysis of the f-MTM and based on (7.54), we have the following recursive formula for the calculation of $q_{\text{fin}}(j)$ [5]:

$$
q_{\text{fin}}(j) = \begin{cases} 1 & \text{if } j = 0 \\ \frac{1}{j}\sum_{k=1}^{K}(N_k - n_k + 1)\alpha_{k,\text{idle}}b_k\delta_k(j)q_{\text{fin}}(j - b_k) + \frac{1}{j}\sum_{k=1}^{K}\sum_{s=1}^{S(k)}(N_k - n_k - \\ \quad n_{kc_1} - \cdots - n_{kc_{S(k)}} + 1)\alpha_{kc_s,\text{idle}}b_{kc_s}\delta_{kc_s}(j)q_{\text{fin}}(j - b_{kc_s}) & j = 1, \dots, C \\ 0 & \text{otherwise} \end{cases}
$$

(7.64)

where
$$
\delta_k(j) = \begin{cases} 1 & (\text{if } 1 \le j \le J_0 + b_k \text{ and } b_{kc_s} > 0) \text{ or } (\text{if } 1 \le j \le C \text{ and } b_{kc_s} = 0) \\ 0 & \text{otherwise} \end{cases},
$$

$$
\delta_{kc_s}(j) = \begin{cases} 1 & \text{if } J_{k_s} + b_{kc_s} \ge j > J_{k_{s-1}} + b_{kc_s} \text{ and } b_{kc_s} > 0 \\ 0 & \text{otherwise} \end{cases}, \text{ and } \alpha_{kc_s,\text{idle}} = v_k\mu_{kc_s}^{-1}.
$$

Note that if $N_k \to \infty$ for $k = 1, \dots, K$, and the total offered traffic-load remains constant, then we have the recursion (2.65) of the CDTM.

7.9.2.2 TC Probabilities, CBP, Utilization, and Mean Number of In-service Calls
The following performance measures can be determined based on (7.64):

- The TC probabilities of service-class k calls with b_k b.u., B_{Tk}, via (6.35).
- The TC probabilities of service-class k calls with their last bandwidth requirement $b_{kc_{S(k)}}$ b.u., $B_{Tkc_{S(k)}}$, via:

$$
B_{Tkc_{S(k)}} = \sum_{j=C-b_{kc_{S(k)}}+1}^{C} G^{-1}q_{\text{fin}}(j)
$$

(7.65)

where $G = \sum_{j=0}^{C} q_{\text{fin}}(j)$ is the normalization constant.
- The CC probabilities of service-class k calls with b_k (without retrial), B_k, via (6.35) but for a system with $N_k - 1$ traffic sources.
- The CC probabilities of service-class k calls with $b_{kc_{S(k)}}$, $B_{kc_{S(k)}}$, via (7.65) but for a system with $N_k - 1$ traffic sources.
- The conditional TC probabilities of service-class k calls with $b_{kc_{S(k)}}$ b.u. given that $j > J_{S(k)-1}$, $B^*_{Tkc_{S(k)}}$, via:

$$
B^*_{Tkc_{S(k)}} = Prob\{j > C - b_{kc_s}|j > J_{S(k)-1}\} = \frac{B_{Tkc_s}}{Prob(j > J_{S(k)-1})} = \frac{\sum_{j=C-b_{kc_s}+1}^{C} q_{\text{fin}}(j)}{\sum_{j=J_{S(k)-1}+1}^{C} q_{\text{fin}}(j)}
$$

(7.66)

- The link utilization, U, via (6.36).
- The average number of service-class k calls in the system accepted with b_k b.u., $\bar{n}_k$, via (6.37), while the mean number of service-class k calls with b_k given that the system state is j, $y_{k,\text{fin}}(j)$, via (7.42).
- The average number of service-class k calls in the system accepted with b_{kc_s} b.u., $\bar{n}_{kc_s}$, via (7.57), while the average number of service-class k calls with b_{kc_s} given that the system state is j, $y_{kc_s,\text{fin}}(j)$, via:

$$y_{kc_s,\text{fin}}(j) = \frac{(N_k - n_k - n_{kc_1} - \ldots - n_{kc_s} - \ldots - n_{kc_{S(k)}} + 1)\alpha_{kc_s,\text{idle}}\delta_{kc_s}(j)q_{\text{fin}}(j - b_{kc_s})}{q_{\text{fin}}(j)}$$

(7.67)

The calculation of $q_{\text{fin}}(j)$ via (7.64), and consequently of all performance measures, requires the determination of an equivalent stochastic system. To avoid it, we adopt the algorithm of Section 7.9.2.3 (see below), which is similar to the algorithm of Section 7.7.2.3 of the f-MTM.

7.9.2.3 An Approximate Algorithm for the Determination of $q_{\text{fin}}(j)$ in the f-CDTM

The algorithm can be described by the following steps [5]:

Algorithm Approximate calculation of $q_{\text{fin}}(j)$ in the f-CDTM

Step 1: Define the corresponding infinite loss model CDTM and calculate $q(j)$ via (2.65).

Step 2: Determine the values of $y_k(j)$ and $y_{kc_s}(j)$ in the CDTM based on (2.68) and (2.69), respectively.

Step 3: Modify (7.64) to the following approximate formula, where the $y_k(j)$ and $y_{kc_s}(j)$ have been determined in step 2 from the corresponding infinite model:

$$q_{\text{fin}}(j) = \begin{cases} 1 & \text{if } j = 0 \\ \dfrac{1}{j}\sum_{k=1}^{K}(N_k - y_k(j-b_k))\alpha_{k,\text{idle}}b_k\delta_k(j)q_{\text{fin}}(j-b_k) + \dfrac{1}{j}\sum_{k=1}^{K}\sum_{s=1}^{S(k)}(N_k - y_k(j-b_{kc_s}) \\ \quad - y_{kc_1}(j-b_{kc_s}) - \ldots - y_{kc_{S(k)}}(j-b_{kc_s}))\alpha_{kc_s,\text{idle}}b_{kc_s}\delta_{kc_s}(j)q_{\text{fin}}(j-b_{kc_s}) \\ \qquad j = 1,\ldots,C \\ 0 & \text{otherwise} \end{cases}$$

(7.68)

Step 4: Determine the various performance measures as follows:
- The TC probabilities of service-class k calls with b_k b.u., B_{Tk}, via (6.35).
- The TC probabilities of service-class k calls with $b_{kc_{S(k)}}$, $B_{Tkc_{S(k)}}$, via (7.65).
- The CC probabilities of service-class k calls with b_k (without retrial), B_k, via (6.35) but for a system with $N_k - 1$ traffic sources.
- The CC probabilities of service-class k calls with with $b_{kc_{S(k)}}$, $B_{kc_{S(k)}}$, via (7.65) but for a system with $N_k - 1$ traffic sources.
- The conditional TC probabilities of service-class k calls with $b_{kc_{S(k)}}$ b.u. given that $j > J_{S(k)-1}$, $B^*_{Tkc_{S(k)}}$, via (7.66).
- The link utilization, U, via (6.36).

- The average number of service-class k calls in the system accepted with b_k b.u., $\bar{n}_k$, via (6.37) where $y_{k,\mathrm{fin}}(j)$ is determined by (7.46).
- The average number of service-class k calls in the system accepted with b_{kc_s} b.u., $\bar{n}_{kc_s}$, via (7.57) where $y_{kc_s,\mathrm{fin}}(j)$ is determined by:

$$y_{kc_s,\mathrm{fin}}(j) = \frac{(N_k - y_k(j-b_{kc_s}) - y_{kc_1}(j-b_{kc_s}) - \ldots - y_{kc_{S(k)}}(j-b_{kc_s}))\alpha_{kc_s,\mathrm{idle}}\delta_{kc_s}(j)q_{\mathrm{fin}}(j-b_{kc_s})}{q_{\mathrm{fin}}(j)} \tag{7.69}$$

Example 7.16 Consider again Example 7.10 ($C = 50, K = 2, b_1 = 10, b_{1r_1} = b_{1c_1} = 8$, $b_{1r_2} = b_{1c_2} = 6, b_2 = 7, b_{2r_1} = b_{2c_1} = 4, \alpha_{1,\mathrm{idle}} = 0.06, \alpha_{1r_1,\mathrm{idle}} = \alpha_{1c_1,\mathrm{idle}} = 0.075, \alpha_{1r_2,\mathrm{idle}} = \alpha_{1c_2,\mathrm{idle}} = 0.1, \alpha_{2,\mathrm{idle}} = 0.2, \alpha_{2r_1,\mathrm{idle}} = \alpha_{2c_1,\mathrm{idle}} = 0.35$). The values of $b_{1c_1} = 8$ and $b_{1c_2} = 6$ are used when $j > J_{1_0} = 30$ and $j > J_{1_1} = 35$, respectively. Similarly, the value of $b_{2c_1} = 4$ is used when $j > J_{2_0} = 37$. The equivalent stochastic system used for the TC calculation in this f-CDTM example is $C = 50019, b_1 = 10000, b_{1c_1} = 8000, b_{1c_2} = 6000, b_2 = 7001, b_{2c_1} = 4005, J_{1_0} = 30000, J_{1_1} = 35000, J_{2_0} = 37001$. We consider three sets of N_1, N_2: (i) $N_1 = N_2 = 12$, (ii) $N_1 = N_2 = 60$, and (iii) $N_1 = N_2 = 600$. Table 7.5 shows the various sets of N_1, N_2 and the corresponding offered traffic-loads, while Table 7.6 shows the state space, which consists of 53 states. The corresponding CDTM system used in the algorithm of Section 7.9.2.3 is $C = 50, K = 2, b_1 = 10, b_{1c_1} = 8, b_{1c_2} = 6, b_2 = 7, b_{2c_1} = 4, \alpha_1 = 0.72, \alpha_{1c_1} = 0.9, \alpha_{1c_2} = 1.2, \alpha_2 = 2.4, \alpha_{2c_1} = 4.2$. For the three different sets of N_1, N_2, we present in Tables 7.7–7.9 the analytical TC probabilities obtained via the equivalent stochastic system and the algorithm of Section 7.9.2.3 together with the corresponding simulation results. At each point (P) of Tables 7.7–7.9, we assume that the values of $\alpha_{1,\mathrm{idle}}, \alpha_{1c_1,\mathrm{idle}}$, and $\alpha_{1c_2,\mathrm{idle}}$ are constant while those of $\alpha_{2,\mathrm{idle}}$ and $\alpha_{2c_1,\mathrm{idle}}$ are increased by $0.4/N_2$ and $0.7/N_2$, respectively, i.e., point 1 is $(\alpha_{1,\mathrm{idle}}, \alpha_{2,\mathrm{idle}}, \alpha_{1c_1,\mathrm{idle}}, \alpha_{1c_2,\mathrm{idle}}, \alpha_{2c_1,\mathrm{idle}}) = (0.72/N_1, 2.4/N_2, 0.9/N_1, 1.2/N_1, 4.2/N_1)$, while point 6 is $(\alpha_{1,\mathrm{idle}}, \alpha_{2,\mathrm{idle}}, \alpha_{1c_1,\mathrm{idle}}, \alpha_{1c_2,\mathrm{idle}}, \alpha_{2c_1,\mathrm{idle}}) = (0.72/N_1, 4.4/N_2, 0.9/N_1, 1.2/N_1, 7.7/N_1)$.

According to Tables 7.7–7.9, the analytical TC probabilities obtained via the algorithm of Section 7.9.2.3 are closer to the simulation results (mean values of 7 runs with 95% confidence interval) than the corresponding results obtained by the equivalent stochastic system.

Table 7.5 Sets of sources and offered traffic-loads per idle source (Example 7.16).

Number of sources	$\alpha_{1,\mathrm{idle}}$ (erl)	$\alpha_{2,\mathrm{idle}}$ (erl)	$\alpha_{1c_1,\mathrm{idle}}$ (erl)	$\alpha_{1c_2,\mathrm{idle}}$ (erl)	$\alpha_{2c_1,\mathrm{idle}}$ (erl)
$N_1 = N_2 = 12$	$0.72/N_1$	$2.4/N_2$	$0.9/N_1$	$1.2/N_1$	$4.2/N_2$
$N_1 = N_2 = 60$	$0.72/N_1$	$2.4/N_2$	$0.9/N_1$	$1.2/N_1$	$4.2/N_2$
$N_1 = N_2 = 600$	$0.72/N_1$	$2.4/N_2$	$0.9/N_1$	$1.2/N_1$	$4.2/N_2$

Table 7.6 The state space, j, j_{eq}, and the blocking states (Example 7.16).

n_1	n_2	n_{1c_1}	n_{1c_2}	n_{2c_1}	j	j_{eq}	B_{T1c_2}	B_{T2c_1}
0	0	0	0	0	0	0		
0	1	0	0	0	7	7001		
0	2	0	0	0	14	14002		
0	3	0	0	0	21	21003		
0	4	0	0	0	28	28004		
0	5	0	0	0	35	35005		
0	5	1	0	0	43	43005		
0	5	1	0	1	47	47010	*	*
0	5	1	1	0	49	49005	*	*
0	6	0	0	0	42	42006		
0	6	0	0	1	46	46011	*	
0	6	0	0	2	50	50016	*	*
0	6	0	1	0	48	48006	*	*
1	0	0	0	0	10	10000		
1	1	0	0	0	17	17001		
1	2	0	0	0	24	24002		
1	3	0	0	0	31	31003		
1	3	1	0	0	39	39003		
1	3	1	0	1	43	43008		
1	3	1	0	2	47	47013	*	*
1	3	1	1	0	45	45003	*	
1	3	1	1	1	49	49008	*	*
1	4	0	0	0	38	38004		
1	4	0	0	1	42	42009		
1	4	0	0	2	46	46014	*	
1	4	0	0	3	50	50019	*	*
1	4	0	1	0	44	44004		
1	4	0	1	1	48	48009	*	*
1	4	0	2	0	50	50004	*	*
2	0	0	0	0	20	20000		
2	1	0	0	0	27	27001		
2	2	0	0	0	34	34002		
2	2	1	0	0	42	42002		
2	2	1	0	1	46	46007	*	
2	2	1	0	2	50	50012	*	*
2	2	1	1	0	48	48002	*	*
2	3	0	0	0	41	41003		
2	3	0	0	1	45	45008	*	
2	3	0	0	2	49	49013	*	*
2	3	0	1	0	47	47003	*	*

(continued)

Table 7.6 (Continued)

n_1	n_2	n_{1c_1}	n_{1c_2}	n_{2c_1}	j	j_{eq}	B_{T1c_2}	B_{T2c_1}
3	0	0	0	0	30	30000		
3	1	0	0	0	37	37001		
3	1	0	1	0	43	43001		
3	1	0	2	0	49	49001	*	*
3	1	0	1	1	47	47006	*	*
3	2	0	0	0	44	44002		
3	2	0	0	1	48	48007	*	*
3	2	0	1	0	50	50002	*	*
4	0	0	0	0	40	40000		
4	0	0	0	1	44	44005		
4	0	0	0	2	48	48010	*	*
4	0	0	1	0	46	46000	*	
4	0	0	1	1	50	50005	*	*

Table 7.7 Analytical and simulation results of the TC probabilities ($N_1 = N_2 = 12$) (Example 7.16).

P	Equivalent stochastic system		Algorithm (Section 7.9.2.3)		Simulation	
	B_{T1c_2} (%)	B_{T2c_1} (%)	B_{T1c_2} (%)	B_{T2c_1} (%)	B_{T1c_2} (%)	B_{T2c_1} (%)
1	1.96	1.07	1.57	0.98	1.57 ± 0.26	0.82 ± 0.07
2	2.78	1.52	2.18	1.37	2.17 ± 0.17	1.17 ± 0.12
3	3.76	2.05	2.92	1.83	2.97 ± 0.21	1.53 ± 0.14
4	4.90	2.66	3.77	2.35	4.07 ± 0.27	1.93 ± 0.22
5	6.19	3.34	4.73	2.91	4.96 ± 0.38	2.36 ± 0.21
6	7.63	4.09	5.78	3.50	5.96 ± 0.31	2.95 ± 0.37

Table 7.8 Analytical and simulation results of the TC probabilities ($N_1 = N_2 = 60$) (Example 7.16).

P	Equivalent stochastic system		Algorithm (Section 7.9.2.3)		Simulation	
	B_{T1c_2} (%)	B_{T2c_1} (%)	B_{T1c_2} (%)	B_{T2c_1} (%)	B_{T1c_2} (%)	B_{T2c_1} (%)
1	4.02	2.23	3.70	2.06	3.00 ± 0.19	1.77 ± 0.08
2	5.89	3.25	5.45	3.00	4.27 ± 0.38	2.67 ± 0.12
3	8.18	4.48	7.61	4.13	6.11 ± 0.40	3.79 ± 0.28
4	10.86	5.92	10.15	5.45	8.06 ± 0.74	5.20 ± 0.27
5	13.87	7.52	13.00	6.93	10.03 ± 0.81	6.83 ± 0.44
6	17.12	9.27	16.12	8.55	12.56 ± 0.76	8.27 ± 0.26

Table 7.9 Analytical and simulation results of the TC probabilities ($N_1 = N_2 = 600$) (Example 7.16).

	Equivalent stochastic system		Algorithm (Section 7.9.2.3)		Simulation	
P	B_{T1c_2} (%)	B_{T2c_1} (%)	B_{T1c_2} (%)	B_{T2c_1} (%)	B_{T1c_2} (%)	B_{T2c_1} (%)
1	4.62	2.57	4.41	2.43	3.74 ± 0.21	2.17 ± 0.09
2	6.82	3.76	6.56	3.58	5.18 ± 0.26	3.40 ± 0.16
3	9.50	5.21	9.20	4.97	7.54 ± 0.43	4.62 ± 0.30
4	12.62	6.88	12.29	6.60	9.72 ± 0.77	6.31 ± 0.32
5	16.09	8.76	15.74	8.43	11.78 ± 0.56	8.40 ± 0.55
6	19.80	10.78	19.45	10.43	14.03 ± 0.86	10.49 ± 0.62

7.10 The Finite Connection Dependent Threshold Model under the BR Policy

7.10.1 The Service System

In the *f-CDTM under the BR policy* (*f-CDTM/BR*), t_k b.u. are reserved to benefit calls of all other service-classes apart from service-class k. The application of the BR policy in the f-CDTM/BR is similar to that of the f-MTM/BR.

7.10.2 The Analytical Model

7.10.2.1 Link Occupancy Distribution
Based on the Roberts method and the algorithm of Section 7.8.2.1 of the f-MTM/BR, the unnormalized values of the link occupancy distribution, $q_{fin}(j)$, in the f-CDTM/BR can be determined as follows:

Algorithm Approximate calculation of $q_{fin}(j)$ in the f-CDTM/BR

Step 1: Define the corresponding infinite loss model CDTM/BR and calculate $q(j)$ via (2.70).

Step 2: Determine the values of $y_k(j)$ and $y_{kc_s}(j)$ $(s = 1, \ldots, S(k))$ in the CDTM/BR based on (2.73) and (2.74), respectively.

Step 3: Modify (7.68) to the following recursive formula, where the $y_k(j)$ and $y_{kc_s}(j)$ have been determined in step 2 from the corresponding infinite model:

$$
q_{fin}(j)=\begin{cases}
1 & \text{if } j = 0 \\
\begin{aligned}
&\frac{1}{j}\sum_{k=1}^{K}(N_k - y_k(j-b_k))\alpha_{k,idle}D_k(j-b_k)\delta_k(j)q_{fin}(j-b_k) + \frac{1}{j}\sum_{k=1}^{K}\sum_{s=1}^{S(k)}(N_k - y_k(j-b_{kc_s})) \\
&-y_{kc_1}(j-b_{kc_1}) - \ldots - y_{kc_{S(k)}}(j-b_{kc_s})\alpha_{kc_s,idle}D_{kc_s}(j-b_{kc_s})\delta_{kc_s}(j)q_{fin}(j-b_{kc_s})
\end{aligned} \\
\qquad\qquad j = 1, \ldots, C \\
0 & \text{otherwise}
\end{cases}
$$

(7.70)

where $D_k(j-b_k)$ and $D_{kc_s}(j-b_{kc_s})$ are determined via (1.65) and (2.58), respectively.

7.10.2.2 TC Probabilities, CBP, Utilization, and Mean Number of In-service Calls

Based on (7.70) and (2.58), we can determine the following performance measures:

- The TC probabilities of service-class k calls with b_k b.u., B_{Tk}, via (6.42).
- The TC probabilities of service-class k calls with $b_{kc_{S(k)}}$, $B_{Tkc_{S(k)}}$, via:

$$B_{Tkc_{S(k)}} = \sum_{j=C-b_{kc_{S(k)}}-t_k+1}^{C} G^{-1} q_{\text{fin}}(j) \tag{7.71}$$

- The CC probabilities of service-class k calls with b_k (without the option of b_{kc_s}), B_k, via (6.42) but for a system with $N_k - 1$ traffic sources.
- The CC probabilities of service-class k calls with with $b_{kc_{S(k)}}$, $B_{kc_{S(k)}}$, via (7.71) but for a system with $N_k - 1$ traffic sources.
- The conditional TC probabilities of service-class k calls with $b_{kc_{S(k)}}$ b.u. given that $j > J_{S(k)-1}$, $B^*_{Tkc_{S(k)}}$, via (7.66), while subtracting the BR parameter t_k from $C - b_{kc_{S(k)}}$.
- The link utilization, U, via (6.36).
- The average number of service-class k calls in the system accepted with b_k b.u., $\bar{n}_k$, via (6.37) where $y_{k,\text{fin}}(j)$ is determined by (7.46).
- The average number of service-class k calls in the system accepted with b_{kc_s} b.u., $\bar{n}_{kc_s}$, via (7.57) where $y_{kc_s,\text{fin}}(j)$ is determined by:

$$y_{kc_s,\text{fin}}(j) = \begin{cases} \dfrac{[N_k - y_k(j-b_{kc_s}) - y_{kc_1}(j-b_{kc_s}) - \ldots - y_{kc_{S(k)}}(j-b_{kc_s})]\alpha_{kc_s,\text{idle}}\delta_{kc_s}(j)q_{\text{fin}}(j-b_{kc_s})}{q_{\text{fin}}(j)} & \text{for } j \leq C - t_k \\ 0 & \text{for } j > C - t_k \end{cases} \tag{7.72}$$

7.11 Applications

Since the finite multirate retry-threshold loss models are a combination of the retry-threshold loss models of Chapter 2 and the EnMLM of Chapter 6, the interested reader may refer to Sections 2.11 and 6.5 for possible applications.

7.12 Further Reading

Similar to the previous section, the interested reader may refer to the corresponding section of Chapter 2 (Section 2.12) and Chapter 6 (Section 6.6). In addition to these sections, interesting extensions of the f-CDTM have been proposed in [7, 8], for WCDMA networks. Compared to [7], in [8], a CAC distinguishes handover traffic from new traffic. More precisely, when the cell load is above a predefined threshold, handover calls are allowed to reduce their bandwidth requirements in order to avoid blocking.

References

1 G. Stamatelos and V. Koukoulidis, Reservation-based bandwidth allocation in a radio ATM network. *IEEE/ACM Transactions on Networking*, 5(3):420–428, June 1997.

2 I. Moscholios, M. Logothetis and P. Nikolaropoulos, Engset multi-rate state-dependent loss models. *Performance Evaluation*, 59(2–3):247–277, February 2005.

3 I. Moscholios and M. Logothetis, Engset multirate state-dependent loss models with QoS guarantee. *International Journal of Communication Systems*, 19(1):67–93, February 2006.

4 I. Moscholios, M. Logothetis and G. Kokkinakis, A simplified blocking probability calculation in the retry loss models for finite sources. *Proceedings of Communication Systems, Networks and Digital Signal Processing – 5th CSNDSP*, Patras, Greece, July 2006.

5 I. Moscholios, M. Logothetis and G. Kokkinakis, On the calculation of blocking probabilities in the multirate state-dependent loss models for finite sources. *Mediterranean Journal of Computers and Networks*, 3(3):100–109, July 2007.

6 J. Kaufman, Blocking with retrials in a completely shared resource environment. *Performance Evaluation*, 15(2):99–113, June 1992.

7 V. Vassilakis, G. Kallos, I. Moscholios and M. Logothetis, Call-level analysis of W-CDMA networks supporting elastic services of finite population. *IEEE ICC 2008*, Beijing, China, May 2008.

8 V. Vassilakis, I. Moscholios, J. Vardakas and M. Logothetis, Handoff modeling in cellular CDMA with finite sources and state-dependent bandwidth requirements. *Proceedings of IEEE CAMAD 2014*, Athens, Greece, December 2014.

8

Finite Multirate Elastic Adaptive Loss Models

In this chapter, the characteristics of the input traffic are the reverse of those in Chapter 7 as far as the bandwidth requirement and allocation are concerned. We consider multirate loss models of quasi-random arriving calls with fixed bandwidth requirements and elastic bandwidth allocation during service. The same traffic characteristics but of random arriving calls are considered in Chapter 3.

8.1 The Elastic Engset Multirate Loss Model

8.1.1 The Service System

In the *elastic EnMLM (E-EnMLM)*, we consider a single link of capacity C b.u. that accommodates elastic calls of K service classes. Calls of each service class k come from a finite source population N_k. The mean arrival rate of service-class k idle sources is $\lambda_{k,\text{fin}} = (N_k - n_k)v_k$, where n_k is the number of in-service calls and v_k is the arrival rate per idle source. The offered traffic-load per idle source of service-class k is $\alpha_{k,\text{idle}} = v_k/\mu_k$ (in erl). Calls of service-class k request b_k b.u. (peak-bandwidth requirement). To introduce bandwidth compression in the model, the occupied link bandwidth j can virtually exceed C up to a limit of T b.u. Then the call admission is identical to the one presented in the case of the E-EMLM (see Section 3.1.1).

Similarly, in terms of the system state-space Ω, the CAC is expressed as in the E-EMLM (see Section 3.1.1). Hence, the TC probabilities of service-class k are determined by the state space $\Omega - \Omega_{\{k\}}$:

$$B_{Tk} = \sum_{\mathbf{n}\in(\Omega-\Omega_{\{k\}})} P(\mathbf{n}) \;\Rightarrow\; B_{Tk} = 1 - \sum_{\mathbf{n}\in\Omega_{\{k\}}} P(\mathbf{n}) \tag{8.1}$$

where $\Omega_{\{k\}} = \{\mathbf{n}\in\Omega : \mathbf{nb} \le T - b_k\}$, $k = 1, ..., K$, $\mathbf{n} = (n_1, ..., n_k, ..., n_K)$ and $\mathbf{b} = (b_1, ..., b_k, ..., b_K)$.

The compression/expansion of bandwidth destroys reversibility in the E-EnMLM and therefore no PFS exists (for $P(\mathbf{n})$), a fact that makes (8.1) inefficient, as Example 8.1 shows.

Example 8.1 Consider a link of $C = 3$ b.u. and $T = 5$ b.u. The link accommodates calls of $K = 2$ service-classes whose calls require $b_1 = 1$ and $b_2 = 2$ b.u., respectively. Let the

Efficient Multirate Teletraffic Loss Models Beyond Erlang, First Edition.
Ioannis D. Moscholios and Michael D. Logothetis.
© 2019 John Wiley & Sons Ltd. Published 2019 by John Wiley & Sons Ltd.
Companion website: www.wiley.com/go/logocode

number of sources be $N_1 = N_2 = 10$, the arrival rate per idle source be $\upsilon_1 = \upsilon_2 = 0.1$ and $\mu_1 = \mu_2 = 1.0$.

(a) Draw the complete state transition diagram of the system and determine the values of j and $r(\mathbf{n})$ for each state $\mathbf{n} = (n_1, n_2)$.
(b) Write the GB equations, and determine the values of $P(\mathbf{n})$ and the TC probabilities of both service-classes.

(a) Figure 8.1 shows the state space Ω that consists of 12 permissible states $\mathbf{n} = (n_1, n_2)$ together with the complete state transition diagram of the system. The values of $r(\mathbf{n})$ are identical to those presented in Table 3.1 for the E-EMLM since the call arrival process does not affect the bandwidth compression mechanism.

(b) Based on Figure 8.1, we obtain the following 12 GB equations:

$(0,0)$: $\quad P(1,0) + P(0,1) - 2P(0,0) = 0$

$(0,1)$: $\quad P(0,0) + P(1,1) + 1.5P(0,2) - 2.9P(0,1) = 0$

$(0,2)$: $\quad 0.6P(1,2) + 0.9P(0,1) - 2.5P(0,2) = 0$

$(1,0)$: $\quad P(0,0) + 2P(2,0) + P(1,1) - 2.9P(1,0) = 0$

$(1,1)$: $\quad P(0,1) + 1.5P(2,1) + 1.2P(1,2) + P(1,0) - 3.8P(1,1) = 0$

$(1,2)$: $\quad 0.9P(1,1) + P(0,2) - 1.8P(1,2) = 0$

$(2,0)$: $\quad 0.9P(1,0) + 3P(3,0) + 0.75P(2,1) - 3.8P(2,0) = 0$

$(2,1)$: $\quad 0.9P(1,1) + 1.8P(3,1) + P(2,0) - 3.05P(2,1) = 0$

$(3,0)$: $\quad 0.8P(2,0) + 3P(4,0) + 0.6P(3,1) - 4.7P(3,0) = 0$

$(3,1)$: $\quad 0.8P(2,1) + P(3,0) - 2.4P(3,1) = 0$

$(4,0)$: $\quad 0.7P(3,0) + 3P(5,0) - 3.6P(4,0) = 0$

$(5,0)$: $\quad 0.6P(4,0) - 3P(5,0) = 0$

The solution of this linear system is:

$P(0,0) = 0.145244 \quad P(0,1) = 0.142633 \quad P(0,2) = 0.079829 \quad P(1,0) = 0.147856$

$P(1,1) = 0.148647 \quad P(1,2) = 0.118673 \quad P(2,0) = 0.067445 \quad P(2,1) = 0.087975$

$P(3,0) = 0.01908 \quad\quad P(3,1) = 0.037275 \quad P(4,0) = 0.004452 \quad P(5,0) = 0.00089$

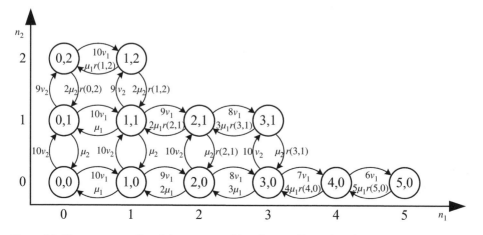

Figure 8.1 The state space Ω and the state transition diagram (Example 8.1).

Based on the values of $P(n_1, n_2)$ and (8.1), we obtain the values of TC probabilities:

$B_{T1} = P(1, 2) + P(3, 1) + P(5, 0) = 0.1568$ (compare with 0.1748 in the E-EMLM)

$B_{T2} = P(0, 2) + P(2, 1) + P(4, 0) + P(1, 2) + P(3, 1) + P(5, 0) = 0.3291$

(compare with 0.3574 in the E-EMLM)

To circumvent the non-reversibility problem in the E-EnMLM, $r(\mathbf{n})$ are replaced by the state-dependent factors per service-class k, $\varphi_k(\mathbf{n})$, which have a similar role to $r(\mathbf{n})$ and lead to a reversible Markov chain [1, 2]. Thus, the compressed bandwidth of a service-class k call, b'_k, becomes $b'_k = \varphi_k(\mathbf{n})b_k$ (which is (3.7)). To ensure reversibility, $\varphi_k(\mathbf{n})$ have the form of (3.8), where $x(\mathbf{n})$ are given by (3.9).

Example 8.2 Consider again Example 8.1 ($C = 3, T = 5, K = 2, b_1 = 1, b_2 = 2$, $N_1 = N_2 = 10, v_1 = v_2 = 0.1, \mu_1 = \mu_2 = 1.0$).

(a) Draw the modified state transition diagram based on $\varphi_k(\mathbf{n})$ and determine the values of $\varphi_k(\mathbf{n})$ for each state $\mathbf{n} = (n_1, n_2)$.
(b) Write the GB equations of the modified state transition diagram, and determine the values of $P(\mathbf{n})$ and the TC probabilities of both service-classes.

(a) Figure 8.2 shows the modified state transition diagram of the system. The values of $\varphi_k(\mathbf{n})$ are identical to those presented in Table 3.2.
(b) Based on Figure 8.2, we obtain the following 12 GB equations:

$(0, 0):$ $P(1, 0) + P(0, 1) - 2P(0, 0) = 0$
$(0, 1):$ $P(0, 0) + P(1, 1) + 1.5P(0, 2) - 2.9P(0, 1) = 0$
$(0, 2):$ $0.75P(1, 2) + 0.9P(0, 1) - 2.5P(0, 2) = 0$
$(1, 0):$ $P(0, 0) + 2P(2, 0) + P(1, 1) - 2.9P(1, 0) = 0$
$(1, 1):$ $P(0, 1) + 1.5P(2, 1) + 1.125P(1, 2) + P(1, 0) - 3.8P(1, 1) = 0$
$(1, 2):$ $0.9P(1, 1) + P(0, 2) - 1.875P(1, 2) = 0$
$(2, 0):$ $0.9P(1, 0) + 3P(3, 0) + 0.75P(2, 1) - 3.8P(2, 0) = 0$
$(2, 1):$ $0.9P(1, 1) + 2P(3, 1) + P(2, 0) - 3.05P(2, 1) = 0$
$(3, 0):$ $0.8P(2, 0) + 3P(4, 0) + 0.5P(3, 1) - 4.7P(3, 0) = 0$
$(3, 1):$ $0.8P(2, 1) + P(3, 0) - 2.5P(3, 1) = 0$
$(4, 0):$ $0.7P(3, 0) + 3P(5, 0) - 3.6P(4, 0) = 0$
$(5, 0):$ $0.6P(4, 0) - 3P(5, 0) = 0$

The solution of this linear system is:

$P(0, 0) = 0.146122$ $P(0, 1) = 0.146122$ $P(0, 2) = 0.087673$ $P(1, 0) = 0.146122$
$P(1, 1) = 0.146122$ $P(1, 2) = 0.116898$ $P(2, 0) = 0.065755$ $P(2, 1) = 0.087673$
$P(3, 0) = 0.017535$ $P(3, 1) = 0.035069$ $P(4, 0) = 0.004091$ $P(5, 0) = 0.000818$

Based on the $P(n_1, n_2)$ and (8.1), we obtain the approximate TC probabilities:

$B_{T1} = P(1, 2) + P(3, 1) + P(5, 0) = 0.1528$ (compare with the exact 0.1568)

$B_{T2} = P(0, 2) + P(2, 1) + P(4, 0) + P(1, 2) + P(3, 1) + P(5, 0) = 0.3322$

(compare with the exact 0.3291)

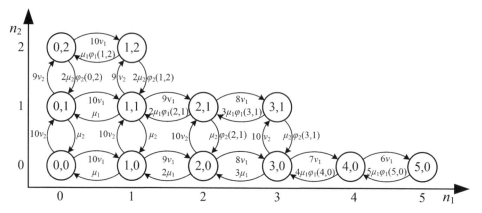

Figure 8.2 The state space Ω and the state transition diagram (Example 8.2).

8.1.2 The Analytical Model

8.1.2.1 Steady State Probabilities

The GB equation (*rate in = rate out*) for state $\mathbf{n} = (n_1, n_2, \ldots, n_k, \ldots, n_K)$ in the E-EnMLM is given by:

$$\sum_{k=1}^{K}(N_k - n_k + 1)v_k\delta_k^-(\mathbf{n})P(\mathbf{n}_k^-) + \sum_{k=1}^{K}(n_k + 1)\mu_k\delta_k^+(\mathbf{n})\varphi_k(\mathbf{n}_k^+)P(\mathbf{n}_k^+) =$$
$$\sum_{k=1}^{K}(N_k - n_k)v_k\delta_k^+(\mathbf{n})P(\mathbf{n}) + \sum_{k=1}^{K}n_k\mu_k\delta_k^-(\mathbf{n})\varphi_k(\mathbf{n})P(\mathbf{n}) \tag{8.2}$$

where $P(\mathbf{n})$, $P(\mathbf{n}_k^-)$, $P(\mathbf{n}_k^+)$ are the probability distributions of the corresponding states $\mathbf{n}, \mathbf{n}_k^-, \mathbf{n}_k^+$, respectively, which are defined as $\mathbf{n}_k^+ = (n_1, \ldots, n_{k-1}, n_k + 1, n_{k+1}, \ldots, n_K)$ and $\mathbf{n}_k^- = (n_1, \ldots, n_{k-1}, n_k - 1, n_{k+1}, \ldots, n_K)$, while:

$$\delta_k^+(\mathbf{n}) = \begin{cases} 1 \text{ if } \mathbf{n}_k^+ \in \Omega \\ 0 \text{ otherwise} \end{cases} \text{ and } \delta_k^-(\mathbf{n}) = \begin{cases} 1 \text{ if } \mathbf{n}_k^- \in \Omega \\ 0 \text{ otherwise} \end{cases}.$$

Assume now the existence of LB between adjacent states. Equations (8.3) and (8.4) are the detailed LB equations of the modified model (which is reversible):

$$(N_k - n_k + 1)v_k\delta_k^-(\mathbf{n})P(\mathbf{n}_k^-) = n_k\mu_k\delta_k^-(\mathbf{n})\varphi_k(\mathbf{n})P(\mathbf{n}) \tag{8.3}$$

$$(N_k - n_k)v_k\delta_k^+(\mathbf{n})P(\mathbf{n}) = (n_k + 1)\mu_k\delta_k^+(\mathbf{n})\varphi_k(\mathbf{n}_k^+)P(\mathbf{n}_k^+) \tag{8.4}$$

for $k = 1, \ldots, K$ and $\mathbf{n} \in \Omega$.

Based on the LB assumption, the probability distribution $P(\mathbf{n})$ has the solution:

$$P(\mathbf{n}) = \frac{x(\mathbf{n})\prod_{k=1}^{K}\binom{N_k}{n_k}a_{k,\text{idle}}^{n_k}}{G} \tag{8.5}$$

where $\alpha_{k,\text{idle}} = v_k/\mu_k$ is the offered traffic-load per idle source of service-class k and G is the normalization constant given by $G \equiv G(\Omega) = \sum_{\mathbf{n}\in\Omega}\left(x(\mathbf{n})\prod_{k=1}^{K}\binom{N_k}{n_k}a_{k,\text{idle}}^{n_k}\right)$.

Note that the probability distribution $P(\mathbf{n})$ does not have a PFS due to the summation of (3.9) needed for the determination of $x(\mathbf{n})$. We now define $q_{\text{fin}}(j)$, as in (6.26).

Consider now two different sets of macro-states: (i) $0 \le j \le C$ and (ii) $C < j \le T$. For the first set, no bandwidth compression takes place and $q_{fin}(j)$ are determined by (6.27) [3]. For the second set, we substitute (3.8) in (8.3) to obtain:

$$(N_k - n_k + 1)a_{k,idle}x(\mathbf{n})P(\mathbf{n}_k^-) = n_k x(\mathbf{n}_k^-)P(\mathbf{n}) \tag{8.6}$$

Multiplying both sides of (8.16) by b_k and summing over k, we have:

$$x(\mathbf{n}) \sum_{k=1}^{K}(N_k - n_k + 1)a_{k,idle}b_k P(\mathbf{n}_k^-) = P(\mathbf{n}) \sum_{k=1}^{K} n_k b_k x(\mathbf{n}_k^-) \tag{8.7}$$

Equation (8.7), due to (3.9) is written as:

$$P(\mathbf{n})C = \sum_{k=1}^{K}(N_k - n_k + 1)a_{k,idle}b_k P(\mathbf{n}_k^-) \tag{8.8}$$

Summing both sides of (8.8) over $\mathbf{\Omega}_j$ and based on (6.26), we have:

$$q_{fin}(j)C = \sum_{k=1}^{K}(N_k - n_k + 1)a_{k,idle}b_k \sum_{\mathbf{n}\in\mathbf{\Omega}_j} P(\mathbf{n}_k^-) \tag{8.9}$$

or

$$q_{fin}(j)C = \sum_{k=1}^{K}(N_k - n_k + 1)a_{k,idle}b_k q_{fin}(j - b_k) \tag{8.10}$$

The combination of (6.27) and (8.10) results in the recursive formula of the E-EnMLM:

$$q_{fin}(j) = \begin{cases} 1 & \text{if } j = 0 \\ \frac{1}{\min(C,j)} \sum_{k=1}^{K}(N_k - n_k + 1)a_{k,idle}b_k q_{fin}(j - b_k) & j = 1, 2, \dots, T \\ 0 & \text{otherwise} \end{cases} \tag{8.11}$$

8.1.2.2 TC Probabilities, CBP, and Utilization
The following performance measures can be determined based on (8.11):

- The TC probabilities of service-class k, B_{Tk}, via:

$$B_{Tk} = \sum_{j=T-b_k+1}^{T} G^{-1} q_{fin}(j) \tag{8.12}$$

  where $G = \sum_{j=0}^{T} q_{fin}(j)$ is the normalization constant.
- The CC probabilities (or CBP) of service-class k, B_k, via (8.12) but for a system with $N_k - 1$ traffic sources.
- The link utilization, U, via:

$$U = G^{-1}\left(\sum_{j=1}^{C} j q_{fin}(j) + \sum_{j=C+1}^{T} C q_{fin}(j)\right) \tag{8.13}$$

The determination of $q_{fin}(j)$ via (8.11) and consequently of all performance measures requires the (unknown) value of n_k (similar to what we have already seen for the proof of (6.27)). To circumvent the complex determination of n_k in each state j via an equivalent stochastic system (as already described in Example 6.5), we adopt an approximate algorithm for the calculation of $q_{fin}(j)$ which is similar to the algorithm of Section 6.2.2.3.

8.1.2.3 An Approximate Algorithm for the Determination of $q_{fin}(j)$

The algorithm comprises the following steps:

Algorithm Approximate calculation of $q_{fin}(j)$ in the E-EnMLM

Step 1: Define the corresponding infinite loss model E-EMLM and calculate $q(j)$ via (3.21).

Step 2: Determine the values of $y_k(j)$ in the E-EMLM, based on (3.25).

Step 3: Modify (8.11) to the following recursive formula, where the values of $y_k(j)$ have been determined in step 2 from the corresponding infinite model:

$$q_{fin}(j) = \begin{cases} 1 & \text{if } j = 0 \\ \frac{1}{\min(C,j)} \sum_{k=1}^{K} (N_k - y_k(j-b_k)) \, \alpha_{k,idle} b_k q_{fin}(j-b_k) & j = 1, \dots, T \\ 0 & \text{otherwise} \end{cases} \qquad (8.14)$$

Step 4: Determine the various performance measures as follows:
- The TC probabilities of service-class k, B_{Tk}, via (8.12).
- The CC probabilities of service-class k, B_k, via (8.12) but for a system with $N_k - 1$ traffic sources.
- The link utilization, U, via (8.13).

Example 8.3 Consider again Example 8.1 ($C = 3, T = 5, K = 2, b_1 = 1, b_2 = 2, N_1 = N_2 = 10, v_1 = v_2 = 0.1, \mu_1 = \mu_2 = 1.0$). Apply the algorithm of Section 8.1.2.3 for the determination of TC probabilities.

Step 1: The corresponding infinite loss model (E-EMLM) has the parameters $C = 3$, $T = 5, K = 2, b_1 = 1, b_2 = 2, \alpha_1 = \alpha_2 = 1$ erl.
Based on (3.21), we have the following normalized values, $Q(j)$:

$Q(0) = Q(1) = 0.1371 \quad Q(2) = 0.2056 \quad Q(3) = 0.1599 \quad Q(4) = 0.1904 \quad Q(5) = 0.17$

Step 2: Based on (3.25), we have for $j = 1, \dots, 5$:

$j = 1 \Rightarrow y_1(1) = 1.0 \quad y_2(1) = 0.0 \qquad\qquad j = 2 \Rightarrow y_1(2) = 0.6667 \quad y_2(2) = 0.6667$
$j = 3 \Rightarrow y_1(3) = 1.2857 \quad y_2(3) = 0.8571 \quad j = 4 \Rightarrow y_1(4) = 1.12 \quad y_2(4) = 1.44$
$j = 5 \Rightarrow y_1(5) = 1.5970 \quad y_2(5) = 1.7015$

Step 3: Based on (8.14), we have the following normalized values of $Q_{fin}(j)$:

$Q_{fin}(0) = 0.14622 \quad Q_{fin}(1) = 0.14622 \quad Q_{fin}(2) = 0.21201$
$Q_{fin}(3) = 0.16344 \quad Q_{fin}(4) = 0.17939 \quad Q_{fin}(5) = 0.15272$

Step 4: The approximate TC probabilities are:

$$B_{T1} = \sum_{j=T-b_1+1}^{T} Q_{\text{fin}}(j) = 0.15272 \text{ (compare with 0.17 in the E-EMLM)}$$

$$B_{T2} = \sum_{j=T-b_2+1}^{T} Q_{\text{fin}}(j) = 0.3321 \text{ (compare with 0.3604 in the E-EMLM)}$$

8.2 The Elastic Engset Multirate Loss Model under the BR Policy

8.2.1 The Service System

We consider again the multiservice system of the E-EnMLM and apply the BR policy (E-EnMLM/BR). A new service-class k call is accepted in the link if, after its acceptance, the occupied link bandwidth is $j \le T - t_k$, where t_k refers to the BR parameter used to benefit calls of other service-classes apart from k (see also the EMLM/BR in Section 1.3.2).

In terms of the system state-space Ω, the CAC is expressed as in the E-EMLM/BR (see Section 3.2.1). Hence, the TC probabilities of service-class k are determined by the state space $\Omega - \Omega_{\{k\}}$:

$$B_{Tk} = \sum_{\mathbf{n} \in (\Omega - \Omega_{\{k\}})} P(\mathbf{n}) \Rightarrow B_{Tk} = 1 - \sum_{\mathbf{n} \in \Omega_{\{k\}}} P(\mathbf{n}) \tag{8.15}$$

where $\Omega_{\{k\}} = \{\mathbf{n} \in \Omega : \mathbf{nb} \le T - b_k - t_k\}$, $k = 1, \dots, K$, $\mathbf{n} = (n_1, \dots, n_k, \dots, n_K)$, and $\mathbf{b} = (b_1, \dots, b_k, \dots, b_K)$.

Example 8.4 Consider again Example 8.1 ($C = 3, T = 5, K = 2, b_1 = 1, b_2 = 2$, $N_1 = N_2 = 10, v_1 = v_2 = 0.1, \mu_1 = \mu_2 = 1.0$). Assume that $t_1 = 1$ and $t_2 = 0$ b.u., so that $b_1 + t_1 = b_2 + t_2$.

(a) Draw the complete state transition diagram of the system and determine the values of j and $r(\mathbf{n})$ for each state $\mathbf{n} = (n_1, n_2)$.
(b) Write the GB equations, and determine the values of $P(\mathbf{n})$ and the TC probabilities of both service-classes.
(c) Draw the modified state transition diagram based on $\varphi_k(\mathbf{n})$ and determine the values of $\varphi_k(\mathbf{n})$ for each state $\mathbf{n} = (n_1, n_2)$.
(d) Write the GB equations of the modified state transition diagram, and determine the values of $P(\mathbf{n})$ and the TC probabilities of both service-classes.

(a) Figure 8.3 shows the state space Ω that consists of 11 permissible states $\mathbf{n} = (n_1, n_2)$ together with the complete state transition diagram of the system. The corresponding values of $r(\mathbf{n})$ and $j = n_1 b_1 + n_2 b_2$ are exactly the same as those presented in Table 3.1 (ignore the last row) for the E-EMLM.

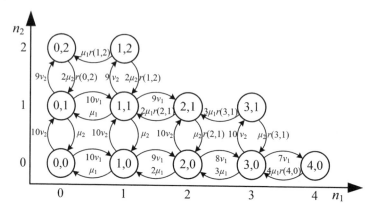

Figure 8.3 The state space Ω and the state transition diagram (Example 8.4).

(b) Based on Figure 8.3, we obtain the following 11 GB equations:

$(0,0)$: $P(1,0) + P(0,1) - 2P(0,0) = 0$

$(0,1)$: $P(0,0) + P(1,1) + 1.5P(0,2) - 2.9P(0,1) = 0$

$(0,2)$: $0.6P(1,2) + 0.9P(0,1) - 1.5P(0,2) = 0$

$(1,0)$: $P(0,0) + 2P(2,0) + P(1,1) - 2.9P(1,0) = 0$

$(1,1)$: $P(0,1) + 1.5P(2,1) + 1.2P(1,2) + P(1,0) - 3.8P(1,1) = 0$

$(1,2)$: $0.9P(1,1) - 1.8P(1,2) = 0$

$(2,0)$: $0.9P(1,0) + 3P(3,0) + 0.75P(2,1) - 3.8P(2,0) = 0$

$(2,1)$: $0.9P(1,1) + 1.8P(3,1) + P(2,0) - 2.25P(2,1) = 0$

$(3,0)$: $0.8P(2,0) + 3P(4,0) + 0.6P(3,1) - 4.7P(3,0) = 0$

$(3,1)$: $P(3,0) - 2.4P(3,1) = 0$

$(4,0)$: $0.7P(3,0) - 3P(4,0) = 0$

The solution of this linear system is:

$P(0,0) = 0.16007 \quad P(0,1) = 0.17231 \quad P(0,2) = 0.13178 \quad P(1,0) = 0.14783$

$P(1,1) = 0.14197 \quad P(1,2) = 0.07098 \quad P(2,0) = 0.06333 \quad P(2,1) = 0.08944$

$P(3,0) = 0.01351 \quad P(3,1) = 0.00563 \quad P(4,0) = 0.00315$

Based on the values of $P(n_1, n_2)$ and (8.15), we obtain the exact values of the TC probabilities:

$B_{T1} = B_{T2} = P(0,2) + P(2,1) + P(4,0) + P(1,2) + P(3,1) = 0.30098$

(compare with 0.3234 in the E-EMLM/BR)

(c) Figure 8.4 shows the modified state transition diagram. The corresponding values of $\varphi_k(\mathbf{n})$ are exactly the same as those presented in Table 3.2 (ignore the last row) for the E-EMLM.

(d) Based on Figure 8.4, we obtain the following 11 GB equations:

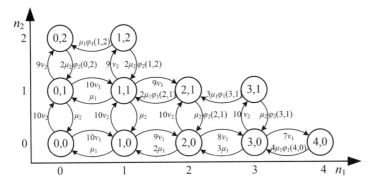

Figure 8.4 The state space Ω and the modified state transition diagram (Example 8.4).

$(0,0)$: $P(1,0) + P(0,1) - 2P(0,0) = 0$

$(0,1)$: $P(0,0) + P(1,1) + 1.5P(0,2) - 2.9P(0,1) = 0$

$(0,2)$: $0.75P(1,2) + 0.9P(0,1) - 1.5P(0,2) = 0$

$(1,0)$: $P(0,0) + 2P(2,0) + P(1,1) - 2.9P(1,0) = 0$

$(1,1)$: $P(0,1) + 1.5P(2,1) + 1.125P(1,2) + P(1,0) - 3.8P(1,1) = 0$

$(1,2)$: $0.9P(1,1) - 1.875P(1,2) = 0$

$(2,0)$: $0.9P(1,0) + 3P(3,0) + 0.75P(2,1) - 3.8P(2,0) = 0$

$(2,1)$: $0.9P(1,1) + 2P(3,1) + P(2,0) - 2.25P(2,1) = 0$

$(3,0)$: $0.8P(2,0) + 3P(4,0) + 0.5P(3,1) - 4.7P(3,0) = 0$

$(3,1)$: $P(3,0) - 2.5P(3,1) = 0$

$(4,0)$: $0.7P(3,0) - 3P(4,0) = 0$

The solution of this linear system is: $P(0,0) = 0.16097$

$P(0,1) = 0.17524$ $P(0,2) = 0.13859$ $P(1,0) = 0.14669$ $P(1,1) = 0.13934$ $P(1,2) = 0.06689$

$P(2,0) = 0.06255$ $P(2,1) = 0.08822$ $P(3,0) = 0.01317$ $P(3,1) = 0.00527$ $P(4,0) = 0.00307$

Based on the values of $P(n_1, n_2)$ and (8.15) we obtain the TC probabilities:

$B_{T1} = B_{T2} = P(0,2) + P(2,1) + P(4,0) + P(1,2) + P(3,1) = 0.30204$

which is quite close to the exact value of 0.30098.

8.2.2 The Analytical Model

8.2.2.1 Link Occupancy Distribution

In the E-EnMLM/BR, the unnormalized values of $q_{fin}(j)$ can be calculated in an approximate way according to the Roberts method (see Section 1.3.2.2). Based on this, we can either find an equivalent stochastic system (requiring enumeration and processing of the state space) or apply the following algorithm (similar to that presented in Section 8.1.2.3):

Algorithm Approximate calculation of $q_{\text{fin}}(j)$ in the E-EnMLM/BR

Step 1: Define the corresponding infinite loss model E-EMLM/BR and calculate $q(j)$ via (3.34a).

Step 2: Determine the values of $y_k(j)$ in the E-EMLM based on (3.25) under the following assumptions, when $j > T - t_k$: (i) $y_k(j) = 0$ and (ii) $\alpha_k b_k q(j - b_k) = 0$.

Step 3: Modify (8.14) to the following recursive formula, where the values of $y_k(j)$ have been determined in step 2 from the E-EMLM:

$$q_{\text{fin}}(j) = \begin{cases} 1 & \text{if } j = 0 \\ \frac{1}{\min(C,j)} \sum_{k=1}^{K} (N_k - y_k(j - b_k)) \, \alpha_{k,\text{idle}} D_k(j - b_k) q_{\text{fin}}(j - b_k) & j = 1, \dots, T \\ 0 & \text{otherwise} \end{cases} \tag{8.16}$$

where $D_k(j - b_k)$ is determined via (3.34b).

Note that if $t_k = 0$ for all k ($k = 1, \dots, K$) then the E-EnMLM results. In addition, if $T = C$, then we have the EnMLM.

8.2.2.2 TC Probabilities, CBP, and Utilization

The following performance measures can be determined based on (8.16):

■ The TC probabilities of service-class k, B_{Tk}, via:

$$B_{Tk} = \sum_{j=T-b_k-t_k+1}^{T} G^{-1} q_{\text{fin}}(j) \tag{8.17}$$

where $G = \sum_{j=0}^{T} q_{\text{fin}}(j)$ is the normalization constant.
■ The CBP (or CC probabilities) of service-class k, B_k, via (8.17) but for a system with $N_k - 1$ traffic sources.
■ The link utilization, U, via (8.13).

Example 8.5 Consider again Example 8.4 ($C = 3, T = 5, K = 2, b_1 = 1, b_2 = 2, t_1 = 1, t_2 = 0, N_1 = N_2 = 10, v_1 = v_2 = 0.1, \mu_1 = \mu_2 = 1.0$). Apply the algorithm of Section 8.2.2.1 for the determination of TC probabilities.

Step 1: The corresponding infinite loss model (E-EMLM/BR) has the parameters $C = 3, T = 5, K = 2, b_1 = 1, b_2 = 2, t_1 = 1, t_2 = 0, \ \alpha_1 = \alpha_2 = 1$ erl. Based on (3.34), we have the following values of $Q(j)$:

$$Q(0) = Q(1) = 0.1463 \quad Q(2) = 0.2195 \quad Q(3) = 0.1707 \quad Q(4) = 0.2033 \quad Q(5) = 0.1138$$

Step 2: Based on (3.25), we have:

$$\begin{aligned} j = 1 &\Rightarrow y_1(1) = 1.0 & y_2(1) = 0.0 \\ j = 2 &\Rightarrow y_1(2) = 0.6667 & y_2(2) = 0.6667 \\ j = 3 &\Rightarrow y_1(3) = 1.2857 & y_2(3) = 0.8571 \\ j = 4 &\Rightarrow y_1(4) = 1.12 & y_2(4) = 1.44 \\ j = 5 &\Rightarrow y_1(5) = 0.0 & y_2(5) = 1.8571 \end{aligned}$$

Step 3: Based on (8.16), we have the $Q_{fin}(j)$, i.e., the normalized values of $q_{fin}(j)$:

$$Q_{fin}(0) = 0.15442 \quad Q_{fin}(1) = 0.15442 \quad Q_{fin}(2) = 0.2239$$
$$Q_{fin}(3) = 0.1726 \quad Q_{fin}(4) = 0.18945 \quad Q_{fin}(5) = 0.10521$$

Step 4: The approximate TC probabilities are:

$$B_{T1} = B_{T2} = \sum_{j=T-b_1-t_1+1}^{T} Q_{fin}(j) = 0.29466 \text{ (compare with 0.3171 in the E-EMLM/BR).}$$

8.3 The Elastic Adaptive Engset Multirate Loss Model

8.3.1 The Service System

In the *elastic adaptive EnMLM (EA-EnMLM)*, we consider a link of capacity C b.u. that accommodates elastic and adaptive calls of K different service-classes. Let K_e and K_a be the set of elastic and adaptive service-classes ($K = K_e + K_a$), respectively. The call arrival process remains quasi-random.

The bandwidth compression/expansion mechanism and the CAC in the EA-EnMLM are the same as those of the E-EnMLM (Section 8.1.1). The only difference is in (3.3), which is applied only on elastic calls (the service time of adaptive calls is not altered).

Example 8.6 Consider again Example 8.1 ($C = 3, T = 5, K = 2, b_1 = 1, b_2 = 2$, $N_1 = N_2 = 10, v_1 = v_2 = 0.1, \mu_1 = \mu_2 = 1.0$) and assume that calls of service-class 2 are adaptive.

(a) Draw the complete state transition diagram of the system and determine the values of j and $r(\mathbf{n})$ for each state $\mathbf{n} = (n_1, n_2)$.
(b) Write the GB equations, and determine the values of $P(\mathbf{n})$ and the exact TC probabilities of both service-classes.

(a) Figure 8.5 shows the state space Ω that consists of 12 permissible states $\mathbf{n} = (n_1, n_2)$ together with the complete state transition diagram of the system. The values of $r(\mathbf{n})$ and $j = n_1 b_1 + n_2 b_2$ are the same as those presented in Table 3.1.
(b) Based on Figure 8.5, we obtain the following 12 GB equations:

$(0, 0):$ $P(1, 0) + P(0, 1) - 2P(0, 0) = 0$

$(0, 1):$ $P(0, 0) + P(1, 1) + 2P(0, 2) - 2.9P(0, 1) = 0$

$(0, 2):$ $0.6P(1, 2) + 0.9P(0, 1) - 3P(0, 2) = 0$

$(1, 0):$ $P(0, 0) + 2P(2, 0) + P(1, 1) - 2.9P(1, 0) = 0$

$(1, 1):$ $P(0, 1) + 1.5P(2, 1) + 2P(1, 2) + P(1, 0) - 3.8P(1, 1) = 0$

$(1, 2):$ $0.9P(1, 1) + P(0, 2) - 2.6P(1, 2) = 0$

$(2, 0):$ $0.9P(1, 0) + 3P(3, 0) + P(2, 1) - 3.8P(2, 0) = 0$

$(2, 1):$ $0.9P(1, 1) + 1.8P(3, 1) + P(2, 0) - 3.3P(2, 1) = 0$

$(3, 0):$ $0.8P(2, 0) + 3P(4, 0) + P(3, 1) - 4.7P(3, 0) = 0$

$(3, 1):$ $0.8P(2, 1) + P(3, 0) - 2.8P(3, 1) = 0$

$(4, 0):$ $0.7P(3, 0) + 3P(5, 0) - 3.6P(4, 0) = 0$

$(5, 0):$ $0.6P(4, 0) - 3P(5, 0) = 0$

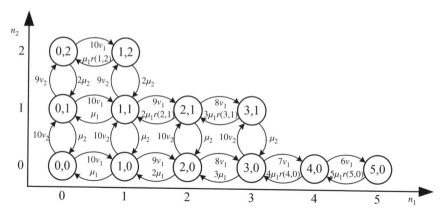

Figure 8.5 The state space Ω and the state transition diagram (Example 8.6).

The solution of this linear system is:

$P(0,0) = 0.159322$ $P(0,1) = 0.159322$ $P(0,2) = 0.071695$ $P(1,0) = 0.159322$
$P(1,1) = 0.159322$ $P(1,2) = 0.081254$ $P(2,0) = 0.071695$ $P(2,1) = 0.083644$
$P(3,0) = 0.019119$ $P(3,1) = 0.029953$ $P(4,0) = 0.004461$ $P(5,0) = 0.000892$

Based on the values of $P(n_1, n_2)$ and (8.1), we determine the exact TC probabilities:

$B_{T1} = P(1,2) + P(3,1) + P(5,0) = 0.11232$ (compare with 0.1568 of the E-EMLM (Example 8.1))
$B_{T2} = P(0,2) + P(2,1) + P(4,0) + P(1,2) + P(3,1) + P(5,0) = 0.26442$
(compare with 0.3291 of the E-EMLM (Example 8.1))

The comparison between the TC probabilities obtained in the EA-EnMLM and the E-EnMLM reveals that the E-EnMLM does not approximate the EA-EnMLM. In addition, the TC probabilities of the EA-EnMLM are lower, a fact that is expected since adaptive calls remain for less time in the system than the corresponding elastic calls.

To circumvent the non-reversibility problem in the EA-EnMLM, $r(\mathbf{n})$ are replaced by the state-dependent factors per service-class k, $\varphi_k(\mathbf{n})$, which have a similar role to $r(\mathbf{n})$ and lead to a reversible Markov chain [4]. Thus the compressed bandwidth of service-class k calls is determined by (3.7), while the values of $\varphi_k(\mathbf{n})$ and $x(\mathbf{n})$ are given by (3.8) and (3.47), respectively.

Example 8.7 Consider again Example 8.6 ($C = 3, T = 5, K = 2, K_e = K_a = 1$, $b_1 = 1, b_2 = 2, N_1 = N_2 = 10, v_1 = v_2 = 0.1, \mu_1 = \mu_2 = 1.0$).

(a) Draw the modified state transition diagram based on $\varphi_k(\mathbf{n})$ and determine the values of $\varphi_k(\mathbf{n})$ for each state $\mathbf{n} = (n_1, n_2)$.
(b) Write the GB equations of the modified state transition diagram, and determine the values of $P(\mathbf{n})$ and the TC probabilities of both service-classes.

(a) The graphical representation of the modified state transition diagram is identical to that of Figure 8.2. The values of $\varphi_k(\mathbf{n})$ are identical to those of Table 3.5 (for the EA-EMLM).

(b) Based on Figure 8.2 and Table 3.5, we obtain the following 12 GB equations:

$(0,0)$: $P(1,0) + P(0,1) - 2P(0,0) = 0$

$(0,1)$: $P(0,0) + P(1,1) + 2P(0,2) - 2.9P(0,1) = 0$

$(0,2)$: $(3/3.4)P(1,2) + 0.9P(0,1) - 3P(0,2) = 0$

$(1,0)$: $P(0,0) + 2P(2,0) + P(1,1) - 2.9P(1,0) = 0$

$(1,1)$: $P(0,1) + (6/3.5)P(2,1) + (6/3.4)P(1,2) + P(1,0) - 3.8P(1,1) = 0$

$(1,2)$: $0.9P(1,1) + P(0,2) - (9/3.4)P(1,2) = 0$

$(2,0)$: $0.9P(1,0) + 3P(3,0) + (3/3.5)P(2,1) - 3.8P(2,0) = 0$

$(2,1)$: $0.9P(1,1) + (10.5/4.7)P(3,1) + P(2,0) - (0.8 + 9/3.5)P(2,1) = 0$

$(3,0)$: $0.8P(2,0) + 3P(4,0) + (3/4.7)P(3,1) - 4.7P(3,0) = 0$

$(3,1)$: $0.8P(2,1) + P(3,0) - (13.5/4.7)P(3,1) = 0$

$(4,0)$: $0.7P(3,0) + 3P(5,0) - 3.6P(4,0) = 0$

$(5,0)$: $0.6P(4,0) - 3P(5,0) = 0$

The solution of this linear system is:

$P(0,0) = 0.157534$ $P(0,1) = 0.150643$ $P(0,2) = 0.06079$ $P(1,0) = 0.164426$

$P(1,1) = 0.157749$ $P(1,2) = 0.077986$ $P(2,0) = 0.080775$ $P(2,1) = 0.085605$

$P(3,0) = 0.024453$ $P(3,1) = 0.033192$ $P(4,0) = 0.005706$ $P(5,0) = 0.001141$

Based on the values of $P(n_1, n_2)$ and (8.1), we determine the TC probabilities:

$B_{T1} = P(1,2) + P(3,1) + P(5,0) = 0.11210$ (compare with the exact 0.11232)

$B_{T2} = P(0,2) + P(2,1) + P(4,0) + P(1,2) + P(3,1) + P(5,0) = 0.27190$

(compare with the exact 0.26442)

8.3.2 The Analytical Model

8.3.2.1 Steady State Probabilities

The GB equation (*rate in = rate out*) for state $\mathbf{n} = (n_1, n_2, \ldots, n_k, \ldots, n_K)$ is given by (8.2) and the LB equations by (8.3) and (8.4).

Similar to the E-EnMLM, we consider two different sets of macro-states: (i) $0 \leq j \leq C$ and (ii) $C < j \leq T$. For the first set, no bandwidth compression takes place and $q_{\text{fin}}(j)$ are determined by (6.27) [4]. For the second set, we substitute (3.8) in (8.3) to have:

$$(N_k - n_k + 1)\alpha_{k,\text{idle}} x(\mathbf{n})P(\mathbf{n}_k^-) = n_k x(\mathbf{n}_k^-)P(\mathbf{n}), \quad k \in K_{\text{e}} \text{ for elastic traffic}$$

$$(8.18a)$$

$$(N_k - n_k + 1)\alpha_{k,\text{idle}} x(\mathbf{n})P(\mathbf{n}_k^-) = n_k x(\mathbf{n}_k^-)P(\mathbf{n}), \quad k \in K_{\text{a}} \text{ for adaptive traffic}$$

$$(8.18b)$$

Multiplying both sides of (8.18a) by b_k and summing over $k \in K_e$, we have:

$$x(\mathbf{n}) \sum_{k=1}^{K_e} (N_k - n_k + 1)\alpha_{k,\text{idle}} b_k P(\mathbf{n}_k^-) = P(\mathbf{n}) \sum_{k=1}^{K_e} n_k b_k x(\mathbf{n}_k^-) \tag{8.19}$$

Similarly, multiplying both sides of (8.18b) by b_k and C/j, and summing over $k \in K_a$, we have:

$$(C/j)\, x(\mathbf{n}) \sum_{k=1}^{K_a} (N_k - n_k + 1)\alpha_{k,\text{idle}} b_k P(\mathbf{n}_k^-) = (C/j)P(\mathbf{n}) \sum_{k=1}^{K_a} n_k b_k x(\mathbf{n}_k^-) \tag{8.20}$$

By adding (8.19) and (8.20), we obtain:

$$P(\mathbf{n}) \left[\sum_{k=1}^{K_e} n_k b_k x(\mathbf{n}_k^-) + \frac{C}{j} \sum_{k=1}^{K_a} n_k b_k x(\mathbf{n}_k^-) \right] =$$
$$x(\mathbf{n}) \left[\sum_{k=1}^{K_e} (N_k - n_k + 1)\alpha_{k,\text{idle}} b_k P(\mathbf{n}_k^-) + \frac{C}{j} \sum_{k=1}^{K_a} (N_k - n_k + 1)\alpha_{k,\text{idle}} b_k P(\mathbf{n}_k^-) \right]$$

$$\tag{8.21}$$

Based on (3.47), (8.21) is written as:

$$P(\mathbf{n}) = \frac{1}{C} \sum_{k=1}^{K_e} (N_k - n_k + 1)\alpha_{k,\text{idle}} b_k P(\mathbf{n}_k^-) + \frac{1}{j} \sum_{k=1}^{K_a} (N_k - n_k + 1)\alpha_{k,\text{idle}} b_k P(\mathbf{n}_k^-)$$

$$\tag{8.22}$$

Summing both sides of (8.22) over $\mathbf{\Omega}_j$ and since $q_{\text{fin}}(j) = \sum_{\mathbf{n} \in \Omega_j} P(\mathbf{n})$, we have:

$$q_{\text{fin}}(j) = \frac{1}{C} \sum_{k=1}^{K_e} (N_k - n_k + 1)\alpha_{k,\text{idle}} b_k q_{\text{fin}}(j - b_k)$$
$$+ \frac{1}{j} \sum_{k=1}^{K_a} (N_k - n_k + 1)\alpha_{k,\text{idle}} b_k q_{\text{fin}}(j - b_k) \tag{8.23}$$

The combination of (6.27) and (8.23) results in the recursive formula of the EA-EnMLM:

$$q_{\text{fin}}(j) = \begin{cases} 1 & \text{if } j = 0 \\ \frac{1}{\min(C,j)} \sum_{k=1}^{K_e} (N_k - n_k + 1)\alpha_{k,\text{idle}} b_k q_{\text{fin}}(j - b_k) + \\ \frac{1}{j} \sum_{k=1}^{K_a} (N_k - n_k + 1)\alpha_{k,\text{idle}} b_k q_{\text{fin}}(j - b_k) & j = 1, 2, \dots, T \\ 0 & \text{otherwise} \end{cases} \tag{8.24}$$

8.3.2.2 TC Probabilities, CBP, and Utilization

The following performance measures can be determined based on (8.24):

- The TC probabilities of service-class k, B_{Tk}, via (8.12).
- The CBP (or CC probabilities) of service-class k, B_k, via (8.12) but for a system with $N_k - 1$ traffic sources.
- The link utilization, U, via (8.13).

The determination of $q_{\text{fin}}(j)$ via (8.24) and consequently of all performance measures requires the complex determination of the (unknown) value of n_k in each state j. To circumvent this, we adopt an approximate algorithm for the calculation of $q_{\text{fin}}(j)$ which is similar to the algorithm of Section 8.1.2.3.

8.3.2.3 An Approximate Algorithm for the Determination of $q_{\text{fin}}(j)$
The algorithm comprises the following steps:

Algorithm Approximate calculation of $q_{\text{fin}}(j)$ in the EA-EnMLM

Step 1: Define the corresponding infinite loss model EA-EMLM and calculate $q(j)$ via (3.57).

Step 2: Determine the values of $y_k(j)$ in the EA-EMLM based on (3.58) and (3.59).

Step 3: Modify (8.24) to the following recursive formula, where the values of $y_k(j)$ have been determined in step 2 from the EA-EMLM [4],[5]:

$$
q_{\text{fin}}(j) = \begin{cases}
1 & \text{if } j = 0 \\
\frac{1}{\min(C,j)} \sum_{k=1}^{K_e} \left(N_k - y_k\left(j-b_k\right) \right) \alpha_{k,\text{idle}} b_k q_{\text{fin}}(j-b_k) + & \\
\frac{1}{j} \sum_{k=1}^{K_a} \left(N_k - y_k\left(j-b_k\right) \right) \alpha_{k,\text{idle}} b_k q_{\text{fin}}(j-b_k) & j = 1, 2, \ldots, T \\
0 & \text{otherwise}
\end{cases}
\tag{8.25}
$$

Step 4: Determine the various performance measures as follows:
- The TC probabilities of service-class k, B_{Tk}, via (8.12).
- The CC probabilities of service-class k, B_k, via (8.12) but for a system with $N_k - 1$ traffic sources.
- The link utilization, U, via (8.13).

Example 8.8 Consider again Example 8.6 ($C = 3, T = 5, K = 2, K_e = K_a = 1$, $b_1 = 1, b_2 = 2, N_1 = N_2 = 10, v_1 = v_2 = 0.1, \mu_1 = \mu_2 = 1.0$). Apply the algorithm of Section 8.3.2.3 for the determination of TC probabilities.

Step 1: The corresponding infinite loss model (EA-EMLM) has the parameters $C = 3$, $T = 5, K = 2, K_e = K_a = 1, b_1 = 1, b_2 = 2, \alpha_1 = \alpha_2 = 1$ erl.
Based on (3.57), we have the following values of $Q(j)$:

$$Q(0) = Q(1) = 0.15033 \quad Q(2) = 0.2255 \quad Q(3) = 0.17539 \quad Q(4) = 0.17121 \quad Q(5) = 0.12723$$

Step 2: Based on (3.58) and (3.59), we have:

$$
\begin{aligned}
j = 1 &\Rightarrow y_1(1) = 1.0 & y_2(1) = 0.0 \\
j = 2 &\Rightarrow y_1(2) = 0.6667 & y_2(2) = 0.6667 \\
j = 3 &\Rightarrow y_1(3) = 1.2857 & y_2(3) = 0.8571 \\
j = 4 &\Rightarrow y_1(4) = 1.2195 & y_2(4) = 1.3902 \\
j = 5 &\Rightarrow y_1(5) = 1.7046 & y_2(5) = 1.6477
\end{aligned}
$$

Step 3: Based on (8.25), we have the following values of $Q_{\text{fin}}(j)$:

$$Q_{\text{fin}}(0) = 0.15947 \quad Q_{\text{fin}}(1) = 0.15947 \quad Q_{\text{fin}}(2) = 0.23122$$
$$Q_{\text{fin}}(3) = 0.17824 \quad Q_{\text{fin}}(4) = 0.15968 \quad Q_{\text{fin}}(5) = 0.11192$$

Step 4: The approximate TC probabilities are:

$$B_{T1} = \sum_{j=T-b_1+1}^{T} Q_{\text{fin}}(j) = 0.11192 \text{ (compare with 0.12723 in the EA-EMLM)}$$
$$B_{T2} = \sum_{j=T-b_2+1}^{T} Q_{\text{fin}}(j) = 0.2716 \text{ (compare with 0.29844 in the EA-EMLM)}$$

8.4 The Elastic Adaptive Engset Multirate Loss Model under the BR Policy

8.4.1 The Service System

We now consider the multiservice system of the *EA-EnMLM under the BR policy* (*EA-EnMLM/BR*). A new service-class k call is accepted in the link if, after its acceptance, the occupied link bandwidth $j \leq T - t_k$, where t_k refers to the BR parameter used to benefit calls of other service-classes apart from k.

In terms of the system state-space Ω, the TC probabilities of service-class k are determined according to (8.15).

Example 8.9 Consider again Example 8.6 ($C = 3, T = 5, K = 2, K_e = K_a = 1,$ $b_1 = 1, b_2 = 2, N_1 = N_2 = 10, v_1 = v_2 = 0.1, \mu_1 = \mu_2 = 1.0$). Assume that $t_1 = 1$ and $t_2 = 0$ b.u., so that $b_1 + t_1 = b_2 + t_2$.

(a) Draw the complete state transition diagram of the system and determine the values of j and $r(\mathbf{n})$ for each state $\mathbf{n} = (n_1, n_2)$.
(b) Write the GB equations, and determine the values of $P(\mathbf{n})$ and the TC probabilities of both service-classes.
(c) Draw the modified state transition diagram based on $\varphi_k(\mathbf{n})$ and determine the values of $\varphi_k(\mathbf{n})$ for each state $\mathbf{n} = (n_1, n_2)$.
(d) Write the GB equations of the modified state transition diagram, and determine the values of $P(\mathbf{n})$ and the TC probabilities of both service-classes.

(a) Figure 8.6 shows the state space Ω that consists of 11 permissible states $\mathbf{n} = (n_1, n_2)$ together with the complete state transition diagram of the system. The corresponding values of $r(\mathbf{n})$ and $j = n_1 b_1 + n_2 b_2$ are exactly the same as those presented in Table 3.1 (ignore the last row).

(b) Based on Figure 8.6, we obtain the following 11 GB equations:

$(0,0):\quad P(1,0) + P(0,1) - 2P(0,0) = 0$

$(0,1):\quad P(0,0) + P(1,1) + 2P(0,2) - 2.9P(0,1) = 0$

$(0,2):\quad 0.6P(1,2) + 0.9P(0,1) - 2P(0,2) = 0$

$(1,0):\quad P(0,0) + 2P(2,0) + P(1,1) - 2.9P(1,0) = 0$

$(1,1):\quad P(0,1) + 1.5P(2,1) + 2P(1,2) + P(1,0) - 3.8P(1,1) = 0$

$(1,2):\quad 0.9P(1,1) - 2.6P(1,2) = 0$

$(2,0):\quad 0.9P(1,0) + 3P(3,0) + P(2,1) - 3.8P(2,0) = 0$

$(2,1):\quad 0.9P(1,1) + 1.8P(3,1) + P(2,0) - 2.5P(2,1) = 0$

$(3,0):\quad 0.8P(2,0) + 3P(4,0) + P(3,1) - 4.7P(3,0) = 0$

$(3,1):\quad P(3,0) - 2.8P(3,1) = 0$

$(4,0):\quad 0.7P(3,0) - 3P(4,0) = 0$

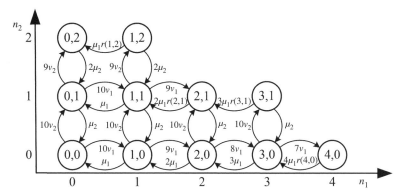

Figure 8.6 The state space Ω and the state transition diagram (Example 8.9).

The solution of this linear system is:

$P(0,0) = 0.169809$ $P(0,1) = 0.176846$ $P(0,2) = 0.095393$ $P(1,0) = 0.162771$

$P(1,1) = 0.152261$ $P(1,2) = 0.052706$ $P(2,0) = 0.074983$ $P(2,1) = 0.089041$

$P(3,0) = 0.016467$ $P(3,1) = 0.005881$ $P(4,0) = 0.003842$

Then based on the values of $P(n_1, n_2)$ and (8.15), we obtain the exact values of the TC probabilities:

$B_{T1} = B_{T2} = P(0,2) + P(2,1) + P(4,0) + P(1,2) + P(3,1) = 0.24686$

(compare with 0.2674 in the EA-EMLM/BR)

(c) The graphical representation of the modified state transition diagram is identical to that of Figure 8.4. The corresponding values of $\varphi_k(\mathbf{n})$ are exactly the same as those presented in Table 3.5 (ignore the last row).

(d) Based on Figure 8.4 and Table 3.5, we obtain the following 11 GB equations:

$(0,0):$ $P(1,0) + P(0,1) - 2P(0,0) = 0$

$(0,1):$ $P(0,0) + P(1,1) + 2P(0,2) - 2.9P(0,1) = 0$

$(0,2):$ $(3/3.4)P(1,2) + 0.9P(0,1) - 2P(0,2) = 0$

$(1,0):$ $P(0,0) + 2P(2,0) + P(1,1) - 2.9P(1,0) = 0$

$(1,1):$ $P(0,1) + (6/3.5)P(2,1) + (6/3.4)P(1,2) + P(1,0) - 3.8P(1,1) = 0$

$(1,2):$ $0.9P(1,1) - (9/3.4)P(1,2) = 0$

$(2,0):$ $0.9P(1,0) + 3P(3,0) + (3/3.5)P(2,1) - 3.8P(2,0) = 0$

$(2,1):$ $0.9P(1,1) + (10.5/4.7)P(3,1) + P(2,0) - (9/3.5)P(2,1) = 0$

$(3,0):$ $0.8P(2,0) + 3P(4,0) + (3/4.7)P(3,1) - 4.7P(3,0) = 0$

$(3,1):$ $P(3,0) - (13.5/4.7)P(3,1) = 0$

$(4,0):$ $0.7P(3,0) - 3P(4,0) = 0$

The solution of this linear system is: $P(0,0) = 0.171718$

$P(0,1) = 0.184889$ $P(0,2) = 0.106053$ $P(1,0) = 0.158546$ $P(1,1) = 0.152355$ $P(1,2) = 0.051801$

$P(2,0) = 0.067855$ $P(2,1) = 0.084059$ $P(3,0) = 0.014369$ $P(3,1) = 0.005003$ $P(4,0) = 0.003353$

Based on the $P(n_1, n_2)$ and (8.15), we obtain the values of the TC probabilities:

$B_{T1} = B_{T2} = P(0, 2) + P(2, 1) + P(4, 0) + P(1, 2) + P(3, 1) = 0.25027$

8.4.2 The Analytical Model

8.4.2.1 Link Occupancy Distribution

In the EA-EnMLM/BR, the unnormalized values of $q_{fin}(j)$ can be calculated in an approximate way according to the Roberts method. Based on this method, we can apply an algorithm similar to that presented in Section 8.3.2.3, which is described by the following steps:

Algorithm Approximate calculation of $q_{fin}(j)$ in the EA-EMLM/BR

Step 1: Define the corresponding infinite loss model E-EMLM and calculate $q(j)$ via (3.60a).

Step 2: Determine the values of $y_k(j)$ in the EA-EMLM/BR based on (3.58) and (3.59) under the following assumptions: (i) $y_k(j) = 0$ when $j > T - t_k$ and (ii) $\alpha_i b_i q(j - b_i) = 0$ when $j > T - t_i$.

Step 3: Modify (8.25) to the following recursive formula, where the values of $y_k(j)$ have been determined in step 2 from the EA-EMLM/BR:

$$q_{fin}(j) = \begin{cases} 1 & \text{if } j = 0 \\ \dfrac{1}{\min(C,j)} \sum\limits_{k=1}^{K_e} \left(N_k - y_k\left(j - b_k\right)\right) \alpha_{k,\text{idle}} D_k(j - b_k) q_{fin}(j - b_k) + \\ \dfrac{1}{j} \sum\limits_{k=1}^{K_a} (N_k - y_k\left(j - b_k\right)) \alpha_{k,\text{idle}} D_k(j - b_k) q_{fin}(j - b_k) & j = 1, 2, \ldots, T \\ 0 & \text{otherwise} \end{cases}$$

(8.26)

where $D_k\left(j - b_k\right)$ is determined via (3.34b).

8.4.2.2 TC Probabilities, CBP, and Utilization

The following performance measures can be determined based on (8.26):

- The TC probabilities of service-class k, B_{Tk}, via (8.17).
- The CBP (or CC probabilities) of service-class k, B_k, via (8.17) but for a system with $N_k - 1$ traffic sources.
- The link utilization, U, via (8.13).

Example 8.10 Consider again Example 8.9 ($C = 3, T = 5, K = 2, K_e = K_a = 1$, $b_1 = 1, b_2 = 2, t_1 = 1, t_2 = 0, N_1 = N_2 = 10, v_1 = v_2 = 0.1, \mu_1 = \mu_2 = 1.0$). Apply the algorithm of Section 8.4.2.1 for the determination of TC probabilities.

Step 1: The corresponding infinite loss model (EA-EMLM/BR) has the parameters $C = 3, T = 5, K = 2, K_e = 1, K_a = 1, b_1 = 1, b_2 = 2, t_1 = 1, t_2 = 0, \alpha_1 = \alpha_2 = 1$ erl. Based on (3.60) we have the following values of $Q(j)$:

$$Q(0) = Q(1) = 0.1594 \quad Q(2) = 0.2392 \quad Q(3) = 0.1860 \quad Q(4) = 0.1816 \quad Q(5) = 0.0744$$

Step 2: Based on (3.58) and (3.59), we have:

$$j = 1 \Rightarrow \quad y_1(1) = 1.0 \qquad y_2(1) = 0.0$$
$$j = 2 \Rightarrow \quad y_1(2) = 0.6667 \quad y_2(2) = 0.6667$$
$$j = 3 \Rightarrow \quad y_1(3) = 1.2857 \quad y_2(3) = 0.8571$$
$$j = 4 \Rightarrow \quad y_1(4) = 1.2195 \quad y_2(4) = 1.3902$$
$$j = 5 \Rightarrow \quad y_1(5) = 0.0 \qquad y_2(5) = 1.8571$$

Step 3: Based on (8.26), we have the following values of $Q_{fin}(j)$:

$$Q_{fin}(0) = 0.16728 \quad Q_{fin}(1) = 0.16728 \quad Q_{fin}(2) = 0.24256$$
$$Q_{fin}(3) = 0.18698 \quad Q_{fin}(4) = 0.16751 \quad Q_{fin}(5) = 0.06838$$

Step 4: The approximate TC probabilities are:

$$B_{T1} = B_{T2} = \sum_{j=T-b_1-t_1+1}^{T} Q_{fin}(j) = 0.23589 \text{ (compare with 0.256 in the EA-EMLM/BR)}$$

Example 8.11 Consider a link of capacity $C = 90$ b.u. that accommodates calls of three service-classes. The first two service-classes are elastic, while the third service-class is adaptive. The traffic characteristics of each service-class of the EA-EnMLM are:

Service-class 1: $N_1 = 200 \quad v_1 = 0.10 \quad b_1 = 1$ b.u.
Service-class 2: $N_2 = 200 \quad v_2 = 0.04 \quad b_2 = 4$ b.u.
Service-class 3: $N_3 = 200 \quad v_3 = 0.01 \quad b_3 = 6$ b.u.

In the case of the EA-EMLM, the corresponding Poisson traffic loads are:

$$\alpha_1 = 20 \text{ erl}, \quad \alpha_2 = 8 \text{ erl}, \text{ and } \alpha_3 = 2 \text{ erl}.$$

Consider also two values of T: (i) $T = 90$ b.u. and (ii) $T = 100$ b.u.

In the case of the EA-EnMLM/BR model, let $t_1 = 5$, $t_2 = 2$ and $t_3 = 0$ in order to achieve TC probabilities equalization between calls of all service-classes. Compare the TC probabilities of all service-classes when v_1 and v_2 increase in steps of 0.01 and 0.005 erl, respectively, while v_3 remains constant, from $(v_1, v_2, v_3) = (0.10, 0.04, 0.01)$ up to $(v_1, v_2, v_3) = (0.15, 0.065, 0.01)$. In the case of the EA-EMLM the last corresponding Poisson traffic loads are $(\alpha_1, \alpha_2, \alpha_3) = (30, 13, 2)$, respectively. Also provide simulation results for the EA-EnMLM and the EA-EnMLM/ BR.

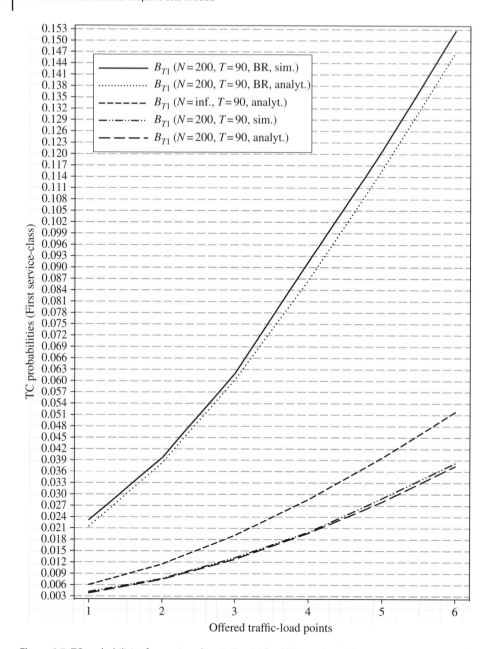

Figure 8.7 TC probabilities for service-class 1 ($T = 90$ b.u.) (Example 8.11).

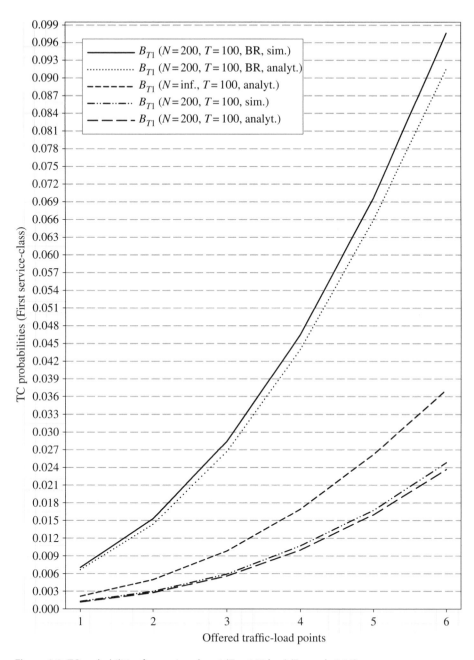

Figure 8.8 TC probabilities for service-class 1 ($T = 100$ b.u.) (Example 8.11).

Figures 8.7–8.8 present the analytical and the simulation TC probabilities of service-class 1 for $T = 90$ and $T = 100$ b.u., respectively. To better compare the corresponding TC probabilities results (while having numerical values), we present in Tables 8.1 and 8.2, only for the first and last point, an excerpt of the results of Figures 8.7 and 8.8, respectively. Similarly, in Figures 8.9–8.10 and 8.11–8.12, we present the corresponding results for service-classes 2 and 3. In the legend of all figures, the term $N = $ inf. refers to the EA-EMLM. Similarly, the term BR in all figures refers to the EA-EnMLM/BR. Simulation results are based on SIMSCRIPT III and are mean values of six runs (no reliability ranges are shown). All figures show that:

(i) Analytical and simulation results are very close to each other.
(ii) The application of the compression/expansion mechanism reduces TC probabilities compared to those obtained when $C = T = 90$ b.u. (compare, e.g., Figures 8.7–8.8, Figures 8.9–8.10, and Figures 8.11–8.12).
(iii) The co-existence of the BR policy and the compression/expansion mechanism reduces TC probabilities compared to those obtained when $C = T = 90$ b.u.
(iv) The TC probabilities obtained by the EA-EnMLM/BR and the EA-EnMLM show that the BR policy favors calls of service-class 3, as expected, and
(v) The results obtained by the EA-EMLM fail to approximate the corresponding results obtained by the EA-EnMLM.

Table 8.1 Excerpt of the results of Figure 8.7, when $T = 90$ (Example 8.11).

(v_1, v_2, v_3)	B_{T1} – sim. ($N = 200$, BR)	B_{T1} – analyt. ($N = 200$, BR)	B_{T1} – analyt. ($N = $ inf.)	B_{T1} – sim. ($N = 200$)	B_{T1} – analyt. ($N = 200$)
$(0.10, 0.04, 0.01)$	0.02320	0.02153	0.00604	0.00420	0.00385
$(0.15, 0.065, 0.01)$	0.15260	0.14692	0.05178	0.03822	0.03743

Table 8.2 Excerpt of the results of Figure 8.8, when $T = 100$ (Example 8.11).

(v_1, v_2, v_3)	B_{T1} – sim. ($N = 200$, BR)	B_{T1} – analyt. ($N = 200$, BR)	B_{T1} – analyt. ($N = $ inf.)	B_{T1} – sim. ($N = 200$)	B_{T1} – analyt. ($N = 200$)
$(0.10, 0.04, 0.01)$	0.00704	0.00668	0.00215	0.00125	0.00117
$(0.15, 0.065, 0.01)$	0.09760	0.09151	0.03716	0.02480	0.02367

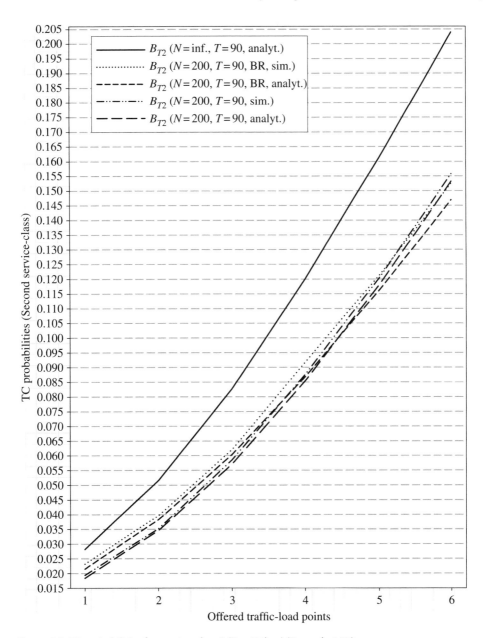

Figure 8.9 TC probabilities for service-class 2 ($T = 90$ b.u.) (Example 8.11).

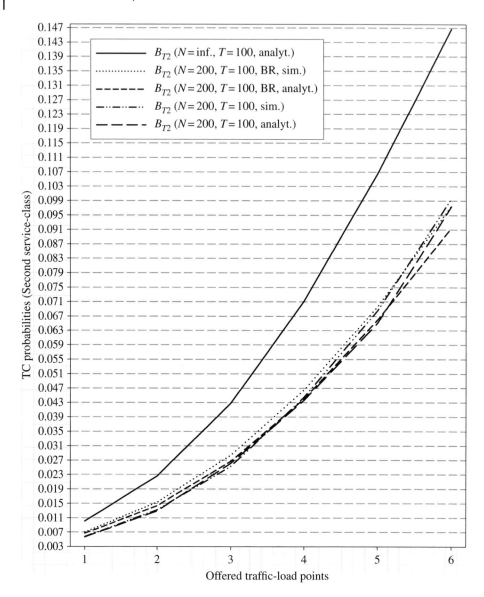

Figure 8.10 TC probabilities for service-class 2 ($T = 100$ b.u.) (Example 8.11).

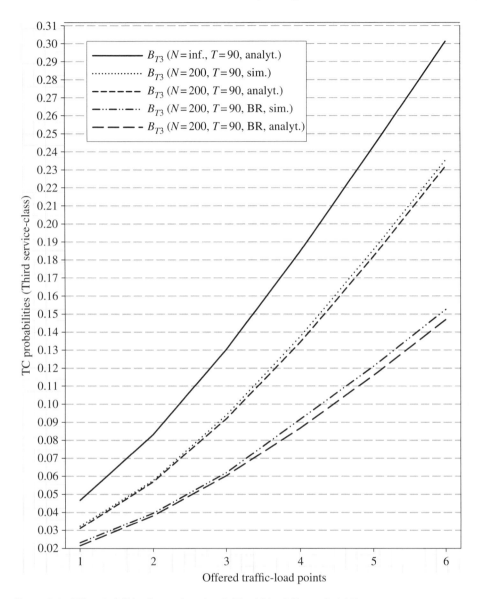

Figure 8.11 TC probabilities for service-class 3 ($T = 90$ b.u.) (Example 8.11).

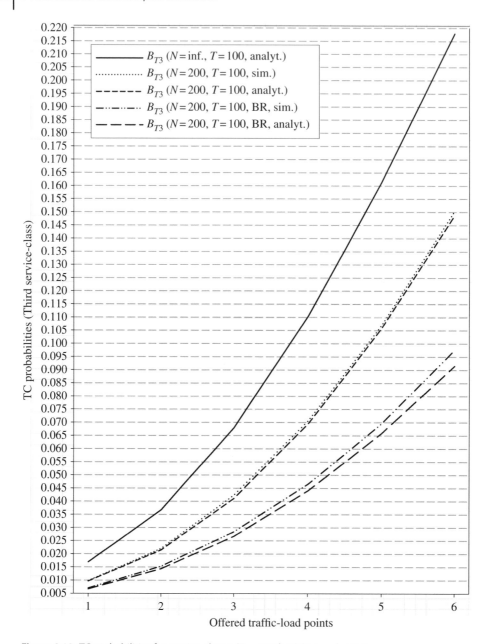

Figure 8.12 TC probabilities for service-class 3 ($T = 100$ b.u.) (Example 8.11).

8.5 Applications

Since the finite multirate elastic adaptive loss models are a combination of the loss models of Chapter 3 and the EnMLM of Chapter 6, the interested reader may refer to Sections 3.7 and 6.5 for possible applications.

In what follows, we continue the discussion started in Section 3.7 by considering the applicability of the models under SDN technology with the advanced 5G features of Cloud-RAN (C-RAN) and the self-organizing network (SON). The latter enables more autonomous and automated cellular network planning, deployment, and optimization [6]. The considered reference architecture which is appropriate for the applicability of the models is presented in Figure 8.13.

This is in line with the C-RAN architecture, although it can also support a more distributed, mobile edge computing (MEC)-like functionality, by incorporating, e.g., the SON features. At the RAN level, the architecture includes an SDN controller (SDN-C) and a virtual machine monitor (VMM) to enable NFV. Three main parts are distinguished: a pool of remote radio heads (RRHs), a pool of baseband units (BBUs), and the EPC. The RRHs are connected to the BBUs via the common public radio interface (CPRI) with a high-capacity fronthaul. The BBUs form a centralized pool of data center resources (denoted as C-BBU). The C-BBU is connected to the EPC via the backhaul connection. To benefit from NFV, we consider virtualized BBU resources (V-BBU) where the BBU functionality and services have been abstracted from the underlying infrastructure and virtualized in the form of VNFs [7]. To realize the virtualization, the VMM manages the execution of BBUs. Finally, the SDN-C is responsible for routing decisions and configuring the packet forwarding elements [8]. Among the BBU functions that could be virtualized in the form of a VNF, we focus on the RRM, which is responsible for CAC and RRA. Various bandwidth/resource sharing policies such as the CS, the BR or the TH could be implemented at the RRM level and enable sharing of V-BBU resources among the RRHs [9]. An analytical framework for the case where all RRHs in the C-RAN form a single cluster can be found in [10]. The analysis for the multi-cluster case is similar and is proposed in [11]. In both [10] and [11], the C-RAN accommodates Poisson arriving calls of a single

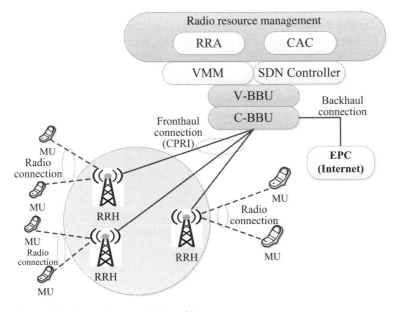

Figure 8.13 The reference C-RAN architecture.

service-class under the CS policy. Guidelines for the extension of the models of [10] and [11] in the case of multiple service-classes are provided in [9]. These guidelines could be the springboard for the analysis of elastic adaptive service-classes of random or quasi-random input under the assumption that each RRH has C subcarriers which can be virtually exceeded up to T subcarriers. The latter is essential in order to include the compression/expansion mechanism for elastic adaptive calls.

We continue with the use of SON technology for the implementation of bandwidth/resource sharing policies (and consequently of the multirate loss models). As an implementation example consider a virtualized RRM function in the C-RAN of Figure 8.13. Traditionally, SON functions refer to self-planning, self-optimization, and self-healing. Implementing the RRM function as a SON function would mainly target the self-optimization objective, although this could also greatly facilitate the self-planning objective. In particular, the goal of self-optimization is as follows. During the cellular network operation, self-optimization intends to improve the network performance or keep it at an acceptable level. The optimization could be performed in terms of QoS, coverage, and/or capacity improvements and is achieved by intelligently tuning various network settings of the BS as well as of the RRM function (e.g., CAC thresholds and RRA parameters). In the literature, the following architectural approaches for implementing the SON functions have been proposed [6]:

(a) Centralized SON (cSON): the SON functions are executed at the network management system (NMS) level or at the element management system (EMS) level. This will be particularly suitable for highly centralized C-RAN solutions.
(b) Distributed SON (dSON): the SON functions are executed at the BS level. They can be implemented either within a BS or in a distributed manner among cooperating BSs. This is beneficial for scenarios that require pushing the network intelligence closer to MUs.
(c) Hybrid SON (hSON): a combination of cSON and dSON concepts (as shown in Figure 8.14). According to this approach, some SON functionality is distributed and executed at the BS level, whereas other SON functionality is centralized at the NMS or EMS level.

Policies such as the CS, BR or the TH (described in this book), although they can be used under all three approaches, may have most benefit under the hSON. Focusing on SON's self-optimization function, we consider the optimization of CAC. The CAC function (part of the dSON) admits or rejects a call, while the cSON function performs the selection of the optimization parameters for the CAC algorithm. These parameters

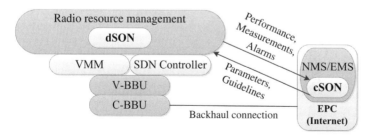

Figure 8.14 Enabling a hybrid SON.

are, for example, the BR parameters. In fact, the BR parameters can be used not only for CAC, but also for determining the allocated bandwidth to calls of each service-class. When the cSON selects the CAC optimization parameters, it considers the overall resource utilization in the cell, the QoS requirements of already accepted calls, and the requirements of the new call. According to the selected bandwidth/resource sharing policy (e.g., the BR policy), its corresponding parameters (e.g., the BR parameters) are sent from the cSON to the dSON/RRM. The cSON sends an updated set of parameters if any changes in the performance guarantees are required (e.g., different acceptable levels of CBP). In the simplified case (e.g., when operating under tight resource or energy constraints) only the current values of the parameters are sent to the dSON/RRM. In particular, the cSON determines the configuration parameters based on a number of objectives (e.g., acceptable CBP). The dSON at the RAN receives the configuration parameters and acts accordingly (e.g., rejects connection requests that do not conform to the specified parameters). If the measurements reported from the dSON to the cSON violate the objectives (e.g., the CBP for a particular service is too high), the cSON will re-calculate and send updated configuration parameters to the dSON. This approach can result in a more autonomous and automated cellular network functionality and enables simpler and faster decision-making and operation.

8.6 Further Reading

Similar to the previous section, the interested reader may refer to the corresponding sections of Chapter 3 (Section 3.8) and Chapter 6 (Section 6.6) in order to study possible extensions of these models.

References

1 V. Koukoulidis, A Characterization of Reversible Markov Processes with Applications to Shared-Resource Environments, PhD thesis, Concordia University, Montreal, Canada, April 1993.

2 V. Iversen, Reversible fair scheduling: The teletraffic theory revisited. *Proceedings of the 20th International Teletraffic Congress, LNCS 4516*, pp. 1135–1148, Ottawa, Canada, June 2007.

3 G. Stamatelos and J. Hayes, Admission control techniques with application to broadband networks. *Computer Communications*, 17(9):663–673, September 1994.

4 I. Moscholios, J. Vardakas, M. Logothetis and M. Koukias, A quasi-random multirate loss model supporting elastic and adaptive traffic. *Proceedings of the 4th International Conference on Emerging Network Intelligence, EMERGING 2012*, Barcelona, Spain, September 2012.

5 I. Moscholios, J. Vardakas, M. Logothetis and M. Koukias, A quasi-random multirate loss model supporting elastic and adaptive traffic under the bandwidth reservation policy. *International Journal on Advances in Networks and Services*, 6(3&4):163–174, December 2013.

6 Self-Organizing Networks (SON); Concepts and Requirements (Release 12), document 3GPP 32.500 v12.1.0, September 2014.

7 Network Function Virtualisation (NFV); Management and Orchestration, document ETSI GS NFV-MAN 001 (V1.1.1), December 2014.

8 T. Chen, M. Matinmikko, X. Chen, X. Zhou, and P. Ahokangas, Software defined mobile networks: Concept, survey, and research directions. *IEEE Communications Magazine*, 53(11):126–133, November 2015.

9 I. Moscholios, V. Vassilakis, M. Logothetis and A. Boucouvalas, State-dependent bandwidth sharing policies for wireless multirate loss networks. *IEEE Transactions on Wireless Communications*, 16(8):5481–5497, August 2017.

10 J. Liu, S. Zhou, J. Gong, Z. Niu, and S. Xu, On the statistical multiplexing gain of virtual base station pools. *Proceedings of IEEE Globecom*, Austin, TX, USA, December 2014

11 J. Liu, S. Zhou, J. Gong, Z. Niu, and S. Xu, Statistical multiplexing gain analysis of heterogeneous virtual base station pools in cloud radio access networks. *IEEE Transactions on Wireless Communications*, 15(8):5681–5694, August 2016.

9

Finite ON–OFF Multirate Loss Models

In this chapter we consider ON–OFF multirate loss models of quasi-random arriving calls with fixed bandwidth requirements. In-service calls do not constantly keep their assigned bandwidth but alternate between transmission periods (ON) and idle periods (OFF). As we discussed in Chapter 5, ON–OFF loss models can be used for the analysis of the call-level behavior of bursty traffic. The finite ON–OFF multirate loss models are based on the EnMLM (see Chapter 6); their recurrent form facilitates their computer implementation.

9.1 The Finite ON–OFF Multirate Loss Model

9.1.1 The Service System

In the *finite ON–OFF multirate loss model (f-ON–OFF)*, we consider a link of capacity C b.u. that accommodates K service-classes of ON–OFF-type calls. Calls of a service-class k ($k = 1, \ldots, K$) come from a finite source population N_k. The mean arrival rate of service-class k idle sources is $\lambda_{k,\text{fin}} = (N_k - n_k^1 - n_k^2)v_k$, where n_k^i is the number of in-service sources of service-class k in state i ($i = 1 \Rightarrow$ state ON, $i = 2 \Rightarrow$ state OFF) and v_k is the arrival rate per idle source. A call of service-class k requires b_k b.u. and competes for the available bandwidth of the system under the CS policy. If the b_k b.u. are available then the call enters the system in state ON, otherwise the call is blocked and lost, and the occupied link bandwidth is characterized as real. The capacity C, named real (real link), corresponds to state ON.

At the end of an ON-period a call of service-class k releases the b_k b.u. and may begin an OFF-period with probability σ_k, or depart from the system with probability $1 - \sigma_k$. While the call is in state OFF, it seizes fictitious b_k b.u. of a fictitious link of capacity C^*. The fictitious capacity C^* corresponds to state OFF. The call holding time of a service-class k call in state ON or OFF is exponentially distributed with mean μ_{ik}^{-1}.

At the end of an OFF-period the call returns to state ON with probability 1 (i.e., the call cannot leave the system from state OFF), while re-requesting b_k b.u. When $C = C^*$, b_k b.u. are always available for that call in state ON, i.e., no blocking occurs while returning to state ON. When $C < C^*$, and there is available bandwidth in the link, i.e., if $j_1 + b_k \leq C$ (where j_1 is the occupied real link bandwidth), the call returns to state ON and a new burst begins; otherwise, burst blocking occurs and the call remains in state OFF for

Efficient Multirate Teletraffic Loss Models Beyond Erlang, First Edition.
Ioannis D. Moscholios and Michael D. Logothetis.
© 2019 John Wiley & Sons Ltd. Published 2019 by John Wiley & Sons Ltd.
Companion website: www.wiley.com/go/logocode

another period. A new service-class k call is accepted in the system with b_k b.u. if it meets the constraints of (5.1) and (5.2).

Based on (5.1) and (5.2), the state space $\mathbf{\Omega}$ of all possible states $\mathbf{j} = (j_1, j_2)$ (where j_2 is the occupied bandwidth of the fictitious link) is given by (5.3). In terms of $\mathbf{\Omega}$, the CAC is identical to that of the ON–OFF multirate loss model (see Section 5.1.1).

9.1.2 The Analytical Model

9.1.2.1 Steady State Probabilities

To describe the analytical model in the steady state we present the following notations [1]:

$\mathbf{n}^i = (n_1^i, \ldots, n_k^i, \ldots, n_K^i)$: the vector of the number of in-service service-class k calls in state i ($i = 1 \Rightarrow$ state ON, $i = 2 \Rightarrow$ state OFF)

$\mathbf{n} = (\mathbf{n}^1, \mathbf{n}^2)$, $\mathbf{n}_{k+}^i = (n_1^i, \ldots, n_k^i + 1, \ldots, n_K^i)$, $\mathbf{n}_{k-}^i = (n_1^i, \ldots, n_k^i - 1, \ldots, n_K^i)$,
$\mathbf{n}_{k+}^1 = (\mathbf{n}_{k+}^1, \mathbf{n}^2)$, $\mathbf{n}_{k+}^2 = (\mathbf{n}^1, \mathbf{n}_{k+}^2)$, $\mathbf{n}_{k-}^1 = (\mathbf{n}_{k-}^1, \mathbf{n}^2)$, $\mathbf{n}_{k-}^2 = (\mathbf{n}^1, \mathbf{n}_{k-}^2)$

$\mathbf{n}_{k+-} = (\mathbf{n}_{k+}^1, \mathbf{n}_{k-}^2)$: a vector that shows a service-class k call transition from state OFF to ON

$\mathbf{n}_{k-+} = (\mathbf{n}_{k-}^1, \mathbf{n}_{k+}^2)$: a vector that shows a service-class k call transition from state ON to OFF

$p_{ik,\text{idle}} \equiv$ the offered traffic-load to state i from service-class k; it is determined by:

$$p_{ik,\text{idle}} = \frac{e_{ik,\text{idle}}}{\mu_{ik}} = \begin{cases} \frac{v_k}{(1-\sigma_k)\mu_{1k}} & \text{for } i = 1 \\ \frac{v_k \sigma_k}{(1-\sigma_k)\mu_{2k}} & \text{for } i = 2 \end{cases} \tag{9.1}$$

where $e_{ik,\text{idle}}$ is the total arrival rate of service-class k calls to state i and is given by:

$$e_{ik,\text{idle}} = v_{ik} + \sum_{j=1}^{2} e_{jk} r_{ji}(\text{k}) = \begin{cases} v_k/(1-\sigma_k), & \text{for } i = 1 \\ v_k \sigma_k/(1-\sigma_k), & \text{for } i = 2 \end{cases} \tag{9.2}$$

v_{ik} is the external arrival rate of service-class k calls to state i determined by:

$$v_{ik} = \begin{cases} v_k & \text{for } i = 1 \\ 0 & \text{for } i = 2 \end{cases} \tag{9.3}$$

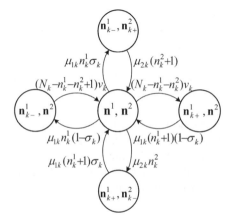

Figure 9.1 The state transition diagram of the f-ON–OFF model.

$r_{ij}(k)$ is the *Prob*{next state is j|current state is i and the service – class is k} and is given by (5.5a) and (5.5b).

Figure 9.1 shows the state transition rates of the f-ON–OFF model (in equilibrium).

Example 9.1 Consider a link of $C = 3$ b.u. and $C^* = 4$ b.u. The link accommodates calls of $K = 2$ service-classes whose calls require $b_1 = 3$ and $b_2 = 1$ b.u., respectively. Let $N_1 = N_2 = 10$, $v_1 = v_2 = 0.1$ calls/sec, $\mu_{11}^{-1} = \mu_{12}^{-1} = \mu_{21}^{-1} = \mu_{22}^{-1} = 1$ sec and $\sigma_1 = \sigma_2 = 0.9$.

(a) Find the total number of permissible states $\mathbf{n} = (\mathbf{n}^1, \mathbf{n}^2) = (n_1^1, n_2^1, n_1^2, n_2^2)$ and determine the values of j_1, j_2 for each state $\mathbf{n}$.
(b) Based on the GB equations, calculate the state probabilities $P(\mathbf{n})$, the occupancy distribution $Q_{\text{fin}}(j_1, j_2)$, and the exact TC probabilities of both service-classes via (5.1) and (5.2).

(a) There are 19 permissible states of the form $\mathbf{n} = (\mathbf{n}^1, \mathbf{n}^2) = (n_1^1, n_2^1, n_1^2, n_2^2)$ already presented in Table 5.1 together with the corresponding values of j_1 and j_2.
(b) Based on Figure 9.1 and Table 5.1, we obtain the following 19 GB equations:

$(0, 0, 0, 0) :\ 0.1P(0, 1, 0, 0) + 0.1P(1, 0, 0, 0) - 2P(0, 0, 0, 0) = 0$

$(0, 0, 0, 1) :\ 0.1P(0, 1, 0, 1) + 0.9P(0, 1, 0, 0) + 0.1P(1, 0, 0, 1) - 2.9P(0, 0, 0, 1) = 0$

$(0, 0, 0, 2) :\ 0.9P(0, 1, 0, 1) + 0.1P(0, 1, 0, 2) - 2.8P(0, 0, 0, 2) = 0$

$(0, 0, 0, 3) :\ 0.9P(0, 1, 0, 2) + 0.1P(0, 1, 0, 3) - 3.7P(0, 0, 0, 3) = 0$

$(0, 0, 0, 4) :\ 0.9P(0, 1, 0, 3) - 4P(0, 0, 0, 4) = 0$

$(0, 0, 1, 0) :\ 0.9P(1, 0, 0, 0) + 0.1P(0, 1, 1, 0) - 2P(0, 0, 1, 0) = 0$

$(0, 0, 1, 1) :\ 0.9P(1, 0, 0, 1) + 0.9P(0, 1, 1, 0) - 2P(0, 0, 1, 1) = 0$

$(0, 1, 0, 0) :\ P(0, 0, 0, 0) + 0.2P(0, 2, 0, 0) + P(0, 0, 0, 1) - 1.9P(0, 1, 0, 0) = 0$

$(0, 1, 0, 1) :\ 0.9P(0, 0, 0, 1) + 1.8P(0, 2, 0, 0) + 0.2P(0, 2, 0, 1) + 2P(0, 0, 0, 2) - 2.8P(0, 1, 0, 1) = 0$

$(0, 1, 0, 2) :\ 0.8P(0, 0, 0, 2) + 3P(0, 0, 0, 3) + 0.2P(0, 2, 0, 2) + 1.8P(0, 2, 0, 1) - 3.7P(0, 1, 0, 2) = 0$

$(0, 1, 0, 3) :\ 0.7P(0, 0, 0, 3) + 4P(0, 0, 0, 4) + 1.8P(0, 2, 0, 2) - 4P(0, 1, 0, 3) = 0$

$(0, 1, 1, 0) :\ P(0, 0, 1, 0) + P(0, 0, 1, 1) - P(0, 1, 1, 0) = 0$

$(0, 2, 0, 0) :\ 0.9P(0, 1, 0, 0) + P(0, 1, 0, 1) + 0.3P(0, 3, 0, 0) - 2.8P(0, 2, 0, 0) = 0$

$(0, 2, 0, 1) :\ 0.8P(0, 1, 0, 1) + 2P(0, 1, 0, 2) + 0.3P(0, 3, 0, 1) + 2.7P(0, 3, 0, 0) - 3.7P(0, 2, 0, 1) = 0$

$(0, 2, 0, 2) :\ 0.7P(0, 1, 0, 2) + 3P(0, 1, 0, 3) + 2.7P(0, 3, 0, 1) - 4P(0, 2, 0, 2) = 0$

$(0, 3, 0, 0) :\ 0.8P(0, 2, 0, 0) + P(0, 2, 0, 1) - 3P(0, 3, 0, 0) = 0$

$(0, 3, 0, 1) :\ 0.7P(0, 2, 0, 1) + 2P(0, 2, 0, 2) - 3P(0, 3, 0, 1) = 0$

$(1, 0, 0, 0) :\ P(0, 0, 0, 0) + P(0, 0, 1, 0) - P(1, 0, 0, 0) = 0$

$(1, 0, 0, 1) :\ P(0, 0, 0, 1) + P(0, 0, 1, 1) - P(1, 0, 0, 1) = 0$

The solution of this linear system is:

$P(0, 0, 0, 0) = 0.000262$ $P(0, 0, 0, 1) = 0.002361$ $P(0, 0, 0, 2) = 0.009561$ $P(0, 0, 0, 3) = 0.022947$

$P(0, 0, 0, 4) = 0.036141$ $P(0, 0, 1, 0) = 0.002361$ $P(0, 0, 1, 1) = 0.021247$ $P(0, 1, 0, 0) = 0.002623$

$P(0, 1, 0, 1) = 0.021247$ $P(0, 1, 0, 2) = 0.07649$ $P(0, 1, 0, 3) = 0.160629$ $P(0, 1, 1, 0) = 0.023608$

$P(0, 2, 0, 0) = 0.011804$ $P(0, 2, 0, 1) = 0.084989$ $P(0, 2, 0, 2) = 0.267714$ $P(0, 3, 0, 0) = 0.031477$

$P(0, 3, 0, 1) = 0.198307$ $P(1, 0, 0, 0) = 0.002623$ $P(1, 0, 0, 1) = 0.023608$

Based on the values of $P(n_1^1, n_2^1, n_1^2, n_2^2)$ we determine the values of $Q_{\text{fin}}(j_1, j_2)$:

$Q_{\text{fin}}(0, 0) = P(0, 0, 0, 0) = 0.000262$

$Q_{\text{fin}}(0, 1) = P(0, 0, 0, 1) = 0.002361$

$Q_{\text{fin}}(0, 2) = P(0, 0, 0, 2) = 0.009561$

$Q_{\text{fin}}(0, 3) = P(0, 0, 0, 3) + P(0, 0, 1, 0)$
$\qquad\qquad = 0.025308$

$Q_{\text{fin}}(0, 4) = P(0, 0, 0, 4) + P(0, 0, 1, 1) = 0.057388$

$Q_{\text{fin}}(1, 0) = P(0, 1, 0, 0) = 0.002623$

$Q_{\text{fin}}(1, 1) = P(0, 1, 0, 1) = 0.021247$

$Q_{\text{fin}}(1, 2) = P(0, 1, 0, 2) = 0.07649$

$Q_{\text{fin}}(1, 3) = P(0, 1, 0, 3) + P(0, 1, 1, 0) = 0.184237$

$Q_{\text{fin}}(2, 0) = P(0, 2, 0, 0) = 0.011804$

$Q_{\text{fin}}(2, 1) = P(0, 2, 0, 1) = 0.084989$

$Q_{\text{fin}}(2, 2) = P(0, 2, 0, 2) = 0.267714$

$Q_{\text{fin}}(3, 0) = P(0, 3, 0, 0) + P(1, 0, 0, 0) = 0.0341$

$Q_{\text{fin}}(3, 1) = P(0, 3, 0, 1) + P(1, 0, 0, 1)$
$\qquad\qquad = 0.221915$

Based on the values of $Q_{\text{fin}}(j)$ and the constraints of (5.1) and (5.2) we obtain the exact TC probabilities:

$$B_{T1} = \sum_{(j_1 > C - b_1) \cup (j_1 + j_2 > C^* - b_1)} Q_{\text{fin}}(j_1, j_2) = \sum_{(j_1 > 0) \cup (j_1 + j_2 > 1)} Q_{\text{fin}}(j_1, j_2) =$$

$$1 - Q_{\text{fin}}(0, 0) - Q_{\text{fin}}(0, 1) = 0.997377 \quad \text{(compare with 0.9987947 in the ON-OFF model)}$$

$$B_{T2} = \sum_{(j_1 > C - b_2) \cup (j_1 + j_2 > C^* - b_2)} Q_{\text{fin}}(j_1, j_2) = \sum_{(j_1 > 2) \cup (j_1 + j_2 > 3)} Q_{\text{fin}}(j_1, j_2) = Q_{\text{fin}}(0, 4) + Q_{\text{fin}}(1, 3) +$$

$$Q_{\text{fin}}(2, 2) + Q_{\text{fin}}(3, 1) + Q_{\text{fin}}(3, 0) = 0.765354$$

(compare with 0.821306 in the ON-OFF model)

Assuming the existence of LB between adjacent states, the following LB equations are extracted from the state transition diagram of Figure 9.1:

$$n_k^1 \mu_{1k} \sigma_k P(\mathbf{n}) = \mu_{2k}(n_k^2 + 1) P(\mathbf{n}_{k-+}) \tag{9.4a}$$

$$\mu_{1k} n_k^1 (1 - \sigma_k) P(\mathbf{n}) = (N_k - n_k^1 - n_k^2 + 1) v_k P(\mathbf{n}_{k-}^1) \tag{9.4b}$$

$$(N_k - n_k^1 - n_k^2) v_k P(\mathbf{n}) = \mu_{1k}(n_k^1 + 1)(1 - \sigma_k) P(\mathbf{n}_{k+}^1) \tag{9.4c}$$

$$\mu_{2k} n_k^2 P(\mathbf{n}) = \mu_{1k}(n_k^1 + 1)\sigma_k P(\mathbf{n}_{k+-}) \tag{9.4d}$$

where $P(\mathbf{n})$, $P(\mathbf{n}_{k-+})$, $P(\mathbf{n}_{k-}^1)$, $P(\mathbf{n}_{k+}^1)$, and $P(\mathbf{n}_{k+-})$ are the probability distributions of the corresponding states $\mathbf{n} = (\mathbf{n}^1, \mathbf{n}^2)$, $\mathbf{n}_{k-+} = (\mathbf{n}_{k-}^1, \mathbf{n}_{k+}^2)$, $\mathbf{n}_{k-}^i = (n_1^i, \dots, n_k^i - 1, \dots, n_K^i)$, $\mathbf{n}_{k+}^i = (n_1^i, \dots, n_k^i + 1, \dots, n_K^i)$, $\mathbf{n}_{k+-} = (\mathbf{n}_{k+}^1, \mathbf{n}_{k-}^2)$.

Equations (9.4b) and (9.4c) describe the balance between the rates of a new call arrival of service-class k and the corresponding departure from the system, while (9.4a) and (9.4d) refer to the ON–OFF alternations of a service-class k call. Based on the LB assumption, the probability distribution $P(\mathbf{n})$ has a PFS which satisfies (9.4a)–(9.4d) and has the form [1]:

$$P(\mathbf{n}) = \frac{1}{G} \prod_{k=1}^{K} \binom{N_k}{n_k^1 + n_k^2} \prod_{l=1}^{n_k^1} \frac{l + n_k^2}{l} \prod_{i=1}^{2} p_{ik,\text{idle}}^{n_k^i} \tag{9.5}$$

where $G \equiv G(\mathbf{\Omega})$ is the normalization constant.

We now define by $b_{i,k,s}$ the b.u. held by a service-class k call in state i according to (5.10). We also define a $(2K \times 2)$ matrix B whose elements are the values of $b_{i,k,s}$ and let $B_{i,k}$ be the (i, k) row of B, where $\mathbf{B}_{i,k} = (b_{i,k,1}, b_{i,k,2})$. In addition, let $\mathbf{j} = \mathbf{n}B$ with $\mathbf{j} = (j_1, j_2)$ where the occupied bandwidth j_s of link s ($s = 1 \Rightarrow$ real link, $s = 2 \Rightarrow$ fictitious link) is given by (5.11).

Having found an expression for $P(\mathbf{n})$ and since the CS policy is a coordinate convex policy (see Section I.12, Example I.30), the probability $P(\mathbf{n}_{k-}^i)$ can be expressed by [1]:

$$(N_k - n_k^i - n_k^t + 1)p_{ik,\text{idle}}\gamma_{ik}(\mathbf{n})P(\mathbf{n}_{k-}^i) = n_k^i P(\mathbf{n}) \tag{9.6}$$

where $i = 1, 2$, $t = 1, 2$ while $t \neq i$, and $\gamma_{ik}(\mathbf{n}) = \begin{cases} 1 \text{ if } n_k^i > 1 \\ 0 \text{ if } n_k^i = 0 \end{cases}$ $(k = 1, \ldots, K)$.

Consider now the set of states $\mathbf{\Omega_j} = \{\mathbf{n} \in \Omega_j : \mathbf{n}B = \mathbf{j}, n_k^i \geq 0, k = 1, \ldots, K, i = 1, 2\}$ whereby the occupied real and fictitious link bandwidths are exactly j_1 and j_2, respectively. Then, the probability $q_{\text{fin}}(\mathbf{j})$ (links occupancy distribution) is denoted as in (5.13).

Summing (9.6) over $\mathbf{\Omega_j}$ we have:

$$N_k p_{ik,\text{idle}} \sum_{\mathbf{n} \in \Omega_j} \gamma_{ik}(\mathbf{n}) P(\mathbf{n}_{k-}^i) - p_{ik,\text{idle}} \sum_{\mathbf{n} \in \Omega_j} (n_k^i + n_k^t - 1)\gamma_{ik}(\mathbf{n}) P(\mathbf{n}_{k-}^i)$$

$$= \sum_{\mathbf{n} \in \Omega_j} n_k^i P(\mathbf{n}) \tag{9.7}$$

The LHS of (9.7) is written as: $N_k p_{ik,\text{idle}} \sum\limits_{\mathbf{n} \in \Omega_j \cap \{n_k^i \geq 1\}} P(\mathbf{n}_{k-}^i) - p_{ik,\text{idle}} \sum\limits_{\mathbf{n} \in \Omega_j \cap \{n_k^i \geq 1\}} (n_k^i + n_k^t - 1)P(\mathbf{n}_{k-}^i)$. Since $\mathbf{\Omega_j} = \{n_k^i \geq 1\} = \{\mathbf{n} : \mathbf{n}_{k-}^i B = \mathbf{j} - \mathbf{B}_{i,k}\}$ we continue by using the following change of variables:

$$n_m^{*i} = \begin{cases} n_m^i & \text{for } m \neq k \\ n_m^i - & \text{for } m = k \end{cases}$$

Thus the LHS of (9.7) can be written as:

$$\text{LHS} = N_k p_{ik,\text{idle}} \sum_{\vec{\mathbf{n}}^{*i} \in \Omega_{j-B_{i,k}}} P(\vec{\mathbf{n}}^{*i}) - p_{ik,\text{idle}} \sum_{\vec{\mathbf{n}}^{*i} \in \Omega_{j-B_{i,k}}} (n_k^{*i} + n_k^t)P(\vec{\mathbf{n}}^{*i}) \tag{9.8}$$

where $\vec{\mathbf{n}}^{*1} = (\mathbf{n}^{*1}, \mathbf{n}^2)$, $\vec{\mathbf{n}}^{*2} = (\mathbf{n}^1, \mathbf{n}^{*2})$, $\mathbf{n}^{*1} = (n_1^{*1}, \ldots, n_k^{*1}, \ldots, n_K^{*1})$, and $\mathbf{n}^{*2} = (n_1^{*2}, \ldots, n_k^{*2}, \ldots, n_K^{*2})$. The first term of (9.8) is equal to $N_k p_{ik,\text{idle}} q_{\text{fin}}(\mathbf{j} - \mathbf{B}_{i,k})$, while the second term is written as:

$$p_{ik,\text{idle}} \sum_{\vec{\mathbf{n}}^{*i} \in \Omega_{j-B_{i,k}}} (n_k^{*i} + n_k^t)P(\vec{\mathbf{n}}^{*i})q_{\text{fin}}(\mathbf{j} - \mathbf{B}_{i,k})/q_{\text{fin}}(\mathbf{j} - \mathbf{B}_{i,k}) =$$

$$p_{ik,\text{idle}} \sum_{\vec{\mathbf{n}}^{*i} \in \Omega_{j-B_{i,k}}} (n_k^{*i} + n_k^t)P(\vec{\mathbf{n}}^{*i}|\mathbf{j} - \mathbf{B}_{i,k})q_{\text{fin}}(\mathbf{j} - \mathbf{B}_{i,k}) =$$

$$p_{ik,\text{idle}} E((n_k^{*i} + n_k^t)|\mathbf{j} - \mathbf{B}_{i,k})q_{\text{fin}}(\mathbf{j} - \mathbf{B}_{i,k})$$

where $E((n_k^{*i} + n_k^t)|\mathbf{j} - \mathbf{B}_{i,k})$ is the expected value of $n_k^{*i} + n_k^t$ given $\mathbf{j} - \mathbf{B}_{i,k}$.

By substituting the "new" first and second terms in (9.8), we have:

$$\text{LHS} = (N_k - E((n_k^{*i} + n_k^t)|\mathbf{j} - \mathbf{B}_{i,k}))p_{ik,\text{idle}}q_{\text{fin}}(\mathbf{j} - \mathbf{B}_{i,k}) \tag{9.9}$$

The RHS of (9.7) can be written as:

$$\text{RHS} = \sum_{\mathbf{n} \in \Omega_j} n_k^i P(\mathbf{n}) = \sum_{\mathbf{n} \in \Omega_j} n_k^i \frac{P(\mathbf{n})}{q_{\text{fin}}(\mathbf{j})} q_{\text{fin}}(\mathbf{j}) = \sum_{\mathbf{n} \in \Omega_j} n_k^i P(\mathbf{n} \mid \mathbf{j}) q_{\text{fin}}(\mathbf{j}) = E(n_k^i \mid \mathbf{j}) \, q_{\text{fin}}(\mathbf{j})$$

(9.10)

for $\mathbf{j} \in \Omega$ and $k = 1, \dots, K$.

Combining (9.9) and (9.10), we have:

$$(N_k - E((n_k^{*i} + n_k^t) \mid \mathbf{j} - \mathbf{B}_{i,k})) p_{ik,\text{idle}} q_{\text{fin}}(\mathbf{j} - \mathbf{B}_{i,k}) = E(n_k^i \mid \mathbf{j}) q_{\text{fin}}(\mathbf{j})$$

(9.11)

Multiplying both sides of (9.11) by $b_{i,k,s}$ and summing over i, k, we have [1]:

$$\sum_{i=1}^{2} \sum_{k=1}^{K} (N_k - E((n_k^{*i} + n_k^t) \mid \mathbf{j} - \mathbf{B}_{i,k})) b_{i,k,s} \, p_{ik,\text{idle}} \, q_{\text{fin}}(\mathbf{j} - \mathbf{B}_{i,k})$$

$$= \sum_{i=1}^{2} \sum_{k=1}^{K} E(n_k^i b_{i,k,s} \mid \mathbf{j}) q_{\text{fin}}(\mathbf{j}) = j_s q_{\text{fin}}(\mathbf{j}) \quad \text{for } \mathbf{j} \in \Omega$$

(9.12)

The estimator $E((n_k^{*i} + n_k^t) \mid \mathbf{j} - \mathbf{B}_{i,k})$ in (9.12) is not known. To determine it, we use a lemma initially proposed in [2] for the determination of a similar estimator in the EnMLM. According to the lemma, two stochastic systems with (i) the same traffic description parameters $(K, N_k, p_{ik,\text{fin}})$ and (ii) exactly the same set of states are equivalent, since they result in the same CBP. The purpose is therefore to find a new stochastic system in which we can determine the estimator $E((n_k^{*i} + n_k^t) \mid \mathbf{j} - \mathbf{B}_{i,k})$. By choosing the bandwidth requirements of calls of all service-classes and the capacities C, C^* in the new stochastic system according to the criteria (i) conditions (a) and (b) are valid and (ii) each state has a unique occupancy $\mathbf{j} = (j_1, j_2)$, then each state $\mathbf{j}$ can be reached only via state $\mathbf{j} - \mathbf{B}_{i,k}$. Thus, the estimator $E((n_k^{*i} + n_k^t) \mid \mathbf{j} - \mathbf{B}_{i,k}) = n_k^{*i} - 1 + n_k^t$ and (9.12) can be written as (for $t = 1, 2, \ t \neq i$):

$$q_{\text{fin}}(\mathbf{j}) = \begin{cases} 1 & \text{for } \mathbf{j} = 0 \\ \dfrac{1}{j_s} \sum\limits_{i=1}^{2} \sum\limits_{k=1}^{K} (N_k - n_k^i - n_k^t + 1) b_{i,k,s} \, p_{ik,\text{fin}} \, q_{\text{fin}}(\mathbf{j} - \mathbf{B}_{i,k}) \\ \quad \text{for } j_1 = 1, \dots, C \text{ (if } s = 1) \quad \text{or} \quad \text{for } j_2 = 1, \dots, C^* - j_1 \text{ (if } s = 2) \\ 0 & \text{otherwise} \end{cases}$$

(9.13)

Equation (9.13) is the two-dimensional recursive formula used for the determination of $q_{\text{fin}}(\mathbf{j})$. The $q_{\text{fin}}(\mathbf{j})$ can be calculated in terms of an arbitrary $q_{\text{fin}}(\mathbf{j} = 0)$ under the normalization condition of $\sum_{\mathbf{j} \in \Omega} q_{\text{fin}}(\mathbf{j}) = 1$. Although (9.13) is simple, it cannot be used for the determination of $q_{\text{fin}}(\mathbf{j})$ unless an equivalent system (mentioned above) is defined by enumeration and processing of the system's state space. The following example reveals the problems that can arise when one tries to use (9.13) prior to the state space enumeration and processing, and how these problems can be overcome.

Example 9.2 Consider a link of $C = 3$ b.u. and $C^* = 3$ b.u. The link accommodates calls of $K = 2$ service-classes whose calls require $b_1 = 3$ and $b_2 = 1$ b.u., respectively. Let $N_1 = N_2 = 5, v_1 = 0.002$ calls/sec, $v_2 = 0.01$ calls/sec, $\mu_{11}^{-1} = 0.5, \mu_{21}^{-1} = 0.6, \mu_{12}^{-1} =$

Table 9.1 State space, (j_1, j_2), $(j_{1,eq}, j_{2,eq})$, and blocking states (Example 9.2).

n_1^1	n_2^1	n_1^2	n_2^2	j_1	j_2	$j_{1,eq}$	$j_{2,eq}$	B_{T1}	B_{T2}
0	0	0	0	0	0	0	0		
0	0	0	1	0	1	0	2	*	
0	0	0	2	0	2	0	4	*	
0	0	0	3	0	3	0	6	*	*
0	0	1	0	0	3	0	5	*	*
0	1	0	0	1	0	2	0	*	
0	1	0	1	1	1	2	2	*	
0	1	0	2	1	2	2	4	*	*
0	2	0	0	2	0	4	0	*	
0	2	0	1	2	1	4	2	*	*
0	3	0	0	3	0	6	0	*	*
1	0	0	0	3	0	5	0	*	*

1.0, $\mu_{22}^{-1} = 1.0$ sec, and $\sigma_1 = \sigma_2 = 0.75$. In Table 9.1 we present the system state-space of this example, consisting of 12 unique states of the form $\mathbf{n} = (\mathbf{n}^1, \mathbf{n}^2) = (n_1^1, n_2^1, n_1^2, n_2^2)$, the respective real and fictitious link occupancies (j_1, j_2), the real and fictitious link occupancies of the equivalent system $(j_{1,eq}, j_{2,eq})$, and the blocking states for each service-class. We observe that the link occupancies are not unique, e.g., $(j_1, j_2) = (0, 3)$ appears twice: for $(n_1^1, n_2^1, n_1^2, n_2^2) = (0, 0, 0, 3)$ and for $(n_1^1, n_2^1, n_1^2, n_2^2) = (0, 0, 1, 0)$. Because of this, we cannot use (9.13) unless we find an equivalent system whose states have unique link occupancy. Also, in both the initial and the equivalent system, the blocking states of each service-class should be the same. Such an equivalent system has $C = C^* = 6$, $b_1 = 5$ and $b_2 = 2$ b.u. The required bandwidth per call of the service-classes of the equivalent system is chosen by a simple heuristic algorithm. This is an iterative procedure where in each iteration the required bandwidth of each service-class is increased unit-by-unit from its initial value and checked whether or not the equivalent system has been found, according to the criteria mentioned above.

Having found an equivalent system, we calculate the $q_{fin}(\mathbf{j})$ via (9.13), and then determine the TC probabilities of each service-class: $B_{T_1} = 0.306$, $B_{T_2} = 0.029$ via (9.14) (see below).

Before we proceed with the determination of the various performance measures, we show the relationship between the f-ON–OFF model and the EnMLM. These models are equivalent in the sense that they provide the same TC probabilities and CBP, when:

(i) $\sigma_k = 0$ (i.e., when state OFF does not exist) for each service-class k ($k = 1, \ldots, K$). In that case the calculation of $q_{fin}(\mathbf{j})$ can be done via (6.27).

(ii) $\sigma_k > 0$ and $C = C^*$. Then we can determine the mean holding time, μ_k^{-1}, of a service-class k call of the f-ON–OFF model via (5.20). In that case, the f-ON–OFF model is equivalent to the EnMLM with traffic parameters, υ_k, b_k and μ_k^{-1} determined by (5.20).

9.1.2.2 TC Probabilities, CBP, and Utilization

The following performance measures can be determined based on (9.13):

- The TC probabilities of service-class k, B_{Tk}, via the formula [1]:

$$B_{Tk} = \sum_{\{j \mid [(b_{1,k,1}+j_1)>C] \cup [(b_{1,k,1}+j_1+j_2)>C^*]\}} G^{-1} q_{\text{fin}}(j) \qquad (9.14)$$

where $G = \sum_{j \in \Omega} q_{\text{fin}}(j)$.
- The CBP (or CC probabilities) of service-class k, B_k, via (9.14) but for a system with $N_k - 1$ traffic sources.
- The link utilization, U_s, via (5.19) where $Q_s(\tau) = \sum_{\{j \mid j_s = \tau\}} G^{-1} q_{\text{fin}}(j)$.

9.1.2.3 BBP

To illustrate the idea behind the formula for the BBP determination we consider Example 9.3.

Example 9.3 Consider again Example 9.2 ($C = 3, K = 2, b_1 = 3, b_2 = 1, N_1 = N_2 = 5, v_1 = 0.002, v_2 = 0.01, \mu_{11}^{-1} = 0.5, \mu_{21}^{-1} = 0.6, \mu_{12}^{-1} = 1.0, \mu_{22}^{-1} = 1.0, \sigma_1 = \sigma_2 = 0.75$) and let $C^* = 4$ b.u. The latter results in the appearance of burst blocking for calls of both service-classes (because $C^* > C$); OFF calls of service-classes 1 and 2 will face burst blocking when $j_1 + b_1 > C$ and $j_2 + b_2 > C$, respectively.

In Table 9.2 we present the system state-space of this example, consisting of 19 unique states of the form $\mathbf{n} = (\mathbf{n}^1, \mathbf{n}^2) = (n_1^1, n_2^1, n_1^2, n_2^2)$, the respective real and fictitious link

Table 9.2 State space, (j_1, j_2), $(j_{1,eq}, j_{2,eq})$, call, and burst blocking states (Example 9.3).

n_1^1	n_2^1	n_1^2	n_2^2	j_1	j_2	$j_{1,eq}$	$j_{2,eq}$	B_{T_1}	B_{T_2}	B_1^*	B_2^*
0	0	0	0	0	0	0	0				
0	0	0	1	0	1	0	2				
0	0	0	2	0	2	0	4	*			
0	0	0	3	0	3	0	6	*			
0	0	0	4	0	4	0	8	*	*		
0	0	1	0	0	3	0	5	*			
0	0	1	1	0	4	0	7	*	*		
0	1	0	0	1	0	2	0	*		*	
0	1	0	1	1	1	2	2	*		*	
0	1	0	2	1	2	2	4	*		*	
0	1	0	3	1	3	2	6	*	*	*	
0	1	1	0	1	3	2	5	*	*	*	
0	2	0	0	2	0	4	0	*		*	
0	2	0	1	2	1	4	2	*		*	
0	2	0	2	2	2	4	4	*	*	*	
0	3	0	0	3	0	6	0	*	*	*	*
0	3	0	1	3	1	6	2	*	*	*	*
1	0	0	0	3	0	5	0	*	*	*	*
1	0	0	1	3	1	5	2	*	*	*	*

occupancies (j_1, j_2), the real and fictitious link occupancies of the equivalent system $(j_{1,\text{eq}}, j_{2,\text{eq}})$ as well as the call and burst blocking states for each service-class. An equivalent system is $C = 6, C^* = 8, b_1 = 5$, and $b_2 = 2$ b.u.

In order to determine the BBP of calls of a service-class k, B_k^*, we need to find the number of service-class k calls in state OFF, n_k^2, when the system is in a burst blocking state, e.g., according to Table 9.2, a burst blocking state of service-class 2 is $(n_1^1, n_2^1, n_1^2, n_2^2) = (1, 0, 0, 1)$ and the corresponding value of $\mathbf{j} = (j_{1,\text{eq}}, j_{2,\text{eq}}) = (5, 2)$.

Multiplying n_k^2 by the corresponding $q_{\text{fin}}(\mathbf{j})$ and the service rate in state OFF μ_{2k}, we obtain the rate whereby service-class k OFF calls would depart from the burst blocking state if it were possible. By summing these rates over the burst blocking state-space $\mathbf{\Omega}^*$, $\mathbf{j} \in \mathbf{\Omega}^* \Leftrightarrow \left\{ (C - b_k + 1 \leq j_1 \leq C) \cap \left(\sum_{s=1}^{2} j_s \leq C^* \right) \right\}$ we obtain the summation $\sum_{(\mathbf{j} \in \mathbf{\Omega}^*)} n_k^2(\mathbf{j}) \, q_{\text{fin}}(\mathbf{j}) \mu_{2k}$.

By normalizing it (taking into account the whole state space $\mathbf{\Omega}$), we obtain the following formula for the BBP calculation:

$$B_k^* = \frac{\sum\limits_{\mathbf{j} \in \mathbf{\Omega}^*} n_k^2 \, q_{\text{fin}}(\mathbf{j}) \mu_{2k}}{\sum\limits_{\mathbf{j} \in \mathbf{\Omega}} n_k^2 \, q_{\text{fin}}(\mathbf{j}) \mu_{2k}} \tag{9.15}$$

where $\mathbf{j} \in \mathbf{\Omega} \Leftrightarrow \left\{ (j_1 \leq C) \cap \left(\sum_{s=1}^{2} j_s \leq C^* \right) \right\}$ and $q_{\text{fin}}(\mathbf{j})$ are calculated by (9.13).

Thus, (9.15) can be seen as the normalized rate of service-class k OFF calls by which OFF calls would depart from the burst blocking states if it were possible.

For the record, the BBP of each service-class in Example 9.3 are $B_1^* = 0.1481$ and $B_2^* = 0.0150$, while the corresponding simulation results (with 95% confidence interval) are $B_{1,\text{sim}}^* = 0.1432 \pm 0.0031$ and $B_{2,\text{sim}}^* = 0.0148 \pm 0.0005$.

9.2 Generalization of the f-ON–OFF Model to include Service-classes with a Mixture of a Finite and an Infinite Number of Sources

Consider a link with a pair of capacities C and C^*, accommodating K_{fin} service-classes of finite ON–OFF sources (quasi-random input) and K_{inf} service-classes of infinite ON–OFF sources (random–Poisson input). Then, the calculation of the link occupancy distribution is done by the combination of (9.13) and (5.17) [3]:

$$q(\mathbf{j}) = \begin{cases} 1 & \text{for } \mathbf{j} = 0 \\ \dfrac{1}{j_s} \sum\limits_{i=1}^{2} \sum\limits_{k=1}^{K_{\text{fin}}} (N_k - n_k^i - n_k^t + 1) b_{i,k,s} p_{ik,\text{fin}} q(\mathbf{j} - \mathbf{B}_{i,k}) \\ \quad + \dfrac{1}{j_s} \sum\limits_{i=1}^{2} \sum\limits_{k=1}^{K_{\text{inf}}} b_{i,k,s} p_{ik} q(\mathbf{j} - \mathbf{B}_{i,k}) \\ \quad \text{for } j_1 = 1, \dots, C \quad (\text{if } s = 1) \quad \text{or for } j_2 = 1, \dots, C^* - j_1 \quad (\text{if } s = 2) \\ 0 & \text{otherwise} \end{cases}$$

$$\tag{9.16}$$

Such a mixture of service-classes does not destroy the accuracy of the model. The TC probabilities calculation can be done via (9.14), while the BBP calculation can be done via (9.15) for the service-classes of finite population and via (5.39) for the service-classes of infinite population.

Example 9.4   Consider two service-classes which require $b_1 = 12$ and $b_2 = 2$ b.u. per call, respectively, and a link of capacity $C = 46$ b.u. Calls of service-class 1 arrive according to a quasi-random process, while calls of service-class 2 arrive according to a Poisson process. The number of sources of service-class 1 is $N_1 = 5$. The traffic description parameters are:

Service-class   1: $v_1 = 0.02, \mu_{11}^{-1} = 0.5, \mu_{21}^{-1} = 0.6, \sigma_1 = 0.9, p_{11,\text{fin}} = 0.1, p_{21,\text{fin}} = 0.108$
Service-class 2: $\lambda_2 = 0.1, \ \mu_{12}^{-1} = 1.0, \mu_{22}^{-1} = 1.0, \sigma_2 = 0.9, p_{12} = 1.0, \ p_{22} = 0.9$

Assuming that $C^* = 46$ (no burst blocking occurs), then the equivalent system used for the TC probabilities calculation is $b_1 = 25, b_2 = 4$, and $C = C^* = 95$. Assuming that $C^* = 51$, then the equivalent system used for the TC probabilities and the BBP determination is $b_1 = 29, b_2 = 5, C = 115$, and $C^* = 125$. Finally, assuming that $C^* = 56$, then the equivalent system is $b_1 = 29, b_2 = 5, C = 115$, and $C^* = 140$. For both service-classes and the different values of C^*, provide (i) analytical TC probabilities results and (ii) analytical and simulation BBP results. For both (i) and (ii), assume that v_1 is constant, while λ_2 increases in steps of 0.1, i.e., point 1 is $(v_1, \lambda_2) = (0.02, \ 0.1)$, point 2 is $(v_1, \lambda_2) = (0.02, \ 0.2)$, ..., and point 7 is $(v_1, \ \lambda_2) = (0.02, \ 0.7)$.

Figures 9.2 and 9.3 show the analytical TC probabilities results of service-class 1 and 2, respectively, for (i) $C = C^* = 46$, (ii) $C = 46, C^* = 51$, and (iii) $C = 46, C^* = 56$, while Figure 9.4 shows the analytical and simulation BBP results for both service-classes and $C^* = 51, 56$. Simulation results are mean values of 10 runs with 95% confidence interval. As Figures 9.2 and 9.3 show, there is a significant decrease in the TC probabilities of both service-classes when we increase the fictitious capacity C^* from 46 to 56. This decrease was anticipated because when C^* increases, more calls may pass to state OFF, releasing bandwidth (in state ON) for new calls. However, the increase in C^* results in the burst blocking increase, as Figure 9.4 shows.

9.3   Applications

An interesting application of the f-ON–OFF model has been proposed in [4], where the OCDMA PON architecture of Figure 9.5 with U ONUs is considered.

All ONUs are connected to the OLT through a passive optical splitter/combiner (PO-SC). The PO-SC is responsible for collecting data from all ONUs and transmitting them to the OLT (upstream direction), as well as for broadcasting data from the OLT to the ONUs (downstream direction). The analysis of [4] concentrates on the upstream direction; however, it can also be applied to the downstream direction. Users that are

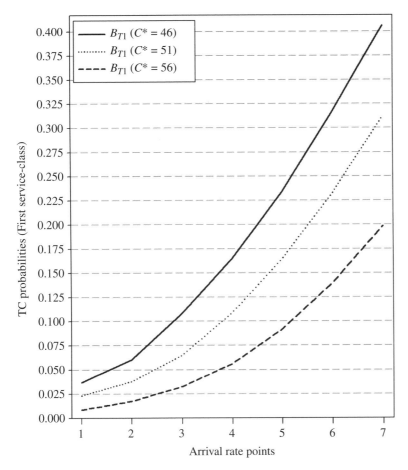

Figure 9.2 TC probabilities for service-class 1 when a) $C^* = 46$, (b) $C^* = 51$, and (c) $C^* = 56$ (Example 9.4).

connected to an ONU alternate between active and passive (silent) transmission periods. The PON uses (L, W, l_a, l_c) codewords, which have the same length L and the same weight W, while the auto-correlation l_a and cross-correlation l_c parameters are defined according to the desired BER at the receiver. The PON supports K service-classes which are differentiated via the parallel mapping technique. Under this technique, the OLT assigns b_k codewords to a service-class k call for the entire duration of the call. More precisely, during the holding time of a service-class k call the data bits of this call are grouped per b_k bits and transmitted in parallel in each bit period. One codeword is used to encode bit "1", while data bit "0" is not encoded. Thus, the call uses a number of these b_k codewords in each bit period and this number is equal to the number of data bits "1" that are transmitted during a bit period. In this way, the complex procedure of assigning codewords in each data bit period is avoided. Furthermore, since b_k bits are transmitted in each data bit period, the data rate of service-class k is $b_k \cdot D$, where D is the basic data rate of a single codeworded call.

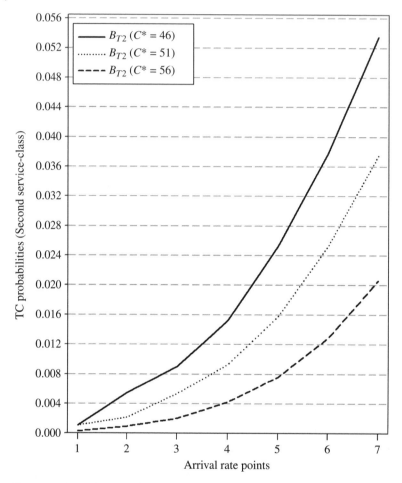

Figure 9.3 TC probabilities for service-class 2 when (a) $C^* = 46$, (b) $C^* = 51$, and (c) $C^* = 56$ (Example 9.4).

When a single codeword is assigned to an active user (active call), the received power of this call at the OLT is denoted by I_{unit} (I_{unit} corresponds to the received power per bit, for a specific value of the BER [5]). Since the PON supports multiple service-classes of different data rates, a number of single codewords is assigned to each service-class, therefore the received power I_k^{act} of an active call of service-class k is proportional to I_{unit}, since b_k data bits are simultaneously transmitted for service-class k during a bit period, therefore:

$$I_k^{\text{act}} = b_k I_{\text{unit}} \tag{9.17}$$

The connection establishment between the end-user and the OLT is based on a three-way handshake (request/ACK/confirmation). Calls of service-class k arrive at ONU u ($u = 1, \ldots, U$) from a finite number of traffic sources $N_{u,k}$; the total number of service-class k traffic sources in the PON is $N_k = \sum_{u=1}^{U} N_{u,k}$. The mean call arrival rate of service-class k is $v_k (N_k - n_k^1 - n_k^2)$, where v_k is the arrival rate per idle source,

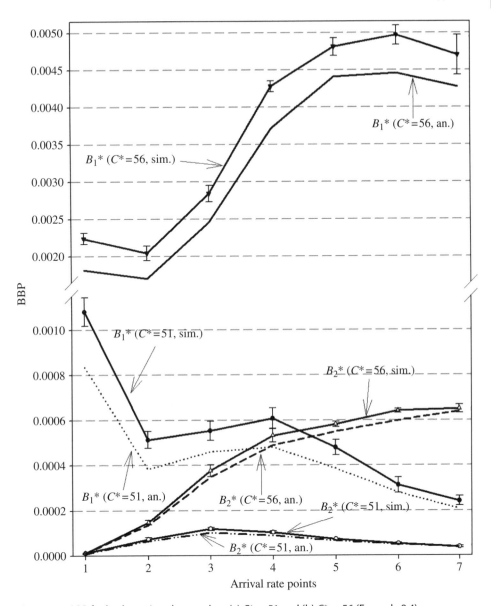

Figure 9.4 BBP for both service-classes when (a) $C^* = 51$ and (b) $C^* = 56$ (Example 9.4).

while n_k^1 and n_k^2 are the numbers of service-class k calls in the PON in the active and passive states, respectively. Calls that are accepted for service start an active period and may remain in the active state for their entire duration, or alternate between active and passive periods. During an active period, a burst of data is sent to the OLT, while no data transmission occurs throughout a passive period. When a service-class k call is transferred from the active to the passive state the total number of in-service codewords is reduced by b_k. When a passive call attempts to become active, it re-requests the same number of codewords (but not necessarily the same codewords) as in the previous

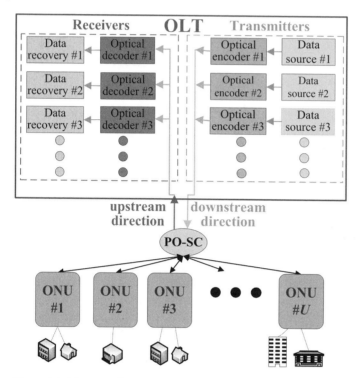

Figure 9.5 A basic configuration of an OCDMA PON.

active state. If the total number of codewords in use does not exceed a maximum threshold (the PON capacity), the call begins a new active period, otherwise burst blocking occurs and the call remains in the passive state for another period. At the end of an active period, the call is transferred to the passive state with probability m_k or departs from the system (the connection is terminated) with probability $1 - m_k$. The active and passive periods of service-class k calls are exponentially distributed with mean $\mu_{i,k}^{-1}$ ($i = 1$ indicates active state, $i = 2$ indicates passive state).

In OCDMA systems, an arriving call should be blocked, after the new call acceptance, if the noise of all in-service calls is increased above a predefined threshold; this noise is called multiple access interference (MAI). We differentiate the MAI from other forms of noise (thermal, fiber-link, beat, and shot noise). The thermal noise and fiber link noise are typically modeled as Gauss distributions $(0, \sigma_{th})$ and $(0, \sigma_{fb})$, respectively, while the shot noise is modeled as a Poisson process (p, p) [6]. The beat noise is modeled as a Gauss distribution $(0, \sigma_b)$ [7]. According to the central limit theorem, we can assume that the total additive noise is modeled as a Gauss distribution (μ_N, σ_N), considering that the number of noise sources in the PON is relatively large. Therefore, the total interference I_N caused by the thermal, the fiber-link, the beat, and the shot noise is modeled as a Gauss distribution with mean $\mu_N = p$ and variance $\sigma_n = \sqrt{\sigma_{th}^2 + \sigma_{fb}^2 + p^2 + \sigma_b^2}$.

Upon a call arrival at an ONU, a CAC located at the OLT decides on its acceptance or rejection according to the total received power at the OLT. More precisely, the CAC estimates the total received power (together with the power of the new call); if it exceeds a maximum threshold I_{max}, the call is blocked and lost. The maximum received power is calculated based on the worst case scenario that all b_k data bits transmitted in parallel are "1", in order to ensure that the BER will never increase above the desired value. The value of I_{max} is also determined by the desired BER at the receiver [5]. This condition is expressed by the following relation:

$$\sum_{k=1}^{K} (n_k^1 I_k^{act} P_{interf}) + I_k^{act} + I_N > I_{max} \Leftrightarrow \frac{I_N}{I_{max}} > 1 - \sum_{k=1}^{K} \left(n_k^1 \frac{I_k^{act}}{I_{max}} P_{interf} \right) - \frac{I_k^{act}}{I_{max}}$$

(9.18)

The summation in (9.18) refers to the received power of all in-service active calls of all K service-classes multiplied by the average probability of interference P_{interf}. This probability is a function of the weight W, the length L, and the maximum cross-correlation parameter l_c of the codewords, as well as of the hit probabilities between two codewords of different users. Specifically, the hit probabilities $p_{l_{c,i}}$ of getting i hits during a bit period out of the maximum cross-correlation value l_c are given by [8]:

$$\sum_{i=0}^{l_c} i \cdot p_{l_{c,i}} = \frac{1}{2} \cdot \frac{W^2}{L}, \quad \text{while} \quad \sum_{i=0}^{l_c} p_{l_{c,i}} = 1$$

(9.19)

where the factor $1/2$ is due to the fact that data bit "0" is not encoded. In the case of $l_c = 1$, the percentage of the total power of a data bit that interferes with a bit of the new call is $1/W$, since 1 out of W "1" of the codewords may interfere. In this case $P_{interf} = (1/W)p_{l_{c,1}} = W/2L$. When $l_c \geq 1$, the probability of interference is given by:

$$P_{interf} = \sum_{i=0}^{l_c} \frac{i}{W} p_{l_{c,i}} = \frac{W}{2L}$$

(9.20)

The condition expressed by (9.18) is also examined at the receiver, when a passive call tries to become active. Based on (9.18), we define the LBP $L_k(n_k^1)$ that a service-class k call is blocked due to the presence of the additive noise, when the number of in-service active calls is n_k^1, as:

$$L_k(n_k^1) = Prob\left(\frac{I_N}{I_{max}} > 1 - \sum_{k=1}^{K} \left(n_k^1 \frac{I_k^{act}}{I_{max}} P_{interf} \right) - \frac{I_k^{act}}{I_{max}} \right)$$

(9.21)

or

$$1 - L_k(n_k^1) = Prob\left(\frac{I_N}{I_{max}} \leq 1 - \sum_{k=1}^{K} \left(n_k^1 \frac{I_k^{act}}{I_{max}} P_{interf} \right) - \frac{I_k^{act}}{I_{max}} \right)$$

(9.22)

Assuming that the total additive noise I_N follows a Gauss distribution (μ_N, σ_N), the variable I_N/I_{max} follows a Gauss distribution ($\mu_N/I_{max}, \sigma_N/I_{max}$) too. Therefore, the RHS of (9.22) is the CDF of the Gauss variable I_N/I_{max} and is denoted as $F_n(x)$:

$$F_n(x) = Prob\left(\frac{I_N}{I_{max}} \leq x \right) = \frac{1}{2} \left(1 + erf\left(\frac{x - \frac{\mu_N}{I_{max}}}{\frac{\sigma_N}{I_{max}} \sqrt{2}} \right) \right)$$

(9.23)

where $erf(\cdot)$ is the well-known error function.

By using (9.22) and (9.23), we can calculate $L_k(n_k^1)$ of service-class k calls by substituting $x = 1 - \sum_{k=1}^{K}(n_k^1 \frac{I_k^{act}}{I_{max}} P_{interf}) - \frac{I_k^{act}}{I_{max}}$:

$$L_k(x) = \begin{cases} 1 - F_n(x) & \text{when} \quad x \geq 0 \\ 1 & \text{when} \quad x < 0 \end{cases} \tag{9.24}$$

Now, let C_1 be the capacity of the (real) shared link, which is the PON capacity. This is discrete because it is expressed by the total number of codewords, which could be assigned to the PON users. When a call is transferred to a passive state, it is assumed that a number of fictitious codewords are assigned to it from a total number of fictitious codewords C_2. That is, each passive call is accommodated in a fictitious shared link of fictitious discrete capacity C_2 [9]. The number of codewords assigned to a passive call is equal to the number of codewords assigned to the call at the active state.

To show the role of the fictitious system in call admission, let j_1 be the number of codewords of all active calls and j_2 be the number of codewords of all passive calls:

$$j_1 = \sum_{k=1}^{K} n_k^1 b_k \quad \text{and} \quad j_2 = \sum_{k=1}^{K} n_k^2 b_k \tag{9.25}$$

If an arriving call is not blocked because of local blocking, then the CAC works as follows, taking into account the hard blocking conditions of (5.1) and (5.2). Let Ω be the set of all permissible states of the whole system (real and fictitious links), then the occupancy distribution of $\mathbf{j} = (j_1, j_2)$, denoted by $q_F(\mathbf{j})$, is given by a two-dimensional approximate recursive formula, which is similar to (9.13):

$$\sum_{i=1}^{2} \sum_{k=1}^{K} (N_k - n_k^1 - n_k^2 + 1) b_{i,k,s} \rho_{ik,F}(\mathbf{j}) q_F(\mathbf{j} - B_{ik}) = j_s q_F(\mathbf{j}) \tag{9.26}$$

where $s = 1$ and $s = 2$ for the real and the fictitious link, respectively, and j_s is the occupied capacity of the system, given by:

$$j_s = \sum_{i=1}^{2} \sum_{k=1}^{K} n_k^i b_{i,k,s} \tag{9.27}$$

and

$$\rho_{ik,F}(\mathbf{j}) = \begin{cases} \frac{v_k[1 - L_k(j_1 - b_k)]}{(1 - m_k)\mu_{1k}} & \text{for} \quad i = 1 \\ \frac{v_k m_k}{(1 - m_k)\mu_{2k}} & \text{for} \quad i = 2 \end{cases} \tag{9.28}$$

9.4 Further Reading

Due to the relationship between the f-ON–OFF model and the EnMLM (see Section 9.1.2.1), the f-ON–OFF model can be extended to include various characteristics of the EnMLM extensions (see, e.g., Chapter 7). Thus, the interested reader may actually study extensions of the EnMLM and consider as a candidate model the f-ON–OFF model, especially when the combination of call blocking and burst blocking is necessary.

References

1 I. Moscholios, M. Logothetis and M. Koukias, An ON–OFF multirate loss model of finite sources. *IEICE Transactions on Communications*, E90-B(7):1608–1619, July 2007.

2 G. Stamatelos and J. Hayes, Admission control techniques with application to broadband networks. *Computer Communications*, 17(9):663–673, September 1994.

3 I. Moscholios, M. Logothetis and M. Koukias, An ON–OFF multi-rate loss model with a mixture of service-classes of finite and infinite number of sources. *Proceedings of IEEE ICC*, Seoul, Korea, May 2005.

4 J. Vardakas, I. Moscholios, M. Logothetis and V. Stylianakis, Performance analysis of OCDMA PONs supporting multi-rate bursty traffic. *IEEE Transactions on Communications*, 61(8):3374–3384, August 2013.

5 C.-S. Weng and J. Wu, Optical orthogonal codes with nonideal cross correlation. *IEEE/OSA Journal of Lightwave Technology*, 19(12):1856–1863, December 2001.

6 W. Ma, C. Zuo and J. Lin, Performance analysis on phase-encoded OCDMA communication system. *IEEE/OSA Journal of Lightwave Technology*, 20(5):798–803, May 2002.

7 X. Wang and K. Kitayama, Analysis of beat noise in coherent and incoherent time-spreading OCDMA. *IEEE/OSA Journal of Lightwave Technology*, 22(19):2226–2235, October 2004.

8 H.-W. Chen, G.-C. Yang, C.-Y. Chang, T.-C. Lin and W. C. Kwong, Spectral efficiency study of two multirate schemes for asynchronous optical CDMA. *IEEE/OSA Journal of Lightwave Technology*, 27(14):2771–2778, July 2009.

9 J. Vardakas, I. Moscholios, M. Logothetis and V. Stylianakis, On code reservation in multi-rate OCDMA passive optical networks. *Proceedings of IEEE CSNDSP*, Poznan, Poland, July 2012.

Part III

Teletraffic Models of Batched Poisson Input

Part III, includes teletraffic loss models of:

(A) Batched Poisson arriving calls with fixed bandwidth requirements and fixed bandwidth allocation during service.

(B) Batched Poisson arriving calls with fixed bandwidth requirements and elastic bandwidth during service.

10

The Erlang Multirate Loss Model With Batched Poisson Arrivals

In this chapter we consider multirate loss models of batched Poisson arriving calls with fixed bandwidth requirements and fixed bandwidth allocation during service. In the batched Poisson process, simultaneous call-arrivals (batches) occur at time-points which follow a negative exponential distribution. A batched Poisson process can model overflow traffic.

10.1 The Erlang Multirate Loss Model with Batched Poisson Arrivals

10.1.1 The Service System

In the *Erlang multirate loss model with batched Poisson arrivals (BP-EMLM)* we consider a link of capacity C b.u. that accommodates K different service-classes under the CS policy. Calls of all service-classes arrive in the link according to a batched Poisson process.

In the batched Poisson process, one basic principle of random arrivals, according to which no simultaneous arrivals occur (Figure 10.1a), is abolished, while another basic principle of random arrivals, according to which arrivals (the batches) occur at time-points following a negative exponential distribution, is kept (Figure 10.1b) [1–4]. The batched Poisson process is important not only because in several applications calls arrive as batches (groups), but also because it can represent, in an approximate way, arrival processes that are more "peaked" and "bursty" (expressed by the peakedness factor z) than the Poisson process. The peakedness factor, z, is the ratio of the variance over the mean of the number of arrivals: if $z = 1$, the arrival process is Poisson, if $z < 1$, the arrival process is quasi-random (see Chapter 6), and if $z > 1$, the process is more peaked and bursty than Poisson. For example, batched Poisson processes are used to model overflow traffic (where $z > 1$) [3].

Calls of service-class k $(k = 1, \ldots, K)$ require b_k b.u. to be serviced and have an exponentially distributed service time with mean μ_k^{-1}. Calls arrive to the link according to a batched Poisson process with arrival rate λ_k and batch size distribution $D_r^{(k)}$, where $D_r^{(k)}$ denotes the probability that there are r calls in an arriving batch of service-class k.

The batch blocking discipline adopted in the BP-EMLM is partial batch blocking. According to the partial batch blocking discipline, a part of the entire batch (one or

Efficient Multirate Teletraffic Loss Models Beyond Erlang, First Edition.
Ioannis D. Moscholios and Michael D. Logothetis.
© 2019 John Wiley & Sons Ltd. Published 2019 by John Wiley & Sons Ltd.
Companion website: www.wiley.com/go/logocode

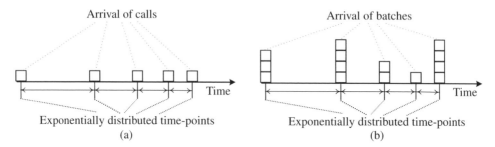

Figure 10.1 Call arrivals according to (a) a Poisson process and (b) a batched Poisson process.

more calls) is accepted in the link while the rest of it is discarded when the available link bandwidth is not enough to accommodate the entire batch. More precisely, if an arriving batch of service-class k contains n calls and the available link bandwidth is m b.u., where $m < nb_k$, then $\lfloor m/b_k \rfloor$ calls will be accepted in the link (where $\lfloor x \rfloor$ is the largest integer not exceeding x) and the other $n - \lfloor m/b_k \rfloor$ calls will be blocked and lost. The complete batch blocking discipline, where the whole batch is blocked and lost, even if only one call of the batch cannot be accepted in the system, is not covered here since it results in complex and inefficient formulas for the calculation of the various performance measures [2, 5–7].

Let n_k be the number of in-service calls of service-class k in the steady state and $\mathbf{n} = (n_1, \dots, n_k, \dots, n_K)$, $\mathbf{b} = (b_1, \dots, b_k, \dots, b_K)$. Due to the CS policy, the set Ω of the state space is given by (I.36). In terms of Ω and due to the partial batch blocking discipline (where each call is treated separately to the other calls of a batch), the CAC is identical to that of the EMLM (see Section 1.2.1).

10.1.2 The Analytical Model

10.1.2.1 Steady State Probabilities
In order to analyze the service system, the first target is to determine the PFS of the steady state probability $P(\mathbf{n})$. In the classical EMLM, the PFS of (1.30) is determined as a consequence of the LB between adjacent states. In the BP-EMLM, the notion of LB as described in the EMLM does not hold; this is shown by the following example.

Example 10.1 Consider a link of $C = 7$ b.u. The link accommodates calls of $K = 2$ service-classes whose calls require $b_1 = 3$ b.u. and $b_2 = 2$ b.u., respectively. Figures 10.2a and 10.2 show the state space Ω and the transitions between all states in the case of the EMLM and the BP-EMLM, respectively. It is obvious, via Figure 10.2b, that in the case of the BP-EMLM there is no LB between adjacent states. However, there exists a form of local flow balance between "upward" and "downward" rates across certain levels that is sufficient to guarantee a PFS for the steady state probability [3]. Such a level is $L_{\mathbf{n}}^{(k)} \overset{k=2}{\underset{\mathbf{n}=(0,1)}{=}} L_{(0,1)}^{(2)}$ (see Figure 10.2b), which separates state $(n_1, n_2) = (0, 1)$ from state $(n_1, n_2 + 1) = (0, 2)$.

To describe the analytical model in the steady state and show that the steady state probability $P(\mathbf{n})$ has a PFS, we present the following notations [3]:

$$\mathbf{n}_k^{+m} = (n_1, n_2, \dots, n_{k-1}, n_k + m, n_{k+1}, \dots, n_K), \quad m = 1, 2, \dots$$
$$\mathbf{n}_k^{-m} = (n_1, n_2, \dots, n_{k-1}, n_k - m, n_{k+1}, \dots, n_K), \quad m = 1, 2, \dots n_k$$

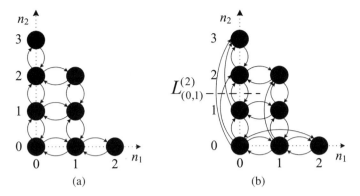

Figure 10.2 The state transition diagram in (a) the EMLM and (b) the BP-EMLM (Example 10.1).

For every state $\mathbf{n}$, we denote the level $L_{\mathbf{n}}^{(k)}$ which separates state $\mathbf{n}$ from state $\mathbf{n}_k^{+1} = (n_1, n_2, \ldots, n_{k-1}, n_k + 1, n_{k+1}, \ldots, n_K)$. Then, the "upward" (due to a new service-class k batch arrival) probability flow across the level $L_{\mathbf{n}}^{(k)}$ is given by [3]:

$$f^{(\mathrm{up})}(L_{\mathbf{n}}^{(k)}) = \sum_{l=0}^{n_k} P(\mathbf{n}_k^{-l})\lambda_k \sum_{m=l+1}^{\infty} D_m^{(k)} \tag{10.1}$$

where $\mathbf{n}_k^{-l} = (n_1, n_2, \ldots, n_{k-1}, n_k - l, n_{k+1}, \ldots, n_K)$ and $P(\mathbf{n}_k^{-l})$ is the corresponding steady state probability.

Equation (10.1) can be also written as follows:

$$f^{(\mathrm{up})}(L_{\mathbf{n}}^{(k)}) = \sum_{l=0}^{n_k} P(\mathbf{n}_k^{-l})\lambda_k \widehat{D}_l^{(k)} \tag{10.2}$$

where $\widehat{D}_l^{(k)} = \sum_{m=l+1}^{\infty} D_m^{(k)}$ is the complementary batch size distribution.

If we set $\mathbf{n}_k^{+1} = (n_1, n_2, \ldots, n_{k-1}, n_k + 1, n_{k+1}, \ldots, n_K)$, then the "downward" probability flow across the level $L_{\mathbf{n}}^{(k)}$ (due to a service-class k call departure) is given by [3]:

$$f^{(\mathrm{down})}(L_{\mathbf{n}}^{(k)}) = (n_k + 1)\mu_k P(\mathbf{n}_k^{+1}) \tag{10.3}$$

Example 10.2 Consider again Example 10.1 ($C = 7, K = 2, b_1 = 3, b_2 = 2$) and let the corresponding batch arrival rates be λ_1 and λ_2.

(a) Determine, via (10.1), the "upward" probability flow across the level $L_{(0,1)}^{(2)}$ due to a new batch arrival of service-class 2.
(b) Repeat the previous calculation for level $L_{(0,2)}^{(2)}$.

(a) Upward probability flow across level $L_{(0,1)}^{(2)}$.

Since $\mathbf{n} = (n_1, n_2) = (0, 1)$ and $\mathbf{n}_2^{-l} = (n_1, n_2 - l) = (0, 1 - l)$, (10.1) can be written as:

$$f^{(\mathrm{up})}(L_{(0,1)}^{(2)}) = \sum_{l=0}^{1} P(\mathbf{n}_2^{-l})\lambda_2 \sum_{m=l+1}^{\infty} D_m^{(2)} \Rightarrow$$

$$f^{(\mathrm{up})}(L_{(0,1)}^{(2)}) = P(0,1)\lambda_2 \sum_{m=1}^{\infty} D_m^{(2)} + P(0,0)\lambda_2 \sum_{m=2}^{\infty} D_m^{(2)} \tag{10.4}$$

The first term of the RHS of (10.4) refers to the case where the system state is $(0, 1)$ and a batch with at least one call (since $m = 1$) arrives in the link. The second term refers to the case where the system state is $(0, 0)$ and a batch with at least two calls (since $m = 2$) arrives in the link. In both cases, we have an "upward" flow across the level $L_{(0,1)}^{(2)}$.

(b) Upward probability flow across the level $L_{(0,2)}^{(2)}$.

Since $\mathbf{n} = (n_1, n_2) = (0, 2)$ and $\mathbf{n}_2^{-l} = (n_1, n_2 - l) = (0, 2 - l)$, (10.1) is written as:

$$f^{(\text{up})}(L_{(0,2)}^{(2)}) = \sum_{l=0}^{2} P(\mathbf{n}_2^{-l})\lambda_2 \sum_{m=l+1}^{\infty} D_m^{(2)} \Rightarrow$$

$$f^{(\text{up})}(L_{(0,2)}^{(2)}) = P(0, 2)\lambda_2 \sum_{m=1}^{\infty} D_m^{(2)} + P(0, 1)\lambda_2 \sum_{m=2}^{\infty} D_m^{(2)} + P(0, 0)\lambda_2 \sum_{m=3}^{\infty} D_m^{(2)} \quad (10.5)$$

Based on (10.2) and (10.3), we have the following local flow balance equation across the level $L_{\mathbf{n}}^{(k)}$ for service-class k calls:

$$f^{(\text{up})}(L_{\mathbf{n}}^{(k)}) = f^{(\text{down})}(L_{\mathbf{n}}^{(k)}), \quad \text{or}$$

$$\sum_{l=0}^{n_k} P(\mathbf{n}_k^{-l})\lambda_k \widehat{D}_l^{(k)} = (n_k + 1)\mu_k P(\mathbf{n}_k^{+1}), \quad k = 1, \dots, K \quad (10.6)$$

The following lemma establishes the sufficiency of the flow balance across the levels $L_{\mathbf{n}}^{(k)}$ for ensuring GB for state n [3]:

Lemma 10.1 If $P(\mathbf{n})$ satisfies $f^{(\text{up})}(L_{\mathbf{n}}^{(k)}) = f^{(\text{down})}(L_{\mathbf{n}}^{(k)})$ for $1 \leq k \leq K$ and all $\mathbf{n} \in \Omega$, then $P(\mathbf{n})$ also satisfies the GB equations.

Proof: Consider a state $\mathbf{n} \in \Omega$ and the difference $f^{(\text{up})}(L_{\mathbf{n}}^{(k)}) - f^{(\text{up})}(L_{\mathbf{n}_k^{-1}}^{(k)})$ which is interpreted as follows (after some simplifications), regarding arrivals from service-class k:

$$f^{(\text{up})}(L_{\mathbf{n}}^{(k)}) - f^{(\text{up})}(L_{\mathbf{n}_k^{-1}}^{(k)}) = \{\text{Probability flow \underline{out of} state } \mathbf{n} \text{ due to a batch arrival}\}$$

$$-\{\text{Probability flow \underline{into} state } \mathbf{n} \text{ due to a batch arrival}\} \quad (10.7)$$

Similarly, we may write, regarding departures from service-class k:

$$f^{(\text{down})}(L_{\mathbf{n}}^{(k)}) - f^{(\text{down})}(L_{\mathbf{n}_k^{-1}}^{(k)})$$

$$= \{\text{Probability flow \underline{into} state } \mathbf{n} \text{ due to a call departure}\} \quad (10.8)$$

$$- \{\text{Probability flow \underline{out of} state } \mathbf{n} \text{ due to a call departure}\}$$

By equating (10.7) and (10.8) and rearranging the terms, we have (for service-class k):

Probability flow <u>into</u> state $\mathbf{n}$ due to a batch arrival +

Probability flow <u>into</u> state $\mathbf{n}$ due to a call departure =

Probability flow <u>out of</u> state $\mathbf{n}$ due to a batch arrival + $\quad (10.9)$

Probability flow <u>out of</u> state $\mathbf{n}$ due to a call departure =

Summing (10.9) over all k ($1 \leq k \leq K$) yields the GB equation for state n:

$$\sum_{k=1}^{K} [f^{(\text{up})}(L_{\mathbf{n}_k^{-1}}^{(k)}) + f^{(\text{down})}(L_{\mathbf{n}}^{(k)})] = \sum_{k=1}^{K} [f^{(\text{up})}(L_{\mathbf{n}}^{(k)}) + f^{(\text{down})}(L_{\mathbf{n}_k^{-1}}^{(k)})] \tag{10.10}$$

Q.E.D.

Example 10.3 Consider a link of capacity $C = 7$ b.u. that accommodates only calls of a single service-class ($K = 1$) which require $b_1 = 2$ b.u. Let the batch arrival rate be λ_1 and the call service rate be μ_1. Consider states $n_1 = 1$ and $n_1 = 2$. The purpose of this example is to show the GB equation of state $n_1 = 2$. To this end, determine the differences $f^{(\text{up})}(L_{(2)}^{(1)}) - f^{(\text{up})}(L_{(1)}^{(1)})$ and $f^{(\text{down})}(L_{(2)}^{(1)}) - f^{(\text{down})}(L_{(1)}^{(1)})$ based on (10.2) and (10.3), respectively. Present graphically the GB equation of state $n_1 = 2$.

The difference $f^{(\text{up})}(L_{(2)}^{(1)}) - f^{(\text{up})}(L_{(1)}^{(1)})$ can be written as:

$$f^{(\text{up})}(L_{(2)}^{(1)}) - f^{(\text{up})}(L_{(1)}^{(1)}) = P(2)\lambda_1 \sum_{m=1}^{\infty} D_m^{(1)} + P(1)\lambda_1 \sum_{m=2}^{\infty} D_m^{(1)} + P(0)\lambda_1 \sum_{m=3}^{\infty} D_m^{(1)}$$
$$- P(1)\lambda_1 \sum_{m=1}^{\infty} D_m^{(1)} - P(0)\lambda_1 \sum_{m=2}^{\infty} D_m^{(1)} \Rightarrow$$

$$f^{(\text{up})}(L_{(2)}^{(1)}) - f^{(\text{up})}(L_{(1)}^{(1)}) = P(2)\lambda_1 \sum_{m=1}^{\infty} D_m^{(1)} - P(1)\lambda_1 D_1^{(1)} - P(0)\lambda_1 D_2^{(1)} \tag{10.11}$$

Similarly, the difference $f^{(\text{down})}(L_{(2)}^{(1)}) - f^{(\text{down})}(L_{(1)}^{(1)})$ is written as:

$$f^{(\text{down})}(L_{(2)}^{(1)}) - f^{(\text{down})}(L_{(1)}^{(1)}) = 3\mu_1 P(3) - 2\mu_1 P(2) \tag{10.12}$$

By equating (10.11) and (10.12) and rearranging the terms (in the form *rate into state (2) = rate out of state (2)*), we have:

$$P(0)\lambda_1 D_2^{(1)} + P(1)\lambda_1 D_1^{(1)} + 3\mu_1 P(3) = P(2)\lambda_1 \sum_{m=1}^{\infty} D_m^{(1)} + 2\mu_1 P(2) \tag{10.13}$$

The purpose of Figure 10.3 is to represent (10.13) graphically (the GB equation of state (2)).

The PFS that satisfies (10.6) and (10.10) is given by [3]:

$$P(\mathbf{n}) = G^{-1}\left(\prod_{k=1}^{K} P_{n_k}^{(k)}\right) \tag{10.14}$$

Figure 10.3 Graphical representation of (10.13) (Example 10.3).

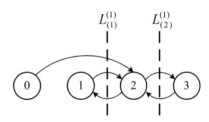

where G is the normalization constant, $G \equiv G(\Omega) = \sum_{\mathbf{n} \in \Omega} \left(\prod_{k=1}^{K} P_{n_k}^{(k)} \right)$, Ω is the state space of the system, $\Omega = \{\mathbf{n} : 0 \leq \mathbf{nb} \leq C, \ k = 1, \ldots, K\}$, $\mathbf{nb} = \sum_{k=1}^{K} n_k b_k$, and

$$P_{n_k}^{(k)} = \begin{cases} \sum_{l=1}^{n_k} \alpha_k \dfrac{P_{n_k-l}^{(k)} \widehat{D}_{l-1}^{(k)}}{n_k} & \text{for } n_k \geq 1 \\ 1 & \text{for } n_k = 0 \end{cases} \tag{10.15}$$

where $\alpha_k = \lambda_k / \mu_k$ is the offered traffic-load (in erl).

An important batch size distribution is the geometric distribution, which is memory-less and a discrete equivalent of the exponential distribution. If calls of service-class k arrive in batches of size s_k, where s_k is geometrically distributed with parameter β_k, i.e., $Pr(s_k = r) = (1 - \beta_k)\beta_k^{r-1}$ with $r \geq 1$, then we have in (10.15), $\widehat{D}_{l-1}^{(k)} = \beta_k^{l-1}$. In that case, the average batch size for service-class k batches will be $1/(1 - \beta_k)$.

Example 10.4 Consider a link of $C = 3$ b.u. The link accommodates calls of $K = 2$ service-classes whose calls require $b_1 = 1$ b.u. and $b_2 = 2$ b.u., respectively. Let $\lambda_1 = \lambda_2 = \mu_1 = \mu_2 = 1$ min^{-1}. Assuming that the batch size distribution is geometrically distributed with parameters $\beta_1 = 0.2$ and $\beta_2 = 0.5$, calculate the values of $P(\mathbf{n})$ and the corresponding values of $Q(j)$ based on the GB equations of (10.10).

The state space Ω of this system consists of six states of the form $\mathbf{n} = (n_1, n_2)$, namely $(0,0)$, $(0,1)$, $(1,0)$, $(1,1)$, $(2,0)$, and $(3,0)$. The GB equation, according to (10.10), for state $(0,0)$ is:

$$(0,0) : \sum_{k=1}^{K} f^{(\text{up})}(L_{\mathbf{n}}^{(k)}) = \sum_{k=1}^{K} f^{(\text{down})}(L_{\mathbf{n}}^{(k)}) \Rightarrow$$

$$f^{(\text{up})}(L_{(0,0)}^{(1)}) + f^{(\text{up})}(L_{(0,0)}^{(2)}) = f^{(\text{down})}(L_{(0,0)}^{(1)}) + f^{(\text{down})}(L_{(0,0)}^{(2)}) \Rightarrow$$

$$\lambda_1 P(0,0) \sum_{m=1}^{\infty} D_m^{(1)} + \lambda_2 P(0,0) \sum_{m=1}^{\infty} D_m^{(2)} = \mu_1 P(1,0) + \mu_2 P(0,1) \Rightarrow$$

$$\lambda_1 P(0,0)\beta_1^0 + \lambda_2 P(0,0)\beta_2^0 = \mu_1 P(1,0) + \mu_2 P(0,1) \Rightarrow$$

$$P(1,0) + P(0,1) - 2P(0,0) = 0$$

Similarly, the rest GB equations are:

$(0,1) : \quad P(0,0) + P(1,1) - 2P(0,1) = 0$

$(1,0) : \quad 0.8P(0,0) + P(1,1) + 2P(2,0) - 3P(1,0) = 0$

$(1,1) : \quad P(0,1) + P(1,0) - 2P(1,1) = 0$

$(2,0) : \quad 0.8P(1,0) + 0.16P(0,0) + 3P(3,0) - 3P(2,0) = 0$

$(3,0) : \quad 0.04P(0,0) + 0.2P(1,0) + P(2,0) - 3P(3,0) = 0$

The solution of this linear system is:

$P(0,0) = 0.2049 \quad P(0,1) = 0.2049 \quad P(1,0) = 0.2049$

$P(1,1) = 0.2049 \quad P(2,0) = 0.1230 \quad P(3,0) = 0.0574$

Based on the values of $P(n_1, n_2)$, we have:

$Q(0) = P(0,0) = 0.2049 \qquad Q(1) = P(1,0) = 0.2049$

$Q(2) = P(0,1) + P(2,0) = 0.3279 \quad Q(3) = P(1,1) + P(3,0) = 0.2623$

The existence of a PFS for the steady-state probabilities leads to an accurate recursive formula for the calculation of the unnormalized link occupancy distribution, $q(j)$ [3]:

$$q(j) = \begin{cases} 1 & \text{if } j = 0 \\ \dfrac{1}{j} \displaystyle\sum_{k=1}^{K} \alpha_k b_k \sum_{l=1}^{\lfloor j/b_k \rfloor} \widehat{D}_{l-1}^{(k)} q(j - l \times b_k) & j = 1, \dots, C \\ 0 & \text{otherwise} \end{cases} \tag{10.16}$$

where $\alpha_k = \lambda_k/\mu_k$, $\lfloor j/b_k \rfloor$ is the largest integer less than or equal to j/b_k and $\widehat{D}_l^{(k)}$ is the complementary batch size distribution given by $\widehat{D}_l^{(k)} = \sum_{m=l+1}^{\infty} D_m^{(k)}$.

The proof of (10.16) is similar to the proof of (1.39) and therefore is omitted.

If calls of service-class k arrive in batches of size s_k, where s_k is given by the geometric distribution with parameter β_k (for all k) then the BP-EMLM coincides with the model proposed by Delbrouck in [8], as shown in [1] and [3]. More precisely, since $\widehat{D}_{l-1}^{(k)} = \beta_k^{l-1}$, (10.16) takes the form:

$$q(j) = \begin{cases} 1 & \text{if } j = 0 \\ \dfrac{1}{j} \displaystyle\sum_{k=1}^{K} \alpha_k b_k \sum_{l=1}^{\lfloor j/b_k \rfloor} \beta_k^{l-1} q(j - l \times b_k) & j = 1, \dots, C \\ 0 & \text{otherwise} \end{cases} \tag{10.17}$$

If $D_m^{(k)} = 1$ for $m = 1$ and $D_m^{(k)} = 0$ for $m > 1$, for all service-classes, then we have a Poisson process and the EMLM results (i.e., the Kaufman–Roberts recursion of (1.39)).

10.1.2.2 TC Probabilities, CBP, Utilization, and Mean Number of In-service Calls

The following performance measures can be determined based on (10.16):

- The TC probabilities of service-class k, B_{Tk}, via the formula:

$$B_{Tk} = \sum_{j=C-b_k+1}^{C} G^{-1} q(j) \tag{10.18}$$

where $G = \sum_{j=0}^{C} q(j)$ is the normalization constant.

- The CBP (or CC probabilities) of service-class k, B_k, via the formula:

$$B_k = (\alpha_k \widehat{D}_k - \overline{n}_k)/\alpha_k \widehat{D}_k \tag{10.19}$$

where $\widehat{D}_k$ denotes the average size of service k arriving batches and is given by $\widehat{D}_k = \sum_{m=1}^{\infty} m D_m^{(k)}$. In the case of the geometric distribution, $\widehat{D}_k = 1/(1 - \beta_k)$.

- The mean number of in-service calls of service-class k, $\overline{n}_k$, via (1.56), where the values of $y_k(j)$ can be determined via:

$$y_k(j) = \alpha_k \frac{\displaystyle\sum_{l=1}^{\lfloor j/b_k \rfloor} \widehat{D}_{l-1}^{(k)} q(j - l \times b_k)}{q(j)}, \quad j = 1, \dots, C \tag{10.20}$$

where $q(j) > 0$ and $y_k(j) = 0$ if $j < b_k$.

Note that (10.20) is an intermediate result for the proof of (10.16) [3]. Indeed, by multiplying both sides of (10.20) with b_k and taking the sum over all service-classes, we have (10.16).

- The link utilization, U, via (1.54).

Example 10.5   In this example we present the difference between TC and CC probabilities. Consider a link of capacity $C = 12$ b.u. that accommodates calls of two services with requirements $b_1 = 1$ and $b_2 = 2$ b.u., respectively. In Figure 10.4 we assume that the link has 6 b.u. available for new calls. At the first time-point, a call of service-class 2 arrives. This call is accepted and the available link bandwidth reduces to 4 b.u. At the second time-point, a batch of service-class 1 arrives consisting of five calls. One out of these calls is blocked and lost. This type of blocking has to do with CC probability (one blocking event, see the CC probability calculation in Figure 10.4). At the third time-point, we assume that there is available bandwidth to accept the whole batch of service-class 1 (two calls) while at the fourth time-point we assume that the whole batch of service-class 2 (two calls) is discarded. This type of blocking has to do with both TC probability (one blocking event, see the TC probability calculation in Figure 10.4) and CC probability (two blocking events, see the CC probability calculation in Figure 10.4). At the fourth to sixth time-points, the comments are similar and thus they are omitted. According to Figure 10.4, the calculation of both CC and TC probabilities gives higher CC probabilities, an expected result since calls arrive following a batched Poisson process.

Example 10.6   Consider again Example 10.4 ($C = 3, K = 2, b_1 = 1, b_2 = 2, \lambda_1 = \lambda_2 = \mu_1 = \mu_2 = 1, \beta_1 = 0.2, \beta_2 = 0.5$).

(a) Calculate the state probabilities $Q(j)$ by applying (10.17).
(b) Calculate the TC and CC probabilities as well as the link utilization via (10.18), (10.19)–(10.20), and (1.54), respectively. Compare the obtained results with those of the EMLM.

(a) Starting with $q(0) = 1$, we recursively calculate $q(j)$ for $j = 1, \dots, 3$:

$j = 1$: $q(1) = q(0) + 0 = 1.0$ $\qquad\qquad\qquad\Rightarrow q(1) = 1.0$
$j = 2$: $q(2) = q(1) + 0.2q(0) + 2q(0) = 3.2$ $\qquad\Rightarrow q(2) = 1.6$
$j = 3$: $3q(3) = q(2) + 0.2q(1) + 0.04q(0) + 2q(1) = 3.84$ $\quad\Rightarrow q(3) = 1.28$

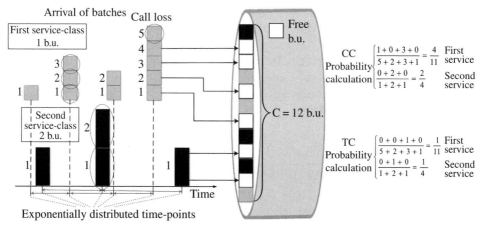

Figure 10.4 Difference between CC and TC probabilities (Example 10.5).

The normalization constant is: $G = \sum_{j=0}^{3} q(j) = 4.88$.
The state probabilities (link occupancy distribution) are:

$$Q(0) = Q(1) = 0.204918 \quad Q(2) = 0.327869 \quad Q(3) = 0.262295$$

(b) TC probabilities:

$$B_{T1} = \sum_{j=C-b_1+1}^{C} G^{-1}q(j) = \frac{q(3)}{G} \Rightarrow B_{T1} = 0.262295$$

$$B_{T2} = \sum_{j=C-b_2+1}^{C} G^{-1}q(j) = \frac{q(2)+q(3)}{G} \Rightarrow B_{T2} = 0.59016$$

To determine the CC probabilities, we should initially determine the values of $y_k(j)$ and $\bar{n}_k$.

$$j = 1: \quad y_1(1) = 1 \qquad y_2(1) = 0$$
$$j = 2: \quad y_1(2) = 0.75 \qquad y_2(2) = 0.625$$
$$j = 3: \quad y_1(3) = 1.4375 \quad y_2(3) = 0.78125$$

$$\bar{n}_1 = \frac{q(1)+0.75q(2)+1.4375q(3)}{G} = \frac{4.04}{4.88} \Rightarrow \bar{n}_1 = 0.827868$$
$$\bar{n}_2 = \frac{0.625q(2)+0.78125q(3)}{G} = \frac{2}{4.88} \Rightarrow \bar{n}_2 = 0.409836$$

Based on the above we have:

$$B_1 = (\alpha_1\hat{D}_1 - \bar{n}_1)/\alpha_1\hat{D}_1 = (1.25 - 0.827868)/1.25 = 0.3377$$
$$B_2 = (\alpha_2\hat{D}_2 - \bar{n}_2)/\alpha_2\hat{D}_2 = (2.0 - 0.409836)/2.0 = 0.79508$$

Utilization: $U = \sum_{j=1}^{C} jQ(j) = 1.6475$ b.u.
The corresponding CBP and link utilization results in the EMLM are:

$$B_1 = 0.25 \quad B_2 = 0.5714 \quad U = 1.61 \text{ b.u.}$$

10.2 The Erlang Multirate Loss Model with Batched Poisson Arrivals under the BR Policy

10.2.1 The Service System

In the *Erlang multirate loss model with batched Poisson arrivals under the BR policy* (*BP-EMLM/BR*) a new service-class k call is accepted in the link if, after its acceptance, the link has at least t_k b.u. available to serve calls of other service-classes.

In terms of the system state-space Ω and due to the partial batch blocking discipline, the CAC is identical to that of the EMLM/BR (see Section 1.3.2.2).

10.2.2 The Analytical Model

10.2.2.1 Link Occupancy Distribution
In the BP-EMLM/BR, the unnormalized values of the link occupancy distribution, $q(j)$, can be calculated in an approximate way according to either the Roberts method (see Section 1.3.2.2) or the Stasiak–Glabowski method (see Section 1.3.2.3). Herein

we present the first method. Both methods have been investigated in [9], where the conclusions show that (i) both methods provide satisfactory results compared to simulation results, (ii) the Roberts method is preferable when only two service-classes exist in the link or when the offered traffic-load is low, and (iii) the Stasiak–Glabowski method can be considered when equalization of blocking probabilities is required, whereas it is preferable when more than two services exist and the offered traffic-load is high.

Based on Roberts method, (10.16) takes the form [9]:

$$
q(j) = \begin{cases} 1 & \text{if } j = 0 \\ \dfrac{1}{j} \sum_{k=1}^{K} \alpha_k D_k(j - b_k) \sum_{l=1}^{\lfloor j/b_k \rfloor} \widehat{D}_{l-1}^{(k)} q(j - l \times b_k) & j = 1, \dots, C \\ 0 & \text{otherwise} \end{cases}
\tag{10.21}
$$

where $D_k(j - b_k)$ is determined via (1.65).

10.2.2.2 TC Probabilities, CBP, Utilization, and Mean Number of In-service Calls

The following performance measures can be determined based on (10.21):

- The TC probabilities of service-class k, B_{Tk}, via the formula:

$$
B_{Tk} = \sum_{j=C-b_k-t_k+1}^{C} G^{-1} q(j)
\tag{10.22}
$$

where $G = \sum_{j=0}^{C} q(j)$ is the normalization constant.
- The CBP (or CC probabilities) of service-class k, B_k, via (10.19).
- The mean number of in-service calls of service-class k, $\overline{n}_k$, via (1.56), where the values of $y_k(j)$ can be determined via:

$$
y_k(j) = \begin{cases} \alpha_k \dfrac{\sum_{l=1}^{\lfloor j/b_k \rfloor} \widehat{D}_{l-1}^{(k)} q(j - l \times b_k)}{q(j)} & \text{for } j \leq C - t_k \\ 0 & \text{for } j > C - t_k \end{cases}
\tag{10.23}
$$

- The link utilization, U, via (1.54).

Example 10.7 Consider again Example 10.4 ($C = 3, K = 2, b_1 = 1, b_2 = 2, \lambda_1 = \lambda_2 = \mu_1 = \mu_2 = 1, \beta_1 = 0.2, \beta_2 = 0.5$) and assume the BR parameters $t_1 = 1, t_2 = 0$.

(a) Calculate the state probabilities $Q(j)$ by applying (10.21).
(b) Calculate the TC and CC probabilities as well as the link utilization via (10.12), (10.19)–(10.20), (10.23), and (1.54), respectively. Compare the results obtained with those of the EMLM/BR.

(a) Starting with $q(0) = 1$, we recursively calculate $q(j)$ for $j = 1, \dots, 3$:

$j = 1:$ $\quad q(1) = q(0) + 0 = 1.0$ $\qquad\qquad \Rightarrow \qquad q(1) = 1.0$

$j = 2:$ $\quad 2q(2) = q(1) + 0.2q(0) + 2q(0) = 3.2$ $\Rightarrow$ $\quad q(2) = 1.6$

$j = 3:$ $\quad 3q(3) = 0 + 2q(1) = 2.0$ $\qquad\qquad\qquad \Rightarrow \qquad q(3) = 0.66667$

The normalization constant is: $G = \sum_{j=0}^{3} q(j) = 4.26667$.
The state probabilities (link occupancy distribution) are:

$$Q(0) = Q(1) = 0.234375 \quad Q(2) = 0.375 \quad Q(3) = 0.15625$$

(b) TC probabilities are:

$$B_{T1} = \sum_{j=C-b_1-t_1+1}^{C} G^{-1}q(j) = \frac{q(2)+q(3)}{G} \Rightarrow B_{T1} = 0.53125$$

$$B_{T2} = \sum_{j=C-b_2-t_2+1}^{C} G^{-1}q(j) = \frac{q(2)+q(3)}{G} \Rightarrow B_{T2} = 0.53125$$

To determine the CC probabilities, we should initially determine the values of $y_k(j)$ and $\bar{n}_k$.

$$j = 1: \quad y_1(1) = 1 \qquad y_2(1) = 0$$
$$j = 2: \quad y_1(2) = 0.75 \quad y_2(2) = 0.625$$
$$j = 3: \quad y_1(3) = 0 \qquad y_2(3) = 1.5$$

$$\bar{n}_1 = \frac{q(1)+0.75q(2)}{G} = \frac{2.2}{4.26667} \quad \Rightarrow \bar{n}_1 = 0.51562$$
$$\bar{n}_2 = \frac{0.625q(2)+1.5q(3)}{G} = \frac{2}{4.26667} \quad \Rightarrow \bar{n}_2 = 0.46875$$

Based on the above we have:

$$B_1 = (\alpha_1\hat{D}_1 - \bar{n}_1)/\alpha_1\hat{D}_1 = (1.25 - 0.51562)/1.25 = 0.5875$$
$$B_2 = (\alpha_2\hat{D}_2 - \bar{n}_2)/\alpha_2\hat{D}_2 = (2.0 - 0.46875)/2.0 = 0.765625$$

Utilization: $U = \sum_{j=1}^{C} jQ(j) = 1.453$ b.u.
The corresponding CBP and link utilization results in the EMLM/BR are:

$$B_1 = B_2 = 0.52 \text{ and } U = 1.44 \text{ b.u.}$$

Example 10.8 Consider a link of capacity $C = 60$ b.u. that accommodates two service-classes whose calls require $b_1 = 1$ b.u. and $b_2 = 12$ b.u., respectively. Consider also the following sets of BR parameters: (i) $t_1 = 3$ and $t_2 = 0$, (ii) $t_1 = 7$ and $t_2 = 0$, and (iii) $t_1 = 11$ and $t_2 = 0$. The third set equalizes the TC probabilities of both service-classes, since $b_1 + t_1 = b_2 + t_2$. The batch size of both service-classes follows the geometric distribution with parameters $\beta_1 = 0.2$ and $\beta_2 = 0.5$. The call service time is exponentially distributed with mean $\mu_1^{-1} = \mu_2^{-1} = 1$. The values of the offered traffic are $\alpha_1 = 10$ erl and $\alpha_2 = 2$ erl. In the first column of Tables 10.1–10.9, α_1 remains constant while α_2 decreases by 0.2. As a reference, Table 10.1 shows the analytical results of TC and CC probabilities (for both service-classes) in the case of the BP-EMLM (CS policy). In Tables 10.2–10.4, for each set of BR parameters and for both service-classes, we present the analytical and simulation results for the TC probabilities in the BP-EMLM/BR. The corresponding results for the CC probabilities are presented in Tables 10.5–10.7. Table 10.8 presents the analytical results of the link utilization for both the BP-EMLM and the BP-EMLM/BR as well as the corresponding simulation results only for the BP-EMLM/BR. All simulation results are mean values of seven runs with 95% confidence interval.

Table 10.1 Analytical results of TC and CC probabilities and link utilization for the BP-EMLM (Example 10.8).

α_2	TC probabilities (%) (analyt. results)		CC probabilities (%) (analyt. results)	
	Service-class 1	Service-class 2	Service-class 1	Service-class 2
2.0	2.52	25.56	3.14	47.84
1.8	2.20	22.99	2.74	45.17
1.6	1.88	20.32	2.35	42.26
1.4	1.57	17.54	1.96	39.08
1.2	1.26	14.69	1.58	35.62
1.0	0.97	11.79	1.22	31.85
0.8	0.70	8.92	0.88	27.76
0.6	0.46	6.16	0.58	23.38

Table 10.2 Analytical and simulation results of the TC probabilities for the BP-EMLM/BR ($t_1 = 3$) (Example 10.8).

α_2	TC probabilities (%)		Simulation (%)	
	Service-class 1	Service-class 2	Service-class 1	Service-class 2
2.0	8.27	24.44	7.46 ± 0.08	24.82 ± 0.19
1.8	7.23	21.98	6.50 ± 0.10	22.32 ± 0.32
1.6	6.20	19.42	5.56 ± 0.13	19.61 ± 0.19
1.4	5.18	16.76	4.75 ± 0.08	16.80 ± 0.26
1.2	4.18	14.04	3.83 ± 0.09	14.27 ± 0.23
1.0	3.22	11.27	2.95 ± 0.07	11.35 ± 0.23
0.8	2.33	8.53	2.12 ± 0.07	8.68 ± 0.23
0.6	1.53	5.89	1.40 ± 0.05	6.26 ± 0.22

Table 10.3 Analytical and simulation results of the TC probabilities for the BP-EMLM/BR ($t_1 = 7$) (Example 10.8).

α_2	TC probabilities (%)		Simulation (%)	
	Service-class 1	Service-class 2	Service-class 1	Service-class 2
2.0	13.88	23.24	14.90 ± 0.13	24.05 ± 0.18
1.8	12.24	20.87	13.10 ± 0.23	21.55 ± 0.18
1.6	10.58	18.40	11.16 ± 0.22	19.16 ± 0.21
1.4	8.93	15.86	9.54 ± 0.14	16.45 ± 0.20
1.2	7.30	13.25	7.65 ± 0.10	13.94 ± 0.31
1.0	5.71	10.62	6.07 ± 0.08	10.98 ± 0.19
0.8	4.19	8.03	4.35 ± 0.10	8.46 ± 0.20
0.6	2.81	5.53	2.93 ± 0.04	5.82 ± 0.26

Table 10.4 Analytical and simulation results of the equalized TC probabilities for the BP-EMLM/BR ($t_1 = 11$) (Example 10.8).

α_2	Analytical results - Equalised TC probabilities (%)	Simulation (%)	
		Service-class 1	Service-class 2
2.0	21.40	22.32 ± 0.25	22.30 ± 0.23
1.8	19.12	19.87 ± 0.22	19.89 ± 0.14
1.6	16.78	17.39 ± 0.16	17.42 ± 0.22
1.4	14.37	14.80 ± 0.18	14.79 ± 0.29
1.2	11.94	12.35 ± 0.18	12.38 ± 0.23
1.0	9.51	9.80 ± 0.12	9.78 ± 0.19
0.8	7.13	7.35 ± 0.05	7.38 ± 0.09
0.6	4.88	5.04 ± 0.14	5.05 ± 0.13

Table 10.5 Analytical and simulation results of the CC probabilities for the BP-EMLM/BR ($t_1 = 3$) (Example 10.8).

α_2	Analytical results (%)		Simulation (%)	
	Service-class 1	Service-class 2	Service-class 1	Service-class 2
2.0	8.74	47.06	8.23 ± 0.07	47.06 ± 0.18
1.8	7.65	44.45	7.17 ± 0.10	44.41 ± 0.14
1.6	6.56	41.61	6.13 ± 0.14	41.77 ± 0.14
1.4	5.49	38.51	5.23 ± 0.08	38.39 ± 0.21
1.2	4.43	35.13	4.22 ± 0.12	35.16 ± 0.10
1.0	3.42	31.44	3.25 ± 0.07	31.61 ± 0.25
0.8	2.48	27.46	2.33 ± 0.08	27.48 ± 0.22
0.6	1.63	23.17	1.56 ± 0.03	23.49 ± 0.25

Table 10.6 Analytical and simulation results of the CC probabilities for the BP-EMLM/BR ($t_1 = 7$) (Example 10.8).

α_2	Analytical results (%)		Simulation (%)	
	Service-class 1	Service-class 2	Service-class 1	Service-class 2
2.0	14.36	46.22	15.57 ± 0.14	46.50 ± 0.05
1.8	12.69	43.66	13.68 ± 0.23	43.80 ± 0.12
1.6	10.99	40.88	11.71 ± 0.22	41.12 ± 0.13
1.4	9.29	37.84	10.02 ± 0.13	37.93 ± 0.18
1.2	7.60	34.54	8.05 ± 0.09	34.77 ± 0.06
1.0	5.96	30.95	6.41 ± 0.08	31.10 ± 0.21
0.8	4.39	27.06	4.60 ± 0.10	27.28 ± 0.22
0.6	2.95	22.88	3.11 ± 0.06	23.18 ± 0.26

Table 10.7 Analytical and simulation results of the CC probabilities for the BP-EMLM/BR ($t_1 = 11$) (Example 10.8).

	Analytical results (%)		Simulation (%)	
α_2	Service-class 1	Service-class 2	Service-class 1	Service-class 2
2.0	22.16	44.93	22.97 ± 0.27	45.13 ± 0.19
1.8	19.82	42.42	20.37 ± 0.22	42.54 ± 0.14
1.6	17.41	39.69	17.86 ± 0.16	39.89 ± 0.25
1.4	14.93	36.75	15.36 ± 0.18	36.71 ± 0.28
1.2	12.42	33.55	12.58 ± 0.26	33.54 ± 0.20
1.0	9.91	30.08	10.23 ± 0.11	30.05 ± 0.20
0.8	7.44	26.35	7.58 ± 0.06	26.36 ± 0.32
0.6	5.11	22.35	5.32 ± 0.08	22.47 ± 0.26

Table 10.8 Analytical results of the link utilization for the BP-EMLM and analytical and simulation results of the link utilization for the BP-EMLM/BR (Example 10.8).

α_2	BP-EMLM	BP-EMLM/BR ($t_1 = 3$)		BP-EMLM/BR ($t_1 = 7$)		BP-EMLM/BR ($t_1 = 11$)	
		Analytical	Simulation	Analytical	Simulation	Analytical	simulation
2.0	37.14	36.82	36.82 ± 0.06	36.52	36.17 ± 0.04	36.16	35.77 ± 0.30
1.8	35.84	35.54	35.42 ± 0.05	35.25	34.95 ± 0.13	34.90	34.62 ± 0.14
1.6	34.38	34.10	34.06 ± 0.09	33.83	33.58 ± 0.11	33.48	33.33 ± 0.08
1.4	32.72	32.47	32.38 ± 0.06	32.22	32.05 ± 0.08	31.89	31.74 ± 0.09
1.2	30.84	30.63	30.62 ± 0.09	30.40	30.20 ± 0.07	30.09	29.97 ± 0.05
1.0	28.70	28.52	28.58 ± 0.06	28.33	28.22 ± 0.09	28.04	28.00 ± 0.08
0.8	26.26	26.12	26.12 ± 0.09	25.96	25.87 ± 0.11	25.71	25.66 ± 0.11
0.6	23.46	23.36	23.36 ± 0.08	23.24	23.22 ± 0.07	23.04	23.03 ± 0.10

Table 10.9 Offered traffic-load versus CC probabilities equalization and the corresponding BR parameters in the BP-EMLM/BR (Example 10.8).

	CC probabilities (%)		BR parameter
α_2	Service-class 1	Service-class 2	t_1
2.0	42.22	42.33	22
1.8	38.68	39.87	22
1.6	37.05	36.86	23
1.4	32.87	34.05	23
1.2	30.38	30.66	24
1.0	27.07	27.37	25
0.8	24.22	23.81	27
0.6	19.88	20.15	29

According to the results of Tables 10.1–10.8 we observe that:

- The BR policy is not fair to calls of service-class 1 because the decrease of TC and CC probabilities of service-class 2 is less significant compared to the increase of TC and CC probabilities of service-class 1. This results in the decrease of the link utilization; compare the link utilization results of Table 10.8 (BR policy).
- The Roberts method provides quite satisfactory results compared to simulation results.
- Although the third set of BR parameters achieves the TC probabilities equalization, the same set cannot achieve the CC probabilities equalization (see Table 10.7). According to (10.19), which holds in the BP-EMLM/BR, the calculation of CC probabilities depends on the offered traffic-load rather than on the BR parameters. For a certain offered traffic-load one can find the BR parameters which almost equalize the CC probabilities. When the offered traffic-load changes, then a new set of BR parameters is needed. To show this, we present in Table 10.9 the BR parameters that almost equalize the CC probabilities of the service-classes.

10.3 The Erlang Multirate Loss Model with Batched Poisson Arrivals under the Threshold Policy

10.3.1 The Service System

In the *Erlang multirate loss model with batched Poisson arrivals under the TH policy* (*BP-EMLM/TH*) we adopt the following TH-type CAC to each individual call upon a batch arrival of service-class k:

(a) Due to the TH policy, the number of in-service calls of service-class k, n_k, should be less than a threshold $n_{k,\max}$, $(n_k < n_{k,\max})$, otherwise the new call cannot be accepted in the link.
(b) If constraint (a) is met, then if $j + b_k \leq C$, the call is accepted in the system, otherwise the call is blocked and lost (due to link bandwidth unavailability).

10.3.2 The Analytical Model

10.3.2.1 Steady State Probabilities
In order to analyze the service system, the first target is to determine the PFS of the steady state probability $P(\mathbf{n})$. Following the analysis of Section 10.1.2.1, it is easy to verify that the GB equation of (10.10) does hold for a state $\mathbf{n} \in \Omega$, where $\Omega = \{\mathbf{n} : 0 \leq \mathbf{nb} \leq C, n_k \leq n_{k,\max}, k = 1, \dots, K\}$. It can also be proved that the PFS of the BP-EMLM/TH is given by (10.14) and (10.15), where (10.15) holds for $n_k \leq n_{k,\max}$ [10].

Example 10.9 Consider again Example 10.4 ($C = 3, K = 2, b_1 = 1, b_2 = 2, \lambda_1 = \lambda_2 = \mu_1 = \mu_2 = 1, \beta_1 = 0.2, \beta_2 = 0.5$). By assuming that $n_{1,\max} = 2$, calculate the values of $P(\mathbf{n})$ and the corresponding values of $Q(j)$ based on the GB equations of (10.10).

The state space Ω of this system consists of five states of the form $\mathbf{n} = (n_1, n_2)$, namely (0,0), (0,1), (1,0), (1,1), and (2,0). The GB equations, according to (10.10), are:

$(0,0):\quad P(1,0)+P(0,1)-2P(0,0)=0$

$(0,1):\quad P(0,0)+P(1,1)-2P(0,1)=0$

$(1,0):\quad 0.8P(0,0)+P(1,1)+2P(2,0)-3P(1,0)=0$

$(1,1):\quad P(0,1)+P(1,0)-2P(1,1)=0$

$(2,0):\quad P(1,0)+0.2P(0,0)-2P(2,0)=0$

The solution of this linear system is:

$P(0,0)=P(0,1)=P(1,0)=P(1,1)=0.217391 \quad P(2,0)=0.130435$

Based on the values of $P(n_1,n_2)$, we have:

$Q(0)=P(0,0)=0.217391 \qquad\qquad Q(1)=P(1,0)=0.217391$

$Q(2)=P(0,1)+P(2,0)=0.347826 \quad Q(3)=P(1,1)=0.217391$

To rely on (10.14) and (10.15) for determining the TC and CC probabilities or link utilization, state space enumeration and processing are required. To circumvent this problem, which is quite complex for many service-classes and large capacity links, we present the following three-step convolution algorithm by modifying the convolution algorithm of [11]:

Algorithm A three-step convolution algorithm for the determination of the occupancy distribution $Q(j)$, in the BP-EMLM/TH

Step 1: Determine the occupancy distribution $q_k(j)$ of each service-class k ($k=1,\dots,K$), assuming that only service-class k exists in the link, as follows:

$$q_k(j)=\begin{cases}\sum_{l=1}^{i}\alpha_k\dfrac{q_k(j-lb_k)\widehat{D}_{l-1}^{(k)}}{i} & \text{for } 1\le i\le n_{k,\max} \text{ and } j=ib_k\\[2mm] 0 & \text{otherwise}\end{cases} \qquad (10.24)$$

To circumvent any numerical problems, we may normalize the occupancy distribution $q_k(j)$ by the corresponding normalization constants, $G_k=\sum_{j=0}^{C}q_k(j)$.

Step 2: Determine the aggregated occupancy distribution $Q_{(-k)}$ based on the successive convolution of all service-classes apart from service-class k:

$$Q_{(-k)}=q_1*q_2*\dots*q_{k-1}*q_{k+1}*\dots*q_K \qquad (10.25)$$

Note that by the term "successive" we mean that we initially convolve q_1 and q_2 in order to obtain q_{12}, then we convolve q_{12} with q_3 to obtain q_{123}, and so on. The convolution operation between two service-classes k and r is determined as:

$$q_k*q_r=\left\{q_k(0)q_r(0),\ \sum_{x=0}^{1}q_k(x)q_r(1-x),\dots,\ \sum_{x=0}^{C}q_k(x)q_r(C-x)\right\}$$

$$(10.26)$$

Step 3: The occupancy distribution $q(j)$, $j = 0, 1, \ldots, C$ is based on the convolution operation of $Q_{(-k)}$ (step 2) and q_k:

$$Q_{(-k)} * q_k = \left\{ Q_{(-k)}(0)q_k(0), \sum_{x=0}^{1} Q_{(-k)}(x)q_k(1-x), \ldots, \sum_{x=0}^{C} Q_{(-k)}(x)q_k(C-x) \right\}$$

(10.27)

Normalizing the values of (10.27), we obtain the occupancy distribution $Q(j)$:

$$
\begin{aligned}
Q(0) &= Q_{(-k)}(0)q_k(0)/G & &\text{for } j = 0 \\
Q(j) &= \left(\sum_{x=0}^{j} Q_{(-k)}(x)q_k(j-x) \right) /G & &\text{for } j = 1, \ldots, C
\end{aligned}
$$

(10.28)

10.3.2.2 TC Probabilities, CBP, Utilization, and Mean Number of In-service Calls

The following performance measures can be determined based on (10.25)–(10.28):

- The TC probabilities of service-class k, B_{Tk}, via the formula:

$$B_{Tk} = \sum_{j=C-b_k+1}^{C} Q(j) + \frac{1}{G} \sum_{x=n_{k,\max}b_k}^{C-b_k} Q_k(x) \sum_{z=x}^{C-b_k} Q_{(-k)}(C - b_k - z)$$

(10.29)

The first sum in (10.29) refers to states j where there is not enough bandwidth for service-class k calls. The other term refers to states $x = n_{k,\max}b_k, \ldots, C - b_k$, where available link bandwidth exists, but nevertheless blocking occurs due to the TH policy. The normalization constant G in the second term of (10.29) refers to the value used in (10.28).

- The CBP (or CC probabilities) of service-class k, B_k, via the formula (10.19).
- The mean number of in-service calls of service-class k, $\overline{n}_k$, via (1.56), where the values of $y_k(j)$ can be determined via:

$$y_k(j) = \frac{\alpha_k \displaystyle\sum_{l=1}^{\min\lfloor j/b_k, n_{k,\max} \rfloor} \widehat{D}_{l-1}^{(k)} \displaystyle\sum_{x=0}^{\min[j-lb_k, \, (n_{k,\max}-l)b_k]} Q_k(x)Q_{(-k)}(j - lb_k - x)/G}{Q(j)}$$

(10.30)

where $Q(j) > 0$ and $y_k(j) = 0$ if $j < b_k$.

The nominator of (10.30) shows the "transfer" of the population of service-class k calls from the previous states $j - lb_k$ to state j due to an arrival of a service-class k batch. The normalization constant G refers to the value used in (10.28).

- The link utilization, U, via (1.54).

Example 10.10 Consider again Example 10.9 ($C = 3, K = 2, b_1 = 1, b_2 = 2$, $n_{1,\max} = 2, \lambda_1 = \lambda_2 = \mu_1 = \mu_2 = 1, \beta_1 = 0.2, \beta_2 = 0.5$).

(a) Apply the convolution algorithm to determine the values of $Q(j)$.

(b) Calculate the TC and CC probabilities as well as the link utilization via (10.29), (10.19), and (1.54), respectively.

(a) The convolution algorithm is:

Step 1: Service-class 1 ($\alpha_1 = 1$ erl, $b_1 = 1$ b.u., $\beta_1 = 0.2$). For $1 \leq i \leq 2$, we have:

$$j = 0 : \qquad q_1(0) = 1.0$$

$$i = 1, j = 1 : \quad q_1(1) = \sum_{l=1}^{1} \alpha_1 q_1(0)\beta_1^0 \qquad\qquad \Rightarrow q_1(1) = 1.0$$

$$i = 2, j = 2 : \quad q_1(2) = \sum_{l=1}^{2} \alpha_1 \frac{q_1(2-l)\hat{D}_{l-1}^{(1)}}{2} = \frac{q_1(1)\beta_1^0 + q_1(0)\beta_1^1}{2} \quad \Rightarrow q_1(2) = 0.6$$

Therefore $G = \sum_{j=0}^{3} q_1(j) = 2.6$ and the normalized values of $q_1(j)$ are:

$$Q_1(0) = \frac{q_1(0)}{G} = 0.3846154 \quad Q_1(1) = \frac{q_1(1)}{G} = 0.3846154 \quad Q_1(2) = \frac{q_1(2)}{G} = 0.2307692$$

Service-class 2 ($\alpha_2 = 1$ erl, $b_2 = 2$ b.u., $\beta_2 = 0.5$). For $1 \leq i \leq 1$, we have:

$$j = 0 : \qquad q_2(0) = 1.0$$

$$i = 1, j = 2 : \quad q_2(2) = \sum_{l=1}^{1} \alpha_2 q_2(0)\beta_2^0 \quad \Rightarrow q_2(1) = 1.0$$

Therefore $G = \sum_{j=0}^{3} q_2(j) = 2.0$ and the normalized values of $q_2(j)$ are:

$$Q_2(0) = q_2(0)/G = 0.5 \quad Q_2(2) = q_2(2)/G = 0.5$$

Step 2: This step also includes step 3 of the algorithm.
Based on (10.26)–(10.28) the normalized values of $Q(j)$ are given by:

$$Q(0) = \frac{Q_1(0)Q_2(0)}{G}$$
$$Q(1) = \frac{Q_1(0)Q_2(1) + Q_1(1)Q_2(0)}{G} = \frac{Q_1(1)Q_2(0)}{G}$$
$$Q(2) = \frac{Q_1(0)Q_2(2) + Q_1(1)Q_2(1) + Q_1(2)Q_2(0)}{G} = \frac{Q_1(0)Q_2(2) + Q_1(2)Q_2(0)}{G}$$
$$Q(3) = \frac{Q_1(0)Q_2(3) + Q_1(1)Q_2(2) + Q_1(2)Q_2(1) + Q_1(3)Q_2(0)}{G} = \frac{Q_1(1)Q_2(2)}{G}$$

Since

$$G = Q_1(0)Q_2(0) + Q_1(1)Q_2(0) + Q_1(0)Q_2(2) + Q_1(2)Q_2(0) + Q_1(1)Q_2(2) = 0.8846154$$

we have the same values with those of Example 10.9:

$$Q(0) = 0.217391 \quad Q(1) = 0.217391 \quad Q(2) = 0.347826 \quad Q(3) = 0.217391$$

(b) TC probabilities:

$$B_{T1} = \sum_{j=C-b_1+1}^{C} Q(j) + \frac{1}{G} \sum_{x=n_{1,max}b_1}^{C-b_1} Q_1(x) \sum_{z=x}^{C-b_1} Q_{(-1)}(C - b_1 - z) = Q(3) + \frac{Q_1(2)Q_2(0)}{G}$$

$$= 0.217391 + \frac{0.2307692 \times 0.5}{0.8846154} \quad \Rightarrow \quad B_{T1} = 0.347825$$

$$B_{T2} = \sum_{j=C-b_2+1}^{C} Q(j) = Q(2) + Q(3) = 0.565217$$

To determine the CC probabilities, we determine the values of $y_k(j)$ and $\overline{n}_k$:

$$j = 1 : \quad y_1(1) = 1 \qquad y_2(1) = 0$$
$$j = 2 : \quad y_1(2) = 0.75 \quad y_2(2) = 0.625$$
$$j = 3 : \quad y_1(3) = 1 \qquad y_2(3) = 1$$

$$\overline{n}_1 = Q(1) + 0.75Q(2) + Q(3) \quad \Rightarrow \quad \overline{n}_1 = 0.695652$$
$$\overline{n}_2 = 0.625Q(2) + Q(3) \qquad\quad \Rightarrow \quad \overline{n}_2 = 0.434782$$

Based on the above we have:

$$B_1 = (\alpha_1 \widehat{D}_1 - \overline{n}_1)/\alpha_1 \widehat{D}_1 = (1.25 - 0.695652)/1.25 = 0.44348$$
$$B_2 = (\alpha_2 \widehat{D}_2 - \overline{n}_2)/\alpha_2 \widehat{D}_2 = (2.0 - 0.434782)/2.0 = 0.78261$$

Utilization: $U = \sum_{j=1}^{C} jQ(j) = 1.565$ b.u.

Example 10.11 Consider a link of $C = 80$ b.u. that accommodates two service-classes. The batch size of both service-classes follows the geometric distribution with parameters $\beta_1 = 0.2$ and $\beta_2 = 0.5$. Calls of service-class 1 require $b_1 = 2$ b.u. and have a threshold parameter at $n_{1,\max} = 25$ calls. The corresponding values for service-class 2 are $b_2 = 7$ b.u. and $n_{2,\max} = 7$ calls. The service time is exponentially distributed with mean $\mu_1^{-1} = \mu_2^{-1} = 1$. Let $\alpha_1 = 5$ erl and $\alpha_2 = 0.5$ erl. Provide analytical results of the TC and CC probabilities for the BP-EMLM/TH, the BP-EMLM, and the BP-EMLM/BR. Let the BR parameters be $t_1 = 5$ b.u. and $t_2 = 0$ b.u.

On the x-axis of Figures 10.5–10.8 the offered traffic load of service-classes 1 and 2 increases in steps of 1.0 and 0.1 erl, respectively. So, point 1 refers to $(\alpha_1, \alpha_2 = (5.0, 0.5)$, while point 10 refers to $(\alpha_1, \alpha_2) = (14.0, 1.4)$. All figures show that (i) the TH policy clearly affects the congestion probabilities of both service-classes, thus it gives the opportunity for a fine TC and CC control aiming at guaranteeing certain QoS to each service-class, and (ii) the BP-EMLM and the BP-EMLM/BR fail to approximate the results obtained from the BP-EMLM/TH.

10.4 Applications

An interesting application of the BP-EMLM has been proposed in [12] for the calculation of various performance measures, including call blocking and handover failure probabilities in a LEO mobile satellite system (MSS). In [12], a LEO-MSS of N_c contiguous "satellite-fixed" cells is considered, each having a fixed capacity of C channels. Moreover, each cell is modeled as a rectangle of length L (e.g., $L = 425$ km in the case of the iridium LEO-MSS [13]) that forms a strip of contiguous coverage on the region of the Earth. Next, a few common assumptions are made. LEO satellite orbits are polar and circular. MUs are uniformly distributed on the Earth surface, while they are considered as fixed. This assumption is valid as long as the rotation of the Earth and the speed of a MU are negligible compared to the subsatellite point speed on the Earth [14]. Moreover, either beam handovers, within a particular footprint, or handovers between adjacent satellites of the same orbit plane may occur. The system of these N_c cells accommodates MUs that generate calls of K service-classes with different QoS requirements. Each service-class k ($k = 1, \ldots, K$) call requires a fixed number of

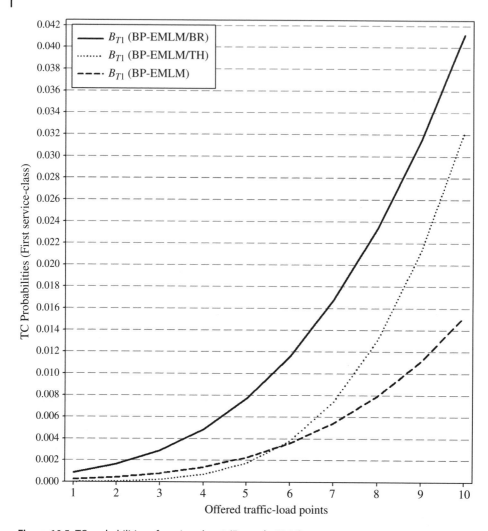

Figure 10.5 TC probabilities of service-class 1 (Example 10.11).

b_k channels for its whole duration in the system. New service-class k calls arrive in the system according to a batched Poisson process with arrival rate λ_k and batch size distribution $D_r^{(k)}$. Due to the uniform MUs distribution, new calls may arrive in any cell with equal probability. The cell that a new call originates is the source cell. Due to the call arrival process of new service-class k calls, we model the arrival process of handover calls of service-class k via a batched Poisson process with arrival rate λ_{hk} and batch size distribution $D_r^{(hk)}$. The arrival of handover calls in a cell is as follows. Handover calls cross the source cell's boundaries to the adjacent right cell having a constant velocity of $-V_{tr}$, where V_{tr} (approx. 26600 km/h in the iridium constellation) is the subsatellite point speed. An in-service call that departs from the last cell (cell N_c) will request a handover in cell 1, thus having a continuous cellular network (Figure 10.9).

Based on the above, let t_c be the dwell time of a call in a cell (i.e., the time that a call remains in the cell). Then, t_c is (i) uniformly distributed in $[0, L/V_{tr}]$ for new calls in their

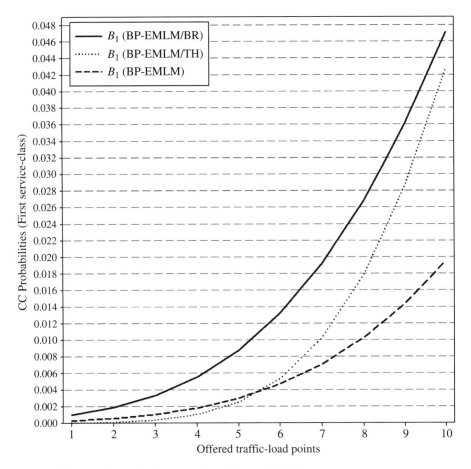

Figure 10.6 CC probabilities of service-class 1 (Example 10.11).

source cell and (ii) deterministically equal to $T_c = L/V_{tr}$ for handover calls that traverse any adjacent cell from border to border. Based on (ii), T_c expresses the interarrival time for all handovers subsequent to the first one. As far as the duration of a service-class k call (new or handover) in the system and the channel holding time in a cell are concerned, they are exponentially distributed with mean T_{dk} and μ_k^{-1}, respectively.

To determine formulas for the handover arrival rate λ_{hk} and the channel holding time with mean μ_k^{-1} of service-class k calls, we define:

(a) The parameter γ_k as the ratio between the mean duration of a service-class k call in the system and the dwell time of a call in a cell [14]:

$$\gamma_k = \frac{T_{dk}}{T_c} \tag{10.31}$$

(b) The time $T_{h1,k}$ as the interval from the arrival of a new service-class k call in the source cell to the instant of the first handover. $T_{h1,k}$ is uniformly distributed in $[0, T_c]$

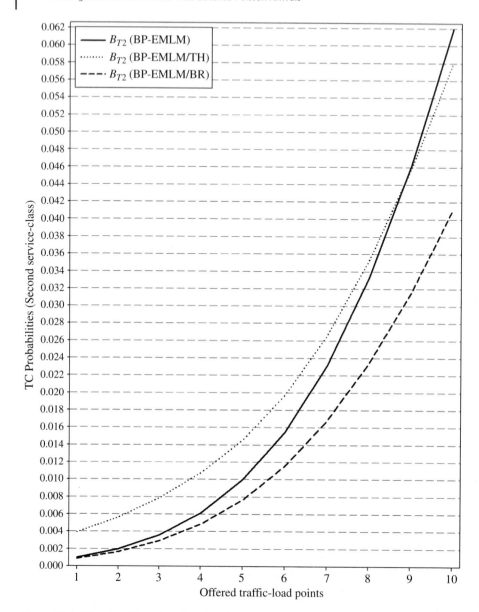

Figure 10.7 TC probabilities of service-class 2 (Example 10.11).

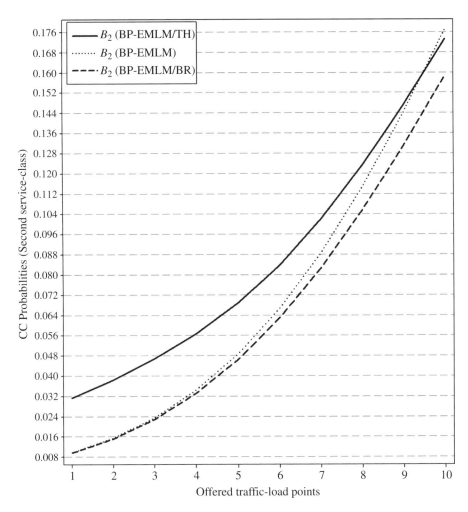

Figure 10.8 CC probabilities of service-class 2 (Example 10.11).

Figure 10.9 A rectangular cell model
for the LEO-MSS network.

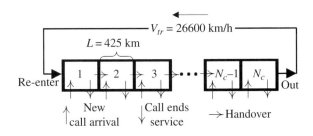

with pdf $f_{T_{h1,k}}(t)$ [15]:

$$
f_{T_{h1,k}}(t) = \begin{cases} \frac{V_{tr}}{L} & \text{for} \quad 0 \le t \le \frac{1}{\gamma_k} T_{dk} \\ 0 & \text{otherwise} \end{cases}
\tag{10.32}
$$

(c) The probabilities $P_{h1,k}$ and $P_{h2,k}$ express the handover probability for a service-class k call in the source and in a transit cell, respectively. These probabilities are different due to the different distances covered by a MU in the source cell and in the transit cells. More precisely, $P_{h1,k}$ is defined as:

$$
P_{h1,k} = \int_0^\infty Prob\{t_{dk} > t \mid T_{h1,k} = t\}f_{T_{h1,k}}(t)dt = \gamma_k(1 - e^{-1/\gamma_k})
\tag{10.33}
$$

where t_{dk} is the service-class k call duration time (exponentially distributed with mean T_{dk}).

The residual service time of a service-class k call after a successful handover request has the same pdf as t_{dk} (due to the memoryless property of the exponential distribution). It follows then that $P_{h2,k}$ can be expressed by:

$$
\begin{aligned}
P_{h2,k} &= Prob\left\{t_{dk} > \frac{L}{V_{tr}}\right\} = 1 - Prob\left\{t_{dk} \le \frac{L}{V_{tr}}\right\} \\
&= 1 - \int_0^{T_c} \frac{1}{T_{dk}}e^{-t/T_{dk}}dt = e^{-1/\gamma_k}
\end{aligned}
\tag{10.34}
$$

The handover arrival rate λ_{hk} can be related to λ_k by assuming that in each cell there exists a flow equilibrium between MUs entering and leaving the cell. In that case, we may write the following flow equilibrium equation (MUs entering the cell = MUs leaving the cell):

$$
\lambda_k(1 - B_k) + \lambda_{hk}(1 - P_{f_k}) = \lambda_{hk} + \lambda_k(1 - B_k)(1 - P_{h1,k}) + \lambda_{hk}(1 - P_{f_k})(1 - P_{h2,k})
\tag{10.35}
$$

where B_k refers to the CBP of new service-class k calls in the source cell and P_{f_k} refers to the handover failure probability of service-class k calls in transit cells. The LHS of (10.35) refers to new and handover service-class k calls that are accepted in the cell with probability $(1 - B_k)$ and $(1 - P_{f_k})$, respectively. The RHS of (10.35) refers to (i) service-class k calls that are handed over to the transit cell (depicted by λ_{hk}), (ii) new calls that complete their service in the source cell without requesting a handover (depicted by $\lambda_k(1 - B_k)(1 - P_{h1,k})$), and (iii) handover calls that do not handover to the transit cell (depicted by $\lambda_{hk}(1 - P_{f_k})(1 - P_{h2,k})$).

Equation (10.35) can be rewritten as:

$$
\frac{\lambda_{hk}}{\lambda_k} = \frac{(1 - B_k)P_{h1,k}}{1 - (1 - P_{f_k})P_{h2,k}}
\tag{10.36}
$$

To derive a formula for the channel holding time of service-class k calls, note that channels are occupied in a cell by either new or handover calls. Furthermore, channels are occupied either until the end of service of a call or until a call is handed over to a transit cell. Since the channel holding time is expressed as $t_{h1,k} = \min(t_{dk}, t_c)$ in the case of the source cell and $t_{h2,k} = \min(t_{dk}, T_c)$ in the case of a transit cell, then the mean value of $t_{hi,k}$, $E_k(t_{hi,k})$ for $i = 1, 2$ is given by:

$$E_k(t_{hi,k}) = T_{dk}(1 - P_{hi,k}) \tag{10.37}$$

Now let P_k and P_k^h be the probabilities that a channel is occupied by a new and a handover service-class k call, respectively. Then:

$$P_k = \frac{\lambda_k(1 - B_k)}{\lambda_k(1 - B_k) + \lambda_{hk}(1 - P_{f_k})} \quad \text{and} \quad P_k^h = \frac{\lambda_{hk}(1 - P_{f_k})}{\lambda_k(1 - B_k) + \lambda_{hk}(1 - P_{f_k})} \tag{10.38}$$

Based on (10.37) and (10.38), the channel holding time of service-class k calls (either new or handover) is approximated by an exponential distribution whose mean μ_k^{-1} is the weighted sum of (10.37) (for $i = 1, 2$) multiplied by the corresponding probabilities P_k (for $i = 1$) and P_k^h (for $i = 2$):

$$\mu_k^{-1} = P_k E_k(t_{h1,k}) + P_k^h E_k(t_{h2,k}) = \frac{\lambda_k(1 - B_K)E_k(t_{h1,k}) + \lambda_{hk}(1 - P_{f_k})E_k(t_{h2,k})}{\lambda_k(1 - B_k) + \lambda_{hk}(1 - P_{f_k})}$$

$$\tag{10.39}$$

Having determined the various input traffic parameters, we can analyze the LEO-MSS via the BP-EMLM assuming that each cell is modeled as a multirate loss system, where all calls compete for the available channels under the CS policy. To facilitate the description of the analytical model in [12], we distinguish new from handover calls and assume that each cell accommodates calls of $2K$ service-classes. A service-class k is new if $1 \leq k \leq K$ and handover if $K + 1 \leq k \leq 2K$.

10.5 Further Reading

Due to the close relationship between the models of this chapter and the EMLM, the EMLM/BR, and the EMLM/TH, the interested reader may refer to the corresponding section of Chapter 1. In addition, due to the fact that the BP-EMLM can be used for the analysis of overflow traffic, it may be a candidate analytical model for various multirate loss systems that carry overflow traffic (e.g., [16–19]). Other extensions of the BP-EMLM that show the applicability of the model in wireless networks appear in [20–22]. In [20], the BP-EMLM is used for the CBP determination in the X2 link of LTE networks. In [21], the BP-EMLM is extended to include multiple access interference, both the notion of local (soft) and hard blocking, the user's activity, as well as interference cancellation for the calculation of congestion probabilities in CDMA networks. An extension of [21] that incorporates the BP-EMLM/BR is proposed in [22].

References

1 E. van Doorn and F. Panken, Blocking probabilities in a loss system with arrivals in geometrically distributed batches and heterogeneous service requirements. *IEEE/ACM Transactions on Networking*, 1(6):664–667, December 1993.

2 G. Choundhury, K. Leung and W. Whitt, Resource-sharing models with state-dependent arrivals of batches, in *Computations with Markov Chains*, W.J. Stewart (ed.), Kluwer, Boston, pp. 255–282, 1995.

3 J. Kaufman and K. Rege, Blocking in a shared resource environment with batched Poisson arrival processes. *Performance Evaluation*, 24(4):249–263, February 1996.

4 J. Morrison, Blocking probabilities for multiple class batched Poisson arrivals to a shared resource. *Performance Evaluation*, 25(2):131–150, April 1996.

5 G. Choundhury, K. Leung and W. Whitt, An inversion algorithm to compute blocking probabilities in loss networks with state-dependent rates. *IEEE/ACM Transactions on Networking*, 3(5):585–601, October 1995.

6 K. Kawanichi, Y. Takahashi and T. Takenaka, Trunk reservation effects on multi-server system with batch arrivals of loss and delay customers. *IEICE Transactions on Communications*, E83-B(1):20–29, January 2000.

7 P. Ezhilchelvan and I. Mitrani, Multi-class resource sharing with batch arrivals and complete blocking. *Proceeding of the International Conference on Quantitative Evaluation of Systems (QEST)*, Lecture Notes in Computer Science, Vol. 10503, Springer, 2017.

8 L. Delbrouck, On the steady state distribution in a service facility with different peakedness factors and capacity requirements. *IEEE Transactions on Communications*, 31(11):1209–1211, November 1983.

9 I. Moscholios and M. Logothetis, The Erlang multirate loss model with batched Poisson arrival processes under the bandwidth reservation policy. *Computer Communications*, 33(Supplement 1):S167–S179, November 2010.

10 I. Moscholios, V. Vassilakis and P. Sarigiannidis, Performance modelling of a multirate loss system with batched Poisson arrivals under a probabilistic threshold policy. *IET Networks*, 7(4):242–247, July 2018.

11 V. Iversen, The exact evaluation of multi-service loss system with access control. *Teleteknik* [English edn], 31(2):56–61, August 1987.

12 I.D. Moscholios, V.G. Vassilakis, P.G. Sarigiannidis, N.C. Sagias and M.D. Logothetis, An analytical framework in LEO mobile satellite systems servicing batched Poisson traffic. *IET Communications*, 12(1):18–25, January 2018.

13 M. Benslama, W. Kiamouche and H. Batatia, Connections management strategies, in *Satellite Cellular Networks*, John Wiley, 2015.

14 G. Maral, J. Restrepo, E. Del Re, R. Fantacci and G. Giambene, Performance analysis for a guaranteed handover service in an LEO constellation with a satellite-fixed cell system. *IEEE Transactions on Vehicular Technology*, 47(4):1200–1214, November 1998.

15 E. Del Re, R. Fantacci and G. Giambene, Performance analysis of dynamic channel allocation technique for satellite mobile cellular networks. *International Journal of Satellite Communications*, 12(1):25–32, January/February 1994.

16 Q. Huang, K. Ko and V. Iversen, Performance modeling for heterogeneous wireless networks with multiservice overflow traffic. *Proceedings of IEEE Globecom*, Honolulu, USA, December 2009.

17 X. Yu and H. Zhu, An efficient method for loss performance modeling of hierarchical heterogeneous wireless networks. *International Journal of Communication Systems*, 27(6):956–968, June 2014.

18 M. Glabowski, S. Hanczewski and M. Stasiak, Modelling of cellular networks with traffic overflow. *Mathematical Problems in Engineering*, 2015, Article ID 286490, 15 pages.

19 M. Glabowski, A. Kaliszan and M. Stasiak, Modelling overflow systems with distributed secondary resources. *Computer Networks*, 108:171–183, October 2016.

20 I. Widjaja and H. Roche, Sizing X2 bandwidth for Inter-connected eNBs. *Proceedings of IEEE VTC Fall*, Anchorage, Alaska, USA, pp. 1–5, September 2009.

21 I. Moscholios, G. Kallos, V. Vassilakis and M. Logothetis, Congestion probabilities in CDMA-based networks supporting batched Poisson input traffic. *Wireless Personal Communications*, 79(2):1163–1186, November 2014.

22 I. Moscholios, V. Vassilakis, G. Kallos and M. Logothetis, Performance analysis of CDMA-based networks with interference cancellation, for batched Poisson traffic under the bandwidth reservation policy. *Proceedings of the 13th International Conference Telecommunications, ConTEL*, Graz, Austria, July 2015.

11

Batched Poisson Multirate Elastic Adaptive Loss Models

In this chapter we consider multirate loss models of batched Poisson arriving calls with fixed bandwidth requirements and elastic bandwidth allocation during service. As we have reached the last chapter of the book, the reader should be able to understand the title of this chapter. As a reminder, in the batched Poisson process (in which now a batch consists of two types of calls, elastic or adaptive), simultaneous call-arrivals (batches) occur at time-points following a negative exponential distribution. Elastic calls can reduce their bandwidth and simultaneously increase their service time. Adaptive calls can tolerate bandwidth compression without altering their service time.

11.1 The Elastic Erlang Multirate Loss Model with Batched Poisson Arrivals

11.1.1 The Service System

In the *elastic Erlang multirate loss model with batched Poisson arrivals* (BP-E-EMLM), we consider a link of capacity C b.u. that accommodates elastic calls of K different service-classes. Calls of each service-class k ($k = 1, \ldots, K$) have the following attributes: (i) they arrive in the link according to a batched Poisson process with rate λ_k and batch size distribution $D_r^{(k)}$, where $D_r^{(k)}$ denotes the probability that there are r calls in an arriving batch of service-class k, (ii) they follow the partial batch blocking discipline (see Chapter 10), and (iii) they request b_k b.u. (peak-bandwidth requirement). To introduce bandwidth compression in the model, the occupied link bandwidth j can virtually exceed C up to a limit of T b.u. Then the call admission is identical to the one presented in the case of the E-EMLM (see Section 3.1.1).

Similarly, in terms of the system state-space $\mathbf{\Omega}$, the CAC is expressed as in the E-EMLM (see Section 3.1.1). Hence, the TC probabilities of service-class k are determined by the state space $\mathbf{\Omega} - \mathbf{\Omega}_{\{k\}}$:

$$B_{Tk} = \sum_{\mathbf{n} \in (\mathbf{\Omega} - \mathbf{\Omega}_{\{k\}})} P(\mathbf{n}) \quad \Rightarrow \quad B_{Tk} = 1 - \sum_{\mathbf{n} \in \mathbf{\Omega}_{\{k\}}} P(\mathbf{n}) \tag{11.1}$$

where $\mathbf{\Omega}_{\{k\}} = \{\mathbf{n} \in \mathbf{\Omega} : \mathbf{n}\mathbf{b} \leq T - b_k\}$ ($k = 1, \ldots, K$), n_k is the number of in-service calls of service-class k in the steady state, $\mathbf{n} = (n_1, \ldots, n_k, \ldots, n_K)$, $P(\mathbf{n})$ is the steady state probability, and $\mathbf{b} = (b_1, \ldots, b_k, \ldots, b_K)$.

Efficient Multirate Teletraffic Loss Models Beyond Erlang, First Edition.
Ioannis D. Moscholios and Michael D. Logothetis.
© 2019 John Wiley & Sons Ltd. Published 2019 by John Wiley & Sons Ltd.
Companion website: www.wiley.com/go/logocode

11.1.2 The Analytical Model

11.1.2.1 Steady State Probabilities

The compression/expansion of bandwidth results in a non PFS for the values of $P(\mathbf{n})$, a fact that makes (11.1) inefficient. In order to analyze the service system and provide an approximate but recursive formula for the calculation of the link occupancy distribution, we assume that local flow balance (as described in Chapter 10) does exist across certain levels that separate two adjacent states of Ω. To this end, we present the following notations [1]:

$$\mathbf{n}_k^{+m} = (n_1, n_2, \dots, n_{k-1}, n_k + m, n_{k+1}, \dots, n_K), \quad m = 1, 2, \dots$$
$$\mathbf{n}_k^{-m} = (n_1, n_2, \dots, n_{k-1}, n_k + m, n_{k+1}, \dots, n_K), \quad m = 1, 2, \dots, n_k$$

The first step in the analysis is to define the levels across which local flow balance will hold. For the state $\mathbf{n}_k^{-1} = (n_1, n_2, \dots, n_k - 1, \dots, n_K)$, with $n_k - 1 \geq 0$, the level $L_{\mathbf{n}_k^{-1}}^{(k)}$ separates $\mathbf{n}_k^{-1}$ from n. Then, the "upward" (due to a new service-class k batch arrival) probability flow across level $L_{\mathbf{n}_k^{-1}}^{(k)}$ is given by [1]:

$$f^{(\text{up})}(L_{\mathbf{n}_k^{-1}}^{(k)}) = \sum_{l=0}^{n_k-1} P(\mathbf{n}_k^{-1-l}) \lambda_k \sum_{m=l+1}^{\infty} D_m^{(k)} \tag{11.2}$$

where $\mathbf{n}_k^{-1-l} = (n_1, n_2, \dots, n_{k-1}, n_k - 1 - l, n_{k+1}, \dots, n_K)$, with $n_k - 1 - l \geq 0$, and $P(\mathbf{n}_k^{-1-l})$ is the corresponding steady state probability.

Equation (11.2) can be also written as follows:

$$f^{(\text{up})}(L_{\mathbf{n}_k^{-1}}^{(k)}) = \sum_{l=0}^{n_k-1} P(\mathbf{n}_k^{-1-l}) \lambda_k \widehat{D}_l^{(k)} \tag{11.3}$$

where $\widehat{D}_l^{(k)} = \sum_{m=l+1}^{\infty} D_m^{(k)}$ is the complementary batch size distribution.

The "downward" (due to a service-class k call departure) probability flow across level $L_{\mathbf{n}_k^{-1}}^{(k)}$ is given by [1]:

$$f^{(\text{down})}(L_{\mathbf{n}_k^{-1}}^{(k)}) = n_k \mu_k r(\mathbf{n}) P(\mathbf{n}) \tag{11.4}$$

where $r(\mathbf{n})$, defined according to (3.2), is the common state dependent factor used to compress/expand the service rate of calls, when their bandwidth is compressed/expanded, since the target is to keep constant the product *service time* by *bandwidth per call*.

Due to the compression/expansion mechanism of calls of service-class k the local flow balance across level $L_{\mathbf{n}_k^{-1}}^{(k)}$ is destroyed, i.e., $f^{(\text{up})}(L_{\mathbf{n}_k^{-1}}^{(k)}) \neq f^{(\text{down})}(L_{\mathbf{n}_k^{-1}}^{(k)})$ or

$$\sum_{l=0}^{n_k-1} P(\mathbf{n}_k^{-1-l}) \lambda_k \widehat{D}_l^{(k)} \neq n_k \mu_k r(\mathbf{n}) P(\mathbf{n}) \tag{11.5}$$

Similar to the E-EMLM, $r(\mathbf{n})$ are replaced by the state-dependent compression factors per service-class k, $\varphi_k(\mathbf{n})$ and $x(\mathbf{n})$ which are defined according to (3.8) and (3.9), respectively.

Having defined $\varphi_k(\mathbf{n})$ and $x(\mathbf{n})$, we make the assumption (approximation) that the following equation holds: $f^{(up)}(L_{\mathbf{n}_k^{-1}}^{(k)}) = f^{(down)}(L_{\mathbf{n}_k^{-1}}^{(k)})$ or

$$\sum_{l=0}^{n_k-1} P(\mathbf{n}_k^{-1-l})\lambda_k \sum_{m=l+1}^{\infty} D_m^{(k)} = n_k \mu_k \varphi_k(\mathbf{n})P(\mathbf{n}) \tag{11.6}$$

Before we proceed with the derivation of a recursive formula for the determination of $q(j)$, note that the GB equation for state $\mathbf{n}_k^{-1}$ is still given by (10.10). In (10.10), the "upward" probability flows are given by (11.3) and the "downward" probability flows are given by (11.4) (if we refer to $r(\mathbf{n})$) or by the RHS side of (11.6) (if we refer to $\varphi_k(\mathbf{n})$).

Example 11.1 Consider a link of $C = 3$ b.u. and let $T = 5$ b.u. The link accommodates calls of $K = 2$ service-classes whose calls require $b_1 = 1$ b.u. and $b_2 = 2$ b.u., respectively. Let $\lambda_1 = \lambda_2 = \mu_1 = \mu_2 = 1 \text{ min}^{-1}$. Assuming that the batch size distribution is geometrically distributed with parameters $\beta_1 = 0.2$ and $\beta_2 = 0.5$, calculate the values of $P(\mathbf{n})$ and the corresponding values of $Q(j)$ based on the GB equation of (10.10) and assuming:

(a) the model with $r(\mathbf{n})$, and
(b) the model with $\varphi_k(\mathbf{n})$ and $x(\mathbf{n})$. Then determine the TC probabilities of both service-classes via (11.1).

The state space Ω of this system consists of 12 states of the form $\mathbf{n} = (n_1, n_2)$. The values of n and $r(\mathbf{n})$ are exactly the same as those of Table 3.1 (Example 3.1). Similarly, the values of $\varphi_k(\mathbf{n})$ and $x(\mathbf{n})$ are exactly the same as those of Table 3.2 (Example 3.3).

(a) Based on the GB equation of (10.10) and (11.3)–(11.4), we have:

$(0,0):$ $\quad P(1,0) + P(0,1) - 2P(0,0) = 0$
$(0,1):$ $\quad 0.5P(0,0) + P(1,1) + 1.5P(0,2) - 3P(0,1) = 0$
$(0,2):$ $\quad 0.5P(0,0) + P(0,1) + 0.6P(1,2) - 2.5P(0,2) = 0$
$(1,0):$ $\quad 0.8P(0,0) + P(1,1) + 2P(2,0) - 3P(1,0) = 0$
$(1,1):$ $\quad 0.8P(0,1) + 0.5P(1,0) + 1.5P(2,1) + 1.2P(1,2) - 4P(1,1) = 0$
$(1,2):$ $\quad P(0,2) + P(1,1) + 0.5P(1,0) - 1.8P(1,2) = 0$
$(2,0):$ $\quad 0.16P(0,0) + 0.8P(1,0) + 3P(3,0) + 0.75P(2,1) - 4P(2,0) = 0$
$(2,1):$ $\quad 0.16P(0,1) + 0.8P(1,1) + P(2,0) + 1.8P(3,1) - 3.25P(2,1) = 0$
$(3,0):$ $\quad 0.032P(0,0) + 0.16P(1,0) + 0.8P(2,0) + 3P(4,0) + 0.6P(3,1) - 5P(3,0) = 0$
$(3,1):$ $\quad P(2,1) + 0.2P(1,1) + 0.04P(0,1) + P(3,0) - 2.4P(3,1) = 0$
$(4,0):$ $\quad 0.8P(3,0) + 0.16P(2,0) + 0.032P(1,0) + 0.0064P(0,0) + 3P(5,0) - 4P(4,0) = 0$
$(5,0):$ $\quad P(4,0) + 0.2P(3,0) + 0.04P(2,0) + 0.008P(1,0) + 0.0016P(0,0) - 3P(5,0) = 0$

The solution of this linear system is:

$P(0,0) = 0.1127$	$P(0,1) = 0.1095$	$P(0,2) = 0.1035$	$P(1,0) = 0.1159$
$P(1,1) = 0.1170$	$P(1,2) = 0.1547$	$P(2,0) = 0.0703$	$P(2,1) = 0.0911$
$P(3,0) = 0.0341$	$P(3,1) = 0.0637$	$P(4,0) = 0.0179$	$P(5,0) = 0.0095$

Based on the values of $P(n_1, n_2)$, we have:

$Q(0) = P(0,0) = 0.1127$ $Q(1) = P(1,0) = 0.1159$

$Q(2) = P(0,1) + P(2,0) = 0.1798$ $Q(3) = P(1,1) + P(3,0) = 0.1511$

$Q(4) = P(0,2) + P(2,1) + P(4,0) = 0.2125$ $Q(5) = P(1,2) + P(3,1) + P(5,0) = 0.2279$

Based on (11.1), the TC probabilities are the following:

$B_{T1} = Q(5) = 0.2279$ $B_{T2} = Q(4) + Q(5) = 0.4404$

(b) Similarly, in the case of $\varphi_k(\mathbf{n})$ and $x(\mathbf{n})$, we have:

$(0,0):$ $P(1,0) + P(0,1) - 2P(0,0) = 0$

$(0,1):$ $0.5P(0,0) + P(1,1) + 1.5P(0,2) - 3P(0,1) = 0$

$(0,2):$ $0.5P(0,0) + P(0,1) + 0.75P(1,2) - 2.5P(0,2) = 0$

$(1,0):$ $0.8P(0,0) + P(1,1) + 2P(2,0) - 3P(1,0) = 0$

$(1,1):$ $0.8P(0,1) + 0.5P(1,0) + 1.5P(2,1) + (18/16)P(1,2) - 4P(1,1) = 0$

$(1,2):$ $P(0,2) + P(1,1) + 0.5P(1,0) - 1.875P(1,2) = 0$

$(2,0):$ $0.16P(0,0) + 0.8P(1,0) + 3P(3,0) + 0.75P(2,1) - 4P(2,0) = 0$

$(2,1):$ $0.16P(0,1) + 0.8P(1,1) + P(2,0) + 2P(3,1) - 3.25P(2,1) = 0$

$(3,0):$ $0.032P(0,0) + 0.16P(1,0) + 0.8P(2,0) + 3P(4,0) + 0.5P(3,1) - 5P(3,0) = 0$

$(3,1):$ $P(2,1) + 0.2P(1,1) + 0.04P(0,1) + P(3,0) - 2.5P(3,1) = 0$

$(4,0):$ $0.8P(3,0) + 0.16P(2,0) + 0.032P(1,0) + 0.0064P(0,0) + 3P(5,0) - 4P(4,0) = 0$

$(5,0):$ $P(4,0) + 0.2P(3,0) + 0.04P(2,0) + 0.008P(1,0) + 0.0016P(0,0) - 3P(5,0) = 0$

The solution of this linear system is:

$P(0,0) = 0.1140$ $P(0,1) = 0.1142$ $P(0,2) = 0.1141$ $P(1,0) = 0.1139$

$P(1,1) = 0.1143$ $P(1,2) = 0.1522$ $P(2,0) = 0.0681$ $P(2,1) = 0.0918$

$P(3,0) = 0.0314$ $P(3,1) = 0.0602$ $P(4,0) = 0.0168$ $P(5,0) = 0.0090$

Based on the values of $P(n_1, n_2)$, we have:

$Q(0) = P(0,0) = 0.1140$ $Q(1) = P(1,0) = 0.1139$

$Q(2) = P(0,1) + P(2,0) = 0.1823$ $Q(3) = P(1,1) + P(3,0) = 0.1457$

$Q(4) = P(0,2) + P(2,1) + P(4,0) = 0.2227$ $Q(5) = P(1,2) + P(3,1) + P(5,0) = 0.2214$

Based on (11.1), the TC probabilities are the following:

$B_{T1} = Q(5) = 0.2214$ (compare with the exact 0.2279)

$B_{T2} = Q(4) + Q(5) = 0.4441$ (compare with the exact 0.4404)

Consider now two different sets of macro-states: (i) $0 \le j \le C$ and (ii) $C < j \le T$. For the first set, no bandwidth compression takes place (i.e., $\varphi_k(\mathbf{n}) = 1$ for all (k) and $q(j)$ can be determined by (10.16) [2]). For the second set, (11.6) based on (3.8) is written as:

$$x(\mathbf{n}) \sum_{l=0}^{n_k-1} P(\mathbf{n}_k^{-1-l}) \alpha_k \sum_{m=l+1}^{\infty} D_m^{(k)} = n_k x(\mathbf{n}_k^{-1}) P(\mathbf{n}) \tag{11.7}$$

where $\alpha_k = \lambda_k / \mu_k$ is the offered traffic-load of service-class k calls (in erl).

Multiplying both sides of (11.7) by b_k and summing over $k = 1, \ldots, K$, we have:

$$x(\mathbf{n}) \sum_{k=1}^{K} \alpha_k b_k \sum_{l=0}^{n_k-1} P(\mathbf{n}_k^{-1-l}) \sum_{m=l+1}^{\infty} D_m^{(k)} = P(\mathbf{n}) \sum_{k=1}^{K} n_k b_k x(\mathbf{n}_k^{-1}) \tag{11.8}$$

Due to (3.9), (11.8) is written as:

$$\sum_{k=1}^{K} \alpha_k b_k \sum_{l=0}^{n_k-1} P(\mathbf{n}_k^{-1-l}) \widehat{D}_l^{(k)} = CP(\mathbf{n}) \tag{11.9}$$

Let $\mathbf{\Omega}_j = \{\mathbf{n} \in \Omega : \mathbf{nb} = j\}$ be the state space where exactly j b.u. are occupied. Then, summing both sides of (11.9) over $\mathbf{\Omega}_j$ and since $\sum_{\mathbf{n} \in \Omega_j} P(\mathbf{n}) = q(j)$, we have:

$$\sum_{\mathbf{n} \in \Omega_j} \sum_{k=1}^{K} \alpha_k b_k \sum_{l=0}^{n_k-1} P(\mathbf{n}_k^{-1-l}) \widehat{D}_l^{(k)} = Cq(j) \tag{11.10}$$

Interchanging the order of summations in (11.10), we have:

$$\sum_{k=1}^{K} \alpha_k b_k \sum_{l=1}^{\lfloor j/b_k \rfloor} \widehat{D}_{l-1}^{(k)} q(j - l \times b_k) = Cq(j) \tag{11.11}$$

since $\sum_{\mathbf{n} \in \Omega_j} \sum_{l=0}^{n_k-1} P(\mathbf{n}_k^{-1-l}) = \sum_{l=1}^{\lfloor j/b_k \rfloor} q(j - l \times b_k)$.

The combination of (10.16) with (11.11) gives the approximate recursive formula of $q(j)$, when $1 \leq j \leq T$ [1]:

$$q(j) = \begin{cases} 1 & \text{if} \quad j = 0 \\ \dfrac{1}{\min(j,C)} \displaystyle\sum_{k=1}^{K} \alpha_k b_k \sum_{l=1}^{\lfloor j/b_k \rfloor} \widehat{D}_{l-1}^{(k)} q(j - l \times b_k) & j = 1, \ldots, T \\ 0 & \text{otherwise} \end{cases} \tag{11.12}$$

where $\alpha_k = \lambda_k/\mu_k$, $\lfloor j/b_k \rfloor$ is the largest integer less than or equal to j/b_k and $\widehat{D}_l^{(k)}$ is the complementary batch size distribution given by $\widehat{D}_l^{(k)} = \sum_{m=l+1}^{\infty} D_m^{(k)}$.

If calls of service k arrive in batches of size s_k where s_k is given by the geometric distribution with parameter β_k (for all k) then (11.12) takes the form:

$$q(j) = \begin{cases} 1, \text{ if} \quad j = 0 \\ \dfrac{1}{\min(j,C)} \displaystyle\sum_{k=1}^{K} a_k b_k \sum_{l=1}^{\lfloor j/b_k \rfloor} \beta_k^{l-1} q \ (j - l \times b_k), \ j = 1, \ldots, T \\ 0, \quad \text{otherwise} \end{cases} \tag{11.13}$$

If $D_m^{(k)} = 1$ for $m = 1$ and $D_m^{(k)} = 0$ for $m > 1$, for all service-classes, then we have a Poisson process and the E-EMLM results (i.e., the recursion of (3.21)).

11.1.2.2 TC Probabilities, CBP, Utilization, and Mean Number of In-service Calls

The following performance measures can be determined based on (11.12):

- The TC probabilities of service-class k, B_{Tk}, via the formula:

$$B_{Tk} = \sum_{j=T-b_k+1}^{T} G^{-1} q(j) \tag{11.14}$$

where $G = \sum_{j=0}^{T} q(j)$ is the normalization constant.

- The CBP (or CC probabilities) of service-class k, B_k, via the formula [1]:

$$B_k = \sum_{j=0}^{T} G^{-1}q(j) \sum_{m=\lfloor (T-j)/b_k \rfloor+1}^{\infty} D_m^{(k)} \tag{11.15}$$

where $D_m^{(k)}$ denotes the probability that there are m calls in an arriving batch of service-class k and $\lfloor (T-j)/b_k \rfloor$ is the maximum integer not exceeding $(T-j)/b_k$. If the batch size is geometrically distributed then (11.15) takes the form:

$$B_k = \sum_{j=0}^{T} G^{-1}q(j)\beta_k^{\lfloor (T-j)/b_k \rfloor} \tag{11.16}$$

The proof of (11.16) is similar to the proof of (10) in [3] (which gives the CC probability in the BP-EMLM where the batch size is geometrically distributed) and therefore is omitted.

- The average number of in-service calls of service-class k, $\bar{n}_k$, via (3.24), where the values of $y_k(j)q(j)$ can be determined via:

$$y_k(j)q(j) = \frac{1}{\min(C,j)}\alpha_k b_k \sum_{x=1}^{\lfloor j/b_k \rfloor} q(j-xb_k)(y_k(j-xb_k)+x) \sum_{m=x}^{\infty} D_m^{(k)}$$
$$+\frac{1}{\min(C,j)} \sum_{i=1,\ i\neq k} \alpha_i b_i \sum_{x=1}^{\lfloor j/b_i \rfloor} q(j-xb_i)y_k(j-xb_i) \sum_{m=x}^{\infty} D_m^{(i)} \tag{11.17}$$

where $q(j) > 0$ and $y_k(j) = 0$ if $j < b_k$. The proof of (11.17) is similar to that of (3.25) (see [4]) and thus is omitted.

- The link utilization, U, via (3.23).

Example 11.2 Consider again Example 11.1 ($C = 3, T = 5, K = 2, b_1 = 1, b_2 = 2$, $\lambda_1 = \lambda_2 = \mu_1 = \mu_2 = 1, \beta_1 = 0.2, \beta_2 = 0.5$).

(a) Calculate the state probabilities $Q(j)$ by applying (11.13).
(b) Calculate the TC and CC probabilities as well as the link utilization via (11.14), (11.16), and (3.23), respectively. Compare the results obtained with those of the BP-EMLM.

(a) Starting with $q(0) = 1$, we recursively calculate $q(j)$ for $j = 1, \ldots, 5$:

$j = 1$: $q(1) = q(0) + 0 = 1.0$ $\Rightarrow$ $q(1) = 1.0$

$j = 2$: $2q(2) = q(1) + 0.2q(0) + 2q(0) = 3.2$ $\Rightarrow$ $q(2) = 1.6$

$j = 3$: $3q(3) = q(2) + 0.2q(1) + 0.04q(0) + 2q(1) = 3.84$ $\Rightarrow$ $q(3) = 1.28$

$j = 4$: $3q(4) = q(3) + 0.2q(2) + 0.04q(1) + 0.008q(0) + 2q(2) + q(0) = 5.848$

$\Rightarrow$ $q(4) = 1.949333$

$j = 5$: $3q(5) = q(4) + 0.2q(3) + 0.04q(2) + 0.008q(1) + 0.0016q(0) + 2q(3) + q(1) = 5.838933$

$\Rightarrow$ $q(5) = 1.946311$

The normalization constant is: $G = \sum_{j=0}^{5} q(j) = 8.775644$.

The state probabilities (link occupancy distribution) are:

$Q(0) = Q(1) = 0.11395$ $\qquad\qquad$ $Q(2) = 0.18232$ $\qquad\qquad$ $Q(3) = 0.145858$

$Q(4) = 0.22213$ $\qquad\qquad\qquad\quad$ $Q(5) = 0.221785$

Compared with the values of $Q(j)$ obtained via $\varphi_k(\mathbf{n})$ in Example 11.1, we see that there exists a slight difference, an indication that local flow balance does not exist.

(b) TC probabilities:

$$B_{T1} = \sum_{j=T-b_1+1}^{T} G^{-1}q(j) = \frac{q(5)}{G} \Rightarrow B_{T1} = 0.221785 \text{ (compare with } 0.262295 \text{ in the BP-EMLM)}$$

$$B_{T2} = \sum_{j=T-b_2+1}^{T} G^{-1}q(j) = \frac{q(4)+q(5)}{G} \Rightarrow B_{T2} = 0.44391 \text{ (compare with } 0.59016 \text{ in the BP-EMLM)}$$

CC probabilities:

$$B_1 = \sum_{j=0}^{T} G^{-1}q(j)\beta_1^{\lfloor (T-j)/b_1 \rfloor} = \frac{q(0)\beta_1^5 + q(1)\beta_1^4 + q(2)\beta_1^3 + q(3)\beta_1^2 + q(4)\beta_1 + q(5)}{G}$$

$$\Rightarrow \quad B_1 = 0.27372 \text{ (compare with } 0.3377 \text{ in the BP-EMLM)}$$

$$B_2 = \sum_{j=0}^{T} G^{-1}q(j)\beta_2^{\lfloor (T-j)/b_2 \rfloor} = \frac{q(0)\beta_2^2 + q(1)\beta_2^2 + q(2)\beta_2 + q(3)\beta_2 + q(4) + q(5)}{G}$$

$$\Rightarrow \quad B_2 = 0.66498 \text{ (compare with } 0.79508 \text{ in the BP-EMLM)}$$

Utilization:

$$U = G^{-1}\left(\sum_{j=1}^{C} jq(j) + \sum_{j=C+1}^{T} Cq(j)\right) = 2.25 \text{ b.u. (compare with } 1.6475 \text{ in the BP-EMLM)}$$

11.2 The Elastic Erlang Multirate Loss Model with Batched Poisson Arrivals under the BR Policy

11.2.1 The Service System

In the *elastic Erlang multirate loss model with batched Poisson arrivals under the BR policy (BP-E-EMLM/BR)* a new service-class k call is accepted in the link if, after its acceptance, the link bandwidth $j \leq T - t_k$, where t_k is the BR parameter of service-class k.

In terms of the system state-space Ω and due to the partial batch blocking discipline, the CAC is identical to that of the E-EMLM/BR (see Section 3.2.1). As far as the TC probabilities of service-class k are concerned, they are determined by (11.1), where $\Omega_{\{k\}} = \{\mathbf{n} \in \Omega : \mathbf{nb} \leq T - b_k - t_k\}$, $k = 1, \ldots, K$.

The compression factor $r(\mathbf{n})$ and the state-dependent compression factor per service-class k, $\varphi_k(\mathbf{n})$ are defined according to (3.2) and (3.8), respectively.

Example 11.3 Consider again Example 11.1 ($C = 3, T = 5, K = 2, b_1 = 1, b_2 = 2, \lambda_1 = \lambda_2 = \mu_1 = \mu_2 = 1, \beta_1 = 0.2, \beta_2 = 0.5$) and assume that $t_1 = 1$ and $t_2 = 0$, so that $b_1 + t_1 =$

$b_2 + t_2$. Calculate the values of $P(\mathbf{n})$ and the corresponding values of $Q(j)$ based on the GB equation of (10.10) while assuming:

(a) the model with $r(\mathbf{n})$ and
(b) the model with $\varphi_k(\mathbf{n})$ and $x(\mathbf{n})$.

Then determine the TC probabilities of both service-classes via (11.1). Note that in (10.10), the "upward" probability flows are given by (11.3), while the "downward" probability flows are given by (11.4) (if we refer to $r(\mathbf{n})$) or by the RHS of (11.6) (if we refer to $\varphi_k(\mathbf{n})$).

The state space $\mathbf{\Omega}$ of this system consists of 11 states of the form $\mathbf{n} = (n_1, n_2)$. The values of n and $r(\mathbf{n})$ are exactly the same as those of Table 3.1 (ignore the last row). Similarly, the values of $\varphi_k(\mathbf{n})$ and $x(\mathbf{n})$ are exactly the same as those of Table 3.2.

(a) Based on the GB equation of (10.10) and (11.3)–(11.4), we have:

$(0,0)$: $P(1,0) + P(0,1) - 2P(0,0) = 0$

$(0,1)$: $0.5P(0,0) + P(1,1) + 1.5P(0,2) - 3P(0,1) = 0$

$(0,2)$: $0.5P(0,0) + P(0,1) + 0.6P(1,2) - 1.5P(0,2) = 0$

$(1,0)$: $0.8P(0,0) + P(1,1) + 2P(2,0) - 3P(1,0) = 0$

$(1,1)$: $0.8P(0,1) + 0.5P(1,0) + 1.5P(2,1) + 1.2P(1,2) - 4P(1,1) = 0$

$(1,2)$: $P(1,1) + 0.5P(1,0) - 1.8P(1,2) = 0$

$(2,0)$: $0.16P(0,0) + 0.8P(1,0) + 3P(3,0) + 0.75P(2,1) - 4P(2,0) = 0$

$(2,1)$: $0.2P(0,1) + P(1,1) + P(2,0) + 1.8P(3,1) - 2.25P(2,1) = 0$

$(3,0)$: $0.032P(0,0) + 0.16P(1,0) + 0.8P(2,0) + 3P(4,0) + 0.6P(3,1) - 5P(3,0) = 0$

$(3,1)$: $P(3,0) - 2.4P(3,1) = 0$

$(4,0)$: $P(3,0) + 0.2P(2,0) + 0.04P(1,0) + 0.008P(0,0) - 3P(4,0) = 0$

The solution of this linear system is:

$P(0,0) = 0.1328$	$P(0,1) = 0.1494$	$P(0,2) = 0.1812$	$P(1,0) = 0.1163$
$P(1,1) = 0.1099$	$P(1,2) = 0.0934$	$P(2,0) = 0.0663$	$P(2,1) = 0.1$
$P(3,0) = 0.0253$	$P(3,1) = 0.0105$	$P(4,0) = 0.0148$	

Based on the values of $P(n_1, n_2)$, we have:

$Q(0) = P(0,0) = 0.1328$

$Q(1) = P(1,0) = 0.1163$

$Q(2) = P(0,1) + P(2,0) = 0.2157$

$Q(3) = P(1,1) + P(3,0) = 0.1352$

$Q(4) = P(0,2) + P(2,1) + P(4,0) = 0.296$

$Q(5) = P(1,2) + P(3,1) = 0.1039$

Based on (11.1) and the state space $\mathbf{\Omega}_{\{k\}} = \{\mathbf{n} \in \mathbf{\Omega} : \mathbf{nb} \leq T - b_k - t_k\}$, $k = 1, \ldots, K$, the TC probabilities are the following:

$B_{T1} = B_{T2} = Q(4) + Q(5) = 0.3999$ (compare with 0.3234 in the E-EMLM/BR)

(b) Similarly, in the case of $\varphi_k(\mathbf{n})$ and $x(\mathbf{n})$, we have:

$(0,0)$: $\quad P(1,0) + P(0,1) - 2P(0,0) = 0$

$(0,1)$: $\quad 0.5P(0,0) + P(1,1) + 1.5P(0,2) - 3P(0,1) = 0$

$(0,2)$: $\quad 0.5P(0,0) + P(0,1) + 0.75P(1,2) - 1.5P(0,2) = 0$

$(1,0)$: $\quad 0.8P(0,0) + P(1,1) + 2P(2,0) - 3P(1,0) = 0$

$(1,1)$: $\quad 0.8P(0,1) + 0.5P(1,0) + 1.125P(2,1) + 1.2P(1,2) - 4P(1,1) = 0$

$(1,2)$: $\quad P(1,1) + 0.5P(1,0) - 1.875P(1,2) = 0$

$(2,0)$: $\quad 0.16P(0,0) + 0.8P(1,0) + 3P(3,0) + 0.75P(2,1) - 4P(2,0) = 0$

$(2,1)$: $\quad 0.2P(0,1) + P(1,1) + P(2,0) + 2P(3,1) - 2.25P(2,1) = 0$

$(3,0)$: $\quad 0.032P(0,0) + 0.16P(1,0) + 0.8P(2,0) + 3P(4,0) + 0.6P(3,1) - 5P(3,0) = 0$

$(3,1)$: $\quad P(3,0) - 2.5P(3,1) = 0$

$(4,0)$: $\quad P(3,0) + 0.2P(2,0) + 0.04P(1,0) + 0.008P(0,0) - 3P(4,0) = 0$

The solution of this linear system is:

$P(0,0) = 0.1340 \qquad P(0,1) = 0.1532 \qquad P(0,2) = 0.1905 \qquad P(1,0) = 0.1149$

$P(1,1) = 0.1067 \qquad P(1,2) = 0.0875 \qquad P(2,0) = 0.0654 \qquad P(2,1) = 0.0988$

$P(3,0) = 0.0247 \qquad P(3,1) = 0.0099 \qquad P(4,0) = 0.0145$

Based on the values of $P(n_1, n_2)$, we have:

$Q(0) = P(0,0) = 0.1340$

$Q(1) = P(1,0) = 0.1149$

$Q(2) = P(0,1) + P(2,0) = 0.2186$

$Q(3) = P(1,1) + P(3,0) = 0.1314$

$Q(4) = P(0,2) + P(2,1) + P(4,0) = 0.3038$

$Q(5) = P(1,2) + P(3,1) = 0.0974$

The corresponding TC probabilities are:

$B_{T1} = B_{T2} = Q(4) + Q(5) = 0.4012$ (compare with the exact 0.3999)

11.2.2 The Analytical Model

11.2.2.1 Link Occupancy Distribution

In the BP-E-EMLM/BR, the unnormalized values of the link occupancy distribution, $q(j)$, can be calculated in an approximate way according to the Roberts method (see Section 1.3.2.2).

Based on Roberts method, (11.12) takes the form [1]:

$$q(j) = \begin{cases} 1 & \text{if} \quad j = 0 \\ \frac{1}{\min(j,C)} \sum_{k=1}^{K} \alpha_k D_k(j - b_k) \sum_{l=1}^{\lfloor j/b_k \rfloor} \widehat{D}_{l-1}^{(k)} q(j - l \times b_k) & j = 1, \ldots, T \\ 0 & \text{otherwise} \end{cases} \qquad (11.18)$$

where $\alpha_k = \lambda_k / \mu_k$, $\lfloor j/b_k \rfloor$ is the largest integer less than or equal to j/b_k, $\widehat{D}_l^{(k)}$ is the complementary batch size distribution given by $\widehat{D}_l^{(k)} = \sum_{m=l+1}^{\infty} D_m^{(k)}$, and $D_k(j - b_k)$ is determined via (3.34b).

If calls of service k arrive in batches of size s_k where s_k is given by the geometric distribution with parameter β_k (for all k) then (11.18) takes the form:

$$q(j) = \begin{cases} 1 & \text{if } \quad j = 0 \\ \frac{1}{\min(j,C)} \sum_{k=1}^{K} \alpha_k D_k(j - b_k) \sum_{l=1}^{\lfloor j/b_k \rfloor} \beta_k^{l-1} q(j - l \times b_k) & j = 1, \ldots, T \\ 0 & \text{otherwise} \end{cases} \qquad (11.19)$$

11.2.2.2 TC Probabilities, CBP, Utilization, and Mean Number of In-service Calls

The following performance measures can be determined based on (11.18):

- The TC probabilities of service-class k, B_{Tk}, via the formula [1]:

$$B_{Tk} = \sum_{j=T-b_k-t_k+1}^{T} G^{-1} q(j) \qquad (11.20)$$

where $G = \sum_{j=0}^{T} q(j)$ is the normalization constant.
- The CBP (or CC probabilities) of service-class k, B_k, via the formula:

$$B_k = \sum_{j=0}^{T-t_k} G^{-1} q(j) \sum_{m=\lfloor (T-t_k-j)/b_k \rfloor +1}^{\infty} D_m^{(k)} + \sum_{j=T-t_k+1}^{T} G^{-1} q(j) \qquad (11.21)$$

If the batch size is geometrically distributed then (11.21) takes the form:

$$B_k = \sum_{j=0}^{T-t_k} G^{-1} q(j) \beta_k^{\lfloor (T-t_k-j)/b_k \rfloor} + \sum_{j=T-t_k+1}^{T} G^{-1} q(j) \qquad (11.22)$$

- The average number of in-service calls of service-class k, $\bar{n}_k$, via (3.24), where the values of $y_k(j) q(j)$ can be determined via (11.17) assuming that $y_k(j) = 0$ when $j > T - t_k$.
- The link utilization, U, via (3.23).

Example 11.4 Consider again Example 11.3 ($C = 3, T = 5, K = 2, b_1 = 1, b_2 = 2$, $\lambda_1 = \lambda_2 = \mu_1 = \mu_2 = 1, \beta_1 = 0.2, \beta_2 = 0.5, t_1 = 1, t_2 = 0$).

(a) Calculate the state probabilities $Q(j)$ by applying (11.19).
(b) Calculate the TC and CC probabilities as well as the link utilization via (11.20), (11.22), and (3.23), respectively. Compare the results obtained with those of the E-EMLM/BR.

(a) Starting with $q(0) = 1$, we recursively calculate $q(j)$ for $j = 1, \ldots, 5$:

$j = 1$:	$q(1) = q(0) + 0 = 1.0$		$\Rightarrow q(1) = 1.0$
$j = 2$:	$2q(2) = q(1) + 0.2q(0) + 2q(0) = 3.2$		$\Rightarrow q(2) = 1.6$
$j = 3$:	$3q(3) = q(2)0.2q(1) + 0.04q(0) + 2q(1) = 3.84$		$\Rightarrow q(3) = 1.28$

$$j = 4 \; : \quad 3q(4) = q(3) + 0.2q(2) + 0.04q(1) + 0.008q(0) + 2q(2) + q(0) = 5.848$$
$$\Rightarrow q(4) = 1.949333$$
$$j = 5 \; : \quad 3q(5) = 2q(3) + q(1) = 3.56 \qquad\qquad \Rightarrow q(5) = 1.186666$$

The normalization constant is: $G = \sum_{j=0}^{5} q(j) = 8.016$.
The state probabilities (link occupancy distribution) are:

$$Q(0) = Q(1) = 0.124751 \quad Q(2) = 0.1996 \quad Q(3) = 0.15968 \quad Q(4) = 0.24318 \quad Q(5) = 0.148037$$

(b) TC probabilities:

$$B_{T1} = B_{T2} = \sum_{j=T-b_1-t_1+1}^{T} G^{-1} q(j) = \frac{q(4) + q(5)}{G} \Rightarrow B_{T1} = B_{T2} = 0.39122$$

(compare with 0.3171 in the E-EMLM/BR)

CC probabilities:

$$B_1 = \sum_{j=0}^{T-t_1} G^{-1} q(j) \beta_1^{\lfloor (T-t_1-j)/b_1 \rfloor} + \sum_{j=T-t_1+1}^{T} G^{-1} q(j) \Rightarrow$$
$$B_1 = \frac{q(0)\beta_1^4 + q(1)\beta_1^3 + q(2)\beta_1^2 + q(3)\beta_1^1 + q(4) + q(5)}{G} = 0.432335$$
$$B_2 = \sum_{j=0}^{T-t_2} G^{-1} q(j) \beta_1^{\lfloor (T-t_2-j)/b_1 \rfloor}$$
$$\Rightarrow B_2 = \frac{q(0)\beta_2^2 + q(1)\beta_2^2 + q(2)\beta_2 + q(3)\beta_2 + q(4) + q(5)}{G} = 0.63323$$

(compare with $B_1 = B_2 = 0.3171$ in the E-EMLM/BR)

Utilization:

$$U = G^{-1} \left(\sum_{j=1}^{C} jq(j) + \sum_{j=C+1}^{T} Cq(j) \right) = 2.177 \text{ b.u. (compare with 2.049 in the E-EMLM/BR)}$$

Example 11.5 Consider a link of capacity $C = 100$ b.u. that accommodates three service-classes of elastic calls which require $b_1 = 1$ b.u., $b_2 = 4$ b.u., and $b_3 = 16$ b.u., respectively. All calls arrive in the system according to a batched Poisson process and the batch size follows the geometric distribution with parameters $\beta_1 = 0.75, \beta_2 = 0.5$, and $\beta_3 = 0.2$, respectively. The service time is exponentially distributed with mean value $\mu_1^{-1} = \mu_2^{-1} = \mu_3^{-1} = 1$. The initial values of the offered traffic-load are $\alpha_1 = 2$ erl, $\alpha_2 = 4$ erl, and $\alpha_3 = 2$ erl. In the x-axis of all figures, we assume that α_2, α_3 remain constant, while α_1 increases in steps of 0.5 erl. The last value of $\alpha_1 = 6$ erl. We consider the following set of BR parameters $t_1 = 15, t_2 = 12$ and $t_3 = 0$. This set achieves TC probabilities equalization among calls of all service-classes. We also consider three different values of T: (a) $T = C = 100$ b.u., where no bandwidth compression takes place (in that case we have the BP-EMLM/BR), (b) $T = 115$ b.u., where bandwidth compression takes place and $r_{min} = C/T = 100/115$, and (c) $T = 130$ b.u., where bandwidth compression takes place and $r_{min} = C/T = 100/130$.

In Figure 11.1 we present the equalized TC probabilities (TC_{eq}) for all values of T. In Figures 11.2–11.4 we present the CC probabilities for the three service-classes, respectively. All figures show that (i) the accuracy of the BP-E-EMLM/BR is absolutely

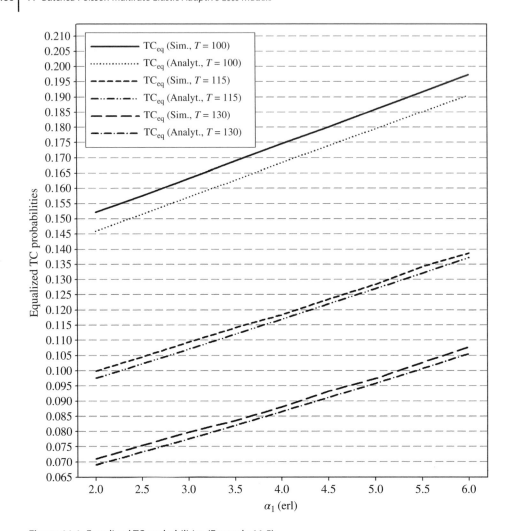

Figure 11.1 Equalized TC probabilities (Example 11.5).

satisfactory compared to simulation (mean values of seven runs with small reliability ranges, not shown in the figures) and (ii) the increase of T above C results in a decrease of both TC and CC probabilities due to the existence of the compression mechanism.

11.3 The Elastic Adaptive Erlang Multirate Loss Model with Batched Poisson Arrivals

11.3.1 The Service System

In the *elastic adaptive Erlang multirate loss model with batched Poisson arrivals (BP-EA-EMLM)* we consider a link of capacity C b.u. that accommodates K service-classes which are distinguished into K_e elastic service-classes and K_a adaptive service-classes: $K = K_e + K_a$. The call arrival process remains batched Poisson.

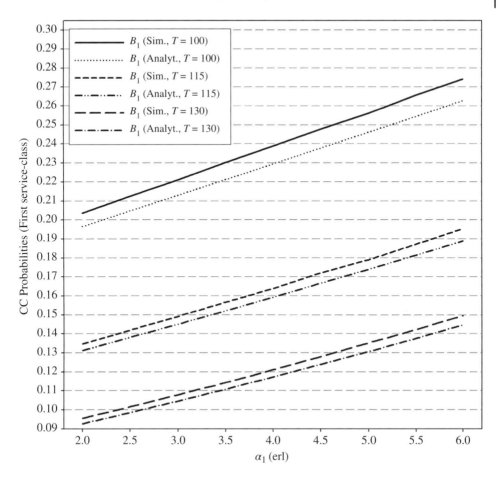

Figure 11.2 CC probabilities for service-class 1 (Example 11.5).

The bandwidth compression/expansion mechanism and the CAC of the BP-EA-EMLM are identical to those presented in the case of the E-EMLM (Section 3.1.1). The only difference is in (3.3), which is applied only on elastic calls (adaptive calls tolerate bandwidth compression without altering their service time). As far as the TC probabilities of service-class k calls are concerned they can be determined via (11.1).

11.3.2 The Analytical Model

11.3.2.1 Steady State Probabilities

Due to the compression/expansion mechanism of calls of service-class k the local flow balance across the level $L_{\mathbf{n}_k^{-1}}^{(k)}$ is destroyed, i.e., (11.5) holds for elastic calls while the corresponding formula for adaptive calls is [5, 6]:

$$\sum_{l=0}^{n_k-1} P(\mathbf{n}_k^{-1-l})\lambda_k \widehat{D}_l^{(k)} \neq n_k \mu_k P(\mathbf{n}), \quad k \in K_{\mathrm{a}} \tag{11.23}$$

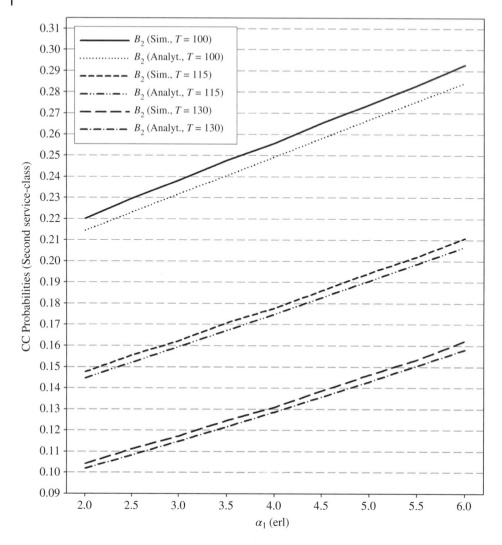

Figure 11.3 CC probabilities for service-class 2 (Example 11.5).

Similar to the BP-E-EMLM, $r(\mathbf{n})$ are replaced by the state-dependent compression factors per service-class k, $\varphi_k(\mathbf{n})$ and $x(\mathbf{n})$, which are defined according to (3.8) and (3.47), respectively.

Having defined $\varphi_k(\mathbf{n})$ and $x(\mathbf{n})$, we make the assumption (approximation) that the following equations hold: $f^{(\text{up})}(L^{(k)}_{\mathbf{n}_k^{-1}}) = f^{(\text{down})}(L^{(k)}_{\mathbf{n}_k^{-1}})$, or

$$\sum_{l=0}^{n_k-1} P(\mathbf{n}_k^{-1-l})\lambda_k \sum_{m=l+1}^{\infty} D_m^{(k)} = n_k \mu_k \varphi_k(\mathbf{n})P(\mathbf{n}), \quad k \in K_e \tag{11.24}$$

$$\sum_{l=0}^{n_k-1} P(\mathbf{n}_k^{-1-l})\lambda_k \sum_{m=l+1}^{\infty} D_m^{(k)} = n_k \mu_k \varphi_k(\mathbf{n})P(\mathbf{n}), \quad k \in K_a \tag{11.25}$$

where the only difference between (11.24) and (11.25) is in k.

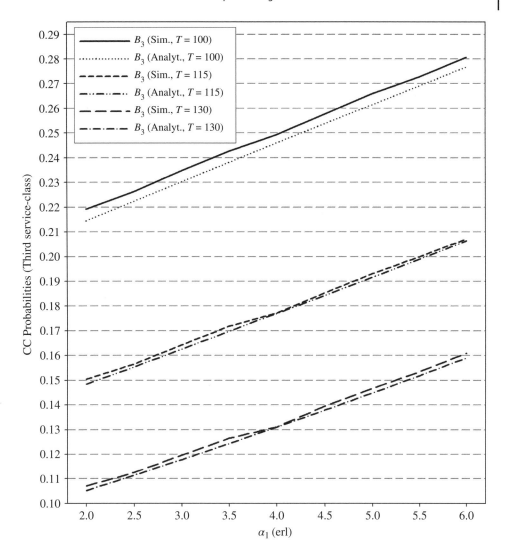

Figure 11.4 CC probabilities for service-class 3 (Example 11.5).

Before we proceed with the derivation of a recursive formula for the determination of $q(j)$, note that the GB equation for state $\mathbf{n}_k^{-1}$ is given by (10.10). In (10.10), the "upward" probability flows are given by (11.3) and the "downward" probability flows are given by (i) (11.5) and (11.23) for elastic and adaptive calls, respectively (if we refer to $r(\mathbf{n})$), or (ii) the RHS of (11.24), (11.25) (if we refer to $\varphi_k(\mathbf{n})$).

Example 11.6 Consider again Example 11.1 ($C = 3, T = 5, K = 2, b_1 = 1, b_2 = 2, \lambda_1 = \lambda_2 = \mu_1 = \mu_2 = 1, \beta_1 = 0.2, \beta_2 = 0.5$) and assume that calls of service-class 2 are adaptive. Calculate the values of $P(\mathbf{n})$ and the corresponding values of $Q(j)$ based on the GB equation of (10.10) and assuming:

(a) the model with $r(\mathbf{n})$, and

(b) the model with $\varphi_k(\mathbf{n})$ and $x(\mathbf{n})$.

Then determine the TC probabilities of both service-classes via (11.1).

The state space Ω of this system consists of 12 states of the form $\mathbf{n} = (n_1, n_2)$. The values of $\mathbf{n}$ and $r(\mathbf{n})$ are exactly the same as those of Table 3.1 (Example 3.1). Similarly, the values of $\varphi_k(\mathbf{n})$ and $x(\mathbf{n})$ are exactly the same as those of Table 3.5 (Example 3.14).

(a) Based on the GB equation of (10.10), we have:

$(0,0):\quad P(1,0) + P(0,1) - 2P(0,0) = 0$

$(0,1):\quad 0.5P(0,0) + P(1,1) + 2P(0,2) - 3P(0,1) = 0$

$(0,2):\quad 0.5P(0,0) + P(0,1) + 0.6P(1,2) - 3P(0,2) = 0$

$(1,0):\quad 0.8P(0,0) + P(1,1) + 2P(2,0) - 3P(1,0) = 0$

$(1,1):\quad 0.8P(0,1) + 0.5P(1,0) + 1.5P(2,1) + 2P(1,2) - 4P(1,1) = 0$

$(1,2):\quad P(0,2) + P(1,1) + 0.5P(1,0) - 2.6P(1,2) = 0$

$(2,0):\quad 0.16P(0,0) + 0.8P(1,0) + 3P(3,0) + P(2,1) - 4P(2,0) = 0$

$(2,1):\quad 0.16P(0,1) + 0.8P(1,1) + P(2,0) + 1.8P(3,1) - 3.5P(2,1) = 0$

$(3,0):\quad 0.032P(0,0) + 0.16P(1,0) + 0.8P(2,0) + 3P(4,0) + P(3,1) - 5P(3,0) = 0$

$(3,1):\quad P(2,1) + 0.2P(1,1) + 0.04P(0,1) + P(3,0) - 2.8P(3,1) = 0$

$(4,0):\quad 0.8P(3,0) + 0.16P(2,0) + 0.032P(1,0) + 0.0064P(0,0) + 3P(5,0) - 4P(4,0) = 0$

$(5,0):\quad P(4,0) + 0.2P(3,0) + 0.04P(2,0) + 0.008P(1,0) + 0.0016P(0,0) - 3P(5,0) = 0$

The solution of this linear system is:

$P(0,0) = 0.1250$	$P(0,1) = 0.1166$	$P(0,2) = 0.0807$	$P(1,0) = 0.1334$
$P(1,1) = 0.1259$	$P(1,2) = 0.1051$	$P(2,0) = 0.0871$	$P(2,1) = 0.0889$
$P(3,0) = 0.0442$	$P(3,1) = 0.0582$	$P(4,0) = 0.0227$	$P(5,0) = 0.0121$

Based on the values of $P(n_1, n_2)$, we have:

$Q(0) = P(0,0) = 0.1250$ $\qquad$ $Q(1) = P(1,0) = 0.1334$

$Q(2) = P(0,1) + P(2,0) = 0.2037$ $\qquad$ $Q(3) = P(1,1) + P(3,0) = 0.1701$

$Q(4) = P(0,2) + P(2,1) + P(4,0) = 0.1923$ $\qquad$ $Q(5) = P(1,2) + P(3,1) + P(5,0) = 0.1754$

Based on (11.1), the TC probabilities are:

$B_{T1} = Q(5) = 0.1754$ (compare with 0.2279 in the BP-E-EMLM)

$B_{T2} = Q(4) + Q(5) = 0.3677$ (compare with 0.4404 in the BP-E-EMLM)

(b) Similarly, in the case of $\varphi_k(\mathbf{n})$ and $x(\mathbf{n})$, we have:

$(0,0):\quad P(1,0) + P(0,1) - 2P(0,0) = 0$

$(0,1):\quad 0.5P(0,0) + P(1,1) + 2P(0,2) - 3P(0,1) = 0$

$(0,2):\quad 0.5P(0,0) + P(0,1) + (3/3.4)P(1,2) - 3P(0,2) = 0$

$(1,0):\quad 0.8P(0,0) + P(1,1) + 2P(2,0) - 3P(1,0) = 0$

$(1,1):\quad 0.8P(0,1) + 0.5P(1,0) + (6/3.5)P(2,1) + (6/3.4)P(1,2) - 4P(1,1) = 0$

$(1,2)$: $P(0,2) + P(1,1) + 0.5P(1,0) - (9/3.4)P(1,2) = 0$

$(2,0)$: $0.16P(0,0) + 0.8P(1,0) + 3P(3,0) + (3/3.5)P(2,1) - 4P(2,0) = 0$

$(2,1)$: $0.16P(0,1) + 0.8P(1,1) + P(2,0) + (10.5/4.7)P(3,1) - (12.5/3.5)P(2,1) = 0$

$(3,0)$: $0.032P(0,0) + 0.16P(1,0) + 0.8P(2,0) + 3P(4,0) + (3/4.7)P(3,1) - 5P(3,0) = 0$

$(3,1)$: $P(2,1) + 0.2P(1,1) + 0.04P(0,1) + P(3,0) - (13.5/4.7)P(3,1) = 0$

$(4,0)$: $0.8P(3,0) + 0.16P(2,0) + 0.032P(1,0) + 0.0064P(0,0) + 3P(5,0) - 4P(4,0) = 0$

$(5,0)$: $P(4,0) + 0.2P(3,0) + 0.04P(2,0) + 0.008P(1,0) + 0.0016P(0,0) - 3P(5,0) = 0$

The solution of this linear system is:

$P(0,0) = 0.1277$	$P(0,1) = 0.1278$	$P(0,2) = 0.0958$	$P(1,0) = 0.1276$
$P(1,1) = 0.1278$	$P(1,2) = 0.1086$	$P(2,0) = 0.0764$	$P(2,1) = 0.0897$
$P(3,0) = 0.0354$	$P(3,1) = 0.0542$	$P(4,0) = 0.0189$	$P(5,0) = 0.0101$

Based on the values of $P(n_1, n_2)$, we have:

$Q(0) = P(0,0) = 0.1277$ $Q(1) = P(1,0) = 0.1276$

$Q(2) = P(0,1) + P(2,0) = 0.2042$ $Q(3) = P(1,1) + P(3,0) = 0.1632$

$Q(4) = P(0,2) + P(2,1) + P(4,0) = 0.2044$ $Q(5) = P(1,2) + P(3,1) + P(5,0) = 0.1729$

Based on (11.1), the TC probabilities are:

$B_{T1} = Q(5) = 0.1729$ (compare with the exact 0.1754)

$B_{T2} = Q(4) + Q(5) = 0.3773$ (compare with the exact 0.3677)

Similar to the BP-E-EMLM, we consider two different sets of macro-states: (i) $0 \leq j \leq C$ and (ii) $C < j \leq T$. For the first set, no bandwidth compression takes place and $q(j)$ can be determined by (10.16) [2]. For the second set, we substitute (3.8) in (11.24) and (11.25) to have:

$$x(\mathbf{n}) \sum_{l=0}^{n_k-1} P(\mathbf{n}_k^{-1-l}) \alpha_k \sum_{m=l+1}^{\infty} D_m^{(k)} = n_k x(\mathbf{n}_k^{-1}) P(\mathbf{n}) \quad k \in K_e \tag{11.26a}$$

$$x(\mathbf{n}) \sum_{l=0}^{n_k-1} P(\mathbf{n}_k^{-1-l}) \alpha_k \sum_{m=l+1}^{\infty} D_m^{(k)} = n_k x(\mathbf{n}_k^{-1}) P(\mathbf{n}) \quad k \in K_a \tag{11.26b}$$

where $\alpha_k = \lambda_k / \mu_k$ is the offered traffic-load of service-class k calls (in erl).

Multiplying both sides of (11.25) by b_k and summing over $k \in K_e$, we have:

$$x(\mathbf{n}) \sum_{k=1}^{K_e} \alpha_k b_k \sum_{l=0}^{n_k-1} P(\mathbf{n}_k^{-1-l}) \sum_{m=l+1}^{\infty} D_m^{(k)} = P(\mathbf{n}) \sum_{k=1}^{K_e} n_k b_k x(\mathbf{n}_k^{-1}) \tag{11.27}$$

Similarly, multiplying both sides of (11.25) by b_k and C/j, and summing over $k \in K_a$, we have:

$$(C/j)x(\mathbf{n}) \sum_{k=1}^{K_a} \alpha_k b_k \sum_{l=0}^{n_k-1} P(\mathbf{n}_k^{-1-l}) \sum_{m=l+1}^{\infty} D_m^{(k)} = (C/j)P(\mathbf{n}) \sum_{k=1}^{K_a} n_k b_k x(\mathbf{n}_k^{-1}) \tag{11.28}$$

By adding (11.27) and (11.28), we have:

$$P(\mathbf{n})\left(\sum_{k=1}^{K_e} n_k b_k x(\mathbf{n}_k^{-1}) + (C/j)\sum_{k=1}^{K_a} n_k b_k x(\mathbf{n}_k^{-1})\right) =$$
$$x(\mathbf{n})\left(\sum_{k=1}^{K_e} \alpha_k b_k \sum_{l=0}^{n_k-1} P(\mathbf{n}_k^{-1-l})\widehat{D}_l^{(k)} + (C/j)\sum_{k=1}^{K_a} \alpha_k b_k \sum_{l=0}^{n_k-1} P(\mathbf{n}_k^{-1-l})\widehat{D}_l^{(k)}\right)$$

(11.29)

Based on (3.47), (11.29) is written as:

$$P(\mathbf{n}) = (1/C)\sum_{k=1}^{K_e} \alpha_k b_k \sum_{l=0}^{n_k-1} P(\mathbf{n}_k^{-1-l})\widehat{D}_l^{(k)} + (1/j)\sum_{k=1}^{K_a} \alpha_k b_k \sum_{l=0}^{n_k-1} P(\mathbf{n}_k^{-1-l})\widehat{D}_l^{(k)}$$

(11.30)

Summing both sides of (11.30) over $\mathbf{\Omega}_j$ and based on the fact that $\sum_{\mathbf{n}\in\mathbf{\Omega}_j} P(\mathbf{n}) = q(j)$, we have:

$$q(j) = \frac{1}{C}\sum_{\mathbf{n}\in\mathbf{\Omega}_j}\sum_{k=1}^{K_e} \alpha_k b_k \sum_{l=0}^{n_k-1} P(\mathbf{n}_k^{-1-l})\widehat{D}_l^{(k)} + \frac{1}{j}\sum_{\mathbf{n}\in\mathbf{\Omega}_j}\sum_{k=1}^{K_a} \alpha_k b_k \sum_{l=0}^{n_k-1} P(\mathbf{n}_k^{-1-l})\widehat{D}_l^{(k)}$$

(11.31)

By interchanging the order of summations in (11.31), we obtain:

$$q(j) = \frac{1}{C}\sum_{k=1}^{K_e} \alpha_k b_k \sum_{\mathbf{n}\in\mathbf{\Omega}_j}\sum_{l=0}^{n_k-1} P(\mathbf{n}_k^{-1-l})\widehat{D}_l^{(k)} + \frac{1}{j}\sum_{k=1}^{K_a} \alpha_k b_k \sum_{\mathbf{n}\in\mathbf{\Omega}_j}\sum_{l=0}^{n_k-1} P(\mathbf{n}_k^{-1-l})\widehat{D}_l^{(k)}$$

(11.32)

or

$$q(j) = \frac{1}{C}\sum_{k=1}^{K_e} \alpha_k b_k \sum_{l=1}^{\lfloor j/b_k\rfloor} q(j - l\times b_k)\widehat{D}_{l-1}^{(k)} + \frac{1}{j}\sum_{k=1}^{K_a} \alpha_k b_k \sum_{l=1}^{\lfloor j/b_k\rfloor} q(j - l\times b_k)\widehat{D}_{l-1}^{(k)}$$

(11.33)

because $\sum_{\mathbf{n}\in\mathbf{\Omega}_j}\sum_{l=0}^{n_k-1} P(\mathbf{n}_k^{-1-l}) = \sum_{l=1}^{\lfloor j/b_k\rfloor} q(j - l\times b_k)$.

The combination of (10.16) with (11.33) gives the approximate recursive formula of $q(j)$, when $1 \leq j \leq T$ [5, 6]:

$$q(j) = \begin{cases} 1 & \text{if} \quad j = 0 \\ \dfrac{1}{\min(j,C)}\sum_{k=1}^{K_e} \alpha_k b_k \sum_{l=1}^{\lfloor j/b_k\rfloor} \widehat{D}_{l-1}^{(k)}q(j - l\times b_k) \\ \quad + \dfrac{1}{j}\sum_{k=1}^{K_a} \alpha_k b_k \sum_{l=1}^{\lfloor j/b_k\rfloor} \widehat{D}_{l-1}^{(k)}q(j - l\times b_k) & \text{if} \quad j = 1, 2, \ldots, T \\ 0 & \text{otherwise} \end{cases}$$

(11.34)

where $\alpha_k = \lambda_k/\mu_k$, $\lfloor j/b_k\rfloor$ is the largest integer less than or equal to j/b_k and $\widehat{D}_l^{(k)}$ is the complementary batch size distribution given by $\widehat{D}_l^{(k)} = \sum_{m=l+1}^{\infty} D_m^{(k)}$.

If calls of service k arrive in batches of size s_k where s_k is given by the geometric distribution with parameter β_k (for all k) then (11.34) takes the form:

$$
q(j) = \begin{cases}
1 & \text{if } j = 0 \\
\dfrac{1}{\min(j,C)} \displaystyle\sum_{k=1}^{K_e} \alpha_k b_k \sum_{l=1}^{\lfloor j/b_k \rfloor} \beta_k^{l-1} q(j - l \times b_k) \\
+ \dfrac{1}{j} \displaystyle\sum_{k=1}^{K_a} \alpha_k b_k \sum_{l=1}^{\lfloor j/b_k \rfloor} \beta_k^{l-1} q(j - l \times b_k) & \text{if } j = 1, 2, \ldots, T \\
0 & \text{otherwise}
\end{cases}
\tag{11.35}
$$

If $D_m^{(k)} = 1$ for $m = 1$ and $D_m^{(k)} = 0$ for $m > 1$, for all service-classes, then we have a Poisson process and the EA-EMLM results (i.e., the recursion of (3.57)).

11.3.2.2   TC Probabilities, CBP, Utilization, and Mean Number of In-service Calls

The following performance measures can be determined based on (11.34):

- The TC probabilities of service-class k, B_{Tk}, via (11.14).
- The CBP (or CC probabilities) of service-class k, B_k, via (11.15) or via (11.16) if the batch size is geometrically distributed.
- The average number of in-service calls of service-class k, $\overline{n}_k$, via (3.24), where the values of $y_k(j)q(j)$ can be determined via (11.36) for elastic traffic and via (11.37) for adaptive traffic:

$$
\begin{aligned}
y_k(j)q(j) = {} & \frac{1}{\min(C,j)} \alpha_k b_k \sum_{x=1}^{\lfloor j/b_k \rfloor} q(j - xb_k)(y_k(j - xb_k) + x) \sum_{m=x}^{\infty} D_m^{(k)} \\
& + \frac{1}{\min(C,j)} \sum_{i=1, i \neq k}^{K_e} \alpha_i b_i \sum_{x=1}^{\lfloor j/b_i \rfloor} q(j - xb_i) y_k(j - xb_i) \sum_{m=x}^{\infty} D_m^{(i)} \\
& + \frac{1}{j} \sum_{i=1}^{K_a} \alpha_i b_i \sum_{x=1}^{\lfloor j/b_i \rfloor} q(j - xb_i) y_k(j - xb_i) \sum_{m=x}^{\infty} D_m^{(i)}
\end{aligned}
\tag{11.36}
$$

$$
\begin{aligned}
y_k(j)q(j) = {} & \frac{1}{j} \alpha_k b_k \sum_{x=1}^{\lfloor j/b_k \rfloor} q(j - xb_k)(y_k(j - xb_k) + x) \sum_{m=x}^{\infty} D_m^{(k)} \\
& + \frac{1}{j} \sum_{i=1, i \neq k}^{K_a} \alpha_i b_i \sum_{x=1}^{\lfloor j/b_i \rfloor} q(j - xb_i) y_k(j - xb_i) \sum_{m=x}^{\infty} D_m^{(i)} \\
& + \frac{1}{\min(C,j)} \sum_{i=1}^{K_e} \alpha_i b_i \sum_{x=1}^{\lfloor j/b_i \rfloor} q(j - xb_i) y_k(j - xb_i) \sum_{m=x}^{\infty} D_m^{(i)}
\end{aligned}
\tag{11.37}
$$

where $q(j) > 0$ and $y_k(j) = 0$ if $j < b_k$.

- The link utilization, U, via (3.23).

Example 11.7   Consider again Example 11.6 ($C = 3, T = 5, K = 2, b_1 = 1, b_2 = 2$, $\lambda_1 = \lambda_2 = \mu_1 = \mu_2 = 1, \beta_1 = 0.2, \beta_2 = 0.5$) where calls of service-class 2 are adaptive.

(a) Calculate the state probabilities $Q(j)$ by applying (11.35).

(b) Calculate the TC and CC probabilities as well as the link utilization via (11.14), (11.16), and (3.23), respectively. Compare the results obtained with those of the BP-E-EMLM.

(a) Starting with $q(0) = 1$, we recursively calculate $q(j)$ for $j = 1, \ldots, 5$:

$j = 1:$ $\quad q(1) = q(0) + 0 = 1.0 \Rightarrow q(1) = 1.0$

$j = 2:$ $\quad 2q(2) = q(1) + 0.2q(0) + 2q(0) = 3.2 \Rightarrow q(2) = 1.6$

$j = 3:$ $\quad 3q(3) = q(2) + 0.2q(1) + 0.04q(0) + 2q(1) = 3.84 \Rightarrow q(3) = 1.28$

$j = 4:$ $\quad q(4) = (1/3)(q(3) + 0.2q(2) + 0.04q(1) + 0.008q(0)) + (1/4)(2q(2) + q(0)) = 1.599333$

$\quad\quad\quad \Rightarrow q(4) = 1.599333$

$j = 5:$ $\quad q(5) = (1/3)(q(4) + 0.2q(3) + 0.04q(2) + 0.008q(1) + 0.0016q(0)) + (1/5)(2q(3) + q(1))$

$\quad\quad\quad = 1.354978 \Rightarrow q(5) = 1.354978$

The normalization constant is: $G = \sum_{j=0}^{5} q(j) = 7.834311$.
The state probabilities (link occupancy distribution) are:

$Q(0) = Q(1) = 0.12764$ $\quad Q(2) = 0.20423$ $\quad Q(3) = 0.16338$ $\quad Q(4) = 0.20414$ $\quad Q(5) = 0.17296$

Compared with the values of $Q(j)$ obtained via $\varphi_k(\mathbf{n})$ in Example 11.6, we see that there exists a slight difference, an indication that local flow balance does not exist.

(b) TC probabilities:

$$B_{T1} = \sum_{j=T-b_1+1}^{T} G^{-1}q(j) = \frac{q(5)}{G} \Rightarrow B_{T1} = 0.17296$$

(compare with 0.221785 in the BP-E-EMLM)

$$B_{T2} = \sum_{j=T-b_2+1}^{T} G^{-1}q(j) = \frac{q(4) + q(5)}{G} \Rightarrow B_{T2} = 0.3771$$

(compare with 0.44391 in the BP-E-EMLM)

CC probabilities:

$$B_1 = \sum_{j=0}^{T} G^{-1}q(j)\beta_1^{\lfloor (T-j)/b_1 \rfloor} = \frac{q(0)\beta_1^5 + q(1)\beta_1^4 + q(2)\beta_1^3 + q(3)\beta_1^2 + q(4)\beta_1 + q(5)}{G} \Rightarrow B_1 = 0.2222$$

(compare with 0.27372 in the BP-E-EMLM)

$$B_2 = \sum_{j=0}^{T} G^{-1}q(j)\beta_2^{\lfloor (T-j)/b_2 \rfloor} = \frac{q(0)\beta_2^2 + q(1)\beta_2^2 + q(2)\beta_2 + q(3)\beta_2 + q(4) + q(5)}{G} \Rightarrow B_2 = 0.62473$$

(compare with 0.66498 in the BP-E-EMLM).

Utilization:

$$U = G^{-1}\left(\sum_{j=1}^{C} jq(j) + \sum_{j=C+1}^{T} Cq(j)\right) = 2.158 \text{ b.u. (compare with 2.25 in the BP-E-EMLM)}$$

11.4 The Elastic Adaptive Erlang Multirate Loss Model with Batched Poisson Arrivals under the BR Policy

11.4.1 The Service System

In the *elastic adaptive Erlang multirate loss model with batched Poisson arrivals under the BR policy (BP-EA-EMLM/BR)* a new service-class k call is accepted in the link if, after its acceptance, the link bandwidth $j \leq T - t_k$, where t_k is the BR parameter of service-class k.

In terms of the system state-space Ω and due to the partial batch blocking discipline, the CAC is identical to that of the E-EMLM/BR (see Section 3.2.1). The only difference is in (3.3), which is applied only on elastic calls. As far as the TC probabilities of service-class k are concerned, they are given by (11.1), where $\Omega_{\{k\}} = \{\mathbf{n} \in \Omega : \mathbf{nb} \leq T - b_k - t_k\}$, $k = 1, \ldots, K$.

The compression factor $r(\mathbf{n})$ and the state-dependent compression factor per service-class k, $\varphi_k(\mathbf{n})$ are defined according to (3.2) and (3.8), respectively, while the values of $x(\mathbf{n})$ are given by (3.47).

Example 11.8 Consider again Example 11.6 ($C = 3, T = 5, K = 2, b_1 = 1, b_2 = 2, \lambda_1 = \lambda_2 = \mu_1 = \mu_2 = 1, \beta_1 = 0.2, \beta_2 = 0.5$) and assume that $t_1 = 1$ and $t_2 = 0$, so that $b_1 + t_1 = b_2 + t_2$. Calculate the values of $P(\mathbf{n})$ and the corresponding values of $Q(j)$ based on the GB equation of (10.10) and assuming:

(a) the model with $r(\mathbf{n})$, and
(b) the model with $\varphi_k(\mathbf{n})$ and $x(\mathbf{n})$.

   Note that in (10.10), the "upward" probability flows are given by (11.3) and the "downward" probability flows are given by (i) (11.4) (if we refer to $r(\mathbf{n})$ and elastic calls) or by the RHS of (11.23) (if we refer to $r(\mathbf{n})$ and adaptive calls) and (ii) by the RHS of (11.24) and (11.25) (if we refer to $\varphi_k(\mathbf{n})$).

The state space Ω of this system consists of 11 states of the form $\mathbf{n} = (n_1, n_2)$. The values of $\mathbf{n}$ and $r(\mathbf{n})$ are exactly the same as those of Table 3.1 (ignore the last row). Similarly, the values of $\varphi_k(\mathbf{n})$ and $x(\mathbf{n})$ are exactly the same as those of Table 3.5.

(a) Based on the GB equation of (10.10), we have:

$(0,0)$: $\quad P(1,0) + P(0,1) - 2P(0,0) = 0$

$(0,1)$: $\quad 0.5P(0,0) + P(1,1) + 2P(0,2) - 3P(0,1) = 0$

$(0,2)$: $\quad 0.5P(0,0) + P(0,1) + 0.6P(1,2) - 2P(0,2) = 0$

$(1,0)$: $\quad 0.8P(0,0) + P(1,1) + 2P(2,0) - 3P(1,0) = 0$

$(1,1)$: $\quad 0.8P(0,1) + 0.5P(1,0) + 1.5P(2,1) + 2P(1,2) - 4P(1,1) = 0$

$(1,2)$: $\quad P(1,1) + 0.5P(1,0) - 2.6P(1,2) = 0$

$(2,0)$: $\quad 0.16P(0,0) + 0.8P(1,0) + 3P(3,0) + P(2,1) - 4P(2,0) = 0$

$(2,1)$: $\quad 0.16P(0,1) + 0.8P(1,1) + P(2,0) + 1.8P(3,1) - 2.5P(2,1) = 0$

$(3,0)$: $\quad 0.032P(0,0) + 0.16P(1,0) + 0.8P(2,0) + 3P(4,0) + P(3,1) - 5P(3,0) = 0$

$(3,1)$: $\quad 0.2P(1,1) + 0.04P(0,1) + P(3,0) - 2.8P(3,1) = 0$

$(4,0)$: $\quad P(3,0) + 0.2P(2,0) + 0.04P(1,0) + 0.008P(0,0) - 3P(4,0) = 0$

The solution of this linear system is:

$P(0,0) = 0.1414$	$P(0,1) = 0.1511$	$P(0,2) = 0.1322$	$P(1,0) = 0.1317$
$P(1,1) = 0.1184$	$P(1,2) = 0.0708$	$P(2,0) = 0.0818$	$P(2,1) = 0.0967$
$P(3,0) = 0.0341$	$P(3,1) = 0.0228$	$P(4,0) = 0.0190$	

Based on the values of $P(n_1, n_2)$, we have:

$Q(0) = P(0,0) = 0.1414$ $\qquad\qquad Q(1) = P(1,0) = 0.1317$

$Q(2) = P(0,1) + P(2,0) = 0.2329$ $\qquad\qquad Q(3) = P(1,1) + P(3,0) = 0.1525$

$Q(4) = P(0,2) + P(2,1) + P(4,0) = 0.2479$ $\qquad\qquad Q(5) = P(1,2) + P(3,1) = 0.0936$

Based on (11.1) and the state space $\Omega_{\{k\}} = \{\mathbf{n} \in \Omega : \mathbf{nb} \leq T - b_k - t_k\}$, $k = 1, \dots,$ K, the TC probabilities are:

$B_{T1} = B_{T2} = Q(4) + Q(5) = 0.3415$ (compare with 0.2674 in the EA-EMLM/BR)

(b) Similarly, in the case of $\varphi_k(\mathbf{n})$ and $x(\mathbf{n})$, we have:

$(0,0):$ $\quad P(1,0) + P(0,1) - 2P(0,0) = 0$

$(0,1):$ $\quad 0.5P(0,0) + P(1,1) + 2P(0,2) - 3P(0,1) = 0$

$(0,2):$ $\quad 0.5P(0,0) + P(0,1) + (3/3.4)P(1,2) - 2P(0,2) = 0$

$(1,0):$ $\quad 0.8P(0,0) + P(1,1) + 2P(2,0) - 3P(1,0) = 0$

$(1,1):$ $\quad 0.8P(0,1) + 0.5P(1,0) + (6/3.5)P(2,1) + (6/3.4)P(1,2) - 4P(1,1) = 0$

$(1,2):$ $\quad P(1,1) + 0.5P(1,0) - (9/3.4)P(1,2) = 0$

$(2,0):$ $\quad 0.16P(0,0) + 0.8P(1,0) + 3P(3,0) + (3/3.5)P(2,1) - 4P(2,0) = 0$

$(2,1):$ $\quad 0.16P(0,1) + 0.8P(1,1) + P(2,0) + (10.5/4.7)P(3,1) - (9/3.5)P(2,1) = 0$

$(3,0):$ $\quad 0.032P(0,0) + 0.16P(1,0) + 0.8P(2,0) + 3P(4,0) + (3/4.7)P(3,1) - 5P(3,0) = 0$

$(3,1):$ $\quad 0.2P(1,1) + 0.04P(0,1) + P(3,0) - (13.5/4.7)P(3,1) = 0$

$(4,0):$ $\quad P(3,0) + 0.2P(2,0) + 0.04P(1,0) + 0.008P(0,0) - 3P(4,0) = 0$

The solution of this linear system is:

$P(0,0) = 0.1441$	$P(0,1) = 0.1616$	$P(0,2) = 0.1471$	$P(1,0) = 0.1267$
$P(1,1) = 0.1185$	$P(1,2) = 0.0687$	$P(2,0) = 0.0731$	$P(2,1) = 0.0934$
$P(3,0) = 0.0294$	$P(3,1) = 0.0207$	$P(4,0) = 0.0167$	

Based on the values of $P(n_1, n_2)$, we have:

$Q(0) = P(0,0) = 0.1441$ $\qquad\qquad Q(1) = P(1,0) = 0.1267$

$Q(2) = P(0,1) + P(2,0) = 0.2347$ $\qquad\qquad Q(3) = P(1,1) + P(3,0) = 0.1479$

$Q(4) = P(0,2) + P(2,1) + P(4,0) = 0.2572$ $\qquad\qquad Q(5) = P(1,2) + P(3,1) = 0.0894$

The corresponding TC probabilities are:

$B_{T1} = B_{T2} = Q(4) + Q(5) = 0.3466$ (compare with the exact 0.3415)

11.4.2 The Analytical Model

11.4.2.1 Link Occupancy Distribution

In the BP-EA-EMLM/BR, the unnormalized values of the link occupancy distribution, $q(j)$, can be calculated in an approximate way according to the Roberts method (see Section 1.3.2.2).

Based on the Roberts method, (11.34) takes the form [5]:

$$q(j) = \begin{cases} 1 & \text{if } j = 0 \\ \dfrac{1}{\min(j,C)} \displaystyle\sum_{k=1}^{K_e} \alpha_k D_k(j - b_k) \sum_{l=1}^{\lfloor j/b_k \rfloor} \widehat{D}_{l-1}^{(k)} q(j - l \times b_k) \\ \quad + \dfrac{1}{j} \displaystyle\sum_{k=1}^{K_a} \alpha_k D_k(j - b_k) \sum_{l=1}^{\lfloor j/b_k \rfloor} \widehat{D}_{l-1}^{(k)} q(j - l \times b_k) & \text{if } j = 1, 2, \dots, T \\ 0 & \text{otherwise} \end{cases} \tag{11.38}$$

where $\alpha_k = \lambda_k/\mu_k$, $\lfloor j/b_k \rfloor$ is the largest integer less than or equal to j/b_k, $\widehat{D}_l^{(k)}$ is the complementary batch size distribution given by $\widehat{D}_l^{(k)} = \sum_{m=l+1}^{\infty} D_m^{(k)}$, and $D_k(j - b_k)$ is determined via (3.34b).

If calls of service k arrive in batches of size s_k where s_k is given by the geometric distribution with parameter β_k (for all k), then (11.38) becomes:

$$q(j) = \begin{cases} 1 & \text{if } j = 0 \\ \dfrac{1}{\min(j,C)} \displaystyle\sum_{k=1}^{K_e} \alpha_k D_k(j - b_k) \sum_{l=1}^{\lfloor j/b_k \rfloor} \beta_k^{l-1} q(j - l \times b_k) \\ \quad + \dfrac{1}{j} \displaystyle\sum_{k=1}^{K_a} \alpha_k D_k(j - b_k) \sum_{l=1}^{\lfloor j/b_k \rfloor} \beta_k^{l-1} q(j - l \times b_k) & \text{if } j = 1, 2, \dots, T \\ 0 & \text{otherwise} \end{cases} \tag{11.39}$$

11.4.2.2 TC Probabilities, CBP, Utilization, and Mean Number of In-service Calls

The following performance measures can be determined based on (11.38):

- The TC probabilities of service-class k, B_{Tk}, via (11.20).
- The CBP (or CC probabilities) of service-class k, B_k, via (11.21) or via (11.22) if the batch size is geometrically distributed.
- The average number of in-service calls of service-class k, $\overline{n}_k$, via (3.24), where the values of $y_k(j)q(j)$ can be determined via (11.36) and (11.37) assuming that $y_k(j) = 0$ when $j > T - t_k$.
- The link utilization, U, via (3.23).

Example 11.9 Consider again Example 11.7 ($C = 3, T = 5, K = 2, b_1 = 1, b_2 = 2$, $\lambda_1 = \lambda_2 = \mu_1 = \mu_2 = 1, \beta_1 = 0.2, \beta_2 = 0.5, t_1 = 1, t_2 = 0$)

(a) Calculate the state probabilities $Q(j)$ by applying (11.39).

(b) Calculate the TC and CC probabilities as well as the link utilization via (11.20), (11.22), and (3.23), respectively. Compare the results obtained with those of the EA-EMLM/BR.

(a) Starting with $q(0) = 1$, we recursively calculate $q(j)$ for $j = 1, \ldots, 5$:

$j = 1$: $\quad q(1) = q(0) + 0 = 1.0$ $\qquad\qquad\qquad\qquad \Rightarrow \quad q(1) = 1.0$

$j = 2$: $\quad 2q(2) = q(1) + 0.2q(0) + 2q(0) = 3.2$ $\qquad \Rightarrow \quad q(2) = 1.6$

$j = 3$: $\quad 3q(3) = q(2) + 0.2q(1) + 0.04q(0) + 2q(1) = 3.84 \Rightarrow \quad q(3) = 1.28$

$j = 4$: $\quad q(4) = (1/3)(q(3) + 0.2q(2) + 0.04q(1) + 0.008q(0)) + (1/4)(2q(2) + q(0))$

$\qquad\qquad = 1.599333$ $\qquad\qquad\qquad\qquad\qquad\qquad \Rightarrow \quad q(4) = 1.599333$

$j = 5$: $\quad q(5) = (1/5)(2q(3) + q(1)) = 0.712$ $\qquad\qquad \Rightarrow \quad q(5) = 0.712$

The normalization constant is: $G = \sum_{j=0}^{5} q(j) = 7.19133$.
The state probabilities (link occupancy distribution) are:

$Q(0) = Q(1) = 0.1391 \quad Q(2) = 0.2225 \quad Q(3) = 0.1780 \quad Q(4) = 0.2224 \quad Q(5) = 0.099$

(b) TC probabilities:

$$B_{T1} = B_{T2} = \sum_{j=T-b_1-t_1+1}^{T} G^{-1}q(j) = \frac{q(4) + q(5)}{G} \Rightarrow B_{T1} = B_{T2} = 0.3214$$

(compare with 0.256 in the EA-EMLM/BR)

CC probabilities:

$$B_1 = \sum_{j=0}^{T-t_1} G^{-1}q(j)\beta_1^{\lfloor(T-t_1-j)/b_1\rfloor} + \sum_{j=T-t_1+1}^{T} G^{-1}q(j) \Rightarrow$$

$$B_1 = \frac{q(0)\beta_1^4 + q(1)\beta_1^3 + q(2)\beta_1^2 + q(3)\beta_1^1 + q(4) + q(5)}{G} = 0.36724$$

$$B_2 = \sum_{j=0}^{T-t_2} G^{-1} q(j)\beta_1^{\lfloor(T-t_2-j)/b_1\rfloor} \Rightarrow B_2 = \frac{q(0)\beta_2^2 + q(1)\beta_2^2 + q(2)\beta_2 + q(3)\beta_2 + q(4) + q(5)}{G} = 0.59117$$

(compare with $B_1 = B_2 = 0.256$ in the EA-EMLM/BR)

Utilization:

$$U = G^{-1}\left(\sum_{j=1}^{C} jq(j) + \sum_{j=C+1}^{T} Cq(j) \right) = 2.082 \text{ b.u. (compare with 1.964 in the EA-EMLM/BR)}$$

Example 11.10 Consider a link of capacity $C = 200$ b.u. that accommodates two elastic and two adaptive service-classes, with the following initial traffic characteristics:

Service-class 1: elastic, $b_1 = 1$ b.u., $\alpha_1 = 7$ erl $\quad$ Service-class 3: adaptive, $b_3 = 10$ b.u., $\alpha_3 = 3$ erl

Service-class 2: elastic, $b_2 = 4$ b.u., $\alpha_2 = 5$ erl $\quad$ Service-class 4: adaptive, $b_4 = 16$ b.u., $\alpha_4 = 1$ erl

We assume that the initial offered traffic-loads α_3 and α_4 remain constant, while α_1 and α_2 increase in steps 1.0 erl and 0.5 erl, respectively, up to final values of $\alpha_1 = 14$ erl and $\alpha_2 = 8.5$ erl. The offered traffic-load point 1, which appears in the x-axis of Figures 11.5–11.11, expresses the initial offered traffic-load, while the subsequent

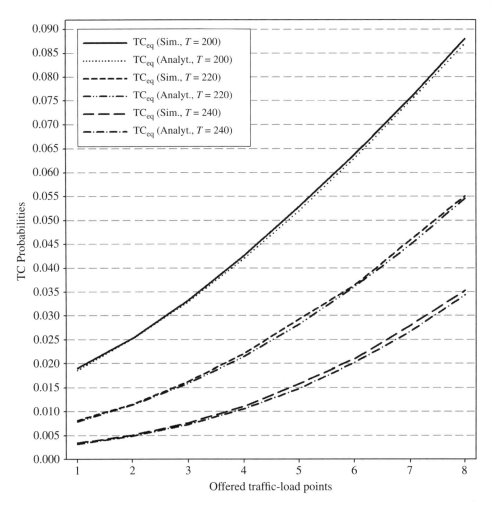

Figure 11.5 Equalized TC probabilities (Example 11.10).

points correspond to the increased traffic-loads. The call service time is exponentially distributed with mean $\mu_1^{-1} = \mu_2^{-1} = \mu_3^{-1} = \mu_4^{-1} = 1$.

To achieve TC probabilities equalization among calls of all service-classes, the BR policy is applied with the following BR parameters: $t_1 = 15$, $t_2 = 12$, $t_3 = 6$ and $t_4 = 0$ b.u.

As far as the batch size distribution is concerned, it follows the geometric distribution for all service-classes with parameters $\beta_1 = 0.75$, $\beta_2 = 0.5$, $\beta_3 = 0.2$, and $\beta_4 = 0.2$, respectively. The corresponding mean batch sizes are 4, 2, 1.25, and 1.25 calls.

For the bandwidth compression mechanism, we consider three values of T: (i) $T = C = 200$ b.u., where no bandwidth compression takes place, and we have the BP-EMLM/BR of [7], (ii) $T = 220$ b.u., where bandwidth compression takes place and $r_{min} = C/T = 200/220$, and (iii) $T = 240$ b.u., where $r_{min} = C/T = 200/240$.

The analytical and simulation results (mean values of 7 runs) of the equalized TC probabilities, TC_{eq}, among the service-classes for each value of T, versus the offered traffic-load, are shown in Figure 11.5. The corresponding CC probabilities for each one

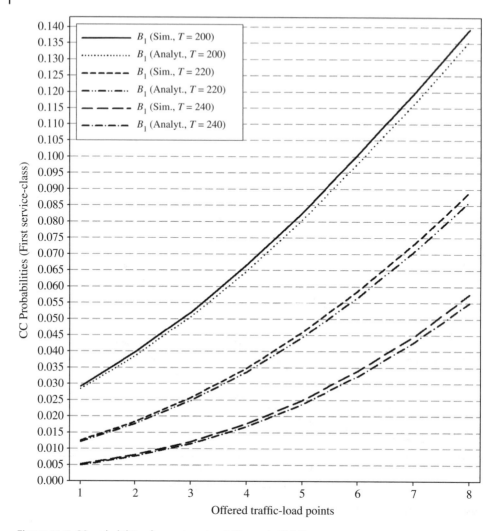

Figure 11.6 CC probabilities for service-class 1 (Example 11.10).

of the four service-classes are shown in Figures 11.6–11.9, respectively. Since CC probabilities refer to the total number of blocked calls out of the total number of arriving calls, there can be no BR parameters that achieve equalized CC probabilities (see also [7]). The analytical and simulation results of the link utilization in b.u. are presented in Figure 11.10. In all cases presented in Figures 11.5–11.9 we observe that (i) the accuracy of the analytical results is absolutely satisfactory compared to simulation results and (ii) CC and TC probabilities decrease as the value of T increases because more calls are admitted in the presence of the bandwidth compression mechanism. The analytical and simulation results of the link utilization in b.u. are presented in Figure 11.10. Since the CC and TC probabilities decrease when $T > C$, the BP-EA-EMLM/BR achieves

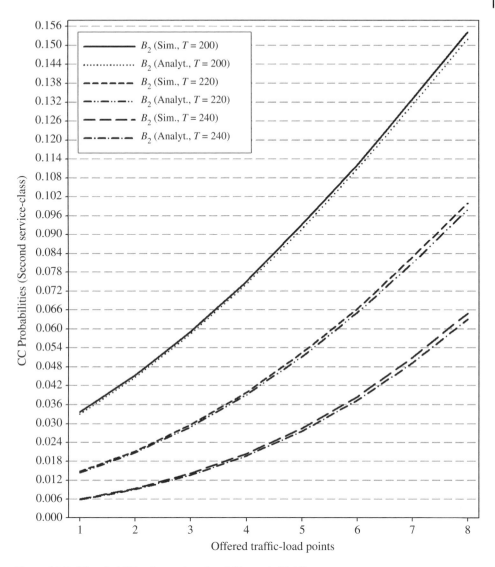

Figure 11.7 CC probabilities for service-class 2 (Example 11.10).

higher link utilization than the BP-EMLM/BR. For further evaluation, in Figure 11.11 we present the analytical results of TC_{eq} and CC probabilities when $T = 240$ b.u. for the aforementioned four service-classes (two elastic and two adaptive) as well as for two more cases: (i) all four service-classes are of elastic type (the BP-E-EMLM of [1] is used) and (ii) all four service-classes are of adaptive type. For presentation purposes and because simulation results are very close to the analytical results, no simulation results are provided, only the analytical results of the first and the fourth service-classes. Figure 11.11 verifies what we intuitively expect: when all service-classes are of elastic

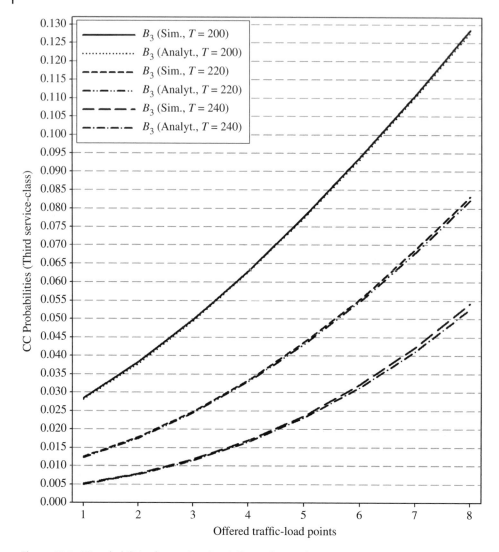

Figure 11.8 CC probabilities for service-class 3 (Example 11.10).

type, higher TC and CC probabilities are expected than in the other two cases. This is because elastic calls expand their service time when their bandwidth is compressed, and therefore remain for longer (on average) in the system than adaptive calls.

11.5 Applications

Since the batched Poisson multirate elastic adaptive loss models are a combination of the elastic adaptive multirate loss models (see Chapter 3) and the batched Poisson multirate

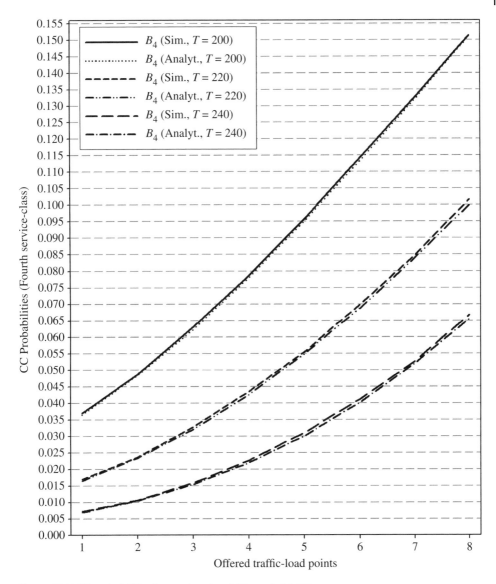

Figure 11.9 CC probabilities for service-class 4 (Example 11.10).

loss models (see Chapter 10), the interested reader may refer to Sections 3.7 and 10.4 for possible applications.

11.6 Further Reading

Similar to the previous section, the interested reader may refer to the corresponding sections of Chapter 3 (Section 3.8) and Chapter 10 (Section 10.5). In addition to these

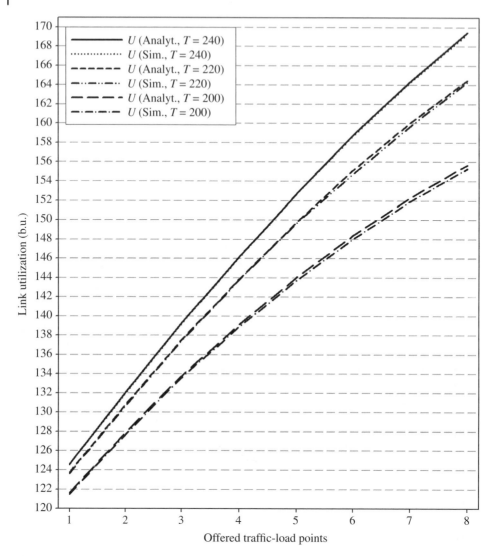

Figure 11.10 Link utilization (in b.u.) (Example 11.10).

sections, a possible interesting extension could be the recent work of [8]. In [8], a self-optimizing 4G wireless network is considered. The network consists of a group of cells that accommodates elastic and adaptive calls of random or quasi-random input and incorporates a mechanism for load balancing between the cells of a group. The determination of CBP is based on approximate formulas whose accuracy has been verified via simulation. The case of bursty traffic in such a network could be studied with the aid of the models in this chapter.

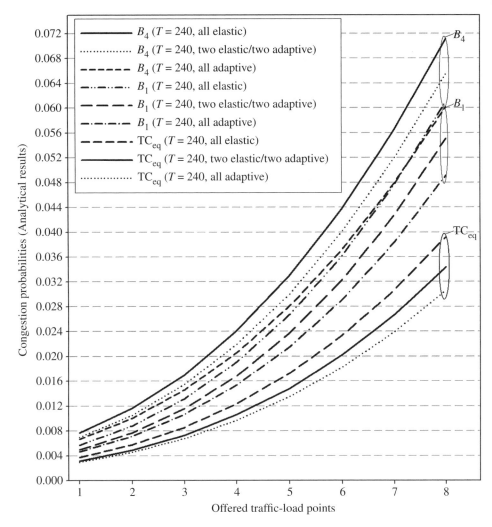

Figure 11.11 Congestion probabilities of all service-classes (elastic/adaptive) (Example 11.10).

References

1 I. Moscholios, J. Vardakas, M. Logothetis and A. Boucouvalas, A batched Poisson multirate loss model supporting elastic traffic under the bandwidth reservation policy. *Proceedings of the IEEE International Conference on Communications, ICC,* Kyoto, Japan, June 2011.
2 J. Kaufman and K. Rege, Blocking in a shared resource environment with batched Poisson arrival processes. *Performance Evaluation,* 24(4):249–263, February 1996.

3 E. van Doorn and F. Panken, Blocking probabilities in a loss system with arrivals in geometrically distributed batches and heterogeneous service requirements. *IEEE/ACM Transactions on Networking*, 1(6):664–667, December 1993.

4 S. Racz, B. Gero and G. Fodor, Flow level performance analysis of a multi-service system supporting elastic and adaptive services. *Performance Evaluation*, 49(1–4):451–469, September 2002.

5 I. Moscholios, J. Vardakas, M. Logothetis and A. Boucouvalas, QoS guarantee in a batched Poisson multirate loss model supporting elastic and adaptive traffic. *Proceedings of the IEEE International Conference on Communications, ICC*, Ottawa, Canada, June 2012.

6 I. Moscholios, J. Vardakas, M. Logothetis and A. Boucouvalas, Congestion probabilities in a batched Poisson multirate loss model supporting elastic and adaptive traffic. *Annals of Telecommunications*, 68(5):327–344, June 2013.

7 I. Moscholios and M. Logothetis, The Erlang multirate loss model with batched Poisson arrival processes under the bandwidth reservation policy. *Computer Communications*, 33(Supplement 1):S167–S179, November 2010.

8 M. Glabowski, S. Hanczewski and M. Stasiak, Modelling load balancing mechanisms in self-optimizing 4G mobile networks with elastic and adaptive traffic. *IEICE Transactions on Communications*, E99-B(8):1718–1726, August 2016.

Appendix A

Interdependency of the Teletraffic Models

As a summary, we present here charts of the teletraffic models covered in this book in order to show the interdependency of the models, as well as when (under what conditions, i.e., changes of their parameters) a transition from one teletraffic model to another occurs, in other words, when each model should be used.

The following parameters/symbols are included in the charts of Figures A.1, A.2, and A.3:

b_{kc_s}	The sth + 1 contingency bandwidth requirement of service-class k
b_{kr_s}	The sth retry bandwidth of service-class k
C	System capacity
C^*	Virtual capacity when the system is in state OFF
J_{ks}	The sth threshold of service-class k
J_s	The sth threshold of the system, common to all service-classes
k	The kth service-class
K_a	Number of adaptive service-classes
K_e	Number of elastic service-classes
$n_{k,\max}$	Maximum number of in-service calls of service-class k
n_k	Number of in-service calls of service-class k
T	Virtual system capacity
t_k	Trunk/bandwidth reservation parameter for service-class k
σ_k	Probability of a service-class k call to pass from an ON to an OFF state
BP-EA-EMLM/BR	Elastic adaptive Erlang multirate loss model with batched Poisson arrivals under the bandwidth reservation policy
BP-EA-EMLM	Elastic adaptive Erlang multirate loss model with batched Poisson arrivals
BP-E-EMLM/BR	Elastic Erlang multirate loss model with batched Poisson arrivals under the bandwidth reservation policy
BP-E-EMLM	Elastic Erlang multirate loss model with batched Poisson arrivals
BP-EMLM/BR	Erlang multirate loss model with batched Poisson arrivals under the bandwidth reservation policy
BP-EMLM/TH	Erlang multirate loss model with batched Poisson arrivals under the threshold policy
BP-EMLM	Erlang multirate loss model with batched Poisson arrivals

Efficient Multirate Teletraffic Loss Models Beyond Erlang, First Edition.
Ioannis D. Moscholios and Michael D. Logothetis.
© 2019 John Wiley & Sons Ltd. Published 2019 by John Wiley & Sons Ltd.
Companion website: www.wiley.com/go/logocode

BR	Bandwidth reservation
CDTM/BR	Connection dependent threshold model under the bandwidth reservation policy
CDTM	Connection dependent threshold model
EA-EMLM/BR	Elastic adaptive Erlang multirate loss model under the bandwidth reservation policy
EA-EMLM/TH	Elastic adaptive Erlang multirate loss model under the threshold policy
EA-EMLM	Elastic adaptive Erlang multirate loss model
EA-EnMLM/BR	Elastic adaptive Engset multirate loss model under the bandwidth reservation policy
EA-EnMLM	Elastic adaptive Engset multirate loss model
E-EMLM/BR	Elastic Erlang multirate loss model under the bandwidth reservation policy
E-EMLM/TH	Elastic Erlang multirate loss model under the threshold policy
E-EMLM	Elastic Erlang multirate loss model
E-EnMLM/BR	Elastic Engset multirate loss model under the bandwidth reservation policy
E-EnMLM	Elastic Engset multirate loss model
EMLM/BR	Erlang multirate loss model under the bandwidth reservation policy
EMLM/TH	Erlang multirate loss model under the threshold policy
EMLM	Erlang multirate loss model
EnMLM/BR	Engset multirate loss model under the bandwidth reservation policy
EnMLM/TH	Engset multirate loss model under the threshold policy
EnMLM	Engset multirate loss model
f-CDTM/BR	Finite connection dependent threshold model under the bandwidth reservation policy
f-CDTM	Finite connection dependent threshold model
f-ON-OFF	Finite ON–OFF multirate loss model
ON–OFF/BR	ON–OFF multirate loss model under the bandwidth reservation policy
ON–OFF	ON–OFF multirate loss model
TH	Threshold

Note:

- From a model of Part II (Figure A.2), we can obtain the corresponding model of Part I (Figure A.1) by assuming that $N_k \to \infty$ for all k.
- Figure A.3 shows the basic connection between the models of Part III and the models of Part I (Figure A.1) through the BP-EMLM and EMLM.
- Based on Figures A.1, A.2, and A.3, we can see some missing teletraffic models, i.e., models which are not included in this book. The reason is twofold: the missing model can be readily conceived by the reader (e.g., the missing model "elastic adaptive finite retry model", can be obtained from the "elastic adaptive retry model"), or/and the accuracy of the missing model is not satisfactory within a typical range of offered traffic load (e.g., the missing model "f-ON-OFF/BR" can be obtained from the "f-ON-OFF", when $t_k > 0$).

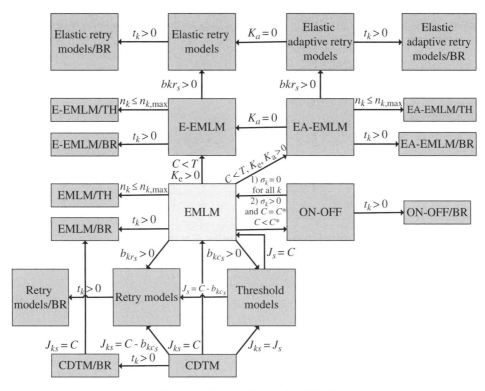

Figure A.1 Interdependency of the teletraffic models of Part I of this book.

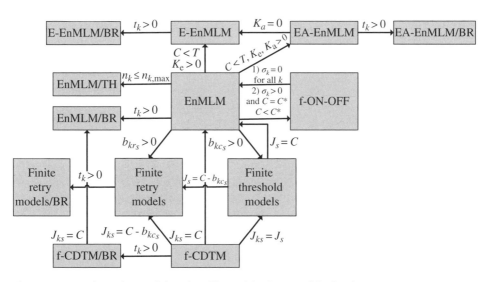

Figure A.2 Interdependency of the teletraffic models of Part II of this book.

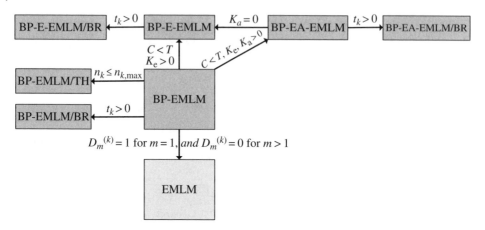

Figure A.3 Interdependency of the teletraffic models of Part III of this book.

Index

Efficient Multirate Teletraffic Loss Models Beyond Erlang, First Edition.
Ioannis D. Moscholios and Michael D. Logothetis.
© 2019 John Wiley & Sons Ltd. Published 2019 by John Wiley & Sons Ltd.
Companion website: www.wiley.com/go/logocode